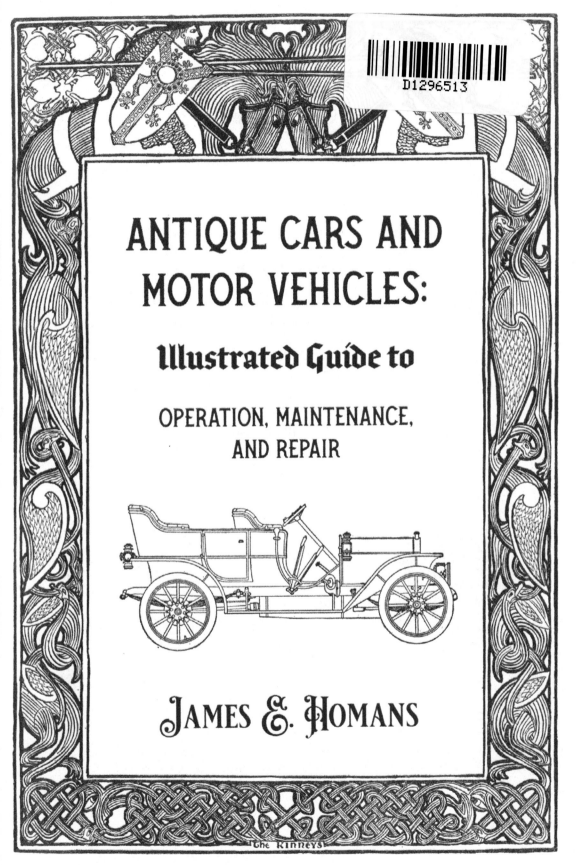

ANTIQUE CARS AND MOTOR VEHICLES:

Illustrated Guide to

OPERATION, MAINTENANCE, AND REPAIR

James E. Homans

Antique Cars and Motor Vehicles:
Illustrated Guide to Operation, Maintenance, and Repair
by James E. Homans

Cover Design by
Mark Bussler

More History Books at
CGRpublishing.com

1939 New York World's Fair:
The World of Tomorrow in
Photographs

The Complete Ford Model T
Guide: Enlarged Illustrated
Special Edition

The Aeroplane Speaks:
Illustrated Historical Guide
to Airplanes

SELF-PROPELLED VEHICLES

A PRACTICAL TREATISE
ON THE
THEORY, CONSTRUCTION, OPERATION,
CARE AND MANAGEMENT
OF ALL FORMS OF
AUTOMOBILES

BY

JAMES E. HOMANS, A. M.

*WITH UPWARDS OF 500 ILLUSTRATIONS AND DIAGRAMS,
GIVING THE ESSENTIAL DETAILS OF CONSTRUCTION
AND MANY IMPORTANT POINTS ON THE SUCCESSFUL
OPERATION OF THE VARIOUS TYPES OF MOTOR CAR-
RIAGES DRIVEN BY STEAM, GASOLINE AND ELECTRICITY.*

1911

TABLE OF CONTENTS.

TABLE OF CONTENTS.

PREFACE.

Since the publication of the first edition of this book the motor vehicle has passed out of the experimental stage and become a practical reality. That it is now a permanent factor in the world of mechanics, in the domain of travel and recreation, and, latterly also, in commercial life, cannot for a moment be questioned. Already the profession of chauffeur, or automobile driver, has taken rank among skilled callings, affording a new and profitable field of effort. The demand for information of a practical character is insistent. This demand the present revised edition attempts to meet.

The motor vehicle is a singularly complex machine. Its construction and operation involve the consideration of an extensive range of facts in several widely separated departments of mechanical knowledge. The study of its construction and operation is a liberal education in itself. It claims a broad territory.

In order to answer every question that must occur to the practical automobilist, one must produce a whole library of books, rather than a single volume of convenient size. Virtually all such questions may be forestalled, however, by clear explanations of the principles governing the design and construction of the machine, and the most conspicuous situations involved in its operation. It must be said, to the credit of both designer and operator, that questions, perplexities and accidents are far fewer at the present time than several years ago. This is due to the general dissemination of knowledge of a practical character, also to the fact that the public has learned to consider the motor vehicle seriously, and award it the attention it deserves.

To the vast realm of motordom the present volume essays to discharge the function of a general introduction; a convenient guide book to the intricacies that must inevitably be encountered; a summary of the facts and principles that it is necessary to understand. As far as possible, the presentation of subjects has been determined by consideration of the needs of the man behind the wheel. Irrelevant matters have been eliminated, and attention has been guided toward present conditions, to the exclusion of all that is experimental and obsolete.

Honest criticism and suggestions would be genuinely appreciated by both the author and the publishers, who would esteem it an assistance in the direction of adequately dealing with a subject that is of great interest and still greater importance at the present time.

For kind assistance in the preparation of this new edition the author begs to render thanks to Mr. Charles E. Duryea; to Mr. E. W. Wright; to several leading authorities and manufacturers who have cheerfully furnished information, as acknowledged in the text; to a number of readers of older editions, who have made intelligent suggestions, and asked even more suggestive questions; and to the reading public, whose generous appreciation has encouraged him to attempt improvement on his former efforts.

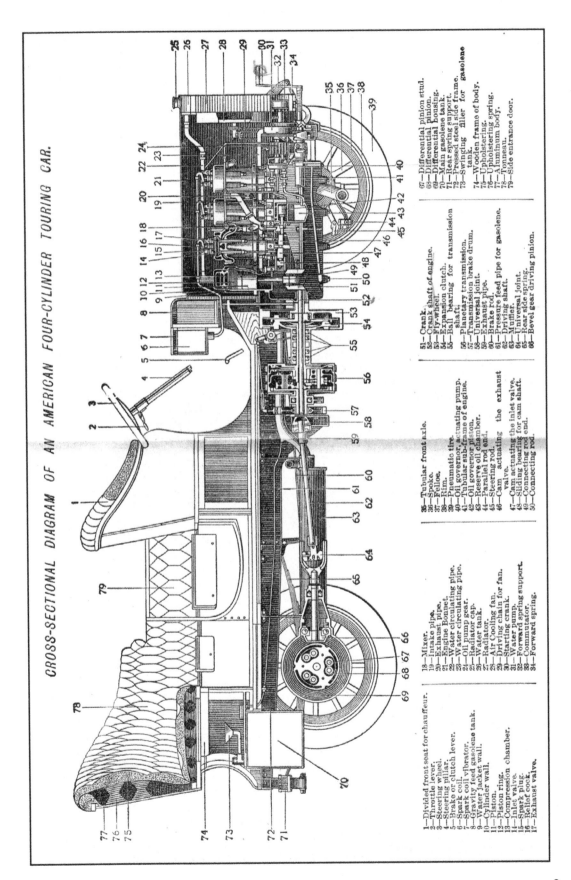

CROSS-SECTIONAL DIAGRAM OF AN AMERICAN FOUR-CYLINDER TOURING CAR.

1—Divided front seat for chauffeur.
2—Throttle lever.
3—Steering wheel.
4—Steering pillar.
5—Brake or clutch lever.
6—Spark coil.
7—Spark coil vibrator.
8—Gravity feed gasolene tank.
9—Water jacket wall.
10—Cylinder wall.
11—Piston.
12—Piston ring.
13—Compression chamber.
14—Inlet valve.
15—Spark plug.
16—Relief cock.
17—Exhaust valve.

18—Mixer.
19—Intake pipe.
20—Exhaust pipe.
21—Engine Bonnet.
22—Water circulating pipe.
23—Water circulating pipe.
24—Oil pump gear.
25—Radiator cap.
26—Water tank.
27—Radiator.
28—Air Cooling fan.
29—Driving chain for fan.
30—Starting crank.
31—Water pump.
32—Forward spring support.
33—Connecting rod end.
34—Forward spring.

35—Tubular front axle.
36—Spoke.
37—Felloe.
38—Rim.
39—Pneumatic tire.
40—Oil governor, actuating pump.
41—Oil governor piston.
42—Tubular sub-frame of engine.
43—Reserve oil chamber.
44—Parallel rod end.
45—Steering rod.
46—Cam actuating the exhaust valve.
47—Cam actuating the inlet valve.
48—Sliding bearing for cam shaft.
49—Connecting rod end.
50—Connecting rod.

51—Crank.
52—Crank shaft of engine.
53—Fly-wheel.
54—Expansion clutch.
55—Ball bearing for transmission shaft.
56—Planetary transmission.
57—Transmission brake drum.
58—Universal joint.
59—Exhaust pipe.
60—Brake rod.
61—Pressure feed pipe for gasolene.
62—Driving shaft.
63—Muffler.
64—Universal joint.
65—Rear side spring.
66—Bevel gear driving pinion.

67—Differential pinion stud.
68—Differential pinion.
69—Differential housing.
70—Main gasolene tank.
71—Rear spring support.
72—Pressed steel side frame.
73—Swinging filler for gasolene tank.
74—Wooden frame of body.
75—Upholstering.
76—Upholstering spring.
77—Aluminum body.
78—Tonneau.
79—Side entrance door.

GOTTLIEB DAIMLER

(1834-1899)

INVENTOR OF THE PRACTICAL HIGH-SPEED GASOLINE MOTOR

AND

"FATHER OF THE AUTOMOBILE"

CHAPTER ONE.

A BRIEF HISTORY OF SELF-PROPELLED ROAD VEHICLES.

Requirements for a Successful Motor Carriage.—Even before the days of successful railroad locomotives several inventors had proposed to themselves the problem of a steam-propelled road wagon, and actually made attempts to build machines to embody their designs. In 1769 Nicholas Joseph Cugnot, a captain in the French army, constructed a three-wheeled wagon, having the boiler and engine overhanging, and to be turned with the forward wheel, and propelled by a pair of single-acting cylinders, which worked on ratchets geared to the axle shaft. It was immensely heavy, awkward and unmanageable, but succeeded in making the rather unexpected record of two and a half miles per hour, over the wretched roads of that day, despite the fact that it must stop every few hundred feet to steam up. Later attempts in the same direction introduced several of the essential motor vehicle parts used at the present day, and with commensurately good results. But the really practical road carriage cannot be said to have existed until inventors grasped the idea that the fuel for the engines must be something other than coal, and that, so far as the boilers and driving gears are concerned, the minimum of lightness and compactness must somehow be combined with the maximum of power and speed. This seems a very simple problem, but we must recollect that even the simplest results are often the hardest to attain. Just as the art of printing dates from the invention of an inexpensive method of making paper, so light vehicle motors were first made possible by the successful production of liquid or volatile fuels.

In addition to this, as we shall presently understand, immense contributions to the present successful issue have been made by pneumatic tires, stud steering axles and balance gears, none of which were used in the motor carriages of sixty and eighty years ago. So that, we may confidently insist, although many thoughtless persons still assert that the motor carriage industry is in its infancy, and its results tentative, we have already most of the elements of the perfect machine, and approximations of the remainder. At the present time the problem is not on what machine can do the required work, but which one can do it best.

A Brief Review of Motor Carriage History.—As might be readily surmised, the earliest motor vehicles were those propelled by steam engines, the first attempt, that of Capt. Cugnot, dating, as we have seen, from 1769-70. In the early years of the nineteenth century, and until about 1840-45, a large number of steam

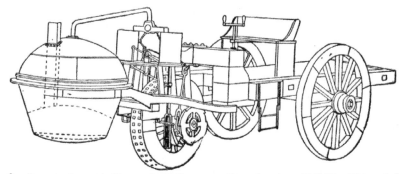

Fig. 1.—Captain Cugnot's Three-wheel Steam Artillery Carriage (1769-70). This cut shows details of the single flue boiler and of the driving connections.

carriages and stage coaches were designed and built in England, some of them enjoying considerable success and bringing profit to their owners. At about the close of this period, however, strict laws regarding the reservation of highways to horse-vehicles put an effectual stop to the further progress of an industry that was already well on its way to perfection, and for over forty years little was done, either in Europe or America, beyond improving the type of farm tractors and steam road rollers, with one or two sporadic attempts to introduce self-propelling steam fire engines. During the whole of this period the light steam road carriage existed only as a pet hobby of ambitious inventors, or as a curiosity for exhibition purposes. Curiously enough, while the progress of railroad locomotion was, in the meantime, rapid and brilliant, the re-awakening of the motor carriage idea and industry, about 1885-89, was really the birth of a new science of constructions, very few of the features of former carriages being then adopted. In 1885 Gottlieb Daimler patented his high-speed gas or mineral spirit engine, the parent and prototype of the wide

variety of explosive vehicle motors since produced and, in the
same year, Carl Benz, of Mannheim, constructed and patented
his first gasoline tricycles. The next period of progress, in the
years immediately succeeding, saw the ascendency of French
engineers, Peugeot, Panhard, De Dion and Mors, whose
names, next to that of Daimler himself, have become common-
places with all who speak of motor carriages. In 1889 Leon
Serpollet, of Paris, invented his famous instantaneous, or "flash,"
generator, which was, fairly enough, the most potent agent in
restoring the steam engine to consideration as means of motor

FIG. 2.—Richard Trevithick's Steam Road Carriage (1802). The centre-pivoted front
axle is about half the length of the rear axle. The cylinder is fixed in the centre of
the boiler. The engine has a fly-wheel and spur gear connections to the drive axle.

carriage propulsion. Although it has not become the prevailing
type of steam generator for this purpose, it did much to turn the
attention of engineers to the work of designing high-power,
quick-steaming, small-sized boilers, which have been brought to
such high efficiency, particularly in the United States. With
perfected steam generators came also the various forms of liquid
or gas fuel burners. The successful electric carriage dates from
a few years later than either of the others, making its appearance
as a practical permanency about 1893-94.

Trevithick's Steam Carriage.—In reviewing the history of
motor road vehicles we will discover the fact that the attempts
which were never more than plans on paper, working models, or
downright failures are greatly in excess of the ones even half-

way practical. From within a few years after Cugnot's notable attempt and failure, many inventors in England, France and America appeared as sponsors for some kind of a steam road carriage, and as invariably contributed little to the practical solution of the problem. In 1802 Richard Trevithick, an engineer of ability, subsequently active in the work of developing railroad cars and locomotives, built a steam-propelled road carriage, which, if we may judge from the drawings and plans still extant, was altogether unique, both in design and operation. The body was supported fully six feet from the ground, above rear driving wheels of from eight to ten feet in diameter, which, turning loose on the axle trees, were propelled by spur gears secured to the hubs. The cylinder placed in the centre of the boiler turned its crank on the counter-shaft, just forward of the axle, and imparted its motion through a second pair of spur gears, meshing with those attached to the wheel hubs. The steering was by the forward wheels, whose axle was about half the width of the vehicle, and centre-pivoted, so as to be actuated by a hand lever rising in front of the driver's seat. This difference in the length of the two axles was probably a great advantage to positive steering qualities, even in the absence of any kind of compensating device on the drive shaft. The carriage was a failure, however, owing to lack of financial support, as is alleged, and, after a few trial runs about London, was finally dismantled.

Gurney's Coaches.—The Golden Age of steam coaches extended from the early twenties of the nineteenth century for about twenty years. During this period much was done to demonstrate the practicability of steam road carriages, which for a time seemed promising rivals to the budding railroad industry. Considerable capital was invested and a number of carriages were built, which actually carried thousands of passengers over the old stage-coach roads, until adverse legislation set an abrupt period to further extension of the enterprise. Among the names made prominent in these years is that of Goldsworthy Gurney, who, in association with a certain Sir Charles Dance, also an engineer, constructed several coaches, which enjoyed a brief though successful career. His boiler, like those then used in the majority of carriages, was of the water-tube variety, and in many respects closely resembled some of the most successful styles made at the present day. It consisted of two parallel horizontal cylindrical drums, set one above the other in the width of the carriage, surmounted by a third, a separator tube, and connected together by a number of tubes, each shaped like the letter U laid on its side, and also, directly, by several vertical tubes. The fire was applied to the lower sides of the bent tubes, under forced draught, thus creating a circulation, but, on account of the small heating surface, the boiler was largely a failure. Mr. Dance did much

Fig. 3.—Sectional Elevation of one of Goldsworthy Gurney's Early Coaches, showing water tube boiler, directly geared cylinders and peg-rod driving wheel.

to remedy the defects of Gurney's boiler with a water-tube generator, designed by himself, in which the triple rows of parallel U-tubes were replaced by a number of similarly-shaped tubes connected around a common circumference by elbow joints, and surmounted by dry steam tubes, thus affording a much larger heating surface for the fire kindled above the lower sides of the bent tubes. Gurney's engine consisted of two parallel cylinders, fixed in the length of the carriage and operating cranks on the revolving rear axle shaft. The wheels turned loose on the axles, and were driven by double arms extending in both directions from the axle to the felloe of the wheel, where they engaged suitably arranged bolts, or plugs. On level roadways only one wheel was driven, in order to allow of turning, but in ascending hills both were geared to the motor, thus giving full power. In Gurney's later coaches and tractors the steering was by a sector,

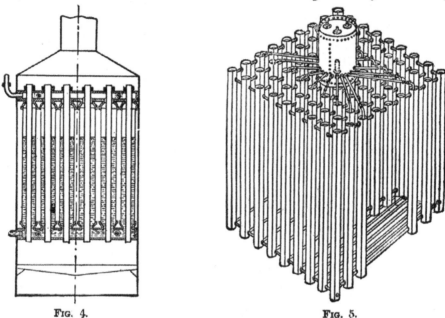

Fig. 4.   Fig. 5.

FIGS. 4-5.—Improved Boilers for Gurney Coaches; the first by Summers & Ogle; the second by Maceroni & Squire.

with its centre on the pivot of the swinging axle shaft and operated by a gear wheel at the end of the revolving steering post. In one of his earliest carriages he attempted the result with an extra wheel forward of the body and the four-wheel running frame, the swinging forward axle being omitted, but this arrangement speedily proving useless, was abandoned.

Improvements on Gurney's Coaches.—Several other builders, notably Maceroni and Squire, and Summers and Ogle, adopted the general plans of Gurney's coaches and driving gear, but added improvements of their own in the construction of the boilers and running gear. The former partners used a water-tube boiler consisting of eighty vertical tubes, all but eighteen of which were connected at top and bottom by elbows or stay-tubes, the others being extended so as to communicate with a central vertical steam drum. Summers and Ogle's boiler consisted of thirty combined water tubes and smoke flues, fitting into square plan, flat vertical-axis drums at top and bottom. Into each of these drums—the one for water, the other for steam—the water tubes opened, while through the top and bottom plates, through the length of the water-tubes, ran the contained smoke flues, leading the products of combustion upward from the furnace. The advantage of this construction was that considerable water could be thus heated, under draught, in small tube sections, while the full effect of 250 square feet of heating surface was realized. With both these boilers exceedingly good results were obtained, both in efficiency and in small cost of operation. Indeed, the reasonable cost of running these old-time steam carriages is surprising. It has been stated that Gurney and Dance's coaches required on an average about 4d. (eight cents) per mile for fuel coke, while the coaches built by Maceroni and Squire often averaged as low as 3d. (six cents). The average weight of the eight and ten-passenger coaches was nearly 5,000 pounds, their speed, between ten and thirty miles, and the steam pressure used about 200 pounds.

Hancock's Coaches.—By all odds the most brilliant record among the early builders of steam road carriages is that of Walter Hancock, who, between the years 1828 and 1838, built nine carriages, six of them having seen actual use in the work of carrying passengers. His first effort, a three-wheeled phaeton, was driven by a pair of oscillating cylinders geared direct to the front wheel, and being turned on the frame with it in steering. Having learned by actual experiment the faults of this construction, he adopted the most approved practice of driving on the rear axle, and in his first passenger coach, "The Infant," he attached his oscillating cylinder at the rear of the frame, and transmitted the power by an ordinary flat-link chain to the rotating axle. He was the first to use the chain transmission.

As Hancock seems to have been a person who readily learned by experience, he soon saw that the exposure of his engines to dust and other abradents was a great source of wear and disablement; consequently in his second coach, "Infant No. 2," he supplanted the oscillating cylinder hung outside by a slide-valve

17

cylinder and crank disposed within the rear of the coach body above the floor. In this and subsequent carriages he used the chain drive, also operating the boiler feed pump from the cross-head, as in most steam carriages at the present day.

Hancock's boiler was certainly the most interesting feature of his carriages, both in point of original conception and efficiency in steaming. It was composed of a number of flat chambers— "water bags" they were called—laid side by side and intercommunicating with a water drum at the base and steam drum at the top. Each of these chambers was constructed from a flat sheet of metal, hammered into the required shape and flanged along the edges, and, being folded together at the middle point,

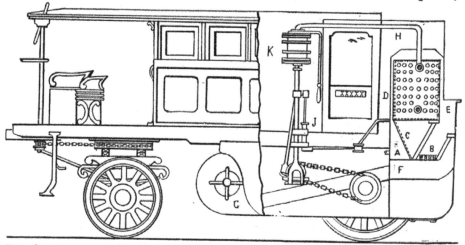

FIG. 8.—Part section of one of Hancock's Coaches, showing Engine and Driving Connections. A is the exhaust pipe leading steam against the screen, C, thence up the flue, D, along with smoke and gases from the grate. B. E is the boiler; H the out-take pipe; K the engine cylinder and, J, the water-feed pump; G is a rotary fan for producing a forced draught, and F the flue leading it to the grate.

the two halves were securely riveted together through the flanged edge. The faces of each plate carried regularly disposed hemispherical cavities or bosses, which were in contact when the plates were laid together, thus preserving the distances between them and allowing space for the gases of combustion to pass over an extended heating surface. The high quality of this style of generator may be understood when we learn that, with eleven such chambers or "water bags," 30 x 20 inches x 2 inches in thickness and 89 square feet of heating surface to 6 square feet of grate, one effective horse-power to every five square feet was realized, which gives us about eighteen effective horse-power for a generator occupying about 11.1 cubic feet of space, or 30 x 20 x 32 inches.

The operation of the Hancock boiler is interesting. The most approved construction was to place the grate slightly to the rear of the boiler's centre, and the fuel, coke, was burnt under forced draught from a rotary fan. The exhaust steam was forced into the space below the boiler, where a good part of it, passing through a finely perforated screen, was transformed into water gas, greatly to the benefit of perfect combustion.

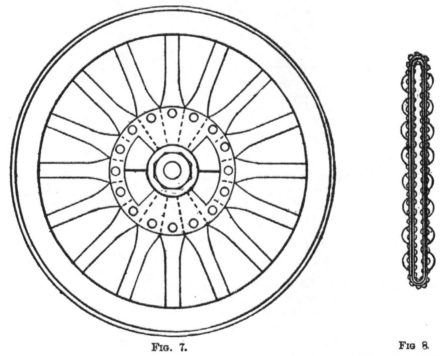

FIG. 7.   FIG 8.

FIG. 7.—Hancock's Wedge Drive Wheel, showing wedge spokes and triangular driving lugs at the nave.
FIG. 8.—One element of the Hancock Boiler, end view.

As early as 1830 Hancock devised the "wedge" wheels, since so widely adopted as models of construction. As shown in the accompanying diagram, his spokes were formed, each with a blunt wedge at its end, tapering on two radii from the nave of the wheel; so that, when laid together, the shape of the complete wheel was found. The blunt ends of these juxtaposed wedges rested upon the periphery of the axle box, which carried a flange, or vertical disc, forged in one piece with it, so as to rest on the inside face of the wheel. This flange was pierced at intervals to hold bolts, each penetrating one of the spokes, and forming the "hub" with a plate of corresponding diameter nutted upon the outer face of the wheel. The through axle shaft, formed in one piece and rotatable, carried secured to its extremities, when the wheel was set in place, two triangular lugs, oppositely disposed and formed on radii from the nave. The outer hub-plate carried

FIG. 9.—Church's Three-wheel Coach (1833), drawn from an old woodcut, showing forward spring wheel mounted on the steering pivot.

similarly shaped and disposed lugs, and the driving was effected by the former pair, turning with the axle spindle, engaging the latter pair, thus combining the advantages of a loose-turning wheel and a rotating axle. Through nearly half of a revolution also the wheel was free to act as a pivot in turning the wagon, thus obtaining the same effect as with Gurney's arm and pin drive wheels. The prime advantage, however, was that the torsional strain was evenly distributed through the entire structure by virtue of the contact of the spoke extremities.

Other Notable Coaches.—According to several authorities, only Gurney, Hancock and J. Scott Russell built coaches that saw even short service as paying passenger conveyances—one of the latter's coaches was operated occasionally until about 1857. There were, however, numerous attempts and experimental structures, all more or less successful, which deserve passing mention as embodying some one or another feature that has become a permanence in motor road carriages or devices suggestive of such features. A coach built by a man named James, about 1829, was the first on record to embody a really mechanical device for al-

Fig. 10.—James' Coach (1829), the "first really practical steam carriage built." Drawn from an old wood cut.

lowing differential action of the rear, or driving, wheels. Instead of driving on but one wheel, as did Gurney, or using clutches, like some others, he used separate axles and four cylinders, two for each wheel, thus permitting them to be driven at different speeds. This one feature entitles his coach to description as the "first really practical steam carriage built." Most of the others, if the extant details are at all correct, must have been, except on straight roads, exceedingly unsatisfactory machines at best. According to the best information on the subject, a certain Hills, of Deptford, was the first to design and use on a carriage, in 1843, the compensating balance gear, or "jack in the box," as it was then called, which has since come into universal use on motor vehicles of all descriptions. As for rubber tires, although a certain Thompson is credited with devising some sort of inflatable device of this description about 1840-45, there seems to have been little done in the way of providing a springy, or resilient, support for the wheels. We have, however, some suggestion of an attempt at spring wheels on Church's coach, which was built in 1833. According to an article in the *Mechanics' Magazine* for January, 1834, which gives the view of this conveyance, as shown in Fig. 9, "The spokes of the wheels are so constructed as to operate like springs to the whole machine—that is, to give and take according to the inequalities of the road." In other respects the vehicle seems to have been fully up to the times, but, judging from its size and passenger capacity, as shown in the cut, it is reasonable to suppose that the use of spring wheels was no superfluous ornamentation. If we may judge further from the cut, the wheels had very broad tires, thus furnishing another element in the direction of easy riding on rough roads.

CHAPTER TWO.

THE MAKE-UP OF A MOTOR CARRIAGE.

Modern Motor Vehicles.—Like other achievements of modern science and industry, motor road vehicles represent long series of brilliant inventions and improvements in several directions. As now constructed they are of three varieties, according to the motive power employed: those propelled by steam, those propelled by explosive engines, using gasoline or some other spirit, those propelled by electric motors. Considerable has been done in the direction of producing efficient compressed air motors, which have been applied to the propulsion of heavy trucks and street railway cars, but for ordinary carriage service small results have thus far been attained. Some inventors have expended their energies in other directions, and several patents have been granted in the United States for coiled spring and clockwork motors, and even for carriages carrying masts and sails. We are not concerned, however, with such eccentric devices, the aim of this book being merely the discussion and explanation of successful, practical devices actually used in the construction and operation of motor carriages.

Conditions of Automobile Construction.—In one way the automobile has a history very like that of the railway carriage. At first both were devised as suitable substitutes for the horse-drawn vehicle, and, as a consequence, began by following certain traditions of construction, which have proved very like hindrances to progress. The first railway passenger coaches were ordinary road wagons, several of which were coupled together, so as to be drawn along a grooved tramway. Later, with the introduction of flanged wheels and heavier constructions, several carriage bodies were mounted on one running truck, which gave the familiar compartment coaches with *vis-a-vis* seats, still used in

England and most of the countries of Continental Europe. Only when the theory of railway car construction departed entirely from the models and traditions of road wagons in the adoption of the American passenger coach, did the day of real progress and comfortable travel begin. In similar fashion many of the greatest constructional problems of automobiles may be most readily solved, both for the designer and the operator, in recognizing the fact that they resemble horse carriages in no other respect than that both have similarly appearing bodies, mounted on four-wheel frames, and run on ordinary highways.

Essential Elements of an Automobile.—While in this age of the world it is impossible to assert that any device is perfected, or that any has reached a finality, it is admissible to assume, for practical purposes, that recognized standards of construction are permanent. Undoubtedly, the automobile of the future will possess many features now unsuspected, but it is with the automobile of to-day that we have to do. We will take up the essential features in turn, therefore, describing their construction and explaining their uses. These may be summed, as follows:

1. The power developed by a motor carried on the running gear is applied to the rear wheels, or to a rotating shaft to which they are secured.

2. The two driven wheels must be so arranged as to rotate separately, or at different speeds, as in turning corners. For this reason, the compensation or balance gear is an essential element.

3. The two forward or steering wheels, studded to pivots at either end of a rigid axle-tree, must be arranged to assume different angles in the act of turning, in order that the steering may be positive and certain.

4. The body of the vehicle must be set relatively low, or the wheel-base, the length between forward and rear wheel-centres, must be relatively long, in order to obtain the best effects in traction, steering and safety.

5. The springs must be of such strength and flexibility as to neutralize vibration, absorb jars and compensate any unevenness in the roadway.

6. The distance between the motor and the driven wheels must be fixed by adjustable radius rods, or reaches, in order that the drive may not be interrupted by the vibrations of travel.

7. The wheels must be shod with pneumatic, or other forms of tires, of sufficient resiliency to protect the machinery, running gear and passengers from the jars, otherwise inevitable at high speeds on ordinary highways.

8. Positive and powerful brakes must be provided, in order to secure effective checking of motion, whenever required.

9. All parts must move with as little friction as possible, in order to save power for traction. For this reason, ball or roller bearings are generally used on all rotating shafts of motor carriages.

10. Convenient and efficient means for ready and generous lubrication of moving parts is a constant necessity.

11. Balance of parts and stable constructions are required to reduce wear and friction.

12. Simplicity of structure, ease of handling and repair. These are the prime requisites of the best automobile.

13. All working parts must be of sufficient size, weight and strength to endure the jars of travel, and to be serviceable under all conditions. There may be some advantages in the light con‑ structions, formerly supposed to be essential, but present-day practice recognizes the evident fact that strength and durability are the more important considerations.

CHAPTER THREE.

COMPENSATION AND COMPENSATING DEVICES.

Automobile Driving and Compensation.—The power of the motor is applied either to the centre-divided rotating rear axle, or to a rotating jack-shaft parallel to it, thence by chain and sprocket to the two wheels, turning loose on a dead rear axle. In both cases the drive is through a device known as the differential or compensating gear. Any device that will admit of a steady drive in straight-ahead running, a difference of speed in the two drive-wheels in turning corners, and a rapid restoration of normal conditions after the turn is completed, is usable for this purpose. There is, however, another necessary function, which may not be omitted,—the differential must also be a "balance gear." That is to say, it must combine with the function of compensation an even or balanced transmission of power to both wheels. Each wheel, so long as it is in motion, must be driven with the same degree of power. At no time, even on short turns when one wheel is stationary, acting as a pivot, is it permissible that, say two-thirds of the power, be sent to one drive-gear, and one-third to the other. The power, transmitted from the centre of the divided axle or jack-shaft, must always be the same in both directions, even though one wheel be stationary.

Compensation and Balancing.—For example, the device shown in Fig. 11 is an excellent specimen of a differential or compensating gear that is not also a balance gear. As may be seen, it consists of a large internal gear wheel, C, within which and rotating about the same axis is a smaller external gear or spur wheel, B,—the two engaging the spur pinions, A, A, as shown. The large internal gear turns on the axle of one wheel, the smaller or spur wheel on the opposite one, and power is applied through the pinions hung on radii of the sprocket. The result is that the power-driven pinions transmit more power to the internal gear, because of its greater diameter, than to the spur gear, thus giving one wheel a tendency to revolve more rapidly than the other. This device was formerly used on foot-propelled tricycles, and is perfectly suitable for a two-track machine of this description, in which the steering wheel is set directly ahead of one of the drivers, so as to progress on the same track.

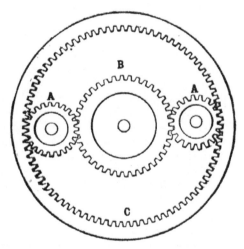

Fig. 11.—A form of Differential Gear formerly used on Tricycles. The studs of the pinions, AA, are set in spokes of the sprocket, turning on their own axes only when either of the wheels of the vehicle, attached respectively to B and C, cease rotating, as in the act of turning.

Automobile Balance Gears.—The most familiar form of balance gear for compensating the drive wheels of motor carriages is the bevel. This is the original form of the device, and was used on steam road wagons as early as 1843. As shown in figs. 12 and 13, the sprocket or drive wheel has secured to its inner rim several studs carrying bevel pinions, which, in turn, engage a bevel gear wheel on either side of the sprocket. These gear wheels, last mentioned, are rigidly attached on either side to the inner ends of the centre-divided axle-bar, one serving to turn the left wheel, the other the right. When power is applied to the sprocket, causing the vehicle to move straight forward, it may be readily understood that the bevel pinions, secured to the sprocket, instead of rotating, which would mean to turn the drive wheels in opposite directions, remain motionless, acting simply as a kind of lock or clutch to secure uniform and continuous rotation of both wheels. So soon as a movement to turn the vehicle is made, at which time the wheels tend to move with different speeds, the resistance of the wheel nearer the centre, on which the turn is made, tending to make it turn more slowly than the other, as anyone may readily observe, these pinions begin rotating on their own axes. Thus, while allowing the pivot wheel

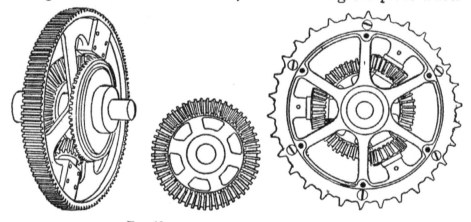

FIG. 12.   FIG. 13.

FIGS. 12 and 13.—Bevel Gear Differentials. The sprocket gear carries three bevel pinions set on studs on three of its radii. These pinions mesh with bevel wheels on either side, which wheels are attached at the two inner ends of the divided axle shaft. The spur drive has two pinions rotating on radii, and shows the action to better advantage.

to slow up or remain stationary, as conditions may require, they continue to urge forward the other at the usual speed. The principle involved in the device may be readily expressed under four heads:

1. When the resistance offered by the two drive wheels and attached gear is the same, as when the carriage is driven forward, the pinions cannot rotate.

2. When the resistance is greater on the one wheel than on the other, they will rotate correspondingly, although still moving forward with the wheel offering the lesser resistance.

3. The pinions may rotate independently on one gear wheel, while still acting as a clutch on the other, sufficient in power to carry it forward.

4. If a resistance be met of sufficient power to stop the rotation of both wheels and their axles, the condition would affect the entire mechanism, and the pinions would still remain stationary on their own axes, just as when in the act of transmitting an equal movement to both wheels.

For light carriage work the sprocket or spur drive generally carries two pinions, as shown in the figure, but in larger vehicles the number is increased to three, four, or six, and the size, pitch

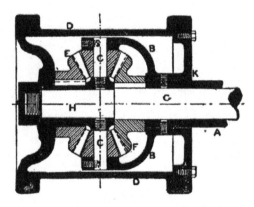

Fig. 14.—The Riker Hub Enclosed Differential. A is the rotating sleeve carrying the drive spur. It is bolted to the yoke carrier, B, and the flange piece, K, as shown. C and C are the studs of the bevel pinions attached to the yoke carrier, B. F is the bevel gear wheel keyed to the rotating through axle shaft, G, whose opposite end is rigidly attached to the other hub. The bevel gear, E, is keyed to the in-flanged portion of the hub. D, turning on the reduced portion, H, of the rotating axle shaft.

and number of the teeth are varied, according to requirements. Of course, it is essential that the equalizing gears be properly chosen for the work they are to perform, in the matter of the number of the pinions and of their teeth, as well as of the metal used, on account of the great strain brought to bear on them. With even the best made bevel-gears there is a danger of end thrust and a tendency to crowd the pinions against the collars, with consequently excessive wear on both. The result is a looseness that demands constant adjustment.

Spur Compensating Gears.—In order to avoid the difficulties encountered with bevel gears, spur-gears were invented, and are now increasing in popularity. In this variety the theory of compensation is the same as with bevel gearing; a divided axle or jack shaft whose two inner ends carry gear wheels cut to mesh with pinions attached to the sprocket pulley. These pinions are, however, set in geared pairs, with their axes at right angles to the radius of the sprocket, which is to say parallel to its axis. As ···ill be seen in the accompanying illustrations, the pinions of each

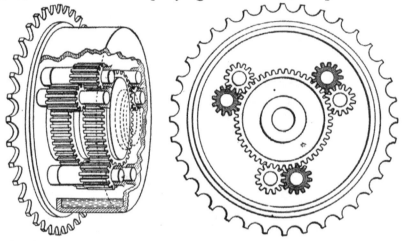

FIG. 15.—One form of Spur Differential or Balance Gear. The two inner ends of the divided axle shaft carry spur wheels, which mesh each with one of every pair of the three pairs of spur pinions shown. As these pinions mesh together both rotate on their axes as soon as turning of the wagon begins.

pair are set alternately on the one side or the other of the sprocket, meshing with one another in about half of their length, the remainder of each being left free to mesh with the axle spurs on the one or other side. The model here has three pairs of pinions, one of each meshing with either of the axle gears. With some differentials the divided axle carries internal gears, with others true spur-wheels. The operation is obvious. When the vehicle is turning, one rear wheel moves less rapidly, causing the pinion with which it is geared to revolve on its mate, which, in turn, revolves on its own axis, although still engaging the gear of the opposite and moving wheel of the vehicle. The motion is thus perfectly compensated, without the wear and thrust inevitable with bevels.

Disadvantages of a Divided Axle Shaft.—The practice of dividing the axle or jack shaft at the centre is a source of weakness which was recognized and provided against long since. Although, theoretically, the shaft is divided at the centre, the construction now usually adopted is to mount one wheel on the axle and the other on a hollow shaft or sleeve which works over it. The solid shaft can then be made as long as the width of the vehicle, the differential gear wheel belonging to it being secured about midway in its length. This hollow shaft or sleeve is about half as long, so that its gear is attached at its inner end and is immedi-

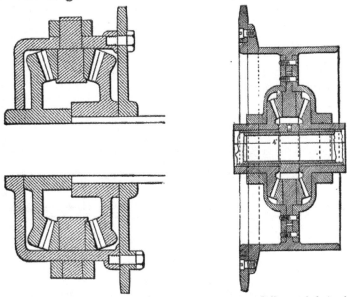

Fig. 16.—Section through the axis of a bevel gear differential train, showing two bevel pinions attached at top and bottom of the sprocket drum, and two bevel gear wheels one on the through axle shaft, the other on a rotating sleeve and through the axis of a bevel gear differential, showing two bevel gears keyed to rotating sleeves over an internal through axle or liner tube.

ately opposite the other, both meshing with the pinions attached to the sprocket. Such a construction involves no other variation from the method of attaching the differential gear-train to the ends of the divided axle than making the eyes of the two gear wheels of different diameters, so as to fit the axle shaft, on the one side, and the hollow axle, or sleeve, on the other. The sprocket is then inserted between them, being held in position by the meshing of the axle gears with the pinions, itself turning loose on the solid through shaft. The inner solid axle shaft **is** secured in position by suitable collars.

Through Axle Shaft and Liner Tube.—Another typical method for securing the strength and solidity of a through axle shaft is to attach both wheels to hollow axles of the same diameter, each of which carries on its opposite or inner end the gear wheel of the differential train. Another tube, called the "liner tube," of the same length as the width of the vehicle, is then inserted in the hollow axles, and the two are brought together so as to bear upon a collar secured to the centre of the liner tube. The sprocket and differential pinion train are inserted and held in place in a fashion similar to that used in the previous device, the inter-meshing of the bevels serving to support it.

With either of these arrangements it is customary to place the differential nearer one wheel.

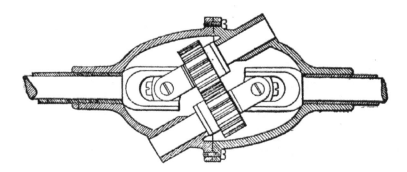

FIG. 17.—A Universal Joint Differential. The sprocket or spur drive turns the sleeve which holds the gear case here shown in section. So long as travel is straight ahead neither pinion rotates on its axis, but as soon as a turn is made rotation begins, thus allowing compensation of the motion of the two wheels of the wagon.

CHAPTER FOUR.

Types of Gear Connection.—In the transmission of power to the driven wheels several methods are followed in practice. These vary according to the size and weight of the vehicle and the character of the motor, also according to the individual preference of the designer. One system is to be preferred to another on account of real or supposed strength and reliability, or of its efficiency in economizing power. Thus it is that a certain system of transmission, declared by one builder fit only for light cars, is used by another on heavy ones, and the opposite is also the case.

At the present time, we may distinguish seven varieties of drives:

1. By chain and sprocket connection from the main shaft—in gasoline carriages, from the second shaft—direct to the differential on the rear axle.

2. By chain and sprocket to each rear wheel separately, from a transverse jack shaft, driven direct from the motor and carrying the differential drum.

3. By longitudinal propeller shaft from the motor to the rear axle, power being transmitted by bevel gears to the differential drum. This method of driving is usually followed between the motor shaft and the jack shaft in the type of transmission just described.

4. By spur gear connections from the motor shaft to the differential drum on the rear axle, as on a few gasoline carriages, some cycles and on nearly all electric vehicles.

5. By spur connection to an external or internal gear on each of the rear wheels from a transverse differential shaft, as in some electric vehicles.

6. By spur connection to an external or internal gear on each of the drive wheels, between each wheel and a separate motor, without using a differential device of any kind, used only on electric vehicles.

7. By using the hub of each wheel as one element of the motor; as in the so-called electric "hub motors," or in cycles where the motor is enclosed within the body of a suspended wire

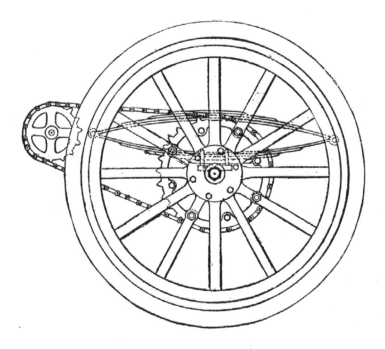

Fig. 18.—Single wheel of a type of car having double-chain drive from a jack-shaft parallel to the dead rear axle

wheel, as in a cage. A similar device has been tried for steam carriages, but without conspicuous success.

Direct drive by a crank on the drive wheel, axle or jack shaft, has been tried in recent times only on one or two bicycles, among them the Holden. The so-called "direct drive" claimed for some modern steam carriages, is really a spur drive; one spur carrying the crank pins of the engine, the other being hung on the differential axis.

Chain and Sprocket Drive.—A type having a chain and sprocket to drive each rear wheel separately is shown in figs. 19, 20. On some large vehicles of early design a single chain connection between the motor main shaft, or the transmission gear, and the differential sprocket on the rear axle, was frequently employed. However, it was early found entirely

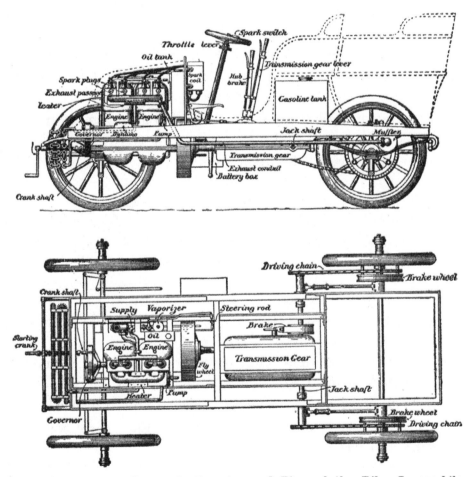

FIGS. 19, 20.—Part Sectional Elevation and Plan of the Riker Locomobile Chassis, showing arrangement of jack shaft, or countershaft, and double chain drive.

unsuitable for any except the lighter types of vehicle. With heavy cars of long wheel base, as at present constructed, it would be absurd.

Jack=Shaft and Separate Wheel Drive.—This construction is found on practically all heavy cars using chain drive. Briefly described, the system includes:

1. A transverse centre-divided jack-shaft driven direct from the motor, or through the transmission gear, by bevels to the differential drum.

2. A sprocket at each end of the jack-shaft for providing chain connection to the hub of each rear wheel.

3. Driven wheels turning loose at the ends of a dead axle-tree, as in a horse carriage, each being driven by a separate chain on a sprocket secured to its hub.

The advantages that may be found in this arrangement are:

1. The superior strength and rigidity of construction to be found in an undivided rigid rear axle.

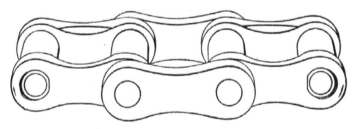

Fig. 21.—Section of a driving chain, showing arrangement of the rollers and side links.

2. The use of shorter chains, involving a greater immunity from ordinary chain troubles, and greater ease of adjustment.

3. Greater ease in removing and repairing the driven wheels.

4. Steadier and better-balanced driving, with a corresponding economy of power.

Troubles with Two=Chain Drive.—Formerly, the use of two chains was found to involve more noise and clatter than is found with one. However, with roller chains, now in nearly universal use on motor vehicles, this annoyance is greatly reduced. Much noise is caused with a loose chain by the jumping of links.

Driving Chains and Their Use.—Two varieties of sprocket driving chain are used on motor vehicles:

1. Roller chains.
2. Block chains.

Both have their advocates, who argue variously the advantages of superior strength or superior driving qualities and noiselessness.

The block chain is made of a series of blocks, properly shaped to fit the periphery of the sprocket, each joined to similar blocks before and after by side links bolted through the body of the block.

The roller chain is made of a series of pairs of rollers, known as centre blocks, similarly joined by side links. Each roller rotates loose on a hollow core, which is turned to smaller diameter at either end, to fit a perforated side piece joining the rollers into pairs. The side-links are set over these side pieces and bolted in place through the cores.

In operation, a block chain with generous slack is liable to meet the sprocket with a continual clapping that at high speed becomes a continuous rattle. The roller chain is largely immune from this trouble. Furthermore, being obviously easier in operation, it economizes power. Some authorities estimate its efficiency in driving as high as 98 per cent. under favorable conditions.

Strength of Driving Chains.—In point of strength a comparison between block and roller chains of the same sizes is interesting, as showing the insuperable superiority of the latter variety. The following tables are supplied by a prominent chain and gear manufacturer. For Diamond non-detachable B-block chains:

Pitch	Width	Breaking Load
1"	5/16, 3/8 or 1/2	1,600 lbs.
1"	5/16, 3/8 or 1/2	2,500 "
1½"	1/2	5,000 "

For three different makes of roller chains, the following figures are given:

Pitch	Width	Diameter of Roller	Breaking Load	
½″	⅛, 3⁄16, or ¼		1,200	lbs.
⅝″	⅛, 3⁄16, or ¼		1,400	"
¾″	5⁄16 or ⅜	15⁄32	4,000	"
15⁄16″	⅜ or ½	9⁄16	4,500	"
1″	⅜ or ½	9⁄16 or ⅝	5,000 or 5,500	"
1¼″	½ or ⅝	⅝ or ¾	5,500 to 7,500	"
1½″	⅝ or ¾	¾ to ⅞	12,000	"
1¾″	1	1	19,000	"
2″	1¼	1⅛	25,000	"

For the sizes of chain here specified, the breaking strength of the roller chain, or the average limit of its pulling power, is shown to be between ½ and ⅔ greater than that of the block chain.

Under ordinary conditions of use, the safe working load of a chain varies between 1-10 and 1-40 the tensile strength. This latter is generally very high. According to the statements of a prominent chain manufacturer:

"A ¾ inch pitch roller chain has sufficient strength to drive a six-ton truck a number of hours. The breaking of this chain will not occur until the pitch of chain and sprocket has elongated, or they become unlike; then the chain climbs the teeth, which act as wedges, exerting enormous strain, quickly wrecking the chain."

Operation of a Driving Chain.—The same authority explains that:

"The rivets of a chain act as a number of auxiliary shafts, and operate under friction in the same manner, but with less favorable conditions than the shaft that drives them. In order to adapt the chain to the load it must carry, he recommends larger sizes than are at present generally used, explaining that the limit of fatigue should approach closely the ultimate strength, and, with these factors attained, the size of chain should be selected which permits sufficient rivet wearing surface. This additional size and weight is objected to by automobile builders, on account of what they term 'clumsiness, weight and expense.' "

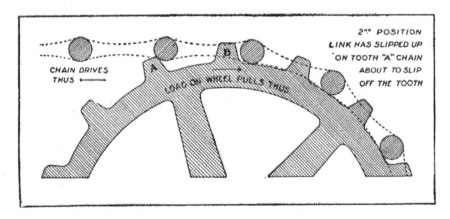

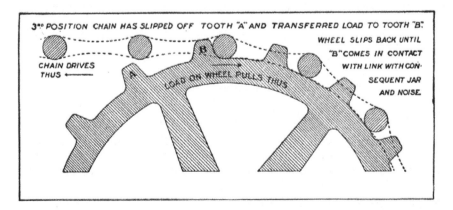

FIGS. 22, 23, 24.—Diagrams illustrating the operation of driving with a roller chain and sprocket.

Double Chain and Bevel Drives.—For commercial and high powered vehicles, there is much in favor of the chain drive, but for machines of light and medium power the propeller shaft and bevel gear is the more desirable.

The chief advantage of the chain drive is great strength with light weight. The rear axle being of the *dead* type is of simpler construction than the divided axle required for the bevel drive and it is perfectly adapted to support the car. Against this is the objectionable noise made by the chain, the difficulty of keeping it clean and lubricated, also the wear and stretching. The bevel drive being enclosed in a tight casing has the advantage of perfect lubrication, with all parts running in oil and freedom from dust. The quiet running of the bevel drive, more than offsets its disadvantages such as the necessary divided live axle with the heavy bracing required so that the imposed weight may not bend or spring it out of line. The popularity of the bevel drive is attested by its general adoption on all types of automobiles except the high powered racing cars and commercial trucks.

Proportions of the Sprocket.—In the design of a chain-transmission system, the proportions of the sprocket are important. According to reliable data:

"The thickness of the sprocket at pitch line should be from 1/32 to 1/16 inch less than the length of the roller, according to pitch of chain. Thickness of tooth on outside diameter should be ½ the length of roller."

The number of teeth is as important a consideration on a sprocket as on a gear wheel. In both cases twelve teeth form the average of good efficiency. This is explained in the following quotation:

"The most satisfactory results are obtained by the use of sprockets having twelve teeth or over. A smaller number may be used, but at a sacrifice of efficiency by elongation from wear of chain, wear of sprockets, and loss of power, experience demonstrates that eight-tooth sprockets are chain-wreckers and power-consumers. Nine teeth will give only fair results, and ten and eleven teeth can only be termed satisfactory when the speed is not high and the conditions of operation are unusually favorable."

Pitches of Chain and Sprocket.—It is impracticable to so design a driving sprocket that the chain rollers shall fit snugly between the teeth. The following quotation from an English authority explains the situation:

"A chain can never be in true pitch with its sprocket. A pair of spur gears tend—to a certain extent—to wear into a good running fit with each other, but a chain, if made to fit its sprocket when new, does not continue to do so a moment after being made, as wear at once throws it out. This being so, it must be put up with, and involves the consequence that a chain can only drive with one tooth at a time, supplemented by any frictional "bite" the other links may have on the base of the tooth interspaces. If the chain be made to fit these accurately, as in Fig. 25 (taking a roller chain in illustration), it is obvious that the least stretch will cause the rollers AA to begin to ride on the teeth as at BB. If, however, the teeth be made narrow compared with the spaces between the rollers, a considerable stretch may occur without this taking place. The roller interspaces, then, should be long, to permit the teeth to have some play in them, while retaining sufficient strength, as shown in Fig. 25 at B.

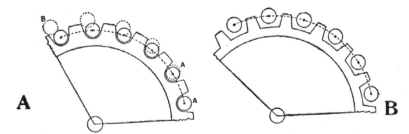

Fig. 25.—Diagrams showing the behavior of a chain on a sprocket of equal pitch, and on one of properly unequal pitch.

"In order that the driving sprocket may receive each incoming link of the chain without its having to slide up the tooth-face, it should be of a somewhat longer pitch than its chain, the result being that the bottom tooth takes the drive, this being permitted by the tooth-play shown in Fig. B. This difference, of course, gradually disappears as the chain stretches. The back wheel sprocket, on the other hand, should take the drive with its topmost tooth, and hence should be of slightly less pitch than the chain, but as the pitch of the latter constantly increases, it may be originally of the same pitch. The only remaining point with regard to design, and one which the owner of a car may easily ensure, is that the number of teeth in the sprockets should be prime to that of the links in the chain.

Even with the best designed sprocket, as each tooth in turn passes out of engagement with the chain, the next roller must be drawn forward through an appreciable distance before engaging a tooth. This causes the snap and rattle, always noticeable in chain-driven vehicles, and is an important factor in waste of driving power. To remedy such defects some have suggested the use of the self-adjusting silent gear chain, so successfully used in other branches of mechanical science. The difficulty here, however, is that such chains must be drawn tighter than those generally used on sprockets, and, unless thoroughly encased, are liable on an automobile to gather dust and grit, which greatly reduce their durability.

Care of Chains.—The principal points to be observed in the use and care of sprocket driving chains are:

1. To maintain the proper tension in order to avoid whipping—which is liable to result in snapping of the chain, particularly a long one—and, at best, involves a loss of driving efficiency. The chain should not be drawn tight, lest a similar disaster result. Some slack must always be allowed.

2. The two sprockets should always be kept in perfect alignment. In the case of double-chain drive from a counter-shaft parallel to the rear axle, care should be exercised to maintain the parallelism, even preferring a somewhat loose chain to a tight one that strains the counter-shaft.

3. If a link shows signs of elongation it should be replaced by a new one at once.

4. Whenever the chain is removed for cleaning or other purpose, it should be carefully replaced, so as to run *in the same direction,* as formerly, and with the same side up. Never turn the chain around or reverse its direction between the sprockets.

5. A new chain should not be put upon a much-worn sprocket.

6. A conspicuous difficulty involved in the use of driving chains is the liability to clog and grind with sand, dust and other abradents. A chain should be occasionally cleaned, therefore, and, what is more important, should be carefully rubbed with graphite preparation, which is the best lubricant for the purpose,

and fills the chinks otherwise open to receive dirt. Furthermore, it prevents dust from adhering to the surface of the chain.

7. After steady use for a more or less extended period, the chain should be removed and thoroughly cleaned. The most approved method is as follows:

Cleaning the Drive Chain.—After removing the chain, cleanse first in boiling water, then in gasoline, in order to remove all grease and dirt whatever. Any break or defect may now be plainly discovered, and should be remedied by inserting new links for those disabled. The common practice is then to boil the chain for about half an hour in mutton tallow, which is thereby permitted to penetrate all chinks between rolling surfaces, forming an excellent inside lubricant. After boiling, the chain is hung up until thoroughly cool, at which time the tallow is hardened. It may then be wiped off clean and treated with a preparation of graphite, or a graphite-alcohol solution on its inner surface.

Some authorities recommend that the chain, after it is cleaned, should be soaked, first, in melted paraffin for an hour at least, and then in a mixture of melted mutton tallow and graphite. After each soaking, it is dried and wiped clean.

With either process, a daily application of graphite chain preparation is most desirable.

Looseness of Chains.—On the point of chain adjustment, the authority quoted above writes as follows:

"Shedding of chains is generally brought about either by excessive looseness or want of alignment between the sprockets and back chain wheels; a sufficient transverse rounding of the tips of the teeth is advisable to diminish the chance of it. A shrowding or flange on each side of the teeth for the side plates of the chain to bear on is certainly desirable, as diminishing the wear on the rollers and giving a certain increase of frictional drive; but it is not always provided. It may be here noted, as a reply to a question occasionally asked by untechnical drivers, that *where there is a differential on the countershaft an inequality in the tightness of the chains does not prevent each of them taking its share of the driving;* and it is more important that the parallelism of the countershaft and back axles shall be maintained than that the chains should be kept equally tight at the sacrifice of this."

Propeller-Shaft Transmission.—Transmission of power by propeller shaft, through bevel gears, to the rear axle, has been adopted by a number of designers, and seems to be gaining favor. It would seem to be the logical outcome of the jack-shaft and double chain system already noticed, since the bevel drive is

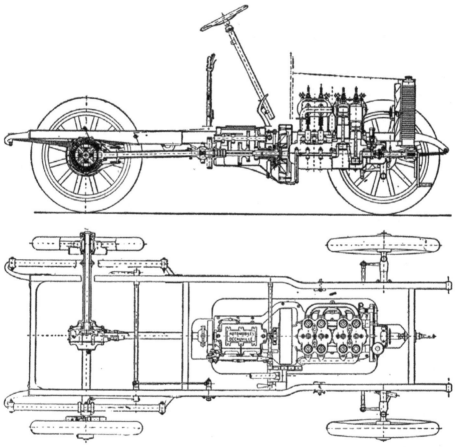

FIGS. 26, 27.—Part Sectional Elevation and Plan of the Decauville Car, showing general arrangement of a propeller shaft drive through bevel gears to the rear axle.

direct to the rear axle, instead of to the transverse jack-shaft. There are several problems and difficulties involved, however, that do not **appear** in other types of transmission.

1. There is naturally greater opportunity for end-thrusts on the rear axle than on a jack-shaft, with a commensurate wear on **the** parts and danger of breakage.

2. Although a universally jointed shaft connects the motor and the driving bevel, the maintaining of perfect steadiness is difficult and various lateral stresses, notably the tendency of the pinion to climb upward or downward over the teeth of the gear, according as the motion is straight ahead or reversed.

As a consequence of these conditions, ball bearings are provided to take the thrust of the large bevel gear on the axle-shaft.

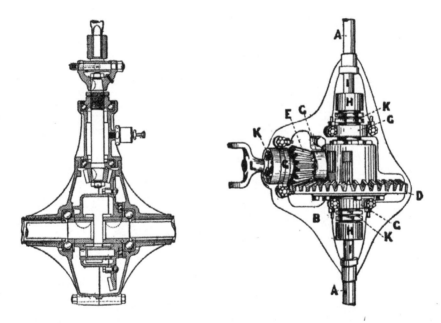

FIG. 28.—Sectional diagram of the bevel-drive of the Pierce Car, showing arrangement of the propeller shaft and location of the thrust bearings.

FIG. 29.—Bevel Driving Apparatus of the Peerless Car, A and B, sleeve and case for axles and gears; D, the driven gear; E, driving pinion; G, ball bearings on E; H, H, universal couplings on the differential; K, K, K, adjustments; L, yoke for flexible driving shaft.

A slip-joint, in addition to the universal coupling on the propeller-shaft, compensates for the varying distance between the speed gear and the axle, under the rise and fall of the springs. In the Packard, and one or two other cars, approximate steadiness of the driving pinion is attained by placing the speed gear directly in front of the rear axle.

The Haynes Propeller Drive.—The Haynes carriage embodies an interesting variation on the common types of bevel drive, having as the driven gear a kind of dished crown gear or sprocket, with teeth around the inturned edge, and, as the driving pinion a roller gear, in which a number of rollers, inclined inward from the periphery, serve instead of teeth. The rotary tendency of the differential case, under stress of the driving pinion, is avoided by the use of a vertical stay-bar projecting through a square yoke in a cross bar above the spring, which serves to direct the stress upward, thus removing all strain from

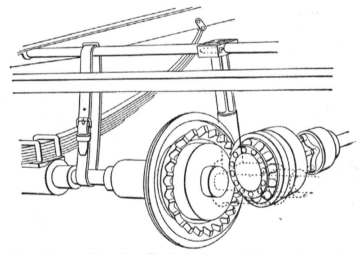

Fig. 30.—The Haynes-Propeller-Shaft Drive, which marks a decided improvement on common types of bevel drive.

the axle casing. Instead of the usual slip-joint, consisting of a sliding square-section shaft, a "four-pronged joint" is used. In this arrangement a flanged hub is keyed to the driving shaft, and carries four steel pins, which project forward, entering four holes in the body of the universal joint. Thus the torque exerts no torsional stress other than a shearing force upon the pins, which has been proved of no serious importance. The advantages claimed for this device are:

1. Superior strength, as found in the comparison between the long, narrow teeth of a bevel gear and the short, thick teeth of the Haynes sprocket.

2. Elimination of thrust, in the fact that two rollers are always in full engagement with the sprocket, one always entering a hollow as another passes out of engagement.

3. Silent operation, by combining the advantages of bevel and roller chain drive, while avoiding their inherent difficulties.

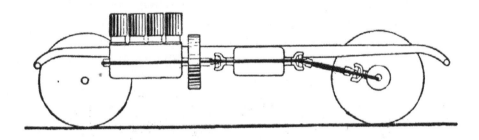

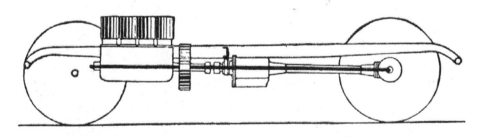

Fig. 31.—Diagrams to illustrate different constructions of shaft drive. The upper figure shows the ordinary construction in which the rear shaft length is at an angle with the engine shaft. The lower figure illustrates the "straight line drive" in which the several shaft lengths are placed in a straight line, thus eliminating friction and wear due to angularity at the universal joint.

The Straight Line Drive.—Several manufacturers of automobiles, of the shaft driven type, have incorporated in their designs what is known as the straight line drive. In this method of power transmission, the parts which make up the driving shaft are all placed in a straight line as shown in the lower diagram of fig. 31. Another construction of shaft drive is illustrated in the upper diagram in which the final length of the shafting is placed at an angle with the other portions. This necessitates a universal joint with more or less friction and wear depending upon the degree of angularity of the two shaft sections. In the figure, the inclination of the rear section is somewhat exaggerated to emphasize the difference in construction.

On account of the action of the supporting springs, a universal joint is necessary as the shaft sections are not in line when the car is light. The construction is such that when the car is loaded, the propeller shaft is in direct line with the crank shaft. Under these conditions the drive is accomplished in a direct line which assures the delivery of the maximum possible power to the rear axle.

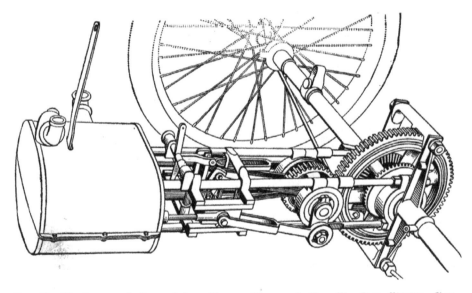

Fɪɢ. 32.—Engine and Spur-drive Connections of the Stanley Steam Carriage. The engine is "direct-connected," driving the differential through a spur gear. A vertical strut suspends the engine from the body of the carriage.

Spur Gear Transmissions.—Transmission of power by spur gears is in very many respects the best method of all. The drive between spurs is steadier, and is attended by smaller loss of power than between bevels. It is impracticable, however, in connection with designs including a main shaft set in the length of the frame, bevels being necessary to change the direction of motion from longitudinal to transverse rotating shafts.

THE DRIVING GEAR.

Spur gear transmission is used on the Stanley car as shown in fig. 32. The engine is placed horizontally in such a position that the steel gear on the crank shaft of the engine engages the main gear of the differential, thus forming a direct power transmission.

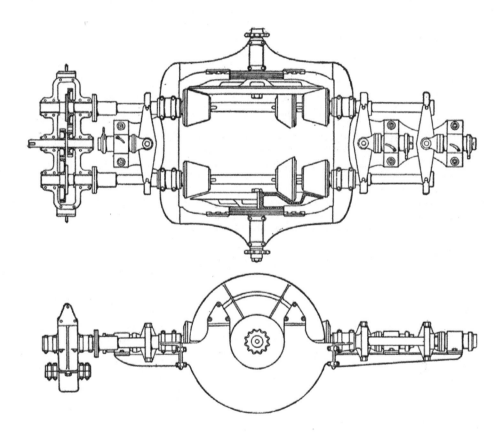

FIG. 33.—Friction drive of the Pittsburg Truck. Power is transmitted by leather fiber cones coming into contact with a bevel cast iron wheel. The front cone gives the reverse motion to the truck, the intermediate cone the high speed, and the rear cone the slow speed.

Although with well-designed spurs over 90 per cent. of the delivered power of the engine may be actually transmitted to the driven shaft, the spur drive will admit of practically no interruption of full engagement between the teeth by thrusts or vibration. Virtually the entire efficiency of the combination depends on maintaining the engagement at the pitch line. If spurs are to be used on automobiles, therefore, it follows that the driven shaft must be above the springs, or the driving shaft below them. The latter alternative is realized in electric vehicles, but the former depends upon some such arrangement of jointed axles or shafts as are embodied on the De Dion or Thornycroft wagons. The famous De Dion rear axle has the section of the shaft carrying the differential hung above the springs, and connected to the road wheels by universal slip-joints, as shown in the figure. The Thornycroft wagon has a similar slip-joint arrangement on a counter-shaft, arranged to afford a steady drive from the engine above the springs to the driving spur in mesh

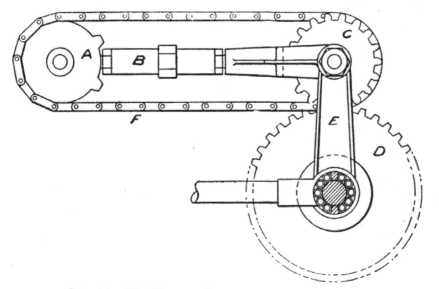

Fig. 34.—The Haynes Spur-gear Transmission.

with the driven spur on the axle sleeve. Such devices are essential, in order to maintain a steady drive between the meshing spurs in spite of the rise and fall of the springs.

Haynes Spur Transmission.—A device formerly used on Haynes carriages accomplishes the end of an uninterrupted spur drive with nearly the same efficiency as the Thornycroft. As shown in the figure, A is the sprocket fixed at one end of the counter-shaft; B, a turnbuckle on the adjustable distance rod between the first counter-shaft and the second counter-shaft carrying the pinion, C; C, a spur pinion keyed to the second counter-shaft, carrying a sprocket driven by a chain from A; D, a spur gear on the rear axle meshing with spur pinion, C, on the second counter-shaft; E, a rigid distance rod for maintaining fixed relations between the spurs, C and D. The advantages of this system are the maintaining of a steady drive without the usual wear and tear on the moving parts consequent on sprocket connections direct from the first counter-shaft, or from the main shaft of the motor. The movements of the distance rod, also, throws no strain upon the springs, as in many other forms of transmission.

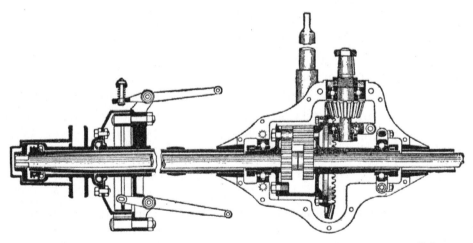

FIG. 35.—The Pierce-Racine rear axle construction. Four point ball bearings are employed throughout as shown in the illustration. The bevel pinion shaft has an inside ball bearing. The bevel gear housing is a steel casting below, with an aluminum casting cover. The lower gear casing member has full circle ends, fixed to the steel axle casings by riveting and keying.

CHAPTER FIVE.

THE STEERING OF A MOTOR VEHICLE.

Steering Gear of Automobiles.—In a horse-drawn vehicle the front axle shaft is centre-pivoted below the body of the carriage and in turning bears on the "fifth wheel." Such an arrangement is the most practical for this class of vehicle, since the tractive power, the horse, can pull in any direction without the use of further appliances than the guiding lines or reins. In motor vehicles, since the motive power is applied to the rear wheels, literally pushing the structure from behind, it is necessary to provide mechanical means for shifting the direction of the forward or steering wheels. The forward axle shaft is rigidly secured across the body of the vehicle, and has no movement whatever. At each end it carries a fork, or yoke, to which is bolted generally at right angles to the axle shaft, so as to form a true knuckle-joint, a boss carrying two branches, one of them conical shape, to fit the axle box of the wheel, which is suitably secured, as in horse-drawn vehicles, so as to rotate freely; the other being an arm, shaped for attaching the transverse steering link bar. This link bar is generally arranged to connect the steering arms of both stud axles on the through axle shaft, the connections for the control handle or wheel, placed conveniently to the driver's hand, varying with different designers.

Pivoted axles, commonly known as Ackerman axles, furnish the readiest and simplest means for steering motor vehicles, at the same time permitting maintenance of stability. The transverse steering link bar attached to an arm at either end is readily manipulated by the driver, and with but small exertion, since the pivots, attached direct to the axles of the wheels, permit a wide angle of variation in the vehicle's direction of travel for a very slight shifting of the steering wheel or handle. The balance of leverage being also in the driver's favor, it is possible to turn the vehicle in any desired direction quickly and with ease.

The Theory of Steering Axles.—The best effect of pivoted steering axles depends upon fixing the steering pivot as near as possible to the centre of the road wheel, in order to enable the greatest arc of operation for the smallest motion of the hand. In this respect the steer wheel of a bicycle is typical, and some light automobiles having the wheels similarly mounted on forks have been notable for easy and efficient operation. But, since this construction is not suitable for heavy carriages, designers have busied themselves devising other methods for accomplishing the same result.

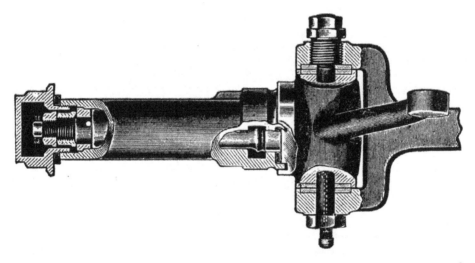

Fig. 36.—A Type of Stud Steering Axle, showing steering arm and pivot and plain bearing axle and box.

1. One of these is to incline the stud axle downward at such an angle as will cause the tire, or periphery, of the wheel to strike the ground at a point coincident with a line drawn through the knuckle pivot. As an additional advantage for this construction, it is claimed that the force of a collision is delivered at or about this line of incidence, rather than on the hub or its axle connection, thus ensuring greater security, and saving the driver a shock.

2. Another device is to incline the pivot axis inward, leaving the axle horizontal, or nearly so, with the result that, as in the

previous case, a line drawn through the pivot strikes the ground at the same point with the periphery of the wheel which is itself in a vertical position.

3. Some such arrangements as the Haynes double yoke pivot may be used with good effect. In this device one yoke is of a piece with the through axle shaft, the other pivot-bolted at each extremity within the first, and carrying the axle spindle at its centre. By this means the centre of the steering pivot may be brought to the theoretically correct position with a much smaller rake of the road wheel than is involved in the first device mentioned.

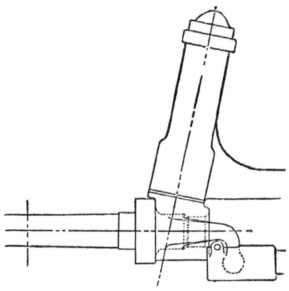

Fig. 37.—Duryea's Inwardly Inclined Steering Pivot. The lines passing through the pivot and across the axle converge to the point of contact of the tire with the ground, thus securing the effect of centre steering.

4. Several attempts have been made to place the steering pivot precisely at the theoretically correct point by use of a hollow steering hub enclosing the pivot. Of these the Riker hub is the best known. In its construction a hollow steel cylinder is penetrated by the end of the transverse axle-tree and pivot bolted to it, so as to be turned in either direction by the steering arm, *H,* fixed at its inner end. Over this cylinder the wheel hub, also hollow, is slid and turns upon it on two trains of ball bearings.

The Clubbe and Southey Hub, Fig. 40, operates on a simpler plan. The fork, or yoke, on the through axle shaft is slightly bent forward at the end, so that a pivot bolt through the eyes pierces a boss attached tangent-wise to a short tubular axle bearing, in which the stud axle, carrying the wheel, revolves freely. The hub is hollow and hemispherical, so as to contain the whole mechanism of the pivot joint, which is slightly forward of the centre, giving a caster action to the wheel in turning. The advantage presumably attained in this caster action is a freer and easier shifting of direction with a given effort at the steering wheel or lever.

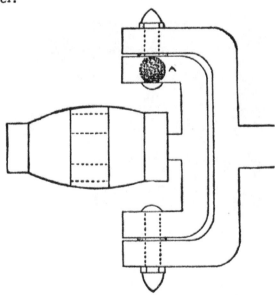

Fig. 38.—The Haynes-Apperson Double Yoke Steering Pivot Axle. The steering arm is attached at A, thus securing the turning effect at approximately the centre of the wheel hub.

The Arc of Steering.—To achieve the end of positive and reliable steering effect, it is necessary that the steer wheels describe concentric arcs in making a turn, with their axle bosses on radii from a common centre, differing in length as the width of the vehicle. This involves that each stud axle inclines from the straight-ahead travel line at an angle different from that of the other. The arcs described by the wheels in turning must be concentric, in order to insure continued travel in the desired direction, without side-slip or harmful resistance, such as must otherwise result. The two wheels, having the same diameter, no matter how much their relative speeds may differ, will by any other arrangement fail to run in the same curved direction.

Turning Arc in Railroad Wheels.—The same principle is applied in railroad cars and locomotives in a manner impracticable with motor carriages. Here, although the wheels are always rigidly attached in pairs at either extremity of rotating through axles, and in fours to the trucks, composed of two parallel through rotating axles with their attached wheels, the differing concentric arcs described by the two rails of the track in round-

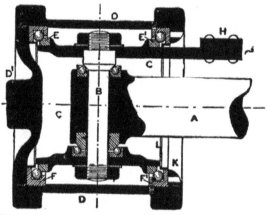

Fig. 39.—Riker's Pivoted Steering Hub. A is the axle shaft; B, the pivot connecting A to the tubular swinging hub, C. E and E' are annular cones which bear on the balls mounted in the ball races, F and F', thus permitting the hub D to rotate independently on the inner tube, C. The steering arm, H, attached to C turns both C and D on the pivot, B.

ing a curve are followed. To accomplish the desired end, railroad car wheels are made with a cone-shaped tread—a double cone, in fact—the base being against the flange of the wheel. In turning a curve, then, the outer wheel, impelled by centrifugal force, rotates on its largest diameter, while the inner wheel, from the same cause, rotates on its smallest. The effect approximated is that of an elongated cone whose point is at the centre of the arc of turning, and its base on the periphery. Thus is approximated the theoretical requirement that the two wheels on an axle should be of different diameters in making a curve. Since, however, the diameters of motor carriage wheels may not be varied by this or any other means, it is obvious that the only other available device is such a variation of the steering angles as has already been mentioned.

The Steering Wheels.—When a carriage's travel is changed from the straight-ahead direction to a curve, the steering wheel moving on the in-track, or smaller arc, must assume a greater angle at the axle than the outer wheel, which moves on the larger of the two concentric arcs. It is evident, moreover, that such variation of axial angles must be accomplished by some device at

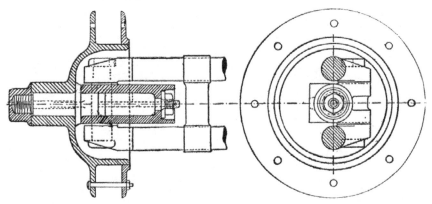

FIG. 40.—The Clubbe and Southey Pivoted Steering Hub. As may be seen, the pivot is to one side of the axle, thus giving the wheel a true caster movement in turning. See Page 45.

the steering arms of the stud axles. If these steering arms be fixed at right angles to the axles, so that the transverse drag-link is of a length theoretically identical with the distance between the wheel treads, any effort to turn the wheels in steering will shift the angles of both arms with the fixed axle-tree equally, hence, causing the axles to assume positions as radii from different centres. The result will be that the outer wheel will describe an arc tending to cross those described by all the other wheels, and may slide or rub, without revolving, as much as one foot in every six. Such a procedure must, of course, retard the progress of the vehicle very seriously, and, from the uncertainty of steering involved, must be particularly troublesome, even dangerous, on narrow turns. It is evident in this case that the outer wheel axle is at too great an angle, or that the inner is at too small an angle.

Steering Constructions.—The simplest method of at once obviating this trouble and also securing the proper angles of the axles is to incline the two steering arms inward from the right angle and make the transverse drag-link shorter than the distance between the axle pivots. If the drag-link be in front of the axletree, the steering arms are inclined outward, making the draglink longer than the distance between axle pivots.

With this arrangement, as may be readily understood, any effort to change the direction of the travel will cause the arm of the outer wheel to approach the right angle with the transverse through axle bar, and cause the arm of the inner wheel to move proportionately away from the right angle. Moreover, since the

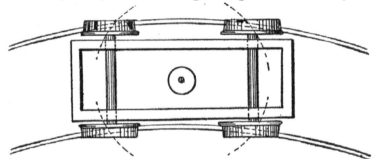

FIG. 41.—Position of the Wheels of a Railroad Car on the Rails in Turning a Curve, showing how the outer and inner wheels turn on different diameters, thus compensating the parallel arcs of travel.

end of the transverse drag-link attached to this inner axle-arm must, in the act of thus widening the angle, be approached nearer and nearer to the immovable through axle bar, it must describe an arc, thus passing through a greater number of degrees than will the opposite or outer end. Consequently, the object of securing a greater angular inclination for the axle of the inner wheel will be accomplished and the proper difference for all usual conditions between the angles of the two approximated. That is, although it generally happens that the angular inclination of the steering arms works best on curves of radii midway between the extremely long and extremely short, it has been found that the difference is not sufficiently great to disturb the parallelism of the described arcs or cause damaging slips or skidding of the rear wheels.

The Steering Angle.—Generally, the steering angle of a motor carriage, which is to say the sum of the inclinations of the two steering arms from the right angle, is between fifty and sixty degrees; giving an inclination for each arm of between twenty-five and thirty degrees. Some of the best makes of carriage have it at or about twenty-five degrees for each arm. As shown in the

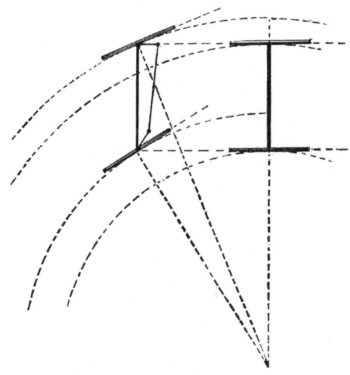

FIG. 42.—Diagram illustrating the Position of the Steering Wheels of a Motor Carriage in Turning. As will be seen, they both are tangential to arcs described on a common centre, as is necessary in order to describe such concentric arcs and give positive steering, when the motive impulse is from behind.

accompanying diagrams, however, various designers have modified the typical arrangement of inclining the steering arms inward and using a drag-link to connect them by such devices as:

1. Placing the arms at right angles and using a link in two sections connected to a fork or bell crank having the total required angle, fifty or sixty degrees, and pivoted at the centre of the fixed axle bar.

2. By dividing the angle betwen the centre-pivoted bell crank and the steering arms, making the former, say thirty degrees and the two latter fifteen degrees each.

The primary object achieved in either of these devices is to ensure the end of ready manipulation of the steering lever. The first-named construction is the one best suited to carriages having the steering pivot in the theoretically correct place—within

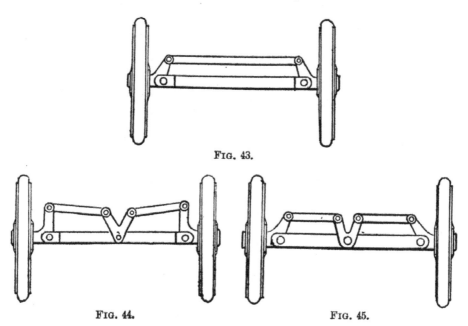

FIG. 43.

FIG. 44.   FIG. 45.

FIGS. 43, 44 and 45.—Top View of Motor Carriage Forward Axles, showing three arrangements of link bars and steering arms. In the first the steering arms are inclined inward at the required angle and connected across the carriage width by a single link. In the second the steering arms are fixed at right angles to the axle-tree, and the angle of inclination is made at a centre pivoted bell crank. In the third the angle of inclination is divided between the steering arms and the central bell crank. Theoretically, the sum of the angles in the third figure is equal to that in the first, and to the angle of the bell crank in the second.

the hub. When for structural reasons the transverse drag-link bar is placed in front of the axle-tree, a position preferred by several manufacturers, the steering arms attached to the bosses of the swinging axles are inclined outward, instead of inward, at the angles found most suitable with reference to the width of the vehicle between the wheel pivots and to the diameter of the wheels.

The construction adopted by some designers of inclining the axle stud inward, as already described, achieves, not only the very desirable end of centre-steering, but also allows a certain inclination, or rake to the steering wheels, as in a bicycle, when making a turn. The rake is a positive advantage to ready steering qualities, when the inclination of the axle pivot is not at so great an angle as to bring unusual side strain on the wheels. Other things being equally favorable, it is also efficient in reducing the steering effort.

The Center of Gravity and the Wheel-base.—There are several questions intimately associated with the problem of correct steering angles. Among these are considerations on the most reliable means for avoiding skidding or side-slip of both rear and front wheels, and on constructions best adapted to maintain balance of the vehicle in making short turns. The progress of motor carriage design in recent years has established the principle that a low center of gravity is a necessity in high-speed cars, in order to avoid the tendency to overturn at a sharp inclination of the steering wheels. The adjustment of the center of gravity has resulted progressively in two tendencies, now prevalent—the long wheel-base and the short clearance between the bottom of the car and the ground. Both conduce to comfortable riding and immunity from overturning. Side-slipping is also avoided in large measure. With very long cars, however, difficulty is experienced in turning sharp corners, or in steering on any but easy curves, except with a very narrow front. These matters will be explained in place.

Skidding.—The term, "skidding," or side-slipping, as generally applied in motor car practice, describes the occasional tendency of the rear wheels to slide sideways to the direction of travel. The result may be disastrous, as well as annoying, since, in the event of colliding with a large or immovable obstacle the wheel may be broken in pieces, or, unless the center of gravity is low, the vehicle will be overturned. The same term is also applied to a similar behavior in the front wheels.

According to authorities, the immediate occasion of side-slip is found in the fact that under certain conditions a wheel revolves more rapidly than it progresses, or progresses more rapidly than it revolves. In either case it slides over the road surface, which does not present sufficient adhesion to promote traction,

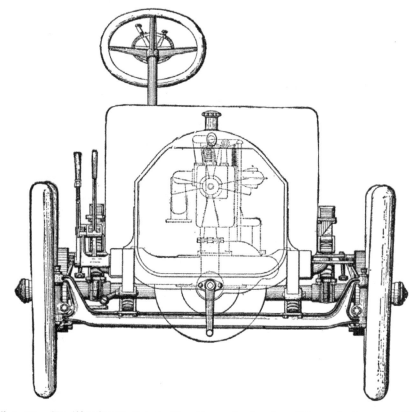

FIG. 46.—To illustrate the inclination of wheels. The cut shows a Matheson car having the front wheels inclined three degrees to balance the "dishing" of the spokes and bring the lowest spoke into a vertical position.

or the balance of rotation and progression. Particularly when the tread of the tire is flattened at contact with the ground, as usually happens with pneumatics, the loss of adhesion results in such a resolution of the propelling power or momentum of the vehicle as will allow of motion in lateral directions, as well as straight ahead.

Skidding occurs under several conditions:

1. When the brake is suddenly thrown in.

2. When the clutch is suddenly thrown in or out.

3. When the steering gear is given a sudden or sharp inclination.

As may be readily understood, either of the former events tend to interrupt the balance of progress and rotation—hence cause skidding. However, the most familiar cause is found in the third instance. Any inclination of the steering wheels produces a side pressure on all the wheels, but a short turn is particularly liable to result in side-slip, from the fact that the propelling power and momentum continue to urge the vehicle forward, leaving a large part of the active energy unresolved into movement on the arc of turning. In such a case, also, as may be readily understood, either rotation or progression is the greater; thus adhesion between the wheel and the roadway is lost.

Protection Against Skidding.—Any device that will promote traction will lessen skidding. We find, therefore, that the most effective apparatus to this end are those that enable the tire, as it were, to bite into the road surface, rendering difficult sliding or slipping in any direction. Such are net-works of rope or chain, hob-nailed tire covers, and conical projections molded into the rubber of the tread. In addition to such surface precautions, there are important considerations in the design and balance of the vehicle structure. The proper location of the center of gravity is now recognized as of extreme importance, and, particularly in very long vehicles, also, the width of the steering apparatus. In former times, when designers were still discussing the proper position for the heaviest weights on the frame, an overloaded forward axle frequently left the rear wheels so lightly burdened as to allow the vehicle to turn end for end on a greasy asphalt street, or a slight inclination of the steering wheels. At present such a catastrophe should be impossible from this cause, on account of better distribution of the load and the use of long wheel-bases.

SELF-PROPELLED VEHICLES.

Duryea's Explanation.—Charles E. Duryea, a prominent American automobile authority, gives the following explanation of the matter:

" In some cases skidding is caused by unequal forces at the rear wheels. For example, if a brake is applied on one the other continues to force the vehicle forward and the vehicle tends to move around the slowest wheel. This may cause skidding of the front end, or it may start skidding at the rear end. If, for any reason, more power is applied to one rear wheel than to the other, the same result follows. If the brakes are suddenly applied while the vehicle is being turned, the wheels may start sliding and, once started, they slide sidewise as readily as any other direction, so that a little deviation in direction of the steering wheels may cause the vehicle to skid. It is readily seen that a change of direction brings the front wheels out of a position straight ahead and causes the rear end to swing sidewise just as an increased resistance on one front wheel would do. Longer wheel base lessens skidding by decreasing the angle between the lines through the centre, and to one of the forward wheels. The gain by increasing the length of the wheel base is not nearly so pronounced as that by narrowing the tread of the front wheels, and this construction is undoubtedly preferable. While rear wheels should be constructed to track with ordinary carriages, front wheels under most conditions should not, for if they track they are liable to refuse to come out of wet car tracks, are almost impossible to get out of deep ruts, and are therefore not so safe as where one or both, because of difference in tread, are kept out of the tracks or ruts. The only objection to front wheels not tracking is in sandy roads, where the depth of the rut will cause one front wheel or the other to skid into the rut, and thus swing the vehicle diagonally across the road in its attempt to move forward."

Analysis of the Diagram.—Mr. Duryea explains his contentions by the accompanying diagram:

"Suppose *aa* to represent the front wheels of a motor vehicle, *bb,* the rear wheels and *c* the centre of gravity. If either front wheel, *a* meets an obstacle throwing an increased resistance to motion on that wheel the mass of the vehicle, acting on the centre of gravity, *c,* together with the driving power on the rear wheels which, in effect, are pushing *c* straight forward, will tend to revolve the entire vehicle; that is to say, the centre of gravity *c* around *a,* because of the fact that a line through the centre of gravity *c* in the direction of motion passes considerably to the side of *a,* which gives rise to the attempt to revolve around *a.* Suppose, for argument, the front wheels to be placed at *dd,* it will readily be seen that any increased resistance on one front wheel tends to stop that corner of the vehicle, and both the inertia of the vehicle, and the push on the rear wheels, carry it forward and sidewise; or, in other words, cause it to skid. This effect is plain with the exaggerated position of the front wheels *dd,* and the same effect although less, exists with the front wheels *aa.* If, however, these wheels are brought close together, the closer the better, or if a single front wheel, *e,* is used, the tendency to skid is very much reduced. In this case a resistance against the front wheel is met directly by both the push of the driving wheels and the inertia of the vehicle and no tendency to skid results.

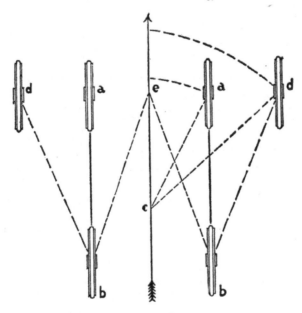

FIG. 47.—Diagram illustrating Duryea's explanation of the influence of the wheel-base on steering and side-slipping.

"Sometimes instead of the hind wheels, it is the front ones that skid, but the same causes act to produce this. For example, if the rear wheels, *bb,* refuse to slide, the increased resistance, such as snow, mud or sand on one front wheel, *d,* will tend to swing that corner of the vehicle sidewise out of its path, taking the other wheel, *d,* with it. This form of skidding is particularly found on roads that slope to one side, where one outer wheel gets in the gutter and slews the front end of the vehicle around. It is no less dangerous than the other, although less seldom found. The exaggerated diagram makes the effect plainly apparent and narrowing the wheels betters the results until they are brought together at a common centre.

"The farther to the rear the centre of gravity, *c,* is located, the less he angles and the greater the immunity from skidding."

The Long Wheel=Base and Steering.—Within the past few years the safety and comfort of passengers has been increasingly identified with the long wheel-base, which secures the desirable ends of a low center of gravity, steadier running and reduced danger of skidding, and is variously alleged to embody advantages in easier steering. That the latter claim holds good on long turns may possibly be true; that it is not the case on short ones is readily discovered. The following explanation from a popular authority serves very well to explain this point:

"When intricate manœuvring is required, and on rough roads generally, too long a wheelbase proves objectionable. In the first place it is found that a given angle of the wheels will not produce as great a change in

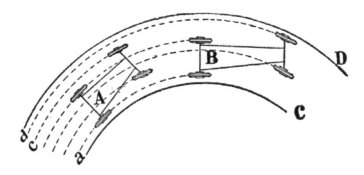

Fig. 48.—Diagram illustrating the effect of a relatively long wheel-base on the turning arc of a motor carriage.

direction when the wheelbase is long as when it is short. This means harder steering, and closer attention on the part of the driver, since very sharp turns cannot be made, and must be avoided by long sweeps, commencing earlier than would be necessary with a short wheelbase. When going very fast, the difficulty is much magnified and great watchfulness is necessary to steer a desired course.

"In going around a curve with a motor car, it will be noticed that the rear wheels do not follow in the tracks of the front wheels, but swing considerably closer to the inside of the curve. The longer the wheelbase, the greater this sidewise displacement of the rear portion of the vehicle, and the wider the space occupied by the car while making the turn. Therefore, with a very long wheelbase, a narrow road in many cases may be barely wide enough for all the wheels of the car when a short turn is made on it, and passing another vehicle may be decidedly dangerous, if not absolutely impossible. * * * * * *

STEERING A MOTOR VEHICLE.

"Perhaps the easiest way in which the lay reader can make the foregoing comparisons between long wheelbases and short wheelbases clear in his mind is to assume the cases of a very short and of an impossibly long wheelbase.

Thus, with a wheelbase only a foot or two long, it is evident that the steering would be very sharp upon the least movement of the front wheels, and that the rear wheels would follow almost in the track of them. On the other hand, with a wheelbase one hundred feet long, it clearly would be impossible to go around a curve on an average road, and a great angle of the steering wheels would be necessary to produce a turn even of wide radius. Of course, these are exaggerated examples, but they serve to suggest an idea that applies very definitely, though in lesser degree, to wheelbases ordinarily long. It is true that modern cars with long wheelbases usually have frames much narrower in the front, to permit of turning the steering wheels at very sharp angles, but this is a means of getting around rather than of doing away with the difficulty."

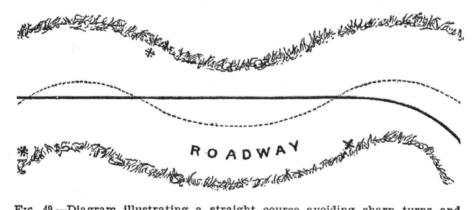

Fig. 49.—Diagram illustrating a straight course avoiding sharp turns and side-slips at points marked by crosses (x x x). Dotted line, course to avoid; straight line, best course to follow.

Avoiding Side=Slip in Driving.—The accompanying diagram, borrowed from the "Motorist's Year Book," exhibits a notable condition in which side-slip may be readily incurred and avoided. The explanation of the diagram is as follows:

"At each of the points marked in the diagram by crosses, if the road is greasy and the curves abrupt, the motorist will stand a chance of side-slip. His straight road, giving no opportunity of lateral pressure on his wheels, will diminish his side-slip risks to one, the last curve wherein the road is shown turning off at a sharp angle. This he must take, of course, but he will do well to take it as broadly as possible. The saving of tires by such a method is surprising, every sharp twist and turn acting destructively, according to its angle of abruptness. It is, of course, supposed that the driver can choose his route, the road being unfrequented, and a fair outlook obtainable, conditions to be found over miles and miles of country driving. Where there is traffic, the rule of the road must be more or less strictly observed; as also in turning corners, beyond which one cannot see.

"In climbing hills, again the automobilist should preserve the straightest possible course. A horsed vehicle zig-zags, in order to spare the horse, by making the wheels act laterally, and so act as brakes to prevent the backward slipping tendency of the vehicle. In driving a car the practice is different. If the course is altered the front wheels exert a lateral pushing action on the road surface and retard the car. As power is valuable upon hills, it should never be wasted in turns, abrupt or gentle, if these can be avoided."

Wheel and Tiller Steering.—The steering gear of a motor carriage is controlled by a tiller or hand wheel at the driver's hand. The difference between the two is very largely a matter of design, except in the heavier types of car; since, after all, the wheel is a multiple lever. In practice, although the balance of leverage is evidently on the side of the driver, even with the simplest form of steering device, the advantages of the wheel are manifold. With the best-designed apparatus to neutralize vibration and prevent any outside stress from reversing the steering, by acting to change the direction of the road wheels, the tiller may be whipped out of the driver's hand. It is also tiring to hold it, even in the straight-ahead position, while, on making a turn, a large arc must often be described. With a wheel the hands may always rest in an easy and natural position, and no ordinary shock can loosen the hold. The driver always has the control in hand.

Irreversible Steering.—In early motor carriages the steering tiller or wheel was connected direct to the axle studs by arrangements closely resembling the simple steering control of a bicycle. The result was, of course, an immense expenditure of strength in effecting changes of direction, not to speak of constant annoyance from jolting and vibration, and the danger that some unexpected obstacle would whip the lever from the hand. The necessity of devising suitable means to render steering irreversible—which is to say, immune from interference by obstacles acting on the road wheels—was very early recognized. Typical methods of achieving this result are shown in accompanying diagrams. In all of these the neutralization of vibration is more or less successfully combined with irreversibility.

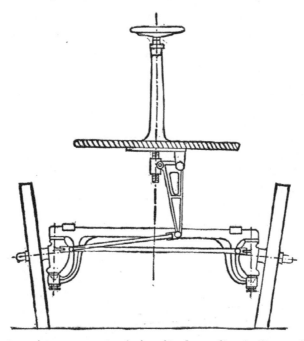

FIG. 50.—Steering Arrangement of the Clarkson-Capel Steam Wagon. The spindle of the steering wheel carries a screw at its end, which works a boss, as the wheel is turned, thus actuating the lever and drag-link attached to the arm of one of the axle pivots.

The Traveling Nut.—The simplest arrangement is the screw and sliding nut device, used on the Clarkson-Capel steam wagon and several others. In this device, as shown in the figure, the pillar or spindle of the steering wheel is threaded at its lower end, and upon it a nut or threaded boss is let on. This nut carries a lug for attaching one arm of a fork or bell crank, whose other arm actuates a drag-link working on the steering arm of one of the axle studs. When the steering pillar is rotated, the nut is caused to move up or down on the thread, operating the bell-crank and link and giving an inclination to the road wheels.

While, as may be plainly seen, the inclination thus imparted to the road wheels is irreversible—since the gearing connected to the sliding boss is locked in any given position—there can be no certain freedom from vibration at the hand wheels.

The Worm and Sector.—In the second type of steering gear the lower end of the steering pillar carries a worm that rotates a toothed sector. On the spindle of this sector is carried an arm that actuates the steering axles through a drag-link in fashion

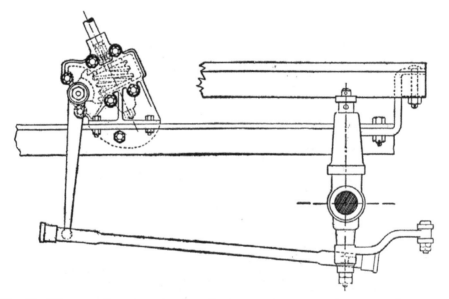

Fɪɢ. 51.—Worm and sector steering device, as developed by Panhard-Levas-sor. The spindle of the steering hand wheel carries a worm gear at its base, which actuates a toothed sector, as shown. This swings an arm and moves the drag-link attached to the arm at the base of the steering head. The transverse drag-link connecting the two steering heads is attached to the arm extending from the front of the carriage. The link between the steering head and the sector arm has ball joints and can adjust the distance as the carriage rises and falls on the springs.

similar to the former device. Ball joints between the drag-link and the arms at either end enable it to compensate the up-and-down motion of the springs. Since the worm can actuate the gear, while the gear cannot actuate the worm, this type of steering is also irreversible; although, as in the former case, vibration may be readily imparted.

The Traveling Nut and Rack.—Combinations of the two foregoing types of steering gear have been produced by several designers. In one of these the worm on the steering pillar causes a threaded boss to work up or down, as in the first type of apparatus. Instead, however, of actuating a bell-crank, it carries a rack, which, in turn, rotates a spur pinion, swinging an arm and drag-link in the manner already explained. Others have arranged the worm and threaded boss, with its rack attachment, in a horizontal position, rotating the worm shaft through bevel gears from the steering pillar. Both these arrangements are very efficient in neutralizing vibration.

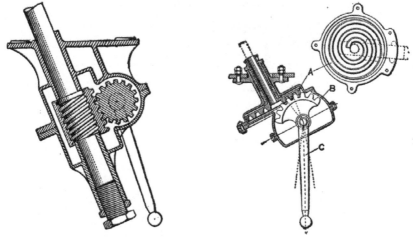

Fig. 52.—Combined Nut and Rack Steering Gear; a device embodying a high degree of immunity from back-lash and a close approximation of perfect irreversibility.

Fig. 53.—Typical Irreversible Steering Device; a spirally grooved gear plate operating a sector.

The Gobron=Brillie Gear.—The Gobron steering apparatus, used on the French-built motor carriage of the same name, is noteworthy as achieving the end of irreversible steering by somewhat different means. As shown in the accompanying figures, A is a hand wheel, at the end of whose spindle, D, is an arm, E, to which is pivoted a toothed sector, B. The arm, E, being moved as the wheel, A, is turned, carries around with it the pivot of the sector, B. This sector meshes with the pinion, C, turning loose on the steering pillar, as shown, and is accordingly rotated through an arc. Thus the arm, F, attached to the pivot of B, on E, has a double motion, which involves that the slightest movement of the wheels, A, is unusually effective in actuating the steering arms, through the link attached, as indicated, to the end of

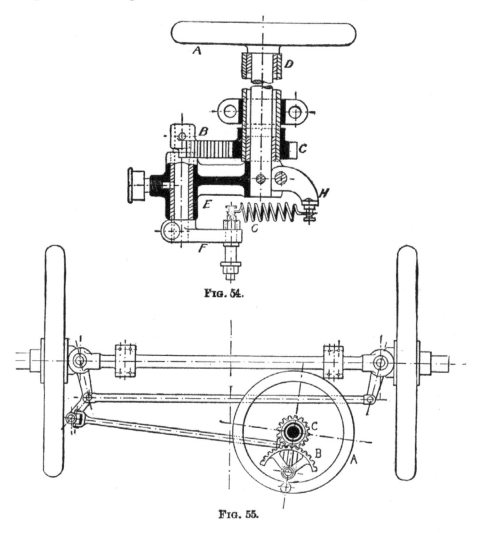

FIG. 54.

FIG. 55.

FIGS. 54 and 55.—The Steering Arrangement of the Gobron-Brillie Carriages.

F. Also, any stress at the wheels is unable to reverse or disturb the movement thus directed. The spring, G, attached to the arm, H, serves to steady the movement and restore F to normal position when required.

CHAPTER SIX.

Unusual Steering and Driving Devices.—The standard, and very probably, the permanent construction for an automobile is to drive to the rear and steer on the forward wheels. However, numerous alternate constructions have been attempted at various times; some proving moderately successful, others failing outright. These may be divided into the following heads:

1. Front driving and steering.
2. Front driving and rear steering.
3. Four-wheel driving and front steering.
4. Four-wheel driving and four-wheel steering.

Front=wheel Driving.—Front-wheel driving, as embodied in the various types of motor wheels and fore-carriages, so common some years since undoubtedly originated in a desire to adapt horse carriages to motor-driving. When embodied in the design of motor vehicles, among which were several well-known electric cabs, the construction was undoubtedly based on a misapprehension of the involved conditions of automobile operation. In both cases the error arose from an idea that horse-traction was thus imitated.

Front-wheel driving involves some kind of device for combining the steering and driving functions, unless, as has occasionally happened, the steering is on the rear wheels. Fig. 57, showing a combined driving and steering device, as used in some of the Hurtu electric cabs, shows one arrangement of gearing for accomplishing the result. Here I is the armature of the motor, NN, the magnets and B, a frame supporting the armature spindle which rotates on the axis, XX. To this spindle is attached the spur pinion, P, which meshes with the pinion, r, turning on the axis, yy, within the boss of the steering pivot. The spur pinion, r, is made in one piece with the bevel pinion, *a*, and this latter engages the toothed bevel ring, *b*, which is clamped to the spokes of the wheel, *RR*. As may be understood, it is possible to swing the wheel, *RR*, on the axis *yy*, fixed in the yoke, *E*, without inter-

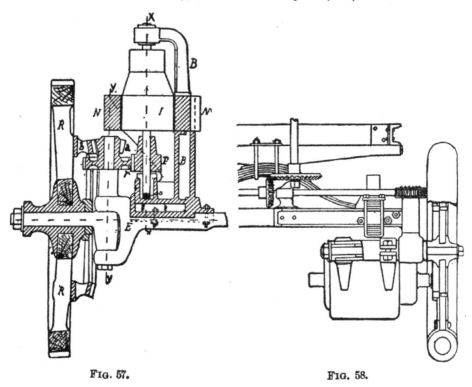

FIG. 57.   FIG. 58.

FIG. 57.—Motor Steering Wheel of the Hurtu Cabs. A drag-link attached to the arm of the pivots can turn the wheels without disturbing the operation of the motor.

FIG. 58.—Steering Motor Wheel Arrangement, by which a worm gear and pinion device, actuated as shown by bevel gears, turns the stud axle entirely around with the attached motor and gearing, without interrupting a steady drive.

fering with the transmission of driving power from the pinion, *a*, to the bevel ring, *b*, thus permitting the vehicle to be steered and driven on the same wheel. Another device, shown in Fig. 58, involves the use of a separate axle for each steering-driver.

Front-driven vehicles travel moderately well on a level roadway, but are quite useless for hill-climbing, from the fact that the centre of gravity is thrown so far back of the engine that the front wheels tend to turn without progressing. When, on the other hand, the rear wheels drive, the centre of gravity falls forward of the axle, and good traction is possible.

Tiller and Wheel Steering.—In the earlier motor vehicles the steering wheels were controlled by a lever or tiller located at the dashboard and extending toward the driver.

In steering with this device the tiller movement is in the reverse direction to that taken by the car. This presents a difficulty, which, to illustrate, suppose the front seat passenger stand up for any reason and while standing to accidentally touch the tiller. The immediate effect is that the course of the car is deflected in the opposite direction to that in which the tiller is moved. This may cause the occupant to lose his balance and to be thrown

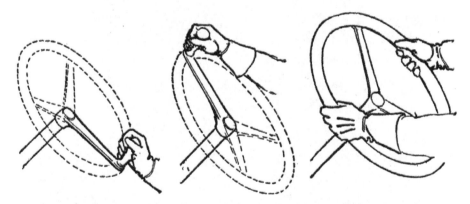

Fig. 59.—Dynamics in Steering. If a wheel be handled by its lowermost point, it acts like a tiller and is unsteady; if handled by its uppermost point it is steady at all times. Grasping the wheel oppositely with both hands is safe for steering under all road conditions.

against the tiller with such force that the car would make a very abrupt turn and probably upset.

At first it was thought the general principle of lever or tiller steering was at fault. In point of fact, it is the direction of the steering motion that is dangerous; reverse the tiller motion to correspond with the direction taken by the car and the forces, previously a cause of danger, become immediately a source of security.

In steering with a wheel, the manner in which it is held and handled is important. Suppose the wheel to be grasped by its lowermost point (fig. 59), then its action is unsteady like that of a short tiller. Again, suppose the wheel to be handled only by its uppermost point, the motion is in the same direction as the car is steered, and it is, therefore, stable. The usual method of holding the wheel, is to grasp it in both hands, one on each side, and when steering the body is leaned in the direction in which the wheel is turned. Hence, if the driver should lean over further than intended, the centrifugal force acting on the driver's body will cause it to sway in such a manner that equilibrium will be restored.

FIG. 60.—An example of rear wheel steering. This system has been supplanted by front wheel steering, because when a carriage is standing near a curb, it is impossible to turn off sharply, as the steering wheel (rear) would run into the curb; and that, when near a ditch or impassible section of the road, in order to turn away from these, the steering wheels (rear) must first run toward them, which may lead to difficulties.

Rear-Wheel Steering.—The objections to rear steering are that, when a carriage is standing near a curb, it is impossible to turn off sharply, as the steering wheel (rear) would run into the curb ; and that, when near a ditch or impassable section of the road, in order to turn away from these, the steering wheels (rear) must first run toward them, which may lead to difficulties.

CHAPTER SEVEN.

THE SUPPORTS OF A MOTOR VEHICLE.

Underframes and Springs.—A few years ago very many automobiles were built with some form of underframe, whose essential elements were perches connecting the front and rear axles, as in most horse carriages, and some form of swivel joint to permit of considerable distortion, in compensation for unevenness on the roadway. The two objects sought in this supposedly necessary structure were strength and flexibility. Very many designers also used complicated frameworks of steel tubing, with the additional object of securing lightness. These elements have now been almost entirely abandoned, except in a few light steam carriages and some electric wagons, since designers have learned by experience that with properly arranged springs a motor vehicle can be strong and flexible, without perches or swivels, and light, without steel tubing.

Advantages of an Underframe.—In one very essential particular, however, the underframe was a desirable complication. In the greater number of cases it embodied an approximation of the essential principle of three-point support for the body and machinery, which is not always perfectly attained in more recent constructions. Thus, the typical underframe for light carriages had longitudinal perches converging in a swivel joint at the centre of the forward axle. Others had two such perches swiveled to the axle. In either case the three-point support was partially provided under conditions involving lateral distortion of the running gear, in spite of the inevitable stiffness of all such frames and the indifferent efficiency of the swivel joints.

Three=Point Support.—Three-point support is desirable from the fact that, whatever the strain and distortion encountered, the three points always fall in one plane. If an object rests evenly upon four points, it is evident that any force acting to remove one of the supports tends to destroy the stability and throw the body into a plane at an angle with the plane of the other three supports. If, on the other hand, its weight be evenly distributed between three points, it is adequately supported on any

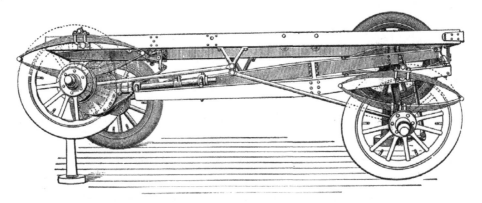

FIG. 61.—Marmon Double Three-Point Support.

plane, and a force, acting unduly on one of the points, cannot draw away the support—rather drawing the supported body in the direction of its moving stress.

One of the most notable applications of the principle of three-point support is found in the Marmon car. Here a triangular under frame is swivelled around the propeller shaft at the rear and supported on the elliptical springs over the front axle. The body frame is supported over the rear springs, and swivelled to the base of the triangular under frame at the front. This arrangement assumes the horizontal position of the engine and body, no matter what obstructions are encountered by the wheels.

Three=Wheel Carriages.—From such facts we are able to apprehend the logical force behind some of the leading arguments for the three-wheeled carriage. As already suggested in a former chapter, it embodies the theoretical requirements of easy steering, and, contrary to first supposition, is less easily upset. Charles E. Duryea, the leading advocate of this type of vehicle, says:

"The future popular two-passenger carriage will be a three-wheeler, because of the many advantages which only need to be known to be appreciated. * * * * * The three-wheeled carriage, if properly designed, rides as easy as a four-wheeler, or so nearly so that the difference cannot be told by a blindfolded observer riding in the two alternately; while the three-wheeler steers more easily, requires less power to propel, starts and stops more quickly, is simpler, lighter, very much better in mud and appreciably better everywhere else."

Commenting on the bicycle traditions, formerly prominent in automobile construction, Mr. Duryea says again:

"Engineers make a mistake who attempt to apply their experience indiscriminately to carriages, for the carriage problem is not a single-plane problem. Both the cycle and its wheels receive strains, and in a single plane, while cycle riders save themselves and the machine by standing on the pedals on rough spots. The automobile rider never does this, while the constant torsions and wrenchings of a four-cornered frame are simply indescribable.

The Chassis and Springs.—At the present day light carriages are most often constructed with long side-spring perches between the axles and have the body supported on a flat frame midway in their length. With heavy carriages the body rests on a rectangular framework of iron or steel that is directly supported on the springs attached to front and rear axles, forming the "chassis," or running gear. With either construction compensation of different levels is possible, as in riding along the side of a slope or going over a rock in one of the wheel tracks, the springs serving the double purpose of absorbing the jars of travel and giving the running gear a necessary degree of distortability.

Construction of Springs.—The leaf springs used in road carriages and railroad cars consist of several layers of steel plates or leaves more often slightly bent, so that, when laid together, they are found forming superposed arcs of so many concentric circles. It is essential to a serviceable spring of this description that the line of the arc be carefully followed from end to end of each plate, and that no attempt be made to straighten or bend back the extremities of the longest leaves. This is true because the spring effect is derived from the temper of the metal in permitting the load to flatten all the arcs at once under a single stress, which .

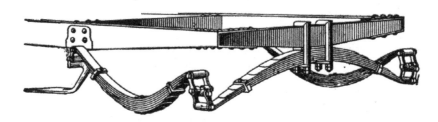

Fig 62..–Three-point suspended spring, or platform spring, one of the latest and most conspicuous improvements in spring suspension designs.

involves that they should slide upon one another in altering their shape, as could not be the case were there any such departure from the line of the arc, as has been mentioned. In that case the several plates would tend to separate and "gape" under a load requiring a degree of compression tending to bring the extremity of any arc to the straight portion of the top leaves. The result would be a loss in spring action, and a probable source of breakage on occasion.

The Construction of Springs.—In constructing laminated leaf springs it is essential that the plates should decrease on a regular scale of lengths, in order that the structure may be of equal strength throughout and of sufficient flexibility for the loads calculated to its dimensions. Where such a spring is thick, consisting of a number of plates, it is a good working rule that the ends of each several plates should touch the sides of a triangle, whose base is drawn between the extremities of the longest plate and whose apex is at or about the theoretical centre point of the spring's movement. This means that, with a well-proportioned spring in its normal shape, the end of each separate plate should be equidistant from that of the one immediately above it and of the one immediately below it. By this construction even distribution of stress is attained without waste or resistance from inactive portions of the length of each plate, as would be the case in a laminated spring flattened at the top plate and having the longitudinal profile shaped to an arc. Such a spring, however,

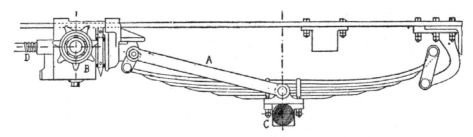

Fɪɢ. 63.—Semi-elliptical Spring and Radius Rod of the Mors Cars. The rod, A, maintains a fixed distance between the sprocket pinion, B, and the wheel axle, C, even when the springs are constantly in action. This carriage also has a device for varying the distance between the countershaft at B, and the engine pulley, by sliding the entire shaft forward or back under impulse from the screw, D. The spring, being hung on links at front and rear, has considerable play, up and down, without disturbing the fixed relation of the axle, C, and the countershaft, B, as determined by the radius rod, A.

would embody bad construction in another particular, since it would neglect one very essential feature of spring construction—curvature of the plates. This curvature is intended to represent the difference between the spring under static and maximum load; at the latter point its leaves should be nearly straightened under stress; beyond that point, as they are bent backward and downward, the point of ultimate strength, involving loss of elasticity and breakage, is rapidly approached. It follows, therefore, that the end of a perfectly elastic and serviceable spring is best attained by such curvature as will allow bending of the plates from each extremity of the top plates, on the support at the centre, without involving endwise compression, as is the case when the curve approaches a semi-circular contour. Consequently, laminated leaf springs are usually constructed to an arc of never more than ninety degrees and often very much less.

According to arrangement, there are three varieties of leaf spring used on automobiles: elliptical, semi-elliptical and scroll.

THE SEMI-ELLIPTICAL SPRING consists of a segment formed by a number of leaves or blades, and is arranged to be attached at the bottom and the two extremities of the arc.

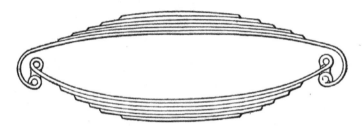

FIG. 64.—Scroll-elliptic Rear Axle Rear Spring used on models of the Packard Light Car.. The C-shaped upper portion is connected by shackles to the elliptical lower half, the effect being to allow the use of fixed distance rods and keep the chain taut, without the use of the usual devices of foreign and American carriages.

THE ELLIPTICAL SPRING is formed by connecting two semi-elliptics or arc-shaped springs at their extremities—generally by bolts passed through perforated bosses formed at the extremities of the longest leaves—and is attached at the apex of each arc by clips or nuts.

THE SCROLL SPRING differs from the semi-elliptic in having one extremity of the arc rolled up and turned inward. It may be attached by a link or a shackle to a flat or semi-elliptical spring —forming a "scroll-elliptic"—or to the body suspended above the axle.

Springs on Motor Carriages.—We may readily understand that motor carriages, being intended primarily for high rates of speed, involve spring conditions found in neither horse-drawn vehicles nor railroad cars. The latter, although traveling at speeds often 100 per cent. greater than the average automobile, run upon an even and comparatively unresistant roadway—the track of steel rails—while the former, although built for the ordinary highways, as are automobiles, are seldom calculated for any but very moderate rates of speed. Railroad cars must thus provide against a **maximum** speed, with a **minimum** road roughness and resistance; horse carriages, on the other hand, must provide against **maximum** roughness and resistance with **minimum** speed; motor carriages must be able to attain high speeds and, at the same time, resist the annoying and destructive effects of roadways, inevitably irregular as to resistance and other conditions

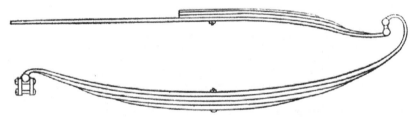

FIG. 65.—Scroll Bottom Carriage Spring, half elliptic, showing **connections** by links and shackles.

of surface. As a general proposition, therefore, we may **assert** that such springs as will promote comfort will prevent undue wear and tear on the motor and parts, which, in fact, makes the end of easy riding for the passengers the prime consideration.

Resistance and Resilience.—To be thoroughly serviceable, a spring should possess two essential qualities in due proportion: resistance and resilience. While a spring should be calculated to give sufficiently to absorb the jars of travel, it should not be so resilient as to rebound with a series of oscillations. This produces a movement that is liable to be extremely annoying, while, at the same time, contributing nothing to protecting the mechanism. As a good general rule, the best spring is one that "moves quickly, when idle or worked on, and slowly, when working"; that is to say, one that absorbs jars by friction between its leaves, rather than transforming them into a series of jumps. The "happy mean," therefore, lies between the extremes of over-sensitiveness and over-rigidity

The Action of Springs.—In this connection it is desirable to remark that good spring action can be obtained only with springs adapted by weight and elasticity for the work required in any given case. The efficiency of a spring can never be increased by oiling between the leaves, since it will not give, except under sufficient load, and, even then, the friction of each leaf upon its neighbor is an essential part in the work of absorbing jars. As some writers have expressed it, the jars of travel are transformed into heat by this friction. At the same time the danger that it will wear out the spring is exceedingly remote.

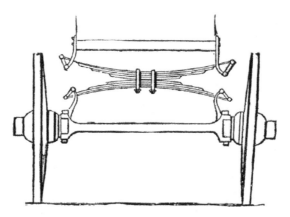

FIG. 66.—Double semi-elliptical spring attachments used on some electric vehicles. The body, being suspended entirely by links on the extremities of the springs, has the full benefit of spring action.

Considerations in Spring Design.—Apart from certain well ascertained figures on the static weight of the load and the size and tensile strength of the springs designed to carry it, there are no reliable data regarding the proper proportions of springs for automobile carriages. As we have said, this is and must continue a matter to be governed most largely by experiment, apart from mathematical calculations, since the constantly varying conditions of automobile travel preclude exact theory. Among these variants may be mentioned high speeds on any and every kind of road and the use of pneumatic tires. The matter is still further qualified by the size of the tires and the degree of inflation, for both of these points are important in modifying the stress to come upon the springs. Indeed, there is no more important factor in the high-speed motor vehicles than the rubber tires, although the properties developed in its practical operation by no means permit its use on vehicles without suspension springs of some description.

The Effects of Pneumatic Tires.—The use of pneumatic tires on a vehicle permits the absorption of considerable vibration and the consequent use of softer springs than are possible with

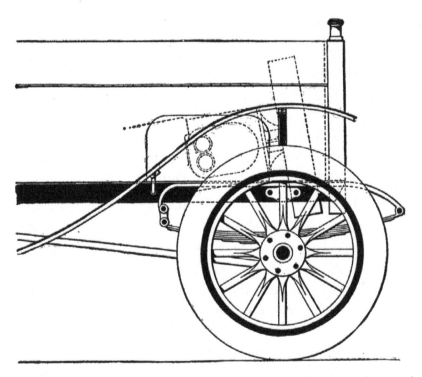

Fig. 67.—Forward running gear of the Northern Car, showing springs connected with a vertical shackle. With this arrangement, it is claimed the return of the spring will be confined to the power of its tension or deflected state. It must return through the shackle on dead center, as it were, and not through the shackle as a hinge.

steel tires. The bouncing motion, frequently developed by pneumatic tires is neutralized by the use of properly adjusted springs, although in the matter of adjustment we must calculate as essential elements the size and degree of inflation of the tires, the weight and dimensions of the springs, and the average speed used. In some respects a heavier spring gives easier riding than a light one, since the latter is apt to bounce disproportionately, even with good pneumatic tires, when the road is somewhat rough.

Condition of Spring Dimensions.—In judging of the dimensions and elasticity of springs suitable for carriage use, the limit of elasticity must be carefully considered with relation to the static and maximum loads to be carried by the vehicle.

THE STATIC LOAD is the dead weight of the vehicle body and frame, together with that of the passengers and other freight, estimated when at rest.

THE MAXIMUM LOAD is the proportionately increased weight of the same items, with relation to the traction effort required when the vehicle is running at its highest speed, under test conditions as to road roughness or hill-climbing requirements.

THE ULTIMATE LOAD is the greatest weight possibly carried with good spring action; the limit of the spring's endurance.

That the springs should be calculated to retain the elasticity, or have the ultimate strength far beyond the maximum load, is obvious, when we consider the office of a spring. In calculating the proportions of springs in the best constructed railroads, it is usually customary to consider the maximum load as twice the static load. Whence it is the general practice to estimate the fitness of a given spring for its work as equivalent to the quotient of the weight of the spring divided by the product of its length, between the extremities of the longest leaf, and the number, width and thickness of the other several leaves.

Proportionate Loads.—The variable nature of carriage roads makes the proportion of static and maximum load much higher for horse-drawn vehicles than for railway cars, except where only the most moderate speeds are to be used; but for automobiles always calculated for high speeds, it never falls below a ratio of 1 to 3, and is often estimated as high as 1 to 5.

Adjusting Weights.—As has been pointed out by several authorities, the difficulty of obtaining springs for automobiles, which shall be serviceable under all conditions, is greatly increased when the weight of the body, motors, etc., is very much in excess of that of the passengers provided for. This is true, since a spring that will subserve the end of easy riding under usual conditions, with extra heavy accessories of this description, would permit no end of jolting and annoying vibration at high speeds on imperfect roads. The fault is difficult to discover except under test conditions.

Placing Springs.—To sum up the general requirements in a few words, we may say that, while pneumatic tires will absorb very many vibrations, thus permitting soft and light springs under the body, the occasional inequalities in the road are liable to occasion a quick succession of annoying jolts, reaching by accumulated forces almost to the limit of spring elasticity, or succeeding one another so rapidly, at high speed, that the springs have little time to recover their normal shape. This seems to indicate that a heavier spring is preferable, or else that spring construction must be in some way varied to give firmer attachments and more evenly distributed elasticity; the time required by the spring to recover itself being the same under all conditions, some springs are thus unfit for high speed work. Many manufacturers prefer semi-elliptical springs to the full elliptical, on the ground that their elasticity is greater for a given weight of spring, and the consensus of opinion on the latter is that the longer the spring, within reasonable limits, the greater the combined elasticity and lightness. When such springs are used as side supports it is general practice to attach one end direct to the longitudinal frame and connect the other by a link, thus allowing ample freedom toward lengthening. When placed transversely over the forward axle both ends are secured to links, the centre being securely clamped.

Rules for Calculating Springs.—As a general proposition, the usefulness of a spring for given work and load is largely a consideration of the total length of the structure between points of attachment. However, the thickness and number of the leaves, and the quality of the steel used—the last-named consideration is of the utmost importance—enter into the formulæ followed in railroad work and carriage designing. These same formulæ are useful to the automobile builder. They may be summarized as follows:

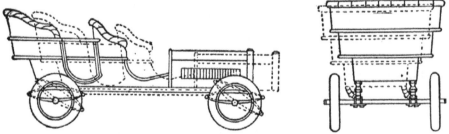

FIGS 68 and 69.—Diagrams illustrating the forward and sidewise lunges of the body of a motor carriage in travel, with indication of the distortion of elliptical springs. See Page 82.

Let B represent the breadth of the plates in inches.

Let T represent the thickness of each in sixteenths of an inch.

Let N represent the number of plates in the spring.

Let S represent the working span, or the distance between the centres of the spring hangers, when the spring is loaded.

Let W represent the working strength of a given spring.

Let E represent the elasticity of the spring in inches per ton.

THE ELASTICITY OR DEFLECTION of a given spring is found by the following formula:

$$1.66 \ \frac{S^3}{N \ B \ T^3} = E \text{ in 16th inch per ton load.}$$

Other authorities give the formula:

$$\frac{S^3}{C \ N \ B \ T^3} = E \text{ in inches per ton load.}$$

Here C represents the constant 40,000 for single and 20,000 for double springs, and T, the thickness of each plate in inches or fractions of an inch.

THE SPAN LENGTH due to a given elasticity and number and size of plates is as follows:

$$\sqrt[3]{\frac{E\ B\ N\ T^3}{1.66}} = S \text{ in inches.}$$

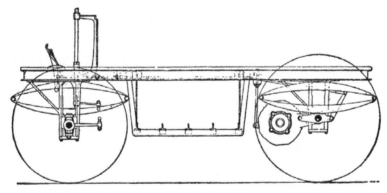

FIG. 70.—The Rainier Pedestal Frame, designed to control the movement of elliptical springs, preventing all distortions in travel.

THE NUMBER OF PLATES due to a given elasticity, span and size of plates:

$$\frac{S^3 \times 1.66}{E\ B\ T^3} = N$$

THE WORKING STRENGTH, or greatest weight a spring can bear, is determined as follows:

$$\frac{B\ T^2\ N}{11.3\ S} = W \text{ in tons (2,240 lbs.) burden.}$$

THE SPAN DUE TO A GIVEN STRENGTH, and number and size of plates:

$$\frac{B\ T^2\ N}{11.3\ W} = S \text{ in inches.}$$

THE NUMBER OF PLATES suited to a given strength, span and size of plates:

$$\frac{11.3\, W\, S}{B\, T^2} = N.$$

The Cut=and=Try Method.—A prominent American manufacturer of carriage springs, the Tuthill Spring Co., underrates the value of formulæ like the above, insisting that experiment alone can completely solve the matter. They make the carrying capacity of a spring dependent upon the following conditions:

1. Upon the length of the spring, because a longer spring is limberer than a shorter spring.

2. Upon the width of the steel, a wider one being stiffer than a narrower one.

3. Upon the number of plates, more plates being stiffer than fewer plates.

4. Upon the opening of the spring (or degree of curve), because the nearer it approximates a straight line the limberer it is.

5. Upon the thickness of the individual plates, because a greater number of thin plates, making a given thickness, is equal to a smaller number of thick plates and will be more elastic.

6. Upon whether a lubricant is used between the leaves or not.

Points on Spring Suspension.—As regards the suspension of springs of horse-drawn vehicles and automobiles, the careful observer will note one point of divergence at once. When elliptic, or semi-elliptic, springs of the ordinary description are used, he will see that in most light horse carriages only two are suspended, one over each of the axle shafts, across the width of the carriage. In automobiles of every build and motive power, while a single spring may be thus attached to the forward axle, the rear axle supports two, one at each side of the frame, and running in the length of the carriage. This is a construction found only in the heavier patterns of horse-drawn carriages, and in both cases it is resorted to for the purpose of neutralizing the forward lunge of the body, inevitable on rough roads with a single transverse elliptical spring. With the horse carriage of the heavier pattern such vibration is annoying and also hurtful to the body, frame and springs. With the automobile, however, the case is even graver; for not only will similar results follow at high speed, but the proper distance between the motor, usually carried in the body above the springs, and the rear axle, will be continually disturbed, with consequent damage to sprocket, chain and gears and loss of a steady drive. Thus, in carriages which have no other provision against this tendency of the rear axle to throw backward or forward under the stress of travel, it is necessary to use a device known as a *distance rod* to maintain a fixed distance between motor and drive axle, when the throw of the springs would otherwise permit it to be disturbed. The better method of overcoming this danger is to set the springs in the length of the carriage, as just described; for thus most of the violent jars in this direction are absorbed, and the fixed relation of motor and axle maintained, without rigid attachments, which would form another notable occasion of accidents. This allows the springs to lengthen under pressure from above or from the direction of travel, and further reinforces against sidewise lunges, which, however, are of far less frequent occurrence.

Attachments for Springs.—The ends of ready lengthening and extra elastic support are to be accomplished by the use of scroll elliptics and semi-elliptics, connected to the carriage body by suitable links. Links are preferable in many places on account of the ready action allowed in several directions, without involving tendency to yield unduly under ordinary conditions. The high speed requirements of motor carriages makes it nearly imperative that leaf springs, either half or full elliptic, should be securely clamped to the supports by clips and nuts, rather than by bolts through bolt holes in the centre. This is true because such bolt holes are liable to prove a source of weakness under high speed conditions and to cause the breaking of springs at the very time when their full strength is most requisite. With clips this danger is wholly averted, and, instead of a weak point at the centre, an additional reinforcement is obtained.

The Alignment of Springs.—In the act of passing over an obstruction, such as a large stone in the roadway, it is evident that the spring above the axle of the wheel that rises must be compressed to an extraordinary degree, unless it is so rigid as to lift the corner of the vehicle body to a corresponding degree. In either event, as is evident, there must be some sidewise distortion of the spring, which, often repeated, must occasion its destruction. Because an automobile is not usually built for rough roads, few provisions have been made against mishaps from this cause. It is a matter, however, that should interest the practical automobilist, particularly a person about to order a machine built for use in a hilly country, or for long-distance touring. In all such cases there should be some means for keeping the springs working in a perfectly vertical line.

Stresses on Springs.—The exact nature of the stresses brought to bear on the springs of a motor carriage are shown diagrammatically in Fig 68. The distortion of a full-elliptical spring, which from its structural elements allows greater action in every direction, is forwards, when some obstacle, met by forward or rear wheel, tends to throw the body by its own momentum, and sidewise, owing to the action of forces precisely similar to those causing side-slipping of the wheels. The effect of an obstacle met by the wheels would be a bending-forward of the upper front and lower rear portions of the elliptical springs, tending to bend the entire structure forward and downward, as shown in the figure. This action is intensified in the case of the rear wheels, because they bear the greater part of the load.

The use of semi-elliptical springs partly neutralizes these tendencies, also reducing the danger of breakage, owing to the facts:

1. That a stiffer spring is required.

2. That a good proportion of the stresses work downward.

A Three=Spring Suspension.—A noteworthy attempt to neutralize the tendencies to hinges, forward and sidewise, is found in
the Hill spring suspension system, shown in Fig. 71. The front
and rear springs are pivoted and linked to the frame by one extremity of each; the opposite extremities are underhung by links
to a semi-elliptical spring—the "equalizing spring"—clipped midway to the side-bar of the body frame. The vehicle body is thus
supported at three points on either side, at the two ends and in the
middle, with the result that any stress exerted at one of the points
will be equalized by being transmitted to the two others. It forms
in fact, a spring running gear. The result is that stresses, which

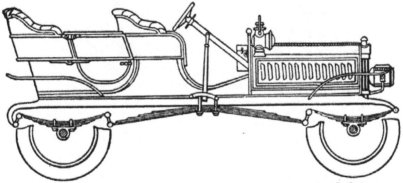

FIG. 71—The Hill three-point-suspended spring device; intended to compensate spring movements and to distribute stresses.

would infallibly distort an ordinary full-elliptical spring, are distributed evenly: the equalizing spring acting in all such cases to
restrain any excessive movement, caused either by the vibrations
of travel or by motor thrust, and compelling the front and rear
springs to lengthen under all stresses.

Pedestal Spring Frames.—Another noteworthy device is that
embodied in the Herschmann steam truck. Instead of the usual
rigid attachment by bolts, the spring has on its lower face a
semi-cylindrical shoe that rests loosely upon a flattened portion
at the top of the axle shaft. The axle works up and down between guides, four in number, at either side of the vehicle, and
formed of angle or L-shaped iron rods. The spring is bolted
between cross-shaped clip plates, the lower of which carries the

shoe above mentioned, and by this means its movement is confined in one vertical plane. With any elevation of one wheel, the axle works against the shoe, merely lifting the spring, without twisting or distorting it sidewise. The Rainier "pedestal frame" similarly provides against other than vertical movement of the springs and axles by two vertical guides extending downward from the steel frame outside the springs. A flattened portion of the axle-tree works up and down between these guides.

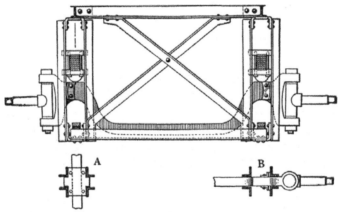

Fig. 72.—The Herschmann spring pedestal device; showing springs resting loose on the axle, their movements being confined to the vertical by guides. All throws of the vehicle body in travel are overcome by this arrangement.

Supplementary Springs.—A recently-introduced device substitutes for the shackle a coil compression spring arrangement, so mounted on a frame that the upper member of a scroll-elliptic, or the spring hanger extending from the body frame, is attached to one end of the coil spring, and the lower member to the other. The coil is compressed under stress of travel absorbing jars, otherwise transmitted to the body and motor.

A devise somewhat similar in effect has been used on models of Mercedes car. An elliptical spring has two small semi-elliptics clipped and bolted inside the arcs of its two members in such position as to meet and engage, when extraordinary stresses tend to depress the main spring, thus absorbing heavy jars and preventing excessive flattening out. The two smaller springs are called the "check springs." One American manufacturer has produced a similar device by the use of a large coiled spring, instead of the two small laminated springs of the Mercedes.

Winton's twin compound spring is an even better solution of the problem of varying loads. Briefly described, it consists of two three-leaf semi-elliptics—the upper somewhat longer than the under—which are joined by shackles at the extremities and attached to the spring supports of the frame. With a light load, under ordinary road conditions, the upper spring alone is in action. When, however, the load increases to a point at which it begins to straighten out, the lower spring begins to receive its share of the load, thereby doubling the resistance of the support. The effect of perfect compensation is thus obtained, along

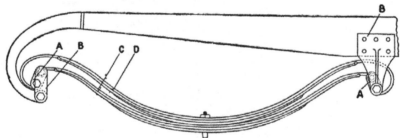

Fig. 73.—Winton's twin compound spring, A and A, links connecting springs, to supports, B and B; C, lower or main spring; D, supplementary spring to take additional loads.

with a practical solution of the serious problem of securing easy riding with either light or heavy load, a thing hitherto impossible. It may be justly claimed that this device combines in unique fashion the essential spring qualities of resistance and resilience.

Absorbing Vibrations.—While, as we have seen, a flexible spring is required for the purpose of deadening the numerous annoying and harmful shocks encountered in operating a car over an uneven roadway, excessive flexibility is liable to intensify such movements. A spring serves its function in bending downward, or straightening, under the stress of a moving load, but it shows itself unequal to the task assigned it, when, by continued vibrations, it merely breaks up or distributes the shock in a series of bounds and jolts, destructive alike to body, machinery and tires, and from which there is no relief or protection.

It is obvious that some device for ensuring the gradual return of the spring to its normal shape, deadening its rebounds and after-movements by absorbing them with some form of friction resistance, is highly desirable. Similar results are achieved in other branches of mechanic arts by the use of "dash-pots," etc. Applied to neutralize the rebound, or after-movements of a motor spring, the result is greater comfort for passengers, smaller injury to machinery and nearly double durability of pneumatic tires.

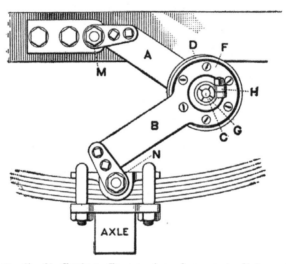

F<small>IG</small>. 74.—The Truffault Spring Suspension for neutralizing shocks due to sudden spring action.

One of the best-known of such devices is the Truffault suspension shown in Fig. 74. It first attained distinction through its adoption on Peugeot cars, and has since done excellent service.

Briefly described, it consists of the two arms, *A* and *B*, joined frictionally by bolt *C*. The arm, *A*, carries a cup-like bronze shell, *D*, and the arm, *B*, a plate, *F*. A cup-like piece of oil-soaked raw-hide is secured between the plate and the shell, being screwed by the nut *G*, on the bolt, *C*. An oil-soaked leather washer separates it from the plate, *F*. This nut is split and is locked in place by the collar, *H*. By screwing sufficiently, the nut, *G*, any desired degree of friction may be obtained. The arms, *A* and *B*, are joined to the frame and the axle by two cone-like frictional joints, which also can be regulated. All these movable frictional parts offer a constant resistance to the vibration of the spring both ways, and it is easy to see that when the wheel strikes an obstruction the arms come together; but instead of flying back as does the free spring, it is retarded by the friction and moves gradually to its normal position, since the friction is always the same, while the tension of the spring diminishes as it approaches its normal position.

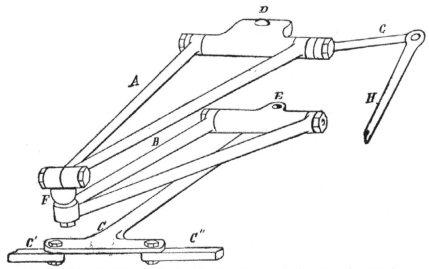

FIG. 75.—The De Dion & Bouton Spring Compensating Steering Device.

Radius Rods.—A spring support involves the use of some device for maintaining a fixed distance between the motor and the driven axle. This generally takes the form of a radius rod attached to a bearing at either end, so as to describe an arc, with the rear axle as a centre, while the springs rise or fall in travel. A turnbuckle permits the length of the rod to be varied according to requirements. With the two-chain drive to the rear wheels, loose on a dead axle, two distance rods, one at each end, are usually provided. With a single-chain drive to a live axle one rod usually suffices. With bevel-gear drive a slip joint on the propeller shaft usually suffices to maintain a fixed distance, although, as must be evident, an extra strain is thereby thrown upon the bevel casing, which is only too liable to break, with the other forms of violence it must endure.

Compensations for the Steering Gear.—Some automobiles include spring compensating devices for the steering gear, although with modern forms of hand-wheel a link swung between ball joints is amply sufficient. On the lighter forms of De Dion carriage a somewhat complicated although highly efficient compensation was used. As shown in an accompanying figure, a V-shaped piece A, constructed of two pieces, is attached to the tubular front cross-piece of the body frame at D, and pivoted on the ball joint at F, to the lower V-shaped piece, B. This is also pivoted at F, and is attached to the axle-tree at E. The T-piece, C, is also pivoted at E rigidly with B, so as to turn sideways with it. It carries the links C′ and C″, which actuate the steering arms of the two stud axles. The link, H, is at-

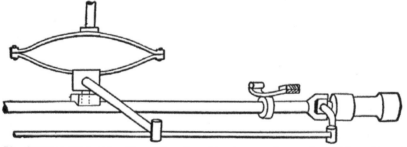

FIG. 76.—Spring Compensating Steering Device used on the Oldsmobile Carriage.

tached to the arm, G, and when moved forward or back by the worm gear and pinion arrangement at the base of the steering-wheel pillar, moves the entire structure, A, B and C, on the pivots, D and E, to the right or left, as desired. The object of the device is to allow of a certain up and down movement, as the springs yield, without disarranging the steering gear or vibrating the steer wheel. In such cases the V-pieces, A and B, move on the ball joint F, thus permitting the points, D and E, to be approached and separated, as the springs move.

In the Oldsmobile, built with longitudinal side springs between the axles, the steering pillar is attached to the front axle through a small elliptic spring, which, bearing against the bottom of the body, is compressed or distended, as it falls or rises, thus enabling the steering to be positive and uninterrupted under all conditions.

CHAPTER EIGHT.

Requirements in Motor Carriage Wheels.—Motor carriage wheels must have five qualities of construction:

1. They must be sufficiently strong for the load they are to carry, and for the kind of roads on which they are to run.

2. They must be elastic, or so constructed that the several parts—hub, spokes and felloes, or rim—are susceptible of a certain flexibility in their fixed relations, thus neutralizing much vibration, and allowing the vehicle greater freedom of movement, particularly on short curves and when encountering obstacles.

3. They must, furthermore, be sufficiently light to avoid absorbing unnecessary power in moving.

4. They must be able to resist the torsion of the motor, which always tends to produce a tangential strain. This is the reason why tangent suspended wire wheels are invariably used in automobiles, instead of the other variety, having radially-arranged spokes.

5. They must have sufficient adhesion to drive ahead without unduly absorbing power in overcoming the tendency to slip on an imperfectly resistant road-bed.

The importance of the two last considerations may be readily understood, in view of the fact that the wheels of motor carriages receive the driving power direct, instead of being merely rotating supports, like the wheels of vehicles propelled by an outside tractive force.

Wooden, Steel and Wire Wheels.—Motor carriage wheels, at the present time, are either wooden, of the so-called "artillery" type, or of steel tubing. A few years ago suspended wire wheels, of the bicycle variety, were extensively applied to motor carriages of all powers, and their claims to superiority were vigorously discussed. They are now so seldom seen that, we may unhesitatingly say, they have been abandoned.

Suspended Wire Wheels.—Like steel tubular framework, also nearly obsolete, the alleged advantages of wire wheels were given as combined lightness and strength. A suspended wire wheel, weight for weight, can undoubtedly carry a heavier load than a wooden wheel, without danger, but it cannot sustain as great stress sidewise, or at right angles to its plane, which is the line of a wheel's greatest weakness, and, in automobile work, of the greatest stress acting upon it.

A wire wheel driven against a curb with sufficient force will have its rim dented, with the result of loosening all its spokes and ruining it. A wooden wheel, on the other hand, may have a gap in it and still be serviceable. It may even run with one or several spokes broken off. A wire wheel being suspended on its spokes—the load being hung between the hub and the perimeter—is bound to suffer in proportion to the number of points of suspension lost. A wooden wheel, being supported at both hub and perimeter by its spokes, has a certain power of compensating or distributing the strain, so that, while a deficiency of support at any one point is of no advantage, it does not always involve destruction.

Steel Tubular Wheels.—Steel tubular wheels, which have been used to a certain extent on automobiles, have the advantage of possessing such strength, particularly in a sidewise direction, as tubular construction possesses, and are immensely superior to wire wheels. Among the advantages claimed are:

1. Superior strength to either wire or wood.

2. True, balanced running, as a pulley on a shaft.

3. Practical immunity from dishing or crushing with the hardest use, or in ordinary accidents.

4. Immunity to rust.

5. Ability to stand the twist and tension of severe strains in the transmission of power.

6. Rims formed from a continuous tube.

7. Perfect alignment of all parts.

Steel wheels are imperfectly elastic, however, and have very little of the desirable spring effect. Thus, while such a wheel, if well made, will endure, without rupture, strains far in excess of those encountered under service conditions, such distortion would result as would unfit it for extended use.

FIG. 77— A typical Wooden Artillery or Wedge Wheel, showing manner of setting the spokes, and the construction of the hub.

Tests conducted, some years since, on one make of steel carriage wheel demonstrated ability to resist a dead weight at the axle up to 3,200 pounds, a sidewise pressure of 1,600 pounds, and a combined pressure at rim and axle up to 3,500 pounds. Beyond these points, however, permanent bending and distortion resulted.

Wooden Artillery Wheels.—Wooden wheels are almost universally used for automobiles at the present time. The type in vogue is the so-called "artillery" wheel, constructed with wedge spokes set together around the nave, and a hub formed of steel plates at front and rear, bolted through the spokes and holding the axle box in place. This is substantially the model originated by Walter Hancock, an early steam carriage builder, and is by far the most solid design of wooden wheel possible. It is, in fact, practically of one piece, having strength to withstand side-wise strains that would speedily wreck a wheel of the type used in horse carriages.

Dishing of Wheels.—Where wooden wheels are used in any kind of vehicle, the effect of elasticity is greatly increased by "dishing"; that is, by inclining the spokes from the exterior plane of the rim to the centre point of the axle spindle, so as to make the wheel a kind of flattened cone. This construction has the effect of transforming the spokes into so many springs, possessing elastic properties, and renders the wheel capable of being deformed under sidewise stress. The shocks of collision with obstacles are thus distributed through the flexibly connected parts, as could not be the case if the wheel were made in one piece or on one plane, and the consequent wear and strain is greatly reduced. The dish of the wheels is usually balanced by slightly inclining the axle spindle from its centre line, thus bringing the lowest spoke to a nearly vertical position with relation to the ground. A great resisting power to shocks produced by obstacles such as is afforded by dished wheels is of far less importance in vehicles designed for good roads as are most automobiles, which need only such inclination of the spokes as will provide for the even distribution of shocks and the maintenance of uniformity in pressure.

Advantages Attained by Dishing.—The significance of the word "dish" is obvious, when we consider that it indicates a diametrical section of about the shape of a saucer or shallow dish. While, as we have seen, this shape furnishes a very desirable spring effect against sidewise strains and shocks, such as are met in swinging around a corner or sliding against a curb—since, although a wheel is always weakest sidewise, it is difficult to thrust a cone inside out—there are several considerations that render it a desirable feature for wagons of all descriptions.

1. The first of these has reference to maintaining a balanced hang to the wheel. Under the conditions of travel a wheel acquires the tendency to crowd on or off the spindle, with the result that it eventually wears loose, as may be frequently found, particularly on heavy carts. Since the spindle is tapered it is necessary that its outer centre should be lower than the inner, and then in order to counteract the outward inclination of the wheel, and consequent tendency to roll outwardly, the spindle end must be also carried forward sufficiently to make the wheel

FIG 78.—Type of Wooden Artillery Wheel constructed with tongue-and-groove joints between the spoke wedges, ensuring greater strength and rigidity.

"gather," which is to say, follow the track. A moderate dish contributes to the end of bringing the tire square to the ground, while at the same time enabling the wheel to rotate without undue wear at the axle.

2. Another constructional advantage involved in the dishing of wooden wheels relates to the method of shrinking on the iron tire. As is known, the tire is first forged to as nearly the required diameter as possible, after which it is heated, so as to

cause it to enlarge its diameter, and in this state placed about the rim of the wheel. When once more cooled it fits tightly. As frequently happens, however, a tire is made somewhat too small for a wheel, which involves that, in the act of shrinking, it will either force the wheel into a polygonal shape or crush one or more of the spokes. By giving the wheel a dish, the shrinkage of the tires merely increases the inclination of the cone from base to apex, the spring of the spokes being quite immaterial, all suffering to about the same extent.

Dished Wheels for Automobiles.—Ever since the motor carriage industry achieved anything like large proportions, the possibility of using dished wheels has been actively discussed. The numerous advantages to be attained have tempted several inventors to devise some suitable means for using them at least on heavy wagons. Among these may be mentioned the De Dion jointed axle and the Daimler driving differential. However, since a large part of the real efficiency of a dished wheel lies in an inclination of its axle, it is easy to see that its application to an automobile presents serious constructional problems. With a divided rear axle shaft of the usual description, it would be impracticable to incline the axles from the differential, except by some form of universal or slip-joint, as in the De Dion carriages. Consequently, until the patents on this device expire, the differential gear cannot be attached above the springs, as is desirable, for many reasons, nor can dished wheels be used.

The Use of Wood Wheels.—Charles E. Duryea enumerates the following advantages to be found in using wooden wheels:

1. The construction, proportions and strength suitable for given requirements have been carefully determined by years of practical experience.

2. Being practically one piece, they do not deteriorate by usage in bad weather and are readily cleaned.

3. If broken, they may be anywhere repaired, all the parts being easily obtainable.

4. They will often give good service even in a bady damaged condition.

5. Experience has shown that they are far more elastic than wire wheels.

6. In wire wheels any attempt to make the hub of proper length to give spread to the spokes under strain results in a clumsy appearance.

7. If the spokes are proportionately strengthened the wire wheel becomes heavier than the wood wheel.

8. The greater number of spokes in a wire wheel, and their proximity at the hub, where dirt and moisture are collected, prevents easy cleaning and promotes rust.

In regard to elasticity Mr. Duryea says:

"As a matter of fact, the wood wheel is far more elastic than the steel wheel, as may be readily seen by watching a light buggy drive over car tracks or rough payments. The rims of the wheels vibrate sideways, sometimes as much as two inches, without damage to the wheel or axle, on which account fewer broken axles will be had when wood wheels are used instead of wire ones. While it is true that the pneumatic tire practically removes the necessity of an elastic wheel, there is no need of refusing to accept a valuable feature."

Dimensions of Automobile Wheels.—As a general proposition we may assert that the larger the wheel the smaller the shocks experienced in passing over inequalities in the road-bed, and the smaller the buffing qualities required in the tires. Thus it is that a wheel five feet in diameter will sink only one-half inch in a rut one foot wide, while a thirty-inch wheel will sink nearly three times as deep, with the result that the resiliency of its tires must be enormously larger, in order to compensate the greater shock experienced. The larger wheel also rises less quickly over obstructions. These are considerations of great importance in motor vehicles, in which any device for the reduction of vibration and concussion is desirable. Furthermore, when a wheel is properly tired, the road resistance to its steady and even rotation is decreased as the square of the increase in its diameter, such a wheel of sixty inches diameter decreasing the resistance in a ratio of between 50 per cent. and 70 per cent., as compared with a wheel of thirty inches diameter.

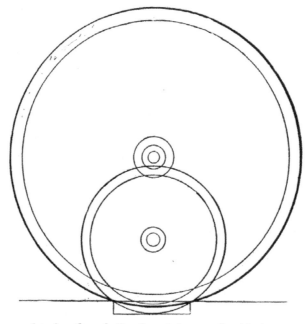

FIG. 79.—Diagram showing the relative drop into a road rut between a small carriage wheel and one twice its diameter.

There are, however, other methods for neutralizing the shocks on rough roads. The end of obtaining a low and easy-running rig may be achieved quite as well by increasing the width of the vehicle, the length of the springs and the size of the tires, as by adding to the height above the ground. Also, the broad tire is superior to the narrow one in the very same particular that it will not sink so quickly into mud and sand, and, by its greater buffing properties, neutralizes the concussion otherwise experienced with small wheels. These and other similar considerations have largely determined the prevalent practice of using wheels of moderate diameter for automobiles.

On the other hand, as many claim, the small wheel is destructive to tires in inverse ratio to its diameter and an increase in proportion would involve a corresponding economy in rubber. In this point, as in others, experiment is a better guide than theory, and if, as some claim, heavy high-speed vehicles can be constructed with wheels of large diameter, they have only to build their vehicle and try it out.

Arguing that it is a distinct advantage to enlarge the diameter of motor carriage wheels for the purposes of obtaining an offset to the concussions experienced on rough roads, to obtain higher speed within certain limits, and to secure greater durability for the tires, particularly when solid rubber tires are used, a prominent American tire-maker writes as follows:

"To prevent traveling on the rim a tire should bind the whole surface of the rim. The higher the wheel the more adhesive surface there is for the tire. When the tire is bound in by lugs the natural kneading and straining of it between the lugs will in time either shear off the lugs or loosen them. Another reason why a large wheel is to be preferred from a tire-maker's point of view is that a large wheel does not turn round so many times in a given distance, and consequently does not wear the tire so fast. If a tire travels very fast under a heavy load the kneading of it causes heating and cracking, which are intensified on the small wheel. Our experience has proved that a large wheel greatly reduces the above difficultes."

Troubles with Large Wheels.—As against theoretical advantages involved in the use of large wheels, there are numerous objections of equal, if not greater, importance. Among these may be mentioned the fact that, the larger the wheel the greater must be its proportional strength and weight of construction, in order to neutralize the ill effects of torsional motor effort, and disproportionate road resistance. Indeed, a moment's reflection will show that a wheel of sixty-inch diameter, built on the same dimensions of hub, spokes and felloes, as a wheel of thirty-inch diameter, will possess considerably more than twice the liability to strain and breakage from the causes above named. If we may assert that such increased liability, as compared with the increase of diameter is on a ratio of three to two, it is obvious that a wheel of sixty-inch diameter must be very nearly three times as heavily and strongly built as a wheel of thirty-inch diameter, in order to insure its durability. We may readily judge, then, at about what point of increased diameter a light pleasure carriage would be equipped with cart wheels. This is only one of the numerous difficulties involved in attempting to use large wheels with a modern high-speed motor.

CHAPTER NINE.

SOLID RUBBER TIRES; THEIR THEORY AND CONSTRUCTION.

The Question of Tires.—All automobiles and cycles, and a large number of horse-drawn vehicles, use rubber tires. The object is twofold:

1. To secure a desirable spring effect.

2. To obtain the requisite adhesion to the road.

While, with properly constructed springs, the first result may be achieved with steel tires, the second is almost impracticable when the power is applied direct to the wheel. Thus, if a light automobile be equipped with steel tires, the wheels will not drive on an imperfectly resistant road-bed, unless most of the load be placed over the rear axle, which, when it is too great in proportion, involves the disadvantage that the steering will be unreliable, the forward wheels tending to skid, instead of turning the vehicle in a positive manner. It is not always practicable to remedy this difficulty, either by strewing sand in front of the wheels or by applying power to all of them. An attempt to produce adhesion by constructing tires with teeth or corrugations, or by giving them extra breadth, would increase the weight for only temporary advantage. The simplest and readiest resort is found in the use of rubber tires.

The Reduction of Vibration.—On the point of reduced vibration in a vehicle, as it is related to the kind of tires used, W. Worby Beaumont says:

"It must also be remembered that the greater comfort of the rider is due to lessened severity of vibration and shock, and this is a relief in which everything above the tires participates. Now, this means a reduction in the wear and tear of every part of the car and motor which can easily be underestimated. The experience of the London cab-owners, whose records of every cost are carefully kept, is a proof of this; and they find that rubber-tired wheels suffer very much less than the iron-tired; every part that could be loosened or broken by constant severe weather or hard vibration remains tight very much longer; the breakage of lamp brackets, hangers and other parts does not occur, and that even the varnish, which being hard and breakable, lasts a great deal longer. The same immunity of the high-speed car is obtained by pneumatics, as compared with solids, and its value is greater in proportion to the greater value of the vehicle."

The Working Unit.—The situation to be met in providing proper supports for a motor carriage may be more readily understood by considering the vehicle and the roadway as the two components of a working unit, precisely like two mutually-moving parts of any machine. In both cases these parts must be calculated and arranged to move, the one upon the other, with the least possible friction and wear. An English authority on motor vans writes as follows:

"The prime fact with which engineers have to deal is that the success or failure of any design mainly depends on the nature of the road on which the van is to be worked. The V-slides of a planing machine are integral parts of the whole. The permanent way of a railroad and the rolling stock constitute together one complete machine. In just the same way the King's highway must be regarded as an integral part of all and every combination of mechanical appliances by which transport is affected on the road. In one word, if we attempt to dissever the road from the van, we shall fail to accomplish anything. Two or three years ago, the maker of a steam van told us that he was surprised to find how little power was required to work his van. He had been running it on wood-paved streets. A week or two later on he was very much more surprised to find that on fairly good macadam after rain he could do next to nothing with the same van. In preparing the designs for any van, the quality of the roads must not for a moment be forgotten; and it will not do to estimate the character of the road by anything but its worst bits. A length of a few yards of soft, sandy bottom on an otherwise good road will certainly bring a van which may have being doing well to grief. Curiously enough we have found this apparently obvious circumstance constantly overlooked. This is not all, however. A road may be level, hard, and of little resistance to traction, and yet be very destructive to mechanism. This type of road is rough and "knobby;" it will shake a vehicle to pieces, and the mischief done by such road augments in a most painfully rapid ratio with the pace of the vehicle. Jarring and tremor are as effectual as direct violence in injuring an auto. Scores of examples of this might be cited. One will suffice. In a motor van a long horizontal rod was used to couple the steering gear to the leading wheels. The rod was broken solely by vibration. It was replaced by a much heavier and stronger bar. That was broken in much the same way, and finally guides had to be fitted to steady the rod and prevent it shaking."

Analogies for a Buffing Support.—In automobile building the principal concern is for the vehicle, which must be constructed so as to endure the most unfavorable conditions of road-

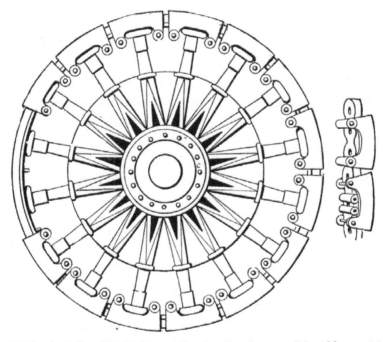

FIG. 80.—Wheel of the "Lifu" Steam Truck, showing a solid rubber cushion tire secured in position and protected by metal shoes around the rim. Although the attachment is so rigid as to prevent creeping, a very effective spring effect is obtained by combination of the cushion tire and shoes. It is effective for heavy service, which would soon destroy an ordinary tire.

bed. The effect on the road is quite secondary. In the construction of railroad locomotives, on the other hand, both components of the working unit, the vehicle and the tramway, must be considered: both must be constructed to interact with a minimal wear and damage. In this connection we may quote Matthias N. Forney, a well-known locomotive authority. In speaking of springs, which in locomotives perform some of the functions delegated to flexible tires in automobiles, he says:

"A light blow with a hammer on a pane of glass is sufficient to shatter it. If, however, on a pane of glass is laid some elastic substance, such as india-rubber, and we strike on that, the force of the blow or the weight of the hammer must be considerably increased before producing the above named effect. If the locomotive boiler is put in place of the hammer, the springs in place of the india-rubber, and the rails in place of the glass, the comparison will agree with the case above."

While in automobiles the effect on the road-bed is inconsiderable, the light and delicately-geared machinery must be protected from damage—the anvil must be shod. Whence it follows that, in the absence of anything like the steel rail surface of a railroad, utility of tires increases directly with their yielding and shape restoring properties. The more readily these functions are exercised, the smaller the wear on all the elements composing the working unit. Furthermore, the necessity in this particular becomes greater in proportion to the weight and contemplated speed capacity of the vehicle, and, beyond the point where pneumatic tires are practical, must be compensated by more efficient springs and lower rates of travel.

Rubber Tires for Automobiles.—There are two varieties of rubber tire in use for every kind of vehicle except cycles: the solid tire and the pneumatic, or inflatable tire. As is generally known, the pneumatic tire was first devised in order to furnish the needed resiliency in bicycles, and for the same purpose it has been found useful in automobiles. It is also superior in point of tractive qualites, "taking hold" of the road-bed far more effectively than the best solid. It has, however, one notable disadvantage, the constant liability to puncture, with the consequent danger of being rendered useless. In order to remedy this defect, inventors and manufacturers have introduced such features as thickening the tread of the tire, increasing its resistance to puncture by inserting layers of tough fabric in the rubber walls, and reinforcing the tread surface in various ways.

At the present time pneumatic tires are almost universally used on automobiles, solids being found only on electric vehicles, intended for use on city streets, or on heavy slow-speed trucks and vans. It is not too much to say, however, that the finality has not yet been reached, and that there are still reputable authorities who hold that, with perfected spring attachments, the solid tire may yet see a wider sphere of usefulness.

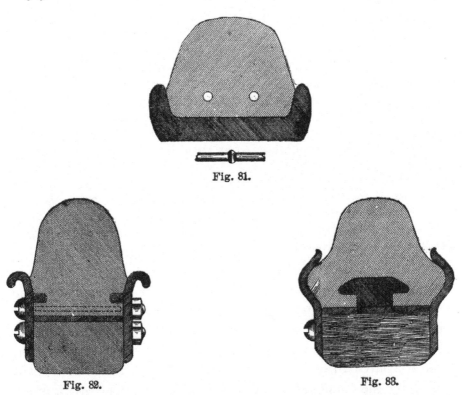

Fig. 81.

Fig. 82.   Fig. 83.

Figs. 81, 82 and 83.—Three varieties of Solid Rubber Tire, showing shape and methods of attaching on the rims. Fig. 81 shows a broad tire, which is attached by forcing over the edges of the channel-shaped rim, to which it is vulcanized, and also secured by endless wires, welded, as shown. Fig. 82 shows a tire secured by bolts through the base, also by annular lugs on the rim sides fitting into channels. Fig. 83 shows an attachment made by connecting at the base by a peripheral T-piece, also by bolts securing sides of channel-shaped rim. All three varieties show rim channels, so shaped as to allow of considerable distortion, laterly, under load.

W. Worby Beaumont writes:

"For high-speed running with comfort over street crossings and level railway crossings, the expensive pneumatic is necessary, but it is a high price to pay for this luxury, and it will only be paid by the few who will pay anything for speed. After a while, when automobile travel settles down to the moderate speeds of the majority, and to the requirements of business, the better forms of solid or nearly solid tire, in which a comparatively small amount of internal movement of the rubber takes place, will probably be most used. A hard pneumatic tire is superior to this for ease at the bad places in roads and over crossings, but greater strength of material suitable for the purpose than is yet available is required to meet all the conditions."

As to the durability of solid tires, under constant use, he says:

"With regard to solid tires, the experience of the London hansom cabs is of much interest. A pair of 1⅝ or 1¾ inch tires will last from a little over six months to, at most, nine months. The most rapid wear is on those cabs which have the best and fastest horses, if we except those cabs that have constantly to run in districts where the road surfaces are destroyed by the prevalence of tramways. * * * * * If thirty miles per day for the hansom driven by men who are, as most are, allowed two horses per day, and assuming 300 days per year, then a year's mileage would be 9,000. They run, however, not more than eight months at best before tire renewal, so that the mileage is not probably more than about 5,500 to 6,000. * * * The mileage of the tires on the four-wheel cabs is much greater, as would be expected, from the smaller weight each wheel carries and the lower speed. The miles traveled per month will also be less."

Structural Requirements in Solid Tires.—The shape and methods of attaching solid tires to the wheel rims must both be determined with reference to the source and pull of the strains likely to affect them. The weight of the vehicle is nearly the greatest source of wear, but even this consideration is closely rivaled by the torsional strain from the engine and in braking, particularly in view of the almost universal use of comparatively small wheels. Indeed, no part of the wheel could suffer greater strain than the tire from the condition last mentioned. In view of the properties of rubber, it may be readily seen that increasing the thickness of the solid tire, in proportion to the increased weight of the vehicle, will largely neutralize the destructive effects due to every cause involved in the structure of the running gear and its load. By this means is obtained a greater width of tread, with a probably smaller total abrasion of the surface from contact with the road-bed, and a greater opportunity for distributing and neutralizing the harmful strains.

The tendency in solid tires is that cuts, due to stones or other sharp obstacles, tend to spread to the centre of the tire across the tread. This is due to the quality of the strains transmitted from the wheels, as above noted, and in order to prevent this tendency from destroying the tire it is necessary to vary the shape. Accordingly, tires are made with bevel edges, rather than on square lines, and the profile is slightly rounded. This conformation, together with good width at the rim, is able to provide for absorbing much of the surplus vibration, while decreasing the ill effects due to the combined action of a heavy load and road resistance.

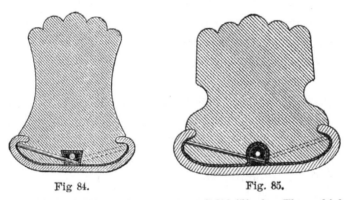

Fig 84. Fig. 85.

FIGS. 84 and 85.—Two Models of the Swinehart Solid Clincher Tire, which derives a good degree of resiliency from its construction with beaded tread and concaved sides.

On the whole it greatly prolongs the life of the tire. The curved surface at the tread and the bevel edges, tending to flatten under the load, provide a sufficient width to ensure good adhesion and the other advantages belonging to a wide tire, while, at the same time, reducing to the minimum the tendency to spread tears and cuts, as above mentioned.

The Present Situation on Solid Tires.—In justice to the earnest efforts of numerous inventors to improve the types and efficiency of solid tires, it must be confessed that the situation has changed materially in the last few years. As shown in Figs. 81, 82 and 83 the prevailing types of tire to a very recent date had a section of approximate rounded triangular shape, which, firmly secured at the sides, all around the rim, possessed a minimum degree of distortability and elasticity. That such tires were "unresilient" and liable to tear is hardly remarkable. Furthermore, that they were subject to serious cutting by stones and other sharp objects seems no less than inevitable. Recent improved tires, departing entirely from such models, have attained a good degree of resiliency and of immunity from such accidents by devices like perforating and concaving the sides of the tire all around above the rim.

The Swinehart solid clincher, shown in Figs. 84 and 85, embodies the excellent features of

1. A Heavily Beaded Tread.
2. Deeply Concaved Sides.
3. Superior Elasticity in the Rubber.

The beaded tread and concaved sides permit of considerable compression under load and the ability of absorbing heavy jolts without serious vibration. As will be readily understood, the construction seems to go far to warranting these claims. The manufacturers confidently assert that their tires are equal to any kind of service up to 35 miles per hour, but claim high efficiency at speeds above 40 miles under a heavy touring car.

CHAPTER TEN.

THE CONSTRUCTION AND TYPES OF PNEUMATIC TIRES.

Advantages of Pneumatic Tires.—The most valuable quality of the pneumatic tire is its resiliency, or the ability to bounce in the act of regaining its normal shape after encountering an obstacle in the road. On encountering a stone, for example, it will yield to a certain extent, absorbing or "swallowing it up," at the same time exerting a pressure sufficient to restore its normal shape. This quality begets two advantages for easy driving:

1. It does away with much of the lifting up of the wheel in passing over obstacles, which is otherwise inevitable.

2. It enables the tire to obtain a better grip on the road-bed.

Commensurate advantages are also derived from this cushioning quality in colliding with obstacles to one side or other of the tread, whence the total pressure exerted through the spokes is greatly reduced and such obstructions exert only a fraction of their usual power to retard the easy and steady operation of the motor and steering gear. In both cases, also, a large part of the shocks and vibrations, usually transmitted direct to the springs, are completely absorbed. No solid tires could furnish anything like such advantages in operation; the usual result, even with the most flexible springs, being that the motor is much shaken or damaged, or its action largely impaired. This is particularly true of the use of solid tires on electric vehicles, the damage resulting, both in point of efficiency and durability, having been estimated by several authorities as high as 30 per cent.

Pneumatic Tires, Speed and Power.—A prominent tire expert furnishes the following data on pneumatic tires, based on experiments:

"I have made tests with 2½ and 3 inch solid rubber tires on automobiles ranging from 16 to 24 horse-power, and on carriages weighing 1 ton to 1½ tons, and have ascertained that both of these automobiles could run safely on a good road at a maximum speed of 42 kilometers, 25 1-10 miles, an hour. When the driver attempted to go beyond this speed (always on a perfect road) the motor was subjected to such fearful vibrations its complete demolition was threatened. Under the same conditions of horse-power, weights and tires, but on what is considered a bad road, it was impossible to attain more than 15 miles an hour. The same autos, with pneumatic tires, made 60 and 70 miles an hour on an average road."

While the average automobilist never contemplates such high speeds as 60 or 70 miles per hour, it is only fair to remark that speed, combined with general road qualities, furnishes the test conditions for the jar-absorbing, vibration-neutralizing, and ad-hesion-increasing properties of pneumatic tires. Furthermore, as the result of numerous experiments, it may be correct to assert that a tire, best fitted to endure test conditions as to speed, is also within certain limits the most suitable type and make to travel under heavy loads, with a minimum of traction effort. For, as most figures seem to indicate, the decrease of traction effort is in ratio with the elasticity of the vehicle's support.

It must not be forgotten that such tests as these were made exclusively with high-speed cars, which, as is generally admitted even at the present day, cannot operate satisfactorily without pneumatics; again, that the tires used were of the ordinary round or conical tread pattern which permit of very little distortion under load and very slight resiliency.

Within recent years several types of solid and semi-solid or cushion tires have been introduced, which seem to furnish sufficient resiliency and traction efficiency for ordinary service. Among these the most noteworthy is the Swinehart tire. As shown in the figure page 105, its features are a corrugated tread and concaved sides. The makers claim for their tires superiority over pneumatics on any except the heaviest high-speed cars, not only in point of traction and speeding, but also in hill-climbing.

Single and Double=Tube Tires.—There are two varieties of pneumatic tire, the single and the double tube. The double-tube tire was first introduced, and in all its various forms consists of an inner, or air tube, made of thin and elastic india-rubber, enclosed in the outer or case tube, built up of strong fabric and a tougher and denser kind of rubber. The case tube is split on its inner face, which bears against the periphery of the wheel, in order to allow the air tube to be readily removed at any time for repair or replacement. The single-tube tire was devised as an improvement, whereby the layers of thread and tough rubber are formed upon and around the delicate air tube, making the two tubes really one. The double-tube tire is most commonly used on automobiles, being preferred on account of several advantages which will be presently mentioned.

Fabric Tires.—Pneumatic tires of both varieties were formerly built up with layers of some tough woven fabric, such as canvas, in which the warp and filler are of the same size, as in ordinary duck and other cloth. This kind of fabric, known as "square woven," has many objectionable features, particularly when the manufacturing process is not most carefully conducted. Unless the most improved methods are employed, the rubber, during vulcanization under heat, develops wrinkles in the canvas fabric, which causes unequal strains on the various plies, or layers, and constitutes the defect known as "buckling." Even without this defect, a woven fabric tire is liable to develop internal chafing between the contiguous threads of each layer, which results in heating, to the eventual deterioration of the entire structure.

Thread Tires.—Experience has proven that strength and immunity from heating demand:

1. That there shall be sufficient clearance between the contiguous threads of a tire fabric to allow a large and firm attachment between the rubber layers above and below each ply.

2. That the possibility of direct contact between individual threads shall be prevented, thus removing the occasion for chafing and heating.

In order to accomplish these results, the so-called thread fabric is used for both varieties of tire.

Single=Tube Thread Tires.—The methods of manufacturing single-tube thread tires is thus explained by Pardon W. Tillinghast, their original inventor:

"A fabric must be employed in which there is no starting point of separation between the fabric and rubber, and one that does not have a substantially smooth surface, or a surface that is continuous in the same plane. The attaching surface of the fabric presented for union with the rubber must be greatly in excess of that furnished by the fabrics in use at the present time. A plurality of plies may be used, some of the plies having

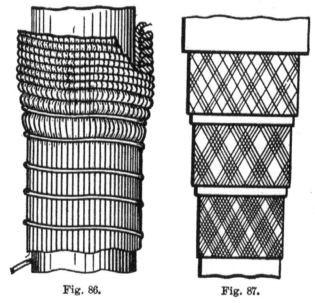

Fig. 86.   Fig. 87.

FIGS. 86 and 87.—The construction of two types of Tillinghast Single-Tube Tires, Fig. 86, shows the formation of the fabric into a succession of loops. Fig. 87 shows the open thread fabric tire in which separate threads are wound, in the manner indicated, over each successive rubber layer or tube.

a more open weave or construction than other plies, and all plies separated by rubber, which will give in effect a single tube or mass of rubber, having fibrous threads extending throughout the mass to prevent bursting, and binding the whole structure into a substantially indestructible body.

"Another means of accomplishing the same end consists essentially of employing a fabric which, when built into a tire, will have the same effect that a bath towel would if it was inclosed and imbedded in the rubber, with the threads sufficiently strong to withstand the inclosed air pressure, the little loops or fibres extending away from the general plane of the main fabric into the surrounding rubber and being vulcanized therein, furnishing an increased surface for union with the rubber; the general surface line of the fabric in each construction is to be broken so that it is not continuous in the same plane, and there is no starting point of separation between the fabric and rubber."

Accompanying figures illustrate the construction of two recent types of tire. One of them is built up with a number of strands of thread running longitudinally on the tube and wound spirally with other threads which hold them securely under inflation. The spiral windings are then pushed along the length of the tube, so as to reduce the distance between the windings

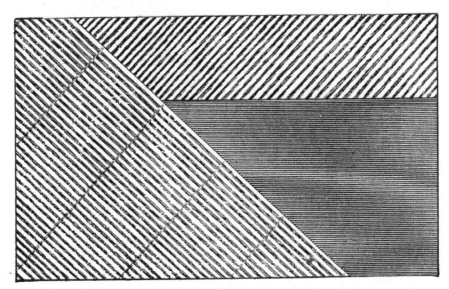

Fig. 88.—Diagram of the successive thread layers in the case-tube of a double-tube thread tire.

from one-quarter inch to less than one-eighth inch, with the result that the intermediate sections of the longitudinal threads are pushed up into series of loops, thus forming stronger attachments for the fabric, when held in the material of the rubber wall built up over this layer of threads. Tillinghast's other method of strengthening the fabric against any cause tending to burst or tear the walls, involves several layers of plies or layers of threads wound on in two diagonal directions, each one being in a more open construction than the last, the closest being on the inmost ply.

Manufacture of Thread Tires.—In the construction of thread fabric double-tube tires, each case tube is built up of plies of strong threads running parallel, and unwoven, except for light cross threads at intervals to hold the main threads in position. Each ply is vulcanized, above and below, to rubber layers, which are applied by heat, under pressure, causing the rubber to be forced between the threads, like plaster between the lathes of a wall, and entirely surrounding them. The entire body of the case

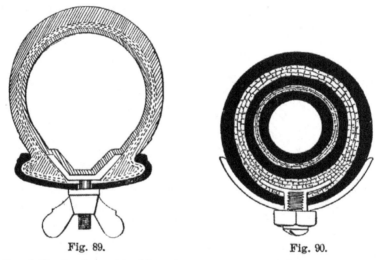

Fig. 89.   Fig. 90.

Figs. 89 and 90.—Sections of double and single-tube pneumatic tires, showing shapes of rims and methods of fastening.

tube is thus in practically one piece, made extra strong and resistant by arranging the threads of each separate ply at right angles with those of the one above or below it. Each thread being thus thoroughly imbedded in rubber, those in consecutive layers cannot come into contact. There is consequently no abrasion or heating, and the threads act, both separately and together, to strengthen the structure in every direction of stress. The end of strength is achieved by using several plies of thread, all inserted under even tension, which cannot be done with square-woven fabric. A further advantage claimed by the advocates of thread fabric is that the rubber more readily and more completely penetrates the interstices between the threads than is possible with the square weave.

Attachments for Tires.—Where single-tube tires are used on automobile wheels the attachment is made by bolts passing through the rim and secured by wing nuts on the inside surface, or by cementing the tire to the rim.

Each bolt is of one piece with a head or plate imbedded in the fabric. While such attachment is sufficiently strong under ordinary conditions, particularly when the tire is thoroughly inflated, it is desirable to spread hard cement in the rim channel, in order to prevent the accumulation of dust and sand, which are always seriously destructive to the tire.

Single-tube tires, attached as described, are very well suited for light vehicles and low speeds, but not at all for heavy, high-speed service. The principal reason is that the attachment, although probably the best possible under the necessary conditions of service, does not altogether neutralize the tendency of the single tube to creep, nor prevent rolling off the rim, should the lugs become loosened or broken. Apart from the dangers of puncture, rim-cutting, etc., shared by both varieties of tire, the single tube, as at present designed, exhibits the tendency to creep to such an extent that the greatest strain is always brought to bear upon the lugs. Being of rounded contour, it is also liable to roll on any attempt to make a sharp corner at high speeds, the attachments at the base often proving insufficient to resist the sidewise stress, and being repeatedly loosened. Thus, although embodying the great advantage of being more easily treated for puncture, the single-tube is practically inferior to the double-tube tire.

Comparison of Tires.—As regards the relative merits of the two varieties of pneumatic tire, we may profitably quote Charles E. Duryea. He states his conclusions as follows:

"The ordinary round tire lying in an arc-shaped rim, as is the common method, cannot utilize its side walls properly when meeting an obstacle, since it is flattened toward the rim and caused to bend at the side abruptly at two places; being bent outward over the edge of the rim and inward at its widest point. The outward bend, together with dirt which may get between tire and rim, tends to chafe the tire on the edge of the rim, a phenomenon commonly known as rim cutting. The other bend cannot stretch the outer layers of fabric, so it must compress the inner fabric and inner rubber, which compression rapidly causes a crack, weakening the tire from the inside, with the result that in a short while the tire begins to swell along the sides and finally bursts. Any rim, therefore, which will hold the tire at the bottom only, and yet preserve it from rolling sidewise on the rim, is conducive to long life of tire, for it leaves the side walls free from short bends and increases the depth of the tire, which increases its beneficial results as well."

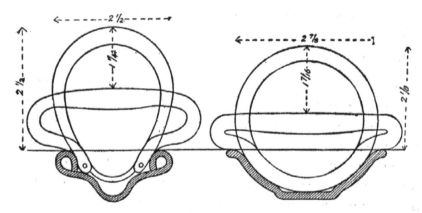

FIG. 91.—Diagram illustrating the relative degree of flattening consequent on deflating a double-tube pneumatic, mechanically secured to base, and a cemented single-tube pneumatic, through one-half diameter above edges of rim. Note the sharp corners of the single tube.

An accompanying figure of a mechanically fastened double-tube tire and of a single-tube cemented tire with arc-shaped rim, shows their shapes when inflated and when deflated to one-half their diameter; demonstrating that since a double-tube tire may be compressed further than a single tube, a small tire of the former variety is as efficient in smoothing the road as a larger one of the latter variety. A proportionate deflation of the two shows a further advantage, in that the walls of a double-tube tire are bent much less for a given compression than those of a single tube, and are forced against the edges of the rim with much less compression. The single-tube tire does not flatten out so widely in proportion to its diameter as does the double tube, which fact is of importance, because added width means added supporting surface, tending to resist further compression as it increases.

Duryea concludes, therefore, that:

"The best automobile tire is the one mechanically fastened so as to relieve the fabric from the strain of holding the tire in position. Its fabric must be as strong as possible, because of the heavy service which means a long fibre closely-woven canvas of the greatest possible strength and the fewest necessary thicknesses which arrangement is less liable to puncture or tear than any thread fabric and is yet as flexible as the necessary strength will permit. Being mechanically fastened, the fabric need not be stretched in the direction of the length of the tire which increases the resilience and lessens the strain and liability of rupture in passing over obstructions."

As may be readily understood, a further advantage gained by using a double-tube tire, mechanically fastened at the base, is that the sidewise strains encountered in turning corners, are not so liable to cause rolling off the rim. In bicycles this danger is largely averted by the rake, or inclination, taken by the wheels in turning corners, which maintains the entire wheel-structure, including the tire, in one plane. But in automobiles this rake cannot be obtained except with the front or steer wheels, the result being that the strain brought upon a tire in turning corners at high speed is enormous. A tire standing high above the rim and rigidly attached at the base is capable of a very considerable sidewise deformation without particularly great danger of rupture or other accident. Howbeit, if the inflation be insufficient, such side strains are very liable to loosen the fastenings, particularly when clamps are used.

Advantages of Double Tubes.—Double-tube tires are practically immune from creeping, on account of the security of their attachment to the wheel rim. They will not roll off, like single tubes, although the attempt to turn sharp corners at high speed strains the fabric excessively, and at times may result in rupture. There are two general methods of attachment: by clinches and by side-flange. In both there is a secure joint between the tire base and the rim at every point around the periphery of the wheel.

Clincher Tires.—A very large proportion of double-tube tires are of the clincher type, being constructed with rubber and fabric flanges on either side of the case tube, which fit snugly into channels formed by inturning the edges of the rim. These chan-

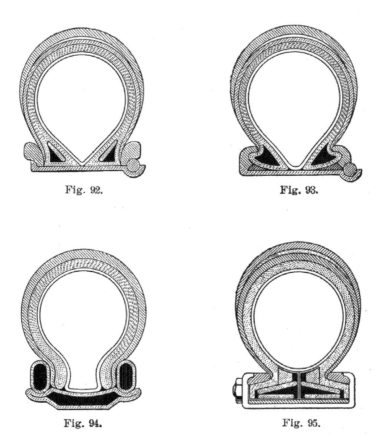

Fig. 92. Fig. 93.

Fig. 94. Fig. 95.

FIGS. 92, 93, 94 and 95.—Four Forms of Double-Tube Pneumatic Tire, showing methods of securing to the rims. Fig. 92, the Goodyear Detachable Side-Flange Tire, with reversible side-rings; Fig. 93, the Goodyear Clincher with side-rings reversed; Fig. 94, the Dunlop Tire, showing tubular side-rings; Fig. 95, the Fisk Tire, showing bottom flanges and retaining rings held to rim by clips and nuts.

nels are the clinches. In removing the case tube it is necessary to insert a flat tool between it and the rim and pry them apart. This operation is tedious and also involves very great strain on the fabric. A careless hand may also cut or bruise the air tube, particularly when it is not protected by a flap.

Side=Flange Tires.—The side-flange tire is gradually supplanting the clincher in very many quarters, embodying, as it does, the advantage of being readily removable, without strain or injury to the fabric or rubber. The original patterns of this variety of tire were held upon the flat rim between two annular plates or flanges, bolted through the felloe. The Goodyear tire, probably the first of its type, was further enforced by strands of braided wire at the base on either side of the opening of the case tube. Its later forms have the wires, but are retained on the rim by two endless steel flange rings and an open steel locking ring, which holds the flanges in position.

The Dunlop Tire.—The latest Dunlop tire is logically in the side-flange class. Its special feature has always been two endless wire rings at either side of the base, which furnishes a sufficiently firm attachment to the rim. Former models of this tire were removable in the same manner as clinchers, by prying over the side of the rim channel. At present, however, removal is accomplished by loosening one of the tubular retaining rings, which is cut and securely held in place by screwing up a turnbuckle.

The Fisk tire has its case tube flanged at the base in somewhat the same fashion as a clincher, but is secured to the flat rim by two metal rings fitting snugly over the flanges and held tightly in place by lugs and bolts.

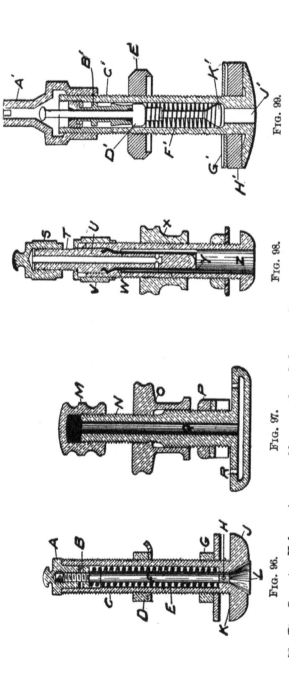

FIG. 96.   FIG. 97.   FIG. 98.   FIG. 99.

FIG. 96.—The Sangster Valve. A, removable screw-threaded cover; B, retaining nut, having notches at edge for passage of air; C, the valve tube; D, lock nut and washer for holding stem to the wheel rim; E, helical spring bearing on B and holding valve, L, in its seat; F, valve stem; G, washer holding valve stem to inner surface of rim; H, passages for admitting air into interior of tire; J, head on inner end of valve stem within tire; K, roughened face of J, making joint with the tire walls under air pressure; L, valve seated in J, and carried on the rod, F.

FIG. 97.—The Welch Valve. This is of the same general description as is used on several double-tube tires. M, the screw cap closing the valve tube; N, the valve tube; O, cap for gripping the wheel rim, on the inner side of which is the nut and washer, P, which presses the wall of the inner tube against the face of the head, R. When the inner tube is fully inflated the holes shown on the upper face of R are closed by pressure of the rubber walls against them.

FIG. 98.—The Wood Valve. S, the screw cap on the valve tube; T, end of the valve tube; U, tube for air from pump; Y, cap holding deflating valve, W, in the seat, loosed when tire is to be deflated; X, nut for holding valve stem to inside of rim; Y, a rubber tube around pipe. U, admitting air to tire when pressure is sufficient through ports at bottom of tube, U; Z, tube admitting air to interior of tire, also head and washer for attaching to inner tire tube.

FIG. 99.—The Schrader Valve. A' is the screw cap on the valve tube; B', the valve seat carried on the binding nut within the tube, C'; D', the valve; E', nut and washer for securing tire to the inner face of the wheel rim; F', spring holding the valve in its seat; G', H', washers bearing against outer face of wheel rim; J', head holding inner surface of tire tube; K', head at the lower end of the valve stem through grooves at the base of which the air enters the tire.

CHAPTER ELEVEN.

Accidents to Pneumatic Tires.—The serviceability of pneumatic tires depends upon a number of considerations, quite apart from any question of their merits as manufactured products. That a tire should embody the best available materials and workmanship must be evident on reflection, and any occasions for disablement arising from faults in these particulars need no lengthy consideration. If the case tube is poorly made, it will heat and crack. If the wall is too thin it will tear or cut. If the walls and tread are too thick and heavy the difficulty of bending under load is increased, sharp corners being formed and the fabric ruptured. If the attachment to the rim is insufficient the tire will creep.

Causes of Excessive Wear in Tires.—A tire may be injured in a number of ways, on account of faulty attachments, carelessness or hard service. Among the commonest forms of wear and tear are:

1. Creeping.
2. Puncture.
3. Rim-cutting.
4. Cracking of the walls.
5. Excessive wear on the walls or **tread**.
6. Chemical action.

The Creeping of Tires.—Creeping is found almost exclusively in single-tube tires. It is due to the fact that the weight of the vehicle, in process of travel, tends to centralize the pressure on the rubber walls, and cause the tire to bulge just forward of the point of contact with the ground. As may be readily recognized, a continued succession of such bulgings tends both to loosen the adhesion of the tire and the rim, and **also to cause the tire to**

push forward from the ground, and thus around the rim, in the effort to relieve and distribute the pressure. As a result, when inflation is insufficient, great strain and pull will be exerted where the valve is joined to the tire, and a rupture often follows at that point. Even were it possible to obviate the last-named accident, it is evident that the service of a tire, thus loosened by the creeping process is impaired. Moreover, it would inevitably roll sideways from the rim before it had been long in use. Also, if loose, it chafes at the rim and wears quickly. The only assurance against

FIG. 100.—Leather-reinforced Pneumatic Tire, showing outside case of leather and spiked leather head.

creeping in a single-tube tire is found in reliable bolt and lug fastenings. Double-tube tires are immune from creeping on account of having complete peripheral attachments in clinches, side flanges, etc.

Puncture of Tires.—The accident known as puncture is such a piercing of the air tube as allows the air to escape and flatten the tire. It is generally caused by a sharp stone or a nail piercing the tread, in which event the air tube must be immediately repaired or else a new one substituted.

Among other possible causes of puncture are:

1. Nipping of the air tube by the tire removing lever; by the lug of the screw bolt; by the edge of the case tube.

2. Sand or other hard substances in the case tube.

Puncture is always an annoying accident, but with the later makes of tire, particularly those equipped with a leather tread, it happens less often than formerly.

Rim=Cutting.—Rim-cutting of pneumatic tires is a mishap arising generally from:

1. Sand or sharp particles lodged between the tire and the edges of the rim, which, particularly when the tire is partially deflated, cut through the outer layer of rubber to the fabric beneath.

2. Overloading, or compelling a tire to carry a weight greater than its dimensions warrant. This causes the tire to flatten, in spite of persistent extra inflating, and the result is nearly always shearing-off at the edges near the points where the flanges engage the clinches.

3. Defective or bent rims. Rims may be unsuitable for given makes of tire, because made for some other style. It is essential that the tire fit the rims perfectly, since, if the attachment is not tight, movement and chafing result, or stones and sand find lodgment; if it is too tight the pressure against the edges of the rim is excessive.

Loose or ill-fitting studs always allow some movement of the tire, and occasion cutting, at least in spots around the rim.

These mishaps occur less frequently at present than those due to bent or rusty rims, which work the same havoc as those that fit poorly. It is particularly necessary to keep the rim in perfect repair, to clean out all evidences of rust, and to remedy any bends or breaks at once.

4. Insufficient inflation is often a cause of cutting, even when the rims are in perfect repair. It is necessary to keep the tires pumped hard at all times. If cutting then results, it is the least possible evidence that the tires are too small for the load they are obliged to carry.

Carriage builders of the present day are able to calculate very accurately the endurance of a tire under a predetermined load. But if the vehicle is used for purposes not contemplated in the original design. it is evident that the tires will not endure. Excessive speeds, like overloading, will work destruction of the best tires. Indeed, both extremes amount to the same thing in the end.

No means has yet been devised to insure tires used on very high-speed machines.

5. Sharp curves or excessive side-slip tend to produce a side pressure that is concentrated at the rim, and, in proportion to the weight of the car, or the speed at which it is driven, are liable to result in cutting of the case tube. Side slipping or skidding is largely neutralized in cars with long wheel-base, but, even with this desirable structural feature, occasions may arise in which rim-cutting results from sudden turns. Once started, a weak point is developed that tends to increase the rent under all favorable circumstances.

Cracking of the Walls.—If a tire is well made any evidence of cracking of the case tube may safely be attributed to driving with insufficient inflation. As the result of a puncture or other mishap, all the air may be exhausted, causing the tire to be completely flattened under the weight of the vehicle. If this does not immediately produce cracking of the case tube, it is a rare good fortune. Long continued pressure of this kind will infallibly tear and destroy the fabric.

The remedy is, of course, to make such repairs as are possible at the time, or else to insert a new air tube. If no extra air tube is at hand, and repairs cannot be made conveniently, the best makeshift is to procure sufficient length of old rope to wind around the circumference of the wheel inside the case tube. This may be done by jacking up the wheel, in precisely the same fashion as if to insert a new air tube, and starting to wind the rope inside the case tube, entirely around the circumference of the wheel, until no more can be inserted. Care should be taken to leave sufficient clearance to insert the flange of the tube in the clinch. There will thus be afforded sufficient support to keep the tire from being flattened for more than half its diameter, thus probably saving the case tube.

Excessive Wear on the Walls or Tread.—Obviously a tire must undergo considerable wear in course of use. With the best possible roads and the highest grade of rubber a more or less rapid deterioration is inevitable. For this, of course, there is no remedy. It is desirable, however, to avoid excessive wear whenever possible.

No tire should be used after the rubber at the tread or side walls has been worn down to the fabric. The result will be that the structure is weakened, offering a smaller resistence to puncture and tearing, also exposing the fibre to the destructive action of water and other corrodents, not to mention the more rapid wear due to abradents, sand, etc.

In case of extraordinary accidents that cut, wear or tear the walls, the case tube should be replaced immediately, in order to prevent an explosive rending of the air tube. This latter is a far more serious mishap than any mere puncture or even cutting, and very frequently precludes the possibility of repair.

With wheels not perfectly parallel, a condition to be found almost exclusively on the front wheels, there is liable to be a very great wear on the treads. This is inevitable, since both wheels must slide in a sidewise direction, quite as much as they can rotate, involving an unnecessary waste of good rubber.

The cause of non-parallelism in the front wheels is generally to be found in a short or bent drag link between the steering arms, and this condition should be carefully searched for before other troubles are suspected.

Sudden braking, although sometimes inevitable, as in attempting to avoid running down a foot passenger or colliding with any object in the road, is a frequent source of wear on rear-wheel tires. Causing the wheels to slide, before the momentum of the car is overcome, it must inevitably cause wear at the tread. For sake of preserving the tires, if for no other reason, the brake of an automobile should be thrown on as gradually as possible.

Direct-acting brakes, or shoe brakes, such as are used on heavy horse wagons with steel tires, are mentioned by some authorities as destructive to the treads of rubber pneumatics. They are practically never used on automobiles at the present day, and need not claim much of our attention. It may be said, however, that their destructive action seems to be in inverse ratio to their bearing surface. With a direct-acting brake of sufficient surface to avoid concentration of strain on a limited area of tread, the wear would be very much less. One authority states that he has used such a shoe brake on a pneumatic tricycle tire for several years without harmful results.

DRIVING AGAINST CURBSTONES is often the occasion of wear upon the side walls of a tire. If frequently repeated the fabric will be exposed, and the destruction of the tire hastened. A driver should always avoid contact with a curbstone, since injuries to the wheels and tires are by no means warranted by the slight advantage gained in point of convenience to passengers.

Chemical Action.—Under the general head of chemical action we may include causes operating to corrode or rot any part of the tire. Chemical deterioration may affect both the rubber and the fabric, and in either case rapidly wrecks the tire. The best and strongest tires are as liable to chemical injury as any others.

THE RUBBER of a tire suffers chemical deterioration from the action of oil, gasoline or acids. These substances, whether carelessly dropped upon the tire or present at any part of the roadway over which it travels, are always destructive in their action. If, therefore, gasoline or oil are accidentally spilled upon a tire, it should be wiped clean as quickly as possible, and care should be exercised not to allow the wheels to stand in accidental puddles of oil on the table floor. Under the action of such substances rubber hardens, losing its elasticity and tenacity, and developing a tendency to wear and chip.

STRONG AND STEADY LIGHT, as well as high or changing temperature, is harmful to rubber. After a tire has been in use for some time it is less liable to suffer from light and heat than a new tire. However, no tire, new or old, should be exposed for extended periods in blazing sunlight. Particularly, it must be said, it should never be left near a window, so that the sun shines through glass. Sunlight, under such conditions, tends to harden the rubber, causing it to develop cracks. Heat acts in similar fashion, although, unless excessive, far more slowly.

PNEUMATIC TIRE TROUBLES.

Extra tires carried on a car should always be kept in cases, such as are provided for the purpose by tire dealers. This rule applies with particular force to the very elastic air tubes, which should be stored in bags in some convenient place away from the light and heat of the sun. Many expensive air tubes have been unnecessarily ruined by lying loose in the wicker baskets at the sides of the tonneau.

Tires in use are not as liable to injury from sunlight as the extra stored tires, for the reason that the dust and mud of travel, while not directly contributing to the advantage of the rubber, seem to neutralize the ill effects of the sun's rays in an efficient manner. This is the best explanation of the fact that used tires are less liable to injury than new ones.

Chemical injury to the fabric or thread lining of a tire consists most usually in rotting from the presence of water or dampness. Injury by oil, acid, etc., is much more remote. On account of the liability of the fabric to be rotted by moisture, it is particularly desirable that the rubber be not allowed to wear away, so as to expose it.

Dampness acts on the fabric of stored tire far more quickly than water will act on canvas wholly immersed in it. Water has the peculiar faculty of penetrating even the minutest chinks or punctures, and is rapidly absorbed by the fibres composing the tire fabric. Only one result can follow: the fabric will be broken down and the case tube correspondingly weakened. Very frequently tires will burst from this cause, after being stored through the winter months.

When in constant use the fabric of a tire is very little in danger of deterioration from water, although dampness in the stable should always be avoided. A tire in use, however, is exposed to an ever graver danger: a cut in the tread of the case tube may admit sand or mud, which, working under the outer layer of rubber, will form a pocket, where water may collect and begin work on the fabric. Any sign of a cut or a *blister*—as lumps covering sand or mud are called—should warn the driver that the tire needs repair.

CHAPTER TWELVE.

Dimensions of Pneumatic Tires.—Nearly the most important consideration in securing the best service from pneumatic tires is that they should be of sufficiently large dimensions for the load they are intended to carry. A large part of the troubles with tires, so conspicuous in former days, was due principally to the fact that they were too small for their loads. That they should be sufficiently inflated is also important. The proper dimensions and air-pressures for double-tube tires, as given by Michelin and other authorities, are found, as follows:

For loads between 350 pounds and a maximum of 600 pounds per wheel, $2\frac{1}{2}$ inches diameter, inflation pressure, 50 pounds.

For loads between 440 and 660 pounds per wheel, $3\frac{1}{3}$ inches diameter, inflation, 70 pounds.

For loads between 550 and 990 pounds per wheel, $3\frac{1}{2}$ inches diameter, inflation, 71 to 78 pounds.

For loads between 660 and 1140 pounds per wheel, 4 inches diameter, inflation, 71 to 78 pounds.

For loads between 880 and 1320 pounds per wheel, $4\frac{2}{3}$ inches diameter, inflation 71 to 78 pounds.

For loads between 1100 and 1650 pounds per wheel, $5\frac{1}{2}$ inches diameter, inflation, 71 to 85 pounds.

The inflation pressure may be indicated by pressure gauges, such as are furnished by some supply houses, but may be judged sufficient when the tire stands firm under the load. A tire too small for the load will likely burst under pressure sufficient to render it firm.

Care of Tires.—In addition to the several principles stated in the foregoing chapter, it is necessary to dwell but little on the matter of caring for tires, so as to prevent, as far as possible, the common mishaps.

1. A tire of proper size for the load carried, if kept properly inflated, is less liable to puncture than when allowed to become soft.

2. It is undesirable to overload a car, so as to bring more than the. maximum pressure, as given above, upon each wheel. The rest of the machinery may endure it: the tires will suffer.

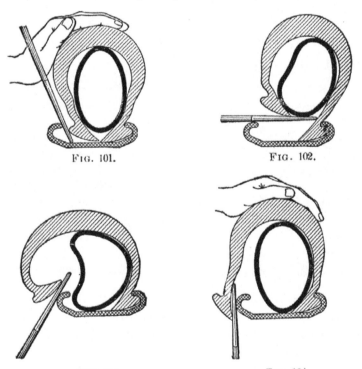

FIG. 101.   FIG. 102.

FIG. 103.   FIG. 104.

FIGS. 101-104.—Showing successive stages in the removal of the shoe or case-tube of a clincher pneumatic tire by the insertion of a tire tool.

This is one very excellent reason why pneumatic tires may not be used on commercial automobiles.

3. Excessive speeds are made possible—at least in the present stage of automobile design—by the use of pneumatic tires. The inevitable consequence, however, is the rapid destruction of the tires. Over-speeding is in this respect equivalent to overloading.

4. Sudden braking, which causes the tires to drag by re-straining the rotation of the wheels, should be avoided, when-ever possible. Tires so treated wear and tear rapidly.

5. Sudden, or short, turns, by distorting, or straining the tires, often results in tearing out and destruction.

6. A tire should never be allowed to rub against a curb stone or other low ridge. Running in a street car track is not the best practice, as it sometimes results in undue wear upon the tire treads, and occasionally causes cutting of the walls.

7. Any evidence of wearing or tearing of the tread or case tube should lead to speedy repair. Tears in the outer rubber cover generally increase in size, allowing sand and moisture

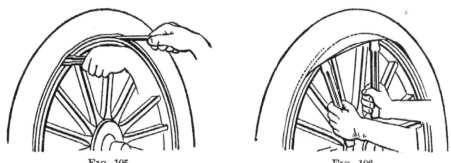

FIG. 105.   FIG. 106.

FIGS. 105-106.—Showing method of removing the case tube with two levers.

to work in, forming "blisters," injuring the fabric and tearing off the outer layer of rubber. It is well to have any tear, small or large, vulcanized as soon as possible, thus saving further trouble and expense. A new tread should be vulcanized on before the fabric of a tire is exposed.

8. Never allow a tire on a vehicle to become deflated. If it leaks, remove it for repair.

9. Particular care should be exercised, in removing and re-turning case tubes, not to rip or pinch the air tube, either with the tire tool or between the ends of the wall, or under the clips.

Repair of Tires.—Formerly books treating of tires included explicit directions for repairing punctured and injured tires.

Most of the rules and directions then given are out of date at the present day. Several reasons may be assigned for this statement:

1. The greater weight of the vehicles now in use causes considerable heating within the tire, particularly when the fabric is not securely united with the rubber in the case tube, or when it rips and tears in the tread. Often the mere movement of the tire generates considerable heat. This condition naturally destroys the effect of most rubber cements, such as are used for attaching patches to the inner tube, or for securing plugs in the case tube.

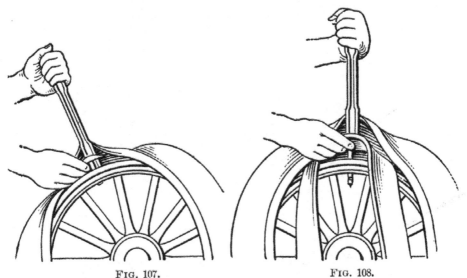

FIG. 107.   FIG. 108.

FIGS. 107-108.—Showing method of removing the air tube with a single (stepped) lever.

2. The work of repairing an air tube is altogether too delicate an operation to be undertaken by any amateur. This is particularly true of large tubes intended to contain high pressures.

3. Experience warrants the statement that the common run of plugs, patches, foolish tire bands and all other repairs effected by the use of cement are worse than useless for present-day tires. Only vulcanizing can effectually remedy dam-

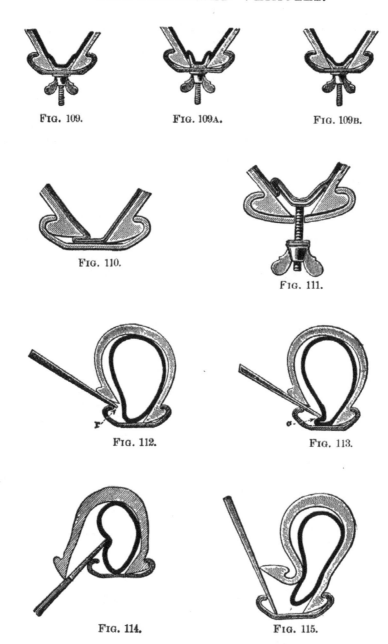

FIG. 109.   FIG. 109A.   FIG. 109B.

FIG. 110.

FIG. 111.

FIG. 112.   FIG. 113.

FIG. 114.   FIG. 115.

FIGS. 109-115.—Diagrams of various mishaps to pneumatic tires. Fig. 109 shows the air tube resting over a perfectly fitting chaplet head; Figs. 109A and 109B, the effects of poorly fitting chaplets, showing liability to pinching of the air tube; Fig. 110, air tube pinched under the edge of case tube; Fig. 111, air tube pinched by attempt to pull down chaplet—in both these cases the air tube is not sufficiently inflated while attaching the case tube; Figs. 112 and 115, the right and wrong way to raise the edge of the case tube over the clinch; Figs. 113 and 114, two ways in which the air tube may be nipped by allowing the tire tool to penetrate too far.

age encountered in any form of tire. Vulcanizing should always be done by a person thoroughly acquainted with working rubber.

An effectual method of guarding against disablement from tire accidents is to carry at least one extra case tube, and several extra air tubes. Both varieties of extra tube should be carefully wrapped and protected from sunlight and moisture. Moisture within the case tube will soon work destruction to the air tube.

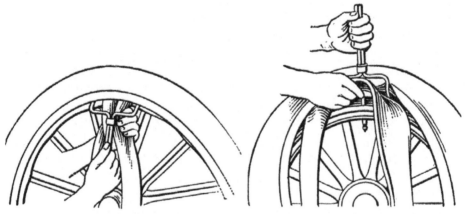

FIG. 116.   FIG. 117.
FIGS. 116-117.—Showing method of removing the air tube with a double lever.

In the event of being caught with no extra air tube, the damaged tube may be removed from the case, which may then be filled as nearly as possible with a coil of half-inch rope, wound around the rim, and stuffed into the case as far as it can be done, so as to prevent too much bending of the walls. The support thus formed will enable the case to be used at a slow speed, until the return home. If the tire is a clincher, the process of stuffing in the rope is tedious. If a side-flange tire is used, the process is far simpler.

CHAPTER THIRTEEN

TYPES AND MERITS OF AUTOMOBILES.

Types of Automobiles.—Within the last three years the construction of automobiles, or motor-propelled road vehicles has been greatly modified and improved in a number of particulars. The troubles that were previously notable are now very nearly overcome, and in the case of steam, electric and gasoline carriages alike the ideal of a perfectly practical machine is rapidly being approximated. Neither has this gradual development of the ideal vehicle involved any such radical changes as some superficial and ill-informed persons have confidently predicted. True to the statements of practical experts, the leading features—such as steering and compensating apparatus, rear-wheel drive, resilient tires, and several other features—have remained the same. Only the details have been altered and improved in the gradual evolution of the practical out of the experimental. Furthermore, the steady tendency is toward a greater uniformity of design, rather than toward any eccentric or novel constructions; toward a perfecting of standard constructions already recognized, rather than toward anything entirely new and peculiar.

In another respect the development of the practical road carriage is notable: and that is, that the largely increased use of the self-propelled vehicle has enabled the builders to afford and supply every new device leading to speed and safety. This liberality in the manufacture of the well known types has been a constant spur to invention to meet the desires of purchasers—the result being, at the date of the issue of this edition of the work, the production of one of the most marvelous mechanisms the world has ever seen.

This remark relates to the several types of vehicles, gasoline, steam and electric. Each type has its advantages and disadvantages. The fact that one form of power is more extensively used than another should not influence the intending purchaser any more than the talk of interested parties. He should be guided by his mechanical inclinations and by the particular service that he will require of the machine. For instance, while an electric vehicle is very desirable for city use or in localities having good roads and battery charging facilities, a steamer is well adapted to touring on all kinds of roads and steep hills. While the radius of travel on one filling of fuel tanks is generally greater for the gasoline car, the steamer can use as fuel both gasoline and kerosene.

Advantages Analyzed.—In a recent number of a well-known automobile journal (*Motor,* New York), the several advantages of the three types of machine are set forth by prominent experts.

Speaking for the steam vehicle, Windsor T. White specifies the following twelve advantages: (1) Practical absence of jar and noise; (2) ease of control—throttling instead of gear shifting by levers; (3) absence of gearing between the engine and the drive axle; (4) flexibility of the steam engine, permitting any speed, from highest to lowest, with nearly even power efficiency; (5) continuous application of power in each cylinder, instead of a power stroke in each two revolutions, as with the four-cycle gasoline engine; (6) ease of lubrication in the comparatively cool cylinder, and absence of trouble from over-oiling; (7) the fact that the steam engine is better understood by the average man than either of the other motive powers; (8) from this reason, the greater ease of having roadside repairs made; (9) a combination of flash generator, automatic fuel regulation, compound engine and direct drive gives the most satisfactory machine for inexpert operators; (10) certain and invariable automatic regulation dependent solely on the physical properties of varying temperature and pressure; (11) complete elimination of boiler troubles, scaling, etc., by the use of the flash generator; (12) complete immunity from burning out, with the combination of flash generator and thermostatic regulation.

Mr. White is speaking, of course, of a carriage using the flash-line system of generation, as embodied in the machines built by his company, which have proved of the greatest advantage for this purpose since the time of Serpollet's first invention of this apparatus in 1889. With other types of generator and regulator the advantages are less conspicuous. Mervyn O'Gorman, an English authority, states the case of the average steam carriage from both sides. As ten advantages: (1) Absence of speed gears;

(2) saving of wear, tear and noise; (3) high power-outputs for short periods for climbing hills and traveling on rough roads; (4) greater speed uphill, and greater average speed for original cost; (5) proportionate fuel consumption and power efficiency; (6) cleanliness equal to petrol motors; (7) absence of the troublesome ignition system, as on petrol motors; (8) absence of exhaust noises, back-shots, pre-ignition, etc.; (9) cheapness in first cost; (10) starting without cranking, therefore stillness of the car in standing. As sixteen disadvantages: (1) The need of extinguishing the fire during stoppages; (2) the consequent trouble of re-igniting the burner; (3) the great loss of fuel, due to not extinguishing; (4) the need for greater attention, owing to the number of adjustments not automatic; (5) limited capacity for carrying fuel and water supply; (6) heavy fuel consumption, generally twice that of gasoline carriages of the same power; (7) heavy water consumption, and the need for constant refills; (8) fouling of the boiler tubes—in some types; (9) vitiation of the air by burned products in greater volume than with gasoline motors; (10) loss of time in starting from a cold boiler; (11) greater dangers from neglect, such as seizing and heating from insufficient lubrication, grave consequences in failure of water system, priming from high water and consequent knocking of the pistons, evil effects of feeding oil into any type of boiler or generator, clogging of valves or failure of pumps; (12) the troubles, due to wind blowing down upon the fire; (13) stoppage of safety valves; (14) necessity of using soft water for boilers; (15) trouble of cleaning the flues; (16) issue of visible steam mixed with oil liable to stain clothes.

Setting forth the advantages of the gasoline carriage, Elmer Apperson enumerates the following twelve points: (1) Availability of fuel, readily obtainable anywhere; (2) convenience in renewing the supply, no fire being present that must be extinguished; (3) economy of fuel, owing (a) to none being used when the machine is standing, (b) to the small amount used when running light, (c) to the high efficiency of the gasoline engine —twenty-five or thirty per cent. as against ten per cent. for the steam engine, and less for the electric motor; (4) perfect throttling system for changing the speed and power ratios; (5) noiselessness, as achieved in the later types of motor; (6) ease of using in winter with non-freezing jacket solutions; (7) the absence of indicating devices to distract the mind of the operator; (8) absence of constant fire, as in a steam machine to "make a volcano of the slightest leak"; (9) rareness of total disablement, as against steam or gasoline machines; (10) extended travel radius, gasoline machines having been run 1,000 miles without a stop, as against the record of 100 miles for a steamer, and the average of 30 or 40 miles per charge for the electric; (11) the greater perfection of the gasoline machine, on account of the thought and labor expended in its development; (12) that it can be built with any style of body, for any kind of service, and holds all records for speed and endurance.

The claims of the electric carriage are set forth by Walter C. Baker under the following twelve heads: (1) The superior material of the electric carriage, together with its durability and attractiveness; (2) the speed range, greater than a horse at low speed and within legal limits at top speed; (3) the small care required in comparison with other types of power, the smallest attention yielding the best results—the battery alone demanding particular care; (4) the ideal source of energy found in the storage battery, which is compact, clean, safe, and able to yield instantly to the will of the operator; (5) freedom from noise, odor or vibration; (6) with all mechanical parts rotating, anti-friction bearings may be used throughout, enabling great results from little power; (7) the slight physical effort required to manage it; (8) absence of oil, fire, water and pumps leaves nothing to freeze, burn, or explode, and requires no pumping at the start; (9) absence of lubricants renders it clean; (10) safety for ladies and convenience for short tours; (11) small number of occasions for failure to run; (12) a single lever to control the motive power, and another for steering, rendering it the simplest of all to manage.

CHAPTER FOURTEEN.

Power Derived from Heat.—Both steam and gas engines are forms of heat motor; since both operate by means of the expansive energy of gases, which have been subjected to the action of heat. A permanent gas, or the vapor from a liquid or solid substance, when exposed to heat tends to expand, and, in expanding, exerts an active pressure in all directions. Thus, if a gas, or a readily volatized liquid, like water or alcohol, contained in a corked vessel, be exposed to heat, the expansion will be exhibited in the expulsion of the cork. In this fact it demonstrated the principle, on which all forms of heat engine operate—that heat may be transformed into mechanical energy through its effects on liquids and gases, promoting the change from fluid to gaseous state and then increasing the volume of the gas. No state of matter is entirely permanent, and, as a general rule, the absorption of a sufficient quantity of heat results in liquefying a solid, and in vaporizing a liquid. Gases subjected to heat, either when ignited, as with inflammable gases, or merely heated as with separated steam, tend to assume greater volumes so long as the temperature is not allowed to fall. On the other hand, modern science has succeeded in producing liquid air and liquid carbonic acid gas by the combination of extremely high pressures and extremely low temperatures. It is sufficient to say that no pressure has yet been found sufficiently high to liquefy air, without the cooperation of a temperature commensurately low. Conversely, also, no known degree of cold can produce this effect, apart from a high pressure acting at the same time.

Principles of Pressure and Temperature in Gases.—A leading property of gases is that, the temperature remaining the same, an increase in volume involves a corresponding decrease in pressure, and, that to maintain even a constant pressure in an expanding gas, the temperature must be raised on a steadily increasing ratio. In other words, a given cubic content of expanding gas, at a constant temperature, shows a lower pressure per square inch as the expansion progresses, and, in order to obtain a given total original efficient pressure the cubic content of the cylinder must increase with the expansion. On the other hand, if a given cubic content of gas be compressed to half its normal volume, without involving an accompanying increase in temperature, the pressure is doubled. In either case, an undue increase of temperature operates to neutralize the stated principle.

From these facts we may deduce the principles that:

1. The inherent pressure of a gas varies inversely with **the** volume and directly with the temperature.

2. The volume of a gas varies inversely with the **pressure and** directly with the temperature.

3. The inherent temperature of a gas varies directly with **the** pressure and inversely with the volume.

To state these principles in another way, we may say:

1. An increased pressure involves a decreased volume **or an** increased temperature.

2. An increased volume involves a decreased pressure **or an** increased temperature.

3. An increased temperature involves an increased volume **and** an increased pressure.

As the operative conditions in a heat engine are immensely irregular no formulae can precisely express the proper temperature, volume or pressure to show working conditions. Since, however, the attributes of the gas at various points in the cycle are in direct proportion to the dimensions of the cylinder, the length of the stroke, the cubic content of the clearance, and other familiar physical and mechanical conditions, very **satisfactory** figures may be found to express the power and capacity of any particular engine.

The Law of Pressure and Volume of Gases.—The physical properties of gases in general are defined by two familiar laws —the first defining the degrees of volume and pressure at constantly maintained temperatures; the second, the ratio of expansion at a constantly increasing temperature. The first, known as *Boyle's Law,* states that

THE VOLUME OF A GAS VARIES INVERSELY AS THE PRESSURE, SO LONG AS THE TEMPERATURE REMAINS THE SAME, OR, THE PRESSURE OF A GAS IS PROPORTIONAL TO ITS DENSITY.

This law has frequently been illustrated by the following experiment:

If we take a hollow cylinder, such as is used on steam engines, having a piston sliding airtight in its length, we will find that the contained, air or other gas, is compressed in front of the piston, as it is forced from one end toward the other of the base, and that this air, or gas, exerts a pressure which increases in ratio as the volume is diminished. This fact may be shown by inserting in the wall of the cylinder a tube containing an airtight piston, upon which bears a spiral spring holding it normally, as at *A* in the accompanying diagram; the pressure there being supposedly equal on both sides of the piston, or equivalent to 15 pounds per square inch. If, now, the area of this small piston be exactly one square inch, and the spring of such a tension as to move upward through one of the spaces between the lines on the diagram behind the large cylinder with each ten pounds of added pressure from below, the result will be as follows: When the piston of the large cylinder has been pushed through one-half its length, the depression of the spring in the smaller one will show that the pressure is just twice what it was at the start, or 30 pounds. At three-quarters the stroke it will show sixty pounds, and at seven-eighths, 120 pounds. If the four smaller cylinders be arranged in the wall of the cylinder, as in the diagram, the difference in pressure at these several points may be graphically represented. Then a curve, drawn so as to pass through the center of each of the smaller pistons, will give an accurate average of pressure for every position of the large piston. On the other hand, as under the operative conditions in a steam engine, it will represent the "curve of expansion," or the decrease in pressure from

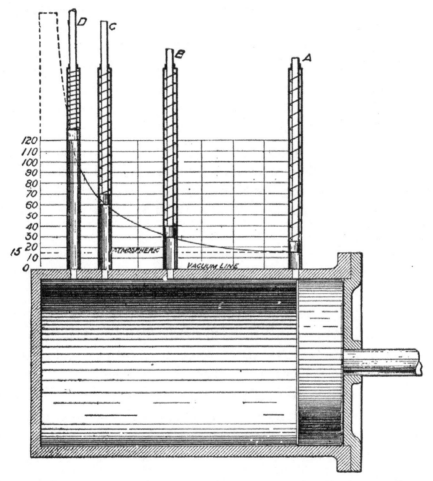

FIG. 118.—Diagrammatic Section of a Cylinder, illustrating the compression and expansion of gases. This cylinder is filled with air at atmospheric pressure which represents a uniform 14.7 pounds to the square inch behind the piston, as shown by the position of the piston in the small cylinder, A. When the piston of the large cylinder is moved through half the length of the stroke, it shows 30 pounds pressure, as shown by the position of the piston in small cylinder, B; when at three-quarters stroke. 60 pounds, as shown by the position of the piston. C: when at seven-eighths stroke, 120 pounds, as shown by position of piston, D. At full stroke it would be 240 pounds. the diagram behind the small piston giving the compression curve from 15 to 240.

the moment of "cut-off," when the inlet valve is closed to the end of the stroke, when the exhaust valve is opened. If, therefore, steam be fed into the cylinder at 200 pounds pressure per square inch, and the inlet be closed when the piston has traversed one-eight of the stroke, the pressure will stand at 100 pounds on quarter-stroke; at 50 pounds on half stroke, and, at 25 pounds on the point of completed stroke, which shows that it is expanded eight times.

Very similar conditions exist in the cylinder of a gas engine, as will be shown later. Here, the expansion of the gas in cylinder is estimated from the moment of maximum pressure, when the fuel charge has reached the height of its temperature, due to its ignition by electric spark or other source of firing.

In both the cases in the diagram, the temperature is supposed to remain constant, while the pressure increases, on the one hand, or decreases on the other. Such compression and expansion would be entirely isothermal, that is, it would take place at a constant temperature.

The Temperature and Volume of Gases.—The "second law of gases," called *Charles* or *Gay Lussac's law*, states that

AT CONSTANT PRESSURE THE VOLUME OF A GAS VARIES WITH THE TEMPERATURE, THE INCREASE BEING IN PROPORTION TO THE CHANGE OF TEMPERATURE AND THE VOLUME OF THE GAS AT ZERO.

By actual experiment it has been ascertained that a gas increases on a ratio of 1-493d part of its volume at 32° Fahrenheit, with each additional degree added to its temperature. This places the "absolute zero," or the point at which a gas would assume its greatest possible density at $-461°$, Fahrenheit, or $-273°$, Centigrade.

Absolute Figures for Temperature.—In temperature and pressure calculations for heat engines, it is customary to use absolute figures, so called, as based upon the data just given. Thus, the absolute temperature is the sum of the sensible thermometric temperature and the constant 461. This latter figure, which is more properly expressed as 460.66, represents the total number of degrees on the Fahrenheit scale from 32° below the freezing point of water to absolute zero of temperature, as calculated by the expansion ratio of gases. Thus in calculating temperatures, we count from absolute zero; instead of 64°, writing 525°; and instead of °32, writing 493°, or, more correctly, 492.66°. The utility of this system lies in the fact that, as a gas has been found to expand by 1-273 of its original volume for each degree, centigrade, or by 1-461 for each degree, Fahrenheit, of increased temperature, we have by the use of absolute figures an approximate expression for both increased heat and increased volume in the same number.

The absolute zero is the point of theoretically complete stability of a gas.

Absolute Figures for Pressure.—Similarly, the *absolute pressure* is given as the sum of the gauge pressure and the constant 15 (more correctly 14.7), representing the total pressure above zero acting against atmosphere. Since, in a gauge, or in the cylinder of a heat engine, the effective power is acting against the pressure of the atmosphere, which is 14.7 lbs. per square inch, the recorded pressure represents the actual pressure less 14.7.

The pressure and temperature of a gas being strictly in ratio, it is possible to determine the temperature, approximately at least from the gauge pressure. The correspondents of temperature and pressure for various gases may be determined by knowledge of their physical properties. For steam they have been completely tabulated, as shown in the following columns, which contain averages by several authorities:

Pressure.	Temperature.	Pressure.	Temperature.	Pressure.	Temperature
15 lbs.	212° F.	55 lbs.	288° F.	100 lbs.	330° F.
20 lbs.	228° F.	60 lbs.	294° F.	105 lbs.	333° F.
25 lbs.	241° F.	65 lbs.	299° F.	120 lbs.	343° F.
30 lbs.	252° F.	70 lbs.	304° F.	135 lbs.	352° F.
35 lbs.	261° F.	75 lbs.	309° F.	150 lbs.	362° F.
40 lbs.	268° F.	80 lbs.	313° F.	165 lbs.	369° F.
45 lbs.	275° F.	85 lbs.	316° F.	180 lbs.	375° F.
50 lbs.	282° F.	90 lbs.	322° F.	195 lbs.	383° F.

Determining the Temperature from the Pressure.—Although saturated steam, or steam having a temperature corresponding to its pressure, is not a perfect gas, the operative conditions in a steam engine are fairly typical for any form of motor operating through the expansive effect of heat upon gases.

In order to explain the process for a cylinder expanding 1-10 pound of steam from 120 pounds per square inch pressure to atmosphere. The following passage quoted from Forney's "Cat-echism of the Locomotive," is sufficient:

"If the piston stand at the point shown in the previous figure, and 1-10 pound of water be put into the cylinder, and heat be applied to it, it would

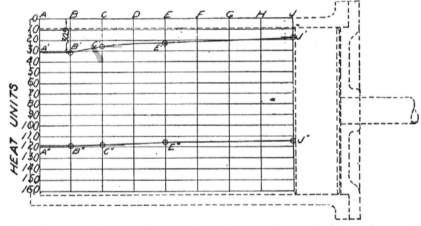

FIG. 119.—Diagram showing the number of heat units required to raise one-tenth pound of steam under the various pressures indicated by the position of the piston, at full stroke, half stroke and seven-eights stroke. In using this diagram it is necessary to note that the heat units are calculated from—1° Fahrenheit, instead of from 39°, as is the general rule.

be necessary to heat the water to 212° before it would boil. To represent this heat, the vertical line, J, is extended below the horizontal line, AJ. To heat 1-10 pound of water to 212° takes 21.2 units of heat,—since one unit of heat is required to raise one pound of water at 39° Fahrenheit to one degree above—which is laid off from J to J' to the scale represented by the horizontal lines. But as is shown in the table in the appendix, after the water begins to boil, 96.6 more units of heat must be added to it to convert it all into steam of atmospheric pressure. This number of units of heat is, therefore, laid off from J to J'. If the piston be moved to E, the middle of the cylinder, and 1-10 pound of water is again put into it, and it is all converted into steam, it will have a pressure of 30 pounds per square inch, as it occupies only half the volume that the same quantity of steam did before. To make water boil under a pressure of 30 pounds, it must be heated to a temperature of 250.4°, which in this case will require 25 units of heat, which is laid down from E to E'. To convert the water into steam, after it begins to boil, will require 93.9 more units of heat, which is also laid down from E to E''. In the same way the total heat to boil and convert 1-10 pound of water into steam at 60 and 120 pounds pressure, as shown in the appendix, is laid down on C C'' and B B'', and the two curves, B' C' E' J' and B'' C'' E'' J'', are drawn through the points which have been laid down. The vertical distance of the one curve from A J represents the heat units required to boil 1-10 pound of water at the pressures indicated by the curve in the previous figure, and the vertical distance of the second curve from A J represents the total units of heat required to convert 1-10 pound of water into steam of a volume indicated by the horizontal distance of any point of the curve from A A'', and when pressure is indicated by the expansion curve above. This curve and the heat diagram may be very conveniently combined by adding the latter below the vacuum line of the former. The relation of the volume pressure and total heat is thus shown very clearly."

Joule's Law of Temperature and Pressure.

—As may be readily understood from what has already been said, the recognized principle in the operation of all forms of heat engine is that

THE WORK-PRODUCING OR DYNAMIC PROPERTY OF A GAS DEPENDS SOLELY UPON ITS TEMPERATURE.

This is, substantially, a statement of *Joule's law,* which compares the temperature of a gas, enabling it to exert a certain amount of power, to the stored energy represented in a body of a certain weight raised to a certain height above the ground. The body, in falling under the force of gravity, obtains a certain degree of acceleration, constantly increasing, by which the weight falling through the given distance is transformed into a force capable of producing a commensurate effect of impact on reaching the earth's surface. This potential energy of a substance, represented either by an acquired temperature or some analogous physical condition, which, under favorable circumstances, would enable the production of a definite amount of work, is known as "entropy." Could the whole power of a heated gas be realized in its expansion—which is to say, could its expansion be perfectly "adiabatic," or "isentropic," involving neither gain nor loss of heat in the process—we should have a theoretically perfect expansion curve on every practical heat engine. This is impossible, however, with the best arrangements yet contrived. Hence it is that the expansion curves of all engines fall far below what is demanded by theory from the original temperature and pressure of the steam, which involves that the final volume and the actual work accomplished are correspondingly diminished.

To quote from an authority on steam engines, "as we cannot take into consideration all the conditions which govern and modify the cycle of any motor, the usual practice is to calculate the power on the assumption that all theoretical conditions are complied with, and then modify the result by a certain co-efficient of efficiency which practice has established for the particular type of motor under consideration."

The Steam Engine Indicator and Its Diagram.—The action of the small cylinders containing springs and pistons as explained in connection with Fig. 118, very well illustrates the operation of the steam engine indicator in tracing the diagram, or "card," which reveals so much on the conditions within the cylinder. The simplest form of this instrument has a cylinder identical with those shown in the figure, except for a pencil carried on the uppermost end of the piston rod, and bearing upon a suitable tablet, which is moved backward and forward with the stroke of the steam piston. This is done by attaching the long arm of a reducing lever to the cross head, and the shorter arm to a link-bar, which holds the card, or tablet, to be inscribed. The line traced by the pencil point will rise or fall, as the pressure within the small cylinder is increased or reduced. The several forms of the indicator most often used at the present day have a rotatable drum, which is attached by a cord to the short arm of the reducing lever, so as to be turned in one direction; being moved in the other direction by a contained spring, which rewinds the cord, so soon as the lever arm moves backward. Thus the records of a great number of strokes may be taken on one sheet of paper.

The records thus made, by knowing the dimensions of the cylinder and the tension, or resisting strength, of the steam-actuated spring, may be very accurately calculated for the entire cycle of the engine.

The Indicator Diagram and the Steam Engine Cycle.—The operative efficiency of an engine may be very well determined from the indicator diagram, which gives a pictorial representation of the internal conditions throughout the entire cycle of operations. As given by a noted authority, already quoted, the steam engine diagram tells eleven different things essential to be known:

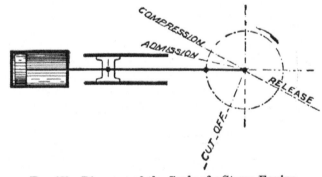

FIG. 120.—Diagram of the Cycle of a Steam Engine.

1. It gives the *initial pressure,* or the pressure at beginning of the stroke.

2. It tells whether the pressure is increased or diminished during the period of admission.

3. It gives the point of cut-off, when the valve is closed and expansion begins.

4. It indicates the rate and pressure of expansion during the whole period of expansion.

5. It gives the "point of release," when the exhaust is opened.

6. It shows the rapidity of the exhaust.

7. It gives the degree of back-pressure on the piston, due to the exhaust having closed, preventing further expansion.

8. It shows the point of closing the exhaust.

9. It shows the *compression* of the residual steam in the clearance after closing the exhaust.

10. It gives the mean power used in driving the engine.

11. In indicates any leakage of valves or piston.

The Indicator Diagram and the Gas Engine Cycle.—In precisely similar fashion, the indicator diagram reveals nine things regarding the operative conditions in the cylinder of a gas engine:

1. It gives the initial pressure from beginning to end of the inlet stroke.

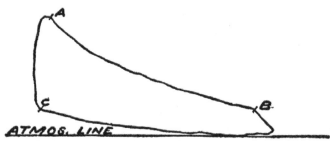

FIG. 12.—Gas Engine Indicator Card. This diagram is an average good card, showing, however, some slight fluctuations in the lines. The explosion line is from C to A; the expansion, from A to B; the exhaust at B. The suction stroke generally approximates the atmospheric line, from which the curve of compression rises to C.

2. It gives the point of closure of the inlet valve, provided the operation is irregular.

3. It gives the curve of compression, registering the highest point of compression pressure.

5. It gives the maximum pressure at the ignition of the charge.

6. It shows whether the ignition is normal or irregular, as shown in Fig. 133.

7. It shows the curve of expansion, indicating whether leakage or other disorder interferes with the full effective pressure.

8. It shows the point of exhaust, enabling a ready computation of the exhaust pressure.

9. It enables a ready estimate of the mean effective pressure.

The Steam Engine Diagram.—The diagram for a high-pressure steam cylinder is given in an accompanying figure. From point, *A,* the pressure rises from the compression maximum of about 50 lbs. to 120 lbs. as the steam enters the cylinder. The cut-off occurs in this cylinder at one-quarter stroke, the expansion starting at point, *C,* and continuing to the opening of the exhaust valve at point, *R.* From this point to *B,* where the exhaust valve closes, the returning in-stroke of the piston drives the steam out through the open exhaust port. The steam then remaining in the cylinder is compressed between points, *B* and *A,* being raised in pressure from a point near atmosphere to 50 lbs. gauge.

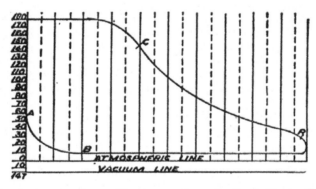

Fig. 122.—The Cycle of a Steam Engine, as shown by the Indicator Card. On this tracing, the admission is shown from A to C; the cut-off at C; the expansion curve from C to R; the release, or opening of the exhaust, at R, exhaust continuing from R to B; closing of the exhaust valve at B; compression of the residual steam in the cylinder clearance, from B to A. The figures on the left-hand vertical line indicate the gauge pressures.

All these stages are more graphically illustrated in the accompanying diagram of the cycle of a steam engine for the steam admitted to one face of the piston. In this figure the dotted circle indicates the path of the crank; the arrow, the direction of rotation. The admission begins a little before the completion of the stroke; the cut-off is set somewhat less than quarter-stroke; release, or opening of the exhaust near the end of the stroke; closing of the valve at the point marked "compression," after which the steam behind the piston is compressed in the clearance until the opening of the inlet valve.

Reading an Indicator Diagram.—The simplest method of reading a diagram, so as to find the power exacted, is to rule equidistant lines from the vertical initial pressure line, so as to divide into ten equal parts, or areas. Ordinates, indicated by the dotted lines, are then ruled between these, and given a value equivalent to the average of pressure represented by the lines on either side, as indicated by the point of contact with the admission line and the expansion curve. Thus in the single high-pressure diagram the first ordinate ruled on the admission line has a value of 155 pounds, which represents 180 less 25 back pressure. The second and third ordinates, according to the figures ruled on the left-hand vertical line, have a value of 180 pounds; the fourth, of 165; the fifth, 128; the sixth, 98; the seventh, 80; the eighth, 68; the ninth, 55; the tenth, 50; showing an expansion of over three volumes from boiler pressure. The sum of the pressures given is 1149, which divided by 10, the number of the ordinates, gives the average of all the pressures acting on the piston during the stroke, or what is known as the *mean effective pressure,* at about 115 pounds.

In similar fashion the diagram for both strokes, inward and outward, of the piston is ruled off and estimated, the figures at the top of the figure indicating the cycle of pressure changes for the right-hand stroke, those at the bottom the cycle for the left-hand, or return, stroke.

Calculating by the Mean Ordinate.—A simpler method for calculating the diagram of a steam or gas engine is to find the mean ordinate of the diagram by the following process: Find the centre of the diagram figure on the base line; erect a line perpendicular to the base from that point; draw another line from the base so that it touches the expansion line at about the point of exhaust valve opening, at such an angle that the two parts on either side of the centre line will be equal measuring from a perpendicular on the explosion line on the one side, and from another touching the "toe" of the tracing on the opposite side. The portion of the centre line thus laid off by intersection is the mean ordinate, which, multiplied by the pressure indicated by the gauge gives the mean effective pressure (M. E. P.).

CHAPTER FIFTEEN.

Gas Engine Cylinder.—The cylinder of a gas engine is open at the end toward the crank, and closed at the opposite end, save for the inlet and exhaust ports, which are opened and closed by valves.

Gas Engine Pistons.—The piston is single-acting—which is to say, acted upon by the power on one face only, or moved by power impulse in one direction only. It is of the type known as "trunk piston," consisting of a cylindrical box of proper size to slide back and forth in the cylinder bore.

The portion of the cylinder length traversed by the piston from end to end of the stroke is called the *sweep.*

That portion at the rear of the cylinder that is never swept by the piston is called the *clearance.*

The valve chamber opens into the clearance, and the ignition apparatus is also located here.

The Clearance.—The clearance determines the degree of compression of the fuel mixture at extreme *in-stroke,* when the piston has reached its furthest point in backward travel.

It is the *combustion space,* or *chamber,* at the moment of igniting the gas.

With the piston sweep, it forms the total *cubical content* of the cylinder, as found at extreme out-stroke, when the piston has reached its utmost forward point of travel.

Piston Construction and Proportions.—The trunk piston is hollow, and within it is pivoted the connecting rod, the opposite end of which is pivoted to the crank pin. Within the piston the connecting rod is pivoted to a pin, variously called the piston pin, wrist pin and gudgeon pin.

The piston is in diameter about .002 inch smaller than the cylinder bore, thus giving a clearance of about .001 inch all around. A snug working fit is obtained by means of packing rings, iron rings so cut that the internal and external circumferences are eccentric, as shown in an accompanying figure, for the purpose of allowing some play for expansion, under the extraordinary heat generated by combustion of the fuel charge.

Piston Rings.—The piston rings fit into grooves cut around the circumference of the piston, and are set in place by being sprung over the junk rings, or the portions of the cylinder cir-

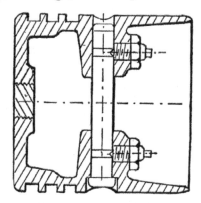

FIG. 123.—Section through a typical Trunk Piston for a Gasoline Engine. Around the circumference, near the rear end, are three circular grooves for inserting the packing rings. Through the central diameter is a perforation for admitting the piston pin, which is held in place by set screws.

The proportions of the piston pin must be carefully calculated for the load it is intended to bear. In general, the length of the piston pin should be equal to that of the crank pin, and its diameter such as to bear an average of 750 pounds for each square inch of its projected area. As given by Roberts, the proper diameter of the pin may be determined as follows:

$$\text{Diameter} = \frac{\text{Cylinder area} \times \text{M. E. P.}}{750 \times \text{length of pin.}}$$

cumference left after cutting the grooves. Three or four rings are set around the piston at the rear end, and, in some engines, there is another around the front end.

Machining Piston Rings.—Piston rings are made of cast iron, and are cut from a pipe-shaped casting. The casting is secured to the lathe chuck, so that a cutting tool can bear against its circumference and separate rings of the proper width. Each ring is then turned in a jig, so that the inner circumference is eccentric with the outer, and a slit is cut in the thinnest section, as shown in the figure. Although formed of a very brittle substance, piston rings have considerable elasticity; being capable of opening sufficiently to be slid over the junk rings of the piston, also allowing of sufficient compression when within the cylinder, to make a tight fit.

Poppet Valves.—The inlet and exhaust ports of a gas engine of the four-cycle type are opened and closed by *poppet* or *mushroom valves*. These consist of metal disks, beveled around one face, so as to fit into a countersink in the port opening, and carried upon *stems* or *spindles*.

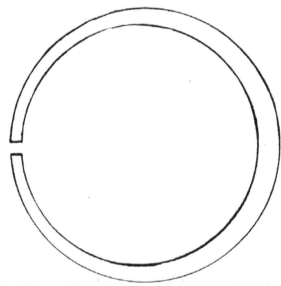

Fig. 124.—Piston Packing Ring for a Gas Engine Cylinder. The inner and outer circumferences are eccentrically arranged, so as to permit of considerable expansion under heat.

The exhaust valve is always operated mechanically from a cam-shaft; the inlet valve may be operated similarly, or may be opened by suction, created by the outward movement of the piston.

Automatic and Positive Inlet Valves.—The automatic inlet valve, operated by suction of the piston against the tension of a spiral spring, has been regularly used on all gas engines until very recently. The positive-operated inlet valve is now gaining favor with designers. The reasons for this change are that the automatic valve often sticks with gummed oil on its seat; that the spring tension may vary, thus changing the fuel pressure in cylinder; that it is noisy; that its operation on high-speed engines is unreliable. As against these defects, the positive inlet valve possesses the advantages of opening and closing as desired, without noise or sticking, and of giving precisely the right pressure in the cylinder, at both high and low speeds.

Valve Springs.—Both valves are held to their seats by compression springs, against the tension of which they are opened.

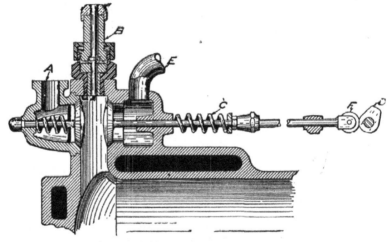

FIG. 125.—Detail Diagram of the Valves and Attachments of a Gas Engine Cylinder. A is the inlet port behind inlet valve held in its seat by a tension spring; B, the spark plug for "jump-spark" ignition; C, the push rod and compression spring of the exhaust valve; D, the cam opening the exhaust; E, the exhaust port; F, the roller at end of valve rod bearing on the cam, D.

When the inlet valves are opened by piston suction, the tension of the spring is regulated, so as to give the desired initial pressure in the cylinder, as will be presently explained. The springs serve to hold the valves securely shut, when their opening is not required.

Elements of a Vehicle Engine.—The essential elements of a vehicle engine are:

1. The carburetter, or vaporizer, in which the liquid hydrocarbon is transformed into vapor.

2. The cylinder, to which the gas is admitted by suction, mixed with a suitable supply of pure air, compressed and ignited.

3. An ignition apparatus for producing the spark or hot surface essential to explosion.

The Crank and Driving Gear.—In the disposition of the crank and driving connections, the explosive motor differs radically from the common type of steam engine. The piston rod in the steam engine slides through the stuffing box in the cylinder head, and the crank is attached to the forward end at the cross head, which works between guides. The gas engine cylinder, being open at the forward end, has no head or stuffing box and no piston rod proper; in fact, the crank and piston rods are combined in one. The crank is hung on the gudgeon pin fixed midway in the length of the hollow trunk piston, and works on the crank-shaft upon which the fly-wheel is secured.

The fly-wheel is positively essential in a gas engine of any size or power. The reason for this lies in the fact that the ordinary four-cycle motor, having but one power stroke in every two revolutions of the crank shaft, requires a heavy fly-wheel to counteract the speed fluctuations and to "store up" energy sufficient to carry the rotation through the three idle strokes of exhaust, supply and compression. For this reason gas engine fly-wheels are made much heavier than those designed for steam engine use. Some one-cylinder gas and gasoline motors are made with two fly-wheels, one on either side of the crank pin, which is, in fact, attached midway on radii of the two wheels or "discs."

In several modern engines the rim of the fly-wheel is made to overhang the bearing, thus, as is claimed, securing better balance.

CHAPTER SIXTEEN.

The Cycle of a Gas Engine.—In the practical operation of a gas engine there are several parts or stages, each characterized by a particular event. The cylinder is charged by an out-stroke of the piston, creating a vacuum behind it and drawing in the mixture of air and gasoline gas formed in the carburetter. The charge is then compressed by the return stroke of the piston, which act secures complete carburization of the contained air, and reduces the mixture to the proper condition to be kindled by the igniting spark or other source of firing. This causes it to explode, or to expand suddenly and with great effect, and drive the piston outward again. The fourth stroke, which is the one immediately following the explosion, is known as the exhaust stroke, from the fact that the piston, moving back again in the cylinder, expels the products of combustion through the exhaust valve. This process completed, the parts are in position for a repetition of the process, the valves for admitting gasoline gas to the cylinder then being opened again.

The Four-Cycle Gas Engine.—These four strokes—two outward and two inward—constitute the "cycle," and, as may be readily understood, there is thus only one power impulse for every two revolutions of the fly-wheel. This power stroke also continues while the crank is traveling through half a revolution, or through an arc of 180 degrees. It is also evident that the cam shaft, for operating the valve system of the cylinder, revolves but once for every two revolutions of the crank shaft, with which it is geared. Thus is secured the opening of the charging, or inlet valve, and of the scavenging, or exhaust, at precisely the proper points in the cycle. The operation of a four-cycle gas engine may be understood in figs. p. 155. Supposing we have a four-cylinder motor, the cranks of whose four pistons

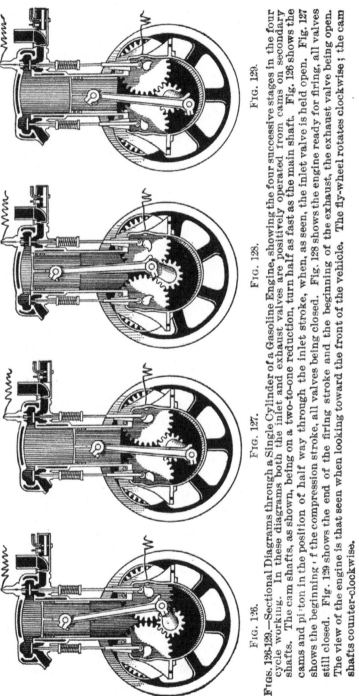

FIG. 126.   FIG. 127.   FIG. 128.   FIG. 129.

FIGS. 126-129.—Sectional Diagrams through a Single Cylinder of a Gasoline Engine, showing the four successive stages in the four cycle working. In these diagrams both the inlet and exhaust valves are positively operated from cams on secondary shafts. The cam shafts, as shown, being on a two-to-one reduction, turn half as fast as the main shaft. Fig. 126 shows the cams and piston in the position of half way through the inlet stroke, when, as seen, the inlet valve is held open. Fig. 127 shows the beginning of the compression stroke, all valves being closed. Fig. 128 shows the engine ready for firing, all valves still closed. Fig. 129 shows the end of the firing stroke and the beginning of the exhaust, the exhaust valve being open. The view of the engine is that seen when looking toward the front of the vehicle. The fly-wheel rotates clockwise; the cam shafts counter-clockwise.

are so fixed that, counting from 1 to 4, we have pistons, cams and valves in positions representing the four cycles. That is to say, the induction, or supply stroke would be occurring in the first cylinder, the compression stroke in the second, the explosion in the third, the exhaust in the fourth. In such an engine the crank is turned by a steady impulse, since a new explosion would occur in each 180 degrees of rotation. At the aspirating or supply stroke, the outward movement of the piston, by creating a partial vacuum, causes the feed valves to open under atmospheric pressure, thus indicating that the pressure within is lower than that of the atmosphere without. At explosion the volume and temperature are raised, and at the end of the exhaust stroke the burned gases are expelled. The supply stroke being completed, and the feed valves closed by force of a spring, there is no considerable increase in volume and pressure due to contact with the hot cylinder walls, nor yet from the residuum of burnt products in the clearance, although, owing to the tension of the valve spring, the pressure of the contained gases is below one atmosphere. The rise in pressure during the supply stroke is from a negative point to generally about 13.50 pounds to the square inch. So soon, however, as the compression stroke begins, the indicator tracing shows a steady rise to 65 or 70 pounds to the square inch, at the completion of the stroke, according to the compression ratio, as will be presently explained.

At the end of the compression stroke the gas mixture in cylinder has attained its greatest density, also its greatest pressure and temperature previous to combustion. It is then ready for firing, which is generally accomplished very shortly before the piston begins the second out-stroke, the explosion serving to bring the gas to the maximum point for volume, pressure and temperature alike. In fact, the effect, as shown by thermometer and indicator tests, is that the temperature in a gas-engine cylinder rises during this stroke from between 500 and 700 degrees, absolute, as noted when the engine is running at good speed, to between 1,500 and 2,000 degrees, on the average, and the pressure from an indicated 65 or 70 pounds to 200 or 230 pounds per square inch.

The fall in both particulars is equally rapid during the succeeding in-stroke, when the burnt gases, under impulse from the piston, are expelled through the open valves.

Regarding the time of firing practice differs considerably. Generally, as stated above, it is slightly before the beginning of the power stroke, in order to allow time for the burning gas to begin expansion. Slow-speed motors are generally fired very slightly after the dead centre. With high-speed motors it varies from about 5 degrees after dead centre to 30 or 40 degrees ahead (as measured on the crank). With a large spark, hot motor and well-mixed fuel, the advanced spark is seldom set more than 15 or 20 degrees ahead.

CHAPTER SEVENTEEN.

The Two Cycle Engine.—To the present time the greater majority of hydro-carbon vehicle engines operate by the four cycle method. There is another form of engine, however, known as the two-cycle, in which the four essential operations, charging, compression, firing, exhaust, are performed in one revolution of the fly-wheel, instead of two. The most familiar form of the two-cycle engine is that shown in the Figures 130-131-132 and its essential features are:

1. An enclosed crank case fitted with a valve arranged to open and admit fuel gas at the front, instead of at the rear of the piston, on the inward, instead of the outward stroke, as in the four part cycle.

2. Inlet and exhaust parts located at points near the extreme outward position of the piston, so as to be uncovered during the outward stroke.

3. A by-pass tube connecting the interior of the cylinder with the crank case, so as to admit fuel gas at the proper point in the cycle.

Since all the essential operations occur during a single revolution of the fly-wheel, every out-stroke of the piston is made under the stress of the exploding fuel charge in the combustion space. The ignited gas continues expanding, driving the piston outward, until the exhaust port begins opening. Exhaust then follows rapidly and is well under way when the inlet port, generally located on the opposite side of the cylinder wall, is uncovered by the outward-moving piston.

The fuel gas in the crank case is slightly compressed by the outgoing piston, and, on the opening of the inlet port, rushes into the combustion space, being deflected upward to the rear end of the cylinder by a screen or deflector plate set in the end of the piston. The inlet of new fuel gas and the exhaust of the burned-out products of the last charge continue until the extreme end of the stroke, and during the next instroke, until the closure, first of the inlet, then of the exhaust port. From this point, the compression of the new charge begins, and on the completion of the instroke the charge is ready for ignition.

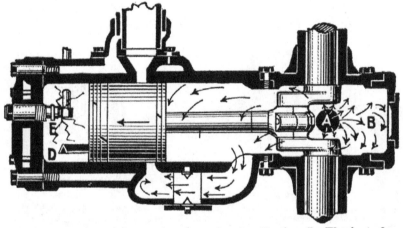

FIG. 130.—Diagram of the Two-part Cycle of a Gas Engine, I. The instroke of the piston, showing the aspiration of fuel gas at A, into crank case, B, and the spark at E in combustion space, D.

Two=Cycle Engines for Motor Vehicles.—Several recent makes of motor vehicle are propelled by two-cycle engines, and, according to reports yield very satisfactory results. The advantages claimed are:

1. A power stroke in every revolution of the fly-wheel for each cylinder—provided the engine has more than one—with twice the consequent power effect per cylinder, as compared with the four-cycle engine.

2. The entire absence of poppet valves, with their springs, stems, push-rods and cam-shafts; thus effecting a greater simplicity of construction and operation.

These considerations should constitute the two-cycle the ideal form of engine for motor carriage purposes. There have been, however, several objections to its use, which, so it is claimed, have been only recently overcome. Prominent among these was the fact that the two-cycle engines, built some years since, seemed incapable of the high speeds required in motor vehicle work; realizing at best not more than between 300 and 400 revolutions, as against an average of 1,000 revolutions for the four-cycle engine, and giving only about 60 per cent. of the power at the same speed. This result was believed to follow on the fact that the cylinder would rapidly choke up with exhaust gas products, which were unable to escape when high speeds were attempted.

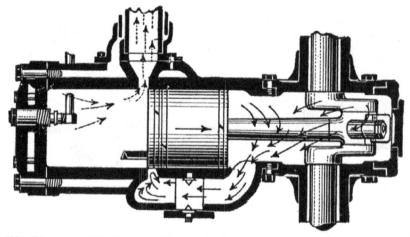

Fig. 131.—Diagram of the Two-part Cycle of a Gas Engine, II. The outstroke of the piston, showing the exhaust of the burned out gases and the compression of the fuel gas in the crank case.

As a consequence, the four-cycle engine has hitherto been considered the only available form for high speed use.

The two-cycle engine has had its widest sphere of use on motor boats, but the highest speed boats are propelled by engines of the four-cycle type. The majority of two-cycle boat engines, however, have been of one and two-cylinder patterns, which are now claimed to be inferior in speed to the four-cylinder.

Essentials of a Two=Cycle Engine.—A successful two-cycle vehicle engine, designed to operate at speeds at all commensurate with the four-cycle vehicle engines, must embody precisely one feature of design, not always easy to realize—provision for rapid exhaust of the burned gases. A prominent gas-engine authority remarks: "The two-cycle engine, at best, is the next thing to an impossibility." By this statement he means that, the act of admitting inflammable fuel mixture into the cylinder, already filled with flaming gas, without igniting it, involves something closely approaching a contradiction in physical conditions. Were it not for the fact that the burning gases actually exhaust faster than the new mixture is admitted under impulse of their inherent expansion, the ignition of the new charge would seem to be nearly

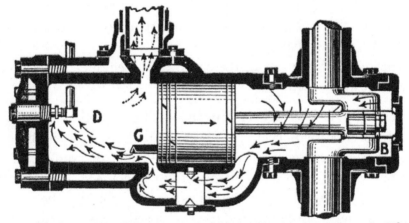

FIG. 132.—Diagram of the Two-part Cycle of a Gas Engine, III. The end of the out-stroke. The gases compressed in the crank case are admitted to the cylinder space, D, through the open inlet port, and past the screen or deflector, C. The passage between cylinder and crank case is controlled by a butterfly valve, which here, as in the other cuts, is shown open.

inevitable. By deflecting the incoming mixture to the rear end of the cylinder, it follows the rapidly expanding exhaust, coming into contact with it only when the expansion has so far reduced the temperature that the danger of pre-ignition is averted. It may be readily seen, however, that the danger of such interference, or, at best, of a contamination of the new charge to a point rendering it unignitable must result, if the speed be increased beyond a certain moderate rate.

The Exhaust of a Two-Cycle Engine.—Many authorities enlarge upon the danger of exhaust gases rushing back from the muffler into the cylinder of a two-cycle engine and producing the condition known as "choking-up" If, therefore, high speeds are to be attempted, the back-pressure of the muffler must be reduced as far as possible, and the exhaust must be rendered correspondingly rapid. These results have been variously achieved, familiarly:

1. By making the exhaust ports twice the width of the inlets, so as to allow the burned gases free egress to the muffler at a much higher speed than is achieved by the incoming mixture.

2. By arranging a rotary fan or blower to hasten the speed and volume of the exhaust, and also assist in cooling the cylinder space, as the new charge enters.

By using the latter device the speed of the engine could be very materially increased.

Governing a Two-Cycle Engine.—The essential features in the control of a two-cycle are a wire gauze screen in the by-pass pipe, for the purpose of preventing back-firing, or crank-case explosions, which would undoubtedly result in some cases; a butterfly valve in the by-pass, for the purposes of throttling the volume of the charge, in order to reduce the speed. The mixture may be modified by controlling the percentage of gasoline, as in other hydro-carbon engines, but the butterfly valve furnishes the most available means for ordinary control.

CHAPTER EIGHTEEN.

THE CONDITIONS OF COMPRESSION AND EXPANSION.

Proportionate Figures for Temperature and Pressure.—In the operation of a gas engine, the fuel gas is confined within the cylinder, so long as it exerts an effect on power and speed. If, then, we know the total cylinder content, we have a constant standard of comparison for calculating the pressure and temperature of a given mixture of gas and air under the several conditions of the cycle. For, although the contained gas occupies the same cubic content at the beginning of the compression stroke and at the end of the firing stroke, it is obvious that its proper volume is vastly increased at the latter moment, as indicated by the raised pressure and temperature. But, following the principles laid down above, we find that the figures are regular and proportionate as between the initial and final volumes, pressures and temperatures.

Initial and Final Figures.—Theoretically, the operations of a gas engine accord with the general laws of gas under the influence of heat and pressure. Accordingly we speak of:

1. *The initial pressure, temperature or volume,* which belong to a gas previous to either compression or expansion. In gas-engine practice initial figures usually refer to the conditions existing at the completion of the supply or aspirating stroke of the cycle.

2. *The final pressure, temperature or volume,* which belong to a gas after either compression or expansion. If we are speaking from the standpoint of expansion the *initial* figures refer to the conditions of explosion; if, on compression, the initial figures refer to the supply stroke. In both cases the final figures refer to the changed conditions found at the end of the operation.

The compression and explosion figures depend upon the conditions existing at the end of the *compression stroke* and at the beginning of the *firing stroke,* respectively.

Ratios of Figures.—Furthermore, all these elements are related according to the following principles:

1. The final volume divided by the initial volume is equal to the final pressure divided by the initial pressure.

2. The final volume divided by the initial pressure is equal to the initial volume divided by the final pressure.

3. The final volume equals the quotient found by dividing the product of the initial pressure and initial volume by the final pressure.

4. The final pressure equals the quotient found by dividing the product of the initial pressure and initial volume by the final volume.

5. The final pressure also equals the quotient found by dividing the product of the initial pressure and final temperature by the initial temperature.

6. The final temperature equals the quotient found by dividing the product of the initial temperature and final pressure by the initial pressure.

In the following formulæ,

Let P′ be the initial pressure.

Let P″ be the final pressure.

Let T′ be the initial temperature.

Let T″ be the final temperature.

Let V′ be the initial volume.

Let V″ be the final volume.

Then, expressing these laws mathematically, we have:

$$\frac{P' \, V'}{P''} = V''; \qquad \frac{P' \, V'}{V''} = P'';$$

$$\frac{P' \, T''}{T'} = P''; \qquad \frac{T' \, P''}{P'} = T''.$$

As previously suggested, definite figures for all these elements may be found only when the cubic content of the cylinder is known. The cubic content of the stroke and clearance areas may, of course, be calculated, when the inside diameter and length of the cylinder and length of the stroke are known. A more practical method suggested by Roberts is to turn the crank to the backward dead centre, close the valves, and fill the cylinder with water. By altering the position of the crank from in-stroke end to out-stroke end, the cubic content of both clearance and total cylinder, including stroke sweep, may be accurately estimated. The water having been weighed before pouring it into the cylinder, the weight of that left over is a ready indication of the weight of that within.

This latter method is particularly convenient where the cylinder has a spherical or enlarged combustion chamber, which would involve mathematical processes of considerable intricacy to estimate its content in cubic feet.

At 39.1° Fahrenheit, water weighs 62.5 pounds per cubic foot. When the water is at a higher temperature, its weight per cubic foot may be found by the following formula, in which T is the temperature shown by thermometer; 461, the constant of absolute temperature, and 500, the absolute temperature of water at 39.1 degrees.

$$\frac{62.5 \times 2}{\dfrac{T + 461}{500} + \dfrac{500}{T + 461}} = \text{Weight per cubic foot.}$$

Here we need only substitute the ascertained temperature figures for T wherever it occurs, reduce the fractions to a common denominator, and perform the indicated additions and divisions.

Measuring the Conditions of Operation.—The factors entering to vary the figures, with the same initial pressures in different engines, are the ratio of compression and the percentage of the clearance volume, as compared with the total cylinder volume.

The Ratio of Compression.—The ratio of compression is found to be equal to the quotient of the total volume of the cylinder from the beginning to the end of the stroke, including also the clearance, divided by the volume of the clearance, which, as is evident, is never decreased during any portion of a stroke.

Applying the rule for calculating the compression ratios of two cylinders, in which the clearance and total content are in proportion of 2 to 4 and 1 to 4, respectively, we derive the following expressions:

$$\frac{2+4}{2} = 3 \qquad \frac{1+4}{1} = 5$$

The Percentage of Clearance.—The percentage of the clearance volume is similarly found by dividing the volume of the clearance by the volume of the piston displacement.

In other words, it is the quotient of the cubic content of the clearance (from the rear of the cylinder to the rearmost reach of the piston at the end of an in-stroke), divided by the cubic content of that portion of the cylinder included between the inmost point of the in-stroke and the outmost point of the out-stroke, as indicated by the position of the rear end of the piston at those two points.

Taking the same two cylinders, having, respectively, clearances of 2 cubic feet and 1 cubic foot, and stroke-sweeps of 4 cubic feet, both, we find the clearance percentage, as follows:

$$\frac{2}{4} = .5 \text{ or } 50\% . \qquad \frac{1}{4} = .25 \text{ or } 25\% .$$

The Compression Pressure.—In order to find the pressure per square inch at the end of the compression stroke, it is necessary only to multiply the figure corresponding to an engine with the given compression ratio and percentage of clearance by the ascertained gauge pressure at the beginning of the stroke, or any other required pressure at the same point. Thus the initial pressure at theoretical unity for a cylinder having a compression ratio of 3 and a clearance percentage of 50 is 4.407, which, multiplied by 13, the gauge or desired pressure, gives 57.29; by 13.2, gives 58.17; by 13.5, gives 59.49; by 14, gives 61.69; by 14.7, gives 64.78.

The Compression Temperature.—The compression temperature is similarly determined by multiplying the found or required absolute temperature at the beginning of the stroke by the figure for one degree for a type of engine having the same compression ratio as the one in question. Thus, for an engine having the ratio

COMPRESSION AND EXPANSION.

Table for Calculating the Compression Pressure and Temperature of a Gas Engine.

A	B	C	D	E	F	G
3.	.4771213	50.	4.407	4.264	146.89	142.13
3.05	.4842958	48.78	4.506	4.358	147.74	142.88
3.1	.4913617	47.62	4.606	4.452	148.58	143.62
3.15	.4983106	46.51	4.707	4.547	149.42	144.36
3.2	.50515	45.45	4.808	4.643	150.25	145.10
3.25	.5118834	44.44	4.910	4.739	151.06	145.82
3.3	.5185139	43.48	5.011	4.835	151.87	146.53
3.35	.5250448	42.55	5.115	4.932	152.67	147.23
3.4	.5314789	41.66	5.217	5.030	153.47	147.93
3.45	.5378191	40.82	5.322	5.128	154.25	148.63
3.5	.544068	40.	5.426	5.226	155.03	149.32
3.55	.5502284	39.22	5.531	5.325	155.80	150.
3.6	.5563025	38.46	5.637	5.424	156.57	150.66
3.65	.5622929	37.74	5.742	5.524	157.32	151.33
3.7	.5682017	37.04	5.848	5.624	158.08	151.99
3.75	.5740313	36.36	5.956	5.724	158.82	152.65
3.8	.5797836	35.71	6.064	5.825	159.56	153.30
3.85	.5854607	35.09	6.171	5.927	160.29	153.94
3.9	.5910646	34.48	6.280	6.029	161.02	154.57
3.95	.5965971	33.9	6.389	6.131	161.73	155.21
4.	.60206	33.33	6.498	6.233	162.45	155.83
4.1	.6127839	32.26	6.718	6.440	163.86	157.07
4.2	.6232493	31.25	6.940	6.648	165.25	158.28
4.3	.6334685	30.3	7.164	6.858	166.62	159.48
4.4	.6434527	29.41	7.390	7.069	167.96	160.66
4.5	.6532125	28.57	7.618	7.282	169.29	161.82
4.6	.6627578	27.77	7.847	7.496	170.59	162.96
4.7	.6720979	27.03	8.078	7.712	171.88	164.09
4.8	.6812412	26.32	8.311	7.929	173.15	165.20
4.9	.6901961	25.64	8.546	8.148	174.41	166.29
5.	.69897	25.	8.783	8.368	175.64	167.37
5.1	.7075702	24.39	9.020	8.590	176.87	168.43
5.2	.7160033	23.81	9.260	8.813	178.07	169.48
5.3	.7242759	23.25	9.501	9.037	179.26	170.52
5.4	.7323938	22.73	9.744	9.263	180.44	171.54
5.5	.7403627	22.22	9.988	9.490	181.60	172.55
5.6	.748188	21.74	10.234	9.719	182.75	173.55
5.8	.763428	20.83	10.73	10.180	185.01	175.50
6.	.7781513	20.	11.233	10.646	187.22	177.42

Column A gives the compression ratio of the cylinder; column B the logarithm of the compression ratio; column C the per cent. of clearance corresponding to any given compression ratio.

Column D gives the figures for the compression pressure corresponding to a theoretical one-pound initial pressure. The figures in this column, corresponding to any given compression ratio, if multiplied by the initial pressure in that cylinder (14.7 minus resistant strength of inlet valve spring), will give the proper compression pressure corresponding to the initial pressure for that cylinder.

Similarly, column E gives the compression pressure corresponding to a theoretical one-pound initial pressure for a scavenging cylinder, whose proper compression pressure may be found by multiplying by the initial pressure.

Columns F and G give the compression temperature for a plain and a scavenging cylinder, respectively, corresponding to a theoretical 100-degree absolute initial temperature. The proper compression temperature for a cylinder of given per cent. clearance and compression ratio may be found by multiplying the figures in either of these columns by $\frac{1}{100}$ of the ascertained absolute compression temperature in the plain or the scavenging cylinder in question. Table from *Power*.

of 3, the theoretical initial temperature is estimated as 1.46°, which, for an initial absolute temperature of 525° (64° + 461) gives 766° (305° + 461), and for 560° (99° + 461) gives 822° (361°+461).

High Compression and Efficiency.—Other things being equal, it might seem reasonable to assert that, the higher the pressure of compression, the greater the rise in temperature at the point of ignition, and, consequently, the greater the power efficiency of the engine. In accordance with this view, we find that, while in many early gas engines the compression pressure was very much below 50 pounds to the square inch, with the more modern and improved patterns it strikes an average in the neighborhood of 70 pounds.

It must not be forgotten, however, that this rule has very definite limitations, and that beyond a certain point of increased compression pressure the efficiency ratio begins to decrease rapidly. This is true, because, although a gas is generally more explosive under pressure, there is always a point at which the rule begins to change. Again, the practical reason, that, to produce a higher compression, a greater amount of power must be absorbed, renders the limitations still more obvious.

High Compression Figures.—Taking a theoretical one-pound pressure and one-degree temperature initial, we have the following figures for varying compression ratios in non-scavenging engines, derived as above:

With a ratio of 3, we have 4.407 for pressure and 1.4689 for temperature; with 4, we have 6.498 and 1.6245, respectively; with 5, we have 8.783 and 1.7564; with 6, in the same way, 11.233 and 1.8722. These figures, multiplied by the ascertained initial pressure and temperature in any particular engine of the same ratio, will give the proper figures for that engine.

Data on Compression Pressure.—On the matter of compression figures this quotation from Hiscox will suffice:

"It has been shown that an ideal efficiency of 33 per cent. for 38 pounds compression will increase to 40 per cent. for 66 pounds, and 43 per cent. for 88 pounds compression. On the other hand, greater compression means greater explosive pressure and greater strain on the engine structure, which in future practice will probably retain the compression between the limits of 40 and 60 pounds.

"In experiments made by Dugald Clerk with a combustion chamber equal to 0.6 of the space swept by the piston, with a compression of 38 pounds, the consumption of gas was 24 cubic feet per indicated horse-power per hour. With 0.4 compression space and 61 pounds compression, the consumption of gas was 20 cubic feet per indicated horse-power per hour; and with 0.34 compression space and 87 pounds compression, the consumption of gas fell to 14.8 cubic feet per indicated horse-power per hour—the actual efficiencies being respectively 17.21 and 25 per cent. This was with a Crossley four-cycle engine."

CHAPTER NINETEEN.

OPERATION AND EFFICIENCY IN A GAS ENGINE.

Definition of Efficiency.—The efficiency of a gas engine is the "ratio of heat turned in to work, as compared with the total heat produced by combustion."

The British Thermal Unit.—The comparison of heat and work in this particular is based upon the *amount, rather than upon the degree,* of heat used. The standard is the so-called *British Thermal Unit,* which may be defined as the amount of heat capable of raising one pound of water through one degree Fahrenheit. This is not a mere question of thermometric temperature. An alcohol lamp and a locomotive furnace may register the same degree on the scale, but the lamp would require a longer period to accomplish the above result—in other words, to generate one thermal unit.

The Efficiency Ratio.—Since all the heat generated by combustion of the gas in cylinder can positively not be utilized as mechanical energy, the efficiency of a gas engine is expressed as a ratio or a fraction. Thus, an engine giving an efficiency of 20 out of each 100 heat units generated would have an efficiency of 20-100ths, or 20 per cent.

The Mechanical Efficiency.—The mechanical efficiency of a heat engine must necessarily be far below the actual heat generated, even with the most perfect machinery imaginable, since it seems practically impossible to fully realize theoretical conditions. Thus, in the operation of a heat engine, there must necessarily be some loss or gain of heat as the gas expands. This, of course, modifies the curve of expansion, and involves a lower mean pressure than is theoretically demanded, should at any time be available for power effort. No expansion in a practical heat engine is perfectly adiabatic; involving that the mean working pressure is always below that required by theory.

The Conditions of Efficiency.—The efficient power of a gas engine is not dependent wholly, or even largely, on relative proportions among the working parts, and, at most, the figures given above are averages for the best obtainable conditions. These conditions are found to consist principally:

1. In the use of the best qualities of fuel.

2. In the production of the best proportions of mixture in fuels.

3. In conditions and means, favorable to rapid and complete ignition of the charge.

4. In efficient means for cooling the cylinder.

Conditions of Fuel Combustion.—In order to secure the proper degree of power efficiency, it is important to consider:

1. Proportioning fuel mixture, since too much or too little of either air or hydrocarbon gas produces the effect of weak or imperfect explosion of the charge.

2. Provision for adequate compression of the charge, in order that, despite the presence of the burned and exhausted gases of previous combustions, there may be uniformity of mixture throughout the mass of fuel gas in cylinder. This is an important element in securing rapid and effective ignition.

The Theory of Fuel Mixtures.—All oils and spirits may be ignited and burned if heated to the required temperature, differing in each case, provided at the same time that air can circulate freely where the heating takes place. The air is required, in order to furnish a sufficient quanity of oxygen for combustion, which, properly speaking, is only the chemical process of absorbing oxygen. The temperature at which an oil or spirit gives off inflammable vapors is called the *flash point,* and the point at which it may be ignited and burned is called the *fire point.* Without a sufficient quantity of air, however, no liquid will either flash or fire, even if confined in a closed vessel heated to very high temperature.

In order to illustrate, the following list of several hydrocarbons, together with their flash and fire points, is quoted from a well-known authority:

	Flash Point.	Fire Point.
Commercial brandy..................	69	92
" whiskey	72	96
" gin	72	101
Kerosene (average quality).	73	104
Petroleum (high test)...............	110-120	140-160

Proportions of Fuel Mixtures.—In the open air the only point to be considered is the temperature for flashing or firing, since atmospheric circulation will always supply the full amount of oxygen for combustion. In a gas-engine cylinder, closed from the outer air, it is necessary to know how much air must be admitted. The most efficient proportions of air and gas, mixed to give a perfect combustion in a closed cylinder, may be considered a matter in many respects relative to the kind of gas employed—some gases require more, some less, for the best effects from combustion.

Figures for Coal Gas.—In general, however, the data on coal gas may be taken as typical for most fuels available in ordinary gas-engine service. With this fuel the figures for good efficiency range between 6 to 1 and 11 to 1 for air and gas, respectively. That is to say, with a mixture of about 5 to 1 or about 12 to 1, for example, the effective pressure due to combustion—if combustion is possible at all—shows a marked falling off, which continues thereafter as the proportion of air in the mixture is either diminished or increased.

Effects of Varying Mixtures.—Between the efficient extremes it has been found that, although the actual indicated explosion pressure decreases in ratio with the increased percentage of air in the mixture, the efficiency steadily increases until the point of 11 to 1 is approximated. This fact is explained by assuming that, in increasing the proportion of air in the mixture, the temperature per unit of gas is raised, although the temperature per unit of the mixture of gas and air is lowered. Since, there-fore, the gas itself is the sole agent of efficiency—the condition necessary to explosion being all that is furnished by the ad-mixture of air—the increase in the proportion of air in the charge, up to the specified limit, increases the total efficiency, even though lowering the pressure of the explosion.

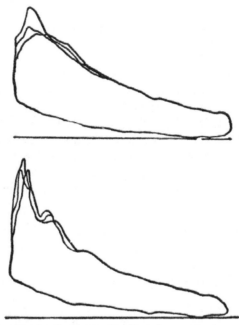

FIG. 133.—Typical Gas-Engine Indicator Cards, taken under actual service conditions. The first diagram is from an engine running under half load; the second from one at full load. Both exhibit the variations in the expansion curve, usually attributed to consecutive explosions. These cards are composites of three successive strokes each.

Causes of Defective Mixture.—As already suggested, an ade-quate degree of compression is as essential to perfect efficiency in a gas engine, from the fact that a more complete mingling of the fuel ingredients is thus secured. In the same engine, how-ever, as shown by indicator cards, several successive firing strokes will show a marked variation in the pressure rise at explosion. Some authorities refer this to the presence of residual burned-out gases in the clearance, which tend to *stratify* the fuel, producing layers of incombustible gas, with the result that several successive weak explosions occur instead of one full and complete explosion.

Advantages of Scavenging.—That the presence of non-combustible burned gases in the cylinder clearance is a fertile source of lost efficiency seems proved by the superior average performance of scavenging engines, in which these residue are largely expelled.

"A mixture of 9 to 1, with no burned gases present, gives a rise of about 2,373 degrees; the same mixture, compressed with the burned gases of a previous explosion in a clearance of 41 2-3 per cent. of the cylinder volume gives a rise of only about 1,843 degrees.

"The resulting temperatures of explosion in the two cases do not differ so greatly as the rise in temperature, because the scavenging engine starts from a lower initial temperature and the rise during compression is not so great. For example, assume an engine with 3.4 compression ratio, running scavenging with an initial pressure of 13.2 pounds and an initial temperature of 580 degrees; and suppose a similar engine running plain, with 13.2 pounds initial pressure and 600 degrees initial temperature. The results are compared below on the basis of a 9 to 1 mixture:

	Ordinary.	Scavenging.
Initial temperature	600	580
Compression temperature	921	858
Rise in temperature by explosion	1,843	2,373
Temperature of explosion	2,764	3,231

"In this comparison the difference in the rise of temperature is nearly 29 per cent. while the difference between the explosion temperatures of the two engines is only scant 17 per cent. A better comparison may be had by considering the pressures; these figure out as follows:

	Ordinary.	Scavenging.
Initial pressure	13.2	13.2
Compression pressure	68.86	66.4
Explosion pressure	206.65	250.0

"Thus, the scavenging engine shows a maximum temperature about 17 per cent. higher than the other engine, while its maximum pressure is a trifle over 21 per cent. greater. * * * * * While excessive explosion pressures are not desirable, it is clearly advantageous, within practical limits, to increase the difference between the maximum forward pressure and that of compression, because it increases the area of the indicator diagram. And as this result is obtained by scavenging, without consuming any more gas, the superiority of a scavenging engine is obvious."

CHAPTER TWENTY.

THE EXHAUST OF A GAS ENGINE.

Losses in the Exhaust.—In the operation of a gas or gasoline engine a large amount of heat and power units are inevitably lost in the exhaust.

The principal reason why this loss may not be avoided is that the gas, after explosion, may not be expanded to atmospheric pressure within the cylinder. At the completion of the power stroke the expansion line stands generally about or above the figure indicated for compression pressure. It is necessary, therefore, to open the exhaust before the completion of the stroke, generally at about $\frac{7}{8}$ stroke. Were the engine otherwise geared, and the piston allowed to receive the pressure of the expanding gas through its full stroke, the gas would not exhaust fast enough to avoid buffing the piston on its return sweep, since through an appreciable distance the continued expansion would balance the rate of escape through the exhaust valve. The effect of this would be to check the speed and power of the engine, with the result of absorbing about as much power as would on the other plan be turned to waste.

The Variation of the Curve of Expansion.—The expansion following explosion is not instantaneous, but continues throughout the stroke, thus constantly keeping up the temperature and pressure, which would, otherwise, tend to fall regularly from maximum to atmosphere. Thus the expansion line on the indicator diagram does not meet the compression line at the end point of the stroke, as should be the case under theoretically perfect conditions. Consequently the exhaust valve must be opened before the completion of the stroke, as above stated.

The Ratio of Expansion.—As may be readily understood, the practice of opening the exhaust valve at about $\frac{7}{8}$ power stroke involves that the expansion ratio differs greatly from the compression ratio, with which, theoretically, it should be identical.

The expansion ratio represents the quotient found by dividing the sum of the total cylinder content (clearance + piston sweep) and that portion of the stroke and clearance content left behind the piston at the moment the exhaust opens, by the cubic content of the clearance. This may be expressed by the following formula:

$$\mathrm{Er} = \frac{\mathrm{C} + \frac{n}{\mathrm{C}}}{\mathrm{B}} = \frac{\text{Volume of Expansion}}{\text{Volume of Clearance}}$$

in which Er is the ratio of expansion.

C " the total cylinder content.

B " the combustion chamber or clearance content.

n " the numerator expressing the portion of the cylinder content left behind the piston at the opening of the exhaust, which, as already stated, is generally ⅞ stroke length, or ⅞ sweep content in cubic measure.

Figures for Exhaust Losses.—The pressures and temperatures voided in the exhaust are in proportion, first place, to the figures realized in explosion, and, secondly, to the expansion ratio of the particular cylinder under test. Both are found to decrease with increasing ratios. Thus, under ordinary conditions, with engines driven by illuminating gas, an explosion temperature of 3,000 and an explosion pressure of 250 for a ratio of 3 give an exhaust temperature of 2,158 and an exhaust pressure of 59.9; for a ratio of 3.5 they give 2,060 and 49.0; for a ratio of 4 they give 1,979 and 41.2; for a ratio of 5 they give 1,851 and 30.8; for a ratio of 6 they give 1,752 and 24.3.

Suppose we assume an expansion ratio of 5.8 in order to get a great expansion, and a compression ratio of 6. Then assume an ordinary engine, because the effect of explosion is not so great and a mixture of 12 volumes of air to 1 of gas, because that is the weakest reliable mixture. Starting with the highest practical initial temperature, 660 degrees, and the lowest practical initial pressure, 13, the following results are obtained:

	Pressure.	Temperature.
Initial	13	660
Compression	146	1,236
Rise	207	1,755
Explosion	353	2,991
Exhaust	35.9	1,765

The Muffler or Silencer.—The exhaust from the cylinder, being commonly expelled at a pressure between two and three times an atmosphere, would naturally make considerable noise and raise dust, were it not for the use of an apparatus called the muffler, or silencer. Although constructed on various designs, the muffler always involves the same theory of "breaking up"

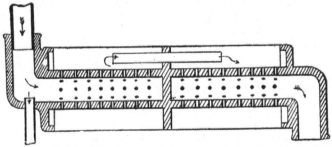

FIG. 134.—The Benz Exhaust Muffler. The arrows indicate the course of the ex-panding exhaust products. Entering at the left, they pass through the perforations in the tube; thence through the smaller tube in the larger chamber; again through the perforations in the right-hand section of the tube, and to atmosphere. The breaking-up of the gas in expansion silences the noise of its exhaust to atmosphere.

the exhaust gas by causing it to pass through fine perforations in the exhaust tube, and of allowing it to expand to nearly atmospheric pressure in one or several successive chambers. Several efficient types of muffler are shown in accompanying diagrams.

Cubic Content of a Muffler.—As indicated by Roberts, the formula for the cubic content of a muffler best calculated to save power gives 3.5 times the square of the cylinder diameter in inches multiplied by the length of the piston stroke in inches, or

$$M = 3.5 \ D^2L.$$

If, therefore, a cylinder have a diameter of $4\frac{1}{2}$ inches and a stroke of 5 inches, we have:

$$M = 3.5 \times (4.5)^2 \times 5 = 3.5 \times 20.25 \times 5 = 354.375 \text{ cu. in.}$$

If two cylinders of this size exhaust into the same muffler, the cubic content should be increased by 50 per cent.; if three cylinders, by 150 per cent.; if four cylinders, by 200 per cent. In other words, under these several conditions, the muffler should be increased by one-half, once and one-half and twice the proper content for a single cylinder.

Losses in the Muffler.—Since, as stated, the principle of a muffler involves imposing obstacles, in the shape of minute perforations, etc., to the free expansion of exhaust gases, it furnishes a large and undesirable back-pressure.

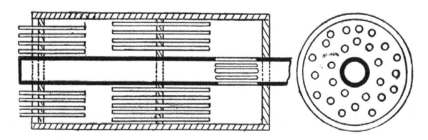

FIG. 135.—The "Loomis" Muffler. The exhaust enters the central tube at the right-hand end, passing out through slits shown in its side to the main chamber, where it is passed through a number of lengths of tubing. Leaving these it emerges to atmosphere through another set of tube lengths.

A French authority states that an engine of 8 I. H. P., running without muffler, gave 6.1 B. H. P. at 967 revolutions per minute, but with muffler gave the same efficiency only on 1,012 revolutions. He also found for a 2.25 I. H. P. engine an efficient output of 2.16 at 2,015 revolutions without muffler, and of 1.91, at 2,057 revolutions with muffler, claiming a loss of 20 kilogram-meters, or 145 foot pounds per second.

These figures are fairly typical for very many mufflers, and, although possibly reduced by some of the more modern models, represent fairly well the kind of obstacles obtruded in the way of the highest mechanical efficiency of the average gas engine.

Preventing Exhaust Losses.—The enormous waste, as indicated by the figures given above, which show that, with average exhaust temperature of 1,760° absolute, or 1,300° F., escaping into an average atmospheric temperature of 70° F., (1.23 × .26) 319.8 heat units, or (319.8 × 778) 248,804 foot-pounds, or over 7.5 horse-power per pound of fuel gas goes through the exhaust valves, is a good argument for seeking some device to utilize at least a part of this lost energy.

Cut-Out Mufflers.—Although there have been many notable improvements, in both the design and operation of mufflers, within the last few years, the situation remains substantially the same in regard to the percentage of power lost in the exhaust.

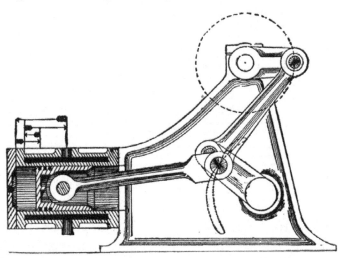

Fig. 136.—Section of the Atkinson Cycle Gas Engine, showing the varying lengths of the strokes—from the top, exhaust, expansion, compression, suction; also, the figure-of-8 path described by the toggle-jointed crank connections, and the path of the crank.

As already stated, it is impracticable to expand the ignited gas to atmospheric pressure ; hence at least 16 per cent. of the total heat energy is inevitably lost on this score. Furthermore, if a muffler is to discharge its function of "muffling," or silencing, the exhaust, some back-pressure is unavoidable. Several manufacturers of mufflers confidently claim that their inventions produce "no back-pressure whatever." It would seem that their mufflers seldom get upon high-powered, high-speed cars, which in racing, and speeding on tour, are commonly driven with the muffler cut out—their drivers being willing to endure the detonations of the exhaust, for the sake of the additional power and mileage capacity. Many mufflers are equipped with a special cut-out attachment, which is used at starting to remove back-pressure as well as in speeding. On a 40-horse-power car as much as 6 horse-powers may be saved by the muffler cut-out.

A Variable=Stroke Engine.—An interesting approximation of theoretical efficiency is found in the Atkinson cycle scavenging engine, which proved able to expand the charge from 185 pounds

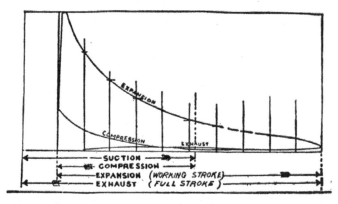

FIG. 137.—Indicator Card for the Atkinson Variable Stroke Four-Part "Two-Cycle" Gas Engine.

at explosion to 10 pounds gauge, at the completion of the power stroke. In this engine the piston rod is connected to a double toggle joint, as indicated in the Figure 186, page 179, which so varied the length of the several strokes of a four-part cycle, as to give a suction stroke through about one-half the sweep length, a return compression stroke to a point about 5-6 the sweep, an impulse stroke from that point clear forward, and an exhausting stroke from end to end of the cylinder. As claimed in a published description, the working effects are that

"The clearance space beyond the terminal exhaust position of the piston is so small that, practically, the products of combustion are entirely swept out of the cylinder during the exhaust stroke, so that each incoming charge has the full explosive strength due to the mixture used."

The accompanying indicator card of an Atkinson engine, of 18 I. H. P., working at 130 revolutions per minute, with a mean pressure of 49 pounds, shows the excellent results achieved by thus varying the length of the several strokes. But such a procedure is impossible in the ordinary four-cycle engine, which finds the only available method of securing approximately complete combustion in varying proportions of the fuel mixture and by scavenging the cylinder.

Although the complications of the Atkinson engine proved it difficult to handle for stationary purposes, there can be no doubt but what it furnishes the elements of an ideal automobile motor, as will doubtless be some day realized.

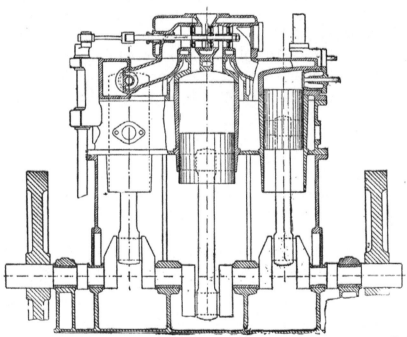

Fig. 138.—Crossley Three-Cylinder Compound Gas Engine. The two end cylinders are high pressure; the central one, low pressure. The exhaust from the two high-pressure cylinders is admitted, alternately, to the low-pressure cylinder by the piston valve, operated by the crank and rotating shaft shown at the left. The exhaust from the low-pressure cylinder passes upward through the port at its top.

Compound Gas Engines.—Compounding for gas engines cylinders has been proven an efficient means for utilizing the common waste of the exhaust. The accompanying figure of the Crossley & Atkinson compound gas engine shows three cylinders —two primary, or high-pressure, between which is a secondary, or low-pressure. The cubic content of the low pressure cylinder is about twice that of either of the high pressure cylinders, thus allowing the exhaust gas to expand very nearly to atmospheric pressure, when fed into it from either of the others. The crank shaft is so arranged that, while the two low pressure pistons are at the dead end of the in-stroke—the one, of compression, the other, of exhaust, for example—the low pressure piston is at the dead end of its out-stroke, or power-stroke. Thus the exhaust gas is fed to the low pressure cylinder from both the high pressure cylinders alternately, and performs a power-stroke once in each revolution of the fly-wheel, always alternately to either of the others. As may be seen from examination of the drawing, connection between the high pressure and low pressure cylinders is had by means of a triple piston valve moved longitudinally on a secondary shaft and so arranged that pure atmospheric air may be admitted to the centre cylinder, when either of the others misses fire.

CHAPTER TWENTY-ONE.

WATER-COOLING FOR THE CYLINDER.

Water=Cooling for Cylinders.—By the far the greater proportion of gas engines—those employed alike for general power purposes and in propelling motor vehicles—have water-cooled cylinders, the water for this purpose being admitted to a jacket or water space cast around the cylinder's circumference This water circulates between the jacket space and the feed tank, either:

1. *By gravity,* in accordance with the laws of liquids, which cause the heated layers to rise from the bottom to the top of the reservoir, and the cooler layers to fall correspondingly.

2. *By forced circulation,* under impulse from a rotary or centrifugal pump, which keeps the water in constant motion.

Air=Cooling for Cylinders.—In recent years air-cooling for automobile engine cylinders has been successfully achieved in a variety of ways:

1. By providing a sufficiently large radiating surface by means of cast flanges or gills, inserted pins and tubes.

2. By using unusually large exhaust valves, so as to cool the combustion space between power strokes.

3. By combining large radiating surfaces with low speeds in multiple-cylinder engines.

4. By the use of auxiliary exhaust ports, combined with surface radiation.

5. By forced draught of air circulating through an air jacket around the cylinder.

The greater majority of air-cooled engines have rotary fans attached, for the purpose of increasing radiation with air currents at high speed.

The Theory of Cylinder Cooling.—The prime necessity involved in efficient means for cooling a gas-engine cylinder is that the temperature of the cylinder is normally maintained below the point at which the lubricating oil will otherwise carbonize. Furthermore, the walls would also become so heated that the fuel charge would be fired out of time, with the result of disarranging the cycle and stopping the engine. Although the "cooling system" is a positive necessity over the combustion space, for the reasons above stated, it forms a serious consideration in estimates on efficiency by absorbing a large proportion of the heat units generated by ignition of the fuel, and thus, under any conditions operating to reduce the total theoretical efficiency, even though by a very small fraction.

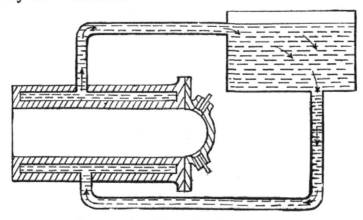

FIG. 139.—Diagram of a Gravity Water-Circulation System for a Gas-Engine Cylinder. As indicated by the arrows, the water from the tank enters the jacket of the cylinder at the lowest point, and being there subjected to the heat of the cylinder walls, rises to the level of the tank water: thus maintaining a continuous circulation.

Jacket Water: Its Rate and Quantity.—On this point Hiscox makes an interesting statement on the proportions of absorbed and efficient heat units, as estimated under typical conditions. He says:

"In regard to the actual consumption of water per horse-power and the amount of heat carried off by it, the study of English trials of an Atkinson, a Crossley, and a Griffin engine showed 62 pounds of water per indicated horse-power per hour, with a rise in temperature of 50° F., or 3,100 heat units carried off in the water out of 12,027 theoretical heat units that were fed to the motor through the 19 cubic feet of gas at 633 heat units per cubic foot per hour.

"Theoretically, 2,564 heat units per hour are equal to one horse-power. Then, 0.257 of the total was given to the jacket water, 0.213 to the indicated power, and the balance, 53 per cent., went to the exhaust, radiation and the reheating of the previous charge in the clearance and in expanding the nitrogen of the air. * * *

"In a trial with a Crossley engine, 42 pounds of water per horse-power per hour were passed through the cylinder jacket, with a rise in temperature of 128° F.—equal to 5,376 heat units to the water from 12,833 heat units fed to the engine through 20.5 cubic feet of gas at 626 heat units per cubic foot."

Gas Consumption and Power Efficiency.—On the point of gas consumption per horse-power under varying conditions, Hiscox states:

"An experimental test of the performance of a gas engine below its maximum load has shown a large increase in the consumption of gas per actual horse-power, with a decrease of load, as the following figures from observed trials show: An actual 12 H. P. engine at full load used 15 cubic feet of gas per horse-power per hour; at 10 H. P., 15½ cubic feet; at 8 H. P., 16½ cubic feet; at 6 H. P., 18 cubic feet; at 4 H. P., 21 cubic feet; at 2 H. P., 30 cubic feet of gas per actual horse-power per hour. This indicates an economy gained in gauging the size of a gas engine to the actual power required, in consideration of the fact that the engine friction and gas consumption for ignition are constants for all or any power actually given out by the engine."

Efficiency and Structural Conditions.—As already stated, an increase in compression, involving a smaller combustion chamber or a longer stroke, ensures a higher temperature and explosive force at ignition. But, in obtaining these ends by a relatively longer piston-sweep, we are met by the difficulty of exposing the ignited gas to a commensurately larger area of heat-absorption through the circulating jacket-water. It is obvious, therefore, that economy in this respect must be obtained by some mechanical or physical variation in the conditions of operation.

Heat Economy: High Speeds.—For example, considerable economy in fuel-consumption may be obtained by increasing the speed of the engine, which, when the cycle is well established, involves that the explosive impulses succeed one another so rapidly that the percentage of heat units absorbed by the jacket water is constantly reduced. Such a reduction of power-output involves, of course, a lower speed, and is accomplished by regulating the gas and air supply. But if, according to the figures quoted above, a 12 H. P. engine at full power consumes 15 cubic feet of gas per horse-power per hour, which is 180 cubic feet per hour, it will at 10 horse-power consume .155 cubic feet, or 86 per cent.; at 8 horse-power, 132 cubic feet, or 75 per cent.; at 6 horse-power, 108 cubic feet, or 60 per cent.; at 4 horse-power, 84 cubic feet, or 46 per cent., and at 2 horse-power, 60 cubic feet, or 33 per cent. The waste in fuel gas under low speed and low power conditions may thus be readily understood—one-sixth of the stated horse-power from one-third of the full gas supply.

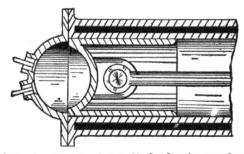

Fig. 140.—Section through a Gas Engine Cylinder having a spherical clearance and a spherical depression on the piston head. The shaded sections at top and bottom indicate the water jackets. The concavities are somewhat greater than are met in general practice. Few builders use the concaved cylinder head.

Heat Economy: Spherical Clearance.—A number of gas engines achieve an economy in the use of heat and power units by having the piston and the combustion chamber of concave profile, so as to form a spherical, spheroidal or elliptical clearance at the end of the in-stroke. That is to say, the rear end of the cylinder is dome-shaped and unjacketed, and the opposing end of the trunk piston is correspondingly hollowed or concaved, thus providing a large uncooled surface at either end of the combustion chamber during the entire cycle. Indeed, while this arrangement permits of a clearance at the end of the in-stroke, of the smallest possible area on the cylinder walls, it provides a total increase in clearance volume on a stated wall surface between 20 and 40 per cent. in engines of ordinary design.

Hiscox estimates that, while the wall surface of a cylindrical clearance space of one-half its unit diameter in length contains 3.1416 square units and 0.3927 cubic unit, the same surface in square unit measure, with a spherical combustion chamber has a volume of 0.5236 cubic unit, representing a gain in volume of 33⅓ per cent. (5236—3927=1309×3=3927). Such superior volume, on equal wall surface, being fully available at the moment of explosion, when the greatest possible degree of heat and pressure is desirable to promote expansion, must vastly increase the effective power of the engine.

Heat Economy: Temperature of Water.—Another consideration of importance in calculating for heat economy in a gas engine is that the temperature of the jacket water should be maintained at a point favorable to moderate absorption of superfluous heat. The temperature of the water must not be too low—the cooling must not be a *freezing* process; since, as is evident from foregoing statements, the efficiency of the engine will fall accordingly. The best practice is to supply water to the jacket at a temperature of a few degrees below the boiling point, permitting it to be returned to the reservoir at a temperature slightly above.

Heat Economy: Rate of Absorption.—A prominent American gas engine authority writes:

"A motor is hotter when the water is boiling rapidly than when it is boiling slowly, and the fact that more heat units are being absorbed by the water proves that the engine is doing harder work and not that it is cooler than before. The writer favors boiling water as the proper temperature and a gravity circulation as the proper circulating method, because this method most nearly insures a fixed temperature for the motor to work under. If kept below the boiling point the temperature of the motor will vary as the work varies. If air-cooled it will vary with the wind or the speed of the vehicle. If circulated by the pump the temperature will vary as the speed of the pump varies, but with the boiling water system it remains reasonably constant and permits the finest adjustment of the mixture and the best results from the sparking."

Heat Economy: Rate of Water Circulation.—The plea for gravity, or thermo-siphonic circulation, just quoted, does not represent the opinions of many experts. Thus, an able writer on gas engines in a leading periodical says:

"The more rapidly the water passes through the jacket, the lower will be the temperature of the issuing jacket water, but the heat units will be greater, within the usual limits of practice. For example, suppose the jacket water passes through at the rate of 16 pounds a minute and rises from 60° F. to 140° F. in passing through. To raise 16 pounds of water 80 degrees requires 1,280 B. T. U. (British thermal units), and as the

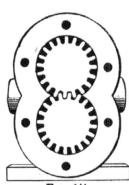 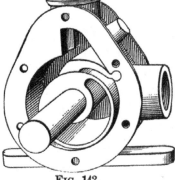

FIG. 141.   FIG. 142.

FIGS. 141-142.—Two Types of Circulating Pump for Use in the Water-Cooling System of Gas Engines. In both cases the water is raised by the use of a rotating watertight piston, being compelled to follow the designed course by the reduction of the space it can occupy around the shaft of the piston.

difference between the average temperature within the cylinder (usually about 1,000° F.) and that of the jacket water (in this case 100°) is 900 degrees, there are 1,422 heat units per minute transmitted through the walls of the cylinder per degree of difference between inner and outer average temperatures.

"Now reduce the rate of flow of the jacket water to 9.57 pounds, and, assuming that the average temperature in the cylinder remains constant, the water will issue at a temperature of 190° F. This means a rise of 130 degrees, and to heat 9.57 pounds of water per minute 130 degrees, will require 9.57 × 130=1,244 heat units per minute, which is 36 less than before. A saving of 36 heat units per minute means

$$\frac{36 \times 778}{33,000} = .8487 \text{ H. P., gross.}$$

"As a matter of fact the flow of water would need to be less than 9½ pounds a minute in order to raise the temperture to 190° F., because as the jacket water increases in temperature, the average temperature in the cylinder increases, making the difference between the two less than if the internal temperature remained constant. This decreases the transmission of heat units to the water. The effect of varying the flow of jacket water cannot be computed accurately, because the internal temperature cannot be computed, and the exact heat conductivity of the cylinder walls is unknown. But, as the foregoing rough example clearly shows, the temperature of the issuing jacket water should be kept as high as practicable by adjusting the rate of flow.

"The limit to the allowable increase in jacket water temperature is set by the cylinder oil. The cylinder walls must not be allowed to become so hot as to decompose the oil, for the very obvious reason that decomposed oil does not lubricate.

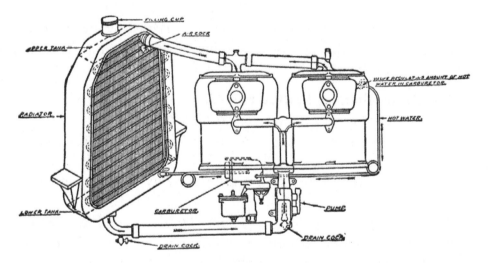

FIG. 143.—An example of a radiator and water cooling system with pump circulation. The cooling is assisted by a fan geared to the engine which induces a current of air through the radiator when the car is standing.

Heat Economy: Regulating Jacket=Water Temperature.—

If we play a hose upon the surface of a gas-engine cylinder, the absorption of heat will be so rapid that motion will cease. Conversely, the efficiency of the engine, within limits, increases with the rise in jacket-water temperature. The limits under ordinary conditions of operation are set at the point when the water begins steaming. It is necessary, therefore, to provide for the radiation of enough thermal units to keep the water from changing its form. For this purpose radiators of the several forms known to automobile construction are used.

Radiators for Cooling Jacket Water.—After leaving the water jacket of the engine, the water is forced through the radiator, before being returned to the tank. Radiators are made in two general styles:

1. Radiators composed of coils of tubing having a number of metal gills or fins let over the tube circumference.

2. Radiators consisting of a flat tank pierced with a multitude of small tubes—like the flues of a boiler. This kind is the well-known Mercedes cellular or "honeycomb" radiator.

Both varieties of radiator are made preferably of copper, a metal having a high heat-conducting capacity.

In both varieties of radiator the water is cooled by air currents passing through the fins or flue-tubes, extracting the heat, in proportion to the available cooling surface exposed.

The Dimensions of Radiators.—The following data are given for the dimensions of radiators of both varieties :

The cooling surface of a *tubular radiator,* stated in square inches, is the product of the length of the tubes by their circumference, plus the area of one fin multiplied by the total number of fins.

The cooling surface of a *cellular radiator,* stated in square inches, is the product of the circumference of one cell or flue multiplied by its length, multiplied by the number of cells or flues.

The usually accepted standard for radiator dimensions requires 5 square feet of cooling surface per indicated horse-power. This gives 9 feet of ⅝-inch tube, or 6 feet of ¾-inch tube per indicated horse-power.

CHAPTER TWENTY-TWO.

AIR-COOLING FOR THE CYLINDER.

Air Cooling for Cylinders.—While, as a general proposition, it may be said that the cooling of a gas-engine cylinder is best accomplished by water-circulation, a number of recent carriages both light and heavy have successfully used air-cooling devices. To within a very few years it has been held that air cooling is impracticable for vehicle motors, and, on the basis of trials made by French builders, the statement has always been made that, while an air-cooled cylinder will work very well on a light high speed vehicle or cycle, it is impossible for automobiles of large

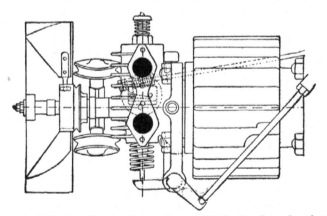

FIG. 144.—Detail Cylinder Head of the Simms Cycle Engine, showing fan wheel, cooling ribs, and peculiar arrangement for opening the exhaust.

power, particularly in climbing hills and in hot weather. Daimler's early motors were air cooled by means of a rotary fan on the crankshaft that created a forced draught through an air jacket surrounding the cylinder, as is shown in a subsequent cut. Later on, automobile builders, such as Mors, Decauville, Darracq, and also Panhard-Levassor, used motors on heavy carriages with the cylinders cooled by peripheral fins or flanges. The principal trouble with these cylinders was that under heavy load the generating of heat was so rapid as to clog the piston, ignite the lubricating oil, or to produce premature explosion of the charge. Largely for this reason, the water-cooling system became universal, except for very light vehicles and cycles intended to be driven at high speeds. In order to assist the work of cooling the cylinder, several builders early adopted the plan of using rotary fans to create a forced draught against the fins cast on the cylinder's walls. Such a device greatly increased the cooling properties of the motor, even when the vehicle was moving at low speed. This was particularly true with the Simms fan-cooled cylinder, on the

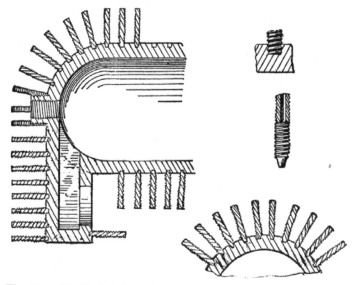

FIG. 145.--The Knox Pin-Cooled Cylinder. In this engine, pins are used for radiating instead of the usual flanges or ribs as on other air-cooled cylinders.

walls of which were cast very deep longitudinal flanges. An English builder, Turell, constructed a three-wheeled carriage propelled by a motor with ribs of this description. It was found however that, with a motor of 2 horse-power, and over, the draught created at high speed was not sufficient for cooling and that the cylinder would quickly become overheated, with the result the exhaust walls would be loosened and the head frequently red hot. It seems to have been reserved for American inventors to design successfully air-cooling systems. One of the most noteworthy of this is the Knox pin-cooled cylinder, in which a large number of brass pins are screwed into suitable holes on the outside of the cylinder's wall. According to claims this device increases the cooling surface nearly 100 per cent., and is exceedingly efficient in utilizing the heat absorbing properties of air under draft.

In connection with the use of corrugated pins on the outside surface of the cylinder, a rotary fan is used, and this, being

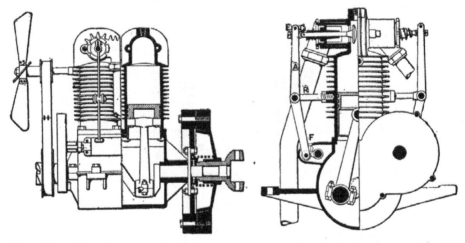

FIG. 146.—The Cameron Air Cooled Engine. The fan shown at the left induces a current of air which passing over the large surface presented by numerous ribs, cools the cylinders. The valves are located above the cylinder bore in opposite chambers and work horizontally. Each valve is operated by a long vertical lever A, pivoted at R. The upper end C bears upon the end of the valve stem and its lower end carries a roller against which bears the camshaft cam D. The upper end of the lever or valve rocker arm is split and takes a threaded piece E, which rests upon the end of the valve stem. By the adjustment of this the timing of the valve is accomplished. The lower end, with its roller is contained within a small cubical-shaped expansion on a detachable plate secured to the side of the crank case, the end of the valve rocker arm working in a slot F in the top of the expansion.

driven direct from the main shaft by a worm gear, always rotates with the speed of the engine, thus providing a sufficient draft for cooling purposes at all speeds. The problem has been differently solved by other American inventors. Thus the builders of the Crest carriage use a cylinder with deep longitudinal flanges, which according to claims and reported tests is very efficient in spite of the fact that the motor is set vertically in the carriage. Briefly described, the flanges are so arranged as to be deepest over the combustion spaces, thus giving the cylinder an approximate pear shape. The success of the air cooling is due to the extremely large radiating surface, due to the use of very wide vertical radiating vanes, to the free passage of air directly behind the valve chamber—this space being

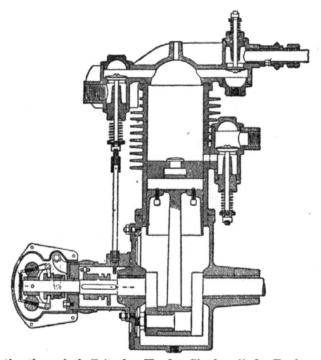

FIG. 147.—Section through the Fritscher-Houdry Single-cylinder Engine, showing the supplementary or "anticipatory" exhaust valve at the point of piston outstroke. The supplementary exhaust used on modern engines is similar to this, only mechanically operated.

usually filled with solid metal—and to the slight tapering of the upper end of the piston. The motor is of the conventional vertical type, excepting that the inlet and exhaust valves are larger in proportion to bore than is usually used. According to claims, apparently verified by independent test, it can safely run at a speed of between 1,900 and 2,000 revolutions per minute.

For air-cooling the cylinders of the Regas engine, a sheet steel jacket carrying numerous copper tubes, each having a longitudinal slot at its base, is slid over the walls. As heat is generated in the operation of the engine, a circulation of air is set up, the hot air being given out at the ends of the tubes, on the principle of the Bunsen burner. In this manner, there is a constant supply of cool air for absorbing the heat of the cylinder and the circulation is maintained without a fan or other mechanical contrivance.

The Franklin system of air cooling is different from any of the fore going devices, and, judging from its numerous imitators,

Fig. 148.—Cylinder of the Regas Engine, showing Bunsen tubes let into steel jacket

embodies the correct principle for cooling a medium to heavy weight gasoline engine. Briefly described, it consists in using a multiple cylinder engine; in the first models four cylinders, and latterly six. The primary effect of using four cylinders is that any desired degree of power may be achieved with shorter strokes and smaller pistons than would be possible with either one or two cylinders. The area of the combustion space being reduced, the heat may be more quickly radiated from the engine. Franklin also uses a supplementary exhaust situated at or near the point of piston out-stroke, so as to be uncovered precisely like the exhaust port in a two-cycle engine. The supplementary exhaust greatly facilitates the expulsion of the burnt out products of combustion. The port opens into a small chamber, normally closed by a poppet valve, which is opened at the proper moment, thus giving an exhaust from both top and bottom of the cylinder. A very similar arrangement was adopted by Fritscher and Houdry as early as 1900, but proved only indifferently effected on a single-cylinder engine.

Other engines, notably the Marion, achieve the end of efficient air cooling by using an exhaust valve of unusually large area. Frayer and Miller enclose the cylinders of their engine with an air jacket through which air is forced by a blower, on a principle precisely similar to water circulation forced by a rotary pump.

Briefly expressed the requirements for effective air cooling are:

1. Radiating surface, large in proportion to the outside area of the cylinder.

2. Large exhaust valves, or some mechanical means for increasing the speed of the exhaust.

3. Combined with these two, a multiple cylinder engine.

CHAPTER TWENTY-THREE.

POWER ELEMENTS OF A GAS ENGINE.

Power Efficiency and Fuel Consumption.—As we have already learned, there are various conditions, both physical and mechanical, that prevent the realization of the full theoretical effect of the heat actually expended in a gas-engine cylinder. Ideally speaking, the efficiency of such an engine should be expressed by this formula:

$$\frac{\text{Temperature rise in degrees}}{\text{Explosion Temperature}} = \frac{T''-T'}{T''}$$

Substituting the average figures previously found, we have this expression:

$$\frac{3000-660}{3000} = \frac{2340}{3000} = .78.$$

This would involve that about 78 per cent., on the average, was the actual *heat efficiency* of a good gas engine. The results, however, are far below this; for, even allowing for all the apparently unavoidable losses in the process of transforming heat into actual work, we find that the real average makes the *actual mechanical efficiency*, in terms of *brake horse-power*, about 80 per cent. of the calculated efficiency, in terms of *indicated horse-power*. Thus:

$$\frac{\text{B. H. P.}}{\text{I. H. P.}} = \frac{8}{10} = .80.$$

This is generally about 17 per cent. of the total heat expended, and seldom more than 20 per cent.

Mechanical Equivalent of Heat.—Now, one horse-power is 33,000 foot-pounds per minute, and 778 foot-pounds equals one thermal unit, which equation expresses the *mechanical equivalent of heat*. Whence, **one** horse-power equals 42.42 thermal units per minute, which is, by the hour, 2,545.2 thermal units. Then a 10 H. P. hour equals 25,452 thermal units and an 8 H. P. hour equals 20,361.60 thermal units. Whence we have:

$$\frac{20361.6}{25452} = .80.$$

If, however, 10 H. P., or 25,452 B. T. U. per hour be assumed equivalent to the I. H. P. of a given engine, which is, as a general average, 26 per cent. of the total heat equivalent supplied to the engine in the shape of fuel, we have it that the total theoretical value of the fuel should be 97,892.31 B. T. U., or 38.46 H. P.

According to one authority, the average heat expenditures found in a number of tests of gas engines is as follows:

To the jacket water.......................... 52 per cent.
To loss in the exhaust........................ 16 " "
To loss in radiator, etc...................... 15 " "
To useful work (B. H. P.)..................... 17 " "

This shows a total of 83 per cent. lost for any efficient mechanical work realized, or useful, at best, only for maintaining necessary interior conditions. Accepting these figures as fairly typical, we find for 10 I. H. P., or 26 per cent., a total of 97,892.31 thermal units, or the heat equivalent of 38.46 H. P. by the hour theoretically, fed to the cylinder in fuel mixture.

Then reducing the above table to terms of heat equivalence, we have:

$$52\% = 50904.00 \text{ B. T. U.} = 20.000 \text{ H. P.}$$
$$16\% = 15662.77 \text{ B. T. U.} = 6.154 \text{ H. P.}$$
$$17\% = 16641.69 \text{ B. T. U.} = 6.538 \text{ H. P.}$$
$$15\% = 14683.85 \text{ B. T. U.} = 5.765 \text{ H. P.}$$

$$100\% = 97892.31 \text{ B. T. U.} = 38.457 \text{ H. P.}$$

Experimental Figures.—Another authority, as quoted by several writers, finds the following results from a series of experiments with a 125 H. P. gas engine: At full load 26 per cent. of the heat energy is converted into mechanical energy, 44 per cent. is lost through the exhaust and by radiation, and 30 per cent. is absorbed by the jacket water, or a total loss of 74 per cent. At three-quarter load, the figures become 25, 38 and 37 per cent., respectively, a total loss of 75 per cent; at one-quarter load, 18, 28,

54, a total loss of 82 per cent.; and, when running free, 10, 32 and 58 per cent., a total loss of 90 per cent. These figures show that the percentage of loss through the exhaust increases as the jacket loss decreases. Other recorded tests show similar figures.

Calorific Values of Fuels.—As we have already learned, some causes of lost efficiency lie in the mechanical constructions at present necessary in gas engines; others, in the inevitable waste due to the operation of physical laws and forces; others, again, in improper mixtures and defective ignition apparatus. Other things equal, however, the kind of fuel used is the most important consideration in securing a high power per pound of fuel. This is particularly emphasized in the fact that the various substances suitable for use as fuels in gas engine cylinders differ greatly in calorific values.

As given by reliable authorities, the calorific values of several common hydrocarbon fuels, as expressed in British thermal units, are as follows:

	Per Pound.	Per Cubic Foot.
Marsh gas (CH_4)	23,594	1,051
Benzine (C_6H_6)	18,448	——
Gasoline	21,900	690
Acetylene (C_2H_2)	21,492	868
Ethylene (C_2H_4)	21,430	1,677
Natural gas	——	900 to 1,000
Illuminating coal gas	——	600 to 800
Water gas (average)	——	710

Determining Calorific Values.—Knowing the specific heat of a given gas at constant volume, the calorific value in thermal units may be discovered as follows, in order to estimate the thermal efficiency of an engine:

$$H = C\,(T'' - T').$$

In this formula H is the calorific value in thermal units; C, the specific heat at constant volume; T'', the temperature of explosion, and T', the initial temperature. The specific heat for a 9 to 1 mixture of air and coal gas being 0.1846; a typical explosion temperature 2,764 degrees, absolute, and an average compression temperature, 921 degrees, we have 340.21 thermal units per pound of the initial charge.

Determining the Explosion Pressure.—The maximum or explosion pressure of a gas engine is equal to the ratio between the compression and maximum temperatures multiplied by the compression pressure. Thus:

$$\frac{Ct}{Et} \times Cp = Ep.$$

Substituting the values given above for a given engine, we have:

$$\left(\frac{2764}{921} = 3\right) \times 68.86 = 206.58 \text{ pounds,}$$

which, as may be seen, is the same as was given in a former chapter:

$$P'' = \frac{T'' \ P'}{T'.}$$

Horse=Power in Terms of Heat Units.—In order to estimate the mechanical efficiency of a given engine we must, as shown above, know the *delivered horse-power.* While there are numerous ways of calculating this, the simplest and readiest formula for a one-cylinder engine is as follows:

$$\frac{D^2 \ L \ R}{18,000} = D. \ H. \ P.$$

This means that the square of the *piston diameter, D,* in inches is to be multiplied by the *length* of the stroke, *L,* in inches and the number of *revolutions* per minute, *R,* of the fly-wheel, and the product divided by 18,000.

The denominator 18,000 is given by Roberts as the proper figure for a four-cycle gasoline engine. For four-cycle engines using coal gas, the denominator would be 19,000. For two-cycle engines using gasoline, the denominator would be 13,500; for other types, 14,000.

The Delivered Horse=Power.—To apply this formula we will take a highly efficient three-cylinder gasoline vehicle motor with proportions as follows: The piston diameter is 4.5 inches; the stroke is 4.5 inches; the number of revolutions per minute is 900. Then, substituting, we have:

$$\frac{20.25 \times 4.5 \times 900}{18,000} = \frac{82,012.5}{18,000} = 4.56 \text{ H. P.}$$

In calculating for more than one cylinder, we have the formula:

$$\frac{D^2 \text{ L R N}}{18,000} = \text{H. P.}$$

in which N is the number of cylinders. Hence, for three cylinders:

$$\frac{82,012.5 \times 3}{18,000} = 13.67 \text{ H. P.}$$

According to the claims of the manufacturer, the engine in question yields no less than 12 D. H. P. by actual brake tests.

The Time Element in Power Estimates.—In the determination of horse-power the *time* element is an important item, because the power to be calculated produces motion, and is not a static pressure to be measured only in terms of pounds weight. It is important also to remember that the power efficiency increases with the rate of motion, being expressed in terms of revolutions per minute of the fly-wheel or crank shaft. Thus, a given engine running with low gas supply or high load may rotate the fly-wheel only 200 times per minute, while, with full gas supply, or at average load, it can produce as many as 2,000 revolutions per minute. Furthermore, the available power decreases as does the number of revolutions per minute, while, as has already been indicated, the rate of gas consumption per unit of work is increased. Thus it is important to know, in making estimates for horse-power whether the engine in question is running free or under load.

Engine Dimensions in Power Estimate.—Next to this, the most important consideration refers to the dimensions of the piston and cylinder and the length of the stroke. For, since these figures indicate the power capacity of the engine, in point of the quantity of fuel consumed, and the power developed by explosion, as acting on the reciprocating parts, they, together with the ascertained rate of motion, are in ratio to a figure equivalent to an average ratio between the operative dimensions of the cylinder—these are given above in Roberts' formula for D. H. P. —and the delivered horse-power. The formula is further verified in the fact that the piston diameter and length of stroke are in discoverable proportion to the D. H. P. and the number of revolutions of the fly-wheel. So that an engine giving, say, 35 D. H. P. at 600 revolutions per minute, with a fuel whose thermic value is known, must have a certain diameter of piston and length of stroke. These facts will be evident from examination of specimen formulæ.

The Indicated Horse=Power.—In making more definite calculations on the power of a gas-engine there are four points to be considered:

1. How great is the mean effective pressure per square inch on the piston during the power stroke?
2. What is the area of the piston?
3. What is the length of the stroke?
4. What is the number of explosions per minute?

The ratio between the product of these factors and 33,000 gives the I. H. P. per minute. Thus:

$$\frac{\text{Pressure} \times \text{area} \times \text{stroke} \times \text{E. P. M.}}{33{,}000} = \text{I. H. P.}$$

To reduce this ratio to a practical formula we take the product of the mean effective pressure of the power stroke; by the area of the piston *in square inches;* by the length of the stroke in feet; by the number of explosions per minute, and divide by 33,000, which figure expresses the number of foot-pounds per minute per horse-power. Thus:

$$\frac{\text{P A S E}}{33{,}000} = \text{I. H. P.}$$

The Mean Effective Pressure.—As may be understood from the term itself, the mean effective pressure is an average for the pressure in pounds per square inch brought to bear upon the piston of a cylinder during the power stroke. It has been well defined as "the difference between the average gauge pressure shown by the expansion line and that shown by the compression line, minus the back pressure of charging or suction." As all these operations are depicted on the indicator diagram an average of its proportions will yield the desired result.

The Brake Horse=Power.—The most satisfactory method of testing the effective power of an engine is by the use of Prony's brake, one form of which is shown herewith. Briefly, it consists

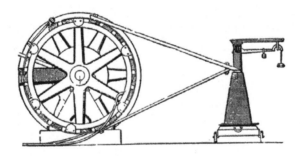

FIG. 150.—Common Form of Prony Brake, for testing the D. H. P. of an engine. An iron band shod with wooden blocks is drawn tightly around the circumference of the fly-wheel. To this two arms are attached, the other ends ot which bear upon the scale platform, as shown. It is necessary that the scale platform be raised to the same height as the centre of the fly-wheel shaft.

of a band of rope or strip iron—the latter is the arrangement shown—to which are fastened a number of wooden blocks, several carrying shoulders to prevent the contrivance from slipping off the wheel rim. Being applied to the circumference of the fly-wheel the brake band is drawn tight, as shown, so that the blocks press against the surface all around. The brake, thus formed, is **prevented from revolving with the fly-wheel, by two arms**, attached near the top and bottom centres of the wheel, and joined at the opposite ends to form a lever, which bears upon an ordinary platform scale, a suitable leg or block being arranged to keep its end opposite to the centre of the shaft. By this arrangement the amount of friction between the brake band and the revolving wheel is weighed upon the scales. For, since the brake fits tightly enough to be carried around by the wheel, but for the arms bearing upon the scale, the amount of frictional power exerted by the wheel in turning free within the blocks may be transmitted and measured, just as would be the case were a machinery load attached, instead of a friction brake.

Formula for Brake Horse Power.—The net work of the engine or horse power delivered at the shaft is determined as follows:

Let W = work of shaft, equals power absorbed per minute.

P = unbalanced pressure or weight in pounds, acting on the lever arm at a distance L.

L = length of lever arm in feet from centre of shaft.

V = velocity of a point in feet per minute at distance L, if arm were allowed to rotate at the speed of the shaft.

N = number of revolutions per minute.

B. H. P. = brake horse power.

Then will $W = PV = 2 \quad LNP$.

Since B. H. B. $= \dfrac{PV}{33000}$,

we have by substituting for V.

B. H. P. $= \dfrac{2 \quad LNP}{33000}$.

CHAPTER TWENTY-FOUR.

CARBURETTERS AND CARBURETTING.

The Carburetter and its Use.—Any device wherein gasoline vapor and air are mixed in proper proportions to form the fuel charge for an internal combustion engine is called a carburetter or vaporizer.

Some writers make a distinction between the two words, applying the word "carburetter," when in addition to a mixing chamber, the device contains a receiving chamber for the gaso-

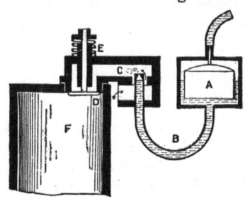

Fig. 151.—The first carburetter having a float feed for maintaining the fuel supply at constant level; introduced by Maybach. A is the hollow float carrying the spindle of the needle valve at its top; B, the tube leading into the inlet valve space; C, the spraying nozzle; D, the inlet valve; E, the inlet valve spring; F, the cylinder space.

line and means of maintaining therein a constant level of the fuel; the word "vaporizer" being applied when the device has no receiving chamber; as, a generator valve.

Gasoline is a liquid which has a very low boiling point and which constantly evaporates even at ordinary temperatures, saturating the air with its vapor. On account of this property of gasoline the carburetter accomplishes the mixing by rapidly bringing a comparatively large volume of air into intimate contact with a quantity of gasoline in the form of, 1, a spray or, 2, by surface contact.

The carburetter should so regulate the supply of air and gasoline that the resulting mixture will always contain the two ingredients in the proper proportions. There must not be too much gasoline vapor, as fuel would be wasted either by being decomposed into soot or unburned on account of there not being enough air to consume it. On the other hand too much air, even though the mixture should ignite, would lower the temperature of combustion and thus diminish the useful expansion. Inability to start the engine, to speed up, or to run as slowly as one would like may all be due to either too little or too much gasoline. Hence the importance of maintaining the supply of gasoline and air in correct proportions.

Varieties of Carburetter.—Classified according to structure and operation, there are three varieties of carburetting apparatus:

1. The *sprayer carburetter,* in which the liquid hydrocarbon is sprayed or atomized through a minute nozzle and mixed with a passing column of air.

2. *The surface carburetter,* operating to produce a fuel mixture when air is passed over the surface of a body of liquid hydrocarbon, or circulated around a gauze, wicking or metal surface saturated with such a liquid.

3. *The ebullition or filtering carburetter,* in which air is forced, under suction, through a body of liquid, from bottom to top, so as to absorb particles of its substance.

Of these types, the *first* and *second* only have been widely used with automobile engines. The sprayer is now the prevailing form.

In the present stage of the carburetter art the non-automatic type of carburetter may be ignored and the automatic carburetter broadly classified into the sprayer and *surface* or *"puddle"* types.

NOTE.—The fuel charge for a gas engine consists of about ten to sixteen parts air to one of gasoline vapor. The proportion varies according to the conditions of the atmosphere, quality of gasoline and engine speed.

Carburetter Principles.—Owing to certain characteristic differences in behavior it will be best to treat the sprayer and surface types separately. First consider the simplest form, or what

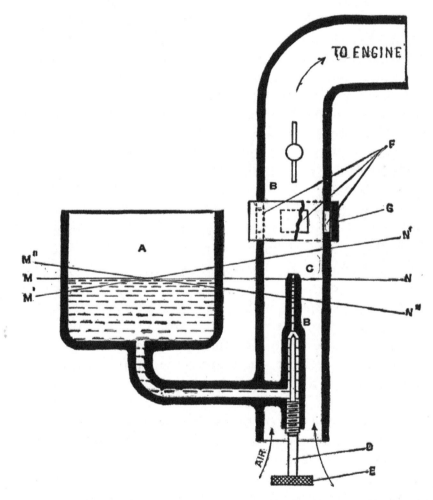

FIG. 152.—A rudimentary, or simple form of spray carburetter illustrating the principles of operation employed in the modern device. A, is the receiving chamber; B, the mixing chamber. A connecting passage conveys fuel to the spray nozzle C, controlled by the needle valve D, by turning the thumb wheel E. Air enters through the primary passage in the base and through the auxiliary ports F, the latter being adjustable by the sleeve G, and the mixture to the engine, controlled by a throttle located above the sleeve.

may be called a rudimentary carburetter having a sprayer and means of regulating the mixture by hand as shown in Fig. 152.

The drawing illustrates a receiving chamber A and a mixing chamber B, the two being connected by a small passageway or duct which terminates at the sprayer C, made adjustable by the needle valve D. The lower end of the mixing chamber B is open to the atmosphere, while the upper end is provided with auxiliary air ports F, having a collar or sleeve G with which to adjust the opening of the ports to the atmosphere.

In explaining the action of this rudimentary carburetter, it is necessary to assume the receiving chamber A to be filled with gasoline to a level MN, very near the elevation of the spray nozzle, and also to assume the supply replenished as it is used so that the fluid level MN is maintained.

Now, suppose the upper end of the mixing chamber to be connected with an engine as indicated. Each intake stroke of the engine will displace a volume of air, causing a partial vacuum in the mixing chamber B; the intensity of the vacuum, as will be seen, depending on the engine speed. Assuming the engine to be working at slow speed with a heavy load and the auxiliary ports F closed by the sleeve G, the gasoline supply may be adjusted by the needle valve E so that the engine will receive from the carburetter a mixture containing the proper proportion of gasoline vapor and air.

If now part of the load on the engine be removed so that it will run say twice as fast, the same amount of air and gasoline for each charge must be received by the engine in one-half the time. Under these conditions the mixture would become too rich, that is, too much gasoline would be fed for the amount of air passing through the inlet at the lower end of the mixing chamber. The excess of gasoline is due to the fact that in order to get twice the amount of air through the inlet the suction has to be more than doubled to compensate for the increased frictional resistance set up by the higher velocity of the air passing through the inlet. The suction, or degree of vacuum in the carburetter, being more than doubled, it naturally follows that more than double the amount of gasoline will pass through the spray nozzle. This excess of vacuum is caused by the expansion of the air in entering the carburetter, increasing its velocity *after expansion* more than two-fold.

In order to maintain the mixture in the same proportions for varying demands, it is necessary to provide some means to keep the suction or degree of vacuum in the mixing chamber constant. The suction may be restored to its normal condition by slightly

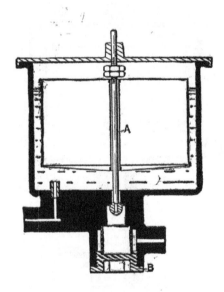

FIG. 153.—A simple form of float feed, with float concentric to inlet valve.

raising the sleeve G so as to partially open the auxiliary air ports F. This allows some air to enter through the auxiliary ports, thus reducing the velocity of the entering air and relieving somewhat the suction at the lower inlet. The amount of opening of the auxiliary air ports necessary for any change of engine speed may be found by experiment.

By placing a throttle valve in the passage B between the auxiliary ports and the engine the load may be altered without any variation in the engine speed by adjusting the throttle opening.

In actual construction, automatic devices are employed to maintain the gasoline in the float chamber* at constant level and to adjust the auxiliary port openings to different engine speeds.

It has been shown that the feeds of gasoline and air do not vary in the same proportion when the suction varies. A second reason for this irregularity is the fact that an initial suction is required to lift the gasoline to the mouth of the nozzle, before spraying can begin. The slightest suction only is required to draw air through the air inlet; there is, however, a cer-

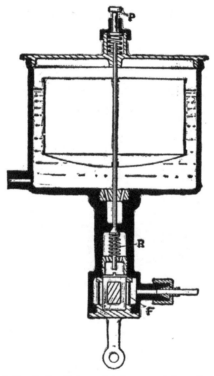

FIG. 154.—A form of float feed in which provision is made for adjusting the fuel level by means of a spring nut R.

tain minimum suction below which no gasoline can be fed, depending on the difference in the level of the supply and the level of the spray nozzle. Hence, the importance of eliminating this difference in level is readily seen. The first requirement of a carburetter may be said to be the maintenance of the gasoline supply in the float chamber at practically the same elevation as that of the spray nozzle.

---

*In discussing the modern carburetter, the term *float chamber* is used instead of receiving chamber as it is generally known by that name, since a float is almost always used to regulate the flow of gasoline into the chamber.

Float Feed.—Of the different devices used to maintain the gasoline supply at constant level in the float chamber, what is known as a *float feed* has been adopted by almost all makers, with the result that at the present day its use is world wide.

Where departures from the system have been made, they usually consist of some form of overflow arrangement whereby the gasoline is maintained at the necessary level by a surplus volume being pumped or otherwise forced into a chamber whence the overflow **returns to the main supply, the height and capacity for the return**

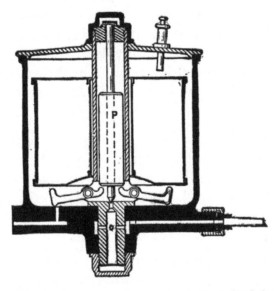

Fig. 155.—This illustrates a construction of float feed in which the fuel level is made adjustable by the use of a variable counterweight P.

of the overflow maintaining the necessary level with reference to the spray nozzle.

A float feed device consists of a cork or hollow metal float placed in the float chamber. It is connected so as to operate the gasoline inlet valve, usually by means of levers. These are arranged in such a manner that, as gasoline enters the float chamber through the inlet valve, the float rises, and in so doing, closes the valve thus shutting off the supply when the gasoline reaches the desired level.

In different makes of carburetters this level varies from about ⅛ to ¼ inch below the top of the spray nozzle; to be accurate, the level should be such that the liquid will form a bubble at the nozzle to be blown off at will, and the exact height should be found by this method when the construction will permit.

There are many forms of float feed. Fig. 153 shows a simple arrangement. The float is constructed concentric with the inlet valve A. In the bottom of the float chamber is a small tube through which the gasoline must flow to the spray nozzle. The object of this tube is to prevent small particles of dirt and bubbles of water that may be in the gasoline from entering the spray nozzle. The plug B at the bottom of the float chamber, where the fuel flows to the spray nozzle, is provided with a fine wire screen to catch any foreign matter that may be in the gasoline in order that it may not lodge in the spray nozzle and impede the flow of the liquid.

Fig. 154 represents a more refined design. The fuel level may be adjusted by means of the spring nut R. At F is located a strainer which can be easily taken out. Fig. 155 shows a construction which is very much employed owing to the great facility with which the fuel level can be adjusted. To this end the counterweight P is either increased or diminished.

In order to obtain uniform results, especially where a car is operated on hilly roads, the float chamber with its float should be constructed concentric with the spray nozzle so that any inclination of the car, in ascending or descending a hill will not disturb the gasoline level with reference to the nozzle. This principle is utilized in the construction of many carburetters as shown in Fig. 156.

The importance of this becomes plain by again referring to Fig. 152. Here, the line MN represents the normal height of the gasoline when the carburetter is level.

Now, suppose the carburetter to be inclined so that the line M'N' or M"N" becomes horizontal. These lines then represent, respectively, the level of the gasoline, with reference to the spray nozzle, for the two inclined positions of the carburetter. Hence, it is evident that the gasoline level would be either too high or too low with respect to nozzle while remaining undisturbed at the float center.

The Float.—This is one of the important parts in the make-up of a carburetter and any imperfection will produce a marked ef-

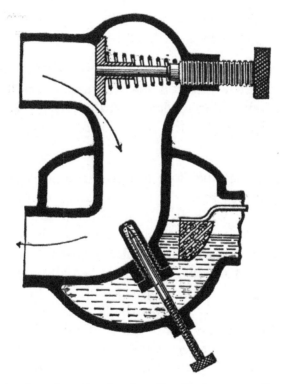

Fig. 156.—Type of carburetter having the float arranged concentric with the spray nozzle. This construction eliminates the disturbance of the fuel level with respect to the nozzle which otherwise would be caused by any inclination of the car.

fect on the quality of the mixture. The material of which the float is made consists usually of cork or metal. Owing to the nature of its work it is a part which sometimes causes trouble; cork floats are liable to become saturated with gasoline thus losing their buoyancy, while those made of metal are liable to leak. Of whatever material it is made, the float should remain constant in weight and buoyancy. When made of metal, the float should be preferably without working joints, and particularly without frictional contacts with levers, which may sooner or later wear through its thin metal and cause a leak.

The float point is usually made adjustable as before shown, so that the level of the liquid may be maintained at the most advantageous point with respect to its proper discharge from the spray nozzle. To secure a constant level the float point must be adjusted for different grades of gasoline, as the level of the float depends upon the specific gravity of the liquid.

Some authorities consider it bad practice to balance floats by weights, in addition to the column of liquid in the float chamber, for, owing to their different densities, the liquid and the weights may interfere in their duties and destroy the perfect balance sought for.

It is advisable that the float chamber should open at the bottom. This facilitates removal of any water, ice or dirt, and removal of float itself, without opening the top and permitting dirt to fall in from above. The float and removable bottom can be replaced with a stream of gasoline flowing upon them, which will wash away particles of dirt, if any accidentally get on the parts while being replaced. With top opening, ice in the bottom of the chamber may not only support the float and prevent its falling to admit gasoline, but may also bind the float so firmly that it cannot be removed to permit removal of ice, which may prove an unpleasant predicament if away from means of warming the carburetter.

Gasoline should enter the float chamber from a single direction, either up or down, so that no pockets exist in which water or dirt may gather.

The inlet needle valve may be kept tight and in perfect working order by occasional grinding and to facilitate this, the construction of the carburetter should be such that the valve is easily accessible. Further, the motion of the car should tend to move the valve to some degree, even though slight, which movement serves to force away any particles of dirt that may lodge on the point during the passage of the liquid. On this account it is best if the float and valve be fixed one to the other so that the point partakes of the motion of the float and liquid in the chamber.

The float chamber is provided with an air vent to prevent the accumulation of any excess pressure which would interfere with the proper flow of the gasoline.

There is on top of the float chamber a pin or "tickler," as it is called. This is a device for depressing the float to obtain an excess of gasoline when such is required for starting the engine. Some motorists regard it as a necessary preliminary to starting, to "tickle the carburetter," but carburetters differ; with some it is necessary that the level in the float feed chamber be high, in others not so high. Some carburetters flood easily, while others never flood. It is as difficult to start on an over rich mixture as it is with a thin one. Any small tickling of the carburetter serves to start the nozzle and create a small amount of mixture. But this process soon floods the carburetter, and as the quantity of air supplied is small and cannot be increased to any great extent before the motor starts, flooding is apt to fill the inlet manifold with almost pure gasoline vapor and the motor will not start.

Many motors will start without touching the carburetter, and in the case of others the process of starting is rendered far easier by the moderate application of attention of this sort.

In priming a carburetter, the tickler should be depressed and held down for a few seconds. This will cause as much, if not more, gasoline to enter in a given space of time, than if the tickler be worked like a pump. The latter operation as frequently performed is liable to injure the float.

Usually the tickler is arranged to pass down to the float through the air vent tube.

Since gasoline has considerable weight, and consequent inertia, the passage to the nozzle should be both short and large, for large passages do not clog easily and, if short, the liquid will respond more promptly to the suction. If the passage be large, the friction is less, on account of reduced velocity of flow.

On the other hand, should this passage be long, the effect of inertia is more marked causing the liquid to respond less quickly to the suction, the strength of which changes rapidly during each intake stroke.

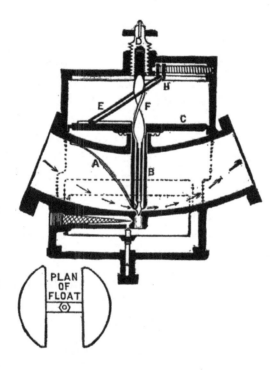

FIG. 157.—The Duryea Carburetter. The gate A is placed in the air passage hinged to the hollow rod B of the piston C. The suction of the engine lifts C and A, opening the air passage as needed. Above C is a radius link E, through which the spiral portion of the gasoline valve spindle F passes. As C raises, this link E turns F, which being threaded in D adjusts the gasoline to the air then passing. This action of E may be adjusted by changing the position of the pivoted end of E carried by the holder H, so that the working point of E makes either a long arc with much needle movement, or a short arc with little needle movement as C rises. The original adjustment for starting is secured by turning D till perfect mixture, slowest speeds and easiest starts are obtained.

On account also of this inertia effect, the liquid does not get started until a considerable volume of air has passed the nozzle, making the early part of the charge too lean. Now, as the suction decreases, the interia of the liquid causes it to continue to flow, making the latter portion of the charge too rich and probably leaving between charges unsprayed drops of liquid which either fall upon the walls of the carburetter, or are drawn into the engine.

Disc Feed.—In the disc feed the air is drawn through a passageway containing a minute fuel opening. This opening is closed by a needle valve which has a disc of very thin sheet metal

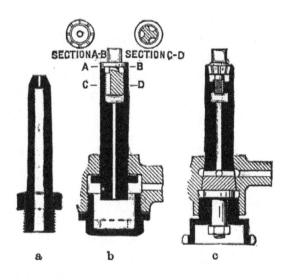

FIG. 158.—Some different forms of spray nozzles: (a), a simple form with single opening; (b), a nozzle consisting of a series of slots; (c), multi-slot nozzle easily removable without the use of tools.

attached to the stem. When no air is passing through the carburetter, the needle valve closes the gasoline nozzle.

As soon as air is drawn through, the current striking against the disc, lifts it from its seat. Gravity and suction then both bring gasoline out of the nozzle to mix with the air. The lift of the valve and its disc are controlled by an adjustable screw which regulates the extent of the movement.

Diaphragm Feed.—This mode of regulating the gasoline supply, depends on the action of reduced air pressure on a dia phragm supported at its circumference, and free to move at the center. The needle valve for controlling the supply of gasoline is held on its seat when no air is passing. As soon as air is drawn through the carburetter, the pressure is reduced on one side of the diaphragm; this causes its center to move. The needle valve being attached to its center, is lifted from its seat, which allows gasoline to flow either by gravity or suction, or both. Sometimes a piston is used instead of a diaphragm, as in the Duryea Carburetter illustrated in fig. 157.

The Spray Nozzle.—In the carburetter, the fuel is discharged into the mixing chamber through a fine orifice called the spray nozzle. This, as its name implies, is intended to deliver the liquid in the form of a fine spray, which is subsequently: 1, vaporized more or less; 2, mixed with the entering air, and 3, carried by the suction into the engine cylinder.

The simplest form of spray nozzle is one having a single opening, as shown in fig. 158-a.

The spraying effect in this simple form is less marked than that obtained with nozzles having a number of slots as illustrated in fig. 158-b. However, with the single nozzle, there is less danger of it becoming clogged. The operation of a multi-slot nozzle is undoubtedly better than one with a single opening, but it is necessary for the construction to be such that it may be readily withdrawn in order to clean the small spray slots.

Fig. 158-c illustrates a construction of this kind which permits the removal of the nozzle without the use of tools, it only being necessary to unscrew the milled nut, and the whole nozzle comes out with it. The amount of liquid passing through the nozzle may be varied by an adjustable needle or metal rod having a conical point. The spraying qualities of the nozzle with a single opening fig. 158-a, are improved, when fitted with a conical pointed needle working from above.

Multiple Nozzles.—Some carburetters are provided with more than one nozzle, two, three or more being employed. Multiple nozzles are well adapted for high powered machines. Carburetters with multiple nozzles are sometimes so constructed that the several nozzles forming the unit, come into action progressively as the power demand increases, producing the same effect as though several separate carburetters were used, each being brought into action successively.

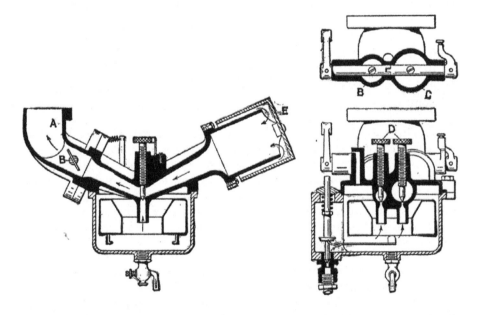

Fig. 159.—The Winton Multiple Nozzle Carburetter. It has two nozzles and is a modification of the surface venturi tube type, consisting of a large and a small tube placed side by side above the float chamber. These tubes are bent downward at their middle so that small puddles of gasoline are formed at their smallest diameters when the engine is idle. When it is running the fuel supply may be regulated by needle valves D. Connection to the engine is made at A. Butterfly valves B and C serve as throttles. When starting C is closed, and all the mixture is drawn through the small opening in B. E serves to muffle the noise of suction and to prevent foreign substances from being drawn into the carburetter.

The needle valve which regulates the supply of fuel at the nozzle should have suitable connections so that it may be adjusted by the operator and enable him, while operating the car, to vary the proportion of the mixture, and thus secure the greatest power by trial, as well as to accommodate the device to the temperature and humidity of different days, and also to the gravity of different grades of fuel. No adjustment, while the car is standing, can compare with adjustments in actual road service in point of accuracy.

Further, the carburetter should be adjustable at low speeds, to secure certain ignition and steady running. Gas engines are apt to misfire at their limits, and the perfect carburetter for automobiles will provide superior conditions at these limits in order to secure the most satisfactory range of service. This necessitates provision also for adjustment at normal or high speeds.

Gasoline, as it is sucked out of the nozzle, made up as it is, of hydrocarbons of differing values, from the point of view of weight and volatility, will hold to the globular form with more or less tenacity, depending upon conditions.

It should be noted that doubling the diameter of these globules increases their surface four times, but their bulk will be increased eight times. Evaporation is proportional to the surface, but if double the quantity reside under a given surface, double the time must be taken to gasify the liquid, subject to a correction in that the spheroids are reducing in diameter as the vapor expands. Hence, the importance of constructing the nozzle so that it shall discharge gasoline in as finely a divided state as possible.

In any one carburetter the perfection of vaporization is proportioned to the fineness with which the liquid is broken up at the nozzle. The shortness of the time within which vaporization must be completed is what causes the above factor of fineness of division to enter. Since the heat transfer between the air and the liquid, or the passage walls and the liquid, is effected chiefly through the agencies of convection and conduction—the former implying a rapid agitation and relative motion between the particles of the two substances, and the latter the exposure by the liquid of the greatest possible surface areas—it is readily seen that the finer the fuel division at the nozzle the more rapid and complete will be the vaporization and the greater the homogeneity of the final mixture.

Those who have constructed transparent mixing chambers for the observance of nozzle action have ascertained that the fuel left the nozzles as a solid stream or in heavy globules and irregular "chunks," not as a fine spray or mist, as it is supposed to do.

A good design of nozzle and needle will do much to correct this faulty action with an increase in power output and fuel economy. However, any nozzle form used will give a wet and uneven discharge with low engine demands, even though a true spray may be delivered with increased demands.

Whatever form be given to the nozzle, the effectiveness with which it can break up the fuel varies as the difference between the pressures at its two ends, and as this pressure difference varies throughout the speed range of the engine, the fineness will also vary. Since the nozzle has a very small opening, even for the largest automobile motors, it is easily stopped up, and the construction should be such as to enable one to remove the nozzle for purposes of cleaning, without too much trouble.

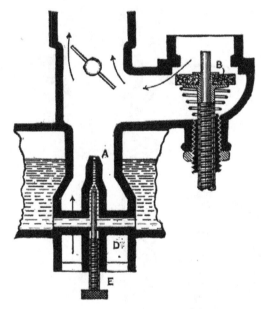

FIG. 160.—The Mixing Chamber with its appendages. Illustrating, in general, the arrangement of parts, the primary and auxiliary air passages; auxiliary valve, spring and adjustment; the spray nozzle with needle valve and the throttle valve. The arrows indicate the direction of the entering air currents and course of mixture.

The Mixing Chamber.—This consists of a small enclosure or passageway containing the spray nozzle. The mixing chamber, as its name implies, is the place where gasoline and air are brought together in proper proportions and commingled to form the fuel charge for the engine. It is provided with a main air inlet and auxiliary air ports as before described but the latter arranged to operate automatically.

The outlet to the engine is fitted with a throttle valve, permitting the quantity of the mixture to be varied as desired.

The construction of the mixing chamber with its appendages follows substantially the arrangement shown in fig. 160. This illustrates a mixing chamber with the spray nozzle A located in the center. The adjustable needle valve E regulates the flow of gasoline to the nozzle. The mixing chamber is open to the atmosphere at its lower end D, through which the primary or main

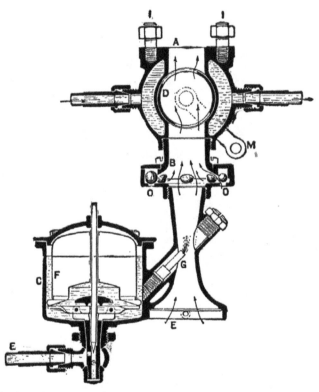

FIG. 161.—The G and A (Grouvelle and Arquembourg) Carburetter. French make of the venturi tube type. In operation, air enters the primary inlet E, mixing with the gasoline at G which is fed from the float chamber C—the fuel level being maintained by the float F. The auxiliary air supply enters at B through the openings O, arranged concentric with the mixing chamber and consisting of a ball cage which is pierced with holes of different sizes, these being stopped by balls of different diameters and weights. As the speed of the engine increases and a greater amount of air is required, the lightest ball lifts, allowing a certain amount of air to slip by it. As the speed is further increased, other balls lift and progressively increase the area of the air space. The outlet A is controlled by a throttle D operated by the lever M. A heating jacket is provided, encircling the throttle as illustrated in the figure.

air supply enters. An auxiliary air supply is admitted through the opening to the right, being controlled by the valve B which is automatic in its action. The lift of this valve may be varied to meet different requirements, by the adjustable threaded spindle.

Under operating conditions the pressure in the mixing chamber is lower than that of the atmosphere. Lowered pressure without a correspondingly lowered temperature tends to cause vaporization which begins as soon as the fuel has left the nozzle. It is impossible to measure or estimate the extent of the vaporization, at the nozzle or through the manifold, due to this pressure reduction, but it is known to be very appreciable in its effect. It should be considered as a condition affecting vaporization, at the nozzle end but slightly, but to a much greater extent after the fuel has become suspended in the air.

The nozzle of average performance will, at medium demands, deliver a thin conical sheet of liquid. This liquid cone is torn away at its edge and carried on by the air column. Some of the fuel torn away is in small enough particles to be considered as spray or mist, and may be taken as contributing directly to the vapor content of the mixture; but the greater part sooner or later strikes some part of the containing walls, and later it is picked up in the form of globules. These globules are continually picked up and thrown out by the air stream in its progress to the cylinders, until some of them are sufficiently small to become permanently entrained or have been completely vaporized.

Bends in the manifold passages aggravate the expulsion of the liquid globules, but they also permit of fuel once thrown out being readily picked up again.

The heavier globules after being thrown out at the turns are again picked up by a following portion of the air column. This action is repeated at each of the turns.

The Mixture.—At first it was thought that the best carburetter was one that gave a constant mixture under all conditions, it being at that time presumed that the Krebs carburetter as shown in fig. 169, gave this result. However, from experience and numerous experiments it has since been conceded that a constant mixture is not advisable from either the standpoint of fuel economy or best operation. Inasmuch as ignition conditions vary with the speed of the engine and the compression values vary similarly with the throttle opening, it follows that the mixture necessary for maximum power at any given speed differs in accordance with the immediate conditions of combustion.

At low speeds the mixture should be richer than at high. This is due to the fact that at low speeds more heat is lost to the cylinder walls, more compression is lost by leakage, and the combustion can therefore be slower, thus sustaining the pressure. At high speeds the compression is higher, due to less leakage and less loss of heat. Therefore, unless the mixture be leaner at high speed there might be danger of pre-ignition.*

A lean and highly compressed charge also burns faster and hence gives better pressures and fuel economy than a richer one.

The quantity of mixture that an engine will take varies greatly with the speed. At slow speeds the volume at approximately carburetter pressure is equal to the cubic content of the cylinders multiplied by the number of power strokes. At high speeds of one thousand revolutions and over the quantity may drop to less than one-half the theoretical amount, depending on the design of the valves, inlet piping and carburetter passages. This peculiarity reacts upon the compression, and hence on the mixture desired for best results. It will thus be seen that the design of the engine has a bearing on the carburetter design, which explains the well known but seemingly mysterious fact that a carburetter giving good results on one engine sometimes fails to maintain its reputation when applied to one of different design.

The design and class of ignition used have also a marked influence. Poorer mixtures can be used, as the spark is hotter, the throttle can be more nearly closed, resulting in increased engine capacity and fuel economy.

---

*The prefix "pre" before ignition means that the fuel charge is ignited before the time of the spark and has no connection with the stroke or crank position as distinguished from its usage when speaking of steam motors: for example, *pre-admission* means that steam is admitted to the cylinder before the beginning of the stroke.

To get the maximum power out of a given sized engine the fuel should be introduced into the cylinders as cold as possible consistent with complete evaporation, intimacy of mixture and completeness of combustion.

The ever varying density and compositions of the fuels used and obtainable introduce many complications into the problem. These differences demand different sizes of nozzles, different float levels, different amounts of heat to be supplied, and different proportions of air for combustion.

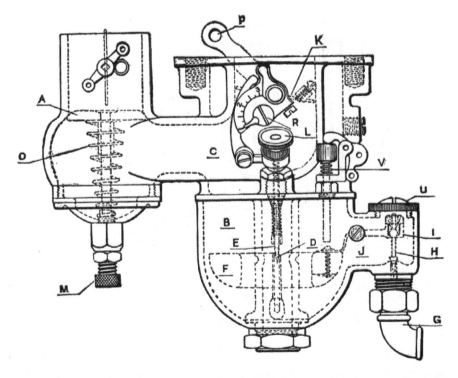

FIG. 162.—The Schebler Carburetter. A compensating air valve A, adjustable by the screw M and spring O, controls the air supply to the mixing chamber C. Above this valve is a shutter which may be partially closed when cranking to increase the suction in order to obtain a rich mixture. The spray nozzle is located at D and the supply regulated by the needle valve E by means of thumb wheel L. The needle valve has two adjustments, one for high speed and one for low. At R is the eccentric high speed adjustment. Throttle valve K is of the butterfly type and is operated by the lever P. Heating is secured by a jacket surrounding the throttle. Gasoline enters the float chamber B through the elbow connection G. The fuel level is maintained by the concentric float F which regulates the supply by the inlet valve H and lever connection J. The float point is adjustable by the needle valve adjusting screw I, accessible by removing cap U. The carburetter is primed by the tickler or flushing pin V.

Owing to the absence of a ready means of ascertaining the quality of the mixture being delivered by a carburetter, the majority of motors in use are operating under more or less disadvantageous conditions, even if carefully and properly regulated at the outset.

Heating for Carburetters.—Vaporization due to pressure reduction is distinguished from vaporization caused by the supplying of heat. In the former action, vaporization can become only partially complete, however far the process of reduction is

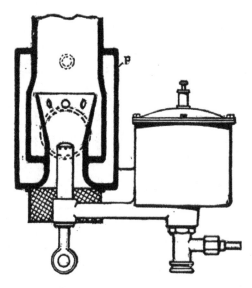

Fig. 163.—A Jacketed Carburetter. The mixing chamber is shown surrounded by a jacket P, for heating the mixture. This is accomplished either by connection with the cooling water, or exhaust from engine. During the summer season, when the atmospheric temperature is high, the heating arrangement may be dispensed with.

carried, since the part of the liquid which vaporizes does so through the abstraction of heat from the remainder, which becomes constantly colder. Vaporization due to pressure reduction by engine suction will continue until the temperature of the liquid becomes so low that vaporization ceases until heat is supplied from some outside source.

Where vaporization is brought about entirely by heat from some outside source the degree to which it may be carried depends wholly upon the amount of heat supplied, since the temperature of the liquid is being constantly raised to or maintained at the proper point.

When a carburetter is rather small, for the engine which it has to supply, it becomes very cold while in operation, as the amount of heat necessary to effect the evaporation of the gasoline is more than is available from the entering air or than could be secured through the metal of the carburetter by conduction. The temperature of the metal becomes so low that water condenses on it, and, in extreme cases, is deported in the form of frost. This indicates a temperature within the carburetter too low for the successful use of inferior fuel, and so low as to possibly affect the intimacy of the resulting mixture even if high test gasoline be used. Moreover, if any water be present in the float chamber, it will be likely to freeze and disturb the flow of the gasoline.

These several undesirable results are produced by the use of a carburetter too small for the engine. To meet these conditions, some makers provide means for heating the air supply. This may be accomplished by arranging the outside end of the air inlet pipe so as to terminate closely to the exhaust manifold or some hot portion of the engine. Not enough attention has been paid to jacketing carburetters to replenish the heat taken up by the evaporation of the' fuel, and, judging from observation of carburetters now in use, it seems that very few engineers have taken the trouble to look into the probable economics that might be effected by proper jacketing. It appears, from the results of experiments that the fuel consumption decreases with an increase ot jacket temperature for a given output, but only up to a certain point. The most effective temperature seems to be about 110° Fahr.

Besides heating the air, carburetters are sometimes jacketed as shown in fig. 163, and the heat supplied to the jacket by two methods. One is by means of hot water, taken from the cooling system by the use of a shunt, and the other by the exhaust gases. Heating the carburetter by cooling water gives good results, but the starting of the motor is more difficult, especially in winter. Heating the carburetters by exhaust gases is open to some objection, as oil and carbon soot are deposited in the heating jacket.

Surface or "Puddle" Carburetters.—In this method of carburetting, a thin layer of air is passed over the surface of the liquid. The surface carburetter consists of a U-shaped mixing chamber, in the base of which a puddle of gasoline about ⅛ inch deep is maintained by float feed as shown in fig. 164. As this puddle is supplied by gravity, a weaker suction will produce a mixture, than where the gasoline must be both lifted and sprayed by suction. This type of carburetter is quite sensitive to changes, both in the float level and in the needle valve adjustment.

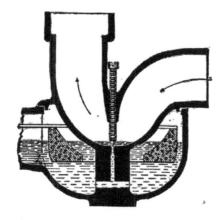

FIG. 164.—The surface or "puddle" type of carburetter. Air flows through the U shaped tube or mixing chamber as indicated by the arrows. The small puddle of gasoline in the bottom of the mixing chamber is mixed with the air by surface contact. The size or cross section of the mixing chamber is usually reduced at the region of the puddle so as to increase the velocity of the inflowing air. The gasoline level in the float chamber is maintained slightly higher than the fuel inlet to the mixing chamber feeding the puddle by gravity. Hence, no initial suction is required to cause a flow of gasoline into the mixing chamber.

An example of surface carburetter construction is shown in the Holley, fig. 165. This carburetter has no auxiliary air inlet and valve. A high air velocity is obtained in the mixing chamber by applying the principle of the venturi tube.

Referring to the figure, which shows the carburetter in two sections, it will be seen that the air enters at A and passes downward and up through a U-shaped tube, which is constricted at its lowest point. In the floor of the U is the gasoline orifice B, which is regulated by a needle valve E. The mixture passes through a butterfly throttle valve and on to the engine by the connection C. The float chamber surrounds the lowest part of the U, and has an annular cork float J, which controls the gasoline valve L, through a lever N pivoted at K. The U-shaped mixing chamber is merely the venturi tube in a special form, allowing a very high air velocity to be obtained at B.

When the engine is at rest there is a puddle of gasoline about ⅛ inch deep in the bottom of the mixing chamber. Consequently

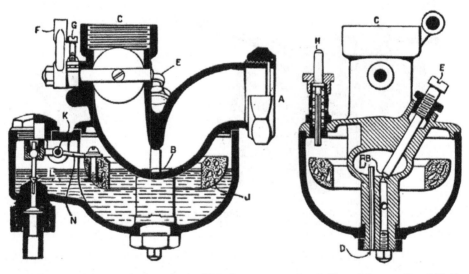

FIG. 165.—The Holley Carburetter. This is an example of the surface or "puddle" type. The fuel level is maintained slightly higher than the inlet orifice which causes a small "puddle" of gasoline to form in the bottom of the U shaped mixing chamber. The operation of this carburetter is described in detail in the text.

when the motor is starting or running very slowly the air does not have to lift the gasoline at all but simply draws over the puddle and is carburetted by surface evaporation. As the throttle is opened and the air velocity increases the puddle is gradually swept away by the strong air current passing over it; at the higher speeds the puddle is wiped out entirely, and a spray of the ordinary sort takes its place.

In starting the engine the float is depressed by the primer H and to prevent the mixing chamber from being flooded to excess a drain pipe D is provided.

The throttle valve is operated by the lever F, and the adjustable stop screw G permits regulation of the opening for minimum speed. The adjustment is through the needle valve E. A dashboard connection is sometimes provided to regulate the opening of this valve.

When there is a dashboard connection the upper end of the needle valve stem has a universal joint, from which a rod extends through the dashboard to a dial and regulating needle as shown in fig. 166.

FIG. 166.—A Surface Carburetter, arranged for dashboard control of fuel needle valve. A universal joint is fitted to the valve stem having an extension connecting with the graduated dial, shown at the right.

A spring ratchet holds the dial where set, and a hinge permits it to accommodate itself to the angle of the rod. This attachment enables the user to adjust the carburetter under running conditions, a matter of an instant, whereas otherwise he might experiment repeatedly. It also makes it possible to adjust for day to day variations in humidity, temperature, and grade of fuel, as well as to start on a rich mixture and cut down when the engine is warmed up. A special adjustment for hills and sand is also possible.

Venturi Carburetters.—When any fluid passes through a pipe of variable cross section or size, the quantity passing any given section in a given time is the same; such being the case, the velocity of the fluid in the various sections is inversely proportional to the areas of the sections. Hence it is evident, from the foregoing facts, that the pressure is greatest at the largest section and least at the smallest.

This is known as the "venturi principle" and has been utilized in the design of some makes of carburetters with good results. In applying this principle to carburetter design, the mixing chamber is shaped like two

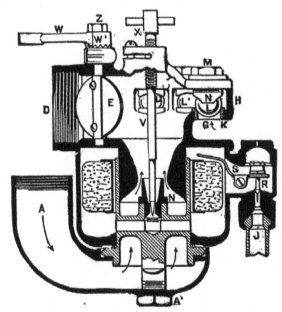

FIG. 167.—The Kingston Carburetter. An example of the venturi type of carburetter. Air enters at A and converges above the nozzle N in the restricted passage which produces the venturi tube effect. D is the exit to the motor controlled by the butterfly throttle E. Auxiliary air enters through five circular openings G, arranged in a semi-circle in the floor of an extension H of the mixing chamber. Each of these five openings consist of a bushing K threaded into the opening in the expansion H, and having its top beveled to receive a ⅝-inch bell metal bronze ball L, which is retained in position by a threaded bushing M, fitting in the top of the extension H. Gasoline enters from the tank through J, controlled by needle valve R, operated through lever S. Complete control of the nozzle N is through the needle valve V, which at the top of the carburetter has a T-piece X, by which it can be raised or lowered, thereby regulating the flow of gasoline. A serrated hub W' of the throttle, permits the handle W to be turned in any direction convenient for the motor by loosening locknut Z. Similarly, the intake pipe A, which is a separate casting, can be turned to any desired position by loosening the nut A'.

hollow truncated cones with their small ends brought together, or in other words like the familiar hour glass. By locating the spray nozzle at the point of least cross section, the conditions are favorable, for securing that marked economy of fuel which results from the use of high air velocities under low pressures. The greater the pressure drop at the nozzle, accompanied by a proportional increase in the air velocity, the better will be the fuel division and vaporization

The very rapid agitation and internal motion of the mixture column, due to the restricted section of the venturi tube, tends to produce a homogeneous fuel charge. A lowering of the pressure, lowers the temperature of the liquid through vaporization, hence, in venturi carburetters where any marked venturi effect is sought, jacketing is advisable.

The advantages of the venturi tube as applied to carburetters may be summed up as follows: Homogeneity of mixture; ease with which the mixing chamber may be jacketed, either by air or water; the mixing chamber may be placed in any plane, thus adapting it to varied motor designs.

Selecting a Carburetter.—Automobile owners often seek to improve the efficiency and increase the power of their motors by the fitting of new carburetters. On account of this, it is well to point out certain truths which may be of service. Before selecting a carburetter, the buyer should have as clear an understanding of its principles as possible. The ideal carburetter requirements are as follows:

1. It must intimately mix in proper proportions the mixture to suit varying engine speeds.

2. If of the spray type, the air velocity at the nozzle should be great enough at slowest engine speeds to overcome the initial lift necessary to bring the fuel to the nozzle level and draw it into the mixing chamber.

3. The nozzle should be accessible for cleaning and should be so shaped, together with the needle valve that it will deliver gasoline in a very finely divided form.

4. The float chamber should be concentric with the nozzle, so that the fuel level at that point will not be disturbed by any inclination of the car.

5. A gauze strainer should be provided at the gasoline inlet and also another at the air inlet.

6. The fuel should flow in a single direction either up or down through the float chamber so no pockets will exist.

7. There should be a vent in the top of the float chamber.

8. The float point should be easily ground and moved by the motion of the float.

9. The float should be adjustable to different grades of fuel.

10. The passage between the float and mixing chambers should be large to prevent clogging.

11. The air passage should be contracted at the nozzle.

12. A removable gauze should be inserted in the mixing chamber to prevent unsprayed liquid reaching the engine.

13. The gasoline inlet valve should be arranged to have dashboard control.

14. There should be means of heating in cold weather or with low gravity fuels.

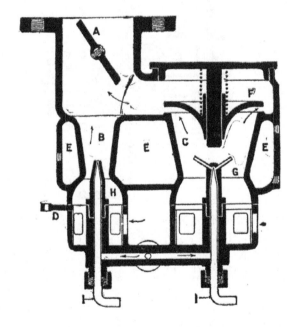

FIG. 168.—The Willet Carburetter. This consists of two carburetters in one, each with its own spray nozzle and adjustment. The small carburetter B is used for low speeds, and a second one C, cutting in on moderate and high speeds. Automatic action is secured by the spring operated valve F. The air supply of carburetter B may be regulated by valve D, having dashboard control. Closing this valve produces a strong suction on the spray nozzle in B, thus drawing a rich mixture to make easy starting possible. The valve is then opened to its normal position, which is wide open. Should the weather be cold and a richer mixture required, this valve may be closed somewhat. The entire carburetter is controlled by the butterfly throttle valve A. Nozzle H has a single opening while G is a multi-nozzle having four outlets. Both mixing chambers may be heated by the jacket E. The fuel flow to nozzle is controlled by the needle valves I.

Size of Carburetter.—In selecting a carburetter the first thing
to be determined is the proper size as success or failure in operating the car depends upon it.   If too large there would be difficulty
in starting and it would be necessary to feed more fuel than would
otherwise be required, because the air velocity through the mixing

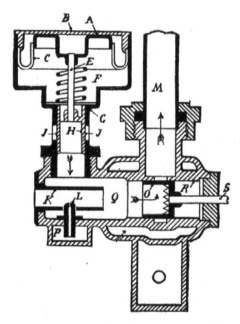

Fig. 169.—The Krebs Carburetter, used on the Panhard-Levassor motors.
Gasoline comes from the float chamber through channel P to the
spray nozzle L, air being admitted at K.   Q is the mixing chamber;
the mixture passes into the feed tube M through the port H, whose
opening is controlled by the position of the serrated perforations in
piston O, moving through bore R, as controlled by the governor
through piston rod S.   When more air than the fixed quantity admitted at K is required, the excess motor suction depresses the small
piston A, held in cylinder F, by the spring E, and sliding in the
elastic diaphragm C. Air is admitted above it through a small port
at B. The depression of piston A, causes the slide H, to move downward in tube G, thus opening the ports I and J, admitting the required amount of air.

chamber would be too low to cause an intimate mixing of the fuel
spray with the air.   Moreover, a very rapid cranking on starting
would be necessary in order to produce sufficient suction in the
mixing chamber to draw gasoline through the nozzle.*

*It must be remembered, that in nearly all carburetters the level of the gasoline in
the float chamber being somewhat lower than the nozzle, an "initial suction" is necessary to get the liquid to the point of discharge and an additional suction to discharge it
into the mixing chamber.

The carburetter size should be determined by the area of the valve opening on the engine and not by the cylinder displacement as the former is a true measure of the engine capacity. A carburetter cannot deliver more charge to a cylinder than the area of the valve opening will allow to pass. Hence, a large carburetter with excess passage area cannot cause an engine to deliver more power than it would with one having a passage equal in area to that of the valve opening.

A carburetter too large would not only waste fuel but reduce the power of the engine by furnishing a weak and non-homogeneous mixture. On the other hand it is obvious that if the carburetter be too small the engine would not develop its rated power, as it could not deliver a full charge at high speed. From the foregoing it follows that the carburetter of proper size should have its passage area equal to the valve opening of the engine.* In multicylinder engines this area is equal to the valve opening multiplied by the number of suction strokes which take place simultaneously, determined from the sequence of cranks, as explained in plate III.

To find the valve opening area, remove an intake valve and measure the diameter of the port it covers, and also the lift of the valve and angle of valve seat. The effective valve opening area is equal to the slant surface of the frustrum of a cone whose upper base diameter is equal to the port diameter, whose slant height is equal to the lift of valve times the sine of the angle of the valve seat and whose lower base diameter is equal to the port diameter plus twice the valve lift times $\cos \Phi \sin \Phi$.

The above values substituted in the following formula will give the required area.

Area valve opening $= \frac{1}{2}$ slant height $\times$ (circumference of upper base $+$ circumference of lower base).

This area is to be multiplied by the number of suction strokes occurring at one time. A carburetter having this area will be of the correct size provided the main and auxiliary passages through the carburetter are smooth surfaced, and as direct as possible. If it be made up of tortuous rough passages, sharp bends, etc., a little excess area should be provided to compensate for the increased frictional resistance resulting therefrom.

*In the exact determination of carburetter size, sufficient excess passage area must be provided to correct for the friction of the mixture through the carburetter and inlet manifold. It is not probable that a carburetter could be found having exactly the same size outlet as the valve opening, hence, the nearest size *larger* is selected which will be amply large to allow for friction. The inlet manifold, of course, must be of the exact size to correspond with the carburetter.

Having determined the required area, a carburetter may be selected having its outlet diameter corresponding as near as possible to this area—taking the nearest larger size. Carburetter makers proportion the outlet to correspond to standard pipe sizes, as given in the table, but it should be noted that internal pipe diameters do not correspond to the nominal diameters as listed. For instance, a pipe listed as ¾ inch has an internal diameter of .82 inch, hence, the correct pipe size should be obtained from the table.

TABLE OF STANDARD PIPE SIZES.

NOMINAL INSIDE DIAMETER.	ACTUAL OUTSIDE DIAMETER.	ACTUAL INSIDE DIAMETER.	INTERNAL AREA.
ins.	ins.	ins.	sq. ins.
½	.840	.622	.304
¾	1.050	.824	.533
1	1.315	1.048	.861
1¼	1.660	1.380	1.496
1½	1.900	1.610	2.036
2	2.375	2.067	3.356
2½	2.875	2.468	4.780
3	3.500	3.067	7.383
3½	4.000	3.548	9.887
4	4.500	4.026	12.730

Adjusting the Carburetter.—It is difficult to state a method which will apply to the adjustment of all makes of carburetters, but it is possible to give a few general instructions.

1. The interior of the float chamber should be examined with a view to removing any dirt or other matter which might interfere with the proper flow of the gasoline.

2. With a spray carburetter, it is sometimes necessary to obtain by priming a mixture for starting. It is, however, possible in doing this to make too lean or too rich a mixture; and if the adjustments be decidedly wrong, the mixture formed on the first few revolutions will be so bad that the engine will stop.

3. Sometimes the float is too high or too low, and the gasoline overflows the spray nozzle continually, or is so low that a con-

siderable suction is required. Now as before stated, the gasoline level should be such that the liquid will form a bubble at the nozzle to be blown off at will. The exact height should be found by this method.

4. After the float chamber has had time to fill, observe whether gasoline drips from the nozzle. If it does, the float valve should be investigated. If pressing it shut, stops the dripping, the float is too high; if the dripping persist, the valve leaks and needs to be reground. Occasionally a float and float valve are so arranged that the valve, although tight in one position, may slant over a trifle and leak from that cause.

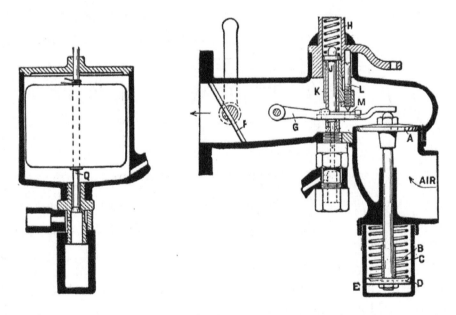

FIG. 170.—The Petrie Carburetter. An air valve A is provided which completely closes the air port when not in operation and also a gasoline valve J which completely closes the gasoline port at the same time. The action of the air valve is resisted by a long spring B. The gasoline valve is lifted from its seat by the action of the air valve through the lever G and the lifter K. It will be noticed that the fulcrum M of the lever G, the point at which the lever G rests upon the air valve A, and the point at which the lifter K rests on the lever G are in a straight line, giving a lift to the gasoline valve J in proportion to the lift of the air valve. To change the proportion between the gasoline and air openings a regulating cap H is provided, by means of which the position of the point L, at which the lifter K rests upon the lever G, may be varied at will, thus varying the lift of the gasoline valve. The air valve is provided with a glycerine dashpot E to make the operation noiseless. The valve stem C extends into the dash pot terminating in the piston D, held in tension by the spring B. The mixture to engine is controlled by the throttle F. To the left is shown a section of the float chamber with needle valve Q arranged concentric to float.

If no dripping occur after standing, depress the float, and on the first sign of dripping crank the engine. If it does not start, prime the carburetter again. In case this fails, shut off the gasoline at the tank, and if there be a drainage outlet from the float chamber draw off a couple of teaspoonsful of gasoline. This weakens the mixture. Repeated cautious experimenting in this manner will soon establish the priming required to start the engine when cold.

5. Gasoline when warm evaporates more rapidly, and caution is required not to prime too much. Many carburetters with a small primary air passage will start the engine without priming, once they are properly adjusted.

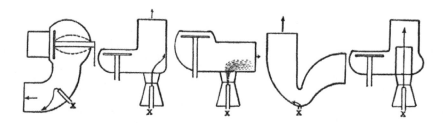

FIG. 171.—A few examples of carburetter design, showing courses followed by the fuel after leaving the nozzle, for different arrangements of parts and passages. The heavy arrowed line leading from the nozzle X indicates the course taken by the mixture as influenced by the design. These diagrams are self explanatory, and show that liquid globules are precipitated against some portions of the mixing chamber wall almost immediately after leaving the nozzle. This tends to disturb the homogeneity of the mixture, and requires that provisions be made for correcting this effect in the remaining portions of the passage.

If the engine should start, but immediately die down, try depressing the float. If the cause of dying down be too weak a mixture, this will keep the engine going.

6. When there is an auxiliary spring controlled air valve, tighten the spring sufficiently to hold it on its seat at low engine speeds and throttle openings. With the engine running light at about 250 to 300 revolutions per minute, adjust the fuel needle valve to such a position that, with the spark just back of center, the speed can be cut down to below 200 revolutions per minute without misfiring.

7. Having made this adjustment, retard the spark fully and with clutch still disengaged, slightly open the throttle. The engine should attain at least its maximum road speed with the throttle about one-eighth open. The auxiliary air valve should begin to open at about 250 r. p. m., but should not open fully for maximum speed with engine running light, as it is not taking full charges.

8. Adjust the spring of the auxiliary valve so that it only partially opens for maximum speed. All the above adjustments are to be made with the clutch disengaged.

9. Now try the car on the road at moderate speeds. Suppose the engine runs in a sluggish manner, vary the gasoline supply without stopping: first reduce, then increase the richness of the

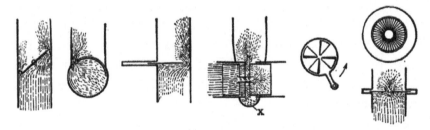

FIG. 172.—Several designs of throttle valves are here shown in a partially open position, where the effects of separation and deflection of the liquid globules are illustrated for each case. It will be seen that all these throttles act as separators when not fully open. The first four throw the liquid upon the walls unevenly. The last one shown to the right, while better distributing the liquid over the walls, is like the rest, an energetic separator. Throttles like number four are rarely found in later designs. Probably all who have had any experience with this type of throttle remember that a drain cock is inserted at X.

mixture and note the affect on the car's performance on level ground. A few trials should give a mixture on which the car will run well; the operation thus obtained, does not prove altogether that the mixture is correct as the car may be running with more throttle opening than is necessary.

10. If the radiator should heat up on level ground and over heats on hills, it indicates too rich a mixture; correct this by adjusting the auxiliary air valve. A change in spring tension has a greater proportional effect at low than at high speeds.

Note whether the valve strikes the stop at moderate speed. If it does, it will not admit sufficient air at high speed, hence, adjust the stop, if possible, so the valve may open further. If it should flutter at high speed, the lift must be reduced to increase the spring tension and diminish the fuel supply to the nozzle.

11. In case there be no needle valve controlling the spray, reduce the primary air inlet so that a larger proportion of the total air stream will go through the auxiliary valve. These changes will weaken the mixture more at high than at low speeds, as it should be for proper working.

12. If in running the car on level ground, the motor be simply weak and not accompanied by heating it indicates that the mixture is too lean. A good test of the mixture is the response to the spark advance. If the mixture be bad, the spark must be advanced considerably to produce any noticeable acceleration, whereas with the correct mixture any change in the advance is felt at once, and the maximum advance is not needed except at maximum speeds. Even more marked is the response to the throttle when the latter is nearly closed.

13. Much depends upon the proper adjustment of the air valve spring. To get the best results in power and economy, the tension of the spring should be almost nothing with the valve upon its seat; and, if the primary air inlet and fuel valve be carefully adjusted as above, it will be found that no more tension is needed to maintain the valve in a closed position while starting the engine. The spring may not be composed of the proper size wire nor have the right number of turns to give the proper initial tension, but, before altering or changing the spring, remove the exhaust piping or manifold and observe the flame colors which are reliable indications of the quality of the mixture. The stiffness of the spring should be such that at the lower and medium speeds the color of the flame will be a dark blue verging upon violet; for other speeds up to the normal or rated speed of the engine, the color should be a somewhat lighter blue, the color gradually fading but at no point losing its decided blue tinge.

This fading of the blue color denotes a gradual weakening of the mixture as it should do for increasing speeds. One necessity, among others before explained, for this gradual weakening of the mixture is that at high piston speeds a slightly weakened mixture burns faster than does one of full strength. This being necessary at high speeds to secure complete combustion before exhaust.

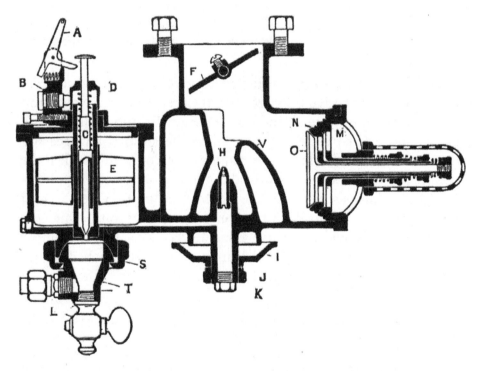

FIG. 173.—The B. G. v. R. Carburetter. In this design the chief features are: an adjustable primary air inlet, a jacketed venturi tube mixing chamber and a triple auxiliary valve. The nozzle H which has no needle valve, is regulated for gasoline flow by loosening set nut J and adjusting the primary air inlet cone I. This cone catches any overflow of gasoline in priming. The nozzle H may be cleaned by removing screw plug K. In operation the auxiliary valve O opens first to supply auxiliary air, and with increasing speeds additional air is admitted the opening of N and M, the three valves acting progressively. These valves are attached to the part P which is removable for inspection. A butterfly throttle is located at F. The float E is arranged concentric with the inlet needle valve C and the float point has spring adjustment, regulated by turning D which is provided with a stop, B. At the upper end is a priming lever A. The float chamber is drained by the cock L   A union S permits its lower part T containing the gasoline connection to be swung into any position most convenient for piping to tank.

A yellow tint in the exhaust indicates too little gasoline in proportion to the amount of air supplied while red indicates too much gasoline. Both these tints, yellow and red, show that the engine is not developing its best power, moreover the red shows a waste of fuel.

When it is impossible to adjust the carburetter so as to get the blue flame color, it is usually due to faulty spraying action of the nozzle. This nozzle defect is further emphasized by fluctuations of the flame color from yellow to red or vice versa, indicating coarseness of fuel division and a resulting non-homogeneous mixture. The nozzle may not be entirely at fault; the mixing is somewhat dependent upon the manner in which the carburetted primary air is brought into contact with that from the auxiliary port; but whatever the whole cause of the trouble may be, the nozzle is chiefly at fault.

14. Sometimes a spring adjusted to give a proper mixture at one speed will not give good results at other speeds. Now, suppose the mixture were found to be originally too rich at high speeds, and was corrected by slackening the spring or increasing the auxiliary valve lift: if the change were only in the lift the mixture at lower speeds has probably not been affected. If, however, the spring has been slackened, the mixture may be too lean at low speeds, owing to the air valve opening too soon. One way to correct this would be to use a spring having a larger number of turns, but a satisfactory result may usually be reached by increasing the spring tension and reducing the spray orifice.

It is quite difficult to make adjustments on the road owing to the motion of the car and the inaccessible position of the carburetter, hence, if the running load be applied to the engine with the car standing, these adjustments can be made more conveniently. A device which has sometimes been employed to secure a running load on the engine with the car standing consists of a rude form of Prony brake. A board, five or six feet in length and somewhat wider than the flywheel face, is either suspended from the side frame of the car or fulcrumed upon a block on the floor. The short end of the lever thus provided bears against the flywheel from the under side and weights up to ten or fifteen pounds placed on the other end provide all the load necessary.

With this apparatus the carburetter may be adjusted to the varied road conditions of power demands while the car is standing.

Changes in carburetter adjustments should not be made hurriedly as the first impression of the nature of a trouble may prove, on further investigation to be wrong. When a fairly good mixture has been obtained, it is advisable to operate the car awhile without further adjustments, noting its behavior and carefully analyzing the carburetter action under all road conditions.

Hand Control.—All attempts at automatic regulation to secure the ideally correct mixture of gasoline and air for every variation in engine speed have not been successful.

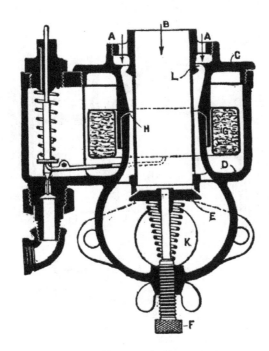

FIG. 174.—The Brock Carburetter   Primary air enters through a ring opening A and flowing downward, as indicated by the arrows meets the gasoline which enters through the slit opening H in the walls of the mixing chamber, the outlet to engine being at K. The gasoline opening H may be adjusted by screwing up or down the top piece C or cover of the float chamber. The float G maintains a level in the float chamber D, approximately $\frac{1}{16}$ inch above the gasoline opening H and in adjusting this opening, screw C down until it seats firmly at H then unscrew about one-eighth turn. At B is the secondary air inlet, controlled by the auxiliary valve E having an adjusting screw F. The float point has spring adjustment as shown.

Whatever may be the claims of carburetter makers, they would be the first to admit that, excellent though the results may be in the hands of the average user, these results at best are but a compromise. Many of the best known European cars have built up reputations by being driven in and winning races on the road, by drivers recruited from the ranks of those who first obtained publicity by track and road racing on motor bicycles having carburetters with hand control. There is no sound reason why a driver, in addition to the throttle, should not have two other levers within reach to alter the quantity of air passing by the nozzle and the quantity of gasoline sprayed into the mixing chamber. Once the correct gasoline supply for the jet is settled at the factory, it would not require to be varied much; therefore an attachment on the dashboard providing exceedingly minute gradations would suffice. Hand control of the gasoline can be used to advantage in ascending steep hills when the engine load limit is nearly reached, necessitating wide open throttle and retarded spark. The automatic auxiliary air supply ought, under these circumstances, to

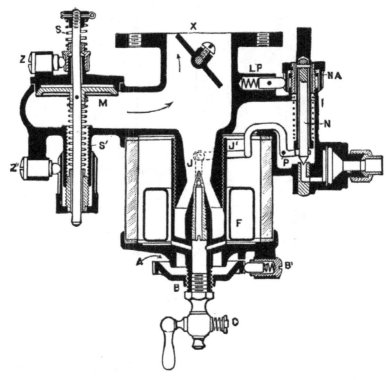

FIG. 175.—The Stromberg Carburetter. The principal features of this carburetter are: a glass float chamber, concentric float, venturi shaped mixing chamber, adjustable primary air inlet, and a two spring adjustment for the auxiliary valve. In operation the gasoline supply is controlled by the float F, through levers J and J'—the latter pivoted at P, and connected to needle valve N. The float point is adjustable by the spring I and nut N A, secured in position by the plunger L P. Primary air enters at A, and is regulated by the adjustable cup B, secured by the plunger B'. The drip cock C, drains the float chamber. The mixture from the venturi tube V, receives supplementary air through the auxiliary valve M, thence it passes to engine through throttle X. The auxiliary valve is controlled by two springs S and S', the lower one acts on moderate speeds and the upper one on high speeds. The springs have adjusting nuts and self locking devices Z and Z'.

promptly close, but the tremendous suction exerted by a four or six cylinder engine on full throttle does keep the air valve open much wider than is essential. The engine asks for the richest possible mixture, and this ought to be supplied, because the certain overheating that will ensue is only temporary, and may be nullified either by stopping the engine when the hill is surmounted or by replenishing the circulating water.

The abolition of hand control for the auxiliary air supply is only for simplicity, for, with or without a variable jet, hand control offers a command of engine flexibility little short of wonderful. It is interesting to watch the spindle of an automatic air valve when the throttle is opened and closed, the car, of course, being at a standstill. The valve will, in nearly every case, be found to gradually open as the engine speed increases in response to the throttle, reaching its full opening at about three-quarters speed. At highest speeds the engine requires considerably more air than is needed at the lower speeds and this is not obtained with automatic control.

A simple device for air hand control may be applied to any car with little trouble. Cut an opening at any suitable place in the pipe between the carburetter and engine and cover it with a sliding collar, valve, flap, or any other device that can be easily opened or closed by a lever on the steering column, the essential feature being that it must be fairly well airtight in the closed position.

With a little experience on the road, the driver will soon discover the point of engine speed determined by the throttle lever at which he can commence to open the extra air supply. If he has never before driven a car so fitted it will be a revelation to him, for this extra air port can be opened wider and wider to an astonishing extent before the engine will misfire to indicate that the mixture is too weak.

This extra air port besides serving as a power increaser, can be made to act as a scavenger and cylinder cooling agent. When descending a long hill, by switching off the spark, entirely closing the throttle and opening the extra air port to its full extent (the top speed gear and clutch are of course kept in engagement so that the car is driving the engine), cold air is drawn into the engine on each suction stroke, clearing out every particle of hot gases and helping materially not only to cool the engine and spark plugs but also to keep the points of the latter much cleaner and freer from carbonized oil than would otherwise be the case.

Carburetter Troubles.—Preliminary to hunting for carburetter troubles, see that there is some gasoline in the tank and that the valve on the pipe leading from same is open. The carburetter is too often blamed for faulty engine performance, which should be attributed to defects in the ignition system. Such symptoms as fouled plugs, black smoke in the exhaust, etc., point at once to the carburetter, but in cases where such obvious signs are wanting, thoroughly inspect the ignition system first.

Gasoline Leaks.—Tanks are liable to become leaky through the opening of the seams by jarring or vibration. Galvanized iron tanks, such as are furnished on some machines, should be discarded when a leak results from rust, as it is practically of no use

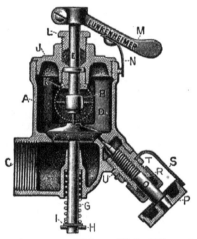

FIG. 176.--A Vaporizer or Generator Valve. This differs from a carburetter in the absence of a float chamber and consists of a mixing chamber containing a check valve and having, 1, an air inlet; 2, a gasoline inlet; and 3, an exit to engine. Its operation is as follows: On the suction stroke, the partial vacuum produced in the mixing chamber A permits the atmospheric pressure to act upon the valve F opening same against the tension of spring G, which is held in position by the washer I and cotter H. At this period, the gasoline port in the valve seat is uncovered and a small amount of gasoline is sprayed into the incoming volume of air and passing into the mixing chamber where the mixing is further assisted, in some designs by baffle walls. At the end of the suction stroke the pressure in the mixing chamber becomes equalized with the atmosphere and the spring causes the valve F to seat, thereby retaining the mixture and shutting off any further injection of gasoline or air. The gasoline supply may be adjusted by the needle valve O operated by the thumb wheel P, which has a flat spot on its circumference on which the spring S bears to retain the adjustment. The spring can be turned to any position by loosening the locknut T. The volume of mixture to the engine is regulated by a sliding throttle D operated by lever M and locked by spring N, which engages notches in a graduated dial. The valve spring G is held in position by cotter H and washer I. A vaporizer when used on a two cycle engine requires no check valve between it and the engine.

to solder it. A heavy gauge copper tank should be substituted. The supply pipe should be made flexible by a loop to avoid strains due to vibration. All soldered connections should be inspected from time to time.

Leaking Float.—Persistent flooding is frequently due to this cause. The presence of liquid inside a metal float is detected by shaking it, and the hole through which it entered, located by heating the float and passing a lighted match over the surface, which will ignite the issuing vapor. To repair, enlarge the hole with an awl, drain and solder. Cork floats sometimes lose their buoyancy by becoming saturated with gasoline; remove and thoroughly dry out by placing the float in a warm place, then apply a coat of shellac.

No Flow of Gasoline.—Sometimes little, if any, gasoline will flow to the nozzle even when the carburetter is flooded in the usual manner. A quantity of dirt in the float sufficient to stop the flow of gasoline, may have gathered on the wire gauze in the

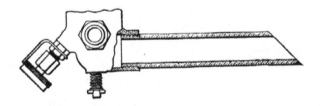

FIG. 177.—An Air Inlet Pipe. This consists of a short length of pipe threaded at one end and screwed into the air inlet of a vaporizer. A saving in fuel is secured by its use as any gasoline or vapor that may be blown into the inlet when the valve seats is retained in the pipe and drawn into the mixing chamber during the next suction stroke. Without any extension of the inlet, this fuel would be blown out into the atmosphere and lost

supply passage. Clean the gauze and also the float valve, spray nozzle and connecting passage. In removing the needle valve to clean the spray nozzle there is no need of losing the adjustment, as after the set screw which locks the adjustment is loosened, the needle may be turned down to a complete close and the number of turns required may be noted from which the old setting may be again obtained.

Flooding.—If not caused by a defective float, examine the float valve for imperfect seating. The leak may usually be stopped by grinding the valve on its seat with a little whiting, or even grinding the seat and valve together without any abrasive, holding the needle and seat in their true relative positions and giving them a motion of rotation with moderate pressure. Carburetters having offset float chambers may flood when the car is not level, as for instance, when standing on a grade.

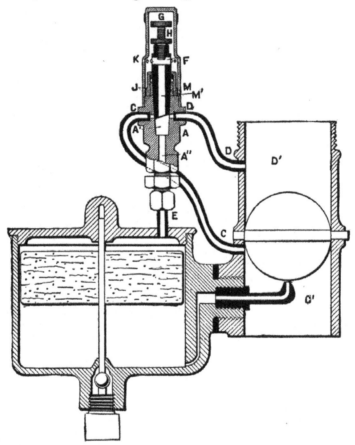

FIG. 178.—The Gillett-Lehman Economizer. This device, which may be applied to any float feed carburetter, automatically governs the air pressure in the float chamber. The main body A turned out of brass, has a central bore; the upper half A' conical in shape, the lower half A" cylindrical. It is tapped at opposite sides for pipe connections C and D, one connecting with the carburetter mixing chamber C' the other with outlet D' to engine. The lower end of A is connected by the nipple E to top of the float chamber which must be air tight. At A' is fitted a tapered brass plug M with a small vertical hole M' through it and a transverse hole F through its top. The lower end of this plug being cut at an angle, permits by turning, adjustment to the openings C and D; the plug being locked in position by cap J. A screw G provided with a locknut H makes the opening F adjustable, and is protected by covering K. The device operates as follows: Being connected to the mixing chamber, in which the vacuum is created by the engine, the atmospheric pressure existing in the float chamber of the carburetter is converted into a partial vacuum—slightly less than the vacuum existing in the suction tube; this vacuum increasing or decreasing in the float chamber in proportion to the increase or decrease in the suction tube, governs the quantity of gasoline issuing at the spray jet.

Flooding may be caused by dirt under the float valve; this may often be removed by depressing the float, thus opening the float valve and flushing. If a carburetter be not well stayed, vibration may keep the float valve off its seat, and continuous flooding result therefrom.

Impure Gasoline.—Many carburetter troubles would be avoided if more care were taken to free gasoline of all dirt before its entrance into the tank. When filling the tank use a strainer funnel. A piece of chamois skin makes an excellent filter; if a wire gauze be used it should have a very fine mesh. In the absence of a strainer funnel, use three or four layers of fine linen fitted inside an ordinary funnel. Never use the same funnel for both gasoline and water.

Stale Gasoline.—When a car is not used for some time the gasoline in the float chamber loses its strength. If the engine should not start close the tank valve and drain the carburetter by opening the pet cock which is usually provided in the bottom of the chamber for this purpose. When empty, close pet cock and open the tank valve, not forgetting to give the float chamber time to fill before trying to start the engine.

Low Grade Gasoline.—This sometimes causes the engine to misfire and not develop its full power. Inferior fuel is generally indicated by a smoky exhaust and a disagreeable odor. Gasoline suitable for automobile use should test 76 degrees. In the absence of a testing outfit pour a little of the liquid on the hand. When it evaporates rapidly and leaves the hand dry and clean it is acceptable, but if it evaporate slowly and leaves a greasy deposit, it should be rejected. This furnishes a fairly reliable indication.

Water in Gasoline.—This is generally indicated when the engine runs irregularly and finally stops. Place a small quantity of the gasoline on a clean knife blade or other smooth metallic surface. The gasoline will evaporate, and if water be present it will collect in small globules unless the water has been purposely *chemically* combined with the gasoline. Gasoline and water chemically combined will burn slowly with a yellowish flame.

Freezing of Carburetter.—When water enters the float chamber it settles to the bottom and in cold weather prevents the action of the float by freezing. It is also liable to enter the spray nozzle and stop it up when it congeals, as it may readily do under some conditions. When heavy demands are made on a carburetter it becomes very cold, as the heat called for to effect evaporation is more than that available from the entering air. Under extreme conditions moisture is deposited in the form of frost, indicating a temperature in the carburetter too low for good working. These conditions are avoided by jacketing or heating the air supply.

Cold Weather.—In extremely cold weather it may be necessary to warm the carburetter and admission pipe by pouring boiling water over them. Saturate a piece of waste with some fresh gaso· line and insert it in the air inlet of the carburetter.

Cranking.—So far as carburetter action is concerned, a few quick turns of the crank will be more likely to start the engine than ten minutes of slow grinding.

Misfiring.—Sometimes caused by either too weak or too rich a mixture. Misfiring allows the unburnt charge to accumulate in the exhaust pipe and muffler; it is sometimes ignited by a later charge and causes a loud report like a gun. Misfiring on slow speed may be caused by too weak a mixture due to having the float set too low, or by leaks on the pipe and connections between the throttle and engine.

After Firing.—This is usually caused by the delayed ignition or combustion of the previous charge, sometimes due to a mixture that is too rich or too weak and hence burns slowly, continuing its combustion after passing into the exhaust.

Weak Explosions.—Regular but weak explosions may be due to either too rich or too poor a mixture, or to the loss of compression. A hiss inside the cylinder indicates a leaky piston ring or that the openings of the piston rings are in line. A little soapy water around the relief cock, spark plug or other opening into the combustion space will indicate a loss of compression by the formation of bubbles.

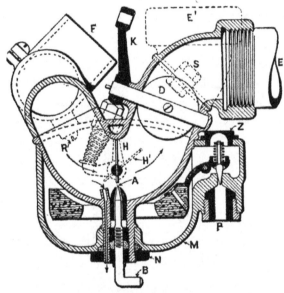

FIG. 179.—The Marvel Carburetter. The particular feature of this carburetter is the damper H, for regulating the fuel flow out of the nozzle A independent of the needle valve adjustment B. The operation is as follows: With damper closed (position H) a strong suction is produced, increasing the strength of the mixture. When the damper is opened as in position H'; the suction is reduced and hence the strength of the mixture likewise. The damper may be swung to and fro through the handle K which also has connection with the throttle valve D. The connection P, to gasoline tank may be swung into any direction by loosening locknut N. By releasing screw R, the hot air connection F may be turned to any convenient angle. Again, by releasing the two nuts S, the engine connection E may be turned to any other position as E' convenient for piping. The float chamber M is removable by unscrewing nut, N. The float point has spring adjustment, accessible by removing cap Z.

Denatured Alcohol.—This consists of ethyl spirit, or the common spirit of wine, mixed with methyl alcohol, or wood spirit and some other hydrocarbon. The object of mingling the spirit with the other ingredients is to prevent its being drunk.

In using alcohol, heat must be supplied to the carburetter for complete vaporization. One type of alcohol carburetter, shown in Fig. 180, is double, the engine being started with gasoline, and run with alcohol as soon as the speed is sufficient to generate a high temperature. The alcohol is then turned on by the rotary cock valve, B.

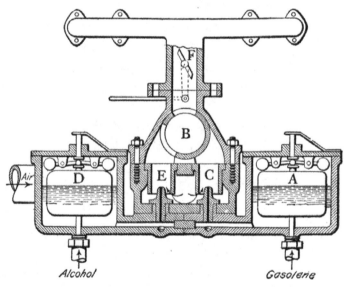

FIG. 180.—A double float-feed carburetter for alcohol and gasoline. A, float in gasoline chamber; B, rotary valve controlling outlet of alcohol or gasoline to engine space, through nozzles, C or E; D, float in alcohol chamber; F, butterfly valve for controlling volume of fuel charge.

Conditions of Using Alcohol Fuel.—The successful use of alcohol as a fuel for a gas engine involves the following conditions:

1. For complete vaporization of the alcohol heat is necessary. For this reason the carburetter is frequently heated by the exhaust or by water jacketing.

2. A higher compression than is commonly used with gasoline is necessary, in order to obtain as high a power efficiency as possible.

3. Reliable sparking devices are essential, in order to produce complete combustion, preventing injurious acid products liable to result from water vapors and incomplete combustion.

Useful Alcohol Data.—The following conclusions regarding the use of alcohol as fuel for engines as compared with gasoline are based on the results of recent experiments:

1. Any engine operating with gasoline or kerosene can operate with alcohol fuel without any structural change whatever, with proper manipulation.

2. It requires no more skill to operate an alcohol engine than one intended for gasoline or kerosene.

3. There seems to be no tendency for the interior of an alcohol engine to become sooty, as is the case with gasoline and kerosene.

4. Alcohol contains approximately 0.6 of the heating value of gasoline, by weight; a small engine requires 1.8 times as much alcohol as gasoline per horse power hour. This corresponds very closely with the relative heating value of the fuels, indicating practically the same thermal efficiency of the two when vaporization is complete.

5. In some cases carburetters designed for gasoline do not vaporize all the alcohol supplied, and in such cases the excess of alcohol consumed is greater than indicated above.

6. The absolute excess of alcohol consumed over gasoline or kerosene will be reduced by such changes as will increase the thermal efficiency of the engine.

7. The thermal efficiency of these engines can be improved when they are to be operated by alcohol, first by altering the construction of the carburetter to accomplish complete vaporization, and second, by increasing the compression very materially.

8. An engine designed for gasoline or kerosene can, without any material alterations to adapt it to alcohol, give slightly more power (about 10 per cent.) than when operated with gasoline or kerosene, but this increase is at the expense of greater consumption of fuel. By alterations designed to adapt the engine to new fuel this excess of power may be increased to about 20 per cent.

9. The different designs of gasoline or kerosene engines are not equally well adapted to the burning of alcohol, though all may burn it with a fair degree of success.

10. Storage of alcohol and its use in engines is much less dangerous than that of gasoline, as well as being decidedly more pleasant.

11. The exhaust from an alcohol engine is less likely to be offensive than the exhaust from a gasoline or kerosene engine, although there will be some odor, due to lubricating oil and imperfect combustion, if the engine be not skillfully operated.

12. With proper manipulation, there seems to be no undue corrosion of the interior due to the use of alcohol.

13. The fact that the exhaust from the alcohol engine is not as hot as that from gasoline and kerosene seems to indicate less possibility of burning the lubricating oil. This is borne out by the fact that the exhaust shows less smoke.

14. In localities where there is a supply of cheap raw material for the manufacture of denatured alcohol, and which are at the same time remote from the source of supply of gasoline, alcohol may immediately compete with gasoline as a fuel for engines.

15. There is no reason to suppose that the cost of repairs and lubrication will be any greater for an alcohol engine than for one built for gasoline or kerosene.

A carburetter designed for alcohol may be used with gasoline, but the reverse conditions are not true. The time required for the evaporation and combustion of alcohol is greater than that required for gasoline, but a higher mean effective pressure is realized with alcohol than with gasoline. Moreover when alcohol is used as a fuel the noise of operation is reduced.

The power efficiency of alcohol has been given as slightly over 1 pint per horse power, according to purity. The figure for gasoline is generally given as about .86 pint per horse power. An interesting test of power efficiency has been made with a motor vehicle used for dragging a plow. With 2 gallons of gasoline 3 roods were plowed; with 2 gallons of kerosene, 3 roods, 35 poles; with two gallons of *alcohol,* 2 roods, 25 poles.

CHAPTER TWENTY-FIVE.

IGNITION.

Introductory.—Ignition is a subject of much importance in automobiling and one that is perplexing to the novice. The engine may operate with an imperfect fuel mixture, if the ignition system be in working order, but any defect in the latter will in nearly every case cause the engine to misfire or stop.

Numerous devices have been tried to fire the charge in gas engines. In the early days, a flame behind a shutter was used, the latter being opened at the proper moment. Sometimes the flame was blown out by a too violent explosion, so this method gave way to a porcelain tube that was kept at white heat by an interior flame. The tube being subject to breakage, spongy platinum, heated by compression, was next tried and found to work, if not too moist from watery vapor in the gas mixture, or if the engine speed were not too high. The heat of high compression was also tried and is in successful use to-day for stationary engines, but seems as yet not to meet automobile requirements.

Electricity is now universally used. Hence, in order to gain a clear understanding of ignition principles it is necessary to have at least an elementary knowledge of electricity of which a short introduction is here given. This should be supplemented by reading the other electrical portions of the book.

Electricity.—The name electricity is applied to an invisible agent known only by the effects which it produces, and the various ways in which it manifests itself.

Electrical *currents* are said to flow through *conductors.* These offer more or less *resistance* to the flow, depending on the material. Copper wire is generally used as it offers little resistance to the flow of the current. It is now thought that the flow takes place along the surface and not through the metal. The current must have pressure to overcome the resistance of the conductor and flow along its surface. This pressure is called *voltage* caused by what is known as *difference of potential* between the source and terminal.

An electric current has often been compared to water flowing through a pipe. The pressure under which the current flows is measured in *volts* and the quantity that passes in *amperes.* The resistance with which the current meets in flowing along the conductor is measured in *ohms.* The flow of the current is proportional to the voltage and inversely proportional to the resistance. The latter depends upon the material, length and diameter of the conductor.

Since the current will always flow along the path of least resistance it must be so guarded that there will be no leakage. Hence to prevent leakage, wires are *insulated,* that is, covered by wrapping them with cotton or silk thread or other non-conducting materials. If the insulation be not effective, the current may leak, and so return to the source without doing its work. This is known as a *short circuit.*

The conductor which receives the current from the source is called the *lead* and the one by which it flows back, the *return.* When wires are used for both lead and return, it is called a *metallic circuit;* when the metal of the engine is used for the return, it is called a *grounded circuit,* the term originating in telegraphy, where the earth is used for the return. In ignition diagrams then the expression "to ground" means *to the metal of the engine.*

An electric current may do work of various kinds, but the one property which makes it available for ignition is the fact that whenever its motion is stopped by interposing a resistance, the energy of its flow is converted into heat. In practice this is accomplished in two ways: 1, by suddenly breaking a circuit, 2, by placing in the circuit a permanent *air gap* which the current must jump. In either case, the intense heat caused by the enormous resistance interposed, produces a spark which is utilized to ignite the charge. The first method is known as the *make and break* or *low tension* and the second, the *jump spark* or *high tension.*

An electric current is said to be: 1, *direct,* when it is of unvarying direction; 2, *alternating,* when it flows rapidly to and fro in opposite directions; 3, *primary,* when it comes directly from the source; 4, *secondary,* when the voltage and amperage of a primary current have been changed by an *induction coil.* A current is spoken of as *low tension,* or *high tension,* according as the voltage is low or high. A high tension current is capable of forcing its way against considerable resistance, whereas, a low tension current must have its path made easy. A continuous metal path is an easy one, but an interruption in the metal, as, the permanent air gap of a spark plug, is difficult to *bridge,* because air is a very poor conductor. Air is such a poor conductor that it is usually spoken of as a *non-conductor.* The low tension current is only able to produce a spark when parts are provided in the path, so arranged that they may be in contact and then suddenly separated. The low tension current will, as the separation occurs, tear off very small metallic particles and use these as a *bridge* to keep the path complete. Such a bridge is called *an arc,* the heat of which is used for ignition.

Magnetism.—The ancients applied the word "magnet," *magnes lapes,* to certain hard black stones which possess the property of attracting small pieces of iron, and as discovered later, to have the still more remarkable property of pointing north and south when hung up by a string; at this time the magnet received the name *lodestone.* The automobile word magneto is derived, as may easily be understood, from the word *magnet.*

Magnets have two opposite kinds of magnetism or magnetic poles, which attract or repel each other in much the same way as would two opposite kinds of electrification. One of these kinds of magnetism has a tendency to move toward the north and the other, toward the south. The two regions, in which the magnetic property is strongest, are called the *poles*. In a long shaped magnet it resides in the ends, while all around the magnet half way between the poles there is no attraction at all. The poles of a magnet are usually spoken of as, *north pole* and *south pole*.

When a current of electricity passes through a wire, a certain change is produced in the surrounding space producing what is known as a *magnetic field*. If the wire be insulated with a covering and coiled around a soft iron rod, it becomes an electro-magnet having a north and south pole, *so long as the current continues to flow*. The magnetic strength increases with the number of turns of the coil, for each turn adds its magnetic field to that of the other turns.

Induction.—If a second coil of wire be wound around the coil of an electro-magnet, but not touching it, an *induced current* is produced in this second coil by what is known as *induction,* each time the current in the inside coil begins or ceases flowing. The inside coil is called the *primary winding* and the outside coil the *secondary winding*. Similarly, the current passing through the inside coil is called the *primary current* and that in the outside coil the *secondary* or *induced current.*

It has been found that by varying the ratio of the number of turns in the two coils the tension or voltage of the two currents is changed proportionately. That is, if the primary winding be composed of ten turns and the secondary of one hundred, the voltage of the secondary current is increased ten times that of the primary. This principle is employed to produce the extremely high tension current necessary with the jump spark method of ignition.

Methods of Producing Electricity.—Currents are produced by, 1, chemical and, 2, mechanical means. In the first method, two dissimilar metals such as copper and zinc called *electrodes* are immersed in an exciting fluid or *dielectric*. When the electrodes are connected at their terminals by a wire or conductor, a chemical action takes place, producing a current which flows from the copper to the zinc. This device is called a *cell,* and the combination of two or more of them connected so as to form a unit, is known as a *battery*. The word battery is frequently used incorrectly for a single cell. That terminal of the electrode from which the current flows is called a *plus* or *positive pole* and the other electrode terminal a *negative pole.*

Cells are said to be *primary* or *secondary* according as they generate a current of themselves or first require to be charged from an external source, storing up a current supply which is afterwards yielded in the reverse direction to that of the charging current.

There are two methods of producing an electric current by mechanical means, 1, by a *dynamo*, and 2, by a *magneto*.

A dynamo has an *electro-magnet* which is known as a *field magnet* to produce a *magnetic field* and an armature which when revolved in the magnetic field develops electric current.

A magneto has a permanent magnet to produce the magnetic field and an armature which is usually arranged to revolve between the poles of the magnet. The basic principles upon which dynamos and magnetos operate are the same. Magnetos are divided into two classes, 1, *low tension* and 2, *high tension* according as they generate a current of low or high voltage. Low tension magnetos are used for make and break ignition and the high tension type for the jump spark system. A low tension magneto in combination with a secondary induction coil may be used to produce a high tension spark.

Primary Cells.—There are various types of primary cells; those known as *dry cells* are most frequently used.

A dry cell is composed of three elements, usually zinc, carbon and a liquid electrolyte. A zinc cup closed at the bottom and open at the top forms the negative electrode; this is lined with several layers of blotting paper or other absorbing material.

The positive electrode consists of a carbon rod placed in the center of the cup; the space between is filled with carbon—ground coke and dioxide of manganese mixed with an absorbent material. This filling is moistened with a liquid, generally sal-ammoniac. The top of the cell is closed with pitch to prevent leakage and evaporation. A binding post for holding the wire connections is attached to each electrode and each cell is placed in a paper box to protect the zincs of adjacent cells from coming into contact with each other, when finally connected together to form a battery.

The average voltage of a dry cell when new is one and one-half volts, while the amperage ranges from about twenty-five to fifty amperes according to size. Now, since it requires about six volts for the proper working of a coil, one cell is not sufficient; hence several must be used.

There are three methods of connecting cells, 1, in *series*, 2, in *parallel* or multiple and 3, in *series multiple*.

A series connection consists in joining the positive pole of one cell to the negative pole of the other as shown in fig. 181; this adds the voltage of each cell. Thus, connecting in series four cells of one and one-half

FIG. 181.—Diagram of a series battery connection: four cells are shown connected by this method. If the cell voltage be one and one-half volts, the pressure between the (+) and (—) terminals of the *battery* is equal to the product of the voltage of a single cell multiplied by the number of cells. For four cells it is equal to six volts.

volts each will give a total of six volts. Fig 182 illustrates a parallel or multiple connection; this is made by connecting the positive terminal of one cell with the positive terminal of another cell and the negative terminal of the first cell with the negative terminal of the second cell. A parallel or multiple connection adds the amperage of each cell; that is, the amperage of the battery will equal the sum of the amperage of each cell. For instance, four cells of twenty-five amperes each would give a total of one hundred amperes when connected in parallel. A series mul-

FIG. 182.—Diagram of a multiple or parallel connection. When connected in this manner the voltage of the battery is the same as that of a single cell, but the amperage of the battery is equal to the amperage of a single cell multiplied by the number of cells.

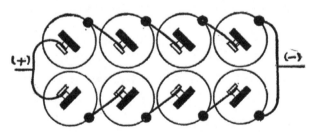

FIG. 183.—Diagram of a series multiple connection. Two sets of cells are connected in series, and the two batteries thus formed, connected in parallel. The pressure equals the voltage of one cell, multiplied by the number of cells in one battery, and the amperage, that of one cell multiplied by the number of batteries.

tiple connection, fig. 183, consists of connecting two sets of cells in series and then connecting the two sets in parallel. In series multiple connections the voltage of each set of cells or battery must be equal, or the batteries will be weakened, hence each battery of a series multiple connection should contain the same number of cells. The voltage of a series multiple connection is equal to the voltage of one cell multiplied by the number of cells in one battery and the amperage is equal to the amperage of one cell multiplied by the number of batteries.

Fig. 184 shows an incorrect method of wiring in series multiple connection. If the circuit be open, the six cells, on account of having more electromotive force than the four cells, will overpower them and cause a current to flow in the direction indicated by the arrows until the pressure of the six cells has dropped to that of the four. This will use up the energy of the six cells, but will not weaken the four cell battery. This action can be corrected by placing a two-way switch in the circuit at the junction of the two negative terminals so that only one battery can be used at a time.

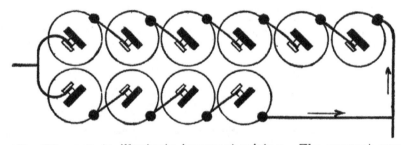

FIG. 184.—Diagram to illustrate incorrect wiring. The current pressure of the six cell battery being greater than that of the smaller unit, current will flow from the former through the latter until the pressure of the six cells is equal to that of the four cells.

Two batteries should be provided and used alternately so that one can recuperate while the other is in use; the stronger should be used in starting.

In renewing dry cells a greater number should never be put in series than originally came with the machine. With a good coil, four to six cells *in series* will give satisfactory service on most machines, and if four cells suffice, then a greater number connected in series will last a shorter length of time. This is because the additional cells increase the voltage beyond that required and likewise cause more current than is necessary, to flow through the coil; this increased current flow of course shortens the life of the battery.

In connecting dry cells heavy copper wire should not be used, because vibration may cause it to break. The terminals should be tightly connected and the spark plugs kept clean. When washing the machine, water should not come in contact with the dry cells, because the paper covers forming the insulation will become moist and the current leak across from one cell to another, resulting in running down the battery.

When a motor will run at high speed without missing explosions, while the car is standing, but will miss under road conditions. it indicates that the battery is weak. If this condition occur, each cell should be tested separately, as often only one of them has weakened, and it is only necessary to replace the weak ones. This should be done at once, as the weak cell will destroy the strength of the others. A weak battery frequently causes trouble in starting, as a better spark is then required than when the motor is warm. Extra milage can be secured from two run down batteries by connecting them in series multiple.

As batteries become weak a slight change of vibrator adjustment will prolong their life. Care should be taken when adjusting coils so as to use as little current as possible. The vibrator should be screwed down sufficiently to give just enough spark to run the motor; the closer the points are the more current will be used. One-third ampere current is the average amount necessary. A half turn of the adjusting screw on a coil will often increase the current consumed by the coil from one-half up to one and one-half amperes or nearly five times the actual amount necessary.

Dry cells will deteriorate when not in use, making it necessary to renew them about every sixty days. It will be economy to do this, as the saving in gasoline will more than offset the additional battery cost; the reason dry cells deteriorate is because the moisture evaporates. Freezing, exposure to heat, and vibration which loosens the sealing, causes the evaporation.

Weak cells can be strengthened somewhat by removing the paper jacket and punching the metal cups full of small holes; and then placing in a weak solution of sal-ammoniac, allowing the cells to absorb all they will take up. This is only to be recommended in cases of emergency when they are hard to get. Each cell when fresh should show from 20 to 25 amperes when tested; the date of manufacture should also be, noted as fresh cells are most efficient.

It is well not to put cells of various voltages or of different makes in the same circuit, for the stronger will discharge into the weakest until all are equal. Dry cells should be tested with an ammeter, care being taken to do it quickly as the ammeter being of a very low resistance short circuits the cell. A voltmeter is not used in testing because while the cells are not giving out current, their voltage remains practically the same, and a cell that is very weak will show nearly full voltage. When no ammeter is at hand the battery current may be tested by disconnecting the end of one of the terminal wires and snapping it across the binding post of the other terminal; the intensity of the spark produced will indicate the condition of the battery.

Secondary Cells.—A second chemical means of producing electricity for ignition is the *storage battery* which consists of two or more secondary cells contained in a carrying case or box usually of wood or hard rubber. A secondary cell is made up of a positive and a negative set of lead plates immersed in an electrolyte of dilute sulphuric acid. The proportion of acid to water is about one part acid to three and one-half parts of water. In preparing the electrolyte, acid should always be added to water— *not water to acid.*

In passing an electric current through a cell the plates undergo a chemical change; when this is complete the cell is said to be *charged.* A quantity of electricity has been stored in the cell, hence the name, *storage battery.* The cell after being charged will deliver a current in a reverse direction because during the discharge a reverse chemical action takes place which causes the plates to resume their original condition. When fully charged the positive plates are coated with peroxide of lead and are brown in color and the negative plates gray.

As the general theory, construction and management of storage batteries are outlined in a later chapter, it will be necessary to say little here regarding them.

The positive and negative poles of a secondary cell are plainly marked + and — or P and N. A cell when fully charged has a pressure of about two and one-half volts.

When current is taken from a cell the voltage drops, and when 1.8 volts is reached, the cell must be recharged. Unless this be done immediately the cell will deteriorate. The secondary cells forming a storage battery should be connected in series. For ignition service the battery capacity generally used is rated at 40 ampere hours. A battery of this capacity is composed of three cells having a total pressure of six volts.

A storage battery should be charged once every two months whether it be used or not. In charging, a direct current should be used—never an alternating one, care being taken to connect the positive wire to the positive terminal and the negative wire to the negative terminal. If connected in the reverse direction serious injury to the battery will result. The simplest method of charging is from an incandescent light circuit, using lamps connected in parallel to reduce the voltage to that of the battery, the current being adjusted by varying the number of lamps in the circuit. The group of lamps is connected in series with the battery to be charged, and the combination connected across the circuit furnishing the current. If the charging source be a 110-120 volt circuit, and the rate required be 6 amperes, twelve 16 c. p. or six 32 c. p. lamps, in parallel, and the group in series with the battery, will give the desired charging rate, unless special high efficiency lamps be used, when more will be required. In case a lower charging rate, say 2 amperes, be used, then a proportionately fewer number of lamps will be needed; but the length of time required to complete the charge will be correspondingly increased.

Instead of lamps, a rheostat is sometimes used. Its resistance should be such as to produce, when carrying the normal charging current, a drop in volts equal to the difference between the pressure of the charging source and that of the battery to be charged; thus, if a battery of three cells giving 6 volts, is to be charged from a 110-volt circuit at a 6-ampere rate, the resistance would be, according to Ohm's law,

$$\frac{110-6 \text{ volts}}{6 \text{ amperes}} = 17.3 \text{ ohms.}$$

The carrying capacity of the rheostat should be slightly in excess of the current required for charging the battery. An ammeter with suitable scale should be inserted in the battery circuit to indicate the quantity flowing. A battery should be charged at the rate given on the name plate on the case, until there is no further rise in its voltage and each cell has been gassing or bubbling freely for at least five hours, and there is also no further rise in the specific gravity of the electrolyte over the same period. The voltage at the end of the charge may be between 2.40 and 2.70 volts per cell, depending on the temperature and age; the higher voltages are obtained on new batteries with the temperature low; on old batteries at high temperatures the lower voltages are obtained.

It therefore must be understood that, in determining the completion of a charge, a fixed or definite voltage is not to be considered, but rather a maximum voltage, as indicated by there being no further rise in the voltage over a period of five hours. It is important that the charge be complete. The temperature of the electrolyte while charging should not be allowed to rise above 100° Fahr. Low temperatures do not injure a battery, but have the effect of temporarily reducing its discharge capacity.

The specific gravity of the electrolyte at the end of the charge should be 1.3. The specific gravity should not be altered when the battery is fully charged. After changing the gravity, the battery should be charged for an hour to thoroughly mix the liquid just added. To add water or electrolyte, or to remove surplus electrolyte, a rubber syringe is employed. A flame should not be brought near the battery during or immediately following the charge.

One of the destroying elements of storage batteries is *sulphation* of the plates. This *sulphate of lead* is deposited on the plates in the form of a very hard grayish coating. It is practically a non-conductor and in consequence plates so affected are rendered useless unless it be removed.

There are many causes for sulphation, among which are, too strong or too hot electrolyte, over discharging, etc. The most common cause of sulphation is over discharging. A battery that is discharged to a low point and then allowed to lie around unused for a considerable time would be destroyed by sulphation or rendered practically useless.

Local sulphation is caused by small particles of the active materials, which have become dislodged from the plates, catching in the separators which are used to prevent the plates from touching and forming a "bridge" between two plates and discharging them entirely. Sediment, which gradually accumulates in the bottom of the jars, should be removed before it reaches the bottom of the plates.

When the plates are sulphated the battery should be given a long slow charge at one-quarter the normal charging rate, till the electrolyte shows the proper specific gravity and the voltage has attained its maximum. The terminals and top of the cell should be kept free from acid, which will cause corrosion.

Verdigris which forms on the terminals is a poor conductor, hence, it should be removed and the terminals kept bright and clean to insure the proper flow of the current. The individual cells of a storage battery should be tested separately in order to determine if there be a weak cell in the circuit as such a cell would reduce the battery output.

Mechanical Generators.—The two methods of producing a current by mechanical means are, 1, by the use of dynamos, or, 2, by magnetos.

In any "field" such as that produced around and inside a coil of wire through which a current flows or between the poles of any magnet either electrical or permanent, there are *invisible lines of force,* which arrange themselves in a definite shape around and between the poles and if they be cut in any way by moving a wire across them, a current is produced in the wire and this current depends largely upon the number of these lines of force which are cut per second. It makes no difference whether

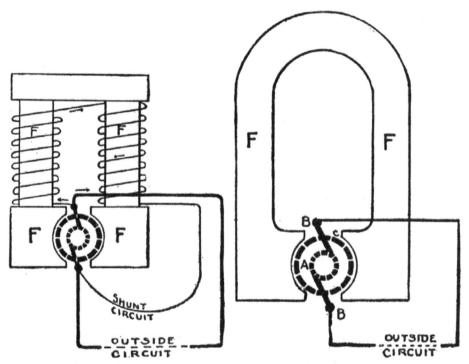

FIG. 185.—Circuit diagrams to illustrate the difference between a dynamo and a magneto. The former has its field magnets F F magnetized by means of a small current flowing around a shunt circuit. In a magneto the field magnets are permanently magnetized. The strength of the magnetic field of a magneto is constant while that of a dynamo varies with the output, hence, a magneto may be run at a widely varying speed and meet ignition requirements, but a dynamo must have its speed maintained approximately constant to keep the voltage within limits.

the wire be held stationary and the magnet and its field moved, or whether the wire itself be removed and the field held stationary. The result is the same so far as producing the current is concerned. The utilization of this principle is the basis upon which the mechanical producers of electricity—dynamos and magnetos—are made.

On account of the very general use of multi-cylinder engines for automobiles a strong impetus has been given to the employment of mechanical generators. When the current is generated by such means, it is not necessary to be economical in its use as the energy absorbed for ignition by a generator is very small.

Dynamos and Magnetos.—A dynamo differs from a magneto chiefly, in that it has field magnets of soft iron or mild steel, wound with wire through which circulates the whole or a portion of the current generated by the machine; a magneto, on the other hand, has field magnets constructed of steel and permanently magnetized.

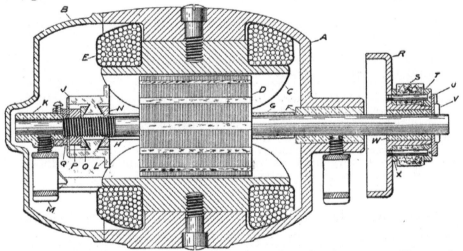

Fig. 186.—Sectional diagram of the Apple Igniting Dynamo. The parts shown are: A, cast iron body containing the moving parts; B, the hinged lid of the body; C, the one pole piece of one of the field magnets; F, brass bearing of the armature spindle; G and H, fibre tubes surrounding the spindle; K, brass spider supporting the spindle; L, commutator; M, wick feed oil cup; N, beveled nut supporting the commutator; O, P, Q, supports of the commutator; R, the driving disc; S, lever friction pinion. This machine can generate a direct current at 8 volts at a speed of between 1,000 and 1,200 revolutions per minute. It is provided with a simple centrifugal governor that automatically interrupts the driving connections when a certain speed has been exceeded.

The circuit diagrams, fig. 185, illustrate this difference. In the dynamos the field magnets FF are magnetized by means of a small current flowing around a shunt circuit; that is, a certain amount of current is taken from the system and used to magnetize the field. The remainder of the current generated is used in the outside circuit.

Dynamos.—The field magnets of a dynamo increase in strength as the current which passes around them increases.

Moreover, as the magnetic strength increases, the voltage of the generated current also becomes stronger. Hence, it is evident that a dynamo is not self-regulating, and if run at too high speed is liable to be overheated or even burned out in its effort to furnish a current beyond its capabilities, on account of this faculty of automatically strengthening its own fields.

Dynamos, therefore, cannot be driven at the widely varying speeds met with in the operation of an automobile. They require to be driven at an approximately uniform speed independent of the speed of the engine, hence a governor is necessary.

Motion is imparted to a dynamo by a very small wheel in frictional contact with the fly wheel of the engine. This frictional wheel is small enough to run the dynamo at full speed when the engine is turned slowly, as in cranking. As the engine speed increases, the governor acts, and maintains the speed of the dynamo unchanged.

A dynamo is generally used in connection with a storage battery for ignition purposes, the current for ignition being supplied by the battery, which in turn is constantly charged by the dynamo to replace the energy drawn from the battery for ignition. An automatic cut out is used which disconnects the dynamo from the battery when the engine stops, to prevent the battery from discharging through the engine. A voltmeter shows the condition of the battery at all times.

Magnetos.—These may be divided, with respect to the manner in which the current is generated, into two types, 1, those having rotating armatures and 2, those having stationary armatures with revolving inductors. Magnetos may be further divided with respect to the kind of current generated, into two classes, 1, low tension and 2, high tension. The latter class may be sub-divided into, 1, true high tension, 2, high tension with self-contained coil and, 3, high tension with separate coil. The last two types are strictly speaking not high tension magnetos.

Inductor Magnetos.—In this class of magnetos the armature is fixed so that it does not revolve and is located with the sector shaped heads of the core at right angles to the line joining the field poles. This position of the core furnishes the least magnetically conducting path. An annular space between the armature and the field poles is provided for the rotation of an *inductor.* This consists of two diametrically opposite cylindrical segments of soft iron supported and carried by a shaft located at the center of the circle described by the segments.

The magnetic condition of the armature core depends entirely upon the position of the inductor. The latter is arranged, 1, to revolve continuously with a gear drive from the engine or, 2, to rotate to and fro through a small arc by link connection to the half time shaft. An example of this type is shown in fig. 194 and later described in the paragraph on "Ignition with inductor magneto."

Low Tension Magnetos.—Generators of this class may be used to supply a current of low voltage for, 1, make and break ignition or for, 2, high tension ignition with induction coils or coil spark plugs. A low tension magneto has an armature winding consisting of about 150 to 200 turns of fairly thick wire, covered with a double layer of insulating material.

One end of the winding is grounded to the armature core and the other, brought to a single insulated terminal. When this terminal is connected to any metal part of the magneto or engine (since the latter is in metallic contact with the base of the magneto), the circuit is complete. The wiring therefore is very simple, which is one of the advantages of the system.

The "live end" of the armature winding is brought out by means of a metallic rod passing lengthways through the shaft of the armature; a hard rubber bushing is provided as insulation between the shaft and the rod. The live end of the winding is located at one end of the armature shaft, from which the current flows to an insulated terminal by means of a metal contact which is pressed against the revolving rod by a spring.

High Tension Magnetos.—The term high tension, as applied to magnetos, by popular usage, includes all magnetos which deliver a high tension current at their terminals.

They may be divided into three distinct classes: 1, those in which the induction secondary wiring is wound directly on the armature; 2, those having a secondary induction coil contained within the magneto, and 3, those having the coil in a separate box usually placed on the dash.

A high tension magneto of the second or third class is quite similar to the low tension type in that it generates a low tension current. This does not, however, pass directly to the cylinders, but instead, delivers the current to a secondary induction coil which consists of 1, a primary winding of a few turns of heavy insulated wire to which the low tension current is delivered and 2, a secondary winding surrounding the primary, and consisting of many turns of very fine insulated wire. The passage of the low tension current through the primary induces a high tension current in the secondary. This induced current has pressure enough to bridge the gap between the terminals of the spark plug.

A condenser is also inserted in the circuit to still further increase the tension of the induced current at the instant of sparking.

The current used for sparking must be delivered to the various cylinders in proper sequence. This is accomplished by a self contained timing device consisting of as many stationary contacts as there are cylinders, each connected by a cable to its cylinder spark plug. A rotary brush successively delivers current to each of these contacts.

Fig. 187 is a circuit diagram of a high tension magneto with a self-contained induction coil. A low tension current is generated in the winding A of the armature, which is rotated between two powerful and permanent magnets. The current flowing from the armature is an alternating one having two points of maximum density in each armature revolution.

As the current leaves the armature, it is offered two paths, 1, the shorter through the interrupter U to ground and 2, the longer through the primary P of the induction coil to ground. A third path through the condenser K is only apparently available; it is obstructed by the refusal of the condenser to permit the passage of the current as the condenser will merely absorb a certain amount of current at the proper moment, that is at the instant of the opening of the interrupter. The interrupter being closed the greater part of the time, allows the primary current to avail itself of the short path it offers. At the instant at which the greatest current intensity exists in the armature, the interrupter is opened mechanically, so that the primary current has no choice but must take the path through the primary P of the induction coil. A

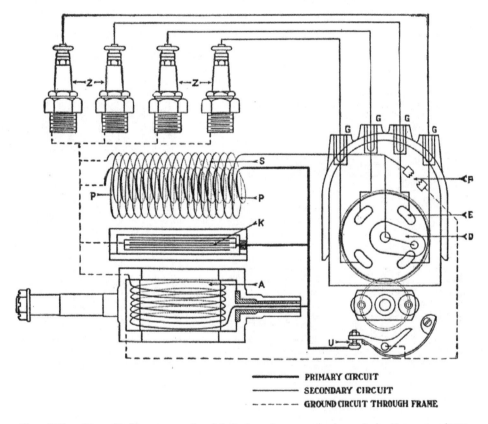

PRIMARY CIRCUIT

SECONDARY CIRCUIT

GROUND CIRCUIT THROUGH FRAME

FIG. 187.—Circuit diagram of a high tension magneto. A is the armature winding; P, primary of transformer; S, secondary of transformer; D, distributing brush carrier; E, contact segments; F, safety spark gap; G, terminals to plugs; U, interrupter; Z, spark plugs. The principles of operation are described in the text.

certain amount of current is at this instant also absorbed by the condenser K. This sudden rush of current into the primary P of the induction coil, induces a high tension current in the secondary winding S of the coil which has sufficient pressure to bridge the air gap of the spark plug.

The sharper the rush of current into the primary winding P, the more easily will the necessary intensity of current for a jump spark be induced in the secondary winding S.

The distribution of the current in proper sequence to the various engine cylinders is accomplished as follows: the high tension current induced in the secondary S of the induction coil is delivered to a distributing brush carrier D that rotates in the magneto at the same speed as the crank shaft of the engine. This brush carrier slides over insulated metal segments E—there being one for each cylinder. Each of these segments E connects

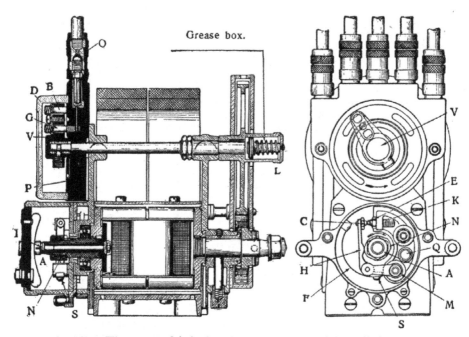

Fig. 188.—The Eisemann high tension magneto with coil in a separate box. Five terminals are shown in the end view; the central one is connected to the coil and the other four to the spark plugs. The two views show the parts as follows: A, cam nut; B, steel contact for high tension distributer; C, platinum contact for make and break lever; D, high tension distributer cover; E, nut for adjustable contact screw; F, spring for make and break lever; G, carbon contact for high tension distributer; H, make and break lever; I, low tension carbon brush; K, adjustable platinum contact screw; L, grease box for large toothed wheel; M, nut; N, cam; O, cable joints; P, distributer plate; Q, metal contact; S, screw for spring for make and break lever; V, high tension distributer.

with one of the terminal sockets that are connected by cable with the spark plugs as shown. At the instant of interruption of the primary current, the distributing brush is in contact with one of the metal segments E and so completes a current to that spark plug connected with this segment.

Should the circuit between the terminal G and its spark plug be broken, or the resistance of the spark plug be too great to permit a spark to jump, then the current might rise to an intensity sufficient to destroy the induction coil. To prevent this, what is known as a safety spark gap F is introduced. This will allow

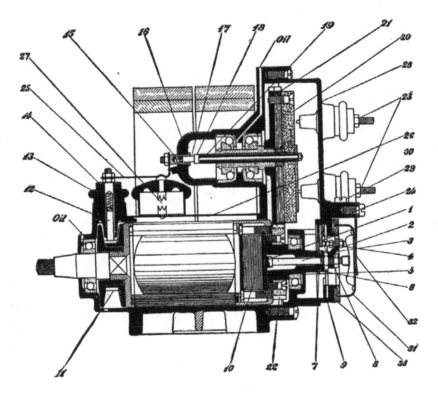

FIG. 189.—The Komet Magneto. The armature is speeded the same as the crank shaft for a four cylinder engine, and for a three or six cylinder engine the armature runs ¾ or 1½ times the crank shaft speed, respectively. The parts of this magneto are as follows: 1, brass plate; 2, brass stud; 3, contact piece; 4, platinum contact screw; 5, hard rubber disc; 6, hard rubber bushing; 7, interrupter spring; 8, platinum point; 9, interrupter disc; 10, condenser; 11, slide ring; 12, carbon brush; 13, carbon spring; 14, hard rubber carbon holder; 15, brass piece; 16, hard rubber cup; 17, carbon; 18, conductor of distributer; 19, hard rubber tube; 20, distributer disc; 21, distributer gear; 22, gear on armature; 23, high tension terminals; 24, timing lever; 25, spring to armature cover; 26, armature cover; 27, safety air gap; 28, distributer cover; 29, screw; 30, bracket; 31, brass cover; 32, spring; 33, fibre ring.

the current to rise only to a certain maximum, after which discharges will take place through this gap F. In construction the spark discharges over this gap are visible through a small glass window conveniently located.

Synchronous Drive.—For ignition purposes, magnetos are generally constructed to deliver an alternating current, that is, a current consisting of a succession of regularly alternating electrical impulses, varying in intensity from a plus maximum to a negative maximum and separated by points of zero pressure dependent upon the armature position with respect to the field. Hence, it is necessary that the generator, unless it run at high speed, should be driven *synchronously,* that is, at a .speed in a definite rate to that of the engine in order that the periods when a spark is desired shall coincide with the periods when sufficient voltage is being developed, as otherwise the sparking periods might occur with a zero point of electrical generation and no spark would be produced.

To meet these conditions the drive must be positive and may consist of either toothed wheel gears or chain and sprocket; the former is more desirable since, with a chain and sprocket drive, there is sufficient lost motion when the chain is loose enough for smooth running, to prevent the accurate timing of the spark.

The friction gear drive or belt and pulley are alike objectionable, from the fact that no slipping or variation is permissible. While some recent forms of high tension magneto are advertised to operate *asynchonously,* that is, not speeded in definite ratio to the engine, the common types are so made that the spark shall occur in the first cylinder at precisely the moment the magneto armature is at a certain point in its rotation. If, therefore, this condition be not strictly observed, the spark will be of defective intensity, and the control of the engine complicated.

Ignition Systems.—There are two systems in general use for igniting the charge by electricity:

1. The low tension or *make and break.*
2. The high tension or *jump spark.*

The low tension system is electrically simple and mechanically complex, while the high tension system is electrically complicated and mechanically simple.

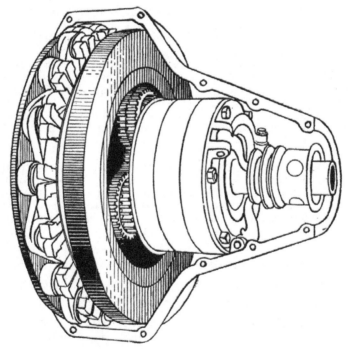

FIG. 190.—Plan view of the Ford combined fly wheel, magneto and planetary change gear. The magneto consists of a stationary spider, shown at the left, which carries 32 coils in which the currents are generated and a series of permanent revolving magnets attached to the fly wheel, the combination producing a low tension current which is used in the ordinary manner with coils, timer and spark plugs.

Low Tension Ignition.—In this system there is a device known as an *igniter,* placed in the combustion space of the engine cylinder. This consists of two electrodes, one of which is stationary and the other movable. The stationary electrode is insulated, while the other having an arm within the cylinder and placed conveniently near is capable of being moved from the outside so that the arm comes into contact with the stationary electrode and separates from the latter with great rapidity. This sudden breaking of the circuit produces an electric arc or *primary spark* caused by the inductance—that is, by the "inertia" or tendency of the current to continue flowing after the separation of the contact points.

The current may be derived from either a primary battery, storage battery or low tension magneto.

While it is possible to produce a spark by simply breaking a battery circuit, it is necessary in order to have a spark of sufficient intensity and duration to introduce into the circuit a *primary induction coil*—this is described in a later section. When a magneto is used, the coil is not necessary as the armature winding serves the same purpose. A magneto furnishing either direct or alternating current may be used; the voltage will depend on the armature speed and the strength of the magnets.

Iridium or platinum is used for contact points of the electrodes, as these metals resist the oxidizing effect of electricity and heat better than others.

In low tension ignition a considerable interval of time is required for the current to rise to its full value and the time of separation of the electrodes should not be sooner than the moment when the maximum current strength has been attained. When a magneto is used the current strength increases with the speed, hence the contact interval can be shorter at high speeds than when a battery is used.

Primary Induction Coils.—When an electric current flows along a coiled conductor, a *counter current* is induced which opposes any rapid change in the current strength. This principle is employed in low tension ignition to intensify the spark when a battery forms the current source. The device which accomplishes this effect is known as a *primary induction coil* and consists of a long iron core wound with a considerable length of low resistance copper wire, the length of the core and the number of turns of the insulated winding determining the efficiency. The current passing through the winding magnetizes the soft iron, and a self-induced current is generated. As soon as the circuit is broken, the magnetic reactance tends to continue the flow of current, despite the break in the circuit, and occasions a spark of great heat and brilliancy. The spark occurs at the moment of breaking the circuit, not at the moment of making.

The Low Tension Circuit.—The elements which compose a low tension or make and break circuit are as follows:

1. A source of current supply consisting of either a primary battery, accumulator or low tension magneto.

2. A primary induction coil when a battery is used.

3. An igniter.

4. A switch for breaking the circuit, and an additional switch to alternate between the battery and the magneto when both means of furnishing the current are provided.

5. Connecting conductors.

Fig. 191 shows a low tension system of a two cylinder engine having all the above elements.

Two sources of current supply are provided—a dry battery and a magneto. One terminal of both the battery and magneto is grounded; the other terminal A of the magneto M is connected to the point S of a threeway switch. The cells comprising the battery J are connected in series and the terminal not grounded is connected to a primary induction coil K and thence to the point T of the threeway switch. By moving the arm of this switch to the right or left, current may be had from the battery or magneto respectively. A conductor C connects the third point of the switch to the stationary or insulated electrode of each igniter, a single throw switch being placed at each igniter which allows either or both cylinders to be thrown out of the circuit at will. The movable electrodes and metal of the engine furnishes the ground return to the battery and magneto.

On a multi-cylinder engine it is evident that no other contact can be made at the moment of break in one cylinder since the current would then flow through any other igniter that might be in contact instead of producing a spark at the break.

The operation of the make and break system is as follows: Starting, say on the battery, the arm of the threeway switch is turned upon point T. The movable electrode D of the first cylinder being in contact with the insulated electrode B by the spring E, the current will flow from the battery J through the coil K, thence through the threeway switch and the single throw switch to the insulated electrode B. The movable electrode D being in contact with the insulated electrode B, the current returns to the battery through D and the metal of the engine, thus completing the circuit. As the cam G revolves in the direction indicated by the arrow, the rod F rises, which allows spring E to bring the movable electrode D into contact with the insulated electrode B, thus completing the circuit previously described. When the nose of cam G passes from under the lower end of F, the latter drops with great rapidity by the action of spring H and in so doing a shoulder at the upper end of F strikes the external arm of D a blow causing the contact point of D to be snapped apart from B. This cycle of operations is repeated by the ignition mechanism of each cylinder in rotation.

At the instant the circuit is broken by the separation of the contact points, the counter current induced in the coil K opposes any rapid change in the current strength, hence, the current continues to flow momentarily after the circuit is broken resulting in a *primary spark*. The action is the same as though the current possessed the property of "inertia," that is, time and resistance, both are necessary to bring it to a state of rest. This inertia effect is intensified by the action of the induction coil. When a magneto is used the armature windings serve the same purpose.

The timing of the spark is accomplished by the adjustable guides L, which serve to vary the horizontal position of the lower ends of the rods F and thus vary the instant at which their ends pass the nose of each cam.

In make and break ignition it is necessary in order to produce a good spark, that the "break" or separation of the contact points

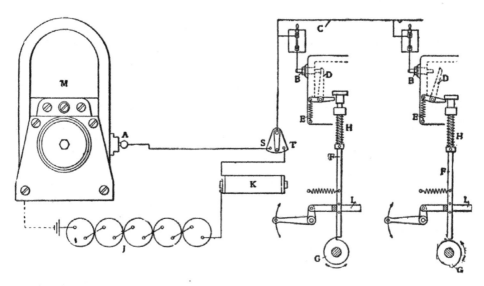

Fig. 191.—A low tension or make and break ignition system. In operation, as the nose of the cam G passes rod F, the latter suddenly drops by the action of spring H. The head of the rod, which has been raised by the cam somewhat above the arm of D, will in its descent strike D a blow which abruptly breaks contact between D and B, thus producing a spark. When not acted upon by the head of the rod F, D is held in contact with B by the Spring E. The system is explained in detail in the text.

of the igniter should take place with extreme rapidity, that is, the spring H should be sufficiently strong to cause the shoulder or rod F, when it falls, to strike the igniter arm a decided blow, thus quickly snapping apart the contact points.

Magnetic Spark Plugs.—The electrical advantages of low tension ignition are somewhat offset by the mechanical complication necessary to operate the igniter. In order to simplify the mechanism, a method has been devised for operating the electrodes of the igniter by magnetism. This is accomplished by a device known as a *magnetic spark plug* illustrated in fig. 192. A list of the parts is given under the figure.

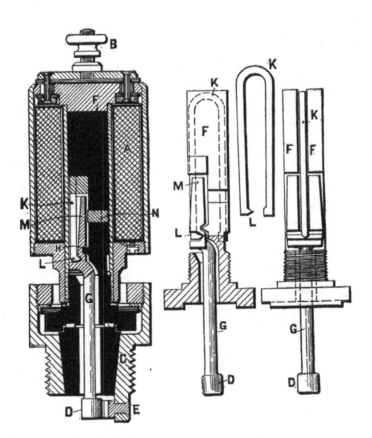

Fɪɢ. 192.—The Bosh magnetic spark plug. This consists of a coil A having one end connected to a terminal B, and the other to the plug casing C. A spark is produced when a separation takes place between the moving contact D and the stationary contact E. Within the plug is a metal core F and a swinging lever G, which lever pivots on the projection H which is a part of the core F. K shows a portion of a hair-pin spring, the end L of which rests in a recess within the lever G, the ordinary tension of the spring tending to hold the lower end of the lever G carrying the contact D against the stationary contact piece E.

The operation of the plug is as follows: when the timing device on the low tension magneto forms a contract for giving a spark to any cylinder, the circuit through the plug is through terminal B and the coil A, thence through C and back to the engine.

The completion of this circuit energizes the core F which tends to pull the upper end M of the lever G towards the right, but it is protected from contact with the core by the non-magnetic brass plug N. The pulling of the upper end of the lever G to the right carries the lower end to the left, separating it from the stationary contact E, thereby breaking the circuit. Immediately the circuit is broken the coil A surrenders its electro-magnetic power, the core F is demagnetized and the end of the hair-pin spring L forces the lower end of the lever G to the right, as the spring L, exerts its pressure beneath the fulcrum H and which brings the contacts D and E together.

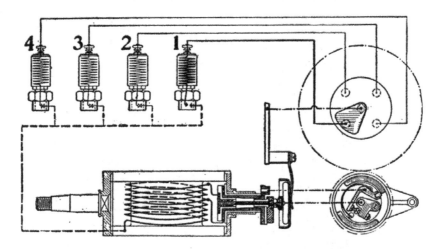

Fig. 193.—Wiring diagram of a low tension system with magnetic spark plugs. A portion of the wiring of the magneto armature is short circuited by the platinum points of the interrupter, and when the circuit is broken, the resulting armature reaction has the effect of raising the armature voltage sufficiently to operate the plugs.

At the bottom of the contact piece there is an insulated fixed stem which is magnetically divided in about the middle by means of a brass part, so that when the current passes through the coil A only the portion of the stem above the brass part can be magnetized and, as a result of this magnetization the upper end M of the interrupter lever G, which directly faces the magnetized part, is attracted, the lower end D simultaneously breaking contact with the contact piece E, thus interrupting the current and producing a spark. In the normal position of the interrupter lever G, the lower end presses against the contact piece E, being kept in that position by the horseshoe shaped spring K, which passes right over the top of the stem and lies in slots in the sides.

The top of the coil is fitted with a terminal screw to which the current from the magneto is led. Current may also be taken from a primary or secondary battery. In this case a *timer* on the engine is necessary to distribute the current to the cylinders in proper sequence.

Fig. 193 shows the magnetic spark plug connections for a four cylinder engine. The current is supplied by a low tension magneto.

A portion of the wiring of the armature is short circuited by the platinum points of the interrupter, and when the circuit is interrupted, the resulting armature reaction has the effect of raising the voltage of the armature sufficiently to operate the magnetic plugs. The rotating distributing bar is adjusted in such a way that it is always in connection with

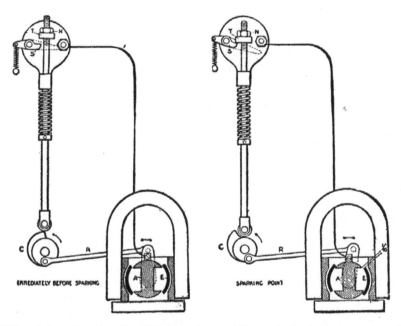

Fig. 194.—A low tension ignition system with an inductor magneto of the oscillating type. The inductor E is rotated to and fro by means of a link R, one end of which is attached to the inductor crank, and the other to the igniter cam C. Two views are shown: immediately before and after sparking. S is the grounded electrode of the igniter; T an adjustable hammer which is secured in position by a lock nut N.

one of the spark plugs at the moment when the contact breaker of the magneto interrupts the circuit, so that the circuit to the plugs is closed and these are magnetized for operation.

The spark is advanced or retarded by rotating the timing lever, in the same manner as with a high tension magneto, and the timing range corresponds to an angle of 50 degrees on the armature shaft. The magneto is switched off in the same manner as a high tension magneto, by making a ground connection. This is done by small plug switches with either a single plug or with a number of plugs equal to the number of cylinders, to enable each cylinder to be switched out separately for testing purposes, from the seat while the car is in motion.

Ignition with Inductor Magneto.—In this system of low tension ignition, the current is furnished by a magneto having a stationary armature and a rotating inductor as before described. The inductor is arranged to either revolve continuously or to oscillate through a small arc. An example of the latter type is shown in fig. 194 which illustrates the Simms-Bosch System.

In the figure, the mechanism is shown in two positions—immediately before and after sparking. The cam which operates the make and break igniter has a link connection to the inductor crank of the magneto which gives an oscillating motion to the inductor. The connection is such that at the instant of "break" the inductor cuts through the greatest number of magnetic lines.

The cam C, on the half time shaft, makes a contact just before sparking, and immediately breaks it again by permitting the hammer T to fall on the cam S. A spark is produced at the instant of break of contact at N.

The winding of the armature A has one end grounded through the base of the magneto, the current returning through the engine to the point S; the other end of the winding is led through an insulated post to the nut N by which it is connected with a stud brought through the cylinder wall, where a wiper, indicated by dotted outline, normally rests against it by means of a spring.

High Tension Ignition.—In this method of producing a spark, a device called a *spark plug* is employed. This consists of two stationary electrodes, one of which is grounded to the engine cylinder and the other insulated. The points of the electrodes are permanently separated from each other by about 1/32 of an inch, the space between the points being known as an *air gap.* This space offers so much resistance to the flow of an electric current that a very high pressure is required to cause the current to burst through the air gap and produce a spark, hence the term "high tension ignition."

Since the spark jumps from one electrode to the other, this method of igniting the charge is also known as the *jump spark* system. The spark itself is properly described by the prefix *high tension* or *secondary*.

In the production of the spark two distinct circuits are necessary, 1, a low tension or *primary* circuit and 2, a high tension or *secondary* circuit. The current which flows through the low tension circuit is called the *primary current* and that which it *induces* in the high tension circuit, the *secondary current.*

IGNITION.

In order to obtain the high pressure required to produce a spark, a device known as a *secondary induction coil* is used which transforms the primary current of low voltage and high amperage into a secondary current of high voltage and low amperage, that is, the quantity of the current is decreased and its pressure increased.

The general principles upon which high tension or jump spark ignition is based are as follows:

An automatic device is placed in the primary circuit which closes and opens it at the time a spark is required. When the circuit is closed, the primary current flows through the primary winding of the coil and causes a secondary current to be induced in the secondary winding. The spark plug being included in the secondary circuit opposes the flow of the current by the high resistance of its air gap. Since the pressure of the secondary current is sufficient to overcome this resistance, it flows or "jumps" across the gap and in so doing intense heat is produced resulting in a spark.

Sometimes the spark is obtained by keeping the primary circuit closed except during the brief interval necessary for the passage of the spark at the plug points. A secondary spark, then, may be produced by either open or closed circuit working, that is, the primary circuit may be kept either opened or closed during the intervals between sparks.

The automatic device which controls the primary current to produce a spark by the first method is called a *contact maker* and by the second method, a *contact breaker*. A closed primary circuit with a contact breaker is used to advantage on small engines run at very high speed as it allows time for the magnetism or magnetic flux in the core of the coil to attain a density sufficient to produce a good spark. The word *timer* is usually applied to any device which controls the primary current, when it controls both the primary and secondary currents, as in *synchronous ignition* it is called a *distributer*. Before explaining the different systems of high tension ignition the several devices used, such as induction coils, spark plugs, etc., will be described in some detail.

Secondary Induction Coils.—In order to obtain the high voltage necessary to produce a secondary spark, a device called a secondary induction coil is used. This transforms the primary low tension current into a secondary high tension current. There are two varieties of these coils:

1. Plain or non-vibrator coil.
2. Vibrator coil.

A plain or single spark coil consists of three parts, 1, an iron core, 2, a primary winding and 3, a secondary winding.

The core of the coil consists of a bundle of soft iron wires, about six or seven inches long and in sufficient number to make the diameter of the core about three quarters of an inch. The reason that a bundle of wires is used for the core instead of a solid rod is that the wire core can be more rapidly magnetized and demagnetized. The core is covered with an insulation of paper, vulcanite or other material, around which is wound the primary coil which consists of two or three layers of coarse insulated wire. Sometimes a light insulation is placed over the primary winding, around which is wound the secondary coil consisting of from ten thousand to fifteen thousand turns of very fine wire insulated by a silk covering. It is usual to place between each layer of the secondary winding, a layer of paraffined paper. This insures the insulation.

The coil is placed in a neat and substantial box and the terminals of the windings are connected to binding posts placed on the outside.

The operation of the coil is as follows: when an electric current is passed through the primary winding, it magnetizes the core which produces a magnetic field in the surrounding space. Any increase or decrease of current in the primary winding induces a current in the secondary winding; *this induced current lasts only during the time of increase or decrease of the primary current.*

Now, the pressure of the current induced in the secondary circuit depends upon the ratio between the number of turns of the two windings,

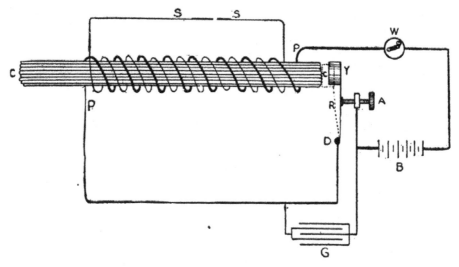

FIG. 195.—Diagram of a vibrator coil. The parts are as follows: A, contact screw; B, battery; C, core; D, vibrator terminal; G, condenser; P, primary winding; S, secondary winding; W, switch; Y, vibrator. When the switch is closed, the following cycle of actions take place: (a) the primary current flows and magnetizes core; (b) magnetized core attracts the vibrator and breaks primary circuit; (c) the magnetism vanishes, inducing a momentary high tension current in the secondary winding; (d) magnetic attraction of the core having ceased, vibrator spring re-establishes contact; (e) primary circuit is again completed and the cycle begins anew.

upon the sizes of wires used and also upon the rate of variation of the current strength in the primary circuit. For instance, if the primary winding contains one hundred turns and the secondary ten thousand turns, the voltage of the secondary circuit will be nearly one hundred times that of the primary.

In a plain coil the primary current is made and broken once for each spark by a *timing device* on the engine. At every "make" the field of force of each turn in the coil grows rapidly, and cuts the neighboring turns, inducing an electromotive force that opposes the increase of the current. On the other hand, at every "break," the primary field rapidly vanishes, the lines again cutting the turns, but in a manner that tends to oppose the decrease of the current.

This opposition to any rapid change in the current strength is called *self-induction.* The current which produces the spark occurs at the time of break and since the strength of this current depends upon the rapidity with which the strength of the primary current falls a timing device is used, which is so constructed that the break will occur very abruptly.

The view has been held by some that a series of sparks occurring with great rapidity is more effective for ignition than the single spark produced by the plain coil. This led to the development and use of the *vibrator coil,* though opinion differs as to the relative merits of the two systems.

A vibrator coil contains in addition to the two windings of the plain coil, a magnetic vibrator and a condenser. The object of the vibrator is to rapidly make and break the primary circuit during the time in which the battery is switched into the circuit by the timer. It consists of a flat steel spring secured at one end, with the other free to vibrate. At a point about midway between its ends contact is made with the point of an adjusting screw, from which it springs away and returns in vibrating. The points of contact of blade and screw are tipped with platinum. One wire of the primary circuit is connected to the blade and the other to the screw, hence, the circuit is made when the blade is in contact with the screw and broken when it springs away.

A condenser is used to absorb the self-induced current of the primary winding and thus prevent it from opposing the rapid fall of the primary current. Every conductor of electricity forms a condenser and its capacity for absorbing a charge depends upon the extent of its surface. Hence, a condenser is constructed of conductive material so arranged as to present the greatest surface for a given amount of material. The usual form of condenser for induction coils is composed of a number of layers of tin foil, separated by paraffin paper, each alternate layer being connected at the ends.

Fig. 195 is a diagram of a vibrator coil, CC represents the core composed of soft iron wires. PP is the primary winding and SS the secondary. There is no connection between these windings and they are carefully insulated. Y is the vibrator or *trembler* and D the centre about which Y vibrates. W is a switch used for opening and closing the primary circuit; B, a battery of five cells. The point of the adjusting screw A rests against a platinum point R soldered upon the vibrator.

If the switch W be closed, the electric current generated by the battery B will flow through the primary winding. This will cause the core CC to become magnetized, and the vibrator Y will at once be drawn towards it. This will break the connection at R. The core, being made of soft iron, immediately upon the interruption of the current, will again lose its magnetism, and the vibrator will return to its original position. This again closes the circuit, after which the operation of opening and closing it is repeated with great rapidity so long as the switch W remains closed.

The cycle of actions may be briefly stated as follows:

1. A primary current flows and magnetizes the core.

2. The magnetized core attracts the vibrator which breaks the primary circuit.

3. The core loses its magnetism and the vibrator springs back to its original position.

4. The vibrator, by returning to its original position closes the primary circuit and the cycle begins again.

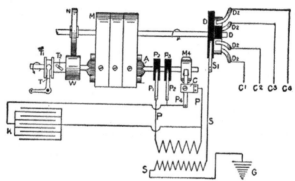

FIG. 196.—Circuit Diagram of the Eisemann High-tension Magneto. A, armature; C, primary circuit breaker; C_1, C_2, C_3, C_4, high-tension leads to cylinders; D, high-tension distributor disc; D_1, D_2, D_3, D_4, distributor wipe contacts; G, primary ground on metal of engine; K, condenser; M, permanent magnets; N, gear on distributor shaft; P, P, primary circuit of induction coil; P_1, P_2, wipe contacts on distributor rings of primary circuit; S, S, secondary circuit; T, bell crank for timing; T_1, spool in which bell crank works; T_2, slotted sleeve on driven shaft; W, gear on driven shaft.

Many types of vibrators are used on induction coils, the most important requirement being that the break occur with great rapidity. In order to render the break as sudden as possible, different expedients have been resorted to, all tending to make the mechanism more complicated, yet having sufficient merit in most cases to warrant their adoption.

In the plain vibrator, the circuit is broken at the instant the spring begins to move, hence the operation must be comparatively slow. In order to render the break more abrupt some vibrators have two moving parts, one of which is attracted by the magnetic core of the coil and moved a certain distance before the break is effected. A vibrator of this type is shown in fig. 197 and described under the illustration.

IGNITION.

When a vibrator coil is used, the success or failure of the ignition system depends largely upon the proper adjustment of the vibrator. The following general instructions for adjusting a plain vibrator should be carefully noted:

1. Remove entirely the contact adjusting screw.

2. See that the surfaces of the contact points are flat, clean and bright.

3. Adjust the vibrator spring so that the hammer or piece of iron on the end of the vibrator spring stands normally about one-sixteenth of an inch from the end of the coil.

4. Adjust the contact screw until it just touches the platinum contact on the vibrator spring—be sure that it touches, but very lightly. Now start the engine; if it misses at all, tighten up, or

FIG. 197.—A hammer vibrator. When at rest, the upward tension of the spring, which carries the Armature A, holds the platinum points in contact and causes the upper spring, C, to leave shoulder of Adjusting screw, D, and rest against the heavy brass plate above it. When the iron core, B, attracts the Armature, A, the downward tension on the upper spring, C, causes the latter to follow the Armature down, holding the platinum points in contact, until the end of the upper spring, C, strikes the lower shoulder of the adjusting screw, D, which gives it a "hammer break." The adjusting screw is held firmly in position by a bronze spiral spring under shoulder D.

screw in the contact screw a trifle further—just a trifle at a time, until the engine will run without missing explosions.

In adjusting the vibrator the coil ought not to use over one-half ampere of current.

Most spark coils have terminals marked "battery," "ground," etc., and to short circuit the timer for the purpose of testing the vibrator it is only necessary to bridge with a screw driver from the "battery" binding post to the "ground" binding post.

A half turn of the adjusting screw on a coil will often increase the strength of the current four or five times the original amount, hence the necessity of carefully adjusting the vibrator. When the adjustment is not properly made it causes, 1, short life of the battery, 2, burned contact points, and 3, poor running of the engine.

In adjusting a multi-unit coil, if any misfiring be noticed, hold down one vibrator after another until the faulty one is located, then screw in its contact screw very slightly.

The number of cells in the circuit should be proportioned to the design of the coil. If the coil be described by the maker as a 4 volt coil, it should be worked by two cells of a storage battery or four dry cells. The voltage of the latter will be somewhat higher, but since their internal resistance is also greater, the current delivery will be about the same. Most coils are made to operate on from 4 to 6 volts. It is a mistake to use a higher voltage than that for which the coil is designed, because it does not improve the spark and the contact points of the vibrator will be burned more rapidly, moreover the life of the battery will be shortened.

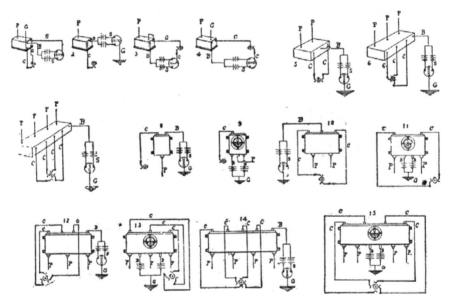

FIG. 198.—Wiring diagrams showing connections of some standard spark coils. Key: B—to Battery; C—to Commutator or Timer; G—to Ground (Engine Frame); P—to Plug; S—to Switch. 1—6 Terminal Standard Non-Vibrator Coil; 2—3 Terminal Standard Vibrator Coil; 3 and 4—4 Terminal Standard Vibrator Coils; 5—Standard Double Vibrator Coil; 6—Standard Triple Vibrator Coil; 7—Standard Quadruple Vibrator Coil; 8—Single Dash Coil; 9—Single Dash Coil with Switch; 10—Double Dash Coil; 11—Double Dash Coil with Switch; 12—Triple Dash Coil; 13—Triple Dash Coil with switch; 14—Quadruple Dash Coil; 15—Sextuple Dash Coil.

Timers.—In order that the spark may occur at the proper instant with respect to the crank position, there must be included in all high tension systems, a device called a *timer* for closing and opening the primary circuit. This causes an induced high tension current to flow at the instant the spark is required.

A timer is simply a revolving switch operated by the engine. It is geared to revolve at one-half the engine speed in the case of a four cycle engine and at full engine speed for a two cycle engine.

All timers consist of a *stationary part* and a revolving part or *rotor*. The former is usually made of a ring of hard rubber, into the inner face of which, is let contact segments forming *insulated contacts;* one of these

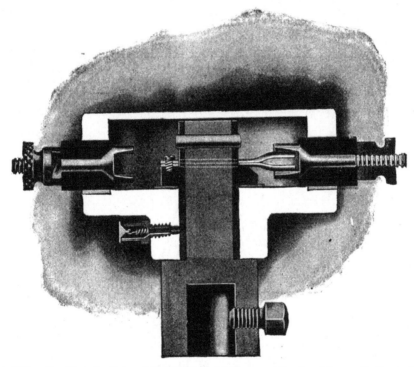

FIG. 199.—Sectional view of the Pittsfield timer. Contact is made by means of phosphor bronze springs which revolve on the timer shaft and engage with stationary contacts, set in the timer ring and insulated by hard rubber. A set screw fitted to the lower end of the revolving part allows it to be placed on the time shaft of any engine.

is provided for each cylinder of the engine. The rotor has an arm which makes contact with all the insulated segments during one revolution. A vertical shaft geared to the engine imparts motion, by direct connection to the rotor and forms, with the rotor arm, the *ground connection* of the primary circuit. The other wire of the primary circuit for each cylinder is connected to each stationary contact.

Hence, during one revolution of the timer arm the primary circuit is made and broken once for each cylinder in the proper sequence.

In order that the spark may be advanced or retarded, that is, made to occur earlier or later, the timer must be so arranged that the stationary contacts may engage at a different time with respect to the engine cycle. This is accomplished by constructing the stationary part of the timer so that it may rotate around the shaft through a small arc. This movement is controlled by a lever on the steering column.

There are several kinds of contacts used in timers, such as, brush, roller, and sliding contacts.

A brush contact consists of a brass brush which bears upon a commutator containing a metal segment with which it makes contact as the commutator revolves.

A roller contact consists of a roller, attached to the end of an arm which is pivoted to the revolving part of the timer; at the other end of the arm is a spring whose tension causes the roller in revolving to bear firmly against the stationary segments.

A sliding contact consists of a spring actuated device on the revolving arm which rubs against the stationary contacts. An example of this type is shown in section in fig 199. The revolving contact consists of two phosphor bronze springs, which make contact by sliding between the two projecting arms of the stationary terminal as shown in the illustration.

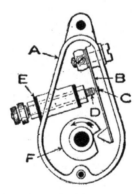

Fig. 200.—A contact maker and mechanical vibrator. The case, A, is usually attached to the gear box of the engine; B is the vibrator blade; C, a platinum contact point; D, an insulated adjusting screw; E, a bushing with insulation; F, the operating cam. As this cam revolves the weight on the end of blade, B, drops into the recess on the cam causing the blade to vibrate and make a number of contacts with D, thus producing a series of sparks when in operation.

Among the special forms of timers, is one with two sets of contact segments and contact brushes, forming practically a double timer on a single shaft and in a single casing. The object of this design is to use one set of segments for all ordinary engine speeds and the other for high speeds, and thus to obviate waste of current at low speeds. It is well known that in order for the coil vibrator to operate properly at the highest speed of the motor the timer segments must be made to subtend a considerable arc, usually forty-five degrees in a timer for a four cylinder engine. This is a larger arc of contact than is required for normal speed. Suppose, for instance, that it suffices for a speed of 2,100 revolutions per minute, then the length of contact at 700 revolutions, which would probably correspond nearly to the average speed of the motor, would be three times as long as necessary, and there would be a corresponding waste of current. Hence, a variable contact arc is necessary for economy of current.

As constructed. one set of segments give a contact of 15° and the other set 45.° Either set may be brought into use by a switch having two positions marked "touring" and "speed," the short segments being used for slow speed and the long segments for high speed.

In addition to the three methods of closing and opening the primary circuit, as just described, this operation is also accomplished by simply touching the contact points. There are two classes of timing devices which work on this principle, viz:

1. Contact makers.
2. Contact breakers.

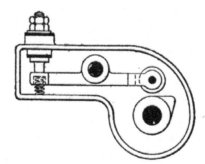

Fig. 201.—A contact breaker. This device keeps the circuit closed at all times except during the brief interval necessary for the passage of the spark at the plug points. Used to advantage on engines running at very high speeds, as it allows time for the magnetic flux in the core of the coil to attain a density sufficient to produce a good spark.

Fig. 200 shows one form of contact maker which serves also to illustrate what is known as a *mechanical vibrator.*

The case A is usually connected to the gear box of the engine. A flat steel spring B is attached to A. An insulated screw D is so adjusted that it does not touch the platinum point C of the blade B unless acted upon by the cam. As the cam F revolves in the direction indicated by the arrow, it comes into contact with a metal nose attached to the end of the blade B.

Shortly before the cam has arrived at the position shown in the figure, the pressure due to the action of the spring causes the nose to suddenly drop into the depression in the cam. Its momentum carries it past its normal position and the point C makes contact with the insulated screw. The metal nose, on account of its weight, will cause the blade B to vibrate, bringing the contact points together several times before the cam again engages the nose. This form of contact maker, is called a mechanical vibrator.

In the plain form of contact maker the circuit is closed and opened once only for each revolution of the cam, which in this case has a projection or nose on its circumference instead of a sharp depression. This engages the contact blade and presses it against the insulated screw to close the circuit.

Since the operation of a contact maker keeps the circuit closed for only a short interval, it has been found necessary, with some forms of high speed engines, to keep the battery and coil in a closed circuit, except during the brief interval necessary for the passage of the spark. This allows the needed time for the magnetic flux of the core of the magnet to attain a sufficient density to induce a secondary current of the required strength. A device known as a *contact breaker* is used for this closed circuit working.

One form of contact breaker is shown in fig. 201. At the left of the figure is an insulated screw. One end of a pivoted lever is kept in contact with the screw by a spring as shown, except at the time of the spark. A roller is attached to the other end of the lever, directly below which is a cam. When the nose of the cam engages with the roller, the contact points quickly separate, thus breaking the circuit and producing a spark.

Distributers.—When one secondary coil only is used with a multi-cylinder engine as in synchronous ignition, a device called a distributer is a necessary part of the system. Its use is to direct the discharge of a single coil to the spark plug of each cylinder in rotation. A distributer consists of a timer for the primary current and a similar device working synchronously, that is, in step with the timer and which switches the secondary current to the various spark plugs in the proper order of firing.

In other words, a distributer is a combination of two timing devices working in unison with each other; one makes and breaks the primary circuit, while the other makes and breaks the secondary circuit and in so doing distributes the current to the several cylinders in correct sequence.

The spark is advanced or retarded by the same method employed with a timer as previously explained.

The primary element of a distributer contains as many stationary contacts as there are cylinders and a revolving arm or *rotor* which in its revolution touches each of the stationary contacts so that the primary circuit is made and broken once for each cylinder during one revolution of the arm.

The secondary element is above and concentric with the primary part. It has a rotor and the same number of stationary contacts as the primary element; the parts of both elements are arranged synmetrically with each other and are contained in a compact cylindrical casing. A shaft geared to the engine operates both the primary and secondary rotors.

The primary rotor is in metallic contact with the shaft and forms with it and the engine a ground return for the primary circuit.

The secondary rotor is carefully insulated. All the primary stationary contacts are connected to one common terminal which receives the primary lead. A binding post is provided for each of the secondary stationary contacts and one for the secondary rotor. These binding posts are usually placed on the top part of the casing.

Fig. 202 is a sectional view of a modern distributer, which differs in some respects from the foregoing description. The primary element

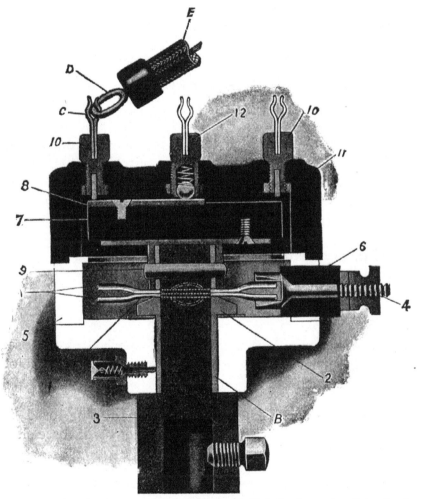

Fig. 202.—Sectional view of the Pittsfield distributer. In this device several revolving contacts are employed instead of one; these consist of a double spring making sliding contact at the portions, A. The parts are: 1, contact springs; 2, shaft; 3, bushing; 4, stationary terminal; 5, timer ring; 6, stationary contact insulation; 7, distributer plate; 8, secondary revolving contact segment; 9, taper pin; 10, secondary stationary terminals; 11, casing; 12, secondary terminal for lead to coil; B, slide bearings; C, hook; D, eye; E, secondary cable. The operation of this distributer is described in the text.

consists of two springs, 1, fastened to the shaft 2. The latter is fitted at its lower end with a bushing 3 containing two set screws to secure it to the timer shaft of the engine. It should be noted that instead of having a stationary contact 4, for each cylinder, only one is provided, but there are additional revolving contacts A so that the current is made and broken once for each cylinder during one revolution of the rotor. To the shaft 2, is fitted a hard rubber distributer plate 7, with segment 8, by taper pin 9. As soon as the springs 1 make contact with the terminal 4, segment 8 comes in contact with one of the terminals 10, inserted in the casing 11. The wiring and operation of the distributer system is later explained under "synchronous ignition."

In some types of distributers an auxiliary spark gap is included in the design. The secondary rotor is arranged so that it does not actually touch the stationary segments but terminates very closely to them, the current being required to jump through the short gap intervening between the arm and segments. This space acts as an *auxiliary spark gap.*

Spark Plugs.—In all high tension ignition systems a *permanent air gap* is placed in the secondary circuit across which the current must jump to produce a spark. The device by which this permanent air gap is maintained is called a *spark plug.* There are several varieties of these as follows:

> Primary or magnetic make and break plugs.
> Secondary plugs.
> Duplex plugs.
> Coil plugs.

The primary plug has already been described in that section of this chapter devoted to low tension ignition devices; the others will now be explained.

Secondary Spark Plugs.—This type of plug used for a secondary or high tension spark plug is made up of three elements as follows:

1. A ground electrode.
2. An insulated electrode.
3. Insulating material separating the two.

The construction of a few typical spark plugs is shown in fig. 203.

In general, the construction is as follows:

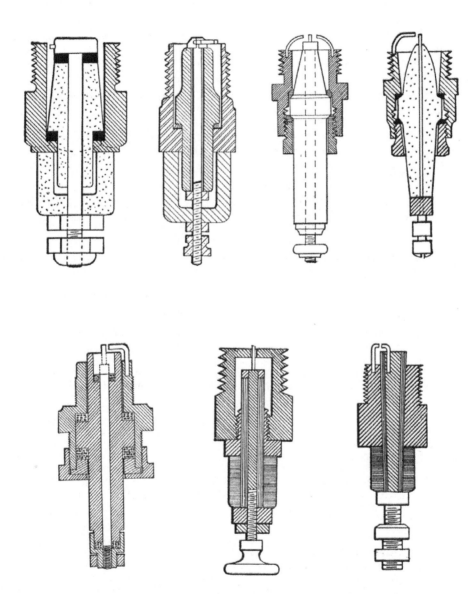

FIG. 203.—Sections of well known spark plugs. The first five have porcelain insulation; the last two, mica.

1. The *ground electrode* is attached to a metal cup which has an external thread so that it may be screwed into the metal of the cylinder, thus forming the ground connection of the secondary circuit.

2. The *insulated electrode* consists of a thin metal rod located in the center of the plug, and whose end is separated from the ground electrode by about one thirty-second of an inch. The space between the terminals of the two electrodes is called the *air gap.*

3. The *insulating material,* forming the third element mentioned, is usually of porcelain or mica and cylindrical in shape. It is retained firmly within the metal cup which separates the two electrodes by a threaded bushing.

Failure of the insulation may occur from several causes. It sometimes happens that:

1. The material becomes covered with a coating of soot which, possessing considerable conductivity, affords an easier path for the current than the air gap.

2. The material becomes saturated with conducting matter, thus reducing its efficiency and causing a liability of short circuits.

Porcelain is well suited for insulating material, since it possesses a very high resistance both to heat and to the electric current. In fact, a high quality of porcelain should not break down with either the heat or the electrical tension encountered in gas engine operation. That porcelains are broken under such conditions is due to uneven heating of the insulating tube or to some unexpected violence. The brittleness of porcelain is the most serious objection to its use. Lower qualities of porcelain are, of course, much more easily broken, and thereby produce short circuiting under ordinary conditions of temperature and electrical tension. Many plugs using porcelain insulation have the porcelain in two or more parts, so as to avoid the troubles arising from uneven temperatures. Heat is liable to break a single long porcelain.

Mica is an ideal insulator, except for the fact that it frequently contains impurities which reduce its insulating efficiency, and also because, owing to its laminated structure, oil and gas may be forced by the pressure of compression between the sheets composing the insulating sheath, thus, in time, producing short circuiting of the current. Most mica insulated plugs having the inner spindle sheathed with concentric coats of mica have also a cap at the end of the sheath to protect it and to insure the attachment of the spindle.

In many modern spark plugs there is an annular clearance between the insulating material and the inside of the metal cups. In some plugs an additional annular clearance is provided between the insulating material and the insulated electrode. This is provided for the purpose of reducing the danger by short circuit by leaving a larger space between the two electrodes than will ordinarily be filled with soot. According to some designers, it also insures a vortex for the gases, circulating in the combustion chamber, under the impulse of the piston strokes, thus expelling a large part of the deposits.

Duplex Spark Plug.—These are designed to work on a metallic circuit, that is, one in which the secondary current is carried by a visible lead and not grounded at any point. This type consists of a double plug constructed so that both electrodes are insulated as illustrated in fig. 204.

Coil Spark Plugs.—A plug of this class consists of an ordinary plug combined with a plain secondary induction coil. The latter is superposed on the plug and contained in a cylindrical casing, the vibrator and condenser being located in a separate box; the object in this case being to minimize the secondary leakage, to have all parts easily accessible, and to simplify the wiring.

FIG. 204.—A duplex or double spark plug. Unlike other plugs, the secondary circuit is carried by visible leads, and is not grounded at any point.

Sparking Pressure.—A current of very high voltage is required to produce a secondary or jump spark on account of the great resistance of the air gap and compression pressure which oppose the current flow.

The required voltage will depend on the length of the air gap and the intensity of the pressure inside the cylinder. For ordinary spark plugs in air the sparking pressure will vary from about 3,000 to 5,000 volts according to the length of the gap, but to produce a spark in an engine cylinder where the mixture has been compressed to four or five times the atmospheric pressure, will require from 10,000 to 20,000 volts.

When a spark plug will not work, the electrodes and insulating material should be thoroughly cleaned with fine sandpaper and the distance between the points adjusted to about one thirty-second of an inch, or the thickness of a ten cent silver piece. To increase the gap between the points, a knife blade can be used to advantage. If the battery be weak, the gap may be made smaller—about one sixty-fourth of an inch.

Spark plugs are often damaged by placing a wrench upon the top or lock nut. The plug should be screwed in just tight enough to prevent leakage. An extra spark plug should be carried as an accessory.

Safety Air Gap.—It is usual to fit high tension magnetos with a device called a safety air gap. Should the resistance of the spark plug become too great to permit a spark to jump, the voltage of the secondary current might rise to an intensity sufficient to destroy the coil. To avoid this, an air gap is introduced in the secondary circuit connected in parallel. This allows the pressure to rise only to a certain maximum after which a discharge will take place through the safety gap.

Auxiliary Air Gap.—This consists of two adjustable electrodes, having their terminals slightly separated and placed in

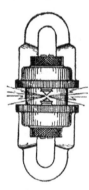

the secondary circuit in series with the plug. Its object is to prevent any leakage of current in case of defective plug insulation by preventing the flow of the secondary current until the voltage has been raised enough to suddenly break down the resistance of the auxiliary gap and also that of the plug. This results in a discharge through the air gap of plug instead of over the sooted surfaces of the plug insulation.

As usually constructed, the auxiliary air gap consists of two adjustable electrodes, set into a short piece of glass tubing as shown in fig. 205.

FIG. 205.— An auxiliary air gap.

High Tension Ignition Circuits.—In any jump spark system, two distinct circuits are necessary:

1. A primary or low tension circuit.

2. A secondary or high tension circuit.

The primary circuit is composed of, 1, a source of current supply, 2, a timer, 3, a switch and 4, the primary winding of an induction coil. These elements are joined in series, the circuit being completed by a ground return.

The secondary circuit includes 1, the spark plug and 2, the secondary winding of the coil. One end of the secondary winding is connected to the insulated electrode of the spark plug; the other end is grounded to the metal of the engine; as illustrated in fig. 207 to be described in detail later.

In high tension ignition, there are several systems among which may be mentioned those using:

1. Plain coils with contact makers or contact breakers.
2. Plain coils with mechanical vibrators.
3. Vibrator coils.
4. Plain coils with master vibrators.
5. Single coils with distributers: *synchronous ignition.*

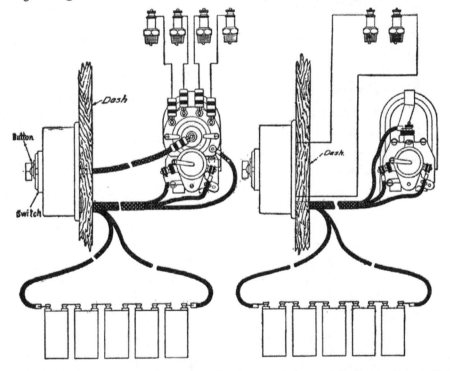

FIG. 206.—Remy wiring diagrams for two and four cylinder motors. This dual ignition system consists of a Remy high tension magneto, battery, coil, and one set of spark plugs. The special coil furnished with the magneto is fitted with a two point switch, used to switch from battery to magneto or vice versa, or disconnect from either to stop the motor. The push button is for starting from the spark with switch turned to the battery side. When the battery is used, the current is simply turned through the coil and distributer of the magneto instead of the magneto current. The speed of the magneto is the same as that of the crank shaft for a two cylinder motor, and twice the crank shaft speed for four cylinders.

6. High tension magnetos.
7. Coil spark plugs.
8. Special igniting devices.

These several systems will now be taken up in the order given with a brief explanation of each.

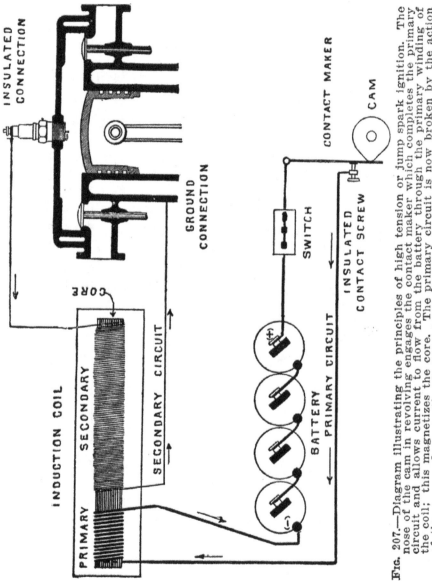

FIG. 207.—Diagram illustrating the principles of high tension or jump spark ignition. The nose of the cam in revolving engages the contact maker which completes the primary circuit and allows current to flow from the battery through the primary winding of the coil; this magnetizes the core. The primary circuit is now broken by the action of the cam and magnetic changes take place in the coil which induce a momentary high tension current in the secondary circuit. The great pressure of this current forces it across the air gap of the spark plug and as it bridges the gap a spark is produced. The arrows indicate the paths of the currents.

Ignition with Plain Coils.—The first high tension system to attain popularity was the single spark system using a plain coil and contact maker. This being the simplest method of producing a secondary spark, it will serve to illustrate the several principles involved in jump spark or high tension ignition.

Fig. 207 is a wiring diagram showing the connections. In the figure the primary and secondary windings of a plain coil are shown separated instead of overlapping, so that the circuits may be easily traced. As before stated, two distinct circuits are necessary to produce a jump spark, 1, the primary, and, 2, the secondary.

The operation is as follows: the primary switch is first closed and then the engine cranked. As the piston approaches the upper dead centre on the compression stroke, the nose of the contact maker cam engages the blade and brings the contact points together, thus completing the primary circuit. Current now flows from the *plus* terminal of the battery, through the switch, thence to the metal of the engine and to the blade of the contact maker. From this point it flows through the insulated screw, lead and primary winding of the coil, and thence through the return wire to the negative terminal of the battery, thus completing the circuit. This is indicated by the arrows.

The action of the cam allows the contact points to touch each other for only a very short time. It should be remembered that the primary and secondary wires do not come in contact with each other, both having an insulating covering.

The momentary current flowing in the primary winding, induces a current of high pressure in the secondary winding, but which flows in a direction *opposite* to that of the primary current as shown by the arrows. This induced current flows from one end of the secondary winding, to the metal of the engine and the ground electrode of the spark plug. It then produces a spark by jumping the air gap, thence it returns from the insulated electrode of the plug to the secondary winding of the coil, completing the circuit.

Instead of a contact maker, this system may be operated by a contact breaker. With this device, the primary circuit remains closed except at the time of the spark. It is evident that the primary current will flow for a much longer interval with a contact breaker than with a current maker. This closed circuit working of the contact breaker is necessary with some forms of engines running at unusually high speeds in order to allow sufficient time, as before explained, for the magnetic flux in the core of the coil to attain a density sufficient to produce a good spark at the plug points.

Ignition with Mechanical Vibrators.—The view held by some that a series of sparks closely following each other is more effective for ignition than a single spark, led first to the introduction of the mechanical vibrator. This system employs a plain coil and is identical with the one just described with the exception that in place of the make or break timing device, a mechanical vibrator is used which gives a succession of sparks for firing each charge.

Ignition with Vibrator Coils.—A more refined method of producing a series of sparks for igniting the charge is by the use of vibrator coils. The magnetic vibrator is a marked improvement on the mechanically operated device as it vibrates with

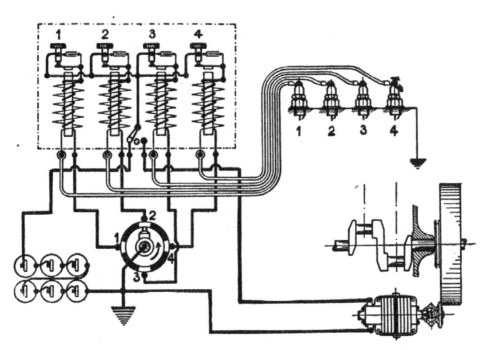

FIG. 208.—Wiring diagram of a dual jump spark system for a four-cylinder, four cycle engine. A dry battery and low tension magneto form the two sources of current supply. The primary, or low tension circuit is shown by heavy lines, the secondary or high tension circuit by fine lines and the leads to spark plugs by the double lines. The dotted rectangle represents the outline of a four unit dash coil.

greater rapidity and is capable of delicate adjustment. This system which is extensively used is illustrated in fig. 208, which is a wiring diagram for a four cylinder engine. The dotted rectangle represents the casing of a quadruple or four unit secondary coil. The heavy lines show the primary circuit, the fine lines, the secondary windings of the coils, and the double lines the leads of insulated wire to the spark plugs.

In the coil connections it should be noted that the adjustable contact screw of each vibrator is connected by a common wire terminating at the two-way switch; also, in each unit, one end of the secondary winding is connected to that end of the primary, leading to the vibrator blade. These common connections simplify the external wiring, as otherwise there would be four binding posts for each unit.

The two-way switch just referred to permits the current supply to be taken from either of two sources, such as a battery and a magneto. Current is supplied by the battery when the switch is in the position shown in the figure. By turning the switch to the right, a current from the magneto will be furnished.

With the battery in the circuit and the timer in the position shown, the operation is as follows:

Current flows from the positive terminal of the battery, to the switch, thence, to the contact screw of coil number two. From here, it flows through the vibrator blade, primary winding of the coil timer and the metal of the engine, and returns to the battery. The primary circuit is alternately opened and closed with great rapidity by the vibrator so long as the rotor of the timer is in contact with terminal 2. During this interval, a series of high tension currents are induced in the secondary circuit producing a succession of sparks.

These currents flow through the secondary winding in a direction opposite to that of the primary current. At each interruption of the primary current, an induced high tension current flows through the secondary winding, to the spark plug, across the gap producing a spark and returns through the metal of the engine, timer and back to the coil.

As the rotor of the timer revolves it touches each of the stationary contacts and in so doing the above cycle is repeated for each cylinder in the order of firing, as wired.

Ignition with a Master Vibrator.—In a multi-unit coil there is a vibrator for each unit, all of which may be operated by a single or master vibrator. The advantage of such a system is that there is but one vibrator to keep in adjustment, since this vibrator serves for all the cylinders; whereas, with one for each unit, all have to be kept in adjustment and the difficulty of keeping the several adjustments is a considerable factor.

In fig. 209 is shown a master vibrator coil. This has but one vibrator V for the four units of the coil, these being designated respectively C, C, C, C, and each consisting of a primary winding P and a secondary winding S.

The primary windings are all united in parallel at the top by a wire W, and with the lower ends connecting respectively with the segments of the timer T. The primary winding MP which operates the vibrator V is in series with this winding, the wire WT connecting from the battery and passing directly through the master primary MP. The four condensers, C1, C2, C3 and C4, are in parallel with the primary windings. Each of the secondary windings S connects direct to the spark plugs, designated respectively H1, H2, H3 and H4.

Fig. 210 illustrates the Splitdorf master vibrator, in which the four coils are designated 1, 2, 3 and 4, and a fifth unit V in the left end of the box, contains the master vibrator. The four primary windings connect direct by the wires P with the timer, and the secondaries are connected direct with the plugs. The internal wirings of all of the primaries are in parallel with the electro magnet in the unit V which operates the master vibrator.

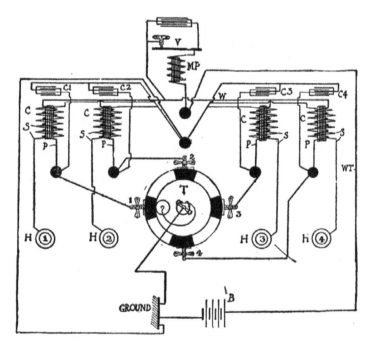

Fig. 209.—Circuit diagram of a master vibrator coil. B, is the battery; C, the unit coils; C1, C2, etc., the condensers; P, the primary windings and S, the secondary windings; H1, H2, etc., the spark plugs; T, the timer; MP, the master primary; V the vibrator; W, the common primary connection; 1, 2, etc., the stationary contacts of the timer.

Synchronous Ignition.—This system employs a distributer and a single coil for a number of cylinders. It is called "synchronous" for the following reason: when a multi-cylinder engine has a coil unit for each cylinder, it requires the adjustment of several vibrators. Now, the time required by the vibrator to act is variable with the adjustment, and with slight differences in construction, hence, of the several vibrators, perhaps no two will act in exactly the same time. Consequently, though in the ordinary multiple coil system the closing of the primary circuits may occur at exactly corresponding moments for all of the cylinders, the production of the spark of ignition will be more or less "out," owing to the variation in the "lag" of the different vibrators.

With a distributer and single coil, the lag is the same for all the cylinders, hence, the application of the word *synchronous.*

Fig. 211 is a wiring diagram showing the connections of a synchronous system; for clearness, the two windings of the coil are shown separated from each other and for the same reason also the primary and secondary elements of the distributer are separated.

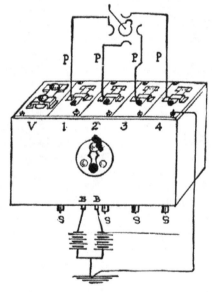

Fig. 210.—The Splitdorf master vibrator coil. As shown in the illustration the several unit coils are indicated by the figures 1, 2, 3 and 4. A fifth unit V at the left contains the master vibrator. The primary wires P connect with the timer and the secondary wires S with the plugs. B B shows the battery connections.

The primary rotor of the distributer being in contact with one of the stationary segments, the path of the primary current is as follows: from the plus terminal of the battery to the metal of the engine, through the primary element of the distributer and the primary winding of the coil; thence to the virbrator blade, contact screw and back to the battery by the return wire as indicated by the arrows. During the time the primary rotor is in contact with the stationary segment, the primary circuit is opened and closed with great frequency by the vibrator. This produces a series of induced currents in a reverse direction through the secondary winding of the coil.

Each secondary segment of the distributer being wired to one of the spark plugs, the rotor during its revolution brings each plug into the secondary circuit in the order indicated in the diagram. As shown, the secondary rotor is in contact with segment number two which causes the induced current to flow from the secondary winding, through the dis-

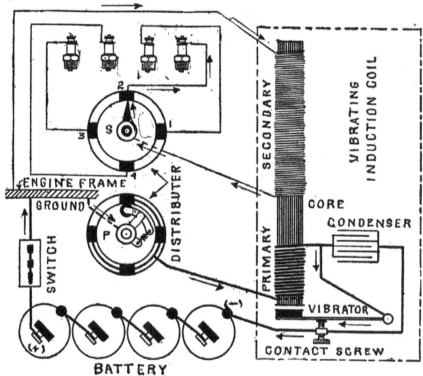

Fig. 211.—Diagram illustrating the principles of synchronous ignition. For clearness the primary and secondary elements of both the coil and the distributer are shown separated. When the primary rotor of the distributer completes the primary circuit, current from the battery flows and the vibrator operates, making and breaking the current with great frequency. A high tension current, made up of a series of impulses, is induced in the secondary circuit and distributed by the rotor arm during its revolution to the several cylinders in the proper order of firing.

tributer, thence to the spark plug, across the gap, through the metal of the engine and back to the coil by the return wire as indicated by the arrows.

One end of the secondary winding is usually connected to one end of the primary winding instead of making a separate connection to the metal of the engine. This simplifies the wiring by having one common ground connection.

In adopting a coil for use with a distributer, the one should be selected which gives the required spark with the least primary current, and which shows freedom from vibrator trouble and the minimum effect on the points after a continuous closed circuit test of at least ten hours. No coil has been produced which will not in time show some pitting of the vibrator points, especially if the direction of the primary current be always the same. A coil worked from a four point distributer will show a given amount of pitting in rather less than a quarter of the time required to produce the same effect if the coil be one of four coils operated from a timer.

It is good judgment to carry a spare coil unit, no matter which system is used, and it should be kept in good condition so that no time need be lost if a change be required.

In connecting up batteries and coils it is recommended that the vibrator screws be made "positive," so that whatever platinum is carried away by the arc may be taken from the screw and deposited upon the contact point of the vibrator. The theory is that the screw is cheaper and easier to replace than is the vibrator, and that, with this arrangement, the vibrator point builds up rather than wears away, requiring only the smoothing off of the extra metal deposited upon it to keep it in condition.

The very slight wear produced upon vibrators operated from non-synchronous alternating current magnetos from which the current is in each direction for one-half of the time, in the aggregate, is well known. Hence, when a battery is used, if the operator would periodically change the direction of the current flow by reversing the two battery wires connecting the one which has gone to the positive pole, to the negative and vice versa, he will find that the wear of the vibrator points is reduced to a minimum.

Magneto Ignition.—There are numerous types of magnetos used for igniting purposes. In the several systems, therefore, different methods of wiring are required. In the true high tension and the self-contained types where the coil and condenser are a part of the magneto, the number of external connections is less than with those having the coil in a separate box. One advantage of magneto ignition is that it does not require hand advance of the spark. The intensity of a magneto current increases with the speed, hence, when running slowly the spark produced in the cylinder will be weak and the charge will be ignited slowly. At high speeds the strength of the current being greater, causes the charge to ignite more rapidly—this charge produces an effect equivalent to advancing the spark.

In starting an engine equipped solely with a magneto, it is necessary to turn the crank much faster than when a battery is used, because the armature must be turned at a certain speed to generate the required current. Due to the refinement of design this factor has been reduced and most magnetos will give a spark sufficient for ignition even if the armature be revolved quite slowly.

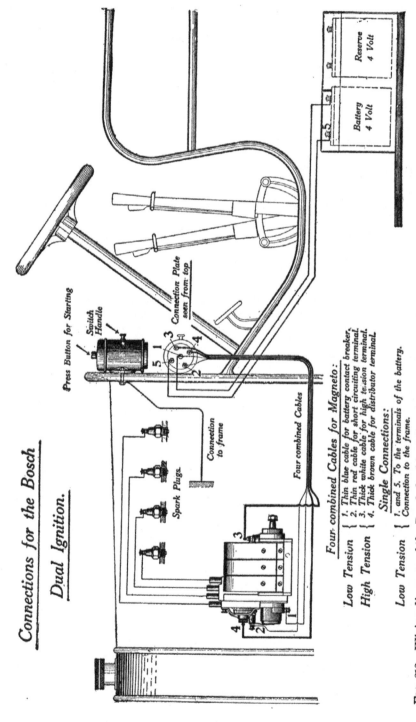

Connections for the Bosch

Dual Ignition.

Press Button for Starting

Switch Handle

Connection Plate seen from top

Spark Plugs.

Connection to frame

Four combined Cables

Battery 4 Volt

Reserve 4 Volt

Four-combined Cables for Magneto:

Low Tension { 1. Thin blue cable for battery contact breaker.
2. Thin red cable for short circuiting terminal.

High Tension { 3. Thick white cable for high tension terminal.
4. Thick brown cable for distributor terminal.

Single Connections:

Low Tension { 1. and 5. To the terminals of the battery.
Connection to the frame.

FIG. 212.—Wiring diagram of the Bosch dual ignition system, using one set of plugs. A special coil is provided with self-contained switch, and a button for bringing a magnetic vibrator into the circuit when desired.

The spark plugs commonly used for battery ignition are not well adapted to a magneto, as the current furnished by the latter is stronger. The greater heat of the current tends to burn the slender points thought necessary, therefore, with a magneto they must be larger for satisfactory working. The gap of a magneto plug should be less than that of a coil plug, because the current, while of greater amperage and heating value, is of less voltage than with a battery system. The gap should not be more than one sixty-fourth of an inch. The most efficient magneto plugs have several points, so that when the distance between one set becomes too great the spark will take place between another set.

In magneto ignition, an important point is that the revolving switch which distributes the secondary current, and the contact breaker should be kept clean.

In fig. 212 is illustrated a magneto ignition system which also has a storage battery for a second source of current.

A Bosch magneto is shown at the left. It is of the true high tension type but differs from the standard rotary armature type in two respects, 1, the high tension connections are slightly altered, and 2, an additional contact breaker is provided for the battery so that the magneto will serve also as a timer for the battery, while the secondary timing device on the magneto is used for both the magneto and the battery current. All other details of the magneto are similar to those of ordinary machines.

For battery ignition a special dash coil is provided, having a self-contained switch and button for bringing a magnetic vibrator into the circuit when desired. The vibrator is only brought into operation for starting the engine from the seat. After starting, the vibrator is cut out and the interruption of the current, effected by mechanical means, hence, there is no *lag* in the operation of the interrupter, as with magnetic vibrators. If there be any mixture in the cylinder, the engine can be started from the seat by pressing the button.

The switch handle which projects through a slot in the casing of the coil, locks in three positions by a spring, the positions being designated respectively, as "Magneto," "Off" and "Battery." The wiring connections are as shown in the illustration.

Ignition with Coil Spark Plugs.—In this system the igniting or firing device consists of a combined spark plug and induction coil; the latter being encased in mica and hermetically sealed. Outside this is a metal cover that protects and supports the whole. The ends of the primary winding are connected to binding posts on top of the casing. The two electrodes of the plug form the terminals of the secondary winding. A master vibrator and condenser are contained in a separate box.

Fig. 213 is a wiring diagram, showing the connections for a four cylinder engine fitted with coil spark plugs. The current supply may be from either battery or magneto as illustrated. It should be noted that in the wiring, only the primary circuit is exposed. The plug shown in the illustration has no ground connection of the secondary terminals, that is, both electrodes are insulated. The connections of the circuit may be easily understood from the figure.

A modification of the plug just described is one having a ground return for both the primary and secondary currents. In other respects the wiring does not differ.

The advantages claimed for the coil plug system is the elimination of secondary leakage due to imperfect insulation or *Hertz wave;* also accessibility secured by the separation of coil and condenser and simplified wiring.

Double Ignition Systems.—Some automobiles are equipped with two independent means of ignition, having no parts in common, thus if anything happen to one system, the other may be brought into use. Double ignition makes a delay on account of ignition troubles, a remote probability; as a guard against disablement, it is one step farther than the dual system in which the two modes of ignition are not independent.

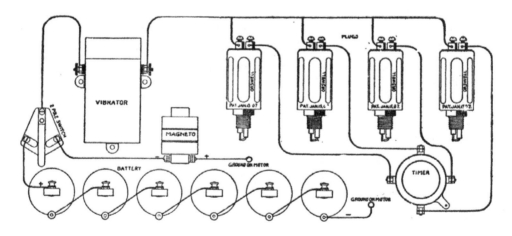

Fig. 213.—Wiring diagram of a coil spark plug system. There is no ground connection for the secondary terminals; as these are connected inside directly to the electrodes of the spark plug, both electrodes being insulated. A condenser and vibrator are placed in the box shown at the left of the figure. In this system only the low tension wiring of the primary circuit is exposed.

There are many combinations to be found in double ignition, one make of car being fitted with both the make and break and the jump spark systems.

Fig. 214 illustrates the double ignition as furnished with the Peerless cars. An Eisemann low tension magneto is used as one source of current supply; the current passes through an induction coil on the dash, giving a high tension current at the spark plugs. In addition to the magneto and entirely separated therefrom is the battery system. All wires are connected with their terminals by spring attachment. By means of a *rubber wire bar*, the method of wiring is improved with respect to shortening the length of wires and retaining them in a desirable position.

Another example of double ignition is that employed on the National cars as shown in fig. 215. One system consists of a synchronous drive, high tension magneto, wired direct to the spark plugs; the other is composed of a storage battery, single coil and distributer.

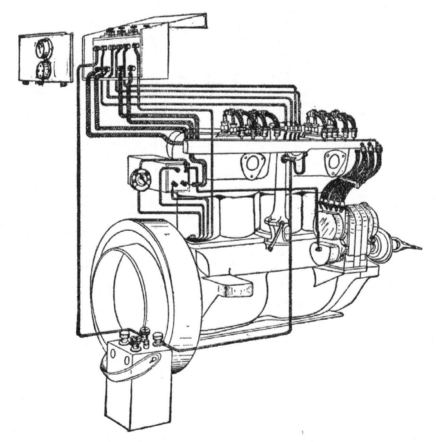

FIG. 214.—A double ignition system with two sets of spark plugs as fitted on Peerless cars. The current which is furnished by an Eisemann low tension magneto passes through an induction coil on the dash, giving a high tension current at the spark plugs. In addition to the magneto, and entirely independent is a battery system of ignition operating the second set of spark plugs. The large number of connections necessary is somewhat simplified by the use of a rubber wire bar as shown.

Special Igniting Devices.—The fact that ignition could be made reliable and certain, as well as more nearly synchronous, by the single spark as caused by the magneto, has influenced several seekers after battery economy with coil ignition to develop and place on the market devices in which a single break in the primary circuit is caused mechanically at each instant at which charge ignition is desired within the several engine cylinders.

These "single-break" coil systems embody, in their most highly

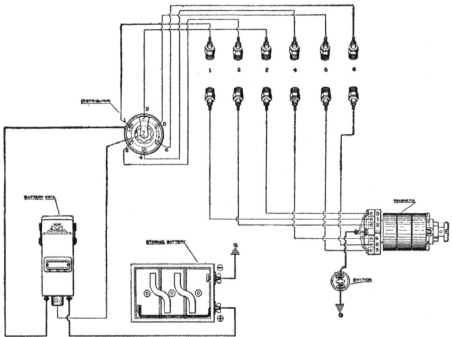

FIG. 215.—Wiring diagram for a six cylinder car, illustrating a double ignition system with two sets of spark plugs. One system consists of a high tension magneto with connections from its distributing terminals to one set of spark plugs; a second system is composed of a battery, vibrating coil, distributer and connections with the second set of plugs.

developed forms, a single plain coil, a secondary timing device for the induced high tension current and a timer or circuit-breaker which causes a sharp break in the circuit of the primary coil winding each time an ignition spark is required. After the coil itself, the circuit breaker is the chief component of single coil systems with distributer, designed to produce but one spark per ignition. Upon it depends the effectiveness of the spark, and in some measure also the current consumed in the coil in producing it.

In consideration of battery economy, it is necessary that the circuit breaker make only a sufficiently long contact to secure the proper building up of the magnetic field about the coil windings, before the occurrence of the break. Because of this, it is usual so to set the adjustable point of the breaker that the contact duration is the minimum with which a proper igniting spark can be secured. In single spark systems, the circuit is both made and broken by mechanical means, and there is therefore no magnetic lag at the period of the break as in vibrator coils.

Formerly dry cells gave satisfaction with one or two cylinder engines, but with the advent of the four and six cylinder engine, it was found that the increased current consumption caused the rapid exhaustion of the battery. On this account the storage cell, of greater first cost but of longer life, was substituted. Since single break igniting devices have been in use, it has been demonstrated that with proper treatment the dry cell battery can be made to give as good service as can any other type of battery.

In view of the increasing use of special igniting devices, a few of these will now be described.

Atwater Kent Spark Generator.—This device produces one contact only for each ignition. The duration of this contact is just long enough to enable the coil to build up for the desired length of spark, and it is the same whether the engine runs fast or slow. By turning the contact screw, which is the only thing adjustable about the apparatus, the duration of contact may be varied within limits,· and a longer or shorter spark produced at will.

Briefly described the Atwater Kent device consists of the following elements:

(*a*) A non-vibrator jump spark coil of highly efficient and durable construction. (*b*) Condenser. (*c*) Mechanical contact maker in the primary circuit, driven by suitable connection from the engine. (*d*) High tension distributer. (*e*) Spark advancing device. (*f*) Button for starting "on the spark." (*g*) Individual cut-outs for testing the cylinders separately.

Of these elements, the contact maker, distributer, and spark advancer are carried by a single vertical shaft, which runs in the left-hand side of the case containing the coil and condenser. This case is bolted on the dash, in easy reach of the driver, and the general arrangement is shown in Fig. 216-1.

The mechanism by which the primary contact is made, is illustrated in figs. 216-2 and 216-3 which show a plan view of the contact maker and portions thereof with the cover removed and the shaft in different positions. The moving parts are the shaft itself, A, fig. 217, the snapper B, and the pivoted contact arm C.

The shaft carries four—or six for a six cylinder engine—milled notches, forming a *ratchet* which engages the claw at the end of the snapper. The latter, which is shown separately in fig. 217 is a light piece of tempered steel which is guided by slots in the bronze base DE, and is

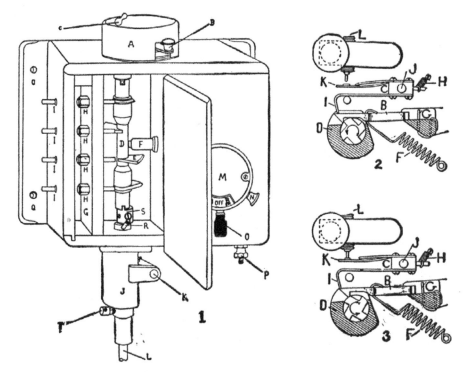

FIG. 216.—1—The Atwater Kent spark generator. 2 and 3—sectional views showing two positions of the contact maker. This device is designed especially to secure economy in the use of the current and is adapted to operate with a dry battery. The generator comprises the following elements: 1, a plain secondary coil; 2, condenser; 3, contact maker; 4, secondary distributer; 5, spark advancing device; 6, starting button; 7, individual cut outs for testing the cylinders separately.

pulled by the spring F, against a spring wire stop G, when released from engagement with the notches on the shaft. The contact arm C, is likewise held normally in the position shown by the tension of spring H.

The shaft, *turning counter clockwise*, draws the snapper into the position shown in Fig. 216-2, and the claw of the snapper when released rides up on the rounded part of the shaft as shown in Fig. 216-3 acting thereby as a wedge between the shaft and the steel hook I of the contact arm, which is pivoted at J. The contact arm is thus oscillated to produce contact between a platinum point in the flat copper spring K, and the stationary insulated contact screw L.

As the snapper continues its motion, it releases the hook I, thereby permitting the contact arm to rebound and break contact. The snapper then comes to rest in its normal position, Fig. 217 and the contact arm resumes its position of rest against the stop. With the engagement of the snapper by the next tooth of the ratchet, the process is repeated.

The timing device is shown in Fig. 216-1. The brass blades which deliver the secondary current to the cable terminals are insulated from the rest of the shaft; and the terminals themselves are protected by weather-proof insulation. As the blades do not touch the terminals, there is no wear. Opposite each terminal is an outside spring button, by pressing which the spark may be grounded for testing the cylinders.

Ignition is advanced or retarded by means of a spiral sleeve beneath the case, which rotates the upper portion of the shaft through a suitable angle. To start "on the spark," the button B, Fig. 216-1 is pressed. This short circuits the contact maker and produces a spark in the cylinder in communication with the distributer at the time.

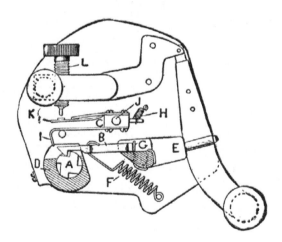

FIG. 217.—Contact maker of Atwater Kent spark generator. The moving parts are the shaft, A, the snapper B, and the pivoted contact arm C. The shaft carries four—or six for a six cylinder engine—milled notches forming a ratchet which engages the claw at the end of the snapper B. The operation of the device is explained in the text.

Pittsfield Acme Igniter.—An outside coil is employed with this device, but it is designed for attachment to the timer shaft in place of the ordinary timer. The period of contact is constant and independent of the speed of the engine. A cam serves to actuate the circuit breaker parts, and the constant period of contact is secured through causing the movable contact point to oscillate under the influence of a pair of flat springs; after its release by the cam.

The action of the oscillating parts will be the same no matter at what speed the actuating cam is run, since contact is made and broken by the action of these flat springs after the cam has released the breaker point carrying part. The cam simply compresses one of the springs, and the circuit is both made and broken by spring action alone. The distributer rotor is driven by the circuit breaker rotor and is mounted within an upper insulating part which fully encloses the circuit breaker.

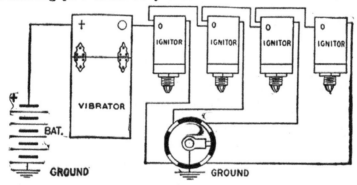

FIG. 218.—The Perfex ignition system. The ignitors consist of coil spark plugs, each having one electrode grounded. A box shown to the left contains the vibrator and condenser. In this method of ignition the primary wiring only is exposed.

American Igniter.—In the operation of this igniter no external coil is used. It is intended for mounting on the timer shaft in the usual manner. The body consists of a cylindrical, insulating, enclosing part into which the secondary coil winding fits. The latter is formed up on a spool of insulating material, and its connections are made through metal blocks which register in the case and complete the secondary circuit without the use of binding posts. The coil core is a hollow cylinder of iron wires, and the primary winding surrounds it, the two forming an integral part of the before mentioned body casing.

The circuit breaker, of the single break type is mounted on the under face of the body and operated by a multiple cam self contained with the ignitor shaft, which latter is carried in annular ball bearings. The cam operates against a roller ended lever which carries a contact point. This point makes the circuit through a second point carried by an adjustable screw. The point itself telescopes into the adjusting screw and is backed by a light spring. This construction causes the light spring to be compressed by the action of the cam, and increases the speed of the parts at the instant of the break, since the break proper is made at a point about midway in the travel of the breaker lever, when its speed is highest.

IGNITION.

Ignition Troubles.—To successfully cope with ignition troubles there are two requisites, 1, a thorough knowledge of the system used and, 2, a well ordered course of procedure in looking for the source of trouble. In many ignition systems, the chief difficulty encountered in the location of defects arises from the fact that faults in different portions of the circuit sometimes make themselves manifest by the same symptoms. If each defect had its individual symptom, locating the trouble would be comparatively easy, but as it is, it is sometimes quite difficult to find the defective parts. In general the following method should be adopted to locate possible derangements:

1. Examine the source of current supply; if a battery, test each cell separately and remove any found to be weak. When a magneto is used, disconnect the drive and turn armature by hand, if the field magnets have not lost their strength the armature should turn perceptibly hard during certain portions of each revolution.

2. Examine the primary circuit for breaks in its continuity, see that all connections are bright and firmly held together by the binding screws; the timer contacts should be clean.

3. The spark plug points should be clean and the air gap the proper length—about one thirty-second of an inch.

4. See that the vibrator contacts are in good condition and the adjustment correct. With this preliminary examination the system may now be tested.

Testing.—Remove the spark plug and lay it on the cylinder without disconnecting the lead to the insulated electrode; the body of the plug only should touch the metal of the cylinder. Crank the engine and note if a spark passes at the gap. The spark should be "fat" if everything be in good condition; if a weak spark be produced it may be due to either a loose terminal, run down battery or badly adjusted vibrator. When no spark can be obtained the entire system must be examined and tested, beginning at the battery. In a multi-cylinder engine a faulty spark plug may be located as follows:

Remove the nuts from the top of the plugs, leaving the high tension wires upon them. Start the engine, and then disconnect and ground all wires except one, then run the engine on one cylinder only. If after a good test at various engine speeds, no misfiring occur, it can be taken for granted that the plug is sound. Proceed in this manner with the remaining plugs.

When a multi-unit coil is used, a faulty plug may be located by holding down all the vibrator blades but one so that only one spark plug operates. By running each cylinder separately by this means it can easily be ascertained which plug is defective. Some coils are provided with little knobs for cutting out cylinders in the manner just described.

Breaks in the Wiring.—An entire break is more easily found than a partial one. To test for an entire break, place the engine upon the sparking point, close primary switch and touch the two

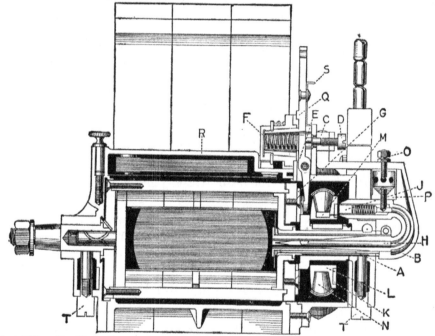

Fig. 219.—Section through the Simms-Bosch high tension magneto. A, armature shaft; B, curved arm carrying high tension lead; C, lug supporting screw; D, adjusting contact breaker, E, against spring, F; G. revolving sleeve carrying face cams; H, high tension lead wire; J, carbon brush of distributer disc; K, insulated ring; L, rotating drum of distributer; M and N, distributer brushes; O and P, safety spark gap; Q, swiveled lever for retarding or advancing the spark time; R, condenser; T, T, spring pushed wick oilers for armature spindle.

terminals of the suspected wire with a test wire. A flow of current indicates a break. A partial break, or one held together by the insulation may sometimes be located by bending the wire sharply at successive points along its length, the engine being at the sparking point and the switch closed as before.

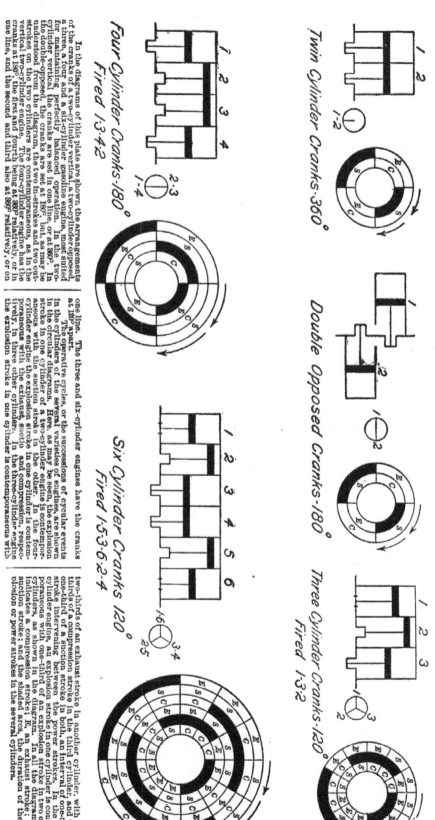

DIAGRAM OF THE CRANKS AND CYCLES OF MULTIPLE-CYLINDER ENGINES.

Twin Cylinder Cranks·360°

Double Opposed Cranks·180°

Three Cylinder Cranks·120°
Fired 1·3·2

Four Cylinder Cranks·180°
Fired 1·3·4·2

Six Cylinder Cranks 120°
Fired 1·5·3·6·2·4

In the diagrams of this plate are shown the arrangements of the cranks of a two-cylinder vertical, a two-cylinder opposed, a three, a four and a six-cylinder gasoline engine, most suited for maintaining perfectly balanced operation. In the two-cylinder vertical the cranks are set in one line, or at 360°. In the double-opposed, the cranks are set at 180°, but, as may be understood from the diagram, the two in-strokes and two out-strokes on the two cylinders are contemporaneous, as in the vertical two-cylinder engine. The four-cylinder engine has the cranks at 180°, the first and fourth being at 360° relatively, or in one line, and the second and third also at 360° relatively, or on one line. The three and six-cylinder engines have the cranks at 180° apart.

The operative cycles, or the successions of cyclar events in the cylinders of the several varieties of engines, are shown in the circular diagrams. Here, as may be seen, the explosion stroke in one cylinder of a two-cylinder engine is contemporaneous with the suction stroke in the other. In the four-cylinder engine the explosion stroke in one cylinder is contemporaneous with the exhaust, suction and compression, respectively, in three other cylinders. In the three-cylinder engine the explosion stroke in one cylinder is contemporaneous with two-thirds of an exhaust stroke in another cylinder, with two-thirds of a compression stroke in the third cylinder, and with one-third of a suction stroke in both, an interval of one-third stroke intervening between the power strokes. In the six-cylinder engine, an explosion stroke in one cylinder is contemporaneous with one-third of an explosion stroke in two other cylinders, as shown in the diagram. In all the diagrams, C indicates a compression stroke; E, an exhaust stroke; S, a suction stroke; and the shaded area, the duration of the explosion or power strokes in the several cylinders.

Primary Short Circuits.—Disconnect the primary wires from the coil, leaving the ends out of contact with anything. Now touch the switch points momentarily, if any spark appear there is a short circuit. A short circuit may sometimes be removed by clearing all wires of contact with metallic bodies and by pulling each wire away from others which were formerly in contact with it.

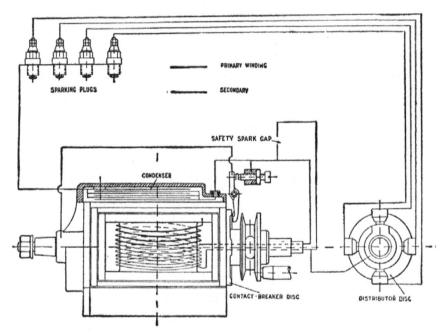

FIG. 220.—Circuit Diagram showing the Simms-Bosch high tension magneto wired up to spark a four cylinder engine. The secondary current as led from the armature winding by a wire, encased in a curbed tube, which emerges from the spindle of the armature. Thence, through a carbon brush bearing upon a flat brass ring, on the front of the secondary distributer, it passes to the contact segment; being conveyed to each spark plug in turn through the four brushes of the secondary distributer. All these details may be readily learned by reference to the diagram of circuits.

Secondary Short Circuits.—Disconnect the secondary lead from spark plug. Under this condition the high tension current may sometimes be heard or seen discharging from the secondary wire to some metallic portion of the car. Water in contact with the secondary wire will sometimes cause a short circuit unless the insulation be of the best quality.

The Primary Switch.—This portion of the primary circuit sometimes causes trouble by making poor contact. This is generally due to the deterioration of the spring portion of the metal which gradually loses its resiliency. Snap switches somtimes fail through the weakening of the springs which hold them in the "on" or "off" position. The contacts of a switch should be kept in good condition.

Primary Connections.—All binding posts and their connections should be clean and bright. The wires should be firmly secured to the binding posts, as a loose connection in the primary circuit is often the cause of irregular misfiring or the stopping of the engine.

Vibration.—Since the wires are subject to constant vibration, a number of strands of fine wire is better than a single heavy wire, as the latter is more liable to be broken. In securing the wire to a binding post care should be taken that all the strands are bound, as a leak will result if a single strand come in contact with any uninsulated metal.

Timers.—The revolving part of a timer may not make good contact with the stationary segments on account of insufficient pressure or dirt: take timer apart, thoroughly clean and increase the spring pressure, if necessary.

Distributers.—These may give trouble by, 1, presence of dirt, 2, loose contacts or, 3, division of the spark; this latter effect is sometimes caused by metallic particles wearing off the revolving part forming a path so that the spark passes from the revolving part to more than one contact segment.

Coils.—The part of a coil which requires most frequent attention is the vibrator. The contact points are subject to deterioration on account of the small spark always present between the points when the coil is in operation. In time, the points become corroded and burned, and therefore require to be re-surfaced by smoothing with a fine file.

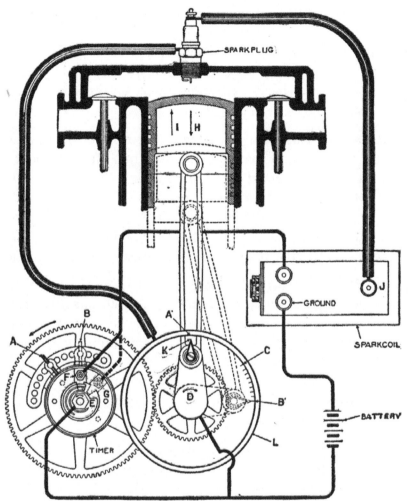

Fig. 221.—A device for testing ignition advance to illustrate the effect of lag in vibrating spark coils. The higher the engine speed the more the spark can be advanced, but no such advance is possible as would be indicated by the position of a timer apparently capable of a movement of 90 degrees or more. This great amount of advance of the timer is necessary to overcome the enormous lag in vibrating spark coils, as it takes just as long to start vibrating, whether the engine be running 100 or 2,000 revolutions. The instrument, as shown above, for demonstrating this advance spark theory consists of a model of a gas engine with its cylinder and piston, connecting rod and crank, but secured to the crank pin is a small pointer K, which rotates within a metal ring L, clearing it about ¼ inch. The wires from the secondary of the spark coil are connected to the insulated metal ring L, and to the crank and pointer K, so the spark will jump from the pointer K to the ring L, while the engine is in operation. The timer should be set in such a position that in turning over the engine slowly by hand in the direction shown by the dotted lined crank a spark will be produced when the crank is at the dead centre. If the engine be now speeded to 1,000 revolutions per minute without moving the timer, the spark will jump across at B or, in other words, will be 90 degrees late. This lateness of the spark is entirely due to the mechanical lag of the vibrator and the magnetic lag of the iron core; hence, the timer must be advanced an equivalent amount to balance up the two. By varying the speed of the engine the spark moves from the position A' to B'.

A faulty connection to the condenser is at once shown by large sparks at the vibrator points. Any repairs to a coil, aside from the vibrator should be done by an expert as the construction is very delicate.

Igniters.—In make and break ignition, failure to get a spark, especially with a weak battery, is frequently due to the tappet spring. This spring must be quite stiff so as to cause the break to take place with considerable rapidity—*the more rapid the break, the better is the quality of the spark.* The contact points of the igniter electrodes are subject to corrosion and wear. When they become pitted the contact surfaces should be filed smooth.

Spark Plugs.—Repeated failure to start when the coil vibrator operates indicates a faulty spark plug. A rich gasoline mixture often leaves a carbon deposit, and being a partial conductor short circuits the plug. The porcelain insulation, on account of its brittleness, may crack inside the sleeve allowing a spark to pass there instead of at the gap. Mica insulation sometimes becomes saturated with oil causing the layers to separate, permitting a short circuit.

Engine Misfires and Finally Stops.—This may be due to the exhaustion of the battery and is indicated by a weak spark and very faint vibrator action.

Engine Suddenly Stops.—This is generally caused by a broken wire or loose switch which does not stay closed. If the engine has only one cylinder, the broken wire may be either in the primary or secondary circuit; if a multi-cylinder engine, the break is in the primary circuit.

Engine does not Start.—Usually caused by: (a) primary switch not closed, (b) battery weak or exhausted, (c) entire or partial break in wire, (d) loose terminal, (e) moisture on spark plug, (f) fouled plug, (h) spark too far retarded or advanced, (i) with magneto ignition, too slow cranking.

Engine runs Fitfully.—Frequently results from a partial break in the wiring, especially in the primary circuit.

Pre=ignition.—Caused by (a) some small particle in the cylinder becoming heated to incandescence (b) the electrodes of the spark plug becoming red hot, (c) intermittent short circuit in the primary.

Engine runs with Switch Open.—Usually caused by, (a) overheated engine or plug points, (b) primary short circuit, (c) defective switch, (d) an incandescent particle inside the cylinder.

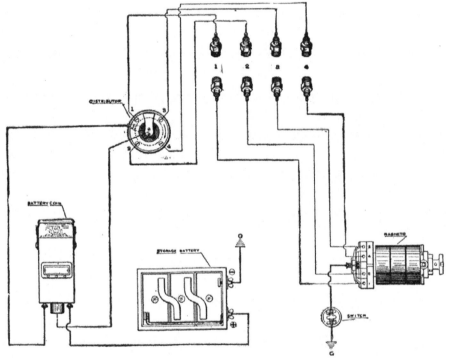

FIG. 222.—Wiring diagram for a four cylinder car, illustrating a double ignition system with two sets of spark plugs. A high tension magneto is connected through its distributing terminals to one set of plugs and current from a battery passes through a single vibrating coil and distributer to the second set, thus furnishing two independent systems.

Engine Misfires.—This may be caused, by (a) weak battery, (b) partial break in conductor, (c) loose or disconnected terminal, (d) intermittent short circuit in the secondary, (e) faulty action of either timer or vibrator contacts, (f) bent vibrator blade, (g) faulty spark plug, (h) air gap too large.

Knocking of Engine.—Too much advance of the spark sometimes produces this effect.

Loss of Power without Misfires.—This may be due to badly adjusted coil contacts, poor spark or incorrect timing.

Explosions in the Muffler.—These are usually caused by misfiring, partially charged storage battery or by one cylinder not working.

Knocking in the Cylinder.—The form of unusual noise commonly described as "knocking" consists of a regular and continuous tapping in the cylinder, which is so unlike any sound usual and normal to operation that, once heard, it cannot be mistaken. Too much advance of the spark sometimes produces this result.

If retarding the spark from the extreme lead fails to overcome the knock, the mixture may be throttled with good probability of success. As mentioned by numerous authorities, the placing of the spark plug in the exact centre of the combustion space occasions a peculiarly sharp knock, which may be stopped by advancing or retarding the spark from the one point of trouble. This explanation of the trouble is questioned by others, and is probably over-rated.

CHAPTER TWENTY-SIX.

Balancing Gasoline Engines.—An important item in the operative efficiency of any type of engine is balance. This involves some mechanical means for rendering all movements perfectly even and for neutralizing thrusts and vibration. Balance is particularly necessary in an internal-combustion engine of any type, since, with a power effort applied only at stated intervals, instead of continually, as in a steam engine, there is a far greater likelihood of irregularity at some point in the cycle. The most probable results of unbalanced movement in a gas engine will be:

1. Vibration, with attendant wear on the supports of the engine.

2. Wear on the moving parts, as between the piston and cylinder bore and at the bearings of the shafts. This must sooner or later result in the disablement of the engine.

3. Loss of efficiency, on account of the creation of numerous stresses which absorb power.

Causes of Unbalanced Motion.—The problem of properly balancing an internal-combustion engine has always been serious, and considerable ingenuity has been exercised in the effort to achieve a perfect solution. The effort to transform reciprocating into rotary motion must inevitably be attended by strains and vibration, which, when proper adjustments are absent, result in wear on the bearings and deformation of the cylinder bore. In a single-cylinder gas engine the vibrations resulting from inertia of the moving parts, moving under varying stress through the several stages of the cycle, are liable to be excessive. It is necessary, therefore, to provide some means for compensating this irregularity, so that, as far as possible, the active energies may be equalized.

Balancing a Single=Cylinder Engine.—Very few single-cylinder gas engines have been constructed with more than an approximate balance. This is true because the only available

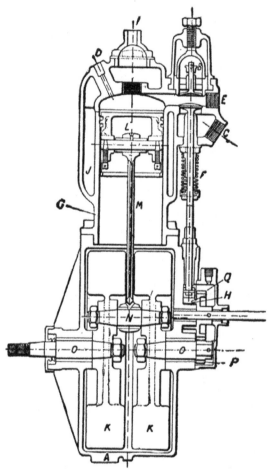

FIG. 223.—Section of the De Dion and Bouton Single-Cylinder Water-Jacketed Carriage Engine. Parts are as follows: A, crank case formed by two cylindrical
pieces bolted together; B, the inlet valve for the fuel mixture from the carburetter; C, the exhaust valve, held closed by a helical spring, F, and opened by
the cam, H; D, the opening for the compression tap; E, the threaded hole for the
sparking plug; F, the spring on the exhaust valve rod; G, the cylinder; I, the
port of exit for the jacket water from jacket, J, the inlet being at a point near
the base of the jacket; K and K are the flywheels, or crank discs, which are
joined together as shown, by the crank pin, N; M is the connecting rod; N is the
crank pin; O and O are the crank shafts, that on the right carrying the pinion,
P, that on the left being threaded for connection to the driving gear; P is a
pinion on the crank shaft meshing with gear, Q.

method is to set balance weights opposite the crank pin; and to
make balance weights balance is a very delicate problem. In

general, the proper weight to be used for good balance must be equal to the weight of the moving parts to which it is opposed. According to the generally accepted theory, the weights to be

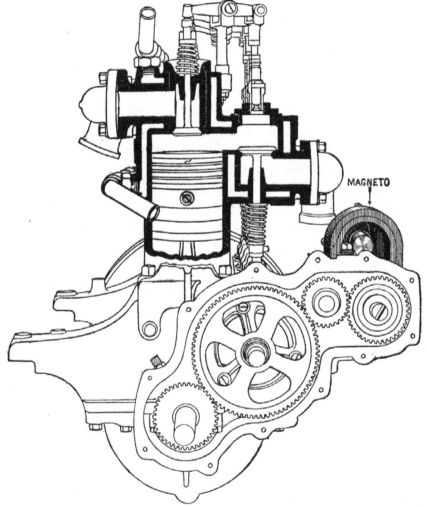

MAGNETO

FIG. 224.—The Mitchell Four-Cylinder Engine. Sectional view, showing front of engine and cross section of cylinder. The valve action is direct for the intake valves. An overhead rocker for the exhaust valve is placed in a cage in the middle of a cylinder head. The rocker is worked by a vertical push rod, having its lower end dropped into a cup in the top end of the cam roller carrying lifter.

considered are those of the crank and crank pin, together with a certain portion of the weight of the connecting rod. In determining the correct portion of the weight to be used, the method usually followed is to set the piston end of the rod on a knife-edge support and to hang the opposite or crank end to a spring-scale balance. This weight, which will naturally be smaller than that of the connecting rod wholly supported by the balance, may be taken as the greatest weight that is mechanically significant.

Arrangement of the Cranks.—It may be safely said, that for success in balancing a single-cylinder vehicle engine, De Dion & Bouton, of France, stand almost alone. In other carriages than theirs, especially those of American manufacture, vibration was at one time an almost inevitable feature. This trouble early led to the construction of motors with several cylinders. Daimler's V-shaped double-cylinder engine was nearly the first meritorious attempt to balance the moving parts of two cylinders. It consisted of two cylinders inclined from the vertical, so as to form an angle of about 30 degrees with the connecting rods working on a common crank. Later on, Daimler engines were made with two vertical parallel cylinders, with cranks at 180 degrees. This arrangement soon proved ineffective to prevent vibration, and, as a consequence, the common crank was restored, both pistons making their out-strokes and in-strokes simultaneously.

Proportions of the Bore and Stroke.—Another element of design that undoubtedly contributes largely to the end of attaining balanced operation is the proper proportioning of the parts. The superior balance of the De Dion single-cylinder engine is to be attributed to the fact that the stroke is short, in proportion to the diameter of the cylinder, quite as much as to the adjustment of moving weights. Very many carriage engines have the stroke length and diameter of bore approximately equal, while in few of them is the stroke very much the longer.

Double=Piston Cylinders.—In addition to adjustment of moving weights, several engines have been designed to balance the reaction produced by explosion of the charge by the use of two pistons in one cylinder, set face to face, so that both are forced outward by the power impulse. In such engines, of which the

Gobron-Brillie is a type, approximate freedom from vibration is accompanied by two other 'advantages—greater velocity of expansion, with consequently greater speed, and immunity from leakage, due to joints and gaskets in the cylinder.

The De Dion Two=Cylinder Engine.—One of the most notable attempts to neutralize vibration in a four-cycle engine is the De Dion balanced double cylinder. In this engine the two cylinders make their out-strokes and in-strokes contemporaneously, as in other double-cylinder engines. Balance is secured, however,

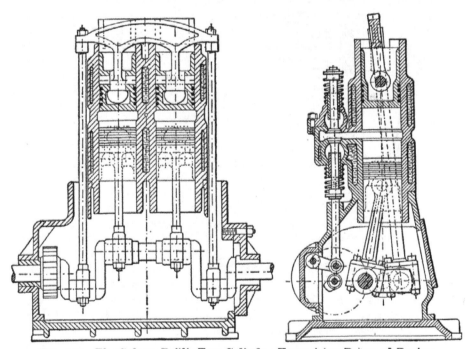

FIG. 225.—The Gobron-Brillie Two-Cylinder, Four-piston Balanced Engine.

by the use of a third cylinder, in which slides a piston, equal in weight with its connecting rod to the weights of the moving parts in the other two. This third cylinder performs none of the functions of power production, its sole purpose being balance of motion. The crank of the third piston is set at 180 degrees to the other two. According to published statements, excellent results were attained in practice with this engine.

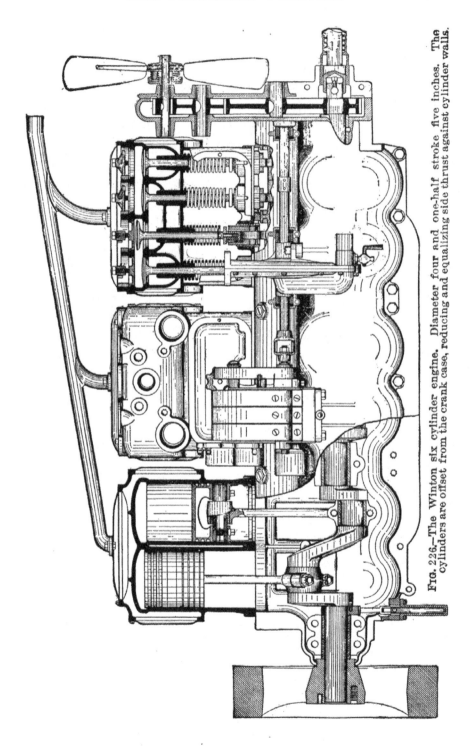

FIG. 226.—The Winton six cylinder engine. Diameter four and one-half stroke, five inches. The cylinders are offset from the crank case, reducing and equalizing side thrust against cylinder walls.

The Three=Cylinder Engine.—The three-cylinder engine, having its cranks set at 120° has been used on several motor vehicles, and has proven itself an improvement on either the single or double cylinder, in point of easily-achieved balance of the working parts. The single-cylinder engine has a power stroke in each two revolutions of the fly-wheel, and the double-cylinder, in each revolution. In the three-cylinder engine, however, a power stroke begins at each 240° of rotation, or three power strokes to a complete cycle of two revolutions as shown in the accompanying folder diagram.

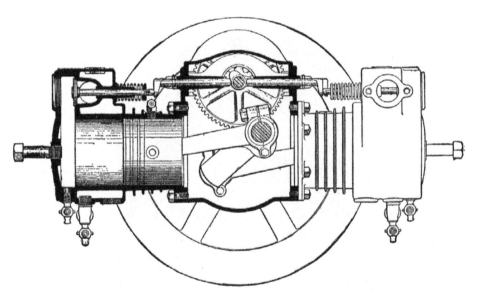

FIG. 227.—Sectional view of the Maxwell double opposed motor. Cylinders 4½ by 4, rated at fourteen horse-power at normal speed. The valve cams and cam shaft are contained in a separate frame which can be removed without change of timing.

The strain put upon the fly-wheel in compressing the charge to the high point used in many modern engines, must be disturbing to perfectly even running, unless the fly-wheel be very heavy and extremely well calculated for its duty. Another advantage, claimed for the three-cylinder engine, is that none of the several stages of the cycle in one of the three cylinders is precisely contemporaneous with any other stage in another cylinder. The effect of successive high-resistance (compression and suction), power-impulse (expansion) and low resistance (exhaust) are distributed or neutralized; thus rendering more even the rotative stress on the crank-shaft, and relieving the fly-wheel of a considerable percentage of its compensating duty. Whether or not these explanations perfectly explain, experience proves the superior balance of the three-cylinder engine, as used by Duryea and several other designers.

Multiple=Cylinder Engines.—The advent of the modern high-powered motor carriage involved the introduction of the

FIG. 228.—The Duryea Three-Cylinder Gasoline Vehicle Engine, with half the crank case sheathing removed, showing cranks, crank shaft, cam shaft, and working parts. The three cylinders have common supply and exhaust tubes; the charge is controlled by a single throttling link, shown at the top, and the igniting circuit has three bridges for the three cylinders. Cranks, as indicated, are at 120 degs.

multiple-cylinder engine, with four, and, latterly, with six cylinders. The reason for this change may be found in several important considerations:

1. The necessity of using larger, consequently heavier, cylinders to produce the increased power.

2. The difficulty of cooling large cylinders on high-speed engines.

3. The superior balance attained by increasing the number of the cylinders, and rendering the power-effect, as nearly as possible constant.

4. The liability to vibration in a gas engine decreases as the square of the number of cylinders; giving a four-cylinder engine 16 times less vibration than a one-cylinder, and a six-cylinder, 36 times less.

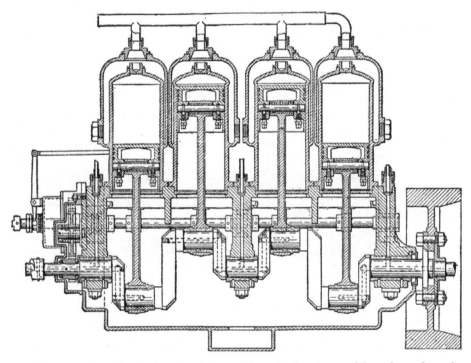

FIG. 229.—A Typical Four-cylinder Engine (Pierce), showing position of cranks and working parts, including secondary shafts.

The Four=Cylinder Engine.—As shown on Faurote's crank and cycle diagram, the four-cylinder engine enables the realization of a nearly-constant power impulse. In other words, a power stroke is occurring in some one of the four cylinders throughout the entire two revolutions of the cycle. Since, however the exhaust opens before the ends of the power stroke, thus rapidly reducing the power-pressure on the piston head, the power effort is neither constant nor uniform. This implies that the balance of the four-cylinder engine is not perfect, particularly at low speeds, when fluctuations in the power effect have relatively greater opportunty to interrupt the steady pull on the shaft. This is shown in a later paragraph.

The Six=Cylinder Engine.—Faurote's diagram also shows the six-cylinder engine and its relative advantages. Here, taking the circle as a complete cycle of two revolutions, or 720°, it may be seen that the value of the power-efforts on the crank shaft is practically constant. As indicated in the diagram, the order of firing in the cylinders is 1st, 5th, 3d, 6th, 2d, 4th. Taking the outermost of the six concentric circles as representing the cycle of the first cylinder, it may be seen that the suction stroke begins at the meridian, or 1°, and, extending through 180°, is followed by the compression stroke. The firing stroke begins at 360°,

Fɪɢ. 230.—Crankshaft of the Olds Six-Cylinder Engine, showing positions of the cranks.

and is completed at 540°. The exhaust opening, being set to occur at about 500°, is slightly preceded by the maximum in the fifth cylinder, which, as may be seen, occurs at 480°. The maximum in the first cylinder, occurring at 360°, involves that the first third of the power stroke in that cylinder is contemporaneous with the last third of the power stroke in the fourth cylinder. The second third of each power stroke is, therefore, the only portion that is not contemporaneous with some part of the power stroke in some other of the cylinders. This arrangement achieves a fairly approximate balance of pressure conditions, high with low, and low with high, throughout the entire cycle for six cylinders.

Multiple=Cylinder Performance.—A suggestive series of experiments on the balance and operation of four and six-cylinder engines is recorded in the following quotation from the well-known English automobilist, S. F. Edge, in a recent issue of *Motor Trader.* Beginning with a comparison of cylinders required to produce a given horse-power efficiency, say 40 horse-power, he estimates in the following manner:

Single cylinder diameter, 10 in.; total force of explosion on piston head, 28,282 lbs.

Double-cylinder diameter, about 6 in.; total force of explosion on piston head, 14,141 lbs.

Triple-cylinder diameter, 5⅝ in.; total force of explosion on piston head, 9,427 lbs.

Four-cylinder diameter, about 5 in.; total force of explosion on piston head, 7,070 lbs.

Six-cylinder diameter, 4 in.; total force of explosion on piston head, 4,713 lbs.

On the basis of these figures, Mr. Edge concludes, as follows:

"I think at the present time the six-cylinder may be taken as ideal. * * * It gives absolutely smooth running, owing to the continuous turning motion, and, at the same time, enormously reduces the cost of up-keep, owing to this regular torque, both on tires and on mechanical parts.

"In order that the steadiness of torque or turning effort in a six-cylinder engine may be fully appreciated, the diagrams given have been constructed from actual tests.

"The first consideration to be taken into account is, of course, the variation of pressure in the cylinder. For the purpose of discovering what actually takes place, a standard 40 horse-power six-cylinder Napier engine was put under test, and a large number of observations made with manograph indicator and pressure recorder. As a mean of all these readings, the indicator diagram [shown in Fig. 231] has been constructed.

"The vertical line is graduated to give pressures in pounds per square inch. From the figure it will be noticed that the compression is carried to about 75 lb. per square inch. The ignition takes place considerably before the end of this stroke, and the pressure rises very rapidly to nearly 450 lb. per square inch. The enormity of this pressure can be better appreciated, when given in total pressure on the piston. The bore of the cylinder is 4 in., the area of the piston 12.56 square inches, and, therefore, the total pressure on each piston is roughly 2 tons.

"The diagram also clearly shows the fall of pressure during the working stroke, and the slight rise and fall above and below the atmospheric pressure during exhaust and suction strokes.

"At the beginning of the suction stroke, for instance, the piston is being pulled along at an ever-increasing rate while the crank travels through approximately 90 degrees. Then, until the end of the stroke the piston tends to keep on moving, and has to be retarded and brought to rest by the crankshaft. In other words, the inertia of the piston and parts moving with it is retarding the crank during the first half of each stroke, and urging it on during the latter half.

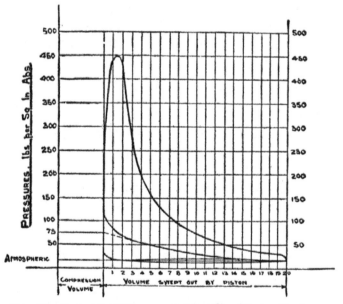

FIG. 231.—Edge's Average Diagram for Gasoline Engine Performances.

"The pressure in the cylinder and the force necessary to accelerate the piston have both been taken into account in the torque diagram for a single-cylinder motor. The turning effort is given in inch-pounds. For example, at point A, 400 inch-lbs. represent a pressure of 200 lbs. on the crank pin, tangential to the crank arm, and acting at a two-inch radius.

"The thick horizontal line represents the average turning-effort during the four strokes, which constitute the cycle. It also shows the effort of the inertia of the piston in giving negative and positive turning efforts at the beginning and end of each stroke. At the end of the compression

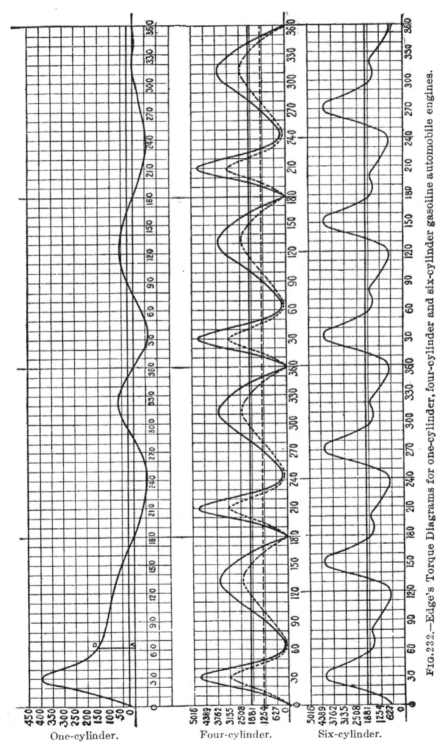

FIG. 232.—Edge's Torque Diagrams for one-cylinder, four-cylinder and six-cylinder gasoline automobile engines.

347

stroke, instead of getting a large negative turning effort, on account of the increased pressure in the cylinder, it will be seen that the torque has only a small negative value. This shows that the inertia of the piston coming to rest at the top of the stroke is nearly sufficient to compress the charge; also, when the crank is on the dead centres, there is no turning effort. It is from this diagram with its large variations that we must start and endeavor to obtain a constant torque.

"The dotted line in the four-cylinder figure is found by superimposing four of these diagrams, corresponding to four cylinders with crank at 180 degrees.

"It is not fair to compare the diagrams for four and six cylinders, for, the cylinders being all the same size, the six-cylinder engine will be giving one and a half times the power of the four, and therefore each vertical height of the dotted figure has been increased one and a half times to the full line, corresponding to larger pistons to equalize the powers of the two engines.

"The most important point to be noticed is that, with six cylinders, there is always a positive turning effort of at least 700 inch lbs. on the crank shaft, and that at no point of the cycle does it approach zero. With four cylinders and cranks at 180 degrees, there must of necessity be four points in the cycle, viz., when the cranks are on the dead centres, at which there can be no turning effort.

"The four-cylinder diagram shows also four other points, at which the torque has only a very small positive value, namely, less than 200 inch lb. This is accounted for by the retarding force of the pistons when being accelerated, after the effect of the explosion has passed. Had this diagram been constructed for any other pistons than the extremely light ones used in the Napier engines, it is extremely probable that at this point the torque would have a considerable negative value. The next rise in the torque is due to the forward pressure of the pistons when nearing the end of the stroke.

"A comparison of the two diagrams will be far more convincing than anything that can be written about them. The total inch-lb. pressures are given for convenience."

Position and Timing of the Valves.—Another matter logically related to the principles governing the balance of a four-cycle engine is the proper timing of the valves. As must be evident on reflection, the valves must open and close precisely at the proper moment, otherwise uneven working and waste of power are inevitable. The timing of the valves is well explained by Fay L. Faurote in the following passage, quoted here by his courtesy:

"The points of opening and closing of valves are designated in two ways: either in terms of degrees around the fly-wheel, or as distance moved by the piston in the cylinder. As it is much easier, after the motor has been assembled, to determine the position of the piston from marks on the fly-

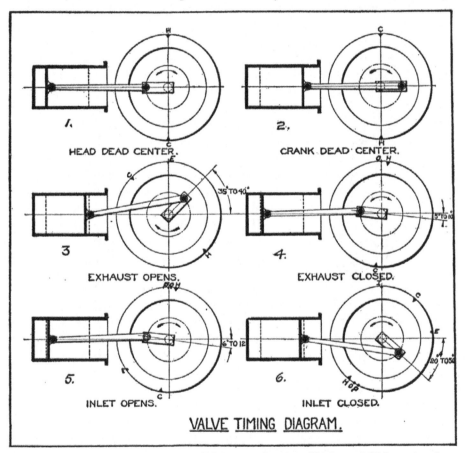

FIG. 233.—Faurote's Valve-Timing Diagram, showing Timing of Valves for One-Cylinder Engine.

wheel, the former method for setting valves has been almost universally adopted.

"As soon as the engine is finished, two marks, diametrically opposite, are located on the rim of the fly-wheel, such that when one is directly over the centre of the main shaft, the piston will be at one end of its stroke, or in other words, when either of these marks is on top, the piston will be on one of its 'dead centres.'

"Referring to Fig. 211, you will note that when the mark, H, passes a vertical line drawn through the centre of the shaft, the piston has just reached the outer end of its stroke, and when the mark, C, comes into this position then the opposite condition is true. These points, as mentioned before, are respectfully the *head* and *crank-end* 'dead centres.'

"Experiments have shown that the exhaust valve should open about 35 or 40 degrees before the crank arrives at the 'crank-end dead centre.' Therefore, No. 3 shows, approximately, relative positions of crank and piston when this opening should occur. In order to mark this position a line is drawn across the fly-wheel at the point, E. Next, as the closing should take place from 5 to 10 degrees late, that is after passing the 'head-end dead centre,' the point, O, is located, as represented in this position.

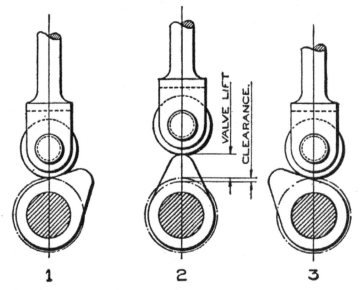

Fig. 234.—The Successive Positions of a Valve-lifting Cam (after Faurote).

The inlet, of course, opens immediately after the exhaust closes, so that the point, P, is next marked off a short distance back of O. Lastly, the time of closing the inlet is determined (this varies from 20 to 50 degrees after crank has passed the 'crank-end dead centre') and the point, I, is settled upon.

"Having located correctly all points of opening and closing of valves, we are ready to proceed with the timing. Glancing at Fig. 234, you will notice that No. 1 shows the cam just about to raise the plunger which operates the valve; No. 2 shows the valve at its highest point, or maximum lift, and No. 3, the position of the cam and roller at the point of closing. You will notice that a small amount of clearance is left, in order to insure a proper seating of the valve, when the cam has left the roller. It will easily be seen that as soon as the cam has turned far enough to cause friction between itself and the roller, the plunger will begin lifting the valve. As long as the roller turns freely it may be assumed that the valve is resting on its seat, but as soon as it appears to turn hard it is taken for granted that the valve is beginning to open. Naturally, when the cam is leaving the roller, the reverse is true.

"Now let us return to our original proposition, and see what use can be made of all this. We will first turn the fly-wheel over with the starting crank until the point, *E,* is directly over the centre of the crank-shaft. According to our calculations, the exhaust valve should be on the point of opening. Place your hand on the roller at the bottom of the valve plunger, and see whether or not it turns freely. If you find that it moves easily, turn the engine a little further in the direction of the arrow. A slight movement should cause the roller to tighten; if it does not, it shows that the cam has not yet come in contact with it, and hence the valve will not open soon enough. In this case turn the wheel back to its former position, and move the cam back around the cam shaft until the valve begins to open at the proper time. Frequently, in doing this, however, you will find that it will be impossible to make the valve close properly, and in that case it is necessary to braze a small piece on the side of the cam to increase its width in order to hold the valve open its required time. Having adjusted the opening, turn the fly-wheel around until the mark, *O,* shows up on top, and proceed in a similar way to find whether or not the roller frees itself at the right moment.

"Assuming that the exhaust valve has been satisfactorily disposed of, let us direct our attention to the inlet. Turn the fly-wheel over as before until the point, *P,* is just over the shaft. Then try the roller to see if it is just beginning to stick. If this is true, we can go on; if not, the same method of procedure has to be followed as in the case of the exhaust valve. When the time for the opening has been adjusted correctly, revolve the wheel until the mark, *I,* comes into position, when, of course, the roller should begin to loosen. After a little practice, by simply changing the shape of the cam, either by filing off or adding to its surface, you will be able to secure the results desired.

"Each engine requires a slightly different valve-timing, so it is impossible to give definite data regarding the above. Each manufacturer furnishes an instruction book which gives detailed information regarding proper valve-timing to be used for any particular size of motor. The diagram (Fig. 233) may be made of considerable assistance by properly substituting the values of angles given in the instruction book."

In timing the valves of a multiple-cylinder engine, this process must, of course, be repeated for each separate cylinder.

CHAPTER TWENTY-SEVEN.

Varieties of Controlling Device.—For the governing of four-cycle engines several different methods have been employed. They are:

1. Hit-and-Miss Governors.
2. Throttle Governors.
3. Ignition Control.

In addition to these may be mentioned such devices as the Winton pneumatic control, which may justly be awarded first place in its class.

Theories of Governing.—Classifying governing apparatus according to the operative theories involved, we have:

1. Valve-lift regulation.
2. Variation of the fuel mixture.
3. Timing of the ignition.

With any one of these means are generally provided for both automatic and intelligent control Although, at the present time, many authorities contend that all control of an automobile engine should be solely in the hand of the driver, automatic governors still hold their place on most of the best-known makes of engine.

Hit=and=Miss Governing.—The original Daimler engines were controlled by what is known as the "hit-and-miss" form of governor. Briefly described, the theory is that, at excessively high speeds, the action of the exhaust valve is interrupted by a mechanism which withdraws the cam-actuated push-rod out of its line, causing it to *miss*. At normal speeds the push-rod always *hits* the end of the valve stem, pushing the valve open against the tension of its spring. In the earlier models of Daimler's V-shaped engine the opening of the exhaust valve was controlled by a feather running in a double eccentric circular cam groove on the face of one of the crank disks, as shown in the half-sectional diagram. By means of a switch actuated by a sliding sleeve and centrifugal ball governor, the feather could be shunted from its course, so as to run in a nearly circular path, thus involving that the attached push-rod neither rises nor falls, and keeping the exhaust valve closed. This involved that the burned-out gases could not escape from the cylinder; also, that

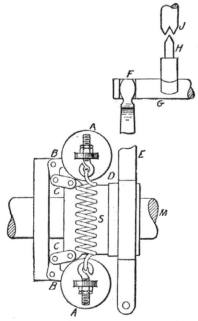

FIG. 235.—One type of Gas Engine Governor, which is an improved variation of the device used on the early Daimler motors. The parts are as follows: A and A, ball weights; B and B, bell cranks actuating the links. C and C, as the balls move outward resisting the tension of spring, S, and sliding sleeve, D, on the shaft, M. E is a lever arm attached to D, which moves the shaft, G, by contact at F, as shown, thus throwing the pick blade, H, out of contact with the end, J, of the exhaust valve rod.

no fresh charge could be taken in, the motor operation being suspended until the speed should fall to the proper rate.

In later models of Daimler engine a hit-and-miss governor of a different description was used, its object being to draw the push-rod away from the line in which it could hit and actuate the valve stem. As shown in an accompanying figure, the cam, *A*, rotated on shaft, *L*, bears upon the roller, *C*, and lifts the arm, *D*, pivoted at *K*, and held in position by a spring, *L*. By lifting arm, *D*, it also lifts pushrod, *B*, which opens the exhaust valve.

When, however, the speed of the motor has increased beyond the predetermined limit a sleeve of varying diameter, sliding on the same shaft, *L*, is slid along, so that the larger diameter is brought to bear against the downward extension, *H*, of the arm, *F*, thus causing *F* to incline on the pivot, *K*, toward the cylinder (at the right as in the cut), hence pushing rod, *B*, by link, *E*, out of range of arm, *D*, as it is moved upward by impulse from cam, *A*. In this case the exhaust valve is not opened.

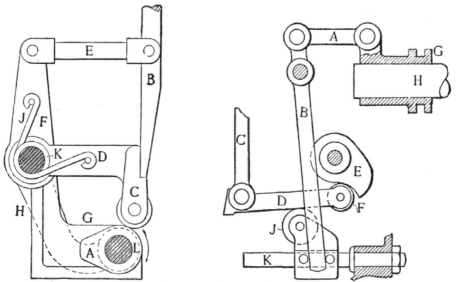

FIG. 236.—Hit and Miss Governor Mechanism of the later Daimler Motors.
FIG. 237.—Mechanism of the Peugeot Variable Exhaust Valve Lift.

Governing by Variable Valve Lift.—The Peugeots introduced another form of exhaust valve control apparatus, which, instead of operating to keep the valve closed, thus involving the difficulties incident on retaining the exhaust gases in the cylinder, gave a varying lift, according to the speed of the engine. As shown in figure 237, *A* is a link attached to spool, *G*, which is slid on shaft, *H*, as the governor works under speed of rotation. *A* actuates the lever, *B*, sliding the roller, *J*, on shaft, *K*, and thus moving the fulcrum of lever, *D*, varies the lift of pushrod, *C*, which receives its motion from cam, *E*, bearing upon roller, *F*.

Governing by Varying Charge Volume.—Instead of interrupting the movement of the exhaust valve, several engineers, notably Winton, Duryea and Mors, adopted the theory of governing by controlling the intake, and thus varying the volume of the fuel charge admitted to the cylinder. By this means the operation of the engine may be maintained at any desired point of speed or power. As shown in the diagram of the Mors engine, the centrifugal governor actuates a horizontal valve shaft, which, in turn, throws levers controlling cocks for varying the fuel supply admitted to the intake valves. A very similar arrangement is embodied on the Duryea three-cylinder engine, with the notable exception that hand control takes the place of automatic governing.

Winton's Pneumatic Governor.—Winton's governor controls the volume of the charge by varying the lift of the inlet valve. It may be operated both automatically and manually, and may be so adjusted that the engine can operate at any desired rate of speed, without interference. Each inlet valve has an elongated stem, which extends backward so as to carry the piston of a small cylinder to the rear of the valve chamber. A reciprocating air pump supplies air to this small cylinder, varying the travel of its piston, according to the speed of the engine. At high speeds the air pump works rapidly, greatly compressing the air before the small piston, and consequently opposing the free opening of the inlet valve; at low speeds, it works slower, allowing greater freedom to the inlet opening. Of course, with the pump working direct from the engine and constantly increasing the air pressure within the small cylinder, the point would soon be reached at which the inlet valve could not open and the operation of the engine must cease. To forestall this difficulty, a "set governor" or regulating cock is provided, for the purpose of allowing a certain proportion of the air to escape from the small cylinder, thus making the rate of speed constant at any desired point. Furthermore, there is another regulating vent cock, controlled by a push button at the driver's foot, which enables him to increase the speed to the point of allowing the air to escape as fast as it comes from the pump, thus removing all obstruction to the lift of the inlet valve.

The details of the Winton governor are given in the accompanying diagram. Here, air compressor piston, *P,* is driven directly from one of the motor pistons, and forces air past the check valve, *V,* into the compressed air cylinder, where it operates to hold the piston to the left, and keeps the intaking valve closed, regardless of the piston suction tending to open the valve by moving it to the right. By means of the regulating cock the pressure may be reduced in the air cylinder, thus permitting the intake valve to open, more or less as the air pressure is more or less

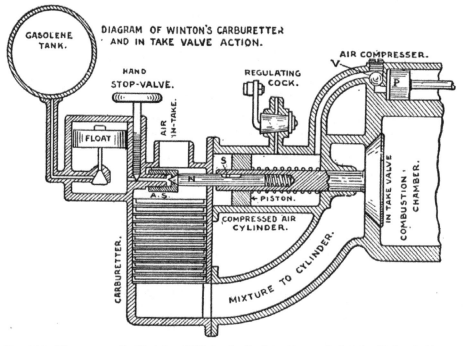

Fig. 238.—Diagrammatic Sketch of Winton's Carburetter and Intake Valve Action, as applied to an Horizontal Cylinder Engine.

reduced in the cylinder. The needle valve, *N,* is seated in and carried by the intake valve stem, is spring pressed to the left by a coiled spring at its right end, is retained by a cross pin, *S,* and co-acts with the adjustable seat, *A, S,* to close or open the passage of gasoline from the float chamber to the carburetter underneath, whence the mixture is drawn to the cylinder through the intake valve. No gasoline can go to the carburetter unless the motor piston is moved, and more or less gasoline goes to the carburetter as the intake valve is lifted more or less. The regulating cock governs the action of the motor by determining the amount of air that is allowed to escape through the vent.

Cadillac Variable Valve=Lift.—An automatic governing device, which varies the lift of the inlet and exhaust valves in a manner analogous to that adopted by Winton is used with the Cadillac four-cylinder engine. In this device, the pressure of a liquid is used to vary the lifts of the variable valve cams fixed on a rotating countershaft, as shown in fig. 239. As here shown, the regulation is accomplished by sliding the cam shaft endwise. The device is described, as follows:

C is a portion of the cam shaft showing two of the cams: A,

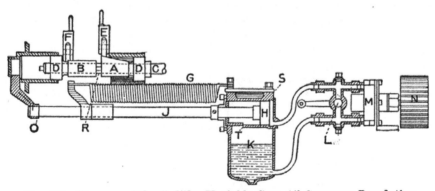

FIG. 239.—Diagram of the Cadillac Variable-Cam Oil-Governor Regulation.

an inlet cam operating the inlet valve through the roll and valve-lifter, E; B, an exhaust cam, operating an exhaust valve through the roll and valve-lifter F. D, D are two bearings for the cam-shaft C, which are also free to move in the bored-out parts of the motor frame. R is a hardened steel finger with its end between the exhaust cam, B, and the inlet cam, A. R is carried on the piston rod, J, which is attached to the piston head, H. The piston and rod, and with them the finger, R, and the cam shaft, C, are all normally held in the position shown by the coil spring, G. With the cam shaft in this position the inlet cam, A, gives the maximum lift to the inlet valve, allowing the motor to develop its full power and speed. M is an oil pump driven by the gear, *N*. The pump, *M*, draws its supply from the well, *K*, and discharges into the closed end of the cylinder, *S*. This discharge is governed by the by-pass, *L*. If L be closed and the motor started, the pump, *M*, discharging into the cylinder, *S*, will force the piston, *H*, out until it uncovers the edge of the discharge port, *T*, and allowing the oil to flow back into the well, *K*. Under these conditions the cam shaft, *C*, is held at the other extreme of its travel so that the inlet cam, *A*, causes a very slight lift of the inlet valve, giving the minimum speed and power from the motor. If the by-pass, *L*, be partly open, the tension of the coil spring, *G*, will carry the cam shaft back, until

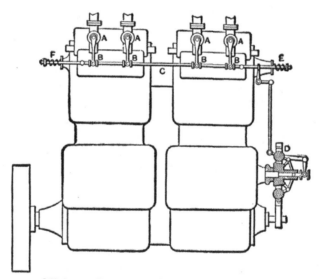

Fɪɢ. 240.–Diagram of Volume Throttling Device on the Mors Engine. A and A are throttle valves on the inlet pipes; B and B, valve levers; C, valve shaft, under control of the governor, D; E and F, springs, used either singly or together, according to control, so as to vary the opening of the inlet. System like the Duryea.

the speed of the motor increases, so that the discharge from the pump, *M*, balances the tension of the spring, *G*, in spite of the opening of the by-pass, *L*. It will be seen that under these conditions, if the load of the motor is increased the reduction in speed will immediately result in an increased lift of the inlet valve, allowing the motor to develop greater power to meet the increased demand. If the load on the motor be decreased, the increase in speed will cause the inlet valve to receive less lift, thus reducing the power of the motor according to the reduced demand upon it.

Varying Mixture and Varying Volume.—Winton claims, as the most conspicuous advantage of his pneumatic control, that the quality or air and gas proportions, of the fuel mixture are constant at any predetermined point of carburetter regulation, and that the volume only is varied, thus supplying fuel as required and effecting a great economy. With reduced volume the

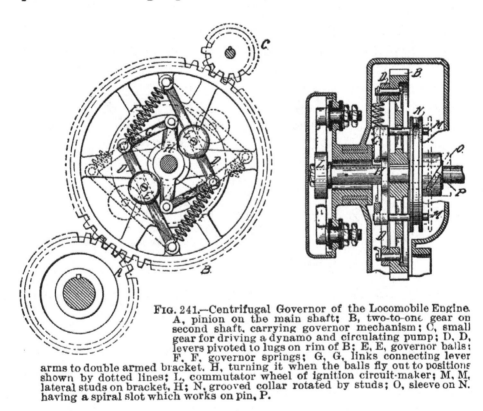

FIG. 241.—Centrifugal Governor of the Locomobile Engine. A, pinion on the main shaft; B, two-to-one gear on second shaft, carrying governor mechanism; C, small gear for driving a dynamo and circulating pump; D, D, levers pivoted to lugs on rim of B; E, E, governor balls; F, F, governor springs; G, G, links connecting lever arms to double armed bracket. H, turning it when the balls fly out to positions shown by dotted lines; L, commutator wheel of ignition circuit-maker; M, M, lateral studs on bracket, H; N, grooved collar rotated by studs; O, sleeve on N. having a spiral slot which works on pin, P.

initial and compression pressures are also reduced. As against "volume throttling," however, very many engineers still adhere to the theory of varying mixture, reducing excessive speeds by allowing greater proportions of air to enter the mixing chamber, and increasing the proportion of gas as the speed falls. This practice involves, of course, that the same volume of fuel mixture is always admitted to the cylinder, and, consequently, that the initial and compression pressures are invariable. The two theories are one in point of reducing the explosion pressure, in order to reduce speed.

The Riker Governor.—The governor used on the Locomobile gasoline engine, for automatically effecting the throttling of the carburetter and the retarding of the spark, is a good example of it class. As shown in the accompanying diagrams, the arms carrying the governor weight actuate links at right angles to their normal position, and cause a sleeve on the governor shaft to turn on the shaft through part of a revolution, according to the speed

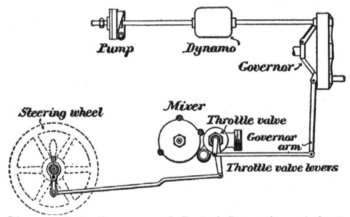

Fig. 242.—Diagram of the Governor and Control Connections of the Locomobile Engine, showing manner of automatically and manually throttling the carburetter.

of the engine. The part rotation of this sleeve serves to retard the spark by shifting the contact of the sparking commutator. At the same time, two pins, attached to the sleeve arms and projecting through the gear into the opposite direction, give a similar turn to the governor shipper loosely let on to the governor shaft. This shipper has a hub with a spiral groove, through which projects a pin fixed into the shaft, as shown. By the part revolution given the shipper by the pins the hub moves backward along the shaft as far as the pin in the groove will allow it, thus actuating a link for throttling the carburetter. As the engine slows down, the sleeve holding the commutator cam returns to its position, and the pins, acting on the shipper, moves the slotted hub into normal position, restoring the full feed of fuel mixture. In starting the engine, the driver reverses the lead, retarding the spark until the full speed is attained, then leaving control to the governor.

Throttling the Fuel Mixture.—In practical operation the fuel mixture is throttled by a valve operated directly by an arm actuated by the centrifugal governor. As shown in the several types of carburetter, described in another chapter, an important

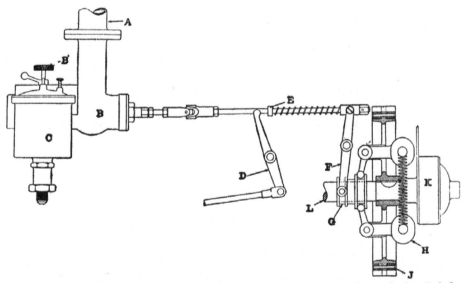

FIG. 243.—Automatic Governor and Hand Throttling Connections of the Toledo Engine. The parts are: A, the suction pipe of the carburetter; B, the carburetter; B', the needle valve on the float chamber; C, the float chamber; D, throttle controller on rod. E; F, the governor lever; G, the sliding governor sleeve; H, governor weight; J, fibre gear on cam shaft; K, sparking commutator; L, cam shaft.

part in the work of governing the engine takes place in the mixing chamber. In all devices for automatically regulating the air-intake of the carburetter, the means adopted is, briefly, some form of sliding or rotating valve for varying the opening of inlet tube. Accurate adjustment of the valve for the particular fuel to be used fixes the maximum and minimum openings at such points that the resulting mixtures of air and fuel gas are always within the explodable limits. The result is that a greater proportion of air is admitted at a high speed, and, consequently, the power effect of the explosion is decreased. As the speed falls, the opening of the air inlet is decreased, and, consequently, the power effect of the explosion is augmented.

Varying the Point of Ignition.—Another effective method of controlling the speed of the engine, is retarding of the spark. In practice, this involves some means for connecting the governor to the rotating member of the "commutator" or contact-breaker, so as to produce the igniting spark at the desired point in the cycle.

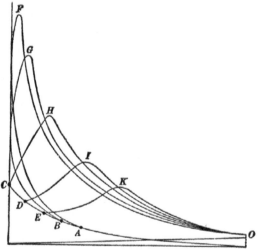

FIG. 244.—Composite Indicator Card for a Gas Engine, showing varying explosion pressures due to varying the time of the spark. A and B are ahead; C on dead centre; D and E, back of centre.

The Correct Time for Ignition.—As with other matters connected with the control of gasoline engines, the time of the spark may be varied only between very definite limits. In general, these limits are between one-third stroke ahead and one-seventh stroke after the dead centre of the crank, according to the kind of fuel, the strength of the mixture and the normal speed of the engine. If it occurs too early, the point of maximum pressure is reached before the compression stroke is completed, and very frequently a "back-kick," or tendency to reversal of the motion follows; certainly a complete waste of the power effort. If it occurs too late, the maximum pressure is reached only when the stroke is far advanced, with the result that a large part of the power effect is lost. It is desirable, however, that the point of maximum pressure should not occur on the dead centre of the crank, since this produces a wholly unnecessary jar and friction on the crank pin, and, as in the two previous cases, wastes the power. Under usual conditions, the point of maximum pressure, or complete ignition, should occur at the beginning of the out-stroke of the piston.

Spark=Timing and Power Effect.—The effects obtained by varying the time of ignition with a constant mixture are shown by the accompanying diagram fig. 244.

Here points *A, B, C, D, E,* are taken at the moment of spark ignition, and the points, *F, G, H, J, K,* at the point of greatest pressure. The point, *A,* is about one-third stroke ahead of dead centre; *B,* about one-fourth ahead; *C,* on the dead centre; *D,* one-sixteenth after; *E,* one-seventh after. The curves, *AF, BG, CH, DJ, EK,* show graphically the relative power effort to be obtained by varying the spark from positive to negative lead.

Spark=Regulation and Speed.—The field for the most frequent application of engine governing by spark regulation is found in the practice of shifting the point of ignition, so as to enable the maintenance of high speeds. This is true for two very definite reasons:

1. With ordinary forms of jump and break spark, the fuel ignites progressively, instead of detonating, or exploding, consequently entailing the lapse of an appreciable period before the maximum pressure is reached.

2. The spark on a high-tension circuit always occurs at a point measurably later than the closure of the primary circuit.

At high speeds, therefore, the time of circuit-closing is advanced in proportion to the number of revolutions per minute, in order to begin the out-stroke as nearly as possible at maximum pressure. This is illustrated in the accompanying diagram from *Technics,* which shows average points for circuit-closure or spark-timing: for hand-starting at *A;* for slow running at *B;* for full load at 400 R. P. M. at *C;* for full load at 1,200 R. P. M. at *D;* for very light load at about 400 R. P. M. at *E.* The situation is set forth, as follows:

"Many attempts have been made to render timing automatic, but up to the present none of these has proved satisfactory. To appreciate the difficulties involved it is necessary to consider all the causes that render variation necessary. It is found that, as an engine runs faster, the point of sparking has to be advanced, so as to cause it to occur earlier, and, when an engine is running very fast, it is necessary for the theoretical

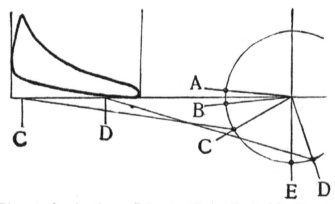

FIG. 245.—Diagram showing Proper Points for Closing the Ignition Circuit at Various Speeds and Loads: A, point of ignition for hand starting; B, point of ignition for very slow running; C, point of ignition for full load at about 400 r.p.m.; D, point of ignition for full load at about 1,200 r.p.m.; E, approximate point of ignition for very light load at about 400 r.p.m.

point of ignition to be even as early as 110° of crank travel before the firing center.

"The principal reason for this is the interval of time between the first ignition of the gas and the instant when maximum pressure is reached; this interval, being approximately constant, renders it necessary to advance the point of ignition as the engine speed increases, if it is desired to keep the point of maximum pressure at the beginning of the working stroke. Two other causes add to this effect—the lag of the trembler on the induction coil, and the lessened compression at high speeds, due to the loss of volumetric efficiency caused by the wire-drawing effect of both induction and exhaust valves. These are slightly compensated for by the quicker burning of the richer mixture, taken in at high speeds, caused by the increased vacuum in the jet chamber. It is evident that the coil lag is a time-element and that the interval between the completion of the electric circuit and the "break," due to the downward movement of the trembler, will be constant for the same coil, and quite independent of the engine speed. This factor is of less importance since the general adoption of high speed tremblers, and is, of course, entirely absent in magneto ignition. The loss of volumetric efficiency results in more burnt gas being left in the cylinder from the previous explosion, and the taking-in of a lessened charge, causing a drop in the compression and consequent slower burning, as the degree of compression has considerable influence on the rate of

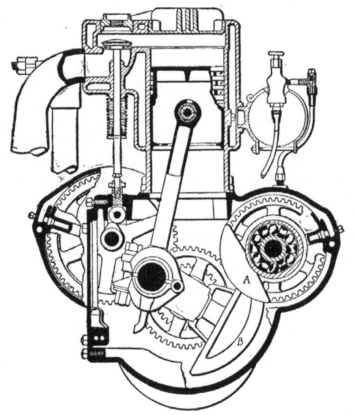

Fig. 246.—End view of Oakland engine showing balance. To the left is the driving mechanism of the valves and to the right are ball-bearing balance weights, A and B. These weights are placed on an eccentric shaft to procure variations in setting. The construction is such that these weights are timed to come into action at the moment when vibration sets in.

burning of an explosive mixture of given quality. The enriching of the mixture at high speeds compensates for this to a certain extent, depending on the efficiency of the valve gear and carburetter, but, of course, this compensation is only at the sacrifice of fuel efficiency.

"From the foregoing remarks it will be evident that if the mixture is throttled, thus lowering the compression, it will be necessary to advance the spark to obtain a correct diagram at the same engine speed; and this effect will generally be intensified, as throttling usually results in a weakened mixture. Any automatic device must, therefore, not only vary the contact to compensate for variation of engine speed, but, if correct ignition and maximum efficiency is desired, also for varying degrees of throttling and alterations of quality of mixture."

Spark and Throttle Governors.—As may be readily understood, governing by retarding the spark is very wasteful of energy, since it results inevitably in exhausting before ignition is complete. For this reason, when spark regulation is used in automatic governing, it is generally in connection with mixture-throttling, which doubly reduces the power effect. In general, however, precisely the same result follows with the use of a weak mixture as with the use of a retarded spark—reduced power effect and slow combustion of the charge. A rich mixture and a positive lead to the spark alike produce increased power effect and rapid combustion. The diagram, shown in Fig. 222, could be produced as the result of varying the fuel mixture, as readily as by shifting the time of the spark-occurrence.

The diagram in Fig. 245 shows that the best effect of the exploding fuel may be obtained only by advancing the spark when desiring to run at high speeds. In order to achieve this end, several cars, notably the Jeffrey Rambler, are equipped with an automatic spark-advance governor.

CHAPTER TWENTY-EIGHT

CLUTCHES AND TRANSMISSIONS.

Essentials of a Gasoline Vehicle.—Every vehicle propelled by a hydro-carbon, or internal-combustion, engine, popularly known as a "gasoline engine," must have a transmission gear, for varying the ratio of speed and power transmitted to the road wheels. The transmission gear is connected to the engine shaft through a clutch, which may be thrown into engagement, to start the vehicle, and thrown out again to stop it.

It is necessary to use some form of throw-out clutch, because it would be difficult to start the engine with the machinery and running gear connected.

It is desirable to use a speed-reducing and changing transmission, between the engine and the road wheels, because the internal-combustion engine is less flexible than the steam engine, and requires a reducing gear to effect a rational economy. Without such a gear, the road wheels may be driven direct from the engine shaft, and changes of speed and power-effect produced by throttling, as already explained. The fact remains, however, that a much more powerful engine would be required than is now used on any vehicle. This is true because, with every throttling of the charge of a gas engine, the initial pressures are reduced, with a consequent reduction of the explosion and the mean effective pressures. In order, therefore, to run at moderate speeds, the engine would have to be throttled down to one-half or one-third its normal power. In ascending hills full power would often be required, and this would be far in excess of what is generally used.

The force of these remarks becomes apparent when we remember that the best efficiency of a gas engine is obtained by maintaining as nearly as possible a constant speed and power output.

The French designer, Vallee, drove his vehicles from the engine shaft through leather belting. Duryea uses a two-speed transmission, doing all his driving, except hill-climbing, on the high gear, and varying the speed by throttling. Both use very high-powered engines, in order to allow a wide range of throttling, from maximum to minimum power without danger of failure.

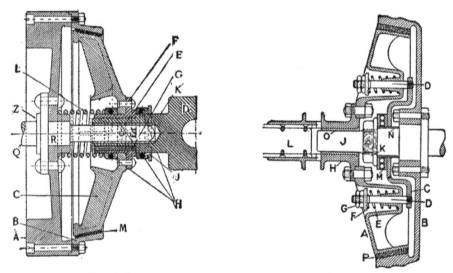

FIG. 247.   FIG. 248.

FIG. 247.—Internal Cone Clutch of the Peerless Car. A, engine fly-wheel; B, female cone; C, male cone; D, universal coupling on male cone; E, bushing on D; F, collar keyed on D; G, key; H, ball bearings for taking up the thrust on disengaging clutch; J, flange on ball cone; K, receptacle on D for operating yoke; L, spiral spring for retaining clutch surface contact; M, leather band riveted on C, giving good friction surface; Q, main shaft; R, portion of shaft turned down to fit fly-wheel; S, portion of shaft turned down to receive clutch sleeve; Z, flange to which fly-wheel is bolted.

FIG. 248.—External Cone Clutch of the Pope-Toledo Car. A, fly-wheel clutch cone; B, fly-wheel; C, fly-wheel clutch stud plate; D, D, clutch spring studs; E, clutch spring; F, spring retainer; G, retainer lock nut; H, sliding sleeve for setting clutch; J, crank shaft end; K, crank shaft nut; L, tail shaft; M, ball thrust collar; N, ball thrust bush; O, sliding sleeve bush; P, clutch cone leather.

Forms of Clutch.—There are four forms of clutch in use on gasoline propelled vehicles:

1. Cone Clutches.

2. Drum and Band Clutches.

3. Expanding Ring Clutches.

4. Compression Disc Clutches.

Requirements in Clutches.—The leading requirements in a serviceable clutch are:

1. Gradual engagement, in order to avoid jerks due to too sudden throwing on of the power.

2. Large contact surfaces.

Forms of Transmission Gear.—There are four forms of transmission gear in use at the present time:

1. Sliding-Spur, or Clash-Gear Transmissions, which may be distinguished in two forms:

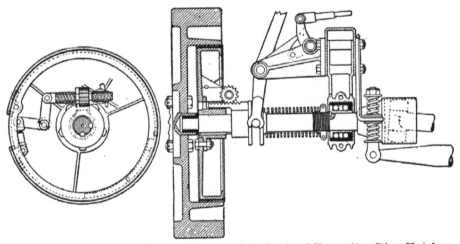

Fig. 249.–End View and Cross Section of the Packard Expanding Ring Clutch.

a. One-lever, sliding-sleeve gears, such as the Panhard-Levassor, Decauville, Riker, Packard and Toledo.

b. One-lever, selective-finger or gridiron slot transmissions, such as the Daimler, Columbia, Knox, and numerous other forms used on modern gasoline cars.

2. Meshing-Spur, or Individual--Clutch Transmissions.

Prominent among these may be mentioned the old Winton and Haynes-Apperson gears.

3. Planetary Transmissions.

Among planetary transmissions may be mentioned the Duryea, Olds and Cadillac.

4. Friction-Disc Transmissions.

In addition to these may be mentioned the belt and pulley transmission of the early Daimler vehicles and others.

Cone Clutches.—The cone clutch is the typical form, and was formerly in practically universal use. As shown in accompanying figures, cone clutches consist of two members: a dish-shaped ring, secured to the face of the fly-wheel, and a truncated cone, carried by a sleeve sliding on the main shaft, and held in close fit by means of a spring. The first member is called the "female cone," the second, the "male cone."

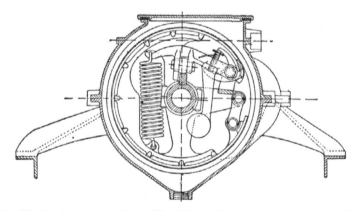

FIG. 250.—Mechanism of the Expanding Ring Clutch of the Columbia Light Car.

There are two varieties of cone clutch: the external cone clutch, in which the male cone is forced against the fly-wheel from the rear; and the internal cone clutch, in which the male cone is contained within the other member and is forced into contact from the front. The latter, or self-contained clutch, is a generally favored pattern. In both forms of cone clutch the contact is between a metal surface and one of leather or fibre. Because it is essential that no oil or grit be allowed to collect on the friction surfaces, the internal cone clutch is preferable, as enabling the surfaces to be more readily protected.

Cone Clutch Efficiency.—In order to achieve good power transmission by means of a clutch, two things are essential:

1. Sufficient friction surface.

2. Proper angularity of the cone.

The angularity generally adopted is between 12° and 15°, generally nearer the latter, which affords a friction surface of about ⅛ the fly-wheel diameter in breadth. To increase or decrease the angle of the cone would neutralize the friction effect.

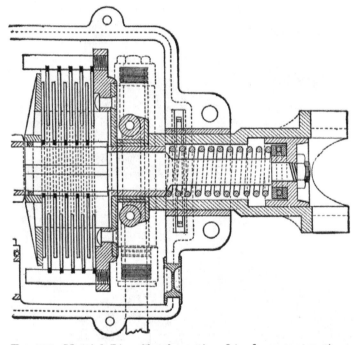

FIG. 251.—MultipleDisc Clutch, sectioned to show construction.

Troubles with Cone Clutches.—Although cone clutches possess the advantage of simple construction, and may be readily thrown in and out of action, they are subject to two grave defects:

1. Unless skillfully handled, the power will be thrown on with a jerk, not gradually, as it should be, thus jarring the machinery and annoying the passengers.

2. The friction surfaces, when worn, are liable to slip on each other, thus losing power and jerking rather than pulling the machinery.

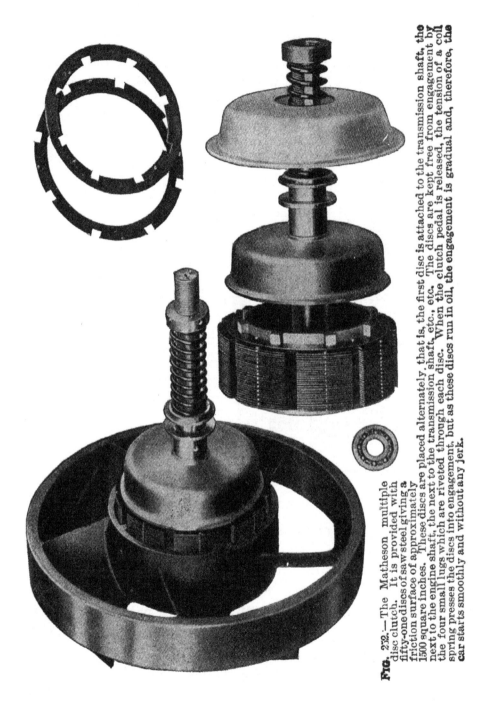

FIG. 232.—The Matheson multiple disc clutch. It is provided with fifty-one discs of saw steel giving a friction surface of approximately 1500 square inches. These discs are placed alternately, that is, the first disc is attached to the transmission shaft, the next to the engine shaft, the next to the transmission shaft, etc., etc. The discs are kept free from engagement by the four small lugs which are riveted through each disc. When the clutch pedal is released, the tension of a coil spring presses the discs into engagement, but as these discs run in oil, the engagement is gradual and, therefore, the car starts smoothly and without any jerk.

In order to avoid the first difficulty several designers have placed small spiral springs at intervals on the surface of the male cone, or between the cones, thus rendering the grip between the surfaces gradual. Such springs may act efficiently, but are objectionable as complicating construction.

Drum and Band Clutches.—Clutches of the drum and band type are really only variations of the form of brakes most common on motor carriages. They are generally used in connection with planetary, or epicyclic, transmissions, and consist simply in leather or fibre rings, which are compressed against the periphery of drums, in order to prevent rotation. They will be described in connection with planetary transmissions.

Expanding Ring Clutches.—Expanding ring clutches are used by several designers as convenient substitutes for the ordinary cone clutches. Mechanically, they are identical with the expanding ring brakes, except for the fact that their use accomplishes the connection into a working unit of two rotating shafts. According to engineering authorities, the cone clutch and the expanding band clutch are similar in theory, the angularity of the cone in the cone clutch being the same as the angle of the operating levers in the band clutch. The friction surfaces of the ring clutch may be both of metal or the ring may be faced with fibre.

Compression Disc Clutches.—The disc clutch is the latest and most satisfactory solution of the clutch problem. Briefly described, it consists of three or more metal discs secured alternately to the clutch shaft and to the face of the engine fly-wheel. By the pressure of a powerful spring the discs are forced together, thus involving a close driving contact, which cannot slip. Unlike other forms of clutch, the disc clutch should be soaked with oil. This contact is gradually made, as is not the case with all other clutches.

Friction=Disc Transmissions.—The friction-disc transmission undoubtedly has a large future. It obviates all the difficulties incident upon the use of sliding spur gears or planetary speed changers, and also does away with clutches of all descriptions. In practical service upon all weights of vehicle it has already demonstrated its ability to transmit power as efficiently as any other device. Briefly described, the friction transmission consists of two elements, the driving friction disc and the driven friction disc. The simplest form, the driven disc is set on a shaft at right angles to the driving disc, and is

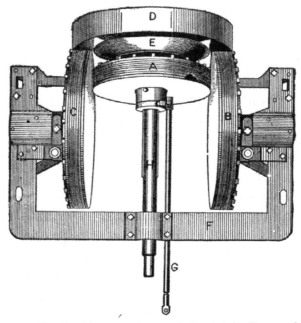

FIG. 253 —A Type of Friction Transmission. A is the driven disc on the transmission shaft; H, B and C are friction idlers driven from driving disc, D; E, is the clutch; F, the transmission frame; G, the lever for changing the speeds by shifting disc A, along shaft, H.

rotated by friction contact between its edge and the face of the driver. When the edge of the driven disc is driven on a circle nearest the periphery of the driver, its speed is greatest. As it is slid along its shaft, toward the centre of the driver, as may be done by means of a squared portion or splines, its speed is constantly decreased. At the center of the driving disc it ceases to rotate. If slid beyond the centre of the driver, its motion is reversed.

Clutch Requirements.—The construction of a clutch must be such that it does not apply the full power of the engine at once, but does so gradually, in order that the car may start slowly and without jerking. If the power were applied suddenly, the machinery might be badly strained, or again, the resistance of the stationary car might be sufficient to overcome the momentum of the engine and cause it to stop between power strokes.

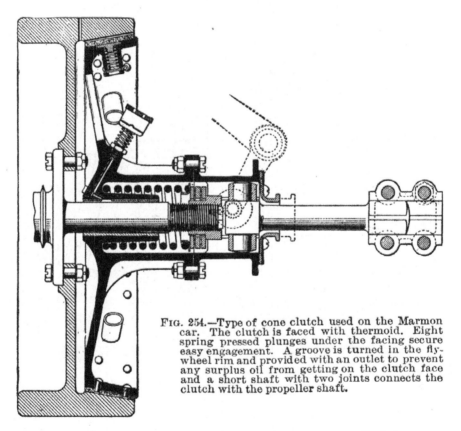

Fig. 254.—Type of cone clutch used on the Marmon car. The clutch is faced with thermoid. Eight spring pressed plunges under the facing secure easy engagement. A groove is turned in the flywheel rim and provided with an outlet to prevent any surplus oil from getting on the clutch face and a short shaft with two joints connects the clutch with the propeller shaft.

A clutch is not necessary on automobiles propelled by steam or electricity as these powers are more flexible, that is, the application of power is not intermittent, as with the gas engine.

A clutch must be capable of transmitting the maximum power of the engine to which it is applied without slip or loss. This is in order to avoid a waste of power. In addition a clutch must be easy to operate, being engaged or disengaged with minimum exertion on the part of the operator.

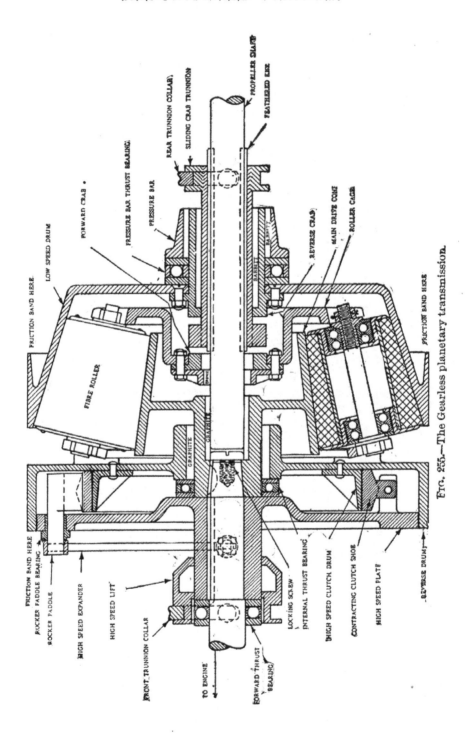

FIG. 255.—The Gearless planetary transmission.

It is essential that the clutch disengage promptly, that there may be no drag or continued rotation of the parts after disengagement. It must be of such design that the co-acting surfaces will operate for extended periods without material wear. Silent operation whether in engaging or releasing, is a desirable quality.

A clutch should be easy of removal for inspection or repairs and should be provided with suitable adjustments so that a certain amount of wear between the surfaces could be compensated for without renewal of surfacing.

It should be as simple as possible, of substantial design and construction, and with as few operating parts, which would be liable to get out of order, as is consistent to preserve proper operation. In event of the parts needing replacement, or of wear being serious enough to require new frictional surfaces, it should be of such construction that the replacements could be made with minimum expense.

The Gearless Transmission.—The transmission of the large Gearless cars, which is their distinguishing feature, is of the planetary type as shown in fig. 255.

There are two speeds forward and reverse without the use of any gears, the high speed being direct, in which the change speed elements revolve together as a unit, with no internal friction nor rolling contact, the entire change speed unit revolving together as a flywheel. It consists of six large special fiber rolls of conical shape revolving on and in an exterior and interior cone. These two cones co-act with a sliding, double faced, solid jaw clutch, which is moved to the extreme forward position to give the low speed forward, and to the extreme rearward position to give the reverse. The internal cone is constantly pressed toward the external cone by means of a spring, so as to always insure "bite" enough to make the six cone rollers revolve without slipping in the low speed and reverse drives.

The gearless transmission has the advantage of no change gear friction whatever on the high speed, or direct drive, and rolling friction engagement in the low speed and reverse.

The coned rollers are held laterally in a cage of large diameter and press against an iron cone made fast to the extension of the motor shaft. On their opposite faces they press against an internally faced cone, also of iron, and which is concentric with the propeller shaft of the car. The cone, roller and cup angles are such that the three elements roll together without any sliding, and hence without sliding friction, save in case of the slipping of the six rollers. To avoid the slipping of the rollers on the cone or in the cup a heavy spring pressure is applied to the cone cup to force it towards the driving cone, this pressure being sufficient to make it impossible for the motor to slide the roller surfaces on the cone or in the cup.

Cork Inserts.—In connection with clutches, cork is used to a considerable extent and with success. It is a peculiar product and performs in accordance with its peculiar characteristics. In the first instance, it has a high co-efficient of friction, so that high pressure is not necessary, and its co-efficient of friction is but little influenced by the question of lubrication. In other words, the cork will hold on a dry surface or if the surface be lubricated and the degree of polish of the surface be not a factor of such marked import as would be the case in the absence of the cork.

High temperatures are not so liable to char cork as they would leather or fibre. This is an important matter in clutches. Even wood will be charred by the heat generated in clutches under certain conditions, which is fair evidence of the fact that the temperature can raise to a point as high as 500 degrees centigrade.

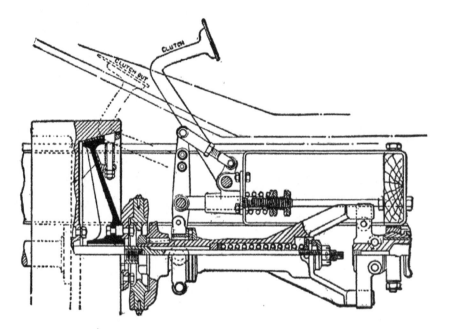

Fig. 256.—Showing method of mounting a cone clutch. The dotted outline of clutch. The dotted outline of clutch pedal shows position for releasing the clutch.

As a rule, the corks are forced into suitable cavities formed for them in one of the metallic frictional surfaces. The corks are previously boiled and thereby softened and then pressed into the cavities. Thus established in a metal surface, they normally protrude above the surrounding surface and engage first when the surfaces are brought together. If sufficient pressure be applied to the clutch they are forced down flush with the metal surface and act with it in carrying the load. Following the release of the load, they again protrude beyond the surrounding metal surface.

Two forms of cork are used, one being the cork in its natural condition, the other prepared as follows: Small pieces are compressed into sheets and blocks of any desired shape under very great pressure and under enough heat to cause the natural gums of the corks to exude and act as a binder.

CHAPTER TWENTY-NINE.

Principles of Operation.—The term *transmission* has come to mean only that portion of the transmission gearing proper which lies between the engine shaft and the propeller shaft or driving chain, and does not include the rest of the driving gear such as the bevel gear, jack shaft or differential.

A transmission is necessary on account of the nature of the gas engine cycle. The piston of a gas engine is operated by an intermittent force, and not, as in the case of a steam engine, by a continuous pressure. A gas engine running at high speed, however, produces a fairly uniform turning effect, so that after it gets under way the intermittent action of the driving force is not so noticeable.

A four cycle engine which receives only one impulse in two revolutions, must give to the flywheel during that impulse, enough momentum to keep the engine going at approximately uniform speed during the exhaust, suction and compression strokes.

In other words, the flywheel must overcome by its momentum, for one and a half revolutions, the resistance of the load and also that due to the back pressure of exhaust, suction and compression.

So far as turning effect is concerned, that is, the number of impulses per revolution, one steam engine cylinder is equivalent to four gas engine cylinders of the four cycle type, therefore, with the latter a heavy flywheel is necessary to transform the highly varying and intermittent driving force into one of nearer constant intensity so that uniform rotation may be approached.

One of the first objects, therefore, of a transmission is to allow the engine to speed up until the energy which it stores up in the fly wheel is sufficient to keep the shaft revolving at a speed showing no great percentage of variation.

Secondly, a transmission is necessary when the engine is required to work under a heavy load which under other circumstances would cause it to slow down, and stall if required to work under such conditions any great length of time.

For instance, it may be assumed, 1, that a man is raising a bucket in a well by winding a rope around the drum of a windlass as shown in fig. 257, and 2, that the bucket must be raised a certain number of feet every minute; then if the bucket of water weigh such an amount as to require all his strength to fulfill these conditions, and that any extra weight added to the bucket would over tax his strength to such an extent as to make further progress impossible, it is evident that some mechanical contrivance is necessary which will enable him to exert the same strength but apply it through a longer period of time.

To make this plain, it may be assumed that he wished to lift a barrel weighing 600 pounds, ten feet. This would be impossible for him to accomplish in a direct manner. If, however, he should build an incline long enough, he would be able to roll it up accomplishing the same work, but taking a longer time. Another way of doing this would be by the use of a lever.

Figs. 257 and 258.—Diagrams illustrating transmission principles. A lever is shown in fig. 257 attached direct to a drum and in fig. 258 gear wheels are shown placed between the lever and drum. If the force applied to the lever be the same in each case, a heavier weight may be raised with the geared lever because the force acts through a greater distance, the gear wheels multiplying the revolutions of the lever necessary to lift the weight a given distance.

Now, returning to the first illustration, instead of turning the drum of the windlass direct by hand, a gear may be placed on the end of the drum and constructed to mesh with a smaller gear attached to the lever as shown in fig. 258.

To illustrate the principles involved, it may be assumed that the large gear on the drum is three times the diameter of the small gear. It will, therefore, require three revolutions of the small gear to one of the large gear, and the pressure exerted will be only one-third of that required if the crank were fastened to the drum direct as shown in fig. 257. In either case, *the work done is the same.*

To compare this with the conditions of automobile operation, the work required to lift the bucket may be represented by the work required to drive the machine, and the man's effort, or force applied to the lever of the windlass, by the pressure exerted on the piston of the engine.

Work is the product of two factors: *force* and *distance* through which the force acts.

The office of the transmission is to keep this first factor—*force* —within proper limits at the engine while allowing it to vary widely at the rear driving wheels of the car.

To illustrate this in the operation of an automobile, a conventional diagram fig. 259, shows an engine shaft placed parallel to the rear axle. Two cone pulleys, one on the engine shaft and one on the rear axle are connected by a belt so that the speed of the engine may be varied by shifting the belt from one side to the other; that is, if the belt be started on the left side of the pulleys where the diameter A is one-third the diameter

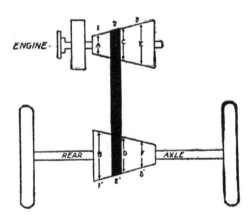

Fig. 259.—Conventional diagram illustrating transmission principles as applied to the automobile. A belt connects two cone pulleys, one on the engine shaft and one on the rear axle. By shifting the belt to the right or left, the speed of the engine is respectively diminished or increased in relation to the speed of the rear axle.

B, the engine will revolve three times for each revolution of the rear axle. Similarly when the belt is in position 2, where diameter C is equal to diameter D, then the engine will revolve at the same rate as the rear axle. Position 3, where diameter E is three times diameter F, the engine will revolve at only one-third the rate of the rear axle.

Position 2 corresponds to the example of the man raising a bucket with the crank fastened direct to the windlass hub (fig. 257), while position 1, corresponds to raising a bucket with the geared lever (fig. 258). The cone and belt transmission allows the speed of the engine to be varied considerably for a given speed of the rear wheels.

Now, for a given amount of *work,* the two factors *force* and *distance* are inversely proportional, that is, if the distance be increased, the force will be diminished a corresponding amount.

In the application of this to the automobile, the factor distance, is represented by the distance traveled by the engine piston during the power strokes, and force, by the pressure exerted on the piston during these strokes.

Since the two factors are inversely proportional, the factor force may be kept within an allowable limit when a heavy load is put on the rear axle by shifting the belt of the transmission to the left so that the speed of the engine is increased in relation to the speed of the rear axle, thus increasing the factor *distance,* and diminishing the factor *force.*

In other words, when a heavy load is put on the rear axle, the speed of the engine may be increased in relation to the speed of the rear axle, by shifting the belt to the left. This operation, 1, reduces the resistance to be overcome by the piston, and 2, stores up more energy in the fly wheel both of which tend to keep the engine moving *during the three non-power strokes of the cycle.*

In the early development of the automobile, a belt transmission somewhat similar to the one just illustrated, was used on the Fouillarion vehicles, built in France, but was displaced later by a system of toothed gear wheels of various diameters to give the several speed ratios between the engine and rear axle.

Types of Transmissions.—There are four forms of transmissions in general use on automobiles:

1. Progressive;
2. Selective;
3. Planetary;
4. Frictional Contact.

Usually, the transmission is constructed to give three speeds forward and one reverse, however, a few of the large sized cars have transmissions giving four speeds forward.

Progressive Transmissions.—With this type of transmission it is necessary, as its name indicates, to make the various speed changes in a definite order, that is, in passing from low to high speed the intermediate speeds must be passed through in regular order.

Fig. 260 is a diagram showing the operation of a three speed progressive transmission. Power is applied from the engine at P and delivered at T to the driving shaft. The shaft T is squared for a portion of its length, and runs in a bearing inside of the gear C. The gears I and L are cut out of the same piece of metal and fitted with a square hole so that they can slide along the shaft P but not revolve independently of it. The gears C′, I′, and L′ are fastened rigidly to the countershaft CS and therefore revolve with it. The gear R is an idler but is so mounted that it may be shifted into mesh with L and L′ when a reverse is desired.

The various speeds operate as follows: If C and C′ only be in mesh and no power is being transmitted to the rear axle, then in order to obtain the low speed, the gear combination IL is shifted so that the gear L will come into mesh with L′. The drive then, is through C, C′, L′, L, and out through the shaft axle T from L′ and L.

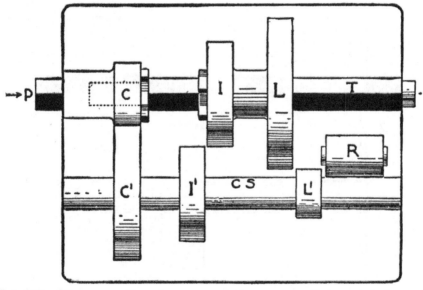

Fig. 260.—Diagram of a three speed "progressive" transmission. The gears C′, I′ and L′ are fastened to the countershaft while I and L slide on the square portion of the main shaft T; R is an idler and is used for reverse. The various speed changes are made by altering the position of the sliding members.

For the intermediate speed the gears are shifted so that I will come into mesh with I′, L of course being moved out of mesh with L′. The drive now is through C, C′, I′ I and out through the shaft T to the rear axle. For the reverse, L and R are shifted so that L meshes with R, and R with L′. The drive, in this case is through C, C′, L′, R, L, the introduction of the fifth gear causing a reverse direction of rotation of the rear axle.

For the highest speed, gears I and L are moved to the left so that they will be in mesh with no other gears, but a clutch cut into the left side of I will fit into the corresponding clutch in the gear C. This serves the purpose of coupling shaft T to shaft P, and the drive is then called "direct." This form of transmission is not used very extensively on account of the excessive shaft length, larger cases and bearings, which must be used.

Selective Transmissions.—This form of transmission, permits the operator to throw in at will, any speed combination within the range of the transmission; thus, it is not necessary in chang-

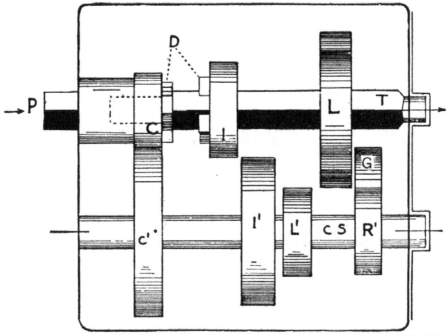

Fig. 261.—Diagram of a three speed "selective" transmission. With this system any of the several speed changes may be made at will without passing through the intermediate speeds as is necessary with a progressive transmission.

ing from low to high speed to pass through the intermediate speed as with the progressive system.

Fig. 261 is a diagram of a three speed selective transmission showing its operation. This gearing consists of two parallel shafts, T and CS, the countershaft CS having keyed to it the gears C′, I′, L′ and R′, the latter a squared shaft T carrying the gears I and L. Gear G is an "idler" used for obtaining the reverse. P is a driving shaft directly connected with the engine through the clutch. Its gear C runs free on the shaft T, and is in mesh with gear C'.

Taking first the low speed position, the drive is from C to C' to L through L'. On the intermediate speed, L is thrown out, and I is thrown into mesh with I'. For high speed the claw

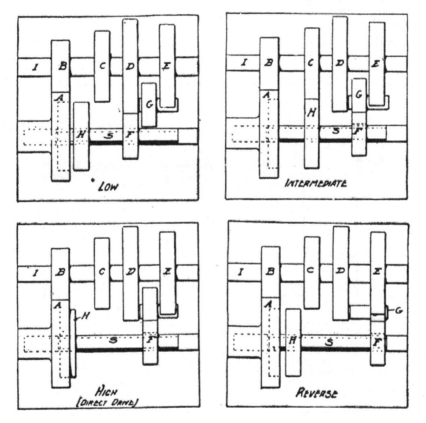

Fig. 262.—Diagram showing the various positions of the change speed gears of a three speed selective transmission. It should be noted that this type is of different construction from that shown in fig. 261. Both are described in detail in the text.

clutch on I is slid into mesh with a corresponding clutch on C. The drive in this case is *direct,* going from P directly out through T, the gears C and I being locked by the clutch. For the reverse, the gears R', G and L are in mesh, and as G makes the fifth gear in the system the direction of rotation is reversed. The gears are shifted by means of one control lever which is placed within easy reach of the driver.

Another three speed selective transmission is shown in fig. 262. This gearing consists of two parallel shafts, I and S, the former having keyed to it the gears B, C, D and E, the latter, a "squared" shaft for carrying the gears H and F. Gear G is an "idler," used for obtaining the reverse. S is a driving shaft directly connected with the engine through the clutch. A runs free on the shaft S, and is in mesh with gear B.

Taking first the low speed position, the drive is from F to D to A through B.

On the intermediate speed, F is thrown out, and H is thrown into mesh with C.

For high speed, the gear H is slid into mesh with an internal gear cut into the rim of A. The drive in this case is direct, going from S directly out through A, the gear H simply serving as a clutch.

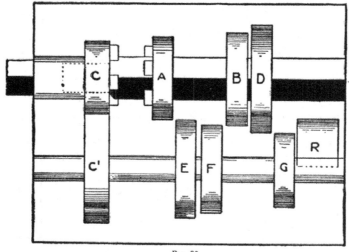

Fig. 95

FIG. 263.—Diagram of a four speed selective transmission. This differs from the three speed only in the fact that four gears are used on the driving shaft instead of three, the various gears being brought into mesh as shown in the illustration.

For the reverse, the gears E, G, and F are in mesh, and as G makes the fifth gear in the system, the direction of rotation is reversed.

In this form of transmission the gears are so arranged that any speed may be obtained without having to go through any of the others, and therefore the one lever selective control may be very easily used. This feature is appreciated by everyone because it makes the operation of changing gears very simple, and allows the car to be easily handled on crowded streets and on different grades.

Some of the larger cars are equipped with selective transmissions giving four speeds forward. A transmission of this type is illustrated in fig. 263.

The four speed selective transmission differs from the three speed only in the fact that four gears are used on the driving shaft instead of three, the various gears being brought into mesh as shown in the illustration.

In the case of a low speed, the drive is through C, C', G and D. The second speed through C, C', F and B. Third, through C, C', E and A. For the reverse, the reverse gear R is thrown into mesh with G and D making the drive through C, C', G R and D.

The various systems used in modern cars are all based on the same principle but differ in minor details according to the ideas of their designers. All of them are enclosed in an oil tight case and run in a bath of oil. The shifting mechanism also differs but the same result is obtained, and it is only on account of various patents which cover these devices that transmissions are not more uniform.

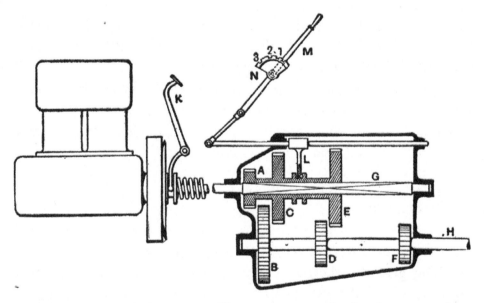

Fig. 264.—A transmission case with cover removed, showing gears in "neutral position." The parts are as follows: A, 1st speed pinion; B, 1st speed gear; C, 2nd speed pinion; D, 2nd speed gear; E, 3rd speed pinion; F, 3rd speed gear; G square portion of driving shaft, carrying A, C and E; H, driven shaft, carrying B, D and F; K, clutch pedal; L, geared striking fork; M, change speed lever; N, change speed quadrant.

The Panhard Sliding Gear Transmission.—As shown in fig. 265, it consists of two shafts, *A* and *C,* the former carrying on a square portion the sliding sleeve, *B,* upon which are four gears of varying diameter. On the shaft, *C,* are keyed four gears, whose diameters vary inversely with those on *A.* At the right-hand extremity of the shaft, *A,* is carried the male cone of the main clutch, which, when held in gear by a pressure of the spring, F, enables the transmission of power direct from the crank to the shaft, A. The clutch may be thrown out by lever, E, which acts to pull the shaft, A, to the left, compressing the spring, F. The sleeve, B, may be shifted on the main shaft by lever, D, which is connected as indicated. When as in the cut, the gear, B^1, is meshed with the gear, C^1, the car will have its slowest speed forward, and the act of shifting the gears to the left from that position will raise the speed at a regularly increasing ratio; the meshing of B^2 and C^2, giving the second speed forward, and the other gears the next two increasing speeds. Similarly, also, in the act of shifting the sleeve from the extreme left position, when gear, B^4, is meshed with gear C^4, there will be a similarly regular decrease of ratio in their speed.

The motion is transmitted from shaft, C, through the bevel gear, G, which, as shown in both sections of the cut, meshes with another bevel on the transverse jack shaft. This bevel, H, and a similar bevel, L, on the case containing the differential gear, are keyed to the sleeve, M, which works over the centre-divided countershaft, at two extremities of which are the sprocket pinions for driving direct to each of the rear wheels. As long as the bevel, G, drives on H, as shown, the motion of the carriage is forward, at any speed determined by the relative positions of the shifting gears on the two shafts, B and C. In order to reverse the motion of the carriage, the sleeve, M, is shifted upon the lever, acting on the spool, K, so that H is pushed out of mesh with G, and L is thrown in. By this process, as is obvious, although the rotation of G continues in the same direction, the movement imparted to L will be the reverse of that previously imparted to H. Thus the reverse has the same number of speed and power combinations as the forward motion.

It is also obvious that, by shifting the sleeve, M, a certain distance, the driving connections to the main shaft, through the

differential, *J*, will be thrown off altogether. This is the operation necessary preceding the throwing on of the brake, the
drum of which is on the countershaft, just beyond the thimble, *H*.

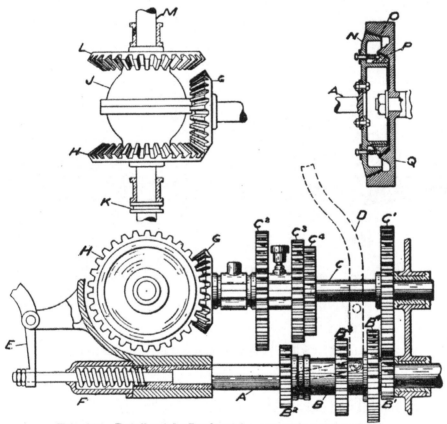

Fig. 265.—Details of the Panhard-Levassor Change Speed Gear.

On the later models of the Panhard carriages a simplified variation of the transmission gear is used, which drives through a
single bevel gear on the jack shaft, constantly in mesh with the
bevel on the secondary driven shaft, or top shaft,—thus requiring
no shifting of the differential to throw the reverse bevel. A
third shaft set parallel to the clutch shaft, carries two spur gears,
as shown in the diagram.

At the position shown in the diagram the lowest forward speed is engaged, through the meshing of the spurs, *A* and *E*. By bringing the hand lever all the way back, the sleeve is moved clear to the right, and *A* and *E* are thrown out of mesh. At the same time, the arm of the sliding gear shifter meets a raised portion of the reverse shaft, as shown, pushes it to the right, depressing

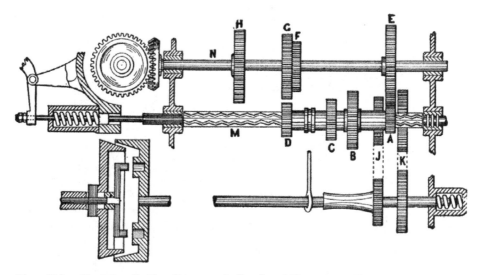

Fig. 266.—Sketch of the Improved Panhard-Levassor Transmission and Clutch.

the spring. The spur, *J*, is then meshed with *E*, and *K* with *A*— the movement of the main clutch shaft being thus transmitted to the top shaft through the engagement and rotation of the third, or reverse, shaft.

The Packard Transmission.—The transmission of the Packard car is of the same general type as the last two mentioned, except that it is operated by two levers, one for shifting the forward gears and one for engaging the reverse.

The Packard car is driven by propeller shaft and bevel gear to the rear axle, and possesses the uncommon advantage of having the transmission to the gear, against the axle, thus saving the trouble and lost motion encountered with a long propeller shaft direct to the driving bevel, and, according to claims, serving to steady the driving bevel.

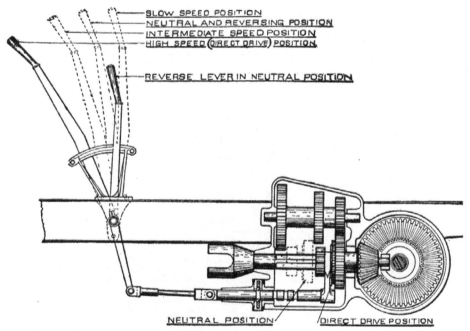

Fig. 267.—Diagram of Control Lovers an l Trans:nission of the Packard Car.

As shown in the accompanying diagram, it consists of three shafts:

1. The drive shaft connected by a universal joint to the of sliding a sleeve holding two spur gears.

2. The bevel pinion shaft carrying a single spur gear at its inner end and bored to serve as a bearing for the drive shaft.

3. The second motion shaft, to which are keyed three spur gears, two of them of diameters suitable to mesh consecutively with the sliding gears on the drive shaft, giving the lowest, intermediate speeds, and the third constantly in mesh with the single gear on the bevel shaft.

The top speed as in the Decauville, and other modern transmissions, is obtained by sliding the two-gear sleeve all the way back (to the right in the diagram), so that its teeth mesh with internal teeth cut in the circumference of the bevel shaft gear, thus making the drive direct from the motor. The reverse is obtained when the gears on the sliding sleeve are in the neutral position (indicated by the dotted outlines in the cut), by operating the short reverse lever, thus causing an idler pinion, hung on a bell crank to be thrown into mesh with the forward (left) end of the drive and top shafts.

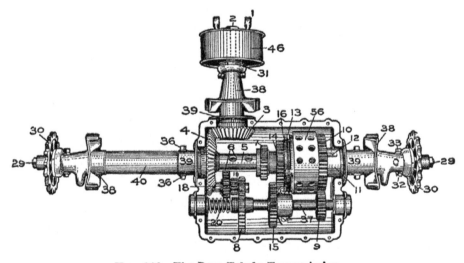

Fig. 268.—The Pope-Toledo Transmission.

The Toledo Transmission.—The transmission gear used on the Pope Toledo car is somewhat different from those previously described. As shown in the accompanying diagram, shaft, 2, driven by the motor, communicates the power to the sliding gear sleeve, 5, through the two bevel gears, 3 and 4 Sleeve, 5, carries sliding gears, 7 and 14, and the male portion of the high-speed gear clutch. These parts are free to move endwise, but are prevented from turning independently by a long feather, 6, on sleeve, 5. The sleeve, 5, is free to turn on the transverse transmission, or jack, shaft, 29. Directly behind this shaft is a second shaft, 37, which carries, gears 8, 9 and 15.

For the first speed forward gear, 7, is meshed with gear, 8, and the motion is transmitted by gear 9, on the second shaft, to gear, 10 on the Jack shaft, 29. The second speed forward is obtained by meshing gears, 14 and 15, and transmitting the motion to jack shaft, 29 as before. To obtain the third, or high, speed, the sleeve carrying gears, 7 and 14, is moved to the right, with the result that gear, 14, acts against pins, 13, disengaging gear, 10, from the counter shaft, and engaging clutch, 16, making the differential, 56, and the countershaft, 29, continuous with sleeve, 5, and thus driving direct from bevel, 4. The reverse is effected when the gear, 7, is moved to the left and meshed with gear, 18, on the reverse shaft, shown below and between sleeve, 5, and countershaft, 37. At the same time, gear, 8, is moved to the left against the pressure of spring, 20, coming into mesh with reverse pinion, 19. The drive is thus from 7 to 18, through 19 to 8, and thence through 9 and 10 to the countershaft, 29. The lever quadrant is notched to show the proper positions for the several speeds described.

Selective Spur Transmissions.—Great troubles with early sliding spur transmissions lay in the facts that, in shifting from high to low gears, all intermediate speeds were engaged; also, that a careless or inexperienced driver was never sure to fully engage two spurs, thus entailing considerable wear and breakage of gear teeth. To meet these objections the "selective-finger" transmission as it is generally called, was devised. The earliest example of this type of gear was that used on Cannstadt-Daimler cars, shown in accompanying diagrams. It was the first car to use the gridiron, or H-shaped, quadrant slot, now so popular. Like later forms of selective transmission, it affected all changes of forward and reverse movements by the use of a single lever. The slot used is typical.

The operation of the common change-speed and reversing lever consists in the use of a double H-shaped slot, or grid sector, so that the lever may be moved backward or forward in any one of three parallel channels, or shifted sideways from one to another by means of a fourth channel cut at right angles to the other three, like the cross line of the letter H.

The hand lever is pivoted to a cross spindle, which may be slid lengthwise in its bearings whenever the hand lever is brought to the middle transverse slot of the grid sector. The four sliding spurs on the square section of the main shaft are in two sections

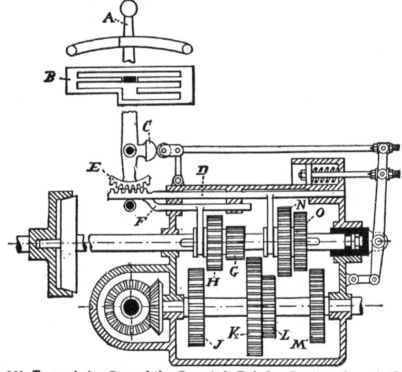

Fig. 269.—**Transmission Gear of the Cannstadt-Daimler Carriage shown in the last** figure. Here, A is the hand lever; B, the gridiron quadrant; C, a dog on the lever for throwing out the clutch in shifting the gears; E, toothed sector at end of A for actuating rack rods D and F (see next figure); G and H, low speed gears on the clutch shaft; J and K, low-speed gears on the second, or driving, shaft; N and O, high-speed gears on the clutch shaft; L and M, high-speed gears on the second shaft. H and G are shifted on square portion of shaft by rack, F; N and O by rack, D.

of two spurs each. Each section is shifted by an arm projecting downward from a horizontal rod bearing a rack on the outer end. Furthermore, these two rack rods are set side by side, so that a toothed sector on the lower extremity of the hand lever may engage either one of the racks, operating either of the two lower speeds when the lever is moving in the left-hand slot, and either of the two higher speeds when it is moving in the second slot. When drawn to the backward position in either slot, it operates the lower of the two speeds, and, in the forward position, the higher of the two. In order to reverse the movement of the carriage, the hand lever is brought to the mid-position on the grid-sector, shifted all the way to the right, and moved forward. This operation is possible because the cross spindle to which the lever is pivoted carries an arm projecting downward at right angles, and terminating in another toothed sector, that, when the lever is slid over to the right, as just explained, engages a third

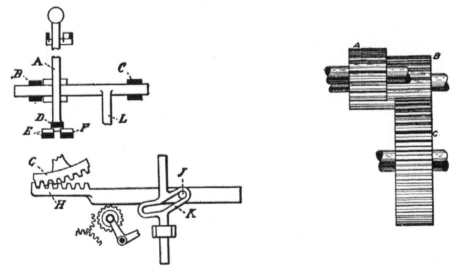

Fɪɢ. 270.--Details of Side-Shifting Change Lever of the Cannstadt-Daimler Car.

rack bar geared to throw in the reverse pinion, B (see figure of reverse gear). The arm, K, in the same figure, carries an upward turned slot in a position to engage a pin on the reverse rack-shaft, so that, when that shaft is slid forward by the interworking of the rack and sector, the arm is lifted and pinion, B, brought into position by the operation of a bell-crank. In addition to the toothed sector set at its lower extremity, the hand lever has an arm at right angles exactly at the pivotal point, so that, when the lever is brought to the transverse slot of the grid-sector, this arm presses upon a bar, thus throwing out the clutch.

The entire operation may be understood from the figures of the reverse apparatus. Here, A is the lever, pivoted between bearings, B and C. D is the toothed sector, which may be shifted to engage either of the rack rods, E or F; L is a downward extension from the pivot rod of A, carrying the sector, G, which may be slid into mesh with rack, H. By sliding rack, H, to the right, as in the cut, pin, J, lifts the rod attached to the curved slot, K, throwing in the reverse pinion. The manner of doing this is shown with the pinions, A and C, meshing with the long reverse pinion, B.

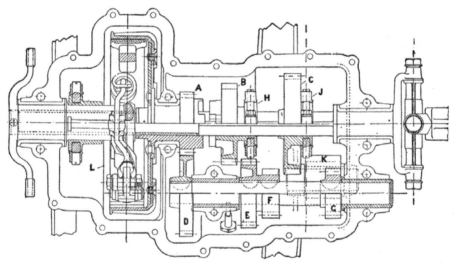

FIG. 271.-Transmission and Clutch of the Columbia Light Car. A, spur gear on the clutch shaft; B and C, spurs on the squared second shaft, the first shifted by fork hung at H, by lever, H (last figure), the second by fork at J by lever, J. D, E, F, G, three-speed pinions keyed to countershaft; K, pinion giving reverse when in mesh with C and G; L, clutch.

The Columbia Transmission.—The selective transmission of the Columbia light car closely resembles that used on the Decauville in the method of obtaining the several speeds and the reverse. As shown in the diagram, the driving shaft consists of two parts; the clutch shaft carrying gear, *A,* and the sleeve shaft carrying gears, *B* and *C.* Gears, *A* and *D,* are constantly in mesh. The low speed is obtained when gears, *F* and *C,* are meshed; the second speed with *E* and *B* meshed; the top speed with *B* moved forward (to the left) so as to engage the claw clutch and make a driving union with *A;* the reverse, when *C* is moved backward (to the right), so as to mesh with idler pinion, *K*, which is permanently meshed with *G*, This transmission differs from the Decauville in the fact that gears, *B* and *C*, are moved independently by forks attached at *H* and *J*, respectively. This transmission is not controlled by a single lever and gridiron quadrant, but by two levers, *H* and *J*, as shown in the diagram of the control.

As the control is typical of modern systems, it is worthy passing notice. The clutch controls foot pedal, *D*, to the left of the

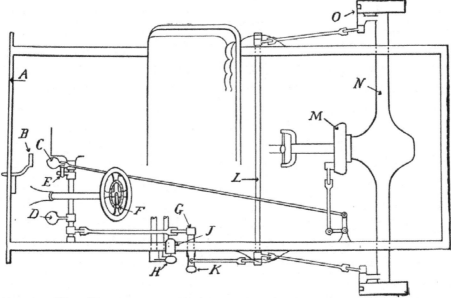

FIG. 272.–Plan Showing Lever and Control System of the Columbia Two-cylinder Light Carriage. A is the dash; B, foot accelerator lever for controlling engine; C, foot break lever; D, clutch lever; E, clutch interlock, requiring that clutch be thrown before brakes are set; F. ignition-timing lever on steering wheel; G, clutch interlock; H, second and third speed lever; J, first speed and reverse lever; K, hub emergency brake lever; L, brake rocker; M, expanding brake on driving shaft; N, rear live axle; O, hub brake.

steering post, opens the friction clutch, when pressed down, and closes it, when allowed to rise. It is fixed on a shaft having a small finger, *E*, interlocking the foot brake lever, *C*, on the right of the steering post, so, that, when the clutch pedal is pressed down, no effect is exerted upon the brake pedal. But owing to a pin projecting in front of the small interlock on the clutch shaft, when the brake pedal is pressed down the clutch pedal is caused to go back and release the clutch. The brake connections run to the rear and connect by a bell crank lever to the expanding brake band on the transmission shaft at *M*. This brake is applied beyond all the universal joints on the propeller shaft so that they receive no braking strains.

The emergency brake lever, *K*, also connects to the clutch pedal by a slip interlock, *G*, so that, when it is pressed down, the clutch pedal is also pulled off. Its connections run aft and connect to band brakes, *O*, on the driving wheel hubs.

The speed change levers, *H* and *J*, are shown on the left side directly in front of the emergency brake lever. As in this vehicle the engine power is very high in proportion to the weight of the vehicle, ordinary service requires that the middle and the high gears are the ones most used. They are thus controlled by one handle, *H*, which is made conspicuous. For such backing and filling as is necessary in turning in close quarters, other handle, *K*, gives the reverse and low gear ahead. To set the medium gear, the conspicuous handle is pulled back as far as it will go; for the high speed it is to be pushed ahead as far as it will go regardless of notches or other indexes. A small snap indicates the off position. Similarly, to set the reverse gear, the second lever is pulled back as far as it will go, and, to set the low gear ahead, it is pushed forward to the end of the slot. One lever cannot be moved unless the other is in the off position.

The Knox=Mercedes Transmission.—A form of transmission introduced on the Mercedes car, and adopted on the Knox vehicles in the United States, represents a type worthy careful attention. As shown in the accompanying diagram, the main shaft, *A*, of large diameter, has four spur gears, *C, D, E,* sliding on fluted keys or feathers integral with the shaft. It is coupled directly to the clutch shaft, and runs in bearings, *PP*. The second motion shaft, *B*, runs in bearings, P^1P^1, and has gears, *F, G, H*, rigidly secured on it. The differential gears are enclosed in the perforated case, *M*, and brake drum, *N*, is firmly secured to the case. Two bevel gears are secured to periphery of M, one of which, *L*, is the direct high gear drive, meshing with pinion,

I, and the other is the drive for lower speeds, meshing with pinion, *J*, on the second motion shaft. Bevel pinion, *I*, is integral with internal gear, *V*, and runs on ball bearings on shaft, *A*, except when it is clutched to this shaft by sliding the gear *E*, into mesh with *V*, by means of fork, *Q*, and shifter bar, *Y²*, giving fourth speed on direct drive. On this drive bevel gears, *J* and *K*, and shaft, *B*, are running idle and gears, *F*, *G*, *H*, are not in mesh. Meshing, *E*, with *H*, gives the third speed.

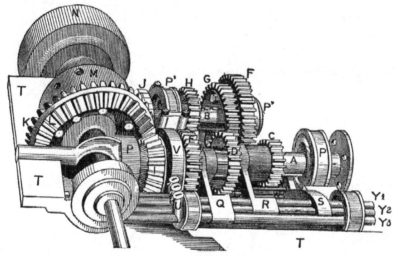

Fig. 273.—The Knox-Mercedes Selective Finger Transmission, showing method of shifting gears by three shifter bars, Y₁, Y₂, Y₃, and of driving through two bevel gears to the jack shaft.

By means of fork, *R*, and shifter bar, *Y²*, *D* is meshed with *G* for second speed or *C* with *F* for first speed, *C* and *D* being integral.

The reverse gear is mounted between two supports on the bottom of case, and is shifted by fork, *S*, and shifter bar *Y¹*, into mesh with, *C* and *F* for the reverse motion.

The bars are shifted by a single hand lever working in a gate quadrant on the selective system. The selector box is dust proof and contains a simple device which positively locks, in their neutral position, all the shifter bars except the one in use. On direct drive none of the gears on the shaft, *B*, are in mesh and bevels, *J* and *K*, are running idle.

The Haynes=Apperson Transmission Gear.—The Haynes-Apperson transmission consists of two parallel shafts, A and B,

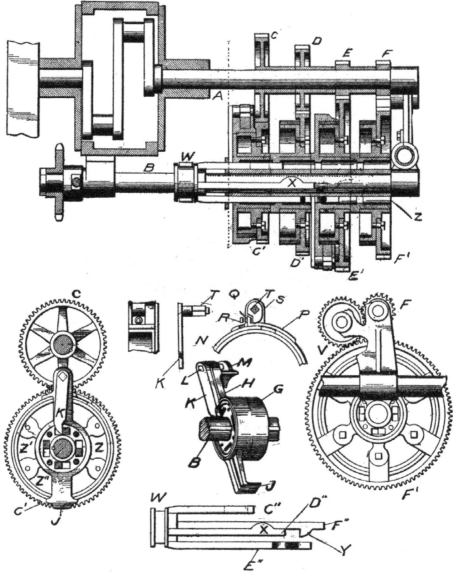

Fig. 274.—The Haynes-Apperson Transmission Gear, shown hung on the crankshaft, as in the lighter cars. The reverse is now accomplished by a chain between F and F', dispensing with the idler, V.

the former being driven direct from the crank, or by belt and pulley from the main shaft, as in the later models of this carriage, and carrying four gears, C, D, E and F, keyed in its length. The countershaft, B, also carries four loose gears, C', D', E' and F', each of which is bolted to a band clutch drum, as illustrated in fig. 274. Each of these brake drums, with its attached gear, turns loose on a separate drum, G, which is keyed to the counter-shaft, all of the attached gears, however, being able to turn through the motion imparted from their mates on the main shaft, without transmitting power to the driving mechanism. As may be readily understood, in order to transmit power through any one of the gears on the countershaft, it is necessary to make it rigid with its drum, G. The driving sprocket is keyed to the end of shaft, B, as shown.

As will be seen in the separate cut, each one of the drums, G carries two arms, H and J, fixed diametrically opposite one another. On the arm, H, is carried a lever arm, K, pivoted at L, and having a short angle of movement by the attachment of its pivot to the bearings, shown at M and N. On the two extremities of the arms, R and J, are carried brackets, which hold the leather brake band against the circumference of the drum turning loose on G. One end of this brake band is riveted to the brake on H, the other to a forged strap, P, having at its extremity the lug, Q, through which works the adjusting screw, R, whose point bears against the dog, S. This dog. S, is carried on the square section, T, of the shaft attached to the lever arm, K, already mentioned; so that a slight movement of the lever, K, to the left, is imparted to the dog, S, whose point bears against the screw, R, on the lug, Q; thus drawing the strap, P, tight around the drum, which is thereby made rigid with the sleeve, G, keyed to the shaft, B. By this means the gear attached to that particular drum imparts the motion transmitted to it from its mate on the shaft, A, to the countershaft, B, such motion varying in speed according to the ratios between the meshed gears. The act of giving the required axial movement to the lever arm, K, is performed as fol-lows:

The sleeve, W, sliding on the countershaft, B, carries four fingers, C'', D'', E'', F'', of differing length, as shown in the figures. In the extremity of each of these fingers is a lug, such as is shown at X and Y, the object of which is to engage the point of the lever, K, on some one of the four arms, H, thus causing it to move its dog, S, and tighten the brake band, as already explained. In order to accomplish this act without interference, the positions of the levers, K, and of the dogs, S, differ in each brake drum. On drum, C', for example, it is at the top of the shaft; in E' it is at the bottom; while in D' and F' it is on the right angle in either direction. For this reason, as may be understood from the cut, the four fingers carried on the sleeve, W, are similarly disposed, in order that their lugs, X or Y, may engage the point of the particular lever, K, which it is intended to actuate, without interference. In order that the fingers, K, may slide through the drums, G, keyed to the shaft, B, four suitable channels penetrate the entire series of drums, G, as shown at Z in one of the cuts.

The sliding sleeve, W, is shifted by a lever working on the thimble on its outer extremity, and by causing its fingers to penetrate the channels, Z, more or less, can give three speeds forward and a reverse. The reverse is accomplished when the lug on the finger, F'', engages the lever, K, on the sleeve, G, belonging to drum and gear, F', which act enables the motion of pinion, F, on shaft, A, to be transmitted through the idler, V, to F', which will of course, rotate in an opposite direction to F, thus reversing the motion of the shaft, B. In more recent models of this gear, F and F' are sprockets and are connected by a chain belt, which accomplishes the end of reversing the travel of the carriage to better advantage than by the use of the idler, V. The lever operating the speed-changing works through a bell crank to spool, W.

The Brush Planetary Transmission.—This transmission has two forward speeds and one reverse as shown in fig. 275. In order to relieve the bearings of unnecessary work, two bronze discs are provided riveted to the low speed and reverse elements indicated as A and B to the right of the figure. Between the discs A and B is placed a ring with finished ends and which fits freely in a bore in the housing. The two members of the housing also have finished ring surfaces which present themselves to the outer surfaces of these bronze rings. The ring, marked C in the drawing, has bolted to it a lever which extends through a slot in the wall of the housing and is connected to the control mechanism by linkage in such a way that it may be made to rotate in either direction within its bore in the housing, depending upon the direction of the motion imparted to the control lever at the side of the car. As shown, there are two short spiral slots cut in the cylindrical surface of the ring C. Into these slots fit two rollers carried on spindles attached to screw plugs inserted in the sides of the case.

The operation is as follows: the bronze discs, A and B, revolve in opposite directions when the engine is running idle, as indicated by the arrows in the detail sketch. If now the ring C be rotated by its linkage in a downward direction, the same as that of the disc A, it will move toward the left at the same time and, as the

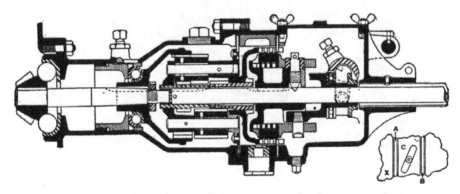

Fig. 275.—Sectional view of the Brush enclosed planetary change gear. This change gear forms a unit with the jack shaft and is suspended from the side frame members by the jack shaft brackets and in front at a single point, thus giving a three point suspension.

motion is continued, will engage the disc A and finally force it into engagement with the stationary surface X of the housing.

If it be rotated in the opposite direction, disc B will be engaged and finally held stationary.

In operating the car, it is usual to fully engage these clutches at once by means of the side lever; but since the case is filled with oil and the rotation of the bronze discs fills the spaces between the engaging surfaces with oil, due to centrifugal action upon the oil, the engagement is not nor cannot be made harsh. The rear transmission member of the change gear is made up of 1, a shaft, 2, a bevel driving pinion and 3, a large internal gear, keyed, riveted and pinned to form a unit.

Transmission Gear Ratios.—When a car is fitted with a selective transmission, the skill of the operator must be such as to enable him to determine the proper gear.

Just what the gear ratio should be is a matter which depends upon the several conditions as: (a) The speed of the motor as it relates to the attainable speed of the car; (b) The ultimate speed of the car; (c) The rate at which acceleration is to be engendered; (d) The design of the motor, taking into account the torque curve of the same; (e) The degree of harmony of the several relations; (f) The competence of tires used.

Fig. 276.—The Locomobile four speed transmission. There are two sliding members moving on the squared shaft: *S2* carries two gears and is moved by the action of the gear lever when in the *outer* slot; *S1* carries one gear and part of a jaw clutch and is moved by the action of the gear lever when in the *inner* slot. 1st and 2nd speeds and reverse are obtained by moving *S2*: 1st speed, gear lever is shifted as far forward as it will go in outer slot (without pressing button on top); this meshes *S2* with *E*. 2nd speed, lever in rear position outer slot; this meshes *S2* with *D*. Reverse lever is moved to extreme forward position in outer slot by pressing button on top; this meshes *S2* with *G*, an idle pinion driven by *F*. Third and fourth speeds are obtained by the movement of *S1*: gear lever in forward position, inner slot, meshes *S1* with *C*, giving third speed; gear lever in rear position, inner slot, causes the jaw clutch on *S* to lock with the clutch pinion *A*, giving four speed and direct drive.

With four speeds the geometrical relation of the three-speed system would be retained and the fourth speed would be interjected between the second and the third of the three-speed system, so that the third speed would become the fourth, in a four-speed system.

If the power of the motor be barely sufficient for the purpose, it is plain that the second speed should be nearer the third speed, and the practice, in general, is to favor the motor in this way. On the other hand, if the motor be of adequate power, it is then that the second speed can be in the geometrical relation, and this is an advantage on very bad roads, in that the low gear is so advantageously related as to afford adequate advantage under the most severe conditions, while the second gear will be high enough to handle quite bad roads at a fair speed in miles per hour of the car. The bevel drive can have several ratios, depending upon circumstances. The ratio is as follows: (a) 3 to 1 in light roadster work; (b) 3½ to 1 in light touring car work; (c) 4 to 1 in heavy touring car work.

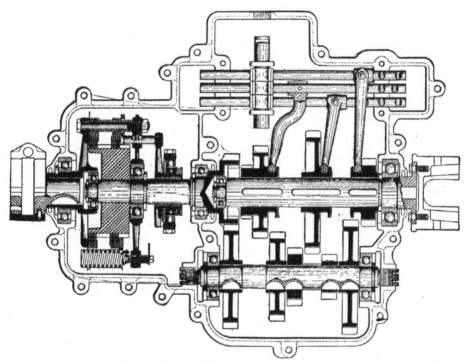

FIG. 277.—The Winton 1910 multiple disc clutch and transmission. The clutch has sixty-seven steel friction surfaces, thirty-three attached to the transmission shaft and thirty-four to the driving spiders which are connected to the flywheel. The transmission is of the selective type, four forward speeds and reverse. Direct drive on the third speed, through internal and external gear combination. Lock-out on fourth speed. The construction is such that it is possible to enter neutral position, but impossible to engage any new set of gears while clutch is engaged.

In a general way it is considered that the sliding gears (assuming three speeds ahead) should be geometrically related in the manner as follows:

First.	MILES PER HOUR Second.	Third.	In a four-speed transmission the third speed would be as follows:
5	10	20	15
6	12	24	18
7	14	28	21
8	16	32	24
9	18	36	27
10	20	40	30
11	22	44	33
12	24	48	36
15	30	60	45
20	40	80	60
25	50	100	75

CHAPTER THIRTY.

ON THE CONSTRUCTION AND OPERATION OF BRAKES ON MOTOR CARRIAGES.

General Requirements in Brakes.—An important subject in connection with the construction and operation of motor vehicles relates to the brakes used for retarding the movement of the carriage when it is desirable to either come to a more or less sudden stop, or to hold the carriage stationary on the side of an incline. Several conditions are essential to the designing of brakes for motor carriages, among which we may mention ease and rapidity of operation and the maximum of braking effect, with the minimum of power exerted at the operating lever.

Varieties of Construction in Brakes.—There are two kinds of brakes in familiar use on vehicles of all descriptions: Shoe brakes, which operate by the pressure of the contact surface or shoe upon the periphery of the wheel tire, and drum brakes, which operate by tightening a band around a drum, either on the hub of the wheel or on the case of the differential gear. Both varieties are used to a considerable extent on motor vehicles, although most authorities agree that shoe brakes are unsuitable for use on wheels tired with pneumatic tubes. The reason given for this opinion is that the constricting effort due to pressing the shoe against the tire is, like the ordinary shocks experienced in travel, largely absorbed by the tire itself, with the result that it is liable to be rent or torn from its attachment to the rim. On the other hand, it has been asserted by at least one well-known manufacturer of motor vehicles that shoe brakes may be safely and satisfactorily used on pneumatic-tired wheels, provided the surface contact of the shoes extend over a sufficiently extensive arc to prevent the strain from being concentrated on small areas of the circumference. This authority asserts that he himself has used a motor tricycle for several years, the wheels of which are equipped with a shoe brake constructed according to his idea. The result is, he states, that the contact surface of the shoe has been worn much more rapidly than the tire surface, which seems to suffer very little, if any, more than would be the case with the use of any other form of brake. Whether his experience in this regard would be borne out in general practice, it is not necessary to inquire, the fact being that nearly all motor vehicles at the present time operate with drum and strap brakes.

Principles of Band Brake Operation.—Among the advantages possibly to be alleged for the drum and band brake we may enumerate the facts that, with ordinary connections, they are much more readily operated and with much greater effect while on any showing involving a minimum of wear on the moving parts. As may be readily understood, the operation of the drum and band brake is a reversed application of the principle of torque, as already explained in connection with the electrical motor. As there explained, if the power acting upon a rotating shaft be equal to the weight of fifty pounds constantly applied, and the pulley attached to the shaft be twice the diameter of the shaft, the available power at the periphery of the pulley will be just one-half that exerted on the periphery of the shaft itself. This statement is equivalent to saying that if a rope carrying a weight of fifty pounds be wound about a pulley, whose diameter is one foot, mounted on a shaft, whose diameter is six inches, it will exactly balance a weight of one hundred pounds on a rope wound about the shaft. The constantly applied power of slightly over twenty-five pounds at the periphery of the pulley will be sufficient to rotate the shaft against a resistance of fifty pounds on the shaft. It thus appears that the braking power, applied around the periphery of the brake drum, is efficient in retarding the momentum of a forward-moving vehicle in very nearly the inverted ratio existing between the diameters of the drum, or pulley, and the rotating shaft to which it is attached. In the practical application of this principle, however, it is obvious that there must be very definite limits to the diameter of the brake drum, or pulley, beyond which it would be undesirable to go. According to the practice adopted by light motor vehicle manufacturers, the average diameters of brake drums range between eight inches and two feet, the principal item of variation in this respect being the weight of the vehicle itself.

Beaumont's Formulæ for Brakes.—It is possible to obtain a very efficient band brake on a very moderate diameter of drum, owing to the fact, which need scarcely be mentioned, that the braking effort is never applied until the motive power is disconnected from the running gear. In a steam vehicle, the first act is to shut off the steam from the cylinder; in a gasoline vehicle, to throw off the main clutch; in an electrical vehicle, to open the circuit of the motor and batteries. The resistance against which the brake must then operate is found to be purely a consideration

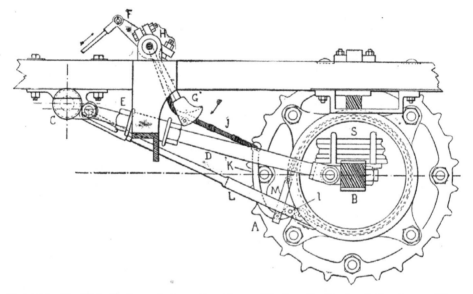

FIG. 278.-**The Hub Brake and Operating Levers Used on the Panhard Carriages.**—The arm, F, being pushed in the direction of the arrow, causes the arm, G, on the same pivot, H, to move in the opposite direction, as indicated by the lower arrow. Through this arm, G, runs the cable, J, as shown, which, pulling on the arm, K, pivoted at *l*, pulls the strap, shown by dotted lines around the drum, S. The other end of the strap attached to the short arm of the lever, K, is thus drawn toward the same point; a tight frictional bind being the result.

of the vehicle's weight, its velocity and the acceleration due to gravity. This principle is already stated by Mr. Beaumont, as follows:

"When it is necessary to determine the brake power to stop a vehicle of a given weight running at a given speed, in a given distance, and, by this means, arrive at something like due comprehension of the necessary parts brought into play to effect this stop, it must first be pointed out to those who overlook the fact, that the strain put upon a brake to effect a stop in a given distance increases as the square of the increase of speed; so that to stop a car running twenty miles per hour requires four times the power necessary to stop it in the same distance when running ten miles per hour. Commonly, all calculations relating to the acceleration of masses at high speed are calculated on the basis of distance covered in feet per second, and hence the work or energy lodged in a mass having a given weight and moving at a given velocity in feet per second is given by the following expression:

$$K = \frac{W \, v^2}{2 \, g}$$

in which K represents the work, or energy, lodged in the moving mass; W represents its weight; v, its velocity, expressed in

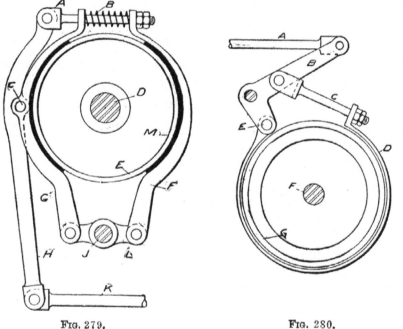

FIG. 279.   FIG. 280.

FIGS. 279 and 280.—Two Forms of Constricting Band Brake. In the first figure, the drum, E, rotates on the spindle, D. Two shoes, F and G, joined to the link, L, pivoted at J, are pressed against the periphery of the drum, E, when the link, K, moves the lever, H, pivoted at C, so as to pull the arm, A, on F, by compressing the spring, B, normally holding them apart.
In the second figure, the band, D, surrounding the drum, G, is drawn tight, when the link, A, operates the bell crank, B, thus producing a pull through its attachments at C and E.

feet per second, and g, the acceleration due to gravity, or 32.2 feet per second."

From the above formula, Mr. Beaumont proceeds to derive other essential elements, such as the efficient power necessarily applied to stop a vehicle of given weight, in a given length of travel.

Reducing the expression for feet per second to miles per hour, according to the usual standard, and, assuming the weight of the vehicle to be one ton (of 2,240 pounds), he reduces the formula, as follows: One mile being 5,280 feet, and one hour, 3,600 seconds,

$$1 \text{ mile per hour} = \frac{5,280}{3,600} = 1.466 \text{ feet per second.}$$

Whence $\dfrac{W \ v^2}{2 \ g} = \dfrac{W \times (1.466)^2}{64.4} = \dfrac{W \times 2.15}{64.4} = W \times 0.0334.$

Then a vehicle weighing one ton, traveling at ten and twenty miles per hour, by the formula,

$$K = W \ V^2 \times 0.0334,$$

in which V represents miles per hour, will be for 10 miles $2,240 \times 100 \times 0.0334 = 7,480$ foot pounds; for 20 miles $2,240 \times 400 \times 0.0334 = 29,920$ foot pounds.

To Find Distance in Which Brakes Will Act on Vehicle's Speed.—Then, taking k as the coefficient of friction between the tires and road surface, which is approximately 0.60 for rubber tires; and taking w as the proportion of the total weight carried by the wheels to which the brake is applied, which may be assumed to be 0.6 of the whole, the maximum distance required to stop the vehicle on the level, on an ordinary road, whose surface resistance is, supposedly, included in the expression, k, may be expressed by l, as follows:

$$l = \frac{W \ V^2 \times 0.0334}{k \ w}$$

Then, for a vehicle weighing one ton, tired with average rubber tires, traveling at a momentum of 10 and 20 miles per hour, respectively, we have:

$$l = \frac{7,480}{0.6 \times 1,344} = 9.3 \text{ feet at 10 miles, and}$$

$$l = \frac{29,920}{0.6 \times 1,344} = 37.1 \text{ feet at 20 miles;}$$

these distances representing the maximum, with a braking effect sufficient to cause the wheels to skid.

To Find the Required Braking Pull.—In order to find the necessary pull, p, on the brake band, the following formula is given:

$$p = k\,w = \frac{W\,V^2 \times .0334}{l},$$

which for one typical vehicle, moving at 20 miles per hour, gives,

$$p = \frac{29,920}{37.1} = 806 \text{ pounds.}$$

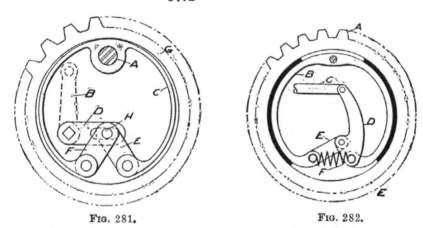

FIG. 281.   FIG. 282.

FIGS. 281 and 282. Two Forms of Expanding Band Brake. In the first figure, the gear, G, has an internal bearing surface, within which is the band, C, pivoted at A, a point separate from G. The arm, B, of the bell crank, B D, being moved to the left, spreads apart the two links, E and F, connected to D at H, thus pressing both ends of the band, C, against the internal bearing surface of G, and producing the necessary braking friction.

In the second figure, the gear, A, similarly arranged with an internal bearing surface, contains the expanding band, B. When the link, C, is pulled, the lever arm, D, double-pivoted at E and F, causes the two ends of the band, B, to press against the internal bearing surface of A, thus creating friction. The spring shown normally holds the two ends of the band apart.

Varieties of Drum and Band Brake.—As shown by accompanying illustrations, there are two general types of drum brake, the first consisting of a drum or pulley, around the circumference of which is a metal strap faced with leather, which is drawn tight whenever it is desired to furnish the resistance necessary to check the rotation of the shaft; and expanding band brakes, in which a similar metal strap, faced with leather or other suitable substance acts against the internal surface of a rotating drum or pulley. The former type is, however, at the present time the most usual construction, although the latter is seeing an increasing popularity.

411

In some forms of constricting band brakes, instead of a metal strap extending entirely around the drum, two shoes pivoted at a certain point, and having their inside faces faced with leather, are tightened against the drum by a suitable lever. In practically all forms of expanding band brake the band is attached to the outside frame, at one point of its circumference, and is suitably tightened by a toggle joint operated by a lever.

The Care of Brakes.—In successfully operating a motor carriage it is particularly essential that the brakes should be maintained in good working order. This involves that the levers and

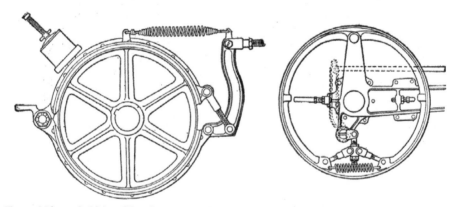

Figs. 283 and 284.—The Locomobile brakes. The running brake consists of a contracting band brake, the pulley of which is located on the differential shaft at the right of the bronze gear case and to which the band is firmly secured. This brake is of the double-acting type, 12 inches in diameter and 4 inches wide. The brake pedal is operated by the right foot and when the brake is engaged the clutch is not automatically disconnected. The halves of the brake band are hinged at the rear and are adjusted in front by two turn-buckles; it has also a set-screw underneath, allowing the band to be adjusted so that it is free around the circumference of the pulley, preventing any binding when not in use. The emergency brakes are located on the rear wheels, being of the internal expansion variety, one to each wheel. These are hinged at the top and when the hand brake lever, placed at the right of the car, is pulled backward, suitable mechanism causes the brake shoes to be expanded against the circumference of the brake drum; when the lever is released, springs draw the bands away from the circumference of the drum.

connections should at all times operate perfectly, and that no worn or loose bearings should be neglected. Furthermore, and most important, the friction surface between the band and the drum should be constantly and carefully guarded from oil deposits, which will certainly render the braking effort useless. If oil collects between the band and the drum surface it may be cut out with gasoline, and the parts then carefully wiped with a suitable rag.

CHAPTER THIRTY-ONE.

ON BALL AND ROLLER BEARINGS FOR MOTOR CARRIAGE USE.

The General Uses of Rotative Bearings.—The practical problems involved in the construction of bicycles and motor carriages have given a great popularity to ball and roller bearings for use in connection with almost every variety of rotating shaft. As we have already seen in several constructions mentioned in previous parts of this volume, ball bearings are used in a large variety of different devices, in order to allow of the greatest possible ease in turning with the smallest friction and wear. The most important use, however, for ball and roller bearings, in both bicycles and motor carriages, is on the axles of the road wheels. For this purpose, although ball bearings are eminently satisfactory on the wheel axles and pedals of bicycles, they are for a number of reasons unsuitable for the heavier weights and higher speeds of motor carriages. Accordingly roller bearings have taken their place almost exclusively in this connection.

Rotating Supports vs. Sliding Surfaces.—The principal object involved in using ball and roller bearings on bicycles and motor carriages is to secure economy of traction effort, with ease and rapidity of driving, as well as a minimum of starting effort at the beginning of travel. A few simple principles will serve to fully explain the reasons for this fact. When we have a plain wheel bearing, such as is used on ordinary horse carriages, consisting of a simple tapered boss, with a similarly shaped hollow axle-box rotating around it, there is a considerable effort necessary at starting from rest, a good proportion of the power being consumed in resisting the friction between the sliding surfaces. This resistance is very largely due to adhesion between the two sliding surfaces, due to cohesion of the lubricating oil or grease. As a matter of fact, it may be easily understood that the sliding action of two round surfaces, one within another, may be readily compared to the sliding of one plane surface upon another. The first difference in point of resistance and effort necessary to overcome inertia, as between two such surfaces, when sliding against one another directly, and when some kind of rollers or rotating supports are interposed, is a matter of the commonest experience. The heaviest objects may be readily moved or slid along the ground when rollers are placed beneath them; also the heaviest loads when carried on wheels of suitable breadth and diameter may be handled with a degree of ease, increasing directly as the ideal conditions are approximated. This principle is the very one that is applied in the practice of substituting ball and roller bearings for ordinary plain bearings. Instead of two plane surfaces having rollers interposed, the two surfaces are given a rounded contour, the one being within the other, and the same rule of increased ease of relative movement applies.

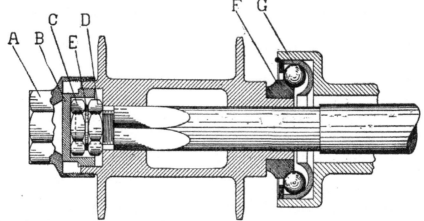

FIG. 285.—One Form of Driving Axle Using Ball Bearings. The hub is secured in place by the nuts and binders shown at A, B, C, D, E. At its inner extremity it carries a cone, F, which works on the ball race, G. The hub is thus suspended on the ball race, which also acts to neutralize end thrusts.

Rotative Bearings vs. Plain Bearings.—The obvious reason for the superior traction qualities obtained by the use of both kinds of rotative bearings is that the friction and resistance between the relatively moving surfaces is so greatly distributed that it is reduced to a practically negligible quantity.

One of the most familiar evidences of loss in power through the friction of the sliding surfaces, in plain bearing wheels, is seen in the fact that the hubs speedily become loose, greatly to the detriment of balanced rotation of the wheels and waste of traction effort. With properly adjusted ball or roller bearings this result is indefinitely delayed, even where it is not entirely obviated, and the wheels on which they are used not only give the best results in point of tractive efficiency, but also in the duration of their period of usefulness.

Ball Bearings and Their Use.—The ball bearing was originally introduced for use on bicycles, and contributed a goodly share to its success, principally for the reasons just specified. On the introduction of the motor carriage, it found a new field of usefulness, although, owing principally to the poor metal used for the balls and the defective designs of ball races, the roller

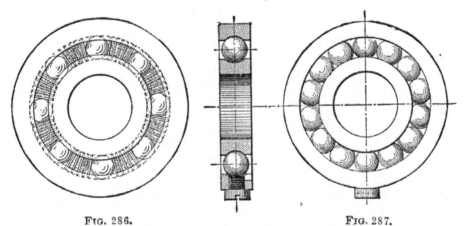

FIG. 286.   FIG. 287.

FIGS. 286 and 287.—Radial Ball-races and Balls. showing most satisfactory method of mounting a ball bearing. Fig. 286 shows the so-called "silent type" of bearing, having the balls separated by felt-packed springs. Fig. 287 shows the "full" type, in which the balls are in contact.

bearing enjoyed a greater popularity for several years. The reappearance of the ball bearing on the motor carriage is to be attributed largely, if not entirely, to fact that balls of superior and uniformly hardened steel have been introduced, which do away with the faults of case hardened steel—liability to crystallizing and crushing, due to inability to support a concentrated load on a single diameter. Formerly, considerable was said about the liability of balls to roll in opposite directions, thus producing friction and speedy wear, faults doubtless due to poor designs of the retaining cones and ball races.

The prevailing type of ball bearing at the present time is the so-called "radial," as shown in accompanying figures, in which the balls are inserted between an internally and an externally grooved ring. For the best results only a single row of balls is used in a journal, and all uncertainty and irregularity in supporting the load are thus eliminated. The radial ball bearing is also capable of taking up moderate end-thrust, although with large end-thrust a special thrust bearing, having the balls running in face grooves between two plates, is used. The type of bearing thus described is capable of showing a nearly uniform friction coefficient.

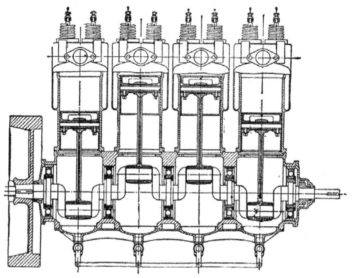

Fig. 288.-Four-cylinder Gasoline Engine, showing the radial ball bearings on the crank shaft.

Roller Bearings and Their Use.—Very largely on account of the defects in the earlier types of ball bearing, roller bearings were for several years used almost exclusively on motor carriages. As has been stated by a prominent manufacturer of roller bearings, we have it that "for heavy weights it would seem that a greater rolling surface must be obtained before we can have a successful bearing, and yet, combined with this greater rolling surface, there must be a purely rolling action to eliminate the wear that results from rubbing and crystallization."

As stated by a noted authority, the peculiar advantage of the roller bearing lies in the fact that in the ideal conditions there is no relative sliding, and, therefore, theoretically, no friction. As also stated by him, however, there are several difficulties in the way of obtaining the theoretically perfect conditions in practical operation. These are: (1) the concentration of the load upon points; (2) the almost insurmountable difficulty of obtaining truly circular cylindrical rollers; (3) the friction on the surfaces of the rollers themselves; (4) the difficulty of adjustment; (5) the lack of parallelism when the rollers are slightly worn; (6) the difficulty of providing for end thrusts or side pressures; (7) the blows and shocks resulting when wearing has occurred on the surfaces of the rollers. He further explains that to any extent whatever, however small, that the surface of contact deviates from the theoretical or geometrical line, the action between the two surfaces deviates from the theoretically perfect rolling contact, involving sliding or frictional contact proportionate to the deformation of the roller.

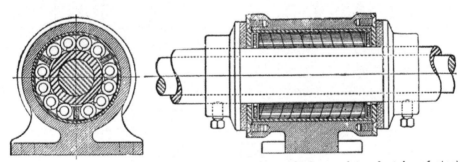

Fig. 289.—The "Hyatt" Flexible Roller Bearing, which consists of strips of steel rolled into coiled springs, forming a strong, though elastic, support, and capable of taking some end thrust.

Constructional Points on Roller Bearings.—Given the best possible process available to the practical machinist for the needs of adequately shaping and hardening rollers, the problem of the best construction becomes almost entirely one of proper assembling of the several parts. As shown by the accompanying illustration, the usual method of mounting roller bearings is to enclose them in a suitable case, in which the several cylindrical rollers are separated, so that, rotating on their own axes, their surfaces do not come into contact. It is a very usual practice to include end thrust ball bearings at the extremities of the roller cylinders, so as to still further reduce the wear and friction incident on the rotation of the several cylinders.

One of the most excellent types of roller bearing for motor carriages is the "American" roller bearing, which, as shown by the accompanying illustrations, consists of a set of main rollers intended directly to sustain the weight, and running in races on the hub and on the axle. These main rollers are separated and guided by intermediate separating rollers, whose office is solely that of separating and guiding. These separating rollers are confined between the centres of the main rollers and overlap their ends, their action being entirely rolling. The supports of these separating rollers are had in three rings held in place by the flange ends of the separators and running in narrow beveled grooves in the separators and in the fixed caps which enclose the entire mechanism. The rolling parts are so arranged that the

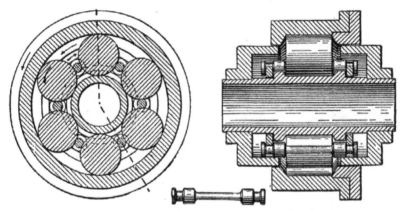

FIG. 290.–Sectional Diagrams of the "American" Roller Bearing. These bearings are beveled at the ends, as indicated, the bevels taking up the end thrusts, and are separated by smaller rollers, one of which is shown below the larger figures. These separating rollers do not come into contact with the rotating axle.

separators engage their supports in perfect harmony with the main rollers, traveling just fast enough to keep up with them in going about the axle, thus avoiding both dragging and pushing.

In this type of bearing the end thrust is entirely taken by bevels, on the principle of the flanges on car wheels, this construction involving that there is no rubbing friction; the action between the ends of the roller and bevels, being purely a rolling one, they are thrust against each other. As claimed by the manufacturers, the separators hold the main rollers far better than any cage could, while the wear upon them is practically negligible, the result being that the main rollers are never allowed to twist around, as is frequently the case in caged bearings.

CHAPTER THIRTY-TWO.

ON THE NATURE AND USE OF LUBRICANTS.

Of Lubricants for Various Purposes.—One of the most important considerations in connection with the operation of a motor vehicle, of any power, relates to the proper lubrication of the moving parts. As is perfectly evident on reflection, it is necessary that all such parts should be supplied with oil or lubricating grease, but it is also a fact, not so well understood, that different kinds of lubricant are necessary to the different kinds of mechanisms.

Of Lubricants for Gasoline Engine Cylinders.—Every reliable dealer in lubricants has a specially prepared grade of oil for a gas engine cylinder, and still another for use in the cylinder of a steam engine, and all agree to the statement, that the kind of lubricant suitable in one case is wholly useless in the other. The primary reason for this distinction is that, as we have seen, the cylinder of a gas engine operates under a far higher temperature than is possible even in a steam engine, and consequently the oils intended for use in the former case must be of such a quality that the point at which they will burn and carbonize from heat is as high as possible. Furthermore, it is essential in a gas engine cylinder that the oil should be constantly supplied, and for the purpose of properly meeting this requirement a number of different kinds of dripping and filtering oil cups have been devised and put into practical use.

Requirements in Gas Engine Lubricants.—As has been repeatedly pointed out by gas engine authorities, the apparently long period spent in finally perfecting the motor was due almost entirely to the fact that the subject of proper lubrication was not fully understood. With the ordinary oils, which are sufficiently suitable for use in the steam engine cylinder, it was impossible to obtain anything like a satisfactory speed and power efficiency, and only when the superior properties of mineral oils were better understood was the present high degree of perfection in any sense obtainable. Even to the present day the question of proper lubricants for gas engines is most essential, and, as has been pertinently remarked, "the saving of a few cents per gallon in purchasing a cheaper grade of oil for this purpose is the most expensive kind of economy imaginable." The general qualities essential in a lubricating oil for use on gas engine cylinders include a "flashing point of not less than 360°, Fahrenheit, and fire test of at least 420°, together with a specific gravity of 25.8 and a viscosity of 175."

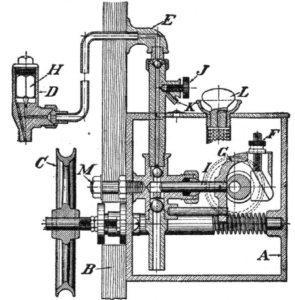

FIG. 291.—Section Through a Type of Power Driven Oil Pump. A, oil reservoir; B, dashboard of car; C, pulley driven by belt from engine shaft; D, gravity valve on distributor; E, outlet elbow; F, set screw to regulate stroke of plunger, I; G, plunger bracket bearing against eccentric, which is on the gear operated by worm, or endless screw, on the shaft of pulley, C; H, weight of gravity valve, D for holding outlet port normally closed, and rising under pressure of oil from pump; I, plunger of pump drawing oil from reservoir, A, through ball valve, and expelling it through ball valve to outlet, E; J, test cap for testing flow of oil; K, oil outlet for test cap; L, filling plug and strainer; M, stud bolt for securing machine to dashboard.

Some Objections to Organic Oils.—While a number of animal and vegetable oils have a flashing point, and yield a fire test sufficiently high to come within the figures specified, they all contain acids or other substances which have a harmful effect on the metal surfaces it is intended to lubricate. In addition to this, their tendency to gum or congeal under certain conditions of temperature or pressure render them unfit for the purpose of gas engine lubrication.

The Use of Graphite as a Lubricant.—Many authorities strongly recommend the use of powdered or flaked graphite in the cylinders of explosive engines for the reason that this substance is one of the most efficient of solid lubricants, especially at high temperatures. It has been found especially useful in some steam engine cylinders and in general on the bearings and moving parts liable to become overheated. According to sev-

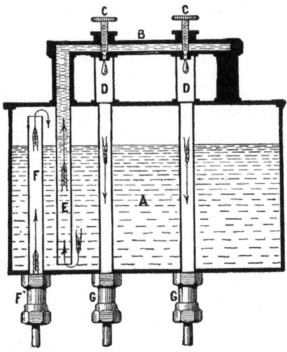

FIG. 292.–Typical Force-feed Lubricator, operating by air or gas pressure, instead of a pump. The parts are: A, oil reservoir; B, distributing pipe; C, C, valve screws for regulating flow of oil to parts, through leaders. D and D; E, standpipe through which oil is forced by air pressure; F, standpipe admitting gas from crank case of engine; F', union for pipe from crank case; G, G, unions for pipes to various parts of the machinery.

eral well-known authorities, it is well adapted for use under both light and heavy pressures when mixed with certain oils. It is also especially valuable in preventing abrasion and cutting under heavy loads and at low velocities.

In using graphite as a lubricant, it is positively essential to remember one thing: It is, as said, very useful *for certain purposes*, when mixed with some liquid oil lubricants. However, it is impossible to use it in connection with oils that are to be filtered through the small orifices of constant feed oil cups, as on the cylinders and bearings of engines. The reason for this is that it will not flow through small holes, even when mixed with very thin oil; and the very cooling of a bearing will cause the graphite, mixed with oil, to clog up the oil hole to an extent that may not be remedied by the reheating of the bearing, after the stoppage of the lubricant. On the same account, it is essential that the diameter. of the oil conduit to any moving part be ascertained to be of suitable shape and proportions before the use of any solid lubricant is attempted.

The Tests and Qualities of Lubricating Oils.—It is perfectly possible to use an oil having a fire test at the point already mentioned in a gas engine cylinder whose temperature at explosion is nearly four times greater, because with a properly ad-

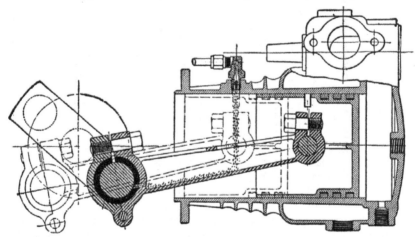

Fig. 293.—Horizontal Cylinder Oiled by Force-feed Oiler Distributor. The piston is oiled when passing under oil port, as shown by the dotted outline. The connecting rod is longitudinally grooved on the upper surface, so as to carry oil to the bearings.

justed water circulation the burning and carbonization of the oil is constantly prevented. The heat-absorbing action of the jacket water is also efficient in retaining at the required point the viscosity of the oil—which is to say, the quality of dripping at a certain ascertained rate through a narrow aperture under pressure. This quality virtually refers to the thinness of the oil. A well-known manufacturer of lubricating oils for gas engine cylinders well states the ideal qualities to be sought, as follows: "There is no danger of this oil burning or smoking in the cylinder and thus causing a carbonaceous deposit, which so seriously interferes with the proper running of the engine. We have repeatedly known of this oil, when put into a cylinder which had not been properly cleaned, cutting out the carbonaceous matter that had accumulated from the use of an inferior oil, after which the cylinder would remain clean and polished by the action of the oil alone." Combined with these ideal elements, the claim is made that this particular variety of oil has a very low "cold test," with the very necessary insurance against congealing, and consequent delay and inconvenience in starting the engine. Its resistance to heat is also placed at such a figure that it will not become unusually thin as will some qualities of oil, the reason being that its viscosity is maintained at the desired point.

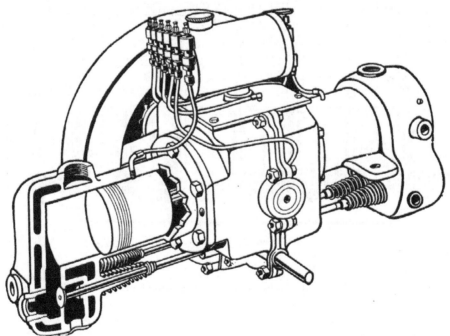

FIG. 294.—Section of the Ford Double-Opposed-Cylinder Horizontal Engine, showing oil leads to the various points from the lubricator operated by compressed air from the crank case.

In choosing lubricants for any of the moving parts of a self-propelled road vehicle it is especially essential to see that the quality of resisting temperatures, both high and low, without change of useful consistency, should be present. An oil that will congeal at ordinary low temperatures, or become thin at ordinary high temperatures, is, of course, entirely unsuitable for this purpose. Furthermore, the quality of flowing freely from well-adjusted oil cups should be assured, since the high speed of automobile engines engendering a constant vibration, affecting more or less the adjustment, involves that the oil supplied should be a subject of constant solicitude. To state the matter in a few words, all competent authorities seem to agree that the conditions of automobile operation require the use of mineral oils on all moving parts and the avoidance of any mixture with animal

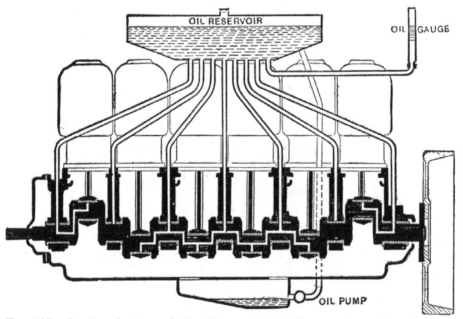

Fig. 295.—Sectional view of the Pierce lubricating system, showing the position of the oil reservoir relatively to the bearings to which it transmits the lubricating fluid and the connection by which the oil overflow is returned to the reservoir.

or vegetable oils, which, although frequently used in stationary engines, cannot but result in inconvenience, not to say disaster, in automobile practice.

Since most manufacturers of motors and vehicles furnish moderately full directions for dealing with the question of lubrication, many of them offering for sale brands of oil which have been carefully tested by themselves, it will be hardly necessary to add more to the principles already laid down.

Points on Lubrication.—The first important consideration involved in preparing a carriage for a run is to see that the moving parts are properly lubricated. Every carriage or motor is sold with directions for providing for this necessity, the rate of oil consumption and the quantity being specifically designated. The

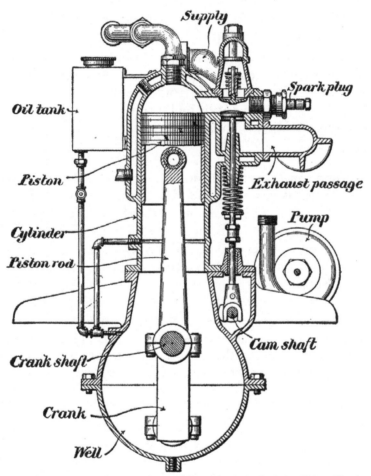

FIG. 205a.-Section Through One Cylinder of an Old Model of the Riker Engine, showing gravity oil feed and splash lubrication. Oil flows from the oil tank to the crank case, and is splashed to the piston sweep by the end of the connecting rod. Excess is caught in the peripheral groove at the end of the piston sweep and returned to the crank case.

principal parts which it is particularly necessary to keep thoroughly oiled are the cylinder pistons, the bearings of the crank shafts and fly-wheels, the differential gear drum and the change speed gearing.

Since on most well-built motors and carriages the moving parts are supplied with lubricating oil by means of sight feed oil cups, of familiar design, it is necessary to do no more than to see that the required level of oil is always maintained. As specified by many motor carriage authorities, it is desirable to thoroughly examine and replenish the oil supply in the adjustable feed cups at the end of about every thirty miles of run. Another consideration of importance in this particular is that before replenishing the supply of oil to such parts as the crank case or the differential gear, the old lubricant should be thoroughly evacuated by means of the vent cocks supplied in each case. The reason for this is that, after a run of from twenty to thirty miles, the oil in the moving parts is apt to be largely contaminated with dust and other impurities, which tend to interfere with its usefulness as a lubricant.

Oil Pumps and Circulation.—With the use of high-speed gasoline engines, it has been found necessary to use a forced circulation of the oil in order to completely lubricate the interior of the cylinder. The most usual method with high-powered multiple-cylinder engines is to employ a positively geared pump to force the oil through adjustable sight-feed conduits to the various moving parts. Such pumps, operating in ratio to the speed of the engine, of course supply lubricant more rapidly as the number of revolutions increases, and slow down as they decrease. Thus, a perfect supply is maintained, as required, on the one hand, and flooding is prevented on the other. There are several efficient types of oil pump on the market, all working on the same principle of forcing the oil to the moving parts in such volumes as may be determined by the adjustment. One or two inventors have produced devices of this kind operated by compressed air forcing the oil out of a tank, the degree of compression being determined by the speed of the engine operating the air pump.

CHAPTER THIRTY-THREE.

PRACTICAL OPERATION OF GASOLINE ENGINES.

Introductory.—The automobile engine, although having reached a high degree of perfection and made of the best materials obtainable, is a piece of machinery requiring the same intelligent attention in its care and management as any other high class machine, in order to obtain the best results in its operation.

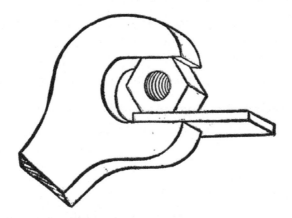

FIG. 296.—Illustrating the adaptation of a large wrench to a small nut. After the wrench is applied to the nut or bolt head, in the ordinary way with one hand, and before beginning to turn it, the wrench jaw is packed with the blade of a screwdriver, or with a bit of metal or hard wood held in the other hand as shown in the cut.

The management of an engine embraces, in addition to the attention given the engine, the adjustment and care of the fuel, cooling and ignition systems. A knowledge of ignition and the carburetter is the chief requisite for successful engine management. A careful study of the chapters devoted to these subjects is especially recommended.

427

Engine Management.—This includes, not only the necessary conditions of operation and control, which are simple to state, but also the numerous disorders and mishaps that may be encountered, as those arising:

1. From faulty construction, which, however, will be seldom experienced with well made automobiles.

2. From careless or ignorant handling, such as:

   a. Insufficient lubrication;
   b. Faulty adjustments;
   c. Exhaustion of the fuel, current or jacket water;
   d. Racing;
   e. Over heating.

3. From any one of a number of disorders in the ignition apparatus.

4. From poor gasoline, or faulty adjustment of the carburetter.

5. From worn or broken parts.

By far the greater proportion of gas engine troubles result from some derangement of the sparking system.

Second in importance come troubles with the fuel mixture. Both electrical apparatus and carburetter may require attention.

Before Starting the Engine.—There are three supplies necessary for the operation of a gas engine:

1. Gasoline;

2. Lubricating oil;

3. Circulating or cooling water.

In filling the gasoline tank, the liquid should always be strained to guard against the carburetter passages becoming clogged by any foreign matter that may be contained in the fuel. A chamois skin or wire netting having a very fine mesh should be used as a filter. In localities where gasoline is very expensive, as in California, number one distillate may be used which works nearly as well as gasoline except that it is necessary to prime the carburetter with the latter in starting when the engine is cold.

It is advisable that gasoline be tested by the consumer before accepting or using. Compact testing outfits are to be had at small cost.

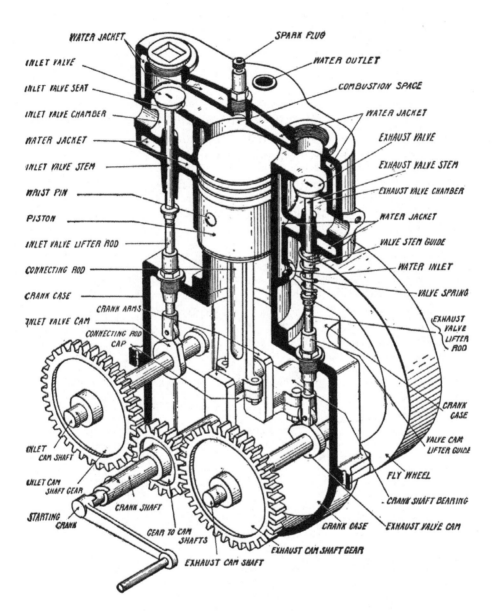

FIG. 297.—Sectional view of a four cycle gas engine, showing the valve gear and other working parts. Both inlet and exhaust valves are mechanically operated. The location of the valves diametrically opposite each other, requires a separate cam shaft for each. These cam shafts are geared to the engine crank shaft and they make one revolution to every two of the engine. When the inlet valve is operated by a spring and the engine suction, only one cam shaft is necessary as illustrated in fig. 313.

After filling the tank, the filler cap should be replaced and care taken that the small hole in the centre of the cap is open so that air may be admitted as the fuel is used, and thus prevent the pressure within the tank becoming less than that of the atmosphere.

The valve on the fuel supply pipe should now be opened and after sufficient time has elapsed for the float chamber of the carburetter to fill, it should be noted that the float pin is up.

When the float pin is up it indicates that the float chamber has received a supply of gasoline from the tank. If the pin remain down, there is some obstruction in the supply pipe preventing the flow of the liquid to the carburetter.

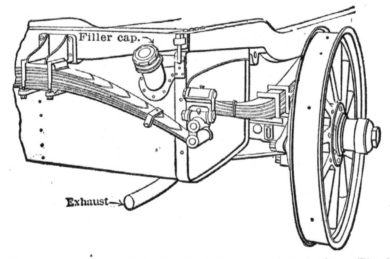

Fig. 298.—Showing usual location of tank and exhaust pipe. The latter passes under the tank and the construction should be such that the pipe is well secured to prevent whip-sawing.

Next, the radiator at the front of the car should be filled with *clean water.* As with the fuel, the same care should be taken with the water, to see that it is free from any foreign matter as the restricted passages of the radiator might become clogged and its efficiency impaired.

After filling the radiator, it is advisable to turn the engine over several times to allow the water to circulate through the cooling system and fill any air pockets that may have formed. This will be indicated by a lowering of the water level in the radiator. In which case more water should be added. If the car be driven in winter, a good non-freezing solution should be used.

It is an excellent plan that both the gasoline and water tanks be tested on each occasion of preparing for a run. Some automobiles have glass gauge tubes fixed to the fuel and water tanks, so

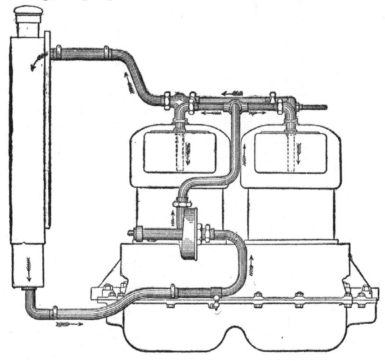

Fig. 299.—The Locomobile cooling system. The cooling water is circulated by a centrifugal pump which draws the water from the bottom of the radiator and forces it upward to the cylinders, whence through vertical stand pipes it is carried clear to the bottom of the water jackets, thus insuring a thorough cooling of the cylinders. The hot water from the motor then passes to the radiator, where it is cooled and delivered back to the pump. A pressure gauge is placed on the dashboard; if the clutch be released temporarily, and the engine speeded up, the pressure gauge will register several pounds, thus indicating that everything in the circulating system is in a satisfactory condition. When no pressure is registered it is an indication that the gauge is out of order or that the water supply needs to be replenished.

that the level of the liquids may be determined at a glance. In others it is a simple matter to test the level by inserting a stick in the filling hole and noting the height to which the liquid rises on it. This may be done with gasoline if the stick be withdrawn quickly and examined before evaporation takes place.

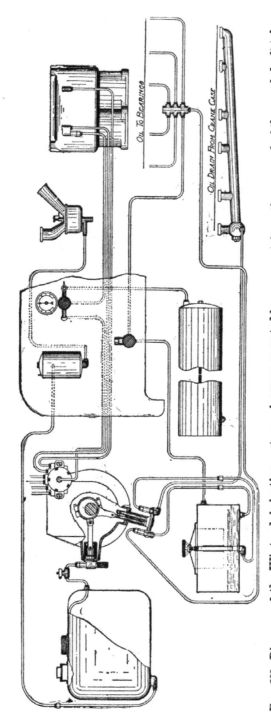

Fig. 300—Diagram of the Winton lubrication system. A pump operated by an eccentric on the rear end of the crankshaft takes oil from the oil tank at left side of motor and delivers it through leaders to the crankshaft main bearings and the front gears. A second pump operated by the same eccentric draws oil from the crank case, where it is deposited by gravitation, and returns it to the oil tank, where it passes through a filter before being used again. There is a sight test on the dash; cylinders are fed by splash, while transmission gears and clutch run in an oil bath.

ENGINE OPERATION.

Oil is a most essential requisite in the operation of automobiles. There are several methods of lubrication in general use, of which may be mentioned:

The gravity system, in which the lubricator is placed at a sufficiently high elevation to permit the oil to flow to the bearings.

The splash system, in which a quantity of oil is placed in the crank case and maintained at such a level that the ends of the connecting rods come in contact with the oil at the lower part of their revolution and splash it upon the working parts.

The pressure system, in which the oil is contained in a reservoir under pressure which forces it to the various bearings by connecting the reservoir to the exhaust by a small pipe or by utilizing the pressure from an enclosed crank case.

The positive system, in which a pump geared to the engine forces a certain amount of oil through the feeds at each stroke of the plunger.

Before starting the engine, all the other working parts requiring lubrication should receive attention and in general, it is well to adhere to the manufacturer's instructions in the performance of this task. The transmission case, the steering gear case and the rear axle housing may be supplied with a mixture of oil and grease which insures lubrication for the gears and bearings. The transmission case requires under ordinary conditions, gear grease mixed with heavy oil about once a month. The bevel gears, differential, steering gear and wheels are sometimes packed with a non-fluid lubricant sufficient for a season's use.

The quality of lubricating oil required for gas engine cylinders is quite different from that used for steam engines. Owing to the high cylinder temperatures a gas engine must have an oil possessing a high fire test. As the average cylinder temperatures may be said to be from 300 to 400 degrees Fahrenheit, an oil should be used having a fire test higher than the latter figure; the flashing point should not be less than 300 degrees. Air cooled engines, being hotter under working conditions than water cooled, require a lubricant capable of withstanding higher temperatures than that required by the latter. The most desirable oils are those free as possible from carbon. Clear oils have less suspended carbon than dark oils.

In addition to the attention required in supplying gasoline, water and oil as just described, it is necessary before starting the engine to make sure:

1. That the brake is set which releases the clutch so that the car cannot start until desired;

2. That all parts of the lubricating system are in working order, all connections opened, and the supply of oil sufficient;

3. That the ignition circuit is closed, which involves examination of all switches, to insure certainty that they are on the "closed" point;

4. That the carburetter control levers be placed in position for ensuring the *richest* mixture under operating conditions, in order

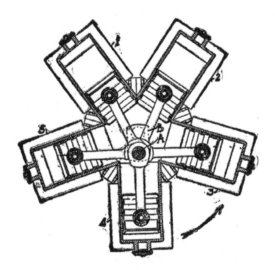

FIG. 301.—The Adams-Farwell engine. This is not a rotary but a revolving engine. It operates upon the four cycle principle, except that the cylinders are allowed to revolve instead of the crank shaft which is keyed to a stationary base. The force of the explosion, being confined between two objects, moves the one offering the least resistance. A is the stationary crank pin and B the shaft centre around which the cylinders revolve. The engine is air cooled and requires no fan on account of the motion of the cylinders.

that, even with the low suction at starting, sufficient power may be obtained for a good headway;

A rich mixture may occasionally fail to ignite at starting, but a weak mixture is more often at fault.

5. That the lever on the spark control quadrant stands at the extreme "back" position, retarding the spark to the limit.

To neglect this may cause "back kick" at cranking, and possibly result in serious injury to the operator.

6. That the throttle be opened partly. It should not be opened any further than is necessary, so that the engine will not race after cranking.

Preparing to Start in Winter Time.—Sometimes gas engines work indifferently in cold weather; a low temperature interferes with effective engine performance in several ways:

1. It renders difficult a rapid vaporization of the fuel.

2. It causes the lubricating oil to thicken, and in some cases to become gummy.

3. It causes freezing of the jacket water, unless precautions be taken to prevent it.

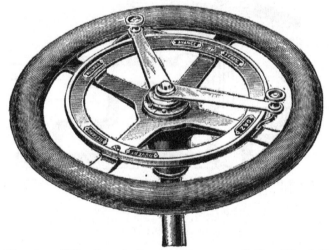

FIG. 302.—Steering Wheel and Control Levers of the Vinot Motor Carriage. The throttle and spark levers work on opposite arcs of the ring. Both turn clockwise for high speed adjustments, and counter clockwise for low speeds.

Carburetting in Cold Weather.—The uncertainty regarding good vaporization is the principal source of failure to operate in winter time, and furnishes an argument in favor of jacketing, or heating the air supply. It is obviously impracticable to heat the ordinary variety of sprayer, except by arranging the air feed pipe to run over or around the muffler, which would doubtless assist matters considerably after the engine is started. The hot exhaust gases are used by some designers for heating the mixing chamber, and the circulating water by others.

Sticking from Gummed Oil.—In cold weather, or after the engine has been inactive for a considerable period, the oil in the cylinder is likely to be thickened, with the result that it is unusually difficult to turn the crank. If a few turns with the electric switch open, do not suffice to loosen the adhesion by friction, the result may be accomplished by squirting a small quantity of gasoline over the piston with a syringe.

Freezing of the Jacket Water.—Nearly the most fatal form of carelessness in the management of a gasoline engine is to allow the cooling water to freeze in the jackets. A frozen water jacket

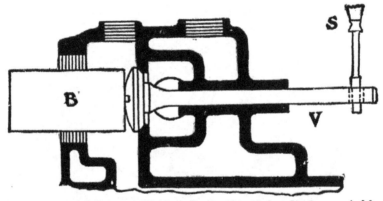

Fig. 303.—Method of grinding valves in horizontal cylinders. A block of steel *B* is held against the head of the valve *V* and the latter rotated on its seat by means of a screwdriver blade *S* inserted in the slot in the stem, the face having been previously trued by a truing tool. In cases where the stem of the valve has no slot, a pair of gas pliers can be used to grip it, being careful in so doing, not to mutilate the threads thereon.

generally bursts, without however, doing certain injury to the arched walls of the cylinder. The engine may be started, therefore, but soon heats up, the jacket water leaking out through the breaks.

Precautions to Prevent Freezing.—In cold weather a careful automobile driver will drain all water from the jackets and circulating system by opening all pet cocks on the cylinder jacket, the pump and feed pipes and the radiator. After the water has entirely run out, the jackets and pipes may be dried by allowing the engine to run for not over a minute, thus vaporizing and expelling all remaining moisture.

Non=freezing Jacket Solutions.—When a motor vehicle is to be run in winter weather, particularly if it is to be left standing with the engine not operating, some kind of non-freezing water solution should be used or the circulating system thoroughly drained. Such a solution is one that lowers the freezing point of

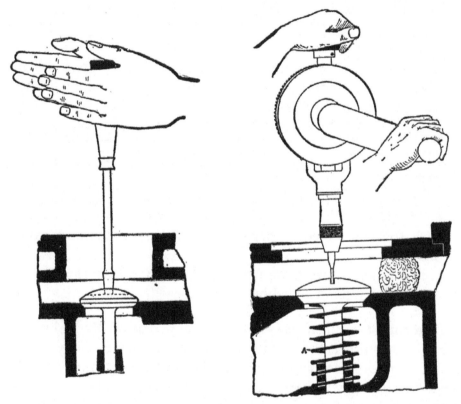

Fig. 304.—Method of using a screwdriver for valve grinding. A handful of waste or a cloth is put in the valve port to protect the cylinder, and the valve face coated with a paste of fine emery powder and oil and put in place. The handle of the screwdriver is now held between the palms of the hands, as in the sketch, and a series of oscillations through a small arc given to the valve by moving the palms in opposite directions. After about thirty of these oscillations have been given, the valve is lifted from its seat, given a half turn, and reseated for further grinding in the same manner. This operation should be continued, with occasional additions of oil and emery, until the valve face and the seat appear to be bright for their full width around the circle.

Fig. 305.—Method of grinding valve with a drill stock. A screwdriver bit is inserted in the chuck and the operation conducted as in the case where a screwdriver is used. Owing to the multiplication between the driving and the driven bevels, the crank should be rocked through a small arc, instead of being rotated. The spring A is fitted within the valve chamber to unseat the valve when it is desired to examine it or when a half turn is to be given the valve on its seat.

the water, allowing it to remain liquid below 32°F. (0°C.). There are several such in use, all recommended by authorities:

1. A solution of water and glycerine: water 70% by weight; glycerine 25% to 30% by weight; sodium carbonate or "washing soda," 2% by weight.

The glycerine is liable to congeal at very low temperatures, but this tendency is largely neutralized by the presence of the soda. With this solution the contents of the jacket and radiator had best be drawn off, and renewed at least once a month.

2. A solution of water and calcium chloride, in proportions of 10 lbs. calcium chloride, dissolved in a pailful of boiling water, forming a saturated solution.

Allow the mixture to boil, and then to settle. Test with litmus paper for acid, which may be neutralized with quicklime. Test occasionally for acid formed by heat.

Before pouring this solution into the tank, it should be carefully strained through a fine cloth, to remove all sediment.

Only the *chemically pure* calcium chloride, sold by responsible chemists, should be used for this solution, and one should carefully avoid using the so-called "chloride of lime," commonly known as calcium hypochlorite.

3. A solution of equal parts by weight of water and wood alcohol.

4. A solution of two parts wood alcohol, 1 part glycerine, 1 part water, is also recommended by Roberts.

Draining the Jackets.—Although any one of the solutions given above prevent freezing of the jacket water, many users find it more satisfactory to drain the jackets through the pet cock on the radiator, when the car is to stand over night, and refill before the next start of the motor. This practice is preferable because the solutions are troublesome and dirty, and at best, do not cool as well as pure water.

Spark and Throttle Adjustments before Starting.—On account of the slow speed at which the engine is turned over in *cranking,* it is necessary that the throttle have a considerable degree of opening and that the spark be fully retarded because of:

1. The weak suction of the piston at slow speed;

2. The need of ensuring a mixture that will ignite under such conditions;

3. The danger of bodily injury from a "back kick" of the engine, which is liable to occur with an early spark at slow speeds, as will be described later.

Cranking.—It may be well to repeat here that the operator should never attempt to crank an engine until:

1. *The brake is set, releasing the clutch;*
2. *The transmission lever is placed in the neutral position;*
3. *The spark fully retarded.*

The neglect of this caution may be followed by serious consequences.

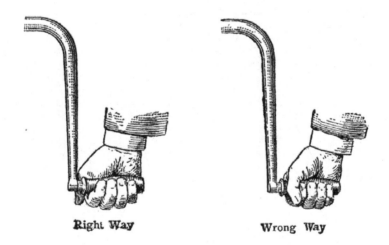

Right Way   Wrong Way

FIGS. 306 and 307.—Illustrating right and wrong methods of cranking an engine. As ordinarily practiced, the hand is so placed that the thumb and fingers encircle it. Such a method is decidedly unsafe should the operator press down on the crank and a back fire occur. The correct method, is to place the thumb on the same side of the handle that the fingers are placed so that the handle is not entirely encircled, allowing the handle to slip out of the grasp when it is being pressed down, and permitting the fingers to release the handle if it is being pulled up, at the time of back fire.

In cranking, the operator faces the car and grasps the crank handle with the four fingers of the right hand, allowing the thumb to lie along the handle. The crank is now raised to its highest position, pressed in toward the car and turned downward.

If, at the beginning of this movement, it turn hard indicating compression, the operator should allow the crank to spring out of engagement with the shaft and revolve backward far enough so that he will pull up against compression.

An engine should never be cranked downward against compression, for in case the spark has not been fully retarded, the pressure of the early explosion may overcome the momentum of the fly wheel and drive the handle violently backward, resulting in at least a seriously sprained wrist.

It is well for the novice to first make two or three turns with the switch off, then a final turn with the switch on when the engine should start.

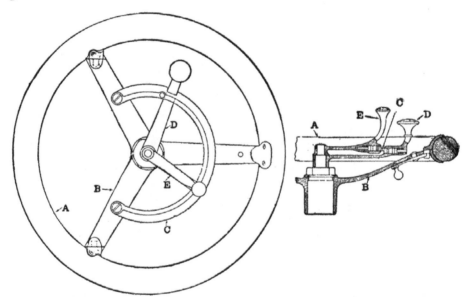

Fig. 308.—Steering Wheel and Attachments of the Pope-Toledo Carriage. A is the wheel rim; B, a spoke or arm of the three-armed spider; C, sector for sliding arms. D and E; D, throttling arm and handle; E, spark regulating handle. The throttle is opened by moving the handle clockwise around the sector; the spark is advanced by moving its handle in the same direction.

Another method for the beginner, consists in turning the handle till he is sure he is pulling upward against compression, then relieving the compression somewhat by partly opening and closing the relief cock, after which the turn is quickly completed.

Some engines are provided with an exhaust valve lifter, which is used to relieve compression during the first few turns in cranking.

If the compression in the cylinders be good, a multi-cylinder engine can usually be started as follows:

The primary switch is first opened and the engine turned over a few times until a fresh charge is obtained in each cylinder. The operator then mounts the seat and after closing the switch, the spark lever is suddenly pushed forward as far as it will go. This operation will usually cause a spark in one of the cylinders and start the engine.

Misfiring During Operation.—Occasionally, the missing of one or more of the cylinders will be noticed during the operation of the engine. This trouble may be recognized by irregularity of motion, gradual slowing down, and, generally, by *after firing,* or explosions in the muffler.

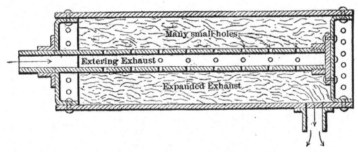

Fig. 309.—A simple form of muffler, as used on many cars and which gives good satisfaction when well designed. It consists of a cylinder and a pipe so contrived that the pipe, which is drilled full of small holes, will admit the exhaust at high pressure, and as it is required to pass through a large number of small holes, it is split up and then expanded. The gas passes to the atmosphere in an even flow, at a pressure slightly above that of the atmosphere. This type of muffler is fairly efficient when well designed.

If the trouble cannot be located in one of the cylinders the inference holds: either that there is some general derangement of the ignition circuit, or that the fuel mixture is not right.

Back Firing and Back Kick.—This is a form of disordered action, sometimes encountered on starting the engine, and most often due to non-observance of necessary rules, as already laid down, for adjusting the engine and auxiliary parts. In back firing the ignition of the charge takes place at such a point in the cycle that the motion of the engine is reversed.

If back firing occur while the operator is holding the crank, it produces a back kick, which is liable to dislocate his shoulder unless the crank throws off automatically.

The term *back firing* is also applied to an explosion occurring during or at the end of the inlet stroke, when the gas in the carburetter mixing chamber is ignited. This is due generally to a loose or defective inlet valve, a pitted inlet valve seat, smoldering carbon residue in the cylinder space, or a spark due to a disarranged ignition circuit. The logical presumption is that the inlet valve needs grinding in its seat, in the same manner as is subsequently explained in connection with the exhaust valve.

Back firing, or ignition at the wrong point in the cycle, with reversed piston movement, must be carefully distinguished from *after firing,* or explosion in the muffler or exhaust pipe. Occasionally the same term is erroneously applied to both mishaps.

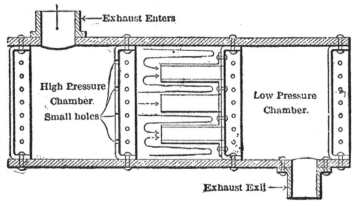

FIG. 310.—Simplex type of muffler, showing three chambers—a high pressure, intermediate, and low pressure chamber, so contrived that the pressure is reduced almost to zero before the exhaust makes its exit to the atmosphere. The volume of the high pressure chamber is equal to that of one of the engine cylinders; the intermediate chamber has twice the volume, and the low pressure chamber three times the volume of the engine cylinder.

Causes of Back Firing.—Back firing, or pre-ignition, may occur under several conditions. Prominent among these are:

1. An early ignition, at or before the backward dead centre of the crank, before the cycle is established, as in the act of cranking the engine for a start. The result is then a *back kick,* as already explained. This can only emphasize the necessity of retarding the spark at starting, so that it will not occur until the piston is at, or very near the dead centre.

2. Over heating of the cylinder walls, due to insufficient heat radiation (in an air cooled engine) or too little jacket water (in a water cooled engine). This should emphasize the necessity of keeping the water supply sufficient for all needs, and of assuring the perfect operation of the circulation system, pump, radiator, etc., before starting the engine.

3. Soot deposits within the combustion space, due to carbonization of excess oil, etc. Such deposits will readily ignite and smolder, and will thus furnish an almost certain source of ignition, during the compression stroke.

Spark and Throttle Adjustments after Starting.—When the engine has speeded up, the adjustments must be changed:

1. The spark must be advanced.

2. The throttle opening must be reduced.

If there be a mechanical governor on the engine, the throttle will shut down automatically, as the engine speeds up.

On account of the spark and throttle adjustments necessary in cranking, the engine when started will begin to race unless it be fitted with a governor, hence, the operator should immediately reduce the throttle opening and advance the spark so the engine will run at its slowest speed while the car is standing. The throttle lever should be pushed all the way back; this does not close the valve entirely but leaves sufficient opening to supply the minimum charge to the engine.

Failure to Start.—Refusal of the engine to take up the cycle, even after prolonged cranking, is a familiar experience in automobile operation. Unless some accident has occurred, or a very unusual strain has been thrown upon the working parts, the inference is that some element of the rather complicated group of mechanisms is out of adjustment, and in most cases the failure to start is due to some faulty adjustment or defect of the carburetter or ignition system.

Causes of Failure to Start.—In cranking, it should be remembered that *a few rapid turns of the crank handle will do more towards starting an engine than ten minutes of slow grinding.*

If an engine show good compression and will not start after four or five turns, it is useless to continue. Assuming that all the preliminaries to starting hitherto specified have been carefully observed, the probable causes of trouble should be sought:

1. *In the spark plug;*
2. *In the secondary wiring;*
3. *In the vibrator of the coil;*
4. *In the interior of the coil;*
5. *In the timing device;*
6. *In the primary wiring;*
7. *In the current source* $\begin{cases} \text{primary or secondary batteries.} \\ \text{magneto or dynamo.} \end{cases}$
8. *In the carburetter.*

The several causes of failure to start the engine as mentioned above, will now be briefly explained in the order given.

Defective Spark Plugs.—The engine will not start when:

1. The plug points are too far apart.
2. The plug is short circuited.
3. The insulating layer of porcelain or mica is broken down.
4. There is much fouling between the plug points.

Fouling may consist of oil or soot. Both give trouble at starting.

Fouling with soot may generally be removed with gasoline. Preventives of fouling are:

1. An annular space between the core insulation and the outer shell, producing a vortex, as is alleged, and allowing piston suction to remove deposits.
2. An auxiliary spark gap, which will generally suffice to insure a spark, but it does not prevent fouling between the spark points. A temporary gap may be made by disconnecting the lead wire of the plug and holding its end at a sufficient distance to allow a visible spark to leap from it to the plug core.

If this prove ineffective, the plug should be unscrewed and examined. Any visible fouling may then be removed by rubbing the insulation with fine sand paper until the bright surface of the porcelain is visible, taking care not to impair the surface.

If no fouling appear the plug may be laid upon the cylinder or frame so that its case only is in contact, and thus grounded, and on cranking the engine, the spark may be seen leaping between the points.

If a spark does not appear, it is probable that, with the ignition circuit in working order, there is some breakage or short circuit in the body of the plug. This, of course, necessitates its removal and the substitution of a new one. If a good spark appear, the search for trouble must be continued to other parts.

In a multi-cylinder engine a defective plug may sometimes be located by touch, that is, if its cylinder has been missing for some time the metal of the plug will be perceptibly cooler than that of the other plugs.

Defects in the Secondary Wiring.—The current, on account of defective insulation may short circuit to some metallic portion of the car or engine. If the secondary lead be disconnected from the spark plug, the current may sometimes be heard or seen in discharging.

Misfiring: Short Circuits.—Very frequently misfiring is caused by a short circuit, which is to say a ground, or an arcing gap between the two sides of the secondary circuit, at some point short of the plug terminals. This will, of course, prevent sparking at the plug, although, owing to the vibration of operation in the other cylinders, the short circuit may occasionally be interrupted and the spark will occur.

Such a short circuit differs from an *auxiliary spark gap,* in that the latter is *in series* with the plug gap, while the former gives a leak *in parallel* to it.

Vibrator Failures.—There may be a defective adjustment of the vibrator, which will prevent it responding to the strength of current in use, or the vibrator may be broken loose.

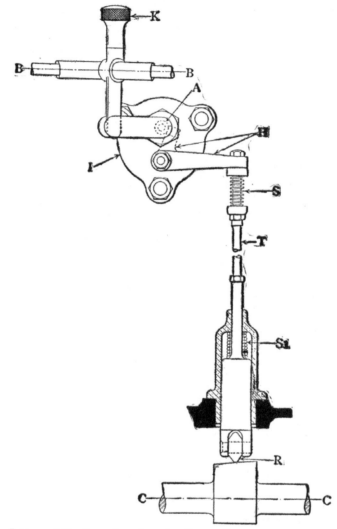

FIG. 311.—Locomobile low tension igniter. *I* is the igniter, the upper end of the tappet rod *T*, is hooked to the hammer lever *H*, and as the tappet rod is given vertical motion, by one of the cams on the cam shaft *C—C*, and rises, the hammer comes in contact with the anvil *A* and stays there until the cam has reached such a position that the tappet rod suddenly falls, causing the hammer to separate sharply from the anvil and the spark to occur, the action being assisted by a strong enclosed spring *SI* at the bottom of the tappet rod. A spring *S* at the top of the tappet rod keeps the electrodes in contact until it is time for the break to occur. Knife blade switches such as *K*, form electrical contact between an insulated bus-bar *B, B,* on the motor and anvils.

As will be evident on reflection and from previous explanations, the spark in the cylinder does not occur at the same point in the piston stroke at high and low speeds, nor, ever necessarily, at the moment the primary circuit is made at the timer. This is due partly to the vibrator and partly to the coil. Some time is always required to saturate the coil, make the break and discharge the core, producing the jump spark.

The average duration of these operations is about .005 second, which, although quite negligible at low speeds, requires progressive advances of the timer as speed increases. The movement of the vibrator also consumes a fraction of a second, its speed being indicated by the pitch of its buzz, but unless the speed be very high, the time for occurrence of the spark is changed. If the vibrator be leaving the core at the moment of circuit making at the contact maker, the time of one vibration must elapse before the occurrence of the spark; if the vibrator be in contact at this moment, the spark follows almost immediately. These facts enforce the desirability of high speed vibration.

In a multiple cylinder engine using a separate coil for each cylinder, the vibrators should be tuned as nearly as possible to the same pitch or rate of vibration; otherwise the sparks will occur at different points of the several respective piston strokes.

In most cases the vibrator requires no adjustment, however, the instructions given for vibrator adjustment in the chapter on ignition may be supplemented by the following:

a. When the adjusting, or back stop screw is turned inward, forcing the vibrator nearer to the pole of the core, the rapidity of vibration will be increased.

b. When the adjusting screw is turned outward, increasing the distance between the vibrator and pole of the core, the rate of vibration will be decreased.

c. There are very definite limits to the proper operation of the core, at either loose or tight adjustment.

d. A fair adjustment for low speeds may prove unsuitable for high speeds, and *vice versa.*

e. A fair adjustment for a strong battery will probably be found unsuitable for a weak battery, and *vice versa.* Therefore, the battery should receive attention, rather than the coil adjustment.

f. With the use of a jump spark coil, this is nearly the strongest argument for a double battery, controlled by a two point switch.

If one cares to risk experiment with coil adjustments, he will soon discover the range of efficient action.

As a general proposition, the following rules hold good for adjustment of the coil:

1. The vibrator should vibrate with sufficient rapidity to give a distinctly musical sound.

2. Rapid vibration, except, of course, one that is excessive, is more efficient and better for the battery than one that is slower.

3. Reducing the rate of vibration increases the efficiency of a weak battery, according to the statements of some authorities.

The truth of the matter is that reducing the rate of vibration produces a stronger spark by permitting the coil to saturate more fully.

A constant sounding of the vibrator indicates a leak or short circuit somewhere, and should be immediately investigated. A short circuit is the quickest means for exhausting a chemical battery. On the other hand, it means speedy destruction for a storage battery, as will be explained later.

Misfiring: Faulty Vibrator Adjustment.—Among the causes which produce misfiring at high speeds may be mentioned a faulty adjustment of the coil vibrator, giving extremely short *makes* of the primary circuit and slow rates of vibration, which cannot keep pace to the requirements of high engine speeds.

Loose circuit connections, shaken out of position as the engine speeds up, and weakened batteries are common causes of this mishap at high speeds.

Defects in the Interior of the Coil.—Electrical faults in this part of the ignition system may be caused by the presence of moisture, oil or dirt and by the condenser not being suited to battery.

The coil generally needs very little attention. Provided the battery be maintained at an approximately even efficiency, and the coil is carefully protected from moisture, oil and dirt, there is virtually no danger of electrical derangement. It may be safely asserted that the majority of cases in which the coil is supposed to be "worn out," are merely examples of irregular or inefficient action of the condenser. Occasionally a spark discharged from the condenser occurs at the moment of breaking contact of the vibrator and screw back stop with the result of burning the contacts. Dirt or oil between the vibrator contacts will produce similar result. In either case there will be no spark at the spark plug. Spark discharges at the vibrator contacts usually result from the condenser not being suited to the battery. When the condenser is of proper size, the spark will be very minute.

Nothing will so rapidly deteriorate a high tension coil as the presence of moisture in its windings. The water frequently soaks through the insulation, short circuiting the current and preventing a spark. A coil, evidently affected by moisture, can not be repaired, except by experienced workmen, and had best be replaced.

In purchasing a coil, it is necessary to see that it is perfectly suitable for the type of battery or generator in use. Induction

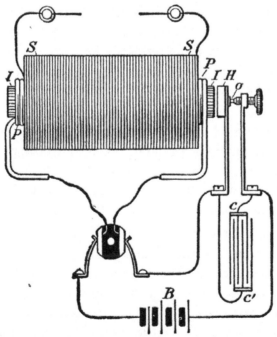

Fig. 312.—Diagram of the Essential Parts of an Induction Coil; B, chemical battery; C, C', condenser terminals; I, laminated iron core; P. primary winding; S, secondary winding; H, head of the vibrator; o, contact point of the back stop screw.

coils, like other electric coils, are wound for use with a certain definite voltage in the primary source. Logically, therefore, the best effect can not be obtained unless the coil and source are mutually suited. This rule holds for all types of source.

Misfiring: Defective Coil.—A broken down coil, or one in which the insulation is weakened, allowing internal leaks and sparking, will cause misfiring for a time, and will very soon be of no use whatever.

Defects in the Timing Device.—This portion of the ignition apparatus should be examined occasionally for:

1. Loose screws or contacts.
2. Thick oil or dirt on contact surfaces.

In a wipe commutator only the thinnest and lightest grade of oil should be used on the contact surface.

Loose or foul contacts constitute a fertile source of ignition failures.

Defects in the Primary Wiring.—The current in this circuit being of low pressure, its flow is easily prevented by loose and corroded terminals, defective switches, or breaks of any kind in the continuity of the wire. Hence, special care should be taken with this part of the ignition system, that:

1. The terminals be kept clean and bright;
2. The connections be firmly made;
3. The spring portions of switches be so adjusted that they bear firmly, making a good contact;
4. Frequent examination be made for partial breaks;
5. The insulation be guarded against breaks, flaws or rubbed areas. By this means leaks and short circuits will be avoided.

Misfiring: Loose Connections.—Loose connections of the wires at a binding screw, may cause misfiring; the looseness may be small, or it may be excessive, and the condition in this respect determines the degree of interference in engine operation. Thus, a loose connection may allow the engine to run from rest to a moderately good speed before trouble begins, or the vibration of operation may interrupt the contact entirely.

Defective Battery.—Ignition failures are often due to a weak, run down, or polarized battery. Dry cells, when used as a source of current for sparking, particularly for extended periods, should be arranged in series in two or more separate batteries, with switches that may cut all out of circuit, except the one in use as current supply. The reason for this is that such cells are subject to deterioration in use, and a **new** battery should always be at hand. Deterioration may result:

1. From extensive use, after which the cell becomes exhausted through consumption of the zinc element, or the electrolyte.

2. From short circuits long continued, which cause the cell to run out of current more rapidly than otherwise. A *temporary* short circuit will not injure a dry cell as seriously as it will some other types of source. Generally, it will polarize it more quickly. A season on open circuit will find it still serviceable.

3. From neglect to open the switch or the primary circuit, on stopping the engine. If, then, there be a leak, or the timer rotor be in engagement with one of the contacts, the current will rapidly run to waste.

Dry cells, so-called, are all of the "open circuit" variety. That is to say, the generation of current produces the condition known as "polarization," or the collection of hydrogen on the electrode attached to the positive lead wire. This condition may be remedied, the cell may be "depolarized," only by leaving it for a period on open circuit, or disconnected.

A polarized cell will show a low current register on the ammeter, but may be restored more or less after resting.

The theory and management of storage cells are set forth in another chapter. Storage cells used on sparking circuits are often charged by the surplus current of the sparking dynamo. When no dynamo is used, they are charged by special attachments to electric feed mains, or by a battery of wet cells of proper voltage.

In order that storage cells should continue of service in the sparking circuit of a gasoline engine, it is necessary to constantly observe the following rules:

1. Each cell should register at full charge about 2.5 volts and should never be used after the voltmeter falls to 1.75.

2. If short circuited at any time, the cell should be immediately disconnected and recharged, as elsewhere specified. Short circuiting is one of the most fatal mishaps that can overtake a storage cell.

Misfiring: Weak Battery.—When the current supply is reduced, as by a weak battery, it may prevent sparking between the plug points, and can be remedied in no better fashion—provided no extra battery be at hand—than by reducing the gap between the points. As a consequence, a weak battery is a frequent cause of misfiring.

Misfiring due to a weak battery may be diagnosed by the occasional apparent violence of the explosions, on account of frequent misses. A weak battery will cause misfiring most conspicuously when the engine has been run up nearly to full speed, and then suddenly drops, owing to irregular ignitions. The reason is, obviously, that the weak battery cannot supply good fat sparks at a rate commensurate with the requirements of rapid operation. With a reduced spark gap and a slow speed, it may be able to cause operation for a limited period.

These principles apply, of course, to chemical batteries. When the current is obtained from a magneto or dynamo, the trouble—if traced to the source—is probably due to loose or worn brushes, a glazed commutator, or a short circuit somewhere in the armature, or around the brush holders.

Defective Generator.—As a rule, troubles with a mechanical generator are liable to arise from glazing or lack of adjustment of the brushes and commutator. Next to this, the oil feed or bearings should be carefully watched and supplied, and the cut-out governor, if one be attached, should be occasionally examined, to be sure that it is in perfect working order.

Glazing.—A troublesome condition that occasionally appears in small dynamos is a glaze on the commutator or contact surfaces of the brushes. This may be removed from the brushes by wrapping a very fine *sandpaper,* sand side up, around the commutator and rotating the spindle, so that the brush ends are thoroughly scoured. It may be removed from the commutator by rubbing the surface with the finest grade of sandpaper. *Emery paper should never be used for this purpose,* since emery, being carbon, is a conductor, and its presence between the segments of the commutator is liable to interfere with the insulation. It also causes rapid wear.

Faulty Action of Carburetter.—The several paragraphs preceding have been devoted entirely to the ignition system which is the source of most failures in starting the engine; second in importance, in this respect, is the carburetter. Success in starting and running the engine depends, to a considerable degree, upon its proper adjustment and control so that it will furnish a mixture of the right proportions to meet varying demands.

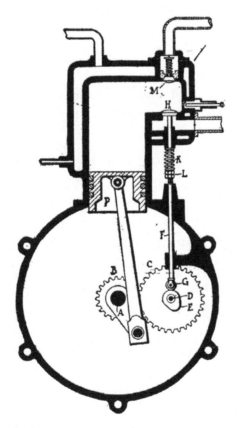

FIG. 313.—Illustrating the operation of a four cycle engine valve gear. The figure shows a spring actuated inlet valve M and a mechanically operated exhaust valve H. The latter is opened when the cam E revolves and raises against the roller G, which is on the bottom of the lifter rod F. The rod F extends upward and rests against the bottom of the stem of the valve H, although between the two or at their point of contact are nut and locknut L for lengthening or shortening the lifter F, and so to vary the time of opening or closing of the valve. The spring K is compressed or squeezed together when the valve is opened and immediately the cam E travels around and allows the roller G to fall; this spring exerts its pressure and closes the valve. The intake valve M is automatically opened by the suction of the engine.

Defective Fuel Mixture.—It frequently happens that too rich a mixture will not ignite readily on cranking and as a consequence, the engine will not start. It is necessary, then, to reduce the mixture, allowing more air to enter the mixing chamber.

If the engine start with a rich mixture, the result is liable to be seen in a heavy and ill smelling smoke from the muffler. The color of this smoke will determine the nature of the trouble.

Dark colored dense smoke indicates an excess of gasoline in the mixture, and may result from one of the following conditions:

1. Imperfect combustion.
2. Defective ignition.
3. Either excessive or defective lubrication.
4. Overheating and consequent flashing of the lubricating oil.
5. A leaky piston.

The two most usual causes of dark smoky exhaust, however, are:

1. Defective carburetter action, due probably to grit under the inlet needle valve, or else to some derangement of the parts.
2. An over rich mixture, which ignites imperfectly.

White dense smoke indicates an excess of oil or a resulting deposit of carbon soot in the cylinder, or a poor oil.

Thin blue, or nearly invisible smoke indicates a normal mixture and good ignition.

An unpleasant odor in the exhaust is frequently mentioned as the one necessary evil of motor carriage operation. It is certainly nothing of the sort, and most often indicates poor lubricating oil or too rich a mixture, which involves wasteful use of fuel. A good mixtrue, perfectly ignited, in a cylinder lubricated with high test oil, should have no very bad odor.

Bad odors and smoke at starting are frequently produced by chemical conditions other than a poor oil or an over rich mixture. They are also common when running at slow speeds. Long continued, however, they constitute a nuisance that demands earnest and careful attention.

Reducing Smoke in the Exhaust.—Smoke from the exhaust being a sure indication of oil flooding or too much gasoline in the fuel mixture, demands attention to the *oil feed* and *carburetter*, as follows:

1. Reduce rate of oil feed, if the smoke indicate oil. If this be the sole trouble, the smoke will decrease after a few revolutions of the fly wheel.

2. Restore the oil feed nearly to normal and adjust the carburetter.

3. Examine the air inlet of the carburetter, and cleanse the gauze screen of any dust. This will restore the air supply.

Dangers of a Smoky Exhaust.—A smoky exhaust, indicating the presence of excess oil or carbon deposits in the cylinder, should serve as a warning in one respect. The soot formed is liable to take fire and smolder, causing pre-ignition, even back-firing, particularly under heavy loads.

If, after other relief measures have been tried, the nuisance persist, the cylinder interior should be cleaned at the earliest opportunity. This, of course, cannot be done until the engine is brought home and can be dismantled at leisure. To forestall further mishaps, the journey should be continued with as weak a mixture as possible.

In cold weather considerable watery vapor appears in the exhaust.

Causes of Defective Mixtures.—An over rich mixture—one containing an excess of gasoline vapor—may be caused by:

1. An air inlet clogged with dust or ice on the gauze.

2. A piece of grit or other object preventing closure of the needle valve.

3. A leaky float, which has become partially filled with liquid gasoline, and is, therefore, imperfectly buoyant.

A leaky float may be repaired by soldering, but authorities recommend that, in this work, a vent be made at some convenient point, and the float cooled by setting on a cake of ice, after which the vent is soldered up, leaving the air within at atmospheric pressure.

A poor mixture may be caused by:

1. An excess of air drawn through some leak in the air pipe.

2. Water in the gasoline.

3. A feed pipe or feed nozzle clogged with lint, grit or other obstructions.

It may occasionally happen, particularly after standing for a long period, that the valve of the carburetter sticks. This will interfere, of course, with proper feed of fuel. To determine whether all parts are in good condition, it is desirable to *flush* or *prime* the carburetter by depressing the protruding end of the valve spindle or the *flusher*. This depresses the float, opens the valve, allowing liquid to enter the chamber, and thus proves that there is no clog or interference.

Under conditions of operation, the carburetter should not be allowed to flood. However, at starting it is often a means of insuring sufficient richness of mixture to enable ignition to take place. A sufficiently rich mixture for starting may be obtained by partially closing by hand the air inlet to the carburetter so that the increased suction will draw a greater quantity of gasoline into the mixing chamber.

The quality of the mixture may generally be determined from the effects on the operation of the engine. If it be not obvious in this manner, it may be determined by actual test.

If the cylinder cock or the spark plug be removed and a lighted match applied the richness of the mixture may be judged by the color of the flame, viz:

1. If the mixture be *too rich,* it will burn *yellow.*

2. If the mixture be *too poor,* it may not burn at all or *faintly blue.*

3. If the mixture be *just right,* it will *explode* and rush out of the opening to the danger of one's fingers.

4. If the mixture seem to be *poor,* injecting a little gasoline from a squirt can, or flooding the carburetter, will prove whether or not the diagnosis be correct.

Misfiring: Defective Mixture.—A defective mixture will frequently occasion misfiring, on account of difficulty of igniting. Such a defective mixture may be one that is either too rich or too weak, and may be produced by a flooded carburetter, or one in which sticking, or some similar disorder, prevents the feeding of sufficient gasoline spray for a good mixture.

In either case the ignition of the charge is slow, if it occur at all, and the result is that unburned gas is discharged into the muffler, producing after firing and reducing the power efficiency.

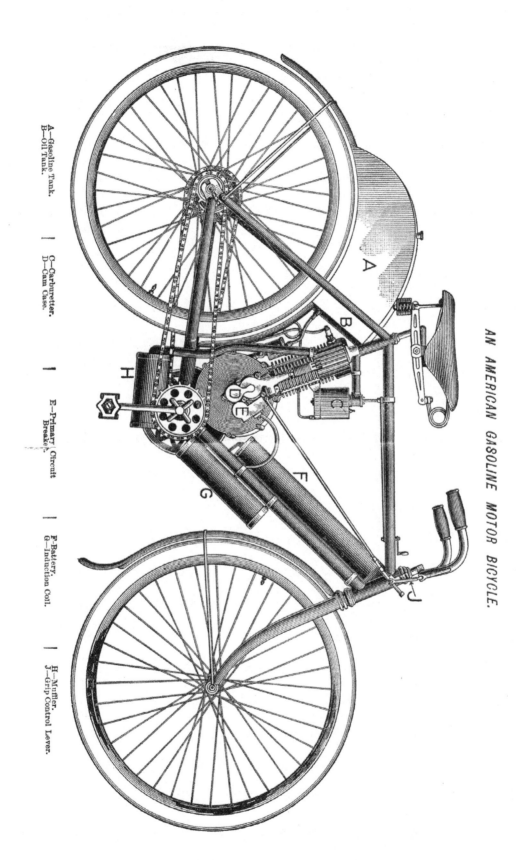

AN AMERICAN GASOLINE MOTOR BICYCLE.

A—Gasoline Tank.
B—Oil Tank.

C—Carburetter.
D—Cam Case.

E—Primary Circuit Breaker.

F—Battery.
G—Induction Coil.

H—Muffler.
J—Grip Control Lever.

After Firing: Defective Mixture.—After firing, or "barking," consists of a series of violent explosions in the muffler, is commonly caused by misfires in one or more cylinders, permitting the accumulation of unburned gas in the muffler, which is ignited by heat of the walls or by the exhaust of firing cylinders. Sometimes it may be due to a mixture that is too rich or too weak, and hence burns slowly, continuing its combustion after passing into the exhaust. It also occurs, not infrequently, when the spark is retarded.

No particular harm results from this rather startling effect, since the explosion can seldom occur until the unburned gas comes into contact with the outer air.

Water in the Carburetter.—This will often prevent starting of the engine, and will always impair its efficiency. Water is very frequently present in gasoline, and, particularly when the tank is low, is liable to get into the pipes and carburetter. Every carburetter has a drain cock at the bottom to let off the water that settles from the gasoline. The natural result of water in the carburetter is impaired or interrupted vaporization of gasoline.

In cold weather, also, the water is liable to freeze, preventing the action of the carburetter parts and clogging the valves. Ice in the carburetter can be melted only by the application of hot water, or some other non-flaming heat, to the outside of the float chamber.

It is not at all necessary to drain the carburetter before every starting, but after a prolonged period of inactivity it is desirable to give the water an opportunity to escape. A strong presumption of water in the carburetter is established when the engine starts, runs fitfully, or irregularly, and finally stops.

Stale or Low Degree Gasoline.—Another condition that will produce some of the same symptoms is low grade or stale gasoline. These two varieties of spirit are practically identical, in effect at least, both being characterized by a lower specific gravity than is required for readily forming a fuel mixture.

Gasoline, or petrol spirit, as it is called in England, should have a specific gravity of about .682, or 76°B. Some English authorities recommend spirit having a specific gravity of from .72 to .74, or between 65° and 59°B, virtually what is known in the United States as high grade benzine. Hydrocarbon spirits of lower degrees on the Baumé scale become increasingly difficult to vaporize.

Gasoline, being a volatile essence distilled from petroleum oil at temperatures ranging between 122° and 257° F., and boiling at between 149° and 194°, on the average, is a compound of several spirits of varying density, gravity and volatility.

It follows, therefore, that, unless stored in an air tight vessel, the lighter constituents are liable to escape, leaving a residue that will show a registry on the Baumé scale below that found easiest to vaporize. This is the process that occurs in the carburetter, if gasoline be allowed to stand in it for any length of time. It is always best, therefore, on storing a vehicle for a protracted period, or, in the event of failure to start the engine, after such extended inactivity, to drain the carburetter.

Of course, if the tank be found to contain only low degree liquid, the only alternative is to empty it and refill with a supply of the proper quality.

Failures with Four Cylinders.—Unless the ignition circuit be elsewhere disarranged—in battery, coil or wiring—failure to start in a four cylinder engine is probably due to causes other than foul or defective spark plugs. It may happen, however, that one, or even two, of the cylinders will fail to ignite. This condition will show symptoms similar to those caused by misfiring, irregular movement and vibration.

Testing for the Missing Cylinder.—In practically all four cylinder engines made at the present day the cranks of the second and third cylinders are in line, and are set at 180° to the cranks of the first and fourth, which are also in one line. Consequently, the pistons of the second and third cylinders make their in strokes · at the same time as the first and fourth make their out strokes. As a rule, the order of ignition is: first, third, fourth, second, which is also the order in which the primary circuit is closed by the timer, closing the circuits through the primary winding of each coil in succession.

In order, therefore, to determine which cylinder, if any, is missing fire, it is necessary only to open the throttle and advance the spark lever to the running position, giving the engine good power, and to cut out three of the four cylinders by depressing their coil vibrators. If the engine continue to run with coils 2, 3 and 4 cut out, cylinder 1 is evidently working properly. Depressing vibrators of 1, 3 and 4 shows whether 2 is working; of 1, 2 and 4, whether 3 is working, and of 1, 2 and 3, whether 4 is working. On discovering the faulty cylinder, its plug may be tested precisely as is the plug of a single cylinder engine.

A precisely similar method may be followed in the search for a missing cylinder of a three or six cylinder engine.

A missing cylinder may also be found by the low temperature of its spark plug exhaust pipe, if the missing be long continued.

Difficulty in Starting.—Sometimes an engine will start badly, but will run well after attaining a high speed. Among the various causes which contribute toward bringing about this condition may be mentioned:

1. *An obstruction* in the jet of the carburetter, causing trouble in starting, when removed by the suction allows the engine to speed up and run well at high speed.

2. *A too weak suction* in starting; this may be remedied by partially closing the air inlet while cranking, or giving the throttle more opening.

3. *Insufficient tension* of the auxiliary air valve spring.

4. *The spark* not sufficiently retarded.

Running Down.—When the engine starts well, runs for a while, then slows down and stops, there are many conditions to which it may commonly be attributed. Among these are:

1. Water or sediment in the carburetter.

2. Loose connections, breakdowns, or any other disarrangement of the ignition, such as would otherwise interfere with starting.

3. A weak or imperfectly recuperated battery—frequently the latter—that suddenly fails to supply current.

4. A leak in the water jacket that admits water to the combustion space.

5. Seizing of the piston in the cylinder on account of failure of the cooling system. This may result, in a water cooled cylinder, from:
   a. Exhaustion of the water;
   b. Stoppage in the pipes or pump;
   c. Breakdown of the pump;
   d. Failure of the oil supply;

In an air cooled cylinder seizing may result from:
   a. Insufficient radiation surface;
   b. Obstructed air circulation.

6. Heated bearings that seize and interfere with operation.

7. Poorly matched or poorly adjusted new parts, particularly pistons, that cause heating and perhaps seizing from friction.

8. Lost compression from broken or stuck valves, leaky piston, etc., as explained in the succeeding paragraph.

Running with Switch Off.—A peculiar condition in engine operation, sometimes encountered, is the running of the engine after the switch has been opened. It occasionally happens that the switch becomes defective, so that it does not break the circuit when in its "off" position. A most common cause for running with open switch is red hot plug points, also the heating to incandescence of some small particle in the cylinder, either loose or attached to the interior surfaces.

Pre=ignition.—An incandescent particle or overheated cylinder will cause an engine to pre-ignite.

Sometimes the rotor arm of the timer wears at the contact point leaving a path of metallic particles on the ring containing the stationary contacts, thus causing the current to flow to the stationary contact via this path and cause ignition to occur before the proper time.

Loss of Power without Misfiring.—The chief cause for an engine to fail to deliver its full power is poor compression. A fuel mixture either too weak or too strong will reduce the power of the engine.

If the bearings be too tight there will be a loss of power due to the additional friction set up; bearings when too tight will heat and a touch of the hand will give indication of their condition.

Another source of loss of power is a defective clutch which slips and does not transmit all the power delivered by the engine.

Brake rods sometimes get out of adjustment, allowing the band to remain in contact with the drum, thus absorbing more or less power.

Low Compression Troubles.—When little or no compression manifests itself as a resistance to the turning of the crank, it is certain that the operation of the engine will be defective, provided it can be started at all. If the engine lose compression after it has started, it will misfire and slow down.

Low compression means absence of a sufficient quantity of gas mixture to give a good power effect. This absence results from a leak in the combustion chamber, due to:

1. A sticking inlet valve—if the inlet be automatic—from an incrustation of oil gum. Sticking may be also due to other causes.

2. Pitted or corroded exhaust valve.

3. A weak spring on the exhaust valve.

4. Loose or open compression tap.

5. A leaky piston, due to:

   a. Worn or broken piston rings.
   b. Piston rings worked around, so as to bring the openings on their circumferences into line.

6. A blown out gasket in the cylinder head.

7. Worn or loose thread at the insertion of the spark plug.

8. A broken valve or valve stem.

9. Worn or scratched sweep wall, due to lack of oil or the presence of grit.

10. A valve stem that is so long as to touch the end of the pushrod when the engine is cold. The remedy for this is to file the end of the valve stem until a card may be inserted between its end and the end of the pushrod.

When the compression is low all the joints and cylinder gaskets should be examined for leaks.

The escape of compression around the spark plug, relief cock or other opening into the cylinder may be detected by the application of a little soapy water; if there be a leak it will be indicated by the formation of bubbles.

A leaky piston is indicated by a hiss inside the cylinder due to worm rings or the openings in the ring having worked around in line with each other. A sharp hiss indicates a broken ring.

Carbonized Cylinders.—An annoyance with which almost every motorist has to contend more or less is the deposit of a hard, indurated form of carbon, similar to gas carbon, upon the walls of the cylinders and valve chambers. This carbon is a product of heat decomposition of the fuel or the lubricant, or both, under pressure, and in the presence of too little air for combustion.

The formation of carbon within the cylinder is generally indicated by the frequent occurrence of pre-ignition, due to projecting points of red hot carbon within the cylinder. Its formation can be avoided almost altogether by close attention to the lubrication, valve and ignition timing, and carburetter adjustments.

Too rich a mixture almost invariably results in carbonization, which also follows upon the use of oils that do not stand high enough temperatures, or that are otherwise of poor quality.

Likewise, delayed opening of either exhaust or inlet valves, in the one case not providing free exit for the exhaust and in the other cutting down the time for combustion, will tend to produce carbonization.

It is not possible to avoid carbonization altogether and even in the best cars, perfectly adjusted, the deposit will slowly accumulate. To keep it to a minimum, the often recommended process of coal oiling the cylinders from time to time is to be advised, but even with this preventative regularly applied it occasionally becomes necessary to take off the cylinders, scrape out the combustion chambers and clean off the valves and pistons.

Carbon when present in lumps will tend to become red hot and thus occasion pre-ignition. Small particles, too, may catch on the valve seats, holding the valves open and causing loss of compression and power; or if the valve heads are of the cast iron type, their breakage by the forced uneven seating. The carbon that catches in the piston rings and their grooves may so bend the rings as to prevent their even contact with the cylinder walls, so essential to good compression, and in addition may badly score the cylinders.

In scraping off these carbon deposits it is necessary to use hard, sharp-edged or pointed tools for scrapers, and to apply them vigorously and thoroughly to every part that presents the objectionable coating.

For cleaning out the ring grooves it usually will be found desirable to expedite the work by grinding a special tool, made to fit so closely as to leave no deposit under its end or by its edges.

Keeping the deposits moist with kerosene will facilitate their removal; soaking them with kerosene for hours or even days will be still better. For surfaces that can be reached in this manner, and that will not be injured by the wear it will cause, finishing may be done with coarse emery cloth, held in the hand or around a stick, if circumstances may require.

It is to be understood that it is a rather long and tiresome job at best, to thoroughly clean all parts of a badly carbonized engine, but the improvement in its power and running afterwards will more than compensate for the work expended by the owner.

A simple and effective method of removing carbon consists of inserting into the cylinder a set of scouring rings and operating the engine for a few minutes on the remaining cylinders.

CHAPTER THIRTY-FOUR.

MOTOR CYCLES.

Requirements of a Motor Cycle.—According to experience in the matter, a motor cycle must be propelled by an air cooled engine, preferably of rather high speed and of somewhat higher power rating than is actually required for the load to be carried. The reasons for both conditions are readily discoverable, since, having dispensed with the water cooling and circulating system

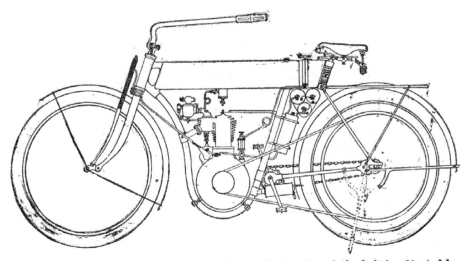

FIG. 314.—A belt drive motor cycle. As shown, the tension of the belt is adjusted by changing the position of the rear wheel axle. Another method of regulating the belt tension is by means of an adjustable idler pulley, illustrated in figs. 327 and 328. The above cut shows the general arrangement of the various parts, such as, carburetter, gasoline tank, ignition system, etc.

for sake of lightness and compactness, it is desirable to avoid such causes of overheating as unusually high speeds, and such low power as would cause the engine to labor under ordinary loads. Some bicycles have been constructed for racing purposes, with an advertised speed of 60 miles per hour and over, several of them having been equipped with an engine guaranteed to develop seven horse power, a rating far in excess of demands for carrying one person over an even roadway. At best, such machines are bulky and heavy, out of all proportion to convenience of handling or for ordinary service. Even with some machines designed for ordinary road service, and having an extreme speed limit of more than 25 or 30 miles per hour, the motor used is guaranteed to develop 2, and even 3 horse-power at between 1,200 and 1,500 revolutions per minute—speeds seldom attempted.

The Framework and Wheels.—The framework and wheels of motor bicycles are, of course, stronger and heavier than in foot propelled machines. The tubes are made with thicker walls, and the joints are more securely reinforced. In several makes the end of security is further assured by struts and trusses, particularly at the fork on the steering post and at the place where the motor is hung. The diamond frame is practically universal,

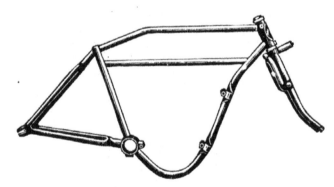

FIG. 315.—A motor cycle frame. The lower member is curved to conform to the shape of the crank case of the engine. The fork consists of two hinged pieces held in place by a spring forming a shock absorbing device.

although several of the earlier types—notably the Wolfmuller and Lawson—used the drop frame. In the Holden bicycle the frame consisted of a single tube, joined to the steering post in front and bent downward to carry the drive wheel in a fork at the rear. The back stays were extended forward to hold the motor and other apparatus, and were further supported from the main tube by a dropping tubular member at front and rear. The pedals in this machine were geared to the forward wheel, as in old fashioned velocipedes.

The Engine.—The one cylinder four cycle engine is the type in general use on motor cycles, although two and four cylinder engines are used on the higher powered machines.

The "V" twin cylinder engine, as shown in fig. 316 is a popular type on account of its simplicity and lightness, there being only one crank and cam shaft for the two cylinders.

The engine is placed in very low position so as to keep the center of gravity or weight low and make the machine easy to balance. With this location, the rider does not have to *straddle a hot engine* and the air strikes directly on the cylinder head of the engine.

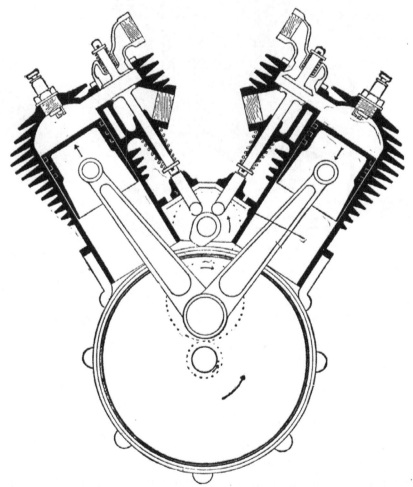

FIG. 316.—Sectional view of a "V" twin cylinder motor cycle engine. This type is in general use on the higher powered machines. Simplicity and lightness are secured in this design as one cam shaft and a single crank suffice for the two cylinders.

467

Arrangement of the Engine.—In the arrangement of the engine on a bicycle there has been a wide diversity of design. In some makes it has been supported on the back stays, between the pedal bearing and the rear wheel; in one make, on an extension of the back stays to rear of the wheel; in several makes it is supported against, or forms a part of the rear or saddle tube

FIG. 317.—The F. N. four cylinder motor cycle engine. The spark plugs are secured to the top of the cylinders, provided laterally with valve chambers cast with them in one piece. At the back end of the crank case is an oil drip cup which collects the oil discharged by the journals of the chank shaft, and sends it back through a conduit into the botom of the crank case. The exhaust valves are fitted with a lifting mechanism. Small levers operating same are connected by a system of rods to a lever on the handle bar, which the rider moves to lift the valves.

member of the "dimond" frame. The favorite position with most machines at the present time is on the forward member of the frame, in front of the pedal bearing, or on a tube arranged beneath, and suitably trussed to hold the weight.

Cooling System and Lubrication.—Motor cycle engines are always air cooled. As the engine has at times to run at very high speed, the average temperature of the cylinder walls is higher than with engines running at more moderate speeds, hence it is important that the cylinder be properly lubricated. A high fire test grade of oil must be used.

The splash system of lubrication is employed; oil is placed in the crank case and the motion of the flywheel and connecting rod end splashes it on all bearings and on the piston and cylinder walls.

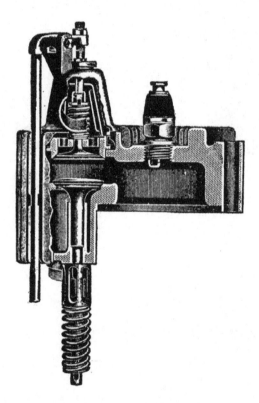

FIG. 318.—Cylinder head and valves of the Indian motor cycle. Both inlet and exhaust valves are placed in the same pocket. The inlet valve of the twin is operated by a lift rod, operated by the cam, and a rocking lever that is mounted on the dome of the valve chamber, and an adjusting screw is provided in the end of this rocking lever to regulate the amount of the opening of the valve. The valve chamber dome is secured in position by a bayonet joint, and may be removed, after disconnecting the induction pipe, by giving it a quarter turn. The inlet valve, with its seat, spring, etc., come out with the dome, from which they are withdrawn by the fingers. The removal of the dome exposes the exhaust valve for inspection.

The Valve Gear.—The valves are offset on one side of the cylinder, being arranged one above the other. The inlet valve is usually of the automatic type while the exhaust is always opened mechanically by a cam.

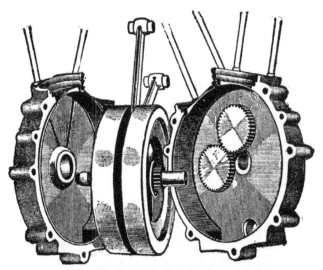

Fig. 319.—Interior view of a twin cylinder crank case with flywheels, connecting rods, and the two to one gears which operate the valve mechanism and the ignition apparatus, whether that be of the battery type or magneto. In this illustration an oil reservoir is shown and in the right hand half of the base is seen the little window through which the oil level can be observed.

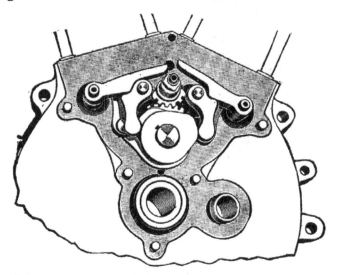

Fig. 320.—Valve gear of the Indian motor cycle. As shown in the illustration, the inlet valve of the front cylinder is about to close, while the exhaust valve of the rear cylinder has just opened. It will be seen that the revolving cam acts on the end of a cam lever, while the cam upon the lever lifts a second lever, or finger, upon which the lower end of the inlet valve operating rod rests. The exhaust valve is operated in the same way, but the levers are of slightly different form, and the end of the cam lever is provided with a steel roller to lessen the friction with the revolving cam, as the power required to operate the exhaust valve is greater than that required for the inlet valve.

It is usual to fit the exhaust valve with a lifter to hold the valve off its seat and thus relieve compression in starting. This is operated by a lever conveniently located. A spiral spring effects the return of the lever to its normal position.

Ignition and Control.—Motor cycles manufactured in America use jump spark ignition, almost without exception. Few of them also have any regulating devices other than levers for varying the time of the spark and the opening of the valves—thus modi-

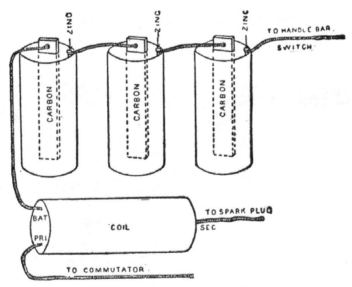

FIG. 321.—Diagram of battery and coil connections for jump spark ignition as applied to a motor cycle. Coils are usually plainly labeled with the abbreviations: "Bat.," "Pri.," "Sec.," indicating that the wires are to be connected to the battery, the primary circuit or contact maker, and the spark plug. The battery and primary wires being for the low tension circuit are easily distinguished from the secondary wire by the small amount of insulation surrounding them.

fying the speed—and a cut out switch located conveniently on the handle bars, for the purpose of stopping the engine. Adjusting the mixture and varying the time of the spark are the typical means provided for changing the speed.

Ignition current is usually obtained from a battery of three dry cells; on the multi-cylinder machines a magneto is frequently used. When a battery is used, a contact maker is provided for controlling the primary current.

471

It is attached to the cam shaft of the engine and the time of spark is regulated by rotating it around the cam shaft. Timing devices of this class are fully described in the chapter on ignition and the method of wiring is illustrated in fig. 321.

The low tension wires may be distinguished by the small amount of insulation surrounding them as compared with the secondary or plug wire.

The primary circuit is completed by a ground connection through the engine and frame. The three terminal cartridge type of coil is generally used as shown in fig. 321. Where the terminals are not marked, it is easy to distinguish the high tension or secondary wire by its size, while almost without exception, the wires at the other end of the coil are to be connected to the battery and contact maker.

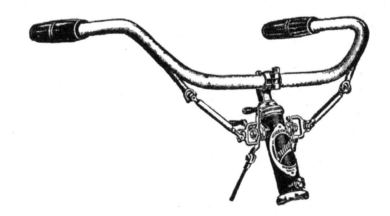

Fig. 322.—Handle bar of the Indian motor cycle with grip control. A twist of the right wrist, operates the spark and exhaust valve. This controls the speed of the machine to a certain extent. When more speed or more power is required, a twist of the left wrist operates the throttle and applies the reserve power which is necessary when steep hills or sand roads are encountered.

In a few cases, a four terminal coil is employed which, though apt to be confusing at first, need not complicate the matter of connecting it up in the machine if only it be remembered that the fourth terminal is nothing more nor less than a ground wire for the secondary coil, and should, therefore be connected to some metal portion of the machine in a secure manner.

Usually some indication on the outside of the case, prevents any danger of confusion.

The method of connecting the wiring for multi-cylinder engines is exactly the same as it would be were each cylinder a separate engine in all respects, save that but one battery is used.

Fig. 323.—Spring fork and handle bar of the Thiem motor cycle. The parts of the fork are: A, main fork; B, auxiliary fork; CC, ball bearing shackles; D, inner shell screwed into fork crown; E, outer shell screwed into swivel collar F; F, swivel collar; G, spring; H, plunger bearing on spring G and forming air tight compartment; I, stem fastened into plunger hand cap J; J, cap screwed into outer shell E; K, collar forming air-tight compartment. It will be noticed that air tight compartments are formed between cap J and collar K, also collar K and Plunger H. As an extra precaution, a rubber washer is placed between J and K and K and H. The parts of the handle bar are: L, handle bar; M, sleeve, revolving; N, sleeve end drop forging; O, ball and socket joints, adjustable; P, rod right thread at one end and left thread at other end; Q, bell crank; R, bell crank. It will be seen that by revolving sleeve M that rod P will move in and out in a horizontal direction. This will cause rod Pa to move through bell crank R and cause rod Pc to move forward or backward and thus moving spark advance or carburetter throttle.

In wiring a multi-cylinder coil then, it is necessary first to connect the proper terminal to the battery and to lead each of the primary wires to the terminals of the contact maker.

Jar Absorbing Devices.—One great disadvantage in motor cycle construction is the practical difficulty of arranging any form of spring or cushion device to take the vibration of the engine.

Several makes of machines include some spring arrangement in the saddlepost for easing the rider, but the framework must be built to endure the vibration of travel on rough roads, and at all speeds. The wear and strain, as may thus be seen, is considerable.

To neutralize this element the engine is provided with heavy flywheels, in order to equalize the movement as far as possible.

One excellent type of high powered, high speed machine, which has won exceptional records in a number of tests and races, has

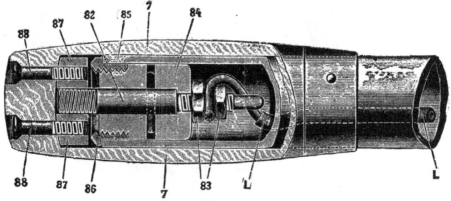

Fig. 324.—Sectional view of the N. S. U. motor cycle switch handle. The ignition current is switched on by turning the handle to the left, and off by turning the handle to the right. The parts are as follows: 7. Switch handle; 82. A metal rod; 83. Terminal nuts; 84. Non-conducting guide block; 85. Set screw, locking to the handle bar; 86. Metal compact ring; 87. Left handed nut switch; 88. Screws, or in later patterns, cast into the same. In assembling these parts, the insulated wire L is carefully drawn through the left side of the handle bar tube and out by the T joint of the same.

an extra large flywheel (between 18 and 21 inches, according to power), and the claims are that this "keeps the engine steady and does away with the heavy vibration in some high powered machines." For machines intended for ordinary speeds such additional weight is hardly necessary.

Valve and Spark Timing.—With some types of engine, the timing of the valves and spark is fixed so that unless wrongly assembled at the factory there is no chance of trouble on this score, excepting, of course, in the event of the rare, but possible breakage of a tooth.

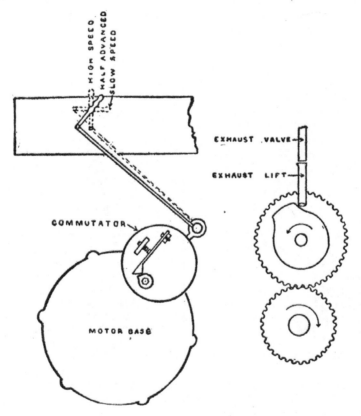

Fig. 325.—Timing motor cycle valves. After removing contact maker and gear case covers and the large gear, 1, the crank is placed on the upper dead centre, and 2, the large gear and cam replaced, the large gear meshing with its driver in such a way that the cam is just breaking away from the lifter as shown in the figure. The gear case cover and contact maker are now replaced. The proper timing of the valve causes it to close on the dead centre.

Fig. 326.—Usual arrangement for spark control on a motor cycle. To time the spark, 1, the spark lever is placed in such a position that the spark will be half way advanced, 2, the crank is turned through one revolution from the point of exhaust closure, 3, the sparking cam is set so that the contact spring is just leaving the contact screw, and tightened in this position.

The gear teeth which mesh in order to give the correct movements are clearly marked either with lines on the ends of the gears or prick punch points, which in any case should be made to register when setting up the motor. Under these conditions the timing of the engine should be a comparatively easy task.

If for any reason it be desired to retime or to verify the timing independently, methods are illustrated in figs. 325 and 326, for performing these operations and described in the text accompanying same.

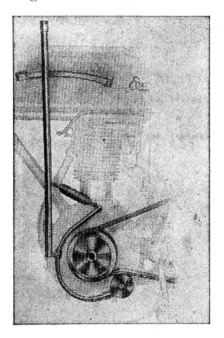 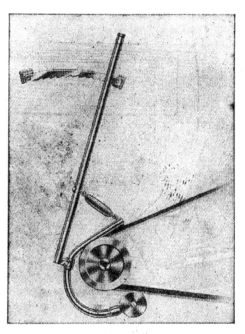

Figs. 327 and 328.—Illustrations showing the operation of a belt drive. The tension of the belt is regulated by the adjustable idler, the two cuts showing the "on" and "off" positions of the latter. The location of the idler in close proximity to the pulley, causes it to be more fully embraced by the belt, thus, increasing the traction area without unduly increasing the belt tension.

The Drive.—There are three methods in general use for transmitting the power of the engine to the rear wheel, viz:

1. Belt drive;
2. Chain drive;
3. Shaft drive.

The belt drive was the first method of power transmission applied to the motor cycle and is still used to a considerable extent. It has the objection of requiring frequent adjustment and must be kept in tight contact to prevent slippage of the small driving pulley on the engine with the consequent loss of power.

The use of round, V-shaped and even flat belts, does not always give satisfaction. The great tension to which the belts have to be subjected in order to ensure proper adhesion, and still more the alternate action of dry and wet weather, cause them to stretch. This drawback frequently necessitates repairs on the road. Finally, the traction exercised by the belt on one of the ends of the hub, hinders the proper working of the latter.

Manufacturers have reduced considerably the defects of belt drive by providing belts of larger and better form.

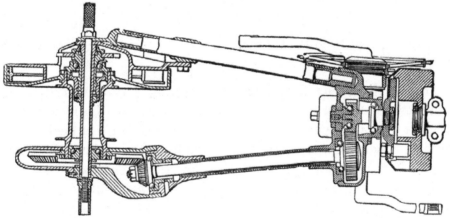

FIG. 329.—The F. N. shaft drive. It consists of a countershaft, the front rear wheel. It is operated as follows: By bringing the hand lever at the top of the frame tube into central position or upright, gives the neutral position allowing engine to run free; by pulling the lever backward the low gear is obtained; by pushing the lever forward the low gear is disengaged and the high gear is brought into action. Two brakes are incorporated in the transmission.

The chain and shaft drive furnish a positive connection between the engine and rear wheel. The chain drive is furnished on a number of the medium priced machines and the shaft drive on the more expensive machines.

While the chain is a satisfactory and inexpensive drive, the shaft with its enclosed gears is entirely protected from dust and does not present any lubricated surfaces to soil the rider's clothing.

Transmissions.—The use of transmissions on motor cycles is, as yet, rather limited; the control of the machine is usually by spark and mixture adjustments and the ignition cut out switch on the handle bar.

It would of course, be impracticable to equip a motor cycle with a transmission giving the number of changes provided for automobiles, however, machines are now to be had, fitted with transmissions giving two speeds and free engine. A compact transmission fulfilling these requirements is shown in fig. 330, in addition, two brakes are incorporated in this transmission as shown in the illustration.

The use of a transmission on a motor cycle, enables the rider, 1, to climb steeper hills, 2, makes it possible to stop and restart at will without dismounting, either on level road or on the steepest hill, by means of the free engine, and 3, to slow down or even come to a dead stop, if "pocketed" in congested street, and restart without pedaling.

Instructions for Starting and Riding Motor Cycles.—In spite of the numerous improvements which have been made in motor cycles in the last few years, they require a great deal of attention, otherwise the machine is liable to become disabled on the road. It is, therefore, important to pay attention to all the parts of the machine. Only then is it possible to obtain full satisfaction in operating.

Before Starting.—As a preliminary to starting, 1, the various parts of the machine should be carefully examined, 2, the gasoline tank and lubricating devices filled, 3, gasoline valve opened, 4, carburetter primed and throttle opened, 5, the exhaust valves raised, 6, ignition cut out plug inserted, 7, handle bar ignition switch opened, and 8, spark well advanced by means of the lever provided for the purpose.

Starting.—In mounting the machine, the pedal on left side of machine should be in the upper position. With right foot on the ground, the machine standing, the rider straddles the saddle and starts the machine by pressure of the left foot on the raised pedal. This method requires less effort than taking a running start or mounting by rear step.

After sufficient momentum has been obtained, 1, close the handle bar ignition switch, and 2, release the valve lifter.

While Riding.—As soon as the engine begins to operate, the spark should be retarded and adjusted together with the throttle to meet the speed requirements. On motor cycles, as a rule, the speed is varied chiefly by the spark position. The control of the machine, at slow speeds, is made more flexible by the use of the handle bar ignition switch.

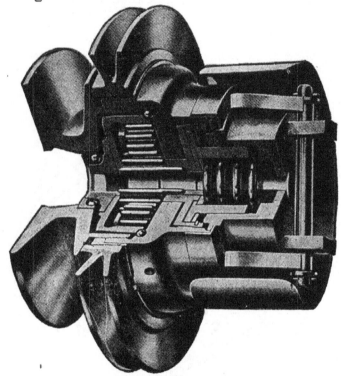

Fig. 330.—The N. S. U. two speed transmission which is attached to the end of which is provided with a pinion engaging with a similar pinion on the crank shaft, while to the other end is secured a bevel pinion engaging with a bevel wheel secured to the hub of the back wheel. The whole is enclosed into a gear case filled with grease which protects it against external influences and ensures efficient lubrication of the parts.

In coasting down hills, 1, the ignition should be cut out with the handle bar switch, 2, throttle closed, and 3, exhaust valves lifted, the latter operation, relieves the drag of the engine and admits fresh air to the cylinders which has a tendency to keep the spark plug points clean and clear the cylinder of carbon deposits.

In operating a motor cycle *it is important that the lubrication of the engine receive frequent attention*—say every ten miles.

The crank case should receive sufficient oil that it may splash up against the piston and cylinder walls.

Occasionally the crank case should be drained, washed out with gasoline and a fresh supply of oil provided.

Stopping.—When it is desired to stop: 1, the ignition is cut out by the handle bar switch, 2, exhaust valves lifted, and 3, brakes applied.

When leaving the machine the gasoline valve should be closed and the *ignition plug removed to prevent the battery becoming exhausted* if the machine stop with contact maker on the spark position.

Fig. 331.—A coaster brake applied to the rear wheel of a motor cycle; operated by a backward movement of the pedals.

Brakes for Motor Cycles.—The question of brakes is an important one with motor cycles and cannot be settled off hand without some consideration of conditions.

In a number of machines, the front wheel brake is omitted, and the braking of the rear wheel largely relegated to the compression of the engine.

In the later development of the motor cycle, the coaster form of brake, incorporated in the rear hub, is the type in general use. An example of this style of brake is shown in fig. 331.

CHAPTER THIRTY-FIVE.

THE OPERATION AND CONSTRUCTION OF STEAM ENGINES FOR AUTOMOBILES.

Steam as a Motive Power.—Vehicles propelled by steam possess certain advantages which are conceded, even by the most ardent advocates of the gas engine. There is a combination of good features inherent in steam propulsion that has met with much favor.

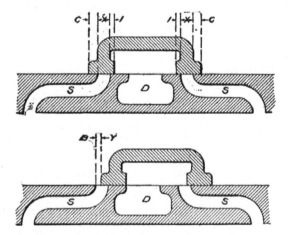

FIG. 332.—Diagrams illustrating the "Lap" and "Lead" of a Steam Cylinder Slide Valve. In both sections, S and S are the steam ports, and D the exhaust. The upper section illustrates the "laps" of a valve; the space between the lines C and X giving the "outside lap," and between the lines X and I the "inside lap" The lower section illustrates the "lead" of a valve; the space between lines B and Y showing the opening of the valve at the beginning of the right-hand stroke.

It is possible with steam to have ample power together with great overload capacity without an extremely heavy plant.

The steam car as manufactured in America is not a copy of foreign ideas, and for some work it has never been approached by any other form of motive power. In hill climbing and speed it is supreme, and the silence in operation and freedom from vibration make it very desirable when maximum comfort in touring is desired.

Among its chief advantages are *flexibility* and *ease of control*. A steam car may be operated at any speed from zero to maximum. All variations of speed can be obtained without gear shifting, as it can be easily varied by changing the amounts of steam admitted to the engine. The engine of

a steam car can never be stalled on account of the absence of dead cen
tres and non-power strokes, the reserve force in the boiler and the ability of such a prime mover to stand an overload of over 100 per cent. This
enables one to obtain the maximum power output under extraordinary
conditions. A two cylinder steam engine produces a torque which can
only be equaled by an eight cylinder, four cycle, or a four cylinder, two
cycle gas engine. Because of this uniform application of energy, the wear
on tires is reduced to a minimum, and the elasticity of the steam and freedom from shock and vibration, reduces considerably wear and tear on
the entire mechanism.

The improved methods of boiler construction, permit the use of steam
of high pressures and of considerable degree of superheat, both of which
tend to decrease the fuel consumption. Either gasoline or kerosene may
be used for fuel. The regulation of the fire and feed water is controlled
by automatic devices, hence, the attention of the driver is not diverted
from the steering wheel and throttle.

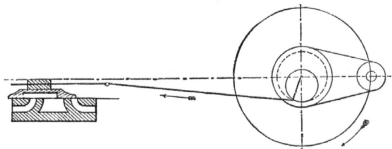

FIG. 333.–Diagram with a single eccentric, illustrating the position of the steam valve,
when the crank pin is at the return dead centre, the throw of the eccentric being
at an angle off the perpendicular. The arrows show the direction of motion.

The Slide Valves of a Steam Cylinder.—The mechanism by
which steam is admitted to the cylinder of a steam engine, consists of a sliding valve of such a shape as to open communication
from one end of the cylinder to the exhaust, while the other end
of the cylinder is receiving steam direct from the steam chest.
This will be readily understood from the accompanying illustration. There are two kinds of valves in common use on steam
carriage engines; the common D-valve shown herewith, and the
piston valve, as shown in a number of engines hereafter to be
described. The object obtained by both valves is the same, although the piston valve is preferred by many engineers because
it is better balanced in its operation, and also because, owing
to its packing rings, it is less liable to leakage. However, with a
well-made valve of either variety, the ends of economy and
durability are equally maintained.

The Operation of the Slide Valve.—The valve controlling the inlet and exhaust ports of a steam cylinder is made of such length that, when in mid-position, it completely closes both inlet ports, neither admitting steam nor allowing it to be exhausted. In the valve shown on the accompanying sectional cut, it is evident that, supposing it to be moved either to the right or to the left, the communication will be opened with the exhaust port on the one side, sooner than with the steam chest on the other, thus permitting with a very slight variation in the length of the stroke, that the exhaust remain open even while the inlet of the steam to the opposite face of the piston is cut off. In calculating the proportions of cylinder valves there are two important items to be considered—the "lap" and the "lead" of the valves. The "lead" of a valve is the amount by which the steam port is open when the piston is at the beginning of the stroke.

The lead may be changed by varying the angular advance of the eccentric. The "lap" of a valve indicates any portion added to the length of the valve, so as to increase the portion of the stroke during which the ports are covered, beyond that length which is positively required to insure the closing of all ports when the valve is in mid-position. There are two kinds of "lap." The "outside lap" is any portion added to the length of the valve beyond that necessary to cover both inlet ports at mid-position. The "inside lap" is any portion added to the hollow or inside portion of the D-valve, over and above what is necessary in order to cover the inner edges of the steam ports, and to close the exhaust port from both sides when the valve is in mid-position. The exhaust valve is closed somewhat before the completion of the stroke, thus allowing the residual steam in the clearance to be compressed somewhat before the opening of the inlet. The most important result obtained in this manner is that the compression produces a temperature, as near as possible, the same as that of the incoming steam, which is an efficient factor in heat economy, although producing some back pressure that slightly reduces the *mean effective pressure.*

From the operations of this valve and cylinder, it must be evident that its stroke cannot be equal to that of the piston in the main cylinder. It cannot, therefore, be operated direct from the crank-shaft of the engine. Accordingly, the most usual method of operating the steam valves of an engine is by an eccentric on the main shaft, which operates the valve rod. This device may be either a single or double eccentric, according to the requirements.

The Eccentric Gear and Link Motion.—An eccentric is a circular piece of metal, a wheel in fact, except for the fact that instead of turning upon its centre, it is attached to the shaft at

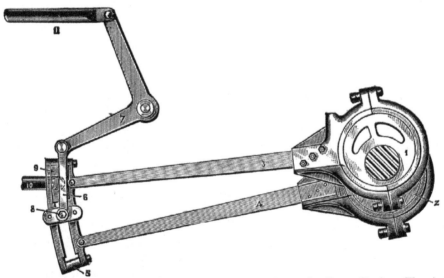

Fig. 334.–Diagram of the Link Motion and Eccentric Gear of a Steam Engine. The parts shown are: (1) backward eccentric; (2) forward eccentric; (3-4) eccentric rods; (5) slotted shifting link; (6) link hanger; (7) reversing arm; (8) link saddle pin; (9) link block; (10) valve stem; (11) reach rod. The position shown in the cut indicates that the backward eccentric is in gear which gives a reverse motion to the engine.

a point near its periphery. Around this disc-shaped piece is attached a circular metal strap, joined to a rod, which may be either attached direct to the valve rod, or, where two eccentrics are used, to one end of the swinging link. The link is an arc-shaped metal piece, usually made with a slot through the greater part of its length. It is hung from its centre point to a link-saddle, which, as shown in the accompanying figure, is bolted to either side of the slot and is suspended from the link hanger either above or below. Within the slot is set a link block, as it is called, so that it may slide in the slot through its entire length, whenever the link is raised or lowered on its hanger. To this link block is attached the valve rod. The general arrangements of the link motion may be understood from the accompanying illustration.

The Operation of the Shifting Link.—As already stated, the link motion was originally intended only for reversing the engine, which is to say to enable the steam to be cut off from

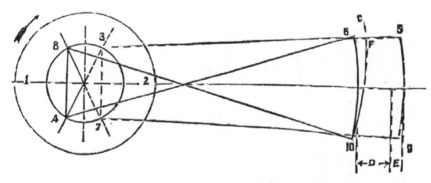

FIG. 335.—Diagram of the Operation of the Link Motion. The centres of the two eccentrics being at 4 and 8, the crank pin at 2, the link at mid-gear, the eccentric rods will be indicated by the full lines, 4-6, 8-10. When the crank pin is at 1, the centres of the eccentrics will be at 3 and 7, and the positions of the rods on the dotted lines, 3-5 and 7-9. The distance, D, indicates the vertical distance between the centres of the eccentrics in the full and dotted-line positions. If from the centre, 8, with the rod as the radius, an arc be drawn to F, the distance, C, shows the position of the link if both rods were "open" with the crank at the cylinder end, 2, instead of at the opposite dead centre, 1. The distance, C, is equal to the distance, E, and the total distance (D + E) that the valve moves is twice the lap, plus twice the lead, plus the distance, or angularity, occasioned by the rods being crossed, when the crank is on the cylinder end dead centre, 2, becoming opened when the crank is at dead centre, 1.

one side of the cylinder and admitted to the other, whenever desired, by shifting the motion of the slide valve. In addition to this function, however, the link motion provides a means for using the steam expansively, when cutting off the supply of live steam at any earlier point in the piston stroke, which act is accomplished by reducing the travel of the slide valve. When the link block is at one end of the slot, the valve receives the motion of the eccentric rod attached to that end of the link, and, consequently, since the links are set at angles somewhat greater than 180 degrees, the one is for the forward motion of the engine, the other for the reversed motion. In the accompanying illustration, the backward eccentric is in gear. By this means, whenever the link is shifted, only the eccentric whose rod stands opposite the link-block imparts its motion to the valve. The other is practically inactive, except for imparting a slight oscillatory motion to the link, which in general practice is negligible. The link which is in gear acts, in reality, like a short-throw crank, or as if it were a single eccentric. From the position of "full-gear"—that is, when the link-block stands at either end of the slot—the travel of the valve may be more or less modified until the centre point of the slot is reached, which point is called

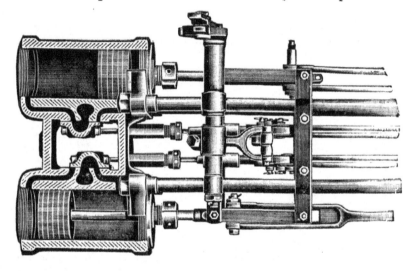

FIG. 336.—View of the Stanley engine with cylinders cut away, to show piston and valve motion. In the position shown, one valve is beginning to open to admit steam to the cylinder; the other valve has passed the point of cut off, the opposite cylinder end being in communication with the exhaust passage. The valves of the Stanley engine are operated by the familiar Stevenson link motion.

mid-gear. There the travel in either direction is so slight that the steam and exhaust ports of the cylinder are not opened. This is in reality the "dead point," and further shifting of the link in the same direction begins the process of reversing by increasing the travel of the valve in the opposite direction. When at mid-gear the valve partakes of the motion of both eccentrics equally, but since their motions describe a cassinian, or flattened figure 8, laid on its side, of which the link-block is the centre, the motion is at its point.

When the link is at full gear, the travel of the valve equals the throw of the eccentric, less the angularity of the eccentric rod. When the link is at mid-gear, the travel of the valve is equal to twice the lap and lead of the valve, plus twice the angularity of the eccentric rods. By the angularity of the

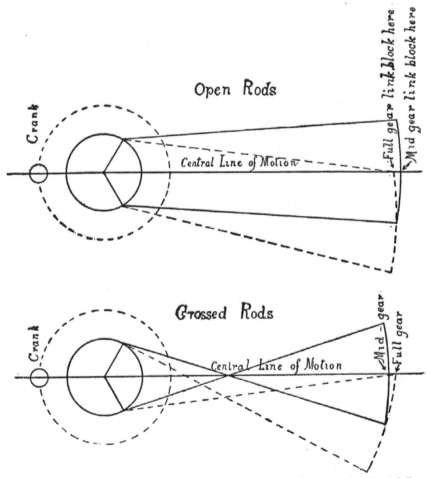

Fig. 337.–Diagram showing the positions of the eccentric throws and rods at full gear and mid-gear, when the rods are "open" and "crossed" with the crank at the forward dead centre, marked 1 in the previous cut.

eccentric rods is meant the distance the centre of the link or the valve would move, should the rod of the geared eccentric be disconnected from it and connected with the other link. The amount of the angularity thus, of course, varies with the length of the rods. The shorter the rods, the greater the travel of the valve, owing to the crossing of the rods during a one-half revolution of the crank. When the eccentric rods of a direct connected link motion are disposed as shown in the accompanying diagram, and the link motion and gear of the crank is at the

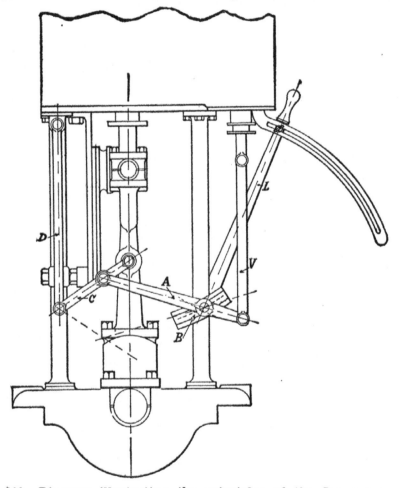

Fig. 338.—Diagram illustrating the principles of the Joy valve gear. Motion is communicated to the valve by a system of levers operated by the connecting rod. The advantages secured by the use of the Joy valve gear are, quick admission and cut off, and constant lead for all degrees of expansion.

dead point marked 1, the rods are said to be open. If they are disposed as shown by the dotted lines in the same figure, and the crank is at the dead point, 2, they are said to be crossed. Open rods give an increasing lead from full gear towards midgear, while crossed rods, give a decreasing lead.

The Joy Valve Gear.—This form of valve gear derives its motion from an arm attached to the connecting rod near the wrist pin. The link is pivoted at its upper end and by moving it forward or backward from the central position, the cut off can be regulated.

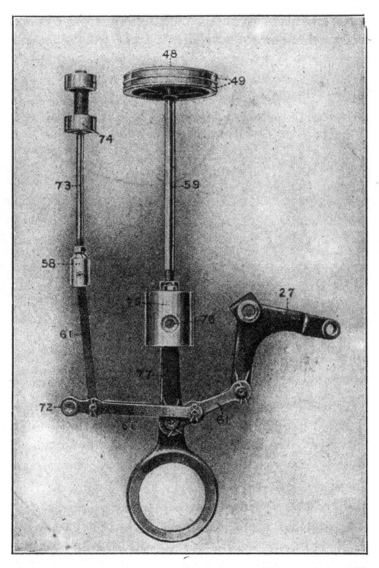

FIG. 339.—The Joy Valve gear as applied to the White engine. The valve gear parts are: 74, valve; 73, valve stem; 58, valve crosshead; 61, valve gear levers; 72, valve slide rollers. The other details shown are: 48, piston; 59, piston rod; 75, crosshead; 76, wrist pin; 77, connecting rod; 27, lever for operating the pumps.

This type of valve gear, is shown in the diagram fig. 338.

The valve rod V is operated by the lever A. There is a block B, provided with a curved slot is used, in which the pin forming the fulcrum of the lever A slides.

The motion is imparted to the lever A directly from the connecting rod by means of the connecting link C, one end of which is pivoted to the connecting rod, the other end to the suspension link D.

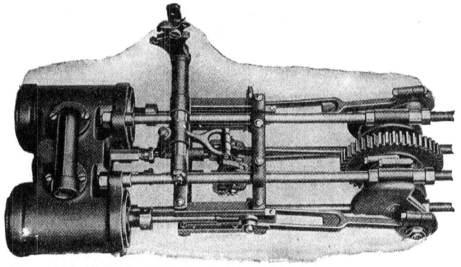

FIG. 340.—View of the Stanley engine, showing main bearing, spur gear, eccentrics, link motion and "hooking up" device. These engines are made in three sizes: 3 x 4; 4 x 5; and 4½ x 6½. The horsepower rating for the several sizes is ten, twenty, and thirty, respectively.

The vertical motion of the connecting link moves the valve an amount equal to its lap and lead, while the horizontal motion causes the ports to open their full opening, by moving the fulcrum up and down in the inclined slot.

By means of the reversing lever L the incline of the block B can be altered, or reversed, to reverse the engine.

The diagram fig. 338 is intended simply to illustrate the principle of the valve gear, the engine shown being of the marine type. The Joy valve gear has been adopted by the White Company and its application to the White engine is shown in figs. 339 and 347.

A feature of this valve gear is that it gives a rapid motion to the valve when opening and closing, thus producing a quick admission and cut off. It gives a constant lead for different cut offs, and a compression more nearly constant than that produced with the Stevenson link motion.

The Joy gear while having many good features has numerous joints which are subject to wear.

The Serpollet Single-Acting Engines.—In the effort to simplify, as far as possible, the construction and operation of steam vehicle motors, intended for use on light carriages, several inventors have contrived excellent types of single-acting engines. Among the advantages to be derived from the use of this type of motor, we may mention dispensing with the stuffing-box and several other constructions, which involves constant danger of wear and difficulty or repair. The Serpollet steam engine very much resembles some types of gasoline motors used on heavy vehicles, both as regards the cylinder and piston and operation of the valves. The cylinders are horizontal, of the double opposed type.

The piston is of the trunk type, consisting of a somewhat elongated hollow cylinder, with the crank rod pivoted on the gudgeon pin somewhat less than midway in its length. The valves in this engine are of the familiar mushroom or poppet type, and are opened by a push rod positively operated from a cam shaft. This shaft is operated by a spur-wheel, which meshes with another spur of the same diameter, mounted on the crankshaft, so that the two turn in even rotation. The exhaust valves are of precisely similar construction and are also positively operated from the same cam-shaft.

Such an engine as this has been constructed with from two to six cylinders, and as may be understood, gives about the same power effect as an engine of the ordinary design and same proportions of stroke, having from one to three cylinders. The cylinders operate on one plane, and are not offset, as in many opposed-cylinder gasoline motors. The steam and exhaust valves are positively operated by a series of cams on a shaft, so that when the steam valve of one is open, its exhaust is closed, involving that the steam valve of the opposite cylinder is closed and its exhaust open. In order therefore to reverse the engine, it is necessary only to slide the row of cams on the square camshaft that carries them, so as to shift the positions and operation of the valves on the two cylinders.

The Piston of a Steam Engine.—The piston of a steam engine, as shown in an accompanying figure, usually consists of a flattened cylindrical piece of slightly smaller diameter than the bore of the cylinder, in which it slides. Steam-tight contact is obtained by springing packing rings into grooves cut in its circumference. The accompanying cut shows three such rings sprung on the piston. The steam admitted through the inlet valve bears upon one face of the piston, and by its expansive energy causes the piston to move.

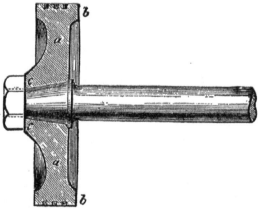

FIG. 341.–The Piston of a small double-acting steam engine, showing method of connecting the piston rod, and the position of the packing rings. The parts are: *a, a,* the body of the piston; *b, b,* the circumference bearing the packing rings; *c, c,* the central boss receiving the coned end of the rod.

The Practical Expansion Ratio for Steam.—In the practical operation of the steam engine, as most generally understood, the steam is fed direct from the boiler to the cylinder, there expanding from its original pressure to a number of volumes, proportioned to the length of the stroke and point of cut-off. The idea of cutting off the supply of steam before the completion of the stroke, and making use of its expansive energy during the remaining portion, constitutes, as we have seen, the first improvement made by Watt. According to Boyle's Law, already quoted, the pressure of the steam is in exactly inverse ratio to its expansion, which is to say that when a body of steam is expanded to twice its original volume, it should have just one-half its original pressure, so long as the temperature be constant. This law is never exactly followed in practice, the general rule, as shown by indicator diagrams, being a rapid fall during the first period of expansion and a more gradual one in the latter

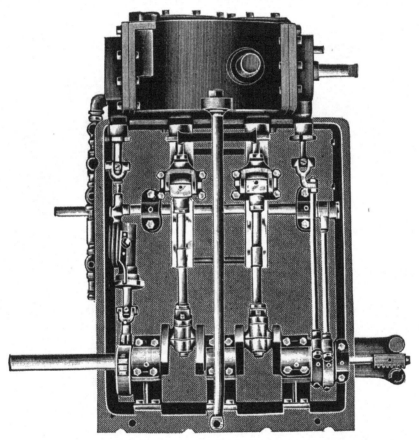

FIG. 342.—The Ofeldt compound engine. The cylinders are cast in one piece and are bolted to one end of the oil box. They are 2½ and 4, with four-inch stroke, and the valve chests are located at each side. The steam enters the H. P. valve chest through a ½ inch connection in the center of the valve chest cover, and exhausts around the cylinders to the L. P. valve chest. The steam exhausts through a ¾ inch connection at corner of valve chest on end of cylinder. The reverse motion is of the special type, only one eccentric being required for each valve. The reverse is set at the end of the crank shaft and extends out through the side of the oil box, where it is connected to a small gear wheel. In either the forward or backward motion the reverse is held in place by the crank shaft. The engine can be reversed when in motion without closing the throttle. Feed water pump is provided operated by an eccentric on the shaft. A simpling connection for starting is made on top of the H. P. cylinder. The valves are the sliding or D type. The engine runs in oil and is rated at fifteen horsepower, a larger size 3½ and 6½ by 5 is rated at thirty horsepower.

period. However, for general purposes, the law is assumed to be perfectly operative, and the rule for calculating the pressure at any point of expansion, is to divide the original absolute pressure by the number of times it has expanded. Thus, steam fed to a cylinder at 100 pounds gauge, or 115 pounds absolute, has a pressure of 57½ pounds when expanded to two volumes, a pressure of 38 1-3 pounds when expanded to three volumes and a pressure of 28¾ pounds when expanded to four volumes.

FIG. 343.—The MacLachlan single acting compound steam engine. It has six cylinders, three 3″ high pressure and three 6″ low pressure with 3½″ stroke and is rated at 30 H. P. with 300 lbs. steam and 600 revolutions. The valves are of the poppet type and the valve gear is such that steam may be cut off at any point of the stroke down to three-fourths. One lever controls the entire operation—simpling, compounding, reversing, starting and the variable cut off.

The following table gives the theoretical efficiency of steam cut off at various other points of the stroke:

Cutting off at	$\frac{1}{10}$	stroke	increases	efficiency	3.3	times.	
"	"	$\frac{1}{8}$	"	"	"	3.07	"
"	"	$\frac{2}{10}$	"	"	"	2.6	"
"	"	$\frac{1}{4}$	"	"	"	2.39	"
"	"	$\frac{3}{10}$	"	"	"	2.2	"
"	"	$\frac{3}{8}$	"	"	"	1.98	"
"	"	$\frac{4}{10}$	"	"	"	1.92	"
"	"	$\frac{1}{2}$	"	"	"	1.69	"
"	"	$\frac{6}{10}$	"	"	"	1.51	"
"	"	$\frac{5}{8}$	"	"	"	1.47	"
"	"	$\frac{7}{10}$	"	"	"	1.35	"
"	"	$\frac{3}{4}$	"	"	"	1.29	"

In the steam engine, these values are considerably reduced on account of losses due to radiation, condensation, leakage, etc. In horse power calculations, therefore, the theoretical mean effective pressure is multiplied by a coefficient or *diagram factor* as it is called which varies for different classes of engines from .6 to .9 as has been determined by numerous tests.

Fig. 344.—The Lane engine. This is a cross compound with steam chests adjacent to each other. Both cylinders have slide valves and the pistons are provided with two snap rings each. The valve gear consists of the Stevenson link motion. The Lane engine is built in two sizes: 3¼ and 5¼ by 3½; 3⅞ and 6¼ by 4. They are rated at twenty and thirty horsepower, respectively.

Fig. 345.—Showing simpling valve on back of the Lane engine. It consists of a small cylinder having ports connecting directly with the high pressure exhaust, the high and low pressure steam chests, and the free exhaust. There is a one-piece plug valve having proper passages through it, and arranged so that the different rotative positions effect the changes of ports for converting the engine from compound (using steam first in small, and afterward in the large cylinder) to single expansion (using high pressure directly in both cylinders).

On Compounding a Steam Engine.—A compound engine is one in which the steam is used several times over in as many separate cylinders, although usually applied to engines operating with two cylinders. The steam is fed from the boiler direct to the first cylinder, in which it is cut off early in stroke, in order that its expansion may be utilized to the greatest possible extent. The exhaust from this cylinder is then fed into the second cylinder, generally two or three times the cubic contents of the first, and is worked expansively to a point as near atmospheric pressure as possible. The most practical and efficient application of this

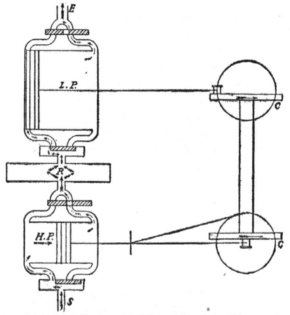

Fig. 346.—Diagram of a "Cross Compound" Steam Engine. The cranks, C and C, are at 90°. The high-pressure steam port is at S; the H. P. exhaust to L. P. cylinder at R, and the exhaust to atmosphere from the low-pressure cylinder, at E.

principle is in the triple and quadruple expansion engines, so largely used in marine work, which, in connection with the vacuum-producing condenser, allows the steam to be worked from the highest available pressure down to near zero. There are two common forms of compound engines of two or three cylinders, which from the arrangements of the working parts, are known as "tandem-compound" and cross-compound." In the tandem-compound engine, the cylinders are placed end to end, the two pistons operating one piston rod. In the

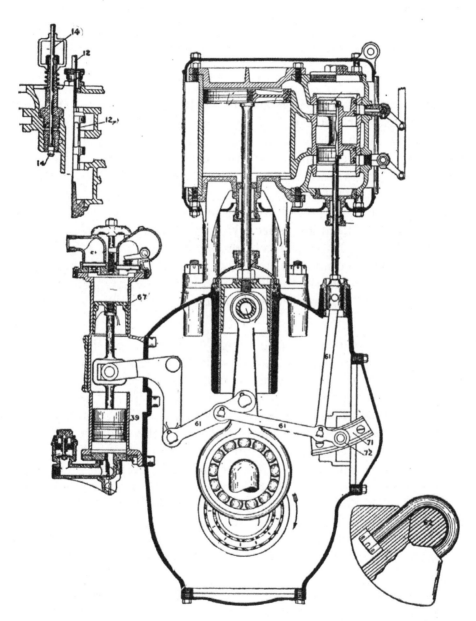

Figs. 347 and 348.—The White Engine and sectional view of "simpling valves." The engine is a double acting compound fitted with the Joy valve gear (61, 71 and 72), and is built in two sizes: 2½ and 4¼ by 3, also 3 and 5 by 4½. The power rating is twenty and forty horsepower respectively. The simpling valves (12 and 14) are used in starting to admit live steam to the low pressure cylinder in case the high pressure piston be on the dead centre. There are two pumps operated by the engine, an air pump 67, and the condenser pump 39.

cross-compound engine the cylinders are placed side by side, the two piston rods operating on a single crank-shaft. The latter model is that most frequently used in compounding steam engines for motor vehicles.

Compound Steam Engines for Light Carriages.—Although many of the earliest types of the American steam carriage still use simple engines, several of the most excellent of the later patterns have adopted compound engines. The principal objection made by many authorities to the use of compound engines on steam road carriages of light weight is that with cylinders of average dimensions, working pressure of between 150 and 200 pounds, in the high pressure cylinder, and a cut-off generally between $\frac{1}{2}$ and $\frac{3}{4}$ stroke, which has been found most economical under ordinary conditions, the low pressure cylinder would be doing little or no work, the whole strain of operation coming on the former, which would practically be working against a vacuum.

A maker of steam carriage engines states, that in order to obtain effective work from both cylinders of a compound engine, the high pressure cylinder must be made about one-half the size of the cylinder used in the simple engine. Then, he asserts, the mean pressure will range from 75 to 100 pounds in the usual running, with cut-off at $\frac{3}{4}$ stroke and the diameters of the two cylinders in ratio of 1 to 3, and the low pressure cylinder will do its share of the work, with the desired economy of power. The difficulty claimed with this arrangement is, that the total reserve power will then be only about one-half that of the simple engine, unless boiler steam can be admitted to both cylinders at any desired time while running, as well as in starting, and the back-pressure be eliminated by exhausting from both to atmosphere.

The higher boiler pressures, made available through improved construction is very favorable to the use of compound engines, permitting a greater expansion range and more economical working.

CHAPTER THIRTY-SIX.

Small Shell Boilers for Carriages.—Many of the best known makes of American steam carriage have vertical fire tube shell boilers. All such boilers are of small dimensions, with a consequently small water capacity. But they have a very extensive heating surface, owing to the insertion of a large number of fire

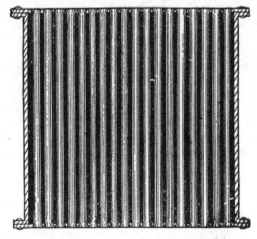

FIG. 349.—Shell Boiler, with flange connections for the tube plates. The shell is strengthened by winding several layers of steel piano wire around the length of the boiler. This cut gives a section on the centre, showing one row of tubes. These are usually made of copper which possesses a superior heat conducting property.

tubes and, according to many showings, seem capable of generating a power pressure far in excess of the usual rule of proportions for surface.

The shells are constructed of seamless steel, formed up or drawn out of solid pieces of the best quality of metal, and by the same method used in making tanks for soda fountains, oxygen-gas outfits, carbon-dioxide machines, etc., many of which are tested up to 3,000, 4,000 and 5,000 pounds per square inch. A wall section of steel made in that way three-sixteenths of an inch thick and having the form of a cylinder twenty inches in diameter, withstands a pressure of more than fifteen hundred pounds per square inch.

In order to get a large heating surface in a shell of small diameter, the tubes are placed very close together and there are a great number of them as shown in fig. 350, hence, the boiler heads are strengthened in such a way that they are even stronger than the shell.

FIG. 350.—The Stanley fire tube boiler. The shell and lower head are of one piece of pressed steel. The bands, as shown in the cut are of thin brass, to hold the asbestos covering in place.

It is claimed by a well-known builder of automobile boilers that it is impossible to explode a boiler as constructed for an automobile, since according to their tests, the tubes will flatten at a pressure of ten hundred pounds and then leak gradually until the pressure falls, without doing other damage.

The fire tube boiler used in the Stanley car has a shell slightly different from the ordinary construction. It is of the same type as originally used on the Locomobile Steamers and is shown in fig. 350. The shell which is of seamless pressed steel, is reinforced by two layers of piano wire wound around its exterior under tension. The lower head is part of the pressed steel shell. The tubes are 33/64 inch outside diameter and are expanded into the heads by means of a taper expander, shown in fig. 351. All tubes are 14 inches long, excepting those in the 26 inch boilers which are 16 inches long. In the 18 inch boilers there are 469 tubes with 66 square feet of heating surface. In the 23 inch boilers there are 751 tubes with 104 square feet of heating surface. In the 26 inch boilers there are 999 tubes with 158 square feet of heating surface.

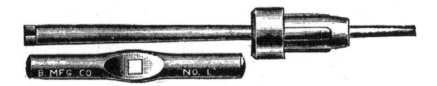

Fɪɢ. 351.—Roller tube expander for expanding tubes of boilers and burners. In expanding a tube, the roller end is inserted in the tube and the central tapered pin turned with an inward pressure. The action of the pin presses the rollers against the tube with great force, thus expanding the latter and making a tight joint.

'As usually constructed, the tubes in shell boilers are spaced the same distance apart, the distance betwen the outside edges of the tubes being only one-quarter of an inch. It will be seen from the dimensions of the Stanley boilers given above, that a large heating surface is obtained with small diameter of shell. Since the tubes are quite short, the entire heating surface is in close proximity to the fire and hence very effective.

Of Tubular Boilers in General.—The wide use of tubular boilers in steam carriages and for other purposes is explained by the fact that in its use the problem of how best to control the circulation, to the ends of quick steaming and higher durability, through more uniform distribution of heat, has been best solved. Although very many varieties of tubular boiler possess high efficiency as generators of steam, none of them attain such great power for absorbing heat but what there is still room for efforts to discover some means of neutralizing waste in this particular.

Small boilers with seamless drawn shells for automobiles are now manufactured in a number of sizes, the standard dimensions and horse power ratings are as follows:

AUTOMOBILE BOILERS.

(Seamless Shells.)

Internal Diam. In.	Thickness of Shells In.	Number of ½ inch Tubes.	Length of Tubes In.	Actual Horse Power.	Approximate Weight in Pounds.
14	$\frac{3}{16}$	309	$13\frac{1}{4}$	$4\frac{4}{10}$	112
16	$\frac{3}{16}$	420	$13\frac{1}{4}$	$5\frac{9}{10}$	146
16	$\frac{1}{4}$	420	$13\frac{1}{4}$	$5\frac{9}{10}$	154
17	$\frac{3}{16}$	480	$13\frac{1}{4}$	$6\frac{8}{10}$	158
17	$\frac{1}{4}$	480	$13\frac{1}{4}$	$6\frac{8}{10}$	174
18	$\frac{3}{16}$	529	$13\frac{1}{4}$	$7\frac{5}{10}$	180
18	$\frac{1}{4}$	529	$13\frac{1}{4}$	$7\frac{5}{10}$	196
19	$\frac{3}{16}$	586	$13\frac{1}{4}$	$8\frac{2}{10}$	203
19	$\frac{1}{4}$	586	$13\frac{1}{4}$	$8\frac{2}{10}$	222
20	$\frac{3}{16}$	676	$13\frac{1}{4}$	$10\frac{1}{10}$	231
20	$\frac{1}{4}$	676	$13\frac{1}{4}$	$10\frac{1}{10}$	257
20	$\frac{1}{4}$	676	$14\frac{1}{4}$	$11\frac{2}{10}$	272
20	$\frac{1}{4}$	676	$15\frac{1}{4}$	$12\frac{1}{10}$	287
20	$\frac{1}{4}$	676	$16\frac{1}{4}$	13	302
23	$\frac{1}{4}$	850	$13\frac{1}{4}$	12	293
23	$\frac{1}{4}$	850	$14\frac{1}{4}$	13	312
23	$\frac{1}{4}$	850	$15\frac{1}{4}$	14	331
23	$\frac{1}{4}$	850	$16\frac{1}{4}$	$14\frac{9}{10}$	350

The sixteen, seventeen, eighteen and nineteen-inch boilers listed above are made with tubes fourteen, fifteen, sixteen seventeen and eighteen inches long, which approximately increases the horse power in proportion as the tubes increase in length.

Heavy Truck Boilers.—Fire tube boilers suitable for commercial vehicles differ from the automobile type, only in that both heads are riveted in, and that the shell is made from heavier stock. The shells are not seamless drawn, but are welded by an electrical process making them homogenous and uniform throughout. Truck boilers are usually made with an extended shell which projects a few inches below the crown sheet to form a casing for the burner. It is, therefore, necessary to cut holes through the side of the shell to accommodate mixing tubes and other burner pipes. Heavy truck boilers with welded shells are regularly manufactured in various sizes as follows:

HEAVY TRUCK BOILERS.
(Welded Shells.)

Internal Diam. In.	Thickness of Shells In.	Number of ½ inch Tubes.	Length of Tubes In.	Actual Horse Power.	Approximate Weight in Pounds.
22	$\frac{5}{16}$	825	$13\frac{1}{4}$	$11\frac{6}{10}$	332
22	$\frac{5}{16}$	825	16	$14\frac{4}{10}$	354
22	$\frac{5}{16}$	825	20	$17\frac{9}{10}$	390
23	$\frac{5}{16}$	850	18	$16\frac{6}{10}$	384
23	$\frac{5}{16}$	850	22	$19\frac{6}{10}$	420
23	$\frac{5}{16}$	850	23	$20\frac{5}{10}$	464
24	$\frac{5}{16}$	951	13	$13\frac{5}{10}$	365
24	$\frac{5}{16}$	951	16	$16\frac{6}{10}$	433
24	$\frac{5}{16}$	951	18	$18\frac{7}{10}$	472
24	$\frac{5}{16}$	951	20	$20\frac{8}{10}$	525
24	$\frac{5}{16}$	951	22	$22\frac{9}{10}$	566
24	$\frac{5}{16}$	951	23	$23\frac{9}{10}$	590
24	$\frac{5}{16}$	951	24	$24\frac{9}{10}$	608
24	$\frac{5}{16}$	951	26	28	659
24	$\frac{5}{16}$	951	28	29	700
24	$\frac{5}{16}$	951	30	$31\frac{1}{10}$	742
28	$\frac{5}{16}$	1320	16	23	675
28	$\frac{5}{16}$	1320	20	$28\frac{4}{10}$	844
30	$\frac{5}{16}$	1470	16	$25\frac{1}{10}$	850
30	$\frac{5}{16}$	1470	20	$32\frac{2}{10}$	890

Boiler Tubes.—In the construction of shell boilers the tubes are made, either of steel plated with copper or zinc, or of seamless drawn copper.

In boiler construction, copper is superior to steel from the fact that it has a much higher thermal conductivity, involving considerably smaller loss of heat in proportion to its exposed surface.

The relative heat conducting power of copper and steel is such that one square foot of copper heating surface is as efficient as 2.13 square feet of steel heating surface. The choice of steel or copper tubes, therefore will depend in part on the boiler efficiency desired.

The working pressure to be carried, also governs the choice between copper and steel for tubes. Copper more easily resists the chemical action of impure water.

Advantages of Controlling Circulation.—By providing suitable arrangements for directing the rising and falling currents, so that interference is obviated, a very desirable end is attained—chemical impurities, held in solution by the water, and precipitated so as to form scale deposits, when it is evaporated, are prevented from locating and hardening; being received into mud drums suitably arranged at the lowest point of the water chamber, where they can be conveniently removed.

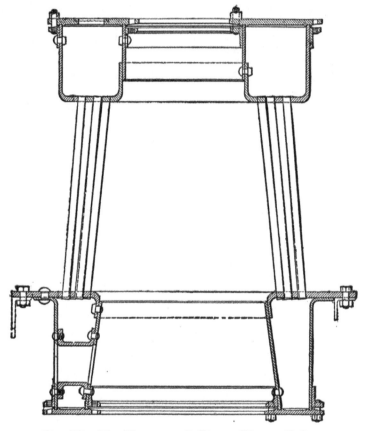

Fig. 352.—The Thornycroft Steam Wagon Boiler.

According to statistics furnished by various authorities these scale deposits, consisting mostly of lime and other non-conducting substances, interfere with the heat-conducting properties of the metal to an enormous extent. A deposit of 1-16 inch involving a loss of 13 per cent. of the fuel; a deposit of ⅛ inch, a loss of 25 per cent.; a deposit of ¼ inch, a loss of 38 per cent.; a deposit of ½ inch, a loss of 60 per cent. The result of allowing such incrustations to increase will be inevitably that the metal surface exposed to the fire is burned out and the boiler ruined.

Water Tube Boilers.—A water tube boiler, consists essentially of, 1, a drum in which is contained both the water and steam. In construction this drum may be either vertical or horizontal. A vertical drum is sometimes spoken of as a *stand pipe*. In sizes suitable for automobiles, the drum is from about five to eight inches in diameter.

In addition to the drum there is, 2, a series of pipes or coils. In the case of a vertical drum, one end of each coil is connected to the lower end of the drum and the other end of the coil, to the upper part of the drum. These coils or pipes are called the *up-flow* coils or *risers,* because the circulation of the water through them is upward.

The reason for this is that water expands as its temperature increases, and consequently, its weight per unit volume is diminished. Hence, the water in the drum being of lower temperature than that in the coils, has a greater density and therefore causes the water to rise in the coils.

In water tube boilers having horizontal drums, a *down flow pipe* is necessary. The upper ends of the coils are connected to the drum usually at the water level. A separate pipe, 3, called the *down flow pipe* is attached to the end of the drum at its lowest point, the other end being connected with the lower end of all the coils. The circulation, due to the varying density of the water is, 1, from the drum, 2, through the down flow pipe, 3, to the coils, and 4, back to the drum which it enters as a mixture of steam and water.

The upflow coils are of small diameter while the down flow pipe is much larger. For the proper flow of the water, the cross sectional area of the down flow pipe should be equal to the sum of all the cross sectional areas of the coils, as must be evident.

Advantages of Water Tube Boilers.—With the water tube boiler, the fact that the full force of the steam pressure cannot bear on any one extended surface involves that in the event of overheating or sinking of the water level, only one or two of the tubes may burst with no very serious consequences.

In the ideal water tube boiler, however, the tubes would run across the draught through a portion of their length, at least, thus making possible a greater absorption of heat, through the breaking of the air currents. This result is immensely increased when the successive rows of tubes are staggered, so as to still further divide up the draught currents.

FIG. 353.—The Ofeldt water tube boiler (automobile type). It consists of a central verticle drum, surrounded by a number of pipe coils which are connected to the drum at its extremities. The drum holds a reserve of water, which, when the boiler is in operation, circulates through the coils absorbing heat from the fire, and re-entering the drum at the top as water and steam. The amount of water in the drum varies from three gallons in the smallest size to eight gallons in the 24-inch boiler. Steam is taken from the top of the drum and passed through a superheater before delivery to engine.

The Ofeldt Water Tube Boilers.—These boilers are built with both horizontal and vertical drums. The vertical drum type is most in use for automobiles while those with horizontal drums are adapted to marine use.

As shown in fig. 353, the first mentioned type consists of a central drum made of standard boiler pipe, the same height as the boiler and five inches or more in diameter, according to the size of the boiler. It has a half inch bottom securely welded.

The stand pipe is covered with a steel cap, on which extend three arms to the boiler cover, holding the boiler proper in the casing. The cap is threaded and securely fitted to the stand pipe. The reserve of water in the stand pipe and coils varies from three gallons in the smallest size to eight gallons in the twenty-four inch size boiler.

The coils are made of one-eighth iron pipe in the small sized boiler, and a combination of one-eighth and one-quarter pipe in the larger sizes. They are coiled at a pitch of 1 1-4 inches to give the proper circulation and prevent the pipes from being clogged. These coils are attached to the stand pipe at the top and bottom with right and left connections.

FIG. 354.—The Ofeldt water tube boiler (marine type). This boiler consists of two horizontal drums connected on each side by numerous vertical *up flow* coils. Between the two series of coils are a set of *down flow* coils connected to the two drums. The cooler water in the upper drum flows down through these coils to the lower drum, thence up through the up flow coils absorbing heat from the fire and re-entering the upper drum as steam and water.

The standard dimensions of the vertical drum type as manufactured are as follows:

Size	Height	Weight	H. P.
15½ inches	17½ inches	145 pounds	4 to 6
16 "	17½ "	145 "	4 " 6
18 "	18 "	165 "	6 " 8
20 "	20 "	210 "	8 " 10
22 "	21 "	300 "	10 " 12
24 "	21 "	345 "	12 " 15
28 "	24 "	525 "	20
32 "	30 "	1000 "	30
36 "	42 "	1500 "	40

These boilers, as listed according to the builders, are rated when used in connection with a single or double, double acting high pressure engine, operating under 250 pounds steam pressure, turning 400 revolutions per minute and *without* vacuum.

When used in connection with compound engines they will give half as much again as the listed ratings, and for marine use in connection with triple expansion engines they will give just double the high pressure rating. Thus the 28-inch boiler 24 inches high is 20 H. P. with a double acting, high pressure engine; with a compound, 30 H. P. and with a triple expansion, 40 H. P. If the boilers are made higher than listed—within a reasonable limit—it will increase the H. P. from one to three for every six inches added to height. The steaming capacity of a boiler also depends upon the fuel. These ratings are made with kerosene as fuel.

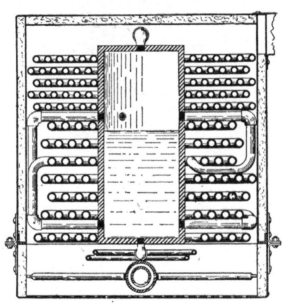

FIG. 355.—The Walker semi-flash steam generator. It consists of a central vertical drum surrounded by pipe coils. The feed water enters the top coil and flows down to the fifth coil, raising its temperature to near the boiling point. From the fifth coil it flows into the bottom of the central drum, thence into six flash steam generating coils and back to the steam space of the drum. From the top of the drum steam is drawn off and carried down to the lowest coil and superheated before delivery to the engine.

Semi=flash Boilers.—Boilers of this type are a combination of the shell and flash boiler. The volume of water carried in the shell gives considerable reserve power, hence, the boiler does not become inoperative in case of a temporary derangement of the feed pump. Two examples of semi-flash boilers are shown in figs. 355 and 357.

The Walker Semi=flash Boiler.—This boiler is provided with a non-tubular shell around which is placed a number of coils of pipe as shown in fig. 355. The five coils at the top are called the *water pre-heating coils.*

Cold water from the feed pump enters the topmost coil and flows down coil by coil, until it reaches the fifth coil.

At this point the water is raised almost to the boiling point. These five coils, thus form a feed water heater. The water passes from the fifth or lowermost of the pre-heating coils into the bottom of the central drum.

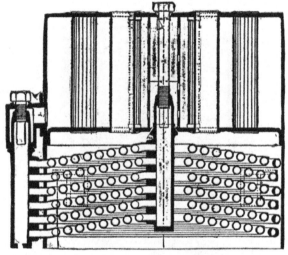

FIG. 356.—The Geneva Carriage Boiler. This boiler consists of several coils of tubing connected at inner and outer extremities to headers, as shown. The water and steam chamber above is constructed like an ordinary flue boiler.

From this central drum, the water, already at the boiling point, is delivered into six flash steam generating coils. These six coils are placed one below the other, directly beneath the five water pre-heating coils above referred to. Each of these flash steam generating coils is independently connected to the central stand-pipe. In shape, these coils are volute. The outer terminal of each of these coils is connected to the bottom of the central drum below the water level, while the inner terminal is carried up and connected to the drum at a point above the level to which the water in the central drum ever rises. By this plan, the hot water which the pre-heating coils deliver into the central drum, is forced to rapidly circulate through these coils and is flashed into steam, which is collected in the top of the central drum.

From the top of the central drum, the steam is drawn off and carried down to the very bottom of the generator and passed through a superheating coil located directly in the fire where the steam is dried and superheated, that is, raised to a temperature higher than that corresponding to its pressure.

The Lane Semi-flash Boiler.—This boiler, shown in fig. 357, consists of one continuous set of coils, superposed on a tubular shell. Connection between the coils and shell includes a *separator*.

The feed water, which enters the uppermost coil, is first heated by the spent gases that are too cool to effectively heat the hotter parts of the boiler below.

The water passes continuously from the upper coil through each succeeding one below, and as it is heated, comes into contact with still hotter surfaces in progressing (as in a flash boiler) till it issues from the bottom coil as steam and water into the centrifugal separator at the side.

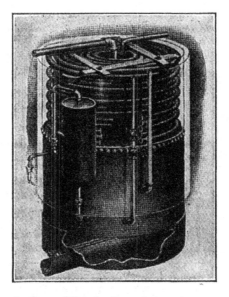

Fig. 357.—The Lane boiler. The feed water enters at the top of the coil and passes continuously from the upper coil through each succeeding one below, coming in contact with still hotter surfaces as it progresses (as in a flash boiler) till it issues from the bottom coil as steam and water into the centrifugal separator at the side. From the top of the separator the steam that has been generated in the coil passes to the upper part of the shell boiler, located beneath the coil, and the water by gravity to the lower part. Steam is drawn from the top head of the shell boiler.

From the top of the separator the steam that has been generated in the coil passes to the upper part of the shell boiler, located beneath the coil, and the water by gravity to the lower part. Steam is drawn from the top head of the shell boiler.

The coils being somewhat removed from the most intense heat are made of brass, a metal that conducts the heat through it more readily than steel.

The shell portion is of pressed steel with lower head and side walls of one piece and seamless. The tubes are one inch in diameter and welded to the lower head.

Serpollet's Flash Boilers.—The first real impulse to the modern steam carriage was the invention by Léon Serpollet in 1889 of the famous "instantaneous generator," known by his name. It consisted of a coil of one and one-half inch lap-welded steel tubing flattened until the bore was of "almost capillary width"—this he later increased to about one-eighth inch—and this, surrounded by a cast-iron covering to protect the steel from corrosion by heat, was exposed to the fire. The result was an extremely rapid generation of steam, the coil being first heated, and the water being vaporized almost as soon as it was injected into the tube.

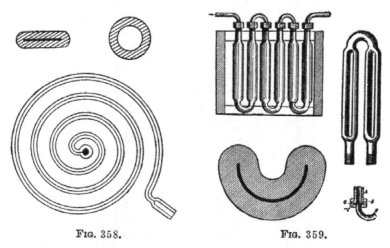

FIG. 358.   FIG. 359.

FIG. 358.—Earliest Form of the Serpollet Flash Generator ; a coil of flattened steel tubing.

FIG. 359.—Second Form of the Serpollet Flash Generator : a series of tubes pressed as shown, bent U-shape and nested ; the extremities being connected by joints and bent unions.

Later, he improved the efficiency of his coil by corrugating its surface. With such a generator of 108 square inches of heating surface more than one boiler horse power could be developed, the average hourly evaporation being forty pounds of water.

The usual working pressure was 300 pounds to the square inch, but each tube could bear a test as high as 1,500 pounds.

One great advantage lay in the fact that the high velocity required by the steam and water in the narrow tube served to keep the surface thoroughly free from sediment and incrustations. For vehicles requiring an additional generative power two such coils were used, one above the other, the water being injected into the lower and the upper one serving to superheat the steam.

To stop the engine it was necessary only to shut off the water feed pump, with the result of stopping the generation of steam at once.

In improved boilers of the Serpollet type a number of straight tubes were united by bent joints and nested, the several layers being connected in series. Moreover, each tube length was flattened, so as to form a U-shape, or crescent, in its cross-section, which arrangement greatly increased its evaporating capacity. But the most efficient form was reached in the design shown in Fig. 361, which shows three superposed sections of tubing; the lowest, four tiers of coil; the second, six tiers of "zigzag," the successive tiers being staggered, as shown; the third, several tiers of flattened tube twisted to angles of about forty-five degrees.

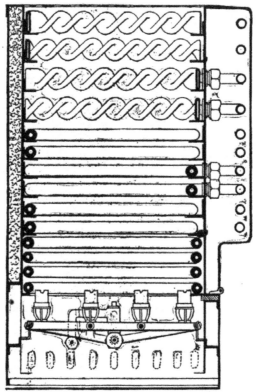

FIG. 360.—Later Form of the Serpollet Flash Generator, consisting of three layers of tubing. The four lowest tiers shown form a coil into which the feed water is injected; the second series of six tiers are arranged "zig-zag," like the nested tubes shown in Fig. 344 ; the third, or topmost, series of four tiers are also arranged " zig-zag," but are flattened and then twisted as shown.

The water is fed to the lowest section, which is immediately exposed to the fire, being thence passed to the second, whose available heating surface is of the greatest possible dimensions, and finally delivered, as superheated steam, from the uppermost twisted coils. The several sections of tubing are connected together *in series* by bends and unions outside the case, as shown, and the entire generator is enclosed in a double sheet-iron casing packed with asbestos. By the arrangement of the tubing, as here shown, the full power of the heater, in both draught and radiated heat, is utilized, as in the type of boiler shown in Fig. 361, but the circulation of the water is perfectly under control and rapid generation of steam assured.

For a six-horse power boiler of this type the outside dimensions, including heater space, are about 2½ x 1½ feet, the total tube length, ninety-five feet, and the heating surface, about twenty-five square feet; giving a generator of convenient size for a four-seat road carriage.

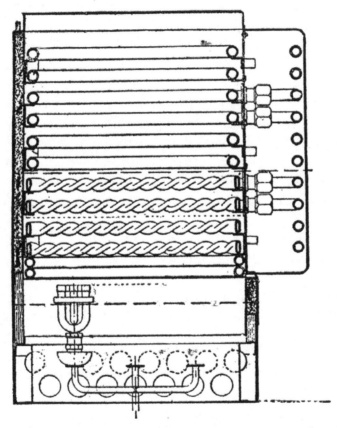

FIG. 361.–Recent Form of the Serpollet Flash Generator. In this type the twisted tubes are placed at the bottom and the "zig-zag" nested tubes at the top. The reason for this arrangement is that twisting the tubes affords a much larger heating surface ; hence these tubes are directly exposed to the fire.

Of Flash Generators in General.—Following along the lines of Serpollet's famous "flash" generator, with its numerous advantages in point of quick steam, high pressure capacity, freedom from scale deposits, and complete immunity from explosion, several designers of steam carriages and wagons have produced improved "boilers" of similar description.

Serpollet's first generator, as applied to his light steam carriage of 1889, was merely a coil of flattened tubing.

Later two such coils, connected in series, formed his generator, and finally the complicated trains of coils and bent tubing.

In the latest generators described the water is fed to the lowest tier of tubing, and the steam is taken off at the top, as in the several types of coiled water tube boilers, already described.

The contrary procedure is followed in most of the really successful flash generators produced by other inventors. The Blaxton generator feeds from the lowest water coil, but the Simpson-Bodman, White Automobile Manufacturing Co., and others feed from the top and superheat the steam in the lowest coils.

This seems to be the more logical process for this type of generator, since, as the water is explosively vaporized by contact with the heated tubes, it follows that the progress should be from the lowest to the highest temperature, vaporizing and superheating the steam, rather than allowing it to follow a course from higher to lower temperature, with the accompanying consequence of loss of heat. By making the tubes of sufficient capacity to vaporize a good quantity of water, surprisingly high temperatures may be obtained in a short time.

The White Flash Generator.—This flash boiler, or generator as it is called, consists of nine coils of steel tubing placed one above the other and connected in series. In both the small and large generators used in the White steam cars the generator tubing is of one-half inch internal diameter, but the length of the tubing differs, of course, for the two sizes.

Fig. 362 shows diagrammatically the circulation of the water and steam through the generator. In operation, water is pumped into the upper coil, and in passing through each coil, it must rise to an elevation higher than the first or upper coil.

In effect, this forms a series of traps, and as is shown in the diagram, the water or steam in order to pass from one coil to that next below, must be forced up to a level above the top coil before it passes down to the next lower coil.

This trapping of the water gives the generator a certain amount of reserve capacity and prevents the water passing directly through the generator to the engine, as it would otherwise be likely to do on a hard pull, and hot water or wet steam would be drawn into the engine cylinders.

It also prevents the steam rising to the top and the water settling to the bottom, as is the natural tendency.

There is but a very small quantity of water and steam in the generator at any given moment (in the larger car the total capacity of the generator is less than one-third of a cubic foot), but the process of making steam is so rapid with the flash system of generation, that the rate of steam production follows the changes in the intensity of the fire without any appreciable lapse of time.

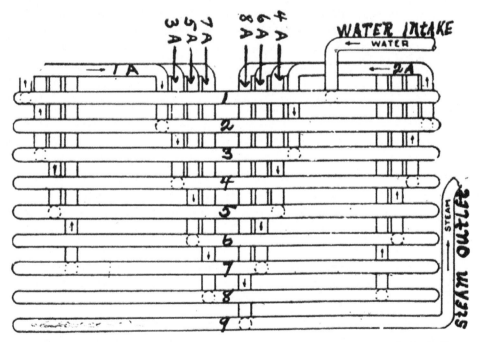

FIG. 362.—Diagram showing circulation through the White flash boiler. In operation, the water is pumped into the upper coil, through the pipe marked "water intake," passing around through coil No. 1, then up through tubing 1A, and down to coil 2, through coil 2 up to tubing 2 A and down to coil 3, through which it passes up through tubing 3 A and back down to and through coil 4, up through tubing 4 A and down through coil 5, up through 5 A down through coil 6, up through 6 A and down and through coil 7, up through 7 A, down and through coil 8, up through 8 A and down into and through coil 9, the last and lowermost coil of tubing, being directly over the fire where the steam is highly superheated, passing out of the generator from this point to the engine. The water or steam, in order to pass from one coil to that next below, must be forced up to a level above the top coil, and must then pass down again. This feature prevents water from descending by gravity, and renders the circulation down through the generator dependent upon the action of the pumps, or in other words a forced circulation.

Seamless Steel Tubing for Flash Boilers.—Improved methods in the manufacture of steel tubing have resulted in an article almost indestructible and has made possible the development and successful application of the flash system of steam generation for automobile propulsion.

Prof. Carpenter of Cornell University has subjected samples of tubing used in flash boilers, to a pressure of 18,900 pounds per square inch without showing any signs of rupture. Owing to the limitations of the testing apparatus on hand, he was unfortunately unable to ascertain the bursting strength.

Seamless steel tubing is now manufactured on an extensive scale, to meet the demands of flash boiler manufacturers and for other purposes where an article possessing great strength is required.

CHAPTER THIRTY-SEVEN.

Of Liquid Fuels in General.—All light steam carriages, and many heavier vehicles as well, use liquid fuel, oil or mineral spirit, to produce heat for their boilers. Such liquid fuel is not burned in liquid form, as is oil in an ordinary lamp, but is vaporized by heat, the vapor or gas thus produced being fed to the burner and ignited, in the same manner as ordinary coal gas used for light or heat in houses. It would be impracticable to carry gas in tanks on steam carriages, since the difficulty of storing and replenishing the supply would be greatly increased. By the use of liquid fuels a vast saving is made possible, both in space and weight, while their consumption in gaseous form is another element of economy.

Advantages in Using Volatile Fuels.—A prominent English authority on motor carriages gives the following five considerations of advantage in the use of liquid fuels:

1. Their combustion is complete, no heat being lost in the form of smoke or soot.

2. They produce no ashes or clinkers, which must be periodically cleaned out. Hence there is no loss of heat or drop in steam pressure, due either to this cause or to the renewal of coal.

3. The flues are never incrusted with soot, which involves the best conditions for use of heat.

4. The temperature of the escaping gases is lower than with a coal fire, since there is no need that the air required for combustion should force its way through a thick layer of burning fuel. Whence the uptake temperature is generally about 400°, Fahrenheit, instead of between 600° and 700°, as with the use of coal fire.

5. Since the fuel is burned in fine particles, in close contact with the oxygen of the air, only a small excess of air over that actually required for combustion is admitted to the burner. The opposite is the case with coal.

As may be readily surmised, the calorific value of liquid fuels is far greater than that of coal. It has been estimated that, taking the two weight for weight, petroleum oil has about twice the heat efficiency of coal. Since, therefore, equal weights of both varieties of fuel occupy about equal spaces, it follows naturally that petroleum products are far more economical and serviceable for use in vehicles of any description, or in boats and ships, where the considerations of weight and space occupied, in ratio to the power, are all-important.

The liquid fuels most commonly used are kerosene and gasoline, both being vaporized by the heat of the burner.

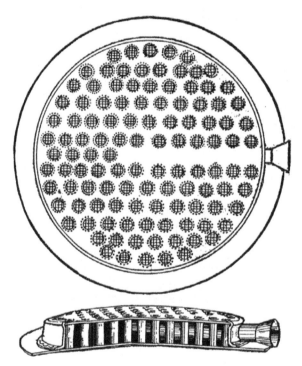

Fɪɢ. 363.—Plan and Part Section of a Typical Gasoline Burner for Steam Carriage Use.

The Gasoline Burner.—Very nearly the typical gasoline burner for steam carriages is shown in an accompanying figure. It consists of a flattened cylindrical chamber, pierced from head to head by a number of short tubes, each of which is expanded into the holes prepared for it and flanged over to make a secure joint, somewhat after the manner of a well-made boiler flue attachment. These air tubes, as they are called, are open to the air at top and bottom, having no communication with the interior of the cylindrical chamber above referred to. The gasoline enters the chamber, from a nozzle at the end of the feed pipe and through a tube entering at one side of the cylinder and extending inward about two-thirds of the diameter. This tube is called the "mixing tube," and its function is to make a mixture of air and gasoline vapor that will burn readily in the atmosphere. Having entered the cylindrical chamber, there is no avenue of escape for the inflammable gas except through the circular series of pin-holes, which surround each one of the air tubes, as may be seen on the cut of the top of this burner. It is at these minute perforations that the gasoline gas is ignited, the combustion being rendered perfect by the air admitted through the air holes previously mentioned.

The Storing and Feeding of Gasoline.—The liquid gasoline for supplying gas to the burner of a steam carriage is carried in a tank, disposed generally to the **rear** of the body, and sufficiently separated from the burner to avoid all dangers that might arise from leaks or overheating. Within this storage tank a good pressure of air is maintained—generally between 50 and 100 pounds to the square inch—from a separate air tank, supplied by a pump. This pressure is sufficient to force the liquid gasoline into the vaporizing tubes, when the supply cock is opened. After it has been vaporized the circulation continues, as controlled by the steam pressure diaphragm regulator, which operates a needle valve on the tube supplying the burner, the amount of gas and liquid gasoline moving between the supply tank and the burner being thus determined. If the fire is blown out in the draughts created by travel, the difficulty may be generally remedied by using higher air pressures in the tank. Some drivers have used as high as 100 pounds and over.

The Automatic Fuel=Feed Regulator.—The fuel-feed regulator, of which there are several serviceable forms, is one of the most necessary attachments of a steam carriage. Generally, it consists of a diaphragm, which, actuated by steam pressure from the boiler, automatically closes, or partly closes, a needle valve, thus regulating the amount of fuel fed to the burner. Several such apparatus are shown in section in Figs. 365-366. There, as may be seen, the diaphragm is fixed across the tube leading from the steam space of the boiler.

Against its inner side bears a solid head, or pressure cap, carrying a rod, at the farther end of which is a needle valve. The

FIG. 364.—The Lane burner. This is made entirely of tubing. The mixing tube exceeds in length the diameter of the burner, thus insuring a uniform mixture of air and vapor. The flames are arranged in straight rows separated by narrow air passages, thus supplying oxygen for combustion to each side of each flame. The cut also shows the vaporizing tubes within the burner casing and the igniting torch below them. The latter is a perforated tube enclosed in an absorbent envelope. The tube is connected with a cup located outside the burner. One valve only is operated to start this burner. There is, however, a second valve in fuel feed pipe, accessible from driver's seat, and also a valve for controlling pilot light, but these are seldom used.

pressure cap is normally held against the diaphragm by a strong spring. When sufficient steam pressure bears upon the diaphragm, the spring is compressed, allowing the rod attached to the head to be pushed inward, thus regulating the needle valve, according to requirement.

The instrument, thus formed, consists of two parts. The one is the pressure chamber containing the spring, whose pressure on the head is regulated by an adjusting screw, through the shaft of which passes the valve rod. The other is the gasoline chamber, into which the fuel for the burner is admitted to the left of the point of the needle valve; its outlet being controlled, as shown, by two hand-wheel valves—one leading to the main burner through the mixing tube, the other being intended to let out a sufficient supply of gasoline to the starting device, which may be a detachable "torch," or auxiliary vaporizer, or some arrangement of drip cup and preliminary generating coil. This arrangement of the valves is shown in different cuts of burners and automatic regulators, being there sufficiently designated. Thus, as shown in the figures, the valve rod, in entering the gasoline end of the regulator, passes through a stuffing box, so as to prevent all leakage at that end.

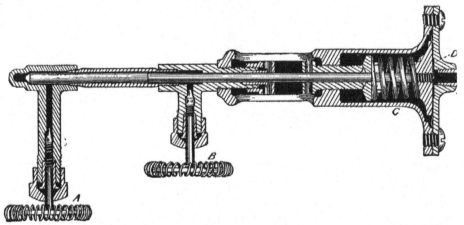

FIG. 365.—Fuel Feed Regulator of a Steam Carriage Burner, intended for Use with "Torch" Burner Kindler or Auxiliary Vaporizer. A is the hand wheel and needle valve regulating the feed to the main burner; B, the hand wheel and valve for operating the torch; C, the spring and header attached to the main valve rod; D, the diaphragm against which steam bears, regulating the main valve according to pressure. The liquid gasoline is admitted at a port on the left-hand extremity of the regulator tube, near the end of the needle valve on the main rod.

Of course, until there is sufficient heat generated to vaporize gasoline for the regular burner and generate steam pressure in the boiler, the automatic regulator cannot operate, as described, and the flow of gasoline to the starting burner or vaporizer is regulated solely by the hand valves.

Another form of regulator, shown in an accompanying cut, used on steam wagons, has the advantage of simplicity in this particular, doing away with both spring and stuffing box. The diaphragm has concentric corrugations, and to its centre is attached a valve rod having longitudinal groovings to permit the fuel to enter the feed tube in such quantities as the pressure on the other face of the diaphragm will permit. Steam pressure, being thus brought to bear, tends to deform the diaphragm; hence compressing the valve rod and decreasing the rate and quantity of fuel feed. The fuel is supplied from the storage tank through the port into the lower chamber of the two formed by the diaphragm, as may be readily understood.

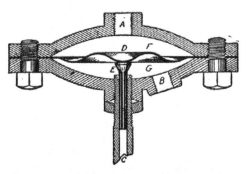

Fig. 366.—Gasoline Burner Regulator, operating with a corrugated diaphragm, like a steam gauge. A is the inlet for steam; B, the inlet for liquid gasoline; C, the port leading to the burner; D, the diaphragm; E, the head on the grooved rod of the valve; F, the steam chamber; G, the gasoline chamber.

Constructional Points on Gasoline Burners.—Several steam carriage burners are formed by riveting together a steel flattened cylindrical pressing and a plane disc, as shown in a former figure, inserting and expanding the draught tubes into suitably arranged perforations, as is done with the flues of boilers. Such a construction is apt to be faulty, however, owing to the fact that the steel plates tend to warp under the influence of heat, causing the draught tubes to leak, and the attachments to wear. The danger of these accidents has moved several inventors and manufacturers to design and produce burners formed with a cast top and steel plate base, or to cast both elements. By the use of castings warping is positively prevented, and leaking at the joints of the draught tubes is obviated.

One of the best-known burners of this construction is that widely known as the "Dayton," which possesses the additional feature of supplying gas for the burner flame through annular openings around each of the draught tubes, instead of using the "pin-hole" design, already described. It is possible to construct with this feature, since the air tubes are cast in one piece with the head and base plates, being afterward reamed out, so as to make them uniform in size. In addition to this air opening, a counter-bore is sunk in the top plate of the burner, and a steel washer is fitted into it, leaving an annular opening for the passage of gas in the inside of the washer. The outside of the washer has a number of small openings in it, so that each air tube is surrounded by two concentric circles of flame. This construction affords a very large heating capacity, and also, as is claimed, prevents the top of the burner from cracking, also less liability

Fig. 367.—The Dayton Burner, showing the Starter Box and Regulator in Position.

of chocking with rust, dust or carbonized particles, which is a frequent source of annoyance with "pin-hole" burners.

An Auxiliary Coil Starting Device.—The starter used with the "Dayton" burner, already described, is shown on page 509, Fig. 367. There, as may be seen, a small box, called a "starter box," is attached at one side of the burner It contains a short coil of tubing, into which liquid gasoline may be admitted by opening the valve which is shown at the side. A few drops of liquid gasoline are then allowed to drip into the "starting cup," beneath the coil, and this, set on fire, will speedily generate sufficient gas to light the pilot burner, from which, in turn, the main

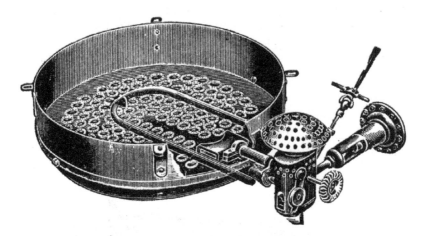

Fig. 368.—The Forg generator and burner. The gasoline supply is carried through a pipe entering on the left hand side and passing over the burner in a loop form, out on the right hand side, where it passes into the generator box. The generator box is made of sheet steel suitably perforated and so arranged that while the fire will burn freely inside of the box, it will not blaze up on the outside.

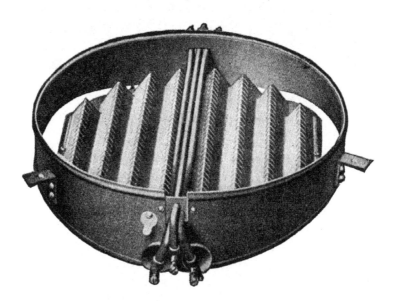

Fig. 369.—Stanley burner, showing vaporizer and mixing tubes. The burner is entirely encased, there being no air inlet except at the mixing tubes, consequently it is not affected by air currents. The pilot light is not shut off by the automatic, but burns continuously until shut off by hand and is just strong enough to hold the steam pressure.

burner may be kindled as soon as the vaporizing tubes are sufficiently heated.

As soon as this point is reached the needle valve to the main burner, shown at the right hand of the starter box, is opened, admitting gas through the nozzle into the mixing tube.

By closing this valve, the main fire may be shut off, as desired, although the pilot light continues burning, until extinguished by shutting off its supply of gas, which is never modified in any way, being out of reach of the automatic regulator controlling the fuel feed to the main burner.

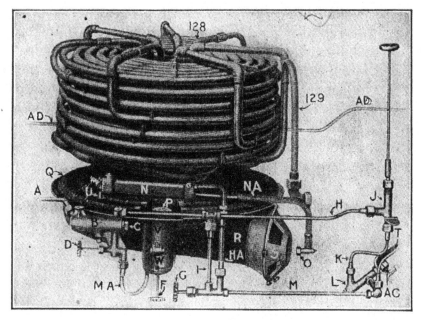

Fig. 370.—The White flash steam generator and burner. Fuel passes through pipe A, then through strainer B. From the strainer it passes through pipe H, valve J, pipe K, valve L, pipes M and HA to vaporizer N. Gas is discharged from the vaporizer through pipe NA and nozzle O into burner induction tube R. Warming up valve G is supplied through pipe I.

The White Burner and Connections.—As shown in fig. 370, the burner is of the Bunsen type, the gasoline vapor drawing back through the mixing tube R, sufficient air for good combustion.

Fuels of the lower specific gravities, such as 65 to 70 (Baume Scale) require more air than those of higher specific gravities, such as 70 to 76. The air supply may be regulated by the air shutter S on the mixing tube. Usually too much air causes the fire to burn very blue and to raise off the burner; too little air causes the fire to burn with a red and yellow flame. The proper flame is blue, a medium between the light and heavy flame just described. If the air supply be not correctly adjusted, it causes the burner to light back to the nozzle and is sometimes accompanied by "howling."

In lighting the sub-burner, the valves D and F should be closed and main fuel valve opened which allows fuel to come through pipe A to the sub-burner V. Valve F should now be opened one turn, door W opened and a lighted match applied inside. After doing this, the supply valve D should be opened slightly, closing it again at once, leaving it open about one second. This operation is repeated until sufficient gasoline runs into the drip cup to be ignited by the match. Sufficient fuel should be kept in the drip cup by opening and closing D to warm up the sub-burner. When the sub-burner becomes hot enough to vaporize the gasoline, fuel will cease to run in the drip cup as it has now become a gas and will pass up through the pilot light grate and burn in the main fire box. Valve D should then be opened at least one turn and left open. As soon as the gasoline in the drip cup is all burnt out, this flame should burn blue and soon heat the grate red hot. This can be seen by looking through the hole in the boiler casing. As soon as the sub-burner gets warmed up, the flame should be adjusted by valve F.

This valve regulates the strength of the flame and should be turned up or down until a steady blue flame is obtained that does not roar. In case the sub-burner goes out, but is still hot enough to vaporize the fuel, it can be relighted by putting a match through the hole in the casing without using the drip cup.

When the sub-burner is to be shut off, valve D is closed and valve F opened wide. This frees the passages in the sub-burner of gas and helps to keep them clear and open. Should the flame in the sub-burner be not sufficiently strong with valve F opened two turns, there is probably some obstruction in the valve and it should be examined and cleaned.

CHAPTER THIRTY-EIGHT.

BOILER ATTACHMENTS AND AUTOMATIC REGULATING DEVICES.

Of Boiler Feeders in General.—There are two different kinds of device for feeding water to steam boilers: plunger pumps operated by the engine or by a separate cylinder; and injectors, which raise and feed the water by a steam jet from the boiler itself. Injectors are largely used for locomotives, marine and stationary boilers, but to the present time almost not at all in steam road carriages. The principal reason for this is that the valves and apertures in an injector, suited for a light carriage boiler, would have to be made so small that they would be constantly clogged with dirt and sediment, hence rendering the instrument inoperative. Furthermore, when in operation, an injector would be liable to fill the boiler too rapidly, while the pressure remained sufficient to raise the water, thus causing priming; and, if shut off until the water level had fallen considerably, would cause damage to the boiler by flooding it, while in an overheated condition.

Plunger Pumps and By=Pass Valves.—The plunger pumps used to feed steam carriage boilers are most often operated from the cross-head of the engine. Consequently, so long as the engine is in motion, water is steadily pumped into the boiler. When, as shown by the water-glass, the level is too high, the by-pass valve may be opened, and the water pumped from and back again to the tank. In some carriages the by-pass is always operated by hand; in others it is also controlled by some kind of automatic arrangement. The automatic control of the by-pass is extremely desirable, particularly since unskilled engineers most often have charge of carriages and are exceedingly liable to forget the small details of management. On the other hand, many automatic devices get out of order altogether too easily, and leave the carriage driver to exercise his skill and judgment at an unexpected moment.

In addition to the danger of flooding the boiler, the opposite embarrassment often occurs—owing to some disarrangement the pump may fail to feed enough water to the boiler, or may not operate at all. Then it is necessary to use a supplementary feeder, generally a hand pump, or a steam pump operated by a separate cylinder. Such supplementary steam pumps and injectors are commonly arranged to start automatically, as required, but may also be started by a hand-controlled valve. Another advantage involved in the use of automatically controlled steam pumps is that water may be fed, as required, to the boiler, after the engine

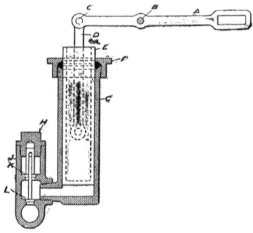

Fig. 371.—Section of a Type of Plunger Feed Pump. As is obvious, the valve opened by suction of the up-stroke is closed by compression of the down-stroke, and *vice versa*. This pump is equipped with a double, or compound, valve, which, as may be seen, secures perfect balance in operation with the simplest possible constructions. The stem of the suction valve enters a bore in the stem of the outlet valve. Referring to the lettered parts: A is the pivoted lever working the pump from the crosshead of the engine; B, the fulcrum point; C, the attachment of the piston rod, D; E, the trunk plunger; F, the packing cap; G, the pump cylinder; H, nut on the valve chamber port; J, the valve chamber; K, water outlet valve; L, water inlet valve.

has ceased motion, and it is desirable to leave the carriage standing with steam up. In this condition, however, a very small amount of water is needed, except under unusual conditions.

Operating the By=Pass Valve.—The driver of a steam carriage must constantly watch the water-glass in order to inform himself as to the water level in the boiler. On noticing that the level is too high, or is rising too rapidly—the proper level is generally about two-thirds up the glass—he opens the by-pass valve by turning a small wheel placed near the throttle lever beside his seat. This act, as already suggested, turns the water forced by the pump back again into the feed tank, a three-way cock controlling its travel.

If, after the water has been led from the boiler for some time, the level begins to sink, it is necessary only to close the by-pass valve, thus resuming the feed. If, from any cause, the pump seems unable to keep up the water level in the boiler, and the reading of the water-glass is verified by the try-cocks, thus showing that it is working perfectly and is unclogged with sediment, a few strokes of the auxiliary hand pump will suffice, if no automatic steam pump be attached to the carriage.

Fɪɢ. 372.—A hand feed water pump for use on cars having tubular boilers working on moderately high steam pressures. The handle is arranged to fold down when not in use.

Fɪɢ. 373.—Hand water pumps for use with flash boilers. It is intended to be placed in front of seat, between the two passengers. The bracket in center being movable, enables the pump to be placed at any height to suit the car. The water connections are for one-quarter inch pipe. The plunger is quite small as the resistance to be overcome—that due to the high working pressure of the flash boiler—is considerable, in fact it would be too great for hand operation if the plunger were large as shown in fig. 372.

Troubles With the Pump.—Since the small water pumps attached to steam carriages are of the simple plunger type, failure to supply sufficient water to the boiler may generally be attributed to loosened packings or to clogged check valves. The rapid sinking of the level in the water-glass will indicate trouble with the pump, except when ascending a high hill. In the latter case the fall of level may reasonably be attributed to the unusual steam consumption. Under usual circumstances, the trouble is due to loosened packings, and this trouble may be remedied by inserting new packings, although particular care should be exercised, so as not to pack the plunger too tightly and cause breakage.

Boiler Attachments: Try-Cocks and Water Glass.—In operating a boiler of any design it is essential both for safety and efficiency that the engineer should be kept constantly informed on the level of the water and the pressure of the steam. For this reason boilers are fitted with try-cocks, water glass and

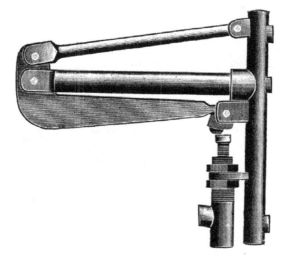

FIG. 374.—The Ofeldt automatic water regulator. This device consists of a column, having an expansion tube attached at right angles. A lever, with the fulcrum braced from the top of the water column, is attached by a joint to the end of the expansion tube, with the lever free to operate the by-pass valve. In operation, the closing and opening of the by-pass valve depend upon the expansion and contraction of the brass tube, when subjected to water at the boiling point and steam, which is over 150 degrees hotter. The water rises in the boiler, at the same time rising in the regulator water column, until it enters the expansion tube, causing the tube to contract and pulling on the lever, thus lifting the free end and opening the by-pass valve. When the water has been evaporated from the expansion tube, permitting the steam to enter, it expands and presses the lever out, thus closing and holding the by-pass valve shut. In actual operation the expansion tube finds the exact position to keep the water in the boiler always at the same level. Should the valve by-pass too much water, or not enough, it can be adjusted to shut off closer or open wider by raising or lowering the valve.

steam gauge, all of which are depicted in accompanying figures. There are usually three try-cocks, as shown, the upper one intended for steam, the second at the working level of the water, and the third at a fixed point above the fire line. In conditions of uncertainty in the action of the water glass the engineer may find out whether the water level is too low by opening the lower cock, or may find if it is too high by opening the two upper ones. In making test it is necessary to leave the cock open sufficiently long to discover whether all steam, all water, or a mixture of both is escaping.

The water glass, or water column, furnishes a ready means for determining the exact height of the water in the boiler.

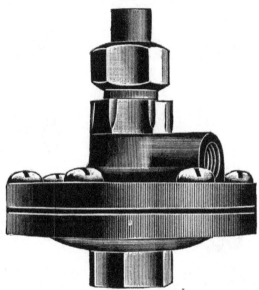

FIG. 375.—The Ofeldt automatic fuel regulator. This consists of two concave brass discs with a steel diaphragm between them, held together with screws, leaving a small space on the under side of the diaphragm for steam and a space for fuel on the upper side. The valve consists of a brass seat in the center of the diaphragm, with a specially made hollow fitting which the valve rests against. This hollow tube is the end of the supply pipe to the burner and can be adjusted to shut off the fire at any desired steam pressure by breaking the union on the upper side of the regulator. In operation, when the steam pressure on the lower part of the diaphragm has reached a point where it is desired to shut off the fire, the diaphragm is pushed upward, pressing the metal seat upward until it closes against the special hollow fitting mentioned before, thus closing the valve. When the boiler pressure decreases, the natural spring of the diaphragm opens the fuel valve and starts the fire again. The fuel enters through the opening on the side and passes down into the space on the upper side of the diaphragm and through the union fitting to the burner. Where a pilot is used, the fuel valve is constructed to shut off all the fuel supply to the main burner. These regulators are ordinarily set for 225 pounds steam pressure and 60 pounds air pressure.

Since it is such an important consideration in boiler operation that the water level should be constantly watched, it is necessary that the water column should be placed where the engineer may constantly observe it. Thus it is that, in steam carriages it is disposed in the side of the body beneath the seat, its condition being readily observable by the driver by reflection in a small mirror set to one side of the dashboard. Lamps are also arranged behind it, so that the level of the water may be observed at night.

The water glass also gives information on the condition of the water within the boiler, as when oil or scum has collected on the surface, causing foaming.

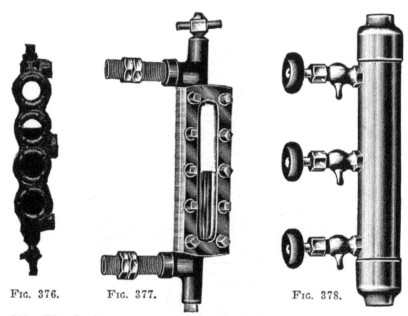

FIG. 376.　　　　FIG. 377.　　　　　　FIG. 378.

FIG. 376.—The Seabury water gauge. This device is designed to withstand any pressure possible with fire tube boilers. Observation of the water is through a series of bull's eyes of Scotch glass one inch thick, fitted into the casting with two packing rings and retained by a brass screw ring. The shape of the glass is such that the water appears a deep black as it comes over the bulls' eyes, the empty compartment above the water appearing white, showing the water level at a glance.

FIG. 377.—Klinger replex water gauge with piston glass one-half inch in thickness. Owing to the peculiar shape of the observation glass, the water appears black while the steam shines with a silvery lustre. By removing the gauge cock at the bottom and the cap at the top the inside surfaces may be cleaned.

FIG. 378.—A water column with try cocks for ascertaining the water level in the boiler. In operation, the cocks should be only partially opened otherwise the water will be raised in the column which will show a false level.

Troubles with the Water Glass.—Troubles with the water glass that must be constantly guarded against are stoppage by sediment and the breaking of the glass tube. The former difficulty may generally be remedied by closing the lower cock and allowing the steam from the upper one to blow through the drain cock shown at the bottom. In case the glass tube be broken it is necessary only to close both cocks, and insert a new tube in the collars, having first removed the nuts and packings at top and bottom. In order to obviate, as far as possible, breakage of the glass it is necessary to avoid too sudden changes of temperature in the column, when first opening the cocks, after getting up steam.

FIGS. 379, 380.—Dial and Interior View of the "American" Duplex Combined Steam and Air Pressure Gauge for Use on Steam Carriages. The dial has two hands; one of them attached to a sleeve which works over the spindle carrying the other, in the same manner as the two hands of a clock are hung. As may be readily understood, the two hands work in opposite directions, one clockwise, the other counter-clockwise, from zero to maximum on their respective scales. The sectional view shows the mechanism by which this result is accomplished: two separate inlets, for steam and air, respectively; two distinct flattened and curved steel tubes, each attached at its end by a link to a lever and toothed sector working on the toothed pinion concentric with the pivot of one of the hands. The two flattened tubes, of course, have different tensile ratios, causing them to tend to straighten at different pressures. Hence the steam hand records a maximum pressure of 240 pounds, while the air hand records a maximum pressure of 100 pounds.

Most of the water glasses used on steam carriage boilers have self-closing valves, which operate to prevent the escape of steam in case the glass is broken. In the use of these valves particular care is needed, since they are very liable to be clogged with sediment or incrustation, causing false indications of the water level and enabling the boiler to be burned out before the driver knows that anything is wrong. Several carriage owners, in the writer's experience, have had these valves removed, and contented themselves with closing the cocks every time the glass is broken. This may be a rather exceptional experience, but it is extremely desirable, if not imperative, to verify the water glass reading by the try-cocks before starting the carriage.

The water glass is an important piece of mechanism, and cannot be too closely observed and cared for. Skilled engine drivers take its record constantly, and so very important is it that no error regarding the water level should be made that some inventors have proposed using colored floats to attract the driver's eye, and enables readier reading of the record. A supply of glass tubes should always be kept on hand in a steam carriage so that breakage may be immediately repaired. Also, every possible pre-

FIG. 381.—A steam pressure gauge for use with flash boilers. It is constructed for indicating pressures up to 1,200 pounds to meet the operative conditions of the flash boilers which carry much higher steam pressure than the ordinary tubular boiler.

caution should be adopted to prevent the accumulation of sediment that might obstruct the free passage of the water into the glass. It is well to clear the tube by flushing with steam at frequent periods.

The Steam Gauge.—As a means of determining the power output, a steam gauge is attached to all well-appointed boilers. This device indicates on a dial the degree of pressure generated within the boiler. Steam gauges are constructed with one of the two varieties of internal mechanism In the first variety the steam bears upon a diaphragm, regulated to yield in proportion to the pressure exerted. The second variety operates through the tendency of a flattened and bent metal tube to straighten out under pressure of the steam or gas within it. As shown in an accompanying figure, a tube, flattened to an ellipsoidal cross section, is connected by one end to a steam pipe leading direct from the boiler. When the cock is opened, steam is admitted to the tube, its pressure tending to change the flat section to one more nearly round, and in the process causing the tube to begin uncoiling it-self in the direction of a straight line conformation. Hence the other end of the tube, attached, as shown, to a link connected to a lever bearing a toothed segment, tends to move, causing the link to move the lever.

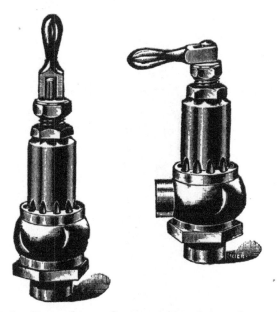

Figs. 382 and 383.—Two views of a type of safety valve suitable for use on fire tube boilers which furnish steam at moderate temperatures. A snap lever is provided as shown for holding valve open. When getting up steam the lever is turned to the vertical position fig. 382. This opens the valve which should remain in this position until all the air is expelled from the boiler and steam begins to issue through the opening when the valve should be closed by turning the lever to the horizontal position as shown in fig. 383.

Safety Valves; Construction, Theory and Operation.—Explosion in a steel-shell, copper-flued carriage boiler is very nearly impossible, and with moderate care and watchfulness the burning out or collapse of the tubes can be prevented.

The unskilled engine-driver is amply protected, if he only exercise reasonable prudence by the automatic burner regulator, the automatic low water alarm, the water glass and steam gauge in plain sight, and lastly by a safety valve adjusted to blow off at the proper pressure.

A safety valve is simply a valve of ordinary description, arranged to close a steam pipe outlet, under pressure of a weight or spring.

The safety valves used on steam carriages are constructed on the same general principles as any of the spring valves used on locomotives, or other boilers. They are usually known as "pop" valves, from the fact that the steam in lifting the valve from its seat usually makes a "pop" or sudden detonation. As a usual thing carriage valves are adjusted to a fixed pressure, which is never disturbed.

FIG. 384.—A pop safety valve designed especially for use with superheated steam. The spring, as is shown in the figure, is not enclosed and is therefore protected from the high temperature of the steam. This is necessary as intense heat soon takes the temper out of the spring and destroys its elastic properties.

The Blow-Off Cock.—This is an important attachment of all boilers, furnishing a ready means of removing the water from the boiler under pressure of its own steam, which is called "blowing-off." It is also used in some carriages for attaching a hose to fill the boiler at starting, or for injecting water for cleaning the interior. It is usually closed with a box nut for receiving a wrench, but sometimes by a cock, as in large boilers.

CHAPTER THIRTY-NINE.

Types of Power Plants.—In the generation and application of steam as a motive power for automobiles, numerous combinations of engines and boilers of different types have been tried, together with varied methods for securing automatic control of the fuel and feed water.

These numerous steam systems, may be classified in several ways, as follows:

1. With respect to the method of generating the steam as:

   a. By shell, water tube or semi-flash boilers, carrying a water level, and furnishing steam at medium pressures.
   b. By flash generators, which do not carry a water level, furnishing steam at high pressures and with considerable degree of superheat.

   NOTE.—The terms, medium pressures and high pressures are used only in a relative sense. All steam pressures carried on automobiles are high when compared to those in use for other requirements. For instance, side wheel steamboats run with 25 to 50 lbs. steam, Corliss engines, 50 to 150 lbs., locomotives, 150 to 225 lbs., triple expansion marine engines, 175 to 300 lbs. For automobile work, 300 to 500 lbs. may be called medium pressures and 500 to 1000 lbs., high pressures. A steam gauge, registering up to 1200 lbs. is shown in Fig. 381.

2. With respect to the manner of working the steam in the engine as:

   a. Simple (sometimes called high pressure);
   b. Compound or two stage expansion.

3. With respect to the disposition of the exhaust steam from the engine, as:

   a. Non-condensing;
   b. Condensing.

4. With respect to the structural features of the engine, as:

   a. Single acting;
   b. Double acting;
   c. Duplex (two simple cylinders);
   d. Multi-cylinder.

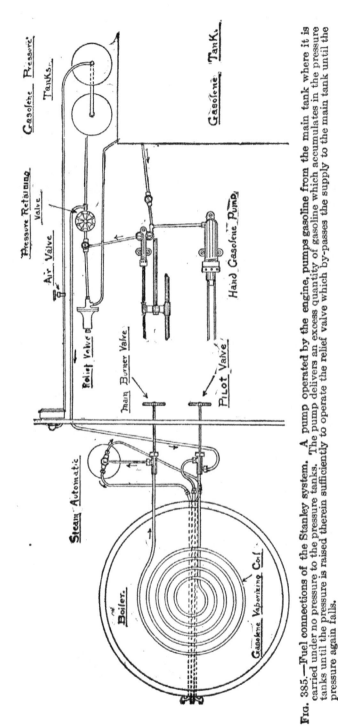

FIG. 385.—Fuel connections of the Stanley system. A pump operated by the engine, pumps gasoline from the main tank where it is carried under no pressure to the pressure tanks. The pump delivers an excess quantity of gasoline which accumulates in the pressure tanks until the pressure is raised therein sufficiently to operate the relief valve which by-passes the supply to the main tank until the pressure again falls.

Of the numerous combinations possible with the different types of engines and boilers, there are three which are in general use:

1. A shell boiler with duplex engine operating at medium pressures.

2. A semi-flash boiler with compound condensing engine operating at medium pressures.

3. A flash boiler with compound condensing engine operating at high pressures.

These three systems will be explained by describing the operation of three well known steamers, viz.:

1. The Stanley;
2. The Lane;
3. The White.

Before explaining the operation of the White Steamer, a short description will be given of a system devised in 1889, by Serpollet—the pioneer in the field of flash steam generation.

STEAM SYSTEMS.

The Stanley System.—The Stanley steamer is propelled by a two cylinder, double acting, high pressure steam engine of the locomotive type, with plain D-slide valves operated by the familiar link motion valve gear. Steam is supplied by a fire tube boiler. Both the engine and boiler are illustrated and described in Chapters thirty-five and thirty-six.

Automatic devices are incorporated in the system which control the fuel and feed water supply.

Fuel Connections.—Gasoline is carried in a tank under no pressure. From this tank it is pumped as used to a receiving reservoir, consisting of two small pressure tanks situated side by

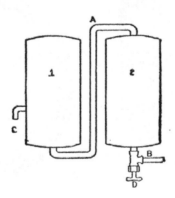

FIG. 386.—The Stanley gasoline pressure tanks. A, is the pipe connecting the two tanks; B, the pipe through which gasoline is pumped; C, the air valve through which air is pumped with the hand air pump; D, a valve for drawing gasoline out of the tank when desired.

side, so piped that the bottom of one is connected with the top of the other, as shown in fig. 386. The main tank, pressure tanks and various pipes and connections comprising the fuel system is shown in the diagram fig. 385. The operation is as follows: Assuming the pressure tanks to be empty, gasoline is pumped by the hand pump until the pressure gauge registers between ten and fifteen pounds.

The effect of this is to nearly fill pressure tank number two with gasoline, the air in this tank being forced by the gasoline into tank number one and is compressed with the resulting pressure as indicated by the gauge.

The pressure in tank one is further increased by attaching the hand air pump to the air valve and pumping till the gauge indicates eighty or ninety pounds which is the working pressure.

If the fire were now lighted, and allowed to burn for some time, the gasoline pressure would gradually drop. In this case it is to be raised again by additional use of the hand pump.

With steam up and the car running, the gasoline is supplied by the power gasoline pump operated by the engine. This pump being proportioned to deliver an excess supply of fuel, an automatic relief valve is provided, adjustable as to pressure, through which the excess passes back into the main tank.

Fig. 387.—Stanley steering wheel, with hands showing how the throttle lever is lightly gripped in the fingers without moving the hand from the wheel.
Fig. 388.—View of Stanley steering wheel, showing the single throttle, locked by its locking screw, and the by pass lever which controls the supply of water to the boiler.

The air in the pressure tank will be gradually absorbed, and more will occasionally have to be supplied by the hand pump. The need of this will be indicated in two ways: 1, when running, the hand on the pressure gauge will be seen to vibrate, and 2, when standing with the pilot burning, the pressure will drop rapidly, owing to too little air for expansion.

To be certain the drop in pressure is due to want of sufficient air, and not to a leaky automatic, the latter is cut out by closing the pressure retaining valve. If now, the pressure continue to fall rapidly, the cause is insufficient air in the pressure tank.

Water Connections.—The system of pumps and piping for the feed water supply is shown in fig. 390. There are two power pumps, one hand pump, by-pass valves and a water indicator.

The two power pumps work continuously when the car is running and have a capacity sufficient to supply the boiler when running up hill or over bad roads. Hence, they must of necessity pump too much water when the car is operated on good roads. To prevent the boiler filling with water under these conditions, a by-pass valve operated by hand is provided which when open, allows the water from the pumps to be returned to the tank instead of into the boiler. By hand control of this valve the desired water level is maintained in the boiler. The pumps are so

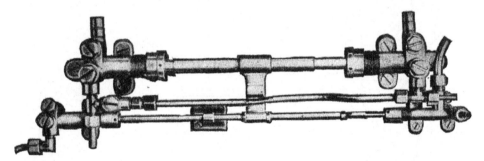

FIG. 389.—Water, gasoline and cylinder oil pumps of the Stanley car. As shown in the illustration, the four plungers form one moving part. The two large pumps are for water, one or both of which may be by-passed by the lever on the steering wheel.

connected that one or both may be by-passed, the by-pass valves being operated by a lever on the steering wheel.

If the pumps become *air bound,* that is, if the pump cylinders and valves become filled with air it will fail to deliver water.

The reason for this is that the air will be simply compressed and re-expanded as the plunger goes in and out, hence, no water would enter the pump.

To remedy this, it is only necessary to open the by-pass for a moment. The pump being thus relieved of boiler pressure, the air will be pumped out through the by-pass and the pump will fill with water and become again operative.

Instead of the ordinary form of glass water gauge, a special water indicator is used as shown in the diagram fig. 391.

541

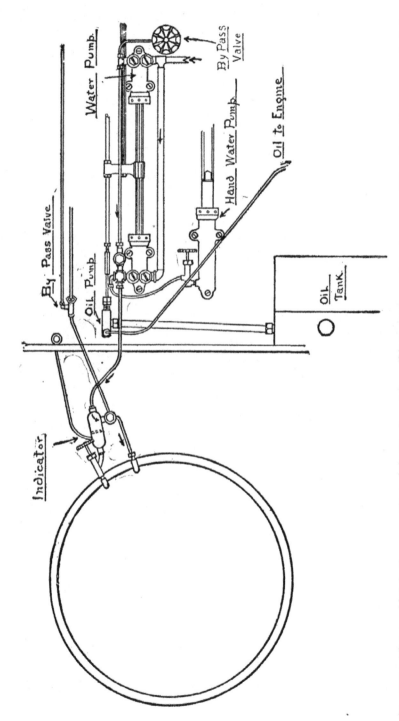

Fig. 390.—Water and lubricating connections of the Stanley system. There are two water pumps, one of them for ordinary use controlled by the by-pass on the wheel, and the other for emergency duty with its by-pass on the footboard. Both water pumps and the oil pumps are driven by the engine. The water pumps have a capacity sufficient to supply the boiler when running up hill and over bad roads. The capacity is therefore too great for ordinary conditions, hence the use of the by-pass operated by hand which allows the water to be returned to the tank when too much is being pumped into the boiler. The oil pump supplies oil to the engine cylinders. Oil enters the pump barrel by gravity and is sent by the plunger through a check valve to the main steam pipe The length of the plunger is adjustable and determines the rate of oil delivery.

The construction of this device is as follows: A water column F is so connected with the boiler at its top and bottom, that the water will stand at the same level in the column as in the boiler.

Connected with the water column at D, about eight or nine inches above the bottom of the boiler, is a casting which may be called the *indicator body,* containing two adjacent chambers G and H, one of which fills from the boiler through the connection D.

Through the other chamber the feed water is pumped, whether going to the boiler or through the by-pass back to the tank. This

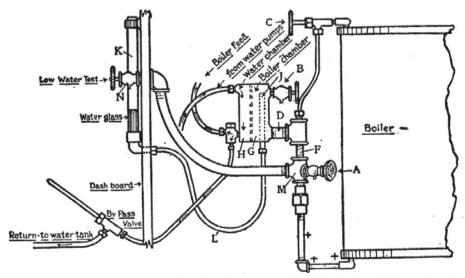

Fig. 391.—Stanley system of indicating water level. A, is a blow off and try cock; B, try cock; C, shut off valve. In cleaning out, cock C is closed and cock A opened when steam is up.

latter chamber may be called the *water chamber,* and the other the *boiler chamber.*

It is evident, that the "boiler chamber" will be filled with water provided the water in the column is above the connection D; otherwise it will be filled with steam.

The indicator proper is a "U" tube, one end of which J is of metal and sealed at the top, and called the "standpipe." This end is inserted some distance up into the "boiler chamber," and is at all times surrounded by either steam or water.

The other end of the "U" tube is a glass tube K, placed vertically on the dashboard. This "U" tube is filled with water so that the standpipe J is filled entirely, and the water when cold stands in the glass an inch or two from the bottom.

The operation of the device is as follows: As long as the chamber G surrounding the standpipe is filled with water and the feed water is being pumped through the other chamber H, it will keep the water in the former chamber comparatively cool, and also the water in the standpipe, and the water will remain at a low point in the glass.

As soon, however, as the water gets below the connection D, the "boiler chamber" will fill with steam, and, as it surrounds the "standpipe" it will vaporize some of the water in it and force the water out of it and up in the glass, thus showing that the water level in the boiler is below the indicator. Whereupon the pump by-pass should again be closed until the water falls in the glass again, which will indicate that the water in the boiler is above the connection D on the indicator.

Usually when the car is standing the indicator will receive sufficient heat to throw the water up into the glass. In this case, if the water in the boiler is above the connection D, it will immediately cool off, and the water will drop again in the glass when the car is run and water is pumped through the "water chamber."

The copper tube L leading from the standpipe extends downward six or seven inches before bending upward again to the water glass bracket, so that the hot water or steam from the standpipe will not pass up into the water glass.

Some three inches below the connection D, mentioned above there is another connection M and a pipe from this leading up through the dashboard, at the end of which is a petcock N, indicated on the sktech. This is called the low water test.

As long as the water covers this connection this petcock will remain comparatively cool, and if opened, water will come out. If, however, the water should get below this connection, the pipe will fill with steam and the end will become burning hot, and if the petcock were opened steam would come out. By this means the operator can determine whether or not the water in the boiler is getting near the point where the fusible plug would melt out.

When the boiler is cold, whether or not it contains water, the water will always be low in the glass. Consequently, before lighting the burner, one of the petcocks should be opened and the siphon valve opened, so as to vent the boiler. If water come out of the petcock, it indicates that the water in the boiler is above that point. If not, it is below that point. The petcock should be kept open long enough to allow any water that might be in the tube to run out, provided it happened to be held there by capillary attraction when the water in the boiler was really below the petcock.

The operator should never start the fire until he is certain that there is water in the boiler.

The connection betwen the bottom of the boiler and the bottom of the water column must be kept clear, otherwise the water might remain in this column, even if there were none in the boiler.

This is cleaned by closing valve C and opening the petcock A, when there is steam in the boiler. This will blow out any sediment that may be in the lower end of the water column.

If the water indicator is to be used in freezing weather, a mixture of glycerine or alcohol and water, one to one, is employed in the "U" tube to prevent freezing.

It is sometimes desirable to test the indicator to see if it be working properly. To do this, the boiler should be well filled with water, say considerably above connection D.

With steam up and petcock B opened, hot water or steam will flow through the boiler chamber of the indicator, and if the indicator be working properly, the water should rise in the glass.

Now, if petcock B be closed and cold water be pumped through the water chamber of the indicator by the hand pump, the boiler chamber will be cooled which will cause the water to again fall in the glass.

The pumping may be done with the by-pass open which saves pumping against the boiler pressure.

The familiar torch method is followed in starting the burner, a small gasoline torch being provided for the purpose. To start the fire successfully, both main burner nozzles and the pilot nozzle should be heated and then the pilot lighted. To do this, the valve is opened one turn and the torch flame immediately pointed into the peek hole, its slide having been previously opened. After the pilot is lighted, this slide should be closed before turning on the main fire. The latter operation should be performed by opening the main valve slowly so that the fire will come on gradually.

The Fusible Plug.—If the water in a fire tube boiler were all evaporated, and the fire kept burning, the boiler would become so heated as to cause it to leak badly.

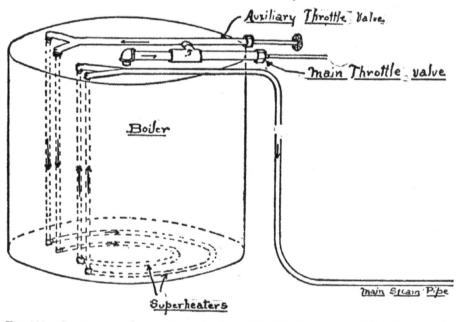

Fig. 392.—Steam connections and superheaters of the Stanley system. The elbows on the superheater, main steam pipe and fusible fitting are made on a taper and driven through the boiler tubes. They are removed by prying under the elbow and hammering at the same time.

To avoid this, the boiler is equipped with a fusible plug. When the water in the boiler gets within three inches of the lower tube sheet, the plug melts, and the noisy escape of steam notifies the operator, who immediately shuts off the fire, both pilot and main burner, thus protecting the boiler from injury. When the plug blows and the fire is shut off, it is a good plan to continue running till the steam pressure is so reduced as to compel a halt. The by-pass is then closed and water pumped into the boiler till it is cool enough to allow the plug to be removed, a new lead inserted and the plug replaced.

The pumping may then be continued till the boiler is one-third full when the fire may be lighted. Usually this can be done without reheating the torch, provided the renewing of the plug has been quickly done. The material in the plug is common lead which melts at 618° Fahr.

The Lane System.—The power plant of the Lane steamer consists of the following elements:

1. Cross compound engine;
2. Condenser;
3. Feed water heater;
4. Semi-flash boiler;
5. Control: automatic regulating devices for fuel and water;
6. Auxiliary Control: hand regulating devices;
7. Fuel and water tanks and connections.

The boiler is designed for a working pressure of 500 pounds, the running pressure being 300 pounds.

It consists, as previously described, of a series of semi-flash coils, a separator, and a fire tube shell, the combination delivering to the engine a supply of steam slightly superheated by the fire tubes which is favorable to economical operation.

Fuel Connections.—The burner is started by the operation of one valve. There is within the burner casing an igniting torch below the vaporizing tubes. This torch consists of a perforated tube enclosed in an absorbent, non-combustible envelope. The tube is connected with a cup conveniently located outside the burner.

In addition to the valve for operating the burner, there is a second valve in the fuel feed pipe, accessible from the driver's seat, and also a valve for controlling the pilot light; these valves are used only occasionally.

The burner is open ⅛ inch between the ⅜ inch diameter burner tubes, so as to ensure a sufficient supply of oxygen for complete combustion, and the 2½ ins. dia. mixing tube is carried 3 ins. outside of the burner casing so as to cool the mixture enough to prevent firing back into the burner and mixing tubes.

The blow out of the burner flame is prevented by reducing the inner mixing tube to 1¼ ins. inside diameter and by fitting a cowl closed on the top, bottom, front and outside, air taken in at the rear of the cowl, which acts both as a wind shield and mud guard.

The Gasoline Tank.—The fuel supply is contained in a cylindrical tank having oval ends. A tank of seventeen gallons capacity is provided for the twenty horse power engine and one holding twenty-two gallons for the thirty horse power engine. A pressure of 60 pounds is maintained in the tank, this pressure being maintained automatically. The air pump is located on the left side of the engine.

The maximum air pressure available is determined by the pump clearance. This clearance space (between the pump valves) can be adjusted through a considerable range by a screw reached from the outside.

An independent steam pump is provided for emergency use.

The Water Connections.—The feed water to the boiler is regularly pumped by a crosshead pump on the engine, which has a capacity in excess of requirements, the level in boiler being regulated by an automatic by pass connected to the delivery pipe from engine pump which, when open, allows the water pumped to return to the tank again, but if closed all the water pumped must go into the boiler.

FIG. 393.—The Lane water indicator as it appears on the dash. It forms a part of the by pass apparatus and its essential feature is an expansion tube. It is connected by pipe to the boiler at the desired water level.

There is also for emergency use an independent steam pump, the reserve power of boiler permitting its use either standing or running, and a hand pump under the foot board.

The Water Tank.—This is located between the condenser and the boiler, and is piped to the engine feed water pump, the water steam pump, and the water hand pump.

Connection with the condenser is near the top of the tank and a water overflow pipe three-quarter inch below the condenser pipe, top end affords a steam exit.

The Water Indicator.—This device for ascertaining the water level in the boiler consists of a dial indicator located on the dash as shown in fig. 393, operated by an automatic by pass illustrated in fig. 394. Its essential feature is an expansion tube´which is located above the hood and in front of the dash and connected by pipe to the boiler at the desired water level.

If water in boiler be below that point the expansion tube will be filled with steam and being hot is consequently in an expanded condition, and by suitable mechanical means it then holds the by pass valve shut and the indicator hand in its corresponding position.

When the water level in the boiler rises above the point of connection, the pipe becomes filled with water and the tube cools. It consequently contracts, opens the by pass valve, and moves the indicator hand.

A second expansion tube acts from a lower point on the boiler and moves the indicator hand still further around if the water level recedes below the normal.

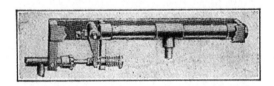

Fig. 394.—The Lane automatic by pass. This is operated thermostatically, that is, by the expansion and contraction of a metal rod brought about by temperature changes which depend on the height of the water in the boiler.

The Condenser.—The exhaust from the engine, instead of being discharged into the atmosphere, as is done in the Stanley system, is led by suitable piping to a condenser in which it is cooled, condensed and returned to the water tank.

The compound type of engine is especially adapted to run condensing, as the steam is exhausted at a lower pressure, than is done with a simple engine. The exhaust steam is not so hot and hence, the proportions of the condenser capable of condensing the steam is less than would be required with a simple engine.

The Lane condenser as shown in fig. 395, consists of five vertical rows of flattened brass tubes opening into a top header to which the exhaust is piped, and to an unobstructed base cavity which is piped to the top of the water tank.

The discharge of this condenser to the water tank is intermittent, a quart or so at each discharge, from the base cavity of the condenser.

This condenser piping avoids a water pump between the condenser and the water tank, though the bottom of the condenser is about 30 ins. below the tank top.

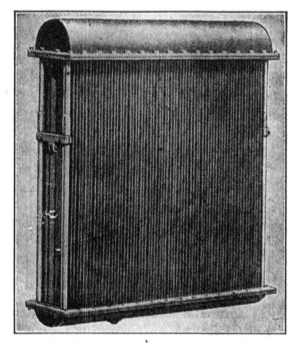

FIG. 395.—The Lane condenser for condensing the exhaust steam from the engine. It is constructed of thin, flat, brass tubes arranged vertically, with their edges toward the front, and air spaces between them. They are all secured to a common header with detachable covers at top and bottom; steam being introduced in the top one and the water piped from the lower one directly back to the dome of the tank. There is a still larger vent from the dome of tank to the atmosphere below the car. There is no pump or outboard relief, the water being returned from condenser to tank by back pressure, which rarely exceeds one pound and is usually much less. Inside the top header is a coil for heating the feed water on its way to the boiler.

Control System.—Before beginning to raise steam the driver tries the gauge cocks screwed directly into the boiler shell; if no water shows at the gauge the hand force pump is worked to fill the boiler to the gauge from the water tank. There are 3 gauge cocks; water at the lower cock indicates enough to raise steam.

To raise steam: 1, the air down draft damper on top of the hood is opened to permit a free passage of air to the burner; 2, a door in the side of the hood at the bottom of the boiler is opened, giving access to the "heater cup" into which about a fluid ounce of alcohol is poured, this going to a horizontal pipe, perforated and asbestos clothed, placed below the gasoline vaporizing tube; 3, the asbestos pipe clothing alcohol wick is lighted, and 4, a hand needle valve between the vaporizer and the burner middle mixing tube is opened, to permit the gasoline vapor injection to the burner main middle tube.

As soon as the gasoline vapor begins to escape from the small holes in the tops of the burner tubes it is fired by the flame of the heating tube and everything is left as it is until the steam gauge shows 300 lbs., and the car is ready to run.

The operation of getting up steam usually takes about ten minutes.

As soon as steam is raised, the top air damper is closed and steam is turned on to the forced draught ejector, which sucks air up through the burner and boiler flues and then forces the product of combustion down to the open lower end of the vertical down draft tube, which is about 5 ins. diameter and extends downward to about the bottom of the burner.

The engine can be started by moving the ratchet retained hand lever on top of the steering wheel, as soon as there is steam pressure enough in the boiler, and after the engine begins working the water level and fuel supply are automatically controlled.

There are two vertical levers: the latched, outside one, is pushed forward to apply the external rear hub drum brake bands through a full length evener. The latched, inside hand lever, works the tumbling shaft to make the link valve motion give an earlier or later cut off, and the reverse.

The forced draft steam valve is opened and closed by a small T-handle on top of the steering wheel.

There is one pedal on the foot board, which is pushed forward to apply the balance gear drum brake band, ordinary brake.

A plunger pedal at the left of the steering column is depressed to change the engine from compound to simple, the engine returning to compound as soon as this plunger pedal is released.

The stop valve between the boiler and throttle is opened and closed by a wooden hand wheel at the front left of the foot board.

A small handle in the middle of the front board rear face controls the boiler water supply independently.

A long vertical glass tube at the right of the front board shows the water level in the tank.

The large, hand worked plunger glass oil cup at the top left of the front board, supplies lubricating oil to the two independent steam pumps.

The Auxiliary Control System.—This is operated by eight valve handles as shown exposed in fig. 396 by the removal of the cover.

It should be understood that this auxiliary control system has nothing to do with the regular control of the car, as handled by the driver when running on the road, but simply controls the auxiliary pump driving and oiling, supplying steam driven water and air pumps and directing the hand pump oil supply.

Fig. 396.—The Lane System, engine placing and control, footboards and auxiliary control cover removed. The illustration shows the inclined engine cylinders, the independent steam water pump and the hand water pump, last resort for supplying the boiler water. The hand cylinder and steam pump oiler, a glass cup with a hand force pump is shown at the upper left of the front board real face. Next to the right is the dial indicator which shows the boiler water level. The next dial shows the air pressure in the gasoline tank, and the third dial is the steam gauge. The glass tube at the right, TG, shows the water level in the water tank. The auxiliary control cover, when removed, discloses 8 handles, top left handle opens the hand oil pump to the independent steam water and air pump steam cylinders, the top row middle handle works the compressed air valve to either send air to the gasoline tank or to the tire inflating tube, or to open air if tire inflating hose be removed. The right hand top valve is the steam pump steam admission. The left handle in the middle row opens the oil lead from the hand pump to the engine steam chest. The middle handle controls the stop valve in the line from the engine driven air pump to the gasoline tank. The right handle in the low line opens steam to the steam water pump. The fusible plug screw T-handle is seen at the left of the front board auxiliary control opening. The metal wheel just below works the stop valve between the fusible plug and the steam boiler. SPP is a plunger pedal which is depressed to change the engine from compound to simple. BP is the ordinary brake pedal.

The emergency water and air pumping, when required, is done by independent steam pumps the air pump being available for both tank pressure and tire inflating, so that the driver is relieved from all pump work.

Cycle of Operation.—With steam up and the car running, the feed pump on the engine forces water to the boiler.

The water passes, first through the feed water heater located in the top of the condenser, where it absorbs heat from the exhaust steam, before entering the boiler preheating coils.

In passing through the preheater coils, the temperature of the water is considerably raised, and it is discharged from these coils into the *separator,* as water and steam.

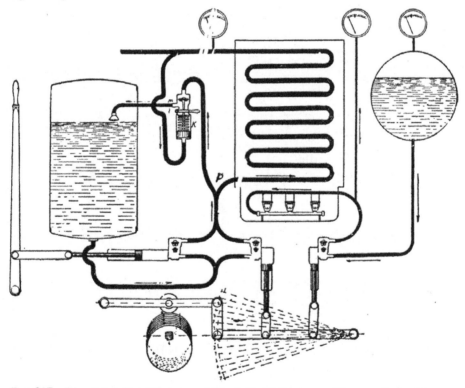

Fɪɢ. 397.—The Serpollet Water and Fuel Feed System. The method of hanging the stepped cam controlling the pump stroke may be here understood.

The water is led from the separator to the bottom of the tubular shell and the steam to the top.

Saturated steam is taken from the top of the shell, whence it is delivered to the engine in a slightly superheated state.

The steam after working expansively in the high pressure cylinder of the engine approaching a state of saturation, is exhausted into a larger or low pressure cylinder where it is again expanded and finally exhausted into the condenser; here it is practically all condensed under ordinary conditions and the water returned to the tank to again begin the cycle as just described.

When the engine is heavily loaded as in ascending steep hills, the condenser may be overtaxed and only condense a portion of the steam. This together with other losses, such as leaks from the stuffing boxes, etc., have to be made up by replenishing the water supply in the tank.

The efficiency of the condenser depends, largely on the temperature of the atmosphere. This is clearly indicated by the difference in its operation in winter and summer.

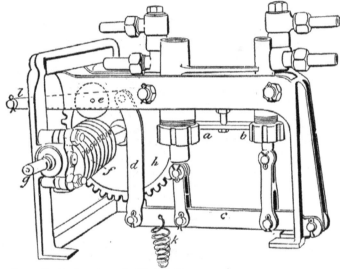

FIG. 398.—Serpollet's Fuel and Water Pumps. The water pump, *a*, and the fuel pump, *b*, are operated from the lever. *c*. This is given an up-and-down movement by the link, *d*, whose stroke is varied by the stepped cam, *f*, on which bears the roller, *e*, on the rod pivoted at *i*. The rotary movement of the cam shaft, *g*, is imparted by the spur wheel, *h*.

Flash Steam Generation: The Serpollet System.—The flash method of producing steam, was introduced by Serpollet in 1889. He invented an instantaneous generator which is described in the chapter on boilers.

The successful operation of a flash generator depends largely on the design of proper automatic devices and connections for regulating the supply of feed water and fuel. The office of these automatics is to so control the generation of steam that a supply, varying to meet the engine demands, may be had at a certain pre determined pressure and degree of superheat.

It is possible to maintain the feed at the proper rate and quantity by automatic pressure regulators, such as are used in connection with steam carriage burners, or else by some system of uniform regulation for fuel and water pumps.

The latter theory was adopted in the Serpollet system being worked out by Gardener.

As shown in the diagram, the fuel is fed to the burner, and the water to the boiler, through pumps, both of which are operated from the same shaft. The fuel pump is smaller than the water pump and its stroke is also shorter, as is obviously necessary. This is accomplished by the use

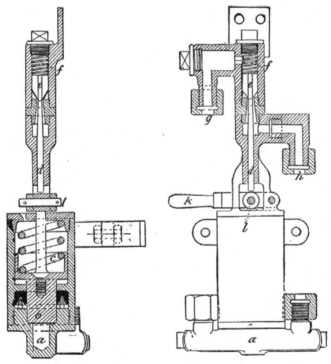

Fig. 399.—The "Safety Valve," or Automatic By-Pass Regulator of the Serpollet Boiler Feed System. The steam, admitted through the tube, *a*, after it has reached a certain pressure, opens the valve, *b*, compressing the spring, *c*. By this action the rod, *d*, forces up the valve, *e*, and the spring, *f*, thus enabling the water from the pump to pass from the pipe, *g*, through the pipe, *h*, to the water tank.

of a stepped cam, consisting of a row of eccentric discs, of varying eccentricity, which, placed upon the rotating shaft, may be slid in either direction, thus varying the lift. By shifting the cam inward toward the driving spur the strokes of both oil and water pumps may be varied from zero to maximum; the cam surface being efficient in giving a greater or shorter inward stroke, and in permitting an outward stroke of equal length under stress of the spiral spring attached below the pump operating lever.

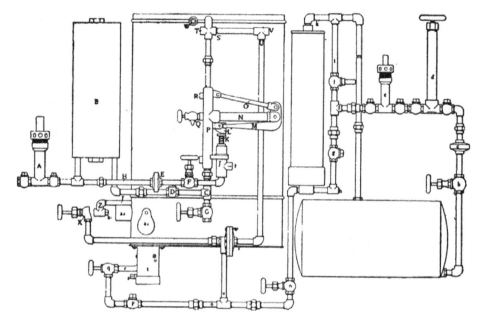

A-Power Feed Water Pump
B-Feed Water Heater
C-Connection for Boiler Feed, Water
    Regulator and Bottom Blow Down
D-Boiler Feed Check Valve
E-Water Regulator Gauze Strainer
F-Globe Valve
G-Boiler Blow Down
H-By-pass Line to Water Regulator Valve
I-Water Regulator Valve
    By-pass Connection
J-Water Regulator Valve
K-Water Regulator Valve Cam
L-Water Regulator Valve Cam
M-Water Regulator Lever
N-Water Regulator Expansion Tube
O-Water Regulator Lever Brace
P-Water Regulator Water Column
Q-Water Regulator Pet Cock
R-Top Connection for Gauge Glass if Desired
S-Water Regulator
    Water Column Connection
T-Connection for Steam Gauge, Pumps, Etc.
U-Steam line to Fuel Regulator
V-Connection for Pop Safety Valve, Etc.
W-Steam Connection for Engine

a-Main Fuel Tank   b-Globe Valve
c-Gauze Strainer   d-Hand Fuel Pump
e-Power Fuel Pump
f-Connection to Automatic Fuel Feed
g-Check Valve
h-Connection to Fuel Gauge
i-Automatic Fuel Feed
j-By-pass Valve of Automatic Fuel Feed
k-Return Line of Leakage by Piston
l-Fuel By-pass Line
m-Return Line to Tank of k and i
n-Globe Valve
o-Branch Fuel Line to Pilot
p-Check Valve with Check Removed and
    Sponge in its place for a Dirt Strainer
q-Pilot Valve   r-Pilot Vaporizer
s-Pilot Nozzle   t-Pilot Box
u-Screw for Holding
    Pilot Vaporizer Straight
v-Fuel Line to Main Burner
w-Automatic Fuel Regulator
x-Main Burner Valve
y-Main Burner Vaporizer
z-Main Burner Elbow
a1-Main Burner Nozzle
a2-Main Burner Mixing Tube
a3-Slide Over Hole for Observing Fire

FIG. 400.—The Ofeldt system of automatic fuel and water regulation as applied to the
Ofeldt boiler. The operation of the water regulator is explained under Fig. 374.
The automatic fuel feed i, consists of a brass tube four inches in diameter by eighteen
to thirty-six inches long, capped on one end and plugged on the other. Inside this
tube is a piston and a spiral spring, the latter being the whole length of the tube. A
safety valve is attached to the by-pass line, which can be set to carry whatever
pressure is desired. A connection is also made to permit whatever fuel leaks by the
piston to return to the tank. A hand fuel pump d, is provided for use when starting
the burner. The operation is as follows: Fuel is forced by a fuel pump e, on crosshead
of engine or else where through connection f to the cylinder and against the piston,
which in turn compresses the spring and the latter gives the pressure to the fuel.
The fuel is forced to the burner through the line containing valve n. A safety valve
j, can be adjusted to carry any pressure desired; i, is the overflow connection to tank.

These operations may be readily understood by a study of Fig. 397, which is sketched from the actual machine.

The liquid fuel and the water, being thus varied in the amounts given forth by the pumps, are forced, the one into the vaporizing tube, passing over the burner, the other into the flattened and nested tubes of the generator. By this means the heat is increased in ratio with the quantity of water injected, and the working pressure may be regulated to any desired limit. When, however, the pressure has arisen above a certain fixed point—it is generally fixed at about 355 pounds per square inch—it is able to open the spring safety valve, k, shown attached to the steam pipe, fig. 399, thus also opening the by pass, m, so that the water from the feed pump is thrown back into the tank.

The water from the pump may be forced through the spring valve, instead of into the generator, by the closing of a check valve at *P*, under steam pressure.

The connections may be readily understood from the diagram, which also shows a hand operated pump for making the initial injection of water into the generator tubes previous to starting the engine.

The construction and operation of the automatic by pass regulator, or "safety valve," may be understood from Fig. 399.

Strictly speaking, a flash generator needs no safety valve, but its operation demands some method of preventing flooding when the pressure is high enough.

The White System.—The method of regulating the supply of water and fuel to the steam generator of the White steamer, presents an inter-relationship of water, gasoline and steam that is highly interesting, exceedingly unique, and, as demonstrated daily by the cars, is most satisfactory. Broadly speaking, the operation of the system, depends on three factors:

1. Water;
2. Gasoline;
3. Steam.

The water carried in the tank must be delivered in proper quantities to the generator, where it is flashed into steam.

Gasoline must be delivered in the proper quantities to the burner so that the correct heat is maintained to generate and superheat the steam.

The steam must be supplied in a highly superheated state, in requisite quantities to meet the varying engine demands.

Since a generator, or flash boiler as it is sometimes called, carries no reserve volume of water or steam, the intensity of the fire and the quantity of feed water supplied, must be continually varied to correspond with operative conditions.

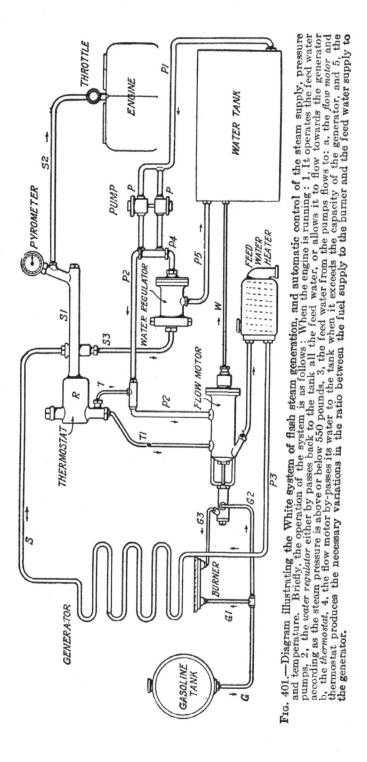

FIG. 401.—Diagram illustrating the White system of flash steam generation, and automatic control of the steam supply, pressure and temperature. Briefly, the operation of the system is as follows: When the engine is running: 1, It operates the feed water pumps, 2, the *water regulator* either by passes back to the tank all the feed water, or allows it to flow towards the generator according as the steam pressure is above or below 550 pounds, 3, the feed water from the pumps flows to: a, the *flow motor* and b, the *thermostat*, 4, the flow motor by-passes its water to the tank when it exceeds the capacity of the generator, and 5, the thermostat produces the necessary variations in the ratio between the fuel supply to the burner and the feed water supply to the generator.

In this system, 1, the steam pressure is made to control the supply of water delivered to the generator, 2, the water pressure controls the gasoline feed, and 3, the steam temperature has a bearing on the water supply. Hence, there is an inseparable interrelationship among the gasoline, water and steam.

The system is diagrammatically illustrated in Fig. 401. In the water system, the water must go from the water tank to the generator; it is drawn from the tank by two positively driven pumps P on the engine through pipe P1. From each pump it follows the piping P2 to the flow motor, whose workings will be considered later; thence to the feed water heater, which is simply a coil of pipe at the engine to heat the water before it goes through pipe P3 to the generator.

The pumps P are constantly working when the engine is running, always pumping the same amount of water per minute, at the same engine speed; however, it is evident that sometimes more steam is needed than at others at the same engine speed, and consequently more water will be needed.

The first device for regulating the flow of water is the *water regulator* into which the water flows by pipe P4. Its entrance to the regulator is governed by a valve, which only opens when the steam pressure gets above 600 pounds.

This opening is accomplished by steam pressure through the pipe S3, acting on a diaphragm which opens the valve, letting the water enter the regulator and escape through the pipe P5 back to the water tank, so that when there is 600 pounds pressure, which is the working figure, the water delivered by the pumps P *does not follow* the course to pipe P2 to the generator, *but is by-passed* through pipes P4 and P5 to the water tank.

With the water delivered to the generator, gasoline must be delivered also in order to have heat to generate steam. The gasoline is carried under pressure in the tank at the rear of the chassis, and starts on its trip to the burner through pipe G, the first branch G1 goes to the pilot light which must be kept burning all the time the car is running.

This pilot light is a small flame whose heat does not enter into changing the water into steam, but serves solely to light the gasoline vapor in the burner, as it must be realized the burner flame is out one minute and on the next, according to the amount of steam required; the automatics of the system shut off and turn on the burner according to the demand, but the pilot light always burns to serve as the match for ignition.

The gasoline, which goes to generate steam, follows pipe G2, into the pointed end of the *flow motor,* where its flow is regulated by a valve, opened and closed according to the water pressure, and finally reaches the burner through the pipe G3. Some gasoline controlling valves are not shown in the diagram, the object of this diagram being merely to show the elements of the system.

Having the water and gasoline at the generator, steam is the product and its course to the engine is next in order. It follows the main pipe S, which, before reaching the engine, has an en-

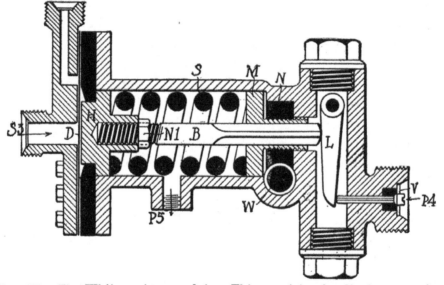

FIG. 402.—The White water regulator. This consists of a diaphragm valve operated by the steam pressure in the generator.

larged section S1 which contains the copper rod of the *thermostat,* and then reaches the engine through the continuation pipe S2.

There is a branch S3 for conveying steam pressure to the water regulator.

The *pyrometer* indicates the temperature of the steam.

In brief, the action of the thermostat is to govern an additional supply of water to the generator. When the temperature of the steam gets too high, it means more water is needed in the generator, and the thermostat delivers this extra water supply as follows: The higher temperature of the steam expands, or lengthens a rod, which through a rocker arm opens a valve, allowing water from the main supply pipe to flow through the pipe T and thence through pipe T1 into the *flow motor*.

As soon as the temperature of the steam drops to normal, the thermostat, through the copper rod, automatically shuts off this water supply. There is a further control on the water by the flow motor, which, at a certain time, by-passes through the pipe W water to the tank.

The exact operation and construction of the water regulator, the thermostat, and the flow motor follow.

The Water Regulator.—This device is shown in fig. 402, and has as its most essential feature a triple diaphragm D against one side of which the steam from the engine bears through the pipe S3. On the other side of the diaphragm is a metal member H, adjustably secured to the shaft B, and which member at its opposite end bears up against the lever L, the lower end of which contacts with the stem of the valve V. This valve V regulates the water entrance P4 from the pumps, so that when the valve opens water enters and escapes by way of pipe P5 to the water tank. The coil spring S normally holds the piece H against the diaphragm so that the valve V closes. However, when the steam pressure through S3 exceeds a certain figure, the diaphragm is forced to the right compressing the spring S and opening the valve V, allowing the water to flow as mentioned. As indicated in fig. 401 the water is by-passed to the water tank.

The Flow Motor.—As shown in fig. 403, this consists of three parts, 1, the right section W in which the water control is adjusted, 2, the small end portion G at the left which controls the gasoline flow to the burner, and 3, the connective portion C.

Water enters direct from the pumps through the opening WE, passing out through WD. Its control of the water is by the piston P which when moved leftward by the water pressure uncovers the groove G, thus allowing the water to pass it and escape through the connection WD. This piston P is in rigid connection with the gasoline controlling valve GV in the left compartment of

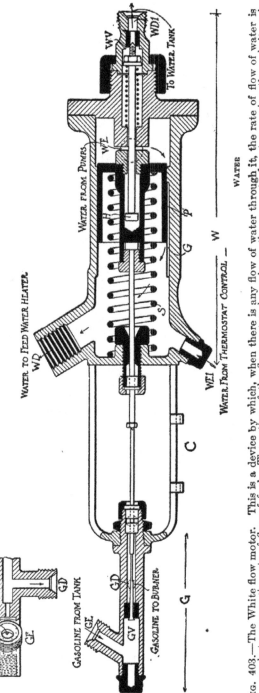

FIG. 403.—The White flow motor. This is a device by which, when there is any flow of water through it, the rate of flow of water is made to govern the rate of flow of fuel. The action of the flow motor depends on the amount of water passing through it and not on the pressure.

the flow motor, so that the valve GV also moves leftward permitting gasoline, which enters from the gasoline tank through the opening GE to escape to the burner through another opening GD.

The faster the engine runs the greater the volume of water delivered by the pumps and the greater the water pressure against the piston P the further will it be moved leftward against the spring S, the more water will pass it, and proportionately the more gasoline will go to the burner.

When the piston P has traveled leftward a certain distance it comes in contact with the end H, which is on the stem of the valve WV, and a further leftward movement of the piston P opens this water valve, which allows water to escape through the by-pass valve WD1 and thence to the water tank. This by-pass valve opens only when too much water is being pumped, and lets a portion go back to the tank. The entrance WE1 is for water admitted from the thermostat control.

The Thermostat.—This device is a regulator, acted on by the temperature of the steam after it leaves the generator, but before it reaches the engine. The operation of the thermostat is shown in Fig. 404. Steam enters through SE from the generator and de-

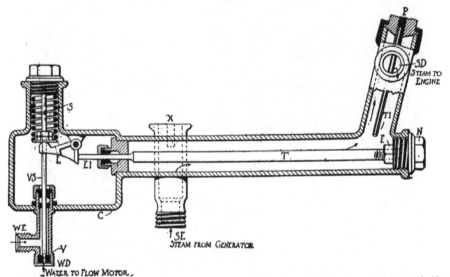

FIG. 404.—The White thermostat for regulating the temperature of the steam. In connection with the thermostat, is a pyrometer in which the temperature of the steam is shown on a gauge.

parts through opening SD to the engine. In its passage it contacts with a copper rod T anchored rigidly at one end E in the casing, and at the end E1 bearing upon a lever L which bears upon a collar on the valve stem VS. The high temperature of the steam lengthens the rod T which through the lever L, opens the valve allowing water to flow to the flow motor and thence to the generator, thus reducing the steam temperature. The flow motor lets gasoline go to the burner in proportion to the water sent to the generator, and if too much water is being pumped, it returns a portion of the water direct to the water tank.

To Start the White Car.—After the water and fuel tanks are filled, air pumped to 30 pounds by the hand air pump, *and the generator pumped full of water,* the sub-burner V, fig. 405, is then lighted.

The sub-burner, will in about five minutes, sufficiently heat the **vaporizer** N to vaporize the fuel for the main burner.

Fig. 405.—Side view of dash of White car. The parts shown are as follows: 42, pyrometer; 43, relief cock lever; 82, cut off pedal adjusting pin; 91, cut off pedal; 93, simpling valve pedal; 94, air pump valve pedal; 95, brake pedal; 103, emergency gear lever; 104, reverse lever; 105, brake lever; 108, cylinder oiler pump; 109, crank case oiler pump; 111, blow off valve; 112, driving shaft; 113, emergency gear rod; 120, flow motor; 209, air and vaporizer gauge; 210, steam gauge; D, main sub-burner valve; F, sub-burner adjusting valve; G, warming up valve; HA, pipe connecting valve G with vaporizer N; J, main burner valve; O, vaporizer nozzle; V, sub-burner casing; W, sub-burner casing door.

To start the main burner, the warming up valve G is slightly opened. This allows the fuel to flow from the main fuel line into the vaporizer N, through pipe HA, without passing through any regulator. Should the vaporizer not be thoroughly heated **a** few drops of raw fuel may drip from the vaporizer nozzle O. If this drop be continuous, valve G should be closed to allow the vaporizer to become hotter.

It is advisable in starting to open and close valve G intermittently four or five times, the interval of opening being about two seconds. By this means any sudden rush of fuel is avoided before the vaporizer gets thoroughly heated.

Fig. 406.—The White dash as seen from the driver's seat. The operating devices shown in the cut are as follows: AA, hand air pump; 42, pyrometer; 43, relief cock lever; 82, cut off pedal adjusting pin; 91, cut off pedal; 93, simpling valve pedal; 94, air pump valve pedal; 95, brake pedal; 108, cylinder oiler pump; 109, crank case oiler pump; 209, air and vaporizer pressure gauge; 210, steam gauge. The small wheel concentric with the steering wheel is the throttle.

With the main fire satisfactorily started, valve G may be left open about one-quarter turn. The safety valve should now be closely watched. This is important, as the steam pressure runs up very quickly and any inattention when the fire is first turned on may result in excessive pressure and cause the safety valve to open. As soon as the pressure reaches 300 pounds, the surplus water collected in the pipe should be blown off through the blow off valve 111 fig. 405, being careful to close this valve as soon as steam appears. The steam pressure is then allowed to again reach 300 pounds. The warming up valve G, is now adjusted so that there is not over twenty pounds showing on the vaporizer pressure gauge 209.

With gear lever 103 in the central or neutral position, so that the engine may run without moving the car, and with cylinder relief cocks opened by lever 43, the engine is started by first pushing the starting pedal 93 all the way forward and then opening slightly the throttle.

The water should be worked out of the engine easily and carefully, by cautious handling of the throttle and by working the reverse lever back and forth from forward to reverse position until the engine is warmed up and will turn over freely. Valve G should now be closed and valve J opened. In warming up the engine, just enough steam should be admitted to the cylinders to keep the engine moving slowly *until all the water is out* when it will run smoothly. Until all the water is out, the engine will run jerkily on account of this water filling the clearance spaces in passing the dead centres, hence, the engine should not be forced by too much throttle opening, but the water should be worked out gradually.

When engine runs smoothly, the relief cocks may be closed by throwing lever 43 over to the right hand position. To get the cylinders thoroughly heated, the foot is transferred from the starting pedal to the cut off pedal 91 and the latter pressed forward so that steam will be admitted for full stroke. The engine should be run thus for about one-half minute and then for two or three minutes with cut off pedal in its normal position, allowing the steam to work expansively.

The air presure is now pumped to 50 pounds, and the sub-burner adjusted to this pressure after which the car may be started.

Summary.—The operation of the White system may be stated briefly as follows:

1. When the engine is running, it operates the feed water pumps.

2. The *water regulator* either by-passes back to the tank all of the water delivered by the pumps, when the steam pressure *exceeds* 550 pounds, or it allows all of the water to flow toward the generator when the steam pressure is *less than* 550 pounds.

That is to say, the water supply is controlled by an "all on" or "all off" action—the required variations being due to changes, automatically brought about in the frequency and durations of these "all on" periods.

3. The feed water from the pumps flows through two branches:

   a. The flow motor branch;
   b. The thermostat branch.

The water going through the flow motor branch moves a piston in the flow motor which in turn, proportionately opens the fuel valve. It also opens the by-pass valve in the flow motor, when the rate of water flow into the flow motor exceeds the capacity of the generator, and by-passes the excess water.

The water going through the thermostat branch, is increased or decreased in amount by the action of the thermostat in opening or closing the water valve of the thermostat. This action produces the necessary variations in the ratio between the fuel supply to the burner and feed water supply to the generator.

The practical result of the automatic actions of the different members of the system is to maintain the steam at a practically uniform high pressure with a considerable degree of superheat under all working conditions.

Flash Steam Data.—The following results were obtained in a series of tests made on the steam plant of the White steamer. For the purpose of testing, the engine was mounted on the frame of a car in the same manner as in the completed motor car, which was, however, supported by solid posts instead of by wheels. The main shaft of the engine was connected to an Alden Prony brake and all the horse power calculations were for *brake* horse power, it being deemed not advisable to use the indicator on account of the small size and high speed of the engine.

During certain of the various tests the boiler pressure averaged 595 pounds, the steam chest pressure varied with the load from 152 pounds to 427 pounds, averaging 303 pounds. The temperature of the steam near the boiler average 783° Fahr., and that in the steam chest 757°. This indicates that the steam leaving the boiler was superheated nearly 300°, that entering the steam chest about 340°, and that exhausted about 28°, so that the steam in its entire passage through the engine remained in a superheated condition.

The actual evaporation from feed water at 78° to steam with the pressure and temperature as shown averaged 10.34 pounds of water per pound of gasoline. The equivalent evaporation "from and at 212°" per square foot of heating surface per hour was 13 pounds for the highest result.

The engine developed a horse power on the brake at its highest load with a consumption of 11.96 pounds of feed water per hour. This remarkably small consumption of feed water shows the value of superheating the steam, it being well known in steam engineering that the saving in feed water due to superheating is a little over one per cent. for each 10° of superheat.

The important facts brought out by the tests are: 1, the feed water consumption of a small compound non-condensing engine using highly superheated steam is very small; 2, when a flash boiler is used, the required amount of heating surface to run the engine is approximately one square foot per brake horse power.

The following table shows the results of some of Prof. Carpenter's tests:

No. of Test.	Revolutions per Minute.	Net Brake Load Lbs.	Brake Horse Power.	Total Lbs.		Water per Brake Horse Power per Hour Lbs.	B. T. U. Above 212° to Engine.				Actual Evaporation per Pound Gasoline.	Actual Evaporation per Square Foot of Heating Surface per Hour.
				Water per Hour Lbs.	Gasoline per Hour Lbs.		Per Lb. of Steam.			B. T. U. per Brake Horse Power per Minute.		
							Saturated Part.	Superheated Part.	Total.			
14	850	72	25.50	320.0	31.125	12.55	1034	198	1232	257	10.30	6.98
15	850	85	30.1	370.0	31.125	12.29	1036	196	1234	252	10.42	8.07
15a	850	85	30.1	370.0	35.5	12.29	1038	196	1234	252	10.42	8.07
15b	850	85	30 1	371.5	35.5	12.30	1035	202	1237	253	10.45	8.11
16	850	96	34.0	408.8	39.25	12.05	1036	200	1236	246	10.40	8.87
17	850	115	40.7	488.0	48.0	11.96	1037	197	1224	244	10.15	10.7
								av. =	1228	av.	10.34	

CHAPTER FORTY.

The Term Electric Vehicle.—This is broadly applicable to a great variety of either passenger or freight carrying machines which are propelled by electric energy supplied from either storage batteries or electric generators installed on the machines themselves, but does not include the storage cars used for electric traction or railway purposes.

The principal types of electric vehicles which are commercially successful at the present time are:

1. Electric automobiles, represented by various types of roadsters, coupes, phætons, cabs, etc., suitable for the use of physicians, business men and others, in city service.

2. Heavy electric trucks and vans for moving merchandise, and for delivering purposes.

3. Gasoline-electric trucks, which represent an attempt to overcome the lack of flexibility of internal combustion engine by combining it with a direct current generator and storage battery.

The Motors.—For electric vehicles these are, in all respects, quite similar to railway motors, except that they are designed to operate safely at several hundred per cent. overload, whenever necessary, as for instance, when propelling the vehicles up a steep hill or incline or over a heavy road, so that in spite of their low power rating, they yield a high percentage of efficiency and are capable of operating under several different pressures, and a corresponding number of different speeds.

The accepted forms of the mechanical part of the transmission or drive are of the *herringbone* gear and the *double reduction* types, while the direct connected spur gear has fallen into general disuse.

The motor is usually hung above the springs, thus being protected from the jars of travel. There are, however, several forms of double reduction using high speed, light motors by means of various combinations of gear and chain, with silent or roller chains or herringbone gears for the first reduction, and single or double roller chains, level gears or herringbone gears for the second reduction.

Light Electric Vehicles.—These are of various types, such as roadsters, Victorias, phætons, runabouts and coupes, and are equipped with batteries which have a capacity ranging from 75 to

Fig. 407.—Heavy truck of the Vehicle Equipment Co. Carrying capacity, 4 tons; speed, 6 miles per hour; travel radius on one charge of battery, 25 miles.

100 miles per charge, with controller arrangements for providing speeds varying from 6 to 26 miles per hour. In these cases the number of cells in each battery may vary from 10 to 30 according to the make and number of plates in each cell. The number of pates in each cell may vary from 11 to 21.

Electric Trucks for City Service.—Under certain traffic conditions and surface requirements, the superior mobility of the gasoline engine truck effects a saving in drivers sufficient to compensate for the higher maintenance charges, but when the number of active trucks are the same in each case, the electric truck becomes more economical on account of its lower maintenace charge.

The gasoline engine truck has the advantage in all classes of service requiring a greater mileage than that which is conveniently obtainable with the electric truck, but the greater portion of city delivery service is well within the limits of the safe operative mileage radius of the electric trucks built at the present time.

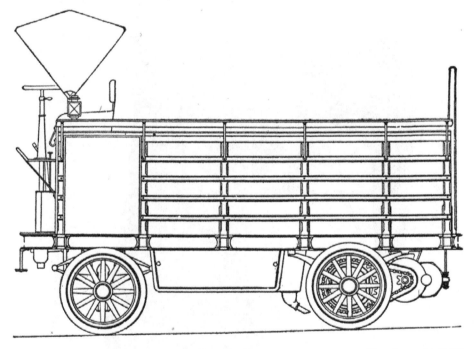

Fig. 408.—Chain and Sprocket Double Reduction for Heavy Trucks. As here shown, the motor is hung above the springs, missing the jars of travel.

Gasoline=Electric Vehicles.—The principal disadvantage of the internal combustion motor or self-propelled vehicles is its lack of flexibility; while on the other hand, the principal disadvantage of the electric vehicle operated by means of storage batteries is its lack of mobility. It is evident that the short coming in each case can be overcome only by combining the internal combustion motor with a direct current generator connected to a storage battery, for supplying the power required by the electric motors.

Such a combination will operate at practically constant speed at all loads, as the generator with the storage battery serves to furnish the necessary overload, or consumes that portion of the energy which is not needed. Furthermore, the transmission will be entirely electrical and will possess the simplicity and flexibility

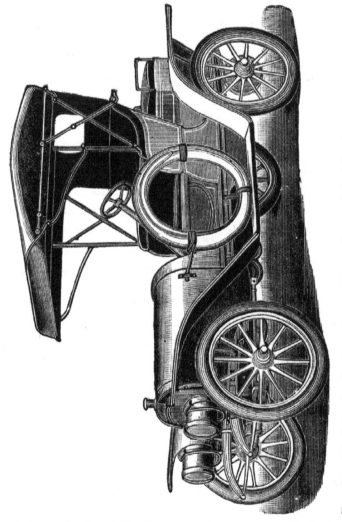

FIG. 409.—The Babcock electric roadster. This car is provided with a battery of forty-two cells, which it is claimed, gives one hundred miles at seventeen miles per hour on one charge. The controller provides for five speeds forward and two reverse. The motor develops fifteen horse-power which will run the car over thirty miles per hour.

of electric control; while the use of motors will eliminate all dif-ferential gears and allow the attainment of various speeds by series-parallel combinations.

A great many vehicles of this type are now being built in the form of omnibuses and trucks for city service and freight and passenger cars for interurban railway service in which they have rendered satisfactory duty.

CHAPTER FORTY-ONE.

PRINCIPLES OF ELECTRICITY.

The Term Electricity.—This is derived from the Greek word *electrom*—amber. It was discovered more than 2,000 years ago that amber when rubbed with an ox's tail possessed the curious property of attracting light bodies. It was discovered afterwards that this property could be produced in a dry steam jet by friction, and in A. D. 1600 or thereabouts, that glass, sealing wax, etc., were also affected by rubbing, producing electricity.

For convenience, electricity is sometimes classified as:

1. *Static electricity,* or electricity *at rest.*
2. *Dynamic electricity,* or electricity *in motion.*
3. *Magnetism,* or electricity *in rotation.*

Static Electricity is a term employed to define electricity produced by friction. It is properly employed in the sense of an electric charge which shows itself by the attraction or repulsion between charged bodies.

When static electricity is discharged, it causes more or less of a current, which shows itself by the passage of sparks or a brush discharge; by a peculiar prickling sensation; by an unusual smell due to its chemical effects; by heating the air or other substances in its path; and sometimes in other ways.

Dynamic Electricity.—A classification used to define current electricity to distinguish it from static electricity. The term *positive* expresses the condition of the point having the higher electric energy or pressure, and, *negative,* the lower relative condition of the other point, and the current is forced through the circuit by the electric pressure at the source, just as a current of steam is impelled through pipes by the generating pressure at the steam boiler.

Units of Electrical Measurement.—These are stated in terms of length, weight and time, which is to say in terms of centimeters, grams and seconds. The units thus established are largely arbitrary, but they have been carefully estimated, so that the proportions between current strength, circuit resistance and voltage may be accurately maintained.

The Ohm, the Unit of Resistance.—The first unit of electrical measurement is the ohm. This unit measures not only the relative resistance of a circuit composed of a conducting wire of a given length and diameter, as compared with wires of different

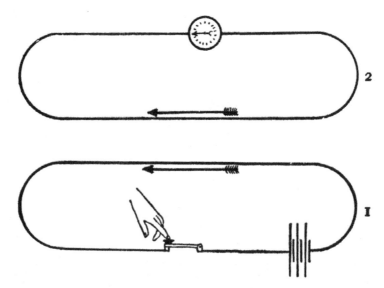

FIG. 410.—Diagram Illustrating the Action of Voltaic Induction Between Two Circuits: the one including a source of electrical energy and a switch; the other including a galvanometer, but having no cell or other electrical source. The direction of the battery current in circuit 1 is indicated by the arrow; the arrow in circuit 2 showing the direction of the induced current.

lengths and diameters, composed of the same material, but also the specific resistance, which refers to the variations in resisting quality found between given wires of the same length and cross-section, made of different materials.

The different resistivity of several different metals, as found in circuits, precisely similar in all points of dimensions, is demonstrated in the fact that, while a unit wire of silver shows a conductivity of 100, and one of copper, 99, a wire of iron gives only 16.80.

The value of the ohm, as fixed by the Electrical Congress, at the Columbian Exposition in 1893, is equivalent to the resistance offered to one volt of E. M. F. by a column of mercury 106.3 centimeters in height (about 41.3 inches), and one square millimeter (.00155 square inch) cross-section, determined at the temperature of melting ice (39° Fahrenheit).

The Ampere, the Unit of Current.—The ampere is the current produced by an electromotive force of one volt in a circuit having a resistance of one ohm. An ampere is that quantity of electricity which will deposit .005084 grain of copper per second.

It is one-tenth the absolute C. G. S. unit of current strength. Current in amperes equals pressure in volts divided by resistance in ohms, or again, electromotive force equals resistance multiplied by current; and again, resistance equals electromotive force divided by the current; thus, it will be seen that these terms are dependent upon each other, and that their relation to each other is expressed by this law. These are written in three ways:

$$1. \quad C. = \frac{E}{R}$$
$$2. \quad E. = C \times R, \text{ or}$$
$$3. \quad R. = \frac{E}{C}$$

If one volt will force one ampere of current through a circuit having one ohm resistance it will take five volts to force five amperes through the same circuit. If this resistance should be increased to five ohms it would take five times five volts for the proper number of volts to force the amperes through, which would be 25 volts. From this it can be seen that it is very easy to obtain any one of these quantities when we have the other two.

The Volt, the Unit of Pressure.—The volt is that electromotive force which can produce a current of one ampere on a circuit having a resistance of one ohm.

There are several specified equivalents for estimating the exact value of one volt E. M. F., but these usually refer to the determined capacity of some given type of galvanic cell.

It is sufficient to say, however, for ordinary purposes, the majority of commercial chemical cells are constructed to yield approximately one volt.

The ordinary Daniell cell used in telegraphy has a capacity of 1.08 volt, and the common type of Leclanché cell gives about 1.50.

The Watt, the Unit of Work.—This represents the rate of energy of one ampere of current under a pressure of one volt, and is equivalent to the product of the voltage multiplied by the amperage.

Other equivalents of the watt make it equal to the product of the resistance by the square of the current, or the quotient of the square of the voltage by the resistance.

Thus, a current of ten amperes at a pressure of 2,000 volts will develop 20,000 watts, as will also another given current of 400 amperes at fifty volts.

Electrical Horse Power.—The operative capacity of an electrical motor is usually stated in terms of watts, or kilowatts (1,000 watts), which may be reduced to horse-power equivalents by dividing by 746, which figure indicates the number of watts to an electrical horse power.

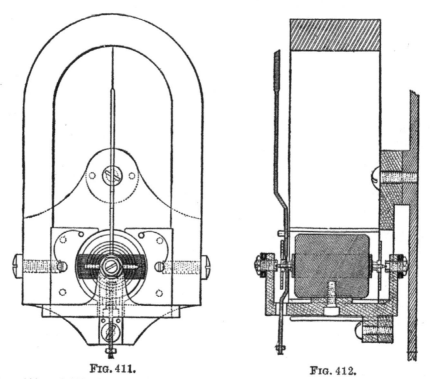

Fig. 411.   Fig. 412.

Figs. 411. and 412.—Sectional Diagrams Illustrating the Construction of Volt and Ammeters. The iron core is secured to the base plate by a screw. The active coil is shown wound around it from end to end.

The Energy Consumption of Electric Vehicles.—The current consumption of electric vehicles operated by storage batteries varies more or less with the different makes, but some idea of the same may be obtained from the results of a test run of 62 miles over dirty and slippery roads recently made in France.

In this run, a number of electric vehicles, each carrying four passengers and weighing, complete, over 2 tons, covered the entire distance at an average speed of 15 miles an hour, with an energy consumption of about 160 watt-hours per ton mile.

The best performance was that of a Vedrine, which required 155 watt-hours per ton mile. Under ordinary conditions this vehicle consumes from 110 to 120 watt-hours per ton mile.

Electricity Meters.—The electrical gauges, ammeters and voltmeters, used on automobiles are constructed on the principle of the D'Arsonval galvanometer, with either a permanent or a variable field.

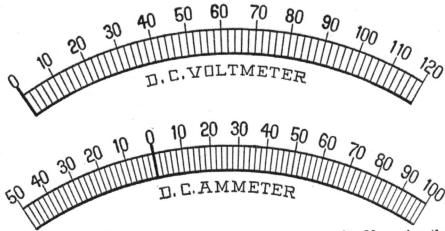

Fig. 413.—Index Scales of a Voltmeter and an Ammeter for Measuring the Pressure and Intensity on a Direct-current Electrical Circuit.

The general features are a small oscillating solenoid whose core is mounted on jeweled bearings, arranged like a dynamo armature between the poles of the permanent horseshoe magnet, with a hand or pointer pivoted at the bearing, so as to indicate the variation in electrical conditions on a graduated scale.

A coiled steel spring attached at the base of the needle acts to restrain and control its movements, thus ensuing reliable indications of current strength or intensity.

Forms of Volt=Ammeter.—For automobile use a voltmeter and an ammeter are usually mounted on one base, with their graduated scale cards sufficiently near together to enable rapid reading of battery conditions. These instruments frequently have the scale traced on glass, so as to be illuminated at night by an incandescent lamp placed behind it.

As shown in figs. 413 and 414, volt-ammeters made by different manufacturers vary in appearance—one type having the two scales arranged side by side, another end to end. The voltmeter indicates the pressure between battery terminals, while the ammeter scale indicates the current strength.

Reading Speed and Power Output.—In running the vehicle the voltmeter scale reading indicates the amount of charge still remaining in the battery—the difference between—and the ammeter rate at which it is being used.

If the speed of a vehicle on a hard level road be determined and the reading noted in connection with it, the ammeter may be used as a very good speed indicator for operation under similar conditions.

The ammeter indicates an overload, which, if above a definite specified figure, would likely damage the battery, as when attempting to start with brakes set, or in beginning the ascent of a heavy grade from a standstill. The amount of power being consumed by the motor is, of course, always the product of the volts by the amperes. Thus, with readings of 80 volts and 16 amperes, 1,280, or about 1.7 horse power, are being constantly used.

Voltmeter Indications.—Although the voltmeter should always register between 1.75 and 2.6 per cell, the former figure indicating the point of discharge—it may happen that an unusually heavy road will bring the needle temporarily below that point. Such indication does not of necessity mean that the battery is exhausted, as on coming upon a better road, it will quickly resume its normal reading.

CHAPTER FORTY-TWO.

Dynamos and Motors.—The machines for converting mechanical movement into electrical current, and for conveying electrical current into mechanical movement, in other words, the dynamo generator and the electric motor, respectively, are the same so far as the general features of their construction are concerned. In operation, however, the motor is the exact reverse of the dynamo.

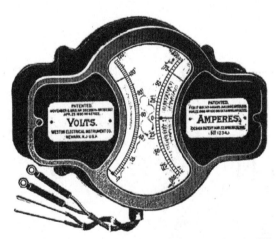

FIG. 414.—Weston Volt-ammeter of the Type used on Electric Vehicles. Other makes of these instruments have the index scales side by side, instead of end to end.

The Essential Parts of Dynamos and Motors.—The essential parts of a dynamo generator and also of an electric motor are:

1. The field magnets constructed like ordinary electromagnets, and having two or any even number of opposed poles with their windings connected in series.

2. The armature rotating between the fields, so as to cut the lines of magnetic force.

3. The pole pieces, which are the exposed ends of the magnet cores.

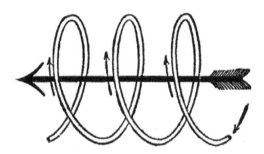

Fig. 415.—Diagram Illustrating the Directions of the Current in the Field Windings and the Induced Current, as found in magnets, solenoids and dynamo operation.

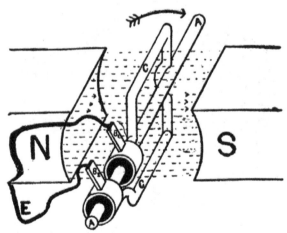

Fig. 416.-Diagram of a Dynamo Electrical Generator, arranged for producing an alternating current, showing the constructional and operative features. Here N and S are the positive and negative poles of the field magnets, between which the lines of force are shown by the dotted lines. A is the armature spindle; B¹ and B², the brushes bearing on the ring drums; C, the coil, or winding, of the armature; E, the outside circuit to which the current is supplied.

4. The commutator or collector.

5. The brushes which rest upon the cylindrical surfaces of the commutator, and as the terminals of the outside circuit, take up and deliver the current generated in the coils of the armature.

The Varieties of Dynamo=Generators.—There are a number of species of dynamo, differing in details, such as the arrangement of the armatures, the winding of the field magnets, etc., according to the use for which they are intended.

Series Motor.—The motors used on electric carriages are generally series wound, that type having been found very well adapted to most ordinary requirements, and from many points of view the most efficient in operation. It also possesses the valuable characteristic of automatically adjusting the consumption of power, as it were, to the load.

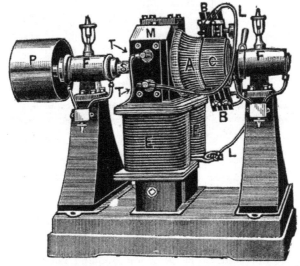

FIG. 417.—A Typical Dynamo-Electrical Generator, with parts lettered. A, the armature; B, B, the brushes; C, the commutator; E, E, the windings of the field magnets; M, the pole piece of the salient field magnet; F, F, bearings of the armature spindle; L, L, the lead wires; P, the pulley; T, T, terminal connections of the outside circuit.

Thus, at a light load it will take small current, while as the resisting torque on the machine increases, power sufficient for demands is constantly absorbed, thus enabling the motor to take extreme overloads with high efficiency.

Shunt and Compound Motors.—With a view to increasing the efficiency or automobile motors, several designers have proposed the use of shunt and compound windings, whose advantages in several particulars have been made apparent in other branches of electrical activity.

Shunt wound motors, in which the field coils, instead of being in series with the armature, are on a shunt between the lead terminals, are very largely used on constant-potential circuits, on account of their ability to regulate the speed, maintaining it at a virtually uniform rate, in spite of the increase in load up to a certain point.

In hill climbing, one-third and even more of the extra energy consumed can be recovered by coasting down the other side with the controller set a notch or two below the coasting speed.

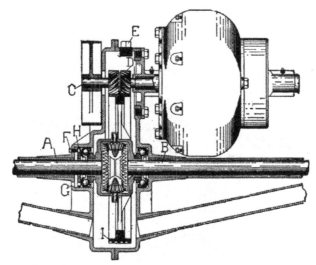

FIG. 418.—Plan Diagram of Single Motor Attached to Rear Axle Through "Herring-bone" Single Reducing Gears. A is the left-hand section of the divided rear axle; B, the right-hand section of the rear axle; C, the brake drum; D, the spiral pinion on the motor shaft driving the worm gear, I, on the differential; E, plug for greasing gears; F, set screw for locking ball race; G, slot for wrench to adjust threaded ring, H, against ball bearings.

The Commutator and Its Use.—In general, the commutator is formed of alternating sections of conducting and non-conducting material, running lengthwise to the axis, upon which it turns. The commutator is used to collect the current produced by the cutting of the lines of magnetic force, so as to cause them all to concur to a desired result, transforming what would naturally be an alternating current into a direct current.

Electric Motor Troubles.—The following digest of common motor troubles is given by Mr. George T. Hauchett in *The Automobile,* and is re-printed by permission:

"While it is not necessary to be an electrician to operate an electrically driven vehicle, it is of great advantage to know what to do when certain troubles occur.

"Let us consider first a single motor equipment provided with a battery which is connected in different ways for the various speeds. Suppose an attempt is made to start, and the vehicle does not respond and the ammeter shows no indication. This almost invariably means open circuit; that is to say, the path for the electricity from the batteries to the motors is not closed. We may find open circuits at any of the following points:

"A. The battery contacts. They may be and often are so badly corroded as to prevent the necessary metal-to-metal contact.

"B. The controller. A connection may be loose or the fingers may not make contact.

Fig. 419.　　　　　　　　　　　　Fig. 420.

Fig. 419.—General Electric Siemens-Halske Type of Vehicle Motor. Four-pole, cylindrical, laminated fields. Capacity, 16 amperes at 80 volts; 1,000 R. P. M. under full load.

Fig. 420.—General Electric Motor for Medium-weight Vehicles. Capacity, 16 amperes at 85 volts; 850 R. P. M. at full load.

"C. The running plug may sometimes be out or not making proper contact.

"D. The motor brushes. May have dropped out or the tension may be so weak that they do not make contact.

"E. The emergency switch may be open.

"Leave the controller till the last. It is but a moment to inspect the other joints and to discover the trouble in them after an hour's fussing with the controller is clearly a waste of time.

"If the motor tries to start, but the current is not sufficient, as shown by the ammeter, poor contact or weak battery may be suspected. Discharged battery will be betrayed by a low voltmeter indication, but if the voltmeter registers the normal amount, poor contact should be sought. Any contacts which are part of the electric circuit, such as binding posts, brushes, switch jaws or controller fingers must be bright metal-to-metal contacts. If they are dirty or corroded the contact may be so bad that the flow of current is seriously reduced or interrupted altogether.

"Improper Connections.—Sometimes the absence of ampere indication and no motion of the vehicle points to a very serious trouble, namely, the improper connection of the batteries. This will be shown by heavy sparks at the controller; in fact, heavy sparks at the controller, absence of ammeter indications and refusal of the vehicle to move, could only be caused by one other difficulty than this, which will be discussed further on.

"When the battery is not properly connected, the motion of the controller causes the sections of battery to exchange current between themselves at a ruinous rate. The terminals of the cells and those to which they should be connected ought to be plainly marked, or, better still, so constructed that it is impossible to go wrong. If the trouble just cited is the fact, one or more sets of terminals of the cells will be found to be connected to the wrong wires.

"If the vehicle fails to move and the flow of current as indicated by the ammeter is enormous, shut off the power at once. Serious damage may ensue if this is not done. Then look to see if:

"A. The brakes are on.

"B. The vehicle is stalled or blocked.

"C. The gears are free and there is no obstacle between the teeth.

"If the motor makes a noticeable attempt to move the trouble is probably something of this mechanical nature.

"Short Circuits.—If, however, large current is indicated and the motor remains absolutely inert, the trouble is electrical, and the inference is that the current does not go through the motor at all. Lift one of the motor brushes and try the vehicle again. If the large current is still indicated, the inference becomes a certainty. This trouble is known as short circuit, that is to say, a spurious path for the current which deflects it out of the motor.

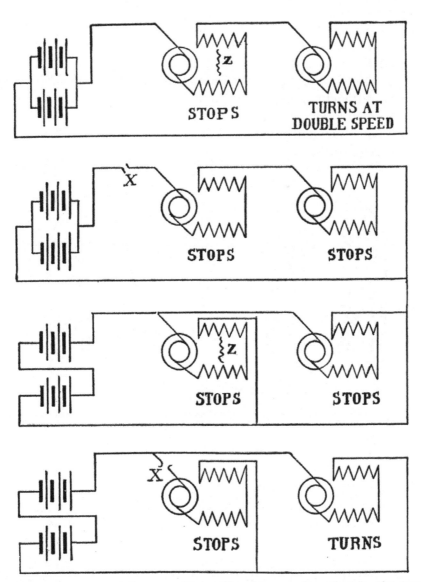

FIG. 421.—Diagram of Common Motor Troubles, as described in the text

In the controller may be sought:

"A. Foreign pieces of metal making contact between portions of the electrical circuit.

"B. Loose fingers which may make contact with wrong parts of the controller or with each other.

"C. Dirt between the fingers or contacts.

"D. Breaks in the insulation permitting the wires to make contact with adjacent metal or with each other.

"If the controller appears to be all right, look in the motor for:

"A. Broken insulation, allowing the bare wires to touch the frame or each other.

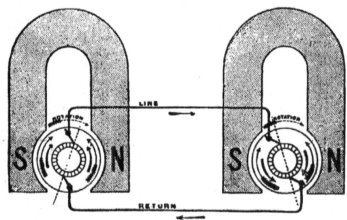

FIG. 422.—Diagram Showing the Operative Conditions of a Dynamo Generator and Electrical Motor. The machine on the left is the dynamo, that on the right the motor.

"B. Dirt between contacts or between live metal and the motor frame.

"C. Foreign materials bridging contacts.

"In such a case it is sometimes of assistance to turn on the current for an instant. The defective place may betray its locality by a smoke or spark.

"If, when the brush is lifted, and the vehicle tried, the excessive current indication disappears, there are but two electrical troubles that are possible:

"A. The magnet coils of the motor may be short circuited.

"B. The ammeter may not be reading correctly.

"The latter trouble is least likely; the former should be sought first.

"A series motor with a short circuited magnet coil will call for a large current but will do nothing with it. Therefore, examine the magnet coil terminals for troubles of this nature.

"A short circuit may exist even if the ammeter does not indicate it. In such a case it is usually found in the controller, which sparks heavily when operated, although the vehicle does not move. This combination of phenomena also indicates improper connection of the batteries, as has been previously explained.

"An excessive call for current is accompanied with a drop in the voltmeter indication.

Fig. 423.—General Electric Motor, Designed for Heavy Vehicle Use, with single or double reduction. Capacity, 30 amperes at 85 volts; 800 R. P. M. at full load.

"**Two=Motor Troubles.**—With a two-motor equipment the difficulties that may arise differ but little. A few which are peculiar to this type may be mentioned. Such motors are sometimes run in two ways. The first notch connects the motors in series, while the higher speed notches connect the motors in parallel. If one of the motors open-circuits on a series notch, the vehicle stops, for the entire motive circuit is broken. If it open-circuits on a parallel notch, that motor stops and the other, with its circuit to the batteries intact, continues to run and may cause the vehicle to make some abrupt and unexpected turns. If either of the motors gets short-circuited, the exact converse takes place. If the accident occurs on a series notch the unimpaired motor continues to run, and, it may be added, at nearly double its previous speed. If it occurs on a parallel notch a short circuit on one motor constitutes a short circuit on the other also, and if the short circuit is sufficiently severe both motors will stop, even though an enormous current may be drawn from the batteries."

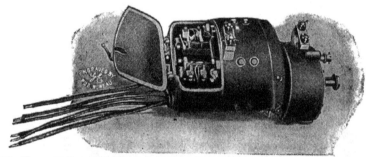

FIG. 424.—Type of General Electric Light Vehicle Motor, with case open, showing commutator and brush apparatus. The pinion end head is arranged for double reduction. Both end heads and gear housing are made of aluminum. Suspension by lugs to body. Capacity, 31½ amperes at 39 volts; 1,800 R. P. M. at full load.

CHAPTER FORTY-THREE.

Introduction.—Storage batteries are generally described as being devices for storing electric energy, which may be utilized subsequently for various purposes. The term accumulators is sometimes applied from the fact that they "accumulate" electric energy when charged from an outside source. Storage batteries are also called secondary batteries to distinguish them from batteries of the primary type.

Secondary batteries are in no sense generators of electricity but are employed to accumulate a given quantity of electric energy, the quantity of which is estimated by the number of hours required to discharge it at a given rate.

The General Theory of Storage Batteries.—The general theory upon which a secondary battery operates was discovered as early as 1801, when Gautherot discovered that if two plates of platinum or silver, immersed in a suitable electrolyte, be connected to the terminals of an active primary cell and current is allowed to flow for any desired period, a small current could be obtained on an outside circuit connecting these two electrodes, as soon as the primary battery had been disconnected. The process which takes place in this case is briefly as follows:

An electrolyte, consisting of a weak solution of sulphuric acid, permits ready conduction of the current from the primary battery, the greater the proportion of acid in certain limits the smaller being the resistance offered.

The effect of the current passing through the electrolyte is the decomposition of the water, which is indicated by the formation of bubbles upon the exposed surfaces of both electrode sheets, these bubbles being formed by oxygen gas on the plate connected to the positive pole of the primary battery and hydrogen on the plate connected to the negative pole of the battery.

Because, however, the oxygen is unable to attack either platinum or silver under such conditions, the capacity of such a device to act as an electrical accumulator is practically limited to the point at which both plates are covered with bubbles. After this point the gases will begin to escape into the atmosphere.

In this simple apparatus, as in the storage cells manufactured at the present day, the prime condition to operation, is that the resistance of the electrolyte should be as low as possible in order that the current may pass freely and with full effect between the electrodes. If the resistance of the electrolyte be too small, the current intensity will cause the water to boil rather than to occasion the electrolytic effects noted above.

As soon as the current from the primary cell is discontinued, and the two electrode plates from the secondary cell are joined by an outside wire, a small current will be caused to flow upon that outside circuit by the recomposition of the acid and water solution. The process is in a very definite sense a reversal of that by which the current is generated in a primary cell.

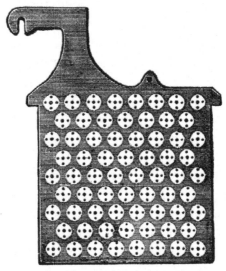

Fig. 425.—One Plate, or "Grid," of a Type of Storage Cell constructed by inserting buttons or ribbons of the proper chemical substances in perforations. Some such cells use crimped ribbons of metallic lead for inserting in the perforations, others pure red lead or other suitable material.

Hydrogen collected upon the negative plate, which was the cathode, so long as the primary battery was in circuit, is given off to the liquid immediately surrounding it, uniting with its particles of oxygen and causing the hydrogen, in combination with them, to unite with the particles of oxygen next adjacent, continuing the process until the opposite positive plate is reached, when the oxygen collected there is finally combined with the surplus hydrogen, going to it from the surrounding solution.

This chemical process causes the current to emerge from the positive plate, which was the anode, so long as the primary battery was in circuit. The current thus produced will continue until the recomposition of the gases is complete; then ceasing because these gases, as before stated, do not combine with the metal of the electrodes.

Plate Material.—The material from which storage battery plates are made depends largely upon the use to which they are to be adapted. Batteries are now being manufactured with plates made of iron and nickel, lead and zinc, and lead and lead, the latter being used almost exclusively.

In batteries of this class the negative plates are made of sponge lead, which has a light gray color and is very soft. The positive plates are of peroxide of lead, being dull chocolate in color and hard in texture.

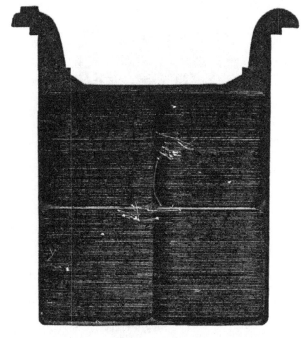

FIG. 426.—"Unformed" Plate of One Pattern of "Gould" Storage Cell. The particular plate shown has total outside dimensions of 6x6 inches. The clear outline of the grooves indicates absence of oxides, due to action of "forming" solutions, or charging current.

Types of Storage Batteries.—In general storage batteries may be divided into two classes:

1. The Plante;
2. The Faure.

The difference is principally in the method of constructing the plates.

In the Plante type, the lead is chemically attacked and finally converted into lead peroxide, probably after it has gone through several intermediate changes. The plates are all formed as positive plates first and then all that are intended for negatives are reversed, the peroxide being changed into sponge lead.

In order to make this type of plate more efficient, and its formation more rapid, the surfaces are finely subdivided, the following methods being those most common: scoring, grooving, laminating, casting, pressing and by the use of a lead wool.

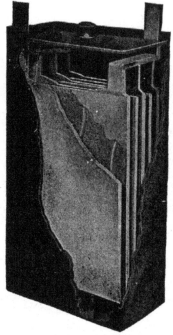

FIG. 427.—One Cell of the "Gould" Storage Battery for Electric Vehicle Use. According to the data given by the manufacturers, this cell, containing four negatives and three positive plates, has a normal charging rate of 27 amperes; a distance rate of 22½ amperes for 4 hours; a capacity of 81 ampere-hours at 3 hours' discharge, and of 90 ampere-hours at 4 hours' discharge. The plates are each 5⅞x7¾ inches, and the total dimensions of the cell, enclosed in its rubber jar, are 2½x6¼x11 inches. Forty such cells are generally used for an average light vehicle battery.

The Faure or pasted type is one which is formed by attaching the active material by some mechanical means to the grid proper. The active material first used for this purpose was red lead, which was reduced in a short time to lead peroxide when connected as the positive or anode, or to spongy metallic lead when connected as the cathode or negative, thus forming plates of the same chemical compound as in the Plante type.

The materials used at the present time by the manufacturers for making this paste are very largely a secret with them, but in general they consist of pulverized lead or lead oxide mixed with some liquid to make a paste.

The Faure plates are usually lighter and of higher capacity than the Plante, but have a tendency to shed the material from the grid, thus making the battery useless.

FIG. 428.—A Typical Storage Cell Enclosed in a Glass Jar. This cell represents one of the best-known makes of the Planté genus. With five plates, as shown, such a cell has a capacity of 80 ampere-hours, at 8 hours' discharge; of 70 ampere-hours, at 5 hours' discharge; of 60 ampere-hours, at 3 hours' discharge, with a discharge rate of 10 amperes in 8 hours; of 14 amperes in 5 hours, and of 20 amperes in 3 hours. The total outside dimensions of this cell are 5⅛x9½x11¼ inches; dimensions of each plate's active surface, 7¾x7¾ inches.

Many ways have been tried for mechanically holding the active material to the grid, the general method being by a special design in the shape of the grid. Some of these designs are solid perforated sheets or lattice work; corrugated and solid recess plates not perforated; ribbed plates with projecting portions; grid cast around active material; lead envelopes; triangular troughs as horizontal ribs.

FIG. 429.—Specimen Negative Plate of a Type of the "Gould" Storage Battery, showing the result of "formation," in the changed appearance of the plate surface.
FIG. 430.—Specimen Positive Plate of a Type of the "Gould" Storage Battery, showing the changed appearance of the plate surface, due to "formation."

Points on Care and Operation.—On the manner of operating and maintaining storage batteries for use in electric vehicles and for other purposes, there are a number of points to be considered.

However, since full directions are always furnished by manufacturers with each set of cells, it is necessary to give only the merest outlines here.

The electrolyte usually consists of 1 part of chemically pure concentrated sulphuric acid mixed with several parts of water. The proportion of water differs with the several types of cell from three parts to eight parts, as specified in the directions accompanying the cells. In making the mixture it is necessary to use an hydrometer to test the specific gravity of both the acid and the solution. The most suitable acid should show a specific gravity of about 1.760, or 66° Baume.

The mixture should be made by pouring the acid slowly into the water, never the reverse. As cannot be too strongly stated, *it is very dangerous to pour the water into the acid;* the latter is corrosive and will painfully burn the flesh.

Distilled or rain water should be used in preparing the electrolyte. When made, the solution should be allowed to cool for several hours or until its temperature is approximately that of the atmosphere (60° being the average). At this point it should have a specific gravity of about 1,200 or 25° Baume. If the hydrometer show a higher reading, water may be added until the correct reading is obtained; if a lower reading, dilute acid may be added with similar intent.

The electrolyte should never be mixed in jars containing the battery plates, but preferably in stone crocks, specially prepared for the purpose. Furthermore, it should never be placed in the cell until perfectly cool.

As soon as possible after placing the electrolyte in the cell, the charging current should be applied.

Connections for Charging.—In charging a storage battery, it is of prime importance that the connections with the generator be properly arranged. This means that the positive pole of the generator should be invariably connected to the positive pole of the secondary battery—which is to say, the pole which is positive in action when the current is emerging from the secondary battery, or the pole that is connected to the positive plates.

An error in making the connections *will result in entire derangement of the battery* and its ultimate destruction.

In charging a storage battery for the first time it is essential that the current should be allowed to enter at the positive pole at about one-half the usual charging rate prescribed; but after making sure that all necessary conditions have been fulfilled, it is possible to raise the rate to that prescribed by the manufacturers of the particular battery.

Portable Instruments used with Batteries.—The following outfit should be obtained for use in charging batteries:

1. Hydrometer Syringe (specific gravity tester);
2. Acid testing set (can be used instead of syringe);
3. Low reading voltmeter and suitable prods;
4. Thermometer.

Period of Charging a New Battery.—With several of the best known makes of the storage battery the prescribed period for the first charge varies between twenty and thirty hours. The manufacturers of a well known cell of the Planté genus prescribe for the first charge, half rate for four hours, after which the current may be increased to the normal power and continued for twenty hours successively.

The strength of current to be used in charging a cell should be in proportion to its own ampere hour capacity.

Thus, as given by several manufacturers and other authorities, the normal charging rate for a cell of 400 ampere hours should be fifty amperes; or one-eighth of its ampere hour rating in amperes of charging current.

Before closing the charging circuit it is essential that the voltage of the generator should be at least ten per cent. higher than the normal voltage of the battery when charged. The fact that a storage cell is fully charged is evident by the apparent boiling of the electrolyte and a free giving-off of gas. It may also be determined by the voltmeter, which will show whether the normal pressure has been attained. At the first charge of the battery the voltage should be allowed to rise somewhat above the point of normal pressure, but thereafter should be discontinued at a specified point.

At the first charging of a cell, when the pressure has reached the required limit, the cell should be discharged until the voltage has fallen to about two-thirds normal pressure, when the cell should again be recharged to the normal voltage (2.5 or 2.6 volts).

Care should be taken in charging a battery not to have a naked flame anywhere in its vicinity.

To either discharge or charge a battery at too rapid a rate involves the generation of heat. Thus, while this is not liable to result in flame under usual conditions, the battery may take fire, if it be improperly connected or improperly used.

Changed Specific Gravity of the Electrolyte.—Another effect resulting from the first charging of a storage cell is a change in the specific gravity of the electrolyte. According to the figures already given, this should be about 1,200, when the solution is first poured into the cells.

At the completion of the first charge, it should, on the same scale, be about 1,225. If it be higher than this, water should be added to the solution until the proper figure is reached; if it be lower, dilute sulphuric acid should be added until the hydrometer registers 1,225.

In charging a storage cell, particularly for the first time, it is desirable to remember that a weaker current than that specified may be used with the same result, provided the prescribed duration of the process be proportionally lengthened. The battery may also be charged beyond the prescribed voltage, ten or twenty per cent. overcharge effecting no injury occasionally; although, if frequently repeated, it seriously shortens the life of the battery.

FIG. 431.—The Exide storage cell. The positive and negative plates are separated by thin sheets of perforated hard rubber, placed on both sides of each positive plate. The electrolyte and plates are contained in a hard rubber jar.

FIG. 432.—An Exide battery of five cells. The box which holds the cells is usually made of oak, properly reinforced, with the wood treated to render it acid proof. The terminals, as shown, consist of metal castings attached to the side of the box and plainly marked.

Another point of importance touches the question of maintaining the charge of the battery. Even if the use be only slight in proportion to the output capacity, the battery should be charged at least once in two weeks, in order to maintain it at the point of highest efficiency. About as often, a battery should be charged at slowest rate, the charging current being adjusted to complete the charge only in twenty or thirty hours.

In charging a storage battery, it is essential to remember the fact that the normal charging rate is in proportion to the voltage of the battery itself.

Thus, a 100-ampere-hour battery, charged from a 110 volt circuit, at the rate of ten amperes per hour, would require ten hours to charge, and would consume in that time an amount of electrical energy represented by the product of 110 (voltage) by 10 (amperes) which would give 1,100 watts.

Old Electrolyte.—The electrolyte may be saved and used when reassembling the battery, provided great care be exercised when pouring it out of the jar, so as not to draw off with it any of the sediment. It should be stored in convenient receptacles, preferably carboys, which have been thoroughly washed and never used for any other purpose.

The electrolyte saved in this manner will not, however, be sufficient to refill the battery, and as some new electrolyte will be required, in general it is recommended that the old supply be thrown away and all new electrolyte (1,200 specific gravity) be used when reassembling.

Charge Indications.—The state of the charge is not only indicated by the density of the electrolyte and the voltage of the cell, but also by the *color of the plates,* which is considered by many authorities as one of the best tests for ascertaining the condition of a battery.

In the case of formed plates, and before the first charging, the positives are of a dark brown color with whitish or reddish gray spots and the negatives are of a yellowish gray. The whitish or reddish gray spots on the positive plates are small particles of lead sulphate which have not been reduced to lead peroxide during the process of forming, and represent *imperfect sulphatation.*

As a general rule the first charging should be carried on until these spots completely disappear. After this the positive plates should be of a dark red or chocolate color at the end of a discharge and of a wet state or nearly black color when fully charged. A very small discharge is sufficient, however, to change them from black to the dark red or chocolate color.

If the battery has been discharged to a potential lower than 1.8 volts, the white sulphate deposits will reappear turning the dark red color to a grayish tint in patches or all over the surface of the plate, or in the form of scales of a venetian red color.

The formation of these scales during charging indicates that the maximum charging current is too large and should be reduced until the scales or white deposits fall off or disappear, after which the current can be increased again.

During charging, the yellowish gray color of the negatives changes to a pale slate color which grows slightly darker at the completion of the charge. The color of the negatives always remains, however, much lighter than that of the positives.

The Capacity of Storage Batteries.—The discharge capacity of a storage battery is stated in ampere-hours, and unless otherwise specified, refers to its output of current at the 8-hour rate. Most manufacturers of automobile batteries specify only the amperage of the discharge at 3 and 4 hours.

As there is no sure way for the automobilist to estimate the discharge capacity of his battery, he is obliged to base such calculations as he makes on the figures furnished by the manufacturers. With the help of his indicating instruments—the voltmeter and ammeter.

It is customary to state the normal capacity of a cell in ampere-hours, based upon the current which it will discharge at a constant rate for eight hours.

Thus a cell which will discharge at 10 amperes for 8 hours *without the voltage falling below* 1.75 *per cell* is said to have a capacity of 80 ampere-hours. It does not follow that 80 amperes would be secured if the cell were discharged in 1 hour. It is safe to say that not more than 40 amperes would be the result with this rapid discharge.

The ampere-hour capacity decreases with the increase in current output. An 80 ampere-hour cell, capable of delivering 10 amperes for 8 hours, would, when discharged at 14 amperes, have a capacity of 70 ampere-hours; when discharged at 20, its capacity would be 60; and when discharged at 40, its capacity will have decreased from 80 to 40 ampere-hours.

Generally speaking, the voltage during discharge is an indication of the quantity of electricity remaining within the cell.

Apart from any considerations of efficiency, the driver of an electric carriage should carefully bear in mind the figures supplied by the manufacturers of the type of battery he uses, in order to judge:

1. How long the present charge will last;

2. Whether he is exceeding the normal rate of discharge, and thus contributing to the unnecessary waste of his battery and incurring other dangers that may involve unnecessary expense.

As a general rule the 1-hour discharge rate is four times that of the normal, or 8-hour discharge, and considerations of economy and prudence suggest that it should never be exceeded, if, indeed, it is ever employed. The 3-hour discharge, which is normally twice that of the 8-hour, is usually the highest that is prudent while the 4-hour discharge is the one most often employed for average high-speed riding; batteries give only the 3 and 4-hour discharge rates in specifying the capacity of their products.

High Charging Rates.—Occasionally it is desirable to charge a battery as quickly as possible, in order to save time, as when belated and far from home with an electric vehicle that has almost reached its limit.

As a general rule, such a procedure should not be adopted unless the battery is thoroughly discharged.

Fig. 433.—Elwell-Parker Motor Generator Set for Charging Vehicle Storage Batteries. This machine has an output capacity of about 15 horse power.

In charging a battery at a high rate, the danger to be avoided is the tendency of the cells to heat.

A battery should never be charged at a high rate unless it be completely exhausted, since it is a fact that the rate of charge that it will absorb is dependent upon the amount of energy already absorbed.

Battery=Charging Apparatus.—A storage battery may be charged from direct current mains having the proper voltage if, as is not always possible, such a circuit be available. Since, however, a current of as great uniformity as possible is required, and existing conditions must be met in each separate case, it is the

FIG. 434.—Waverley Motor-generator Charging Set for Use on a Single-phase Alternating Current Circuit of 100 to 110 Volts (60 Cycles). This apparatus will give a current of 15 amperes at 65 volts in charging a 24-cell battery, or 10 amperes in charging a 30-cell battery.

rule to use a motor-generator set with a regulating switchboard.

Such an apparatus consists of a direct current dynamo, driven direct from the shaft of a motor, which, in turn, is energized by current from the line circuit.

With a direct current on the line, a direct-current motor may be used; but with an alternating current an induction motor is required. The speed of the motor is governed by a rheostat, and the output of the dynamo is thus regulated as desired.

Method of Operating.—An idea of the procedure involved in the use of such an apparatus may be obtained from the following items furnished by the General Electric Company's outfits:

1. Pull down the tripping handle of the circuit breaker and close the two outside poles which connect the motor circuit. The tripping shaft is then automatically locked so that the breaker will not be open. Then push the core of the low voltage coil (right-hand coil) up as far as it will go.

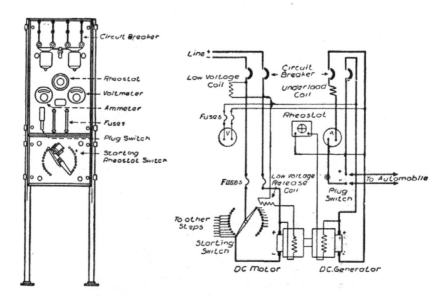

FIGS. 435, 436.–Switchboard and Motor-generator Circuit Connections for Charging a Battery from Direct Current Mains.

2. Start the motor.

3. Regulate the generator to give about the desired charging voltage.

4. Connect cable to automobile and attach to panel by means of plug switch.

5. Raise the core of the underload coil (left-hand coil) up as high as it will go, and while holding in this position close the other two poles of the circuit breaker. The closing of these two poles releases the lock on the tripping shaft so that the breaker will then operate on either underload or low voltage.

6. Regulate generator voltage until ammeter indicates the normal ampere charging rate of the storage battery.

Charging Through the Night.—If, after a late evening run, the vehicle will be wanted early the next morning, the battery may be charged during the night without an attendant being present; but in doing this great care must be taken not to excessively overcharge.

A careful estimate of the amount of current required should be made and the rate of charge based on this estimate.

If, say, 72 ampere hours be required to recharge, and the time available is nine hours, the average rate of charge must be 8 amperes.

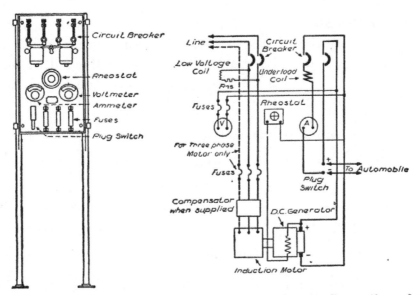

FIGS. 437. 438.–Switchboard and Motor-generator Circuit Connections for Charging a Battery from Alternating Current Mains. The connections of a third wire are shown, for use in case a three-phase circuit is available.

If charging from a 110-volt circuit, the rate at the start should be about 10 amperes; if from a 500-volt circuit, about 9 amperes; as, in charging from a source with constant voltage, such as a lighting or trolley circuit, the rate into the battery will fall as the charge progresses. This also applies if the charging be done, without attendance, from a mercury arc rectifier.

Charging Batteries Out of Vehicles.—When a battery is being overhauled or is out for cleaning, it may be more convenient or suitable to charge it while out of the vehicle.

In such a case the cells must be connected together in series and to the charging source in relatively the same manner as if they were in the vehicle; that is, the positive (+) terminal of one group of cells must be connected to the negative (—) terminal of the next group, and the two free terminals, one positive and the other negative, must be connected respectively to the positive and negative terminals of the charging circuit, but not until all of the groups have been connetced in series.

Great care must always be taken to have the polarities correct and the wire or cable for the connections of ample size to carry, without heating, the heaviest current used in charging. The size used in the vehicle will be proper.

The operation of charging is then carried on in precisely the same manner as if the battery were in the vehicle.

Short Circuiting.—A form of derangement that may occasionally affect the vehicle batteries is short circuiting. It may be caused by some of the active material—if the cell be of the pasted variety—scaling off and dropping between the plates, or by an over collection of sediment in the bottom of the cell.

Should the operator suspect trouble with his battery he may discover a short circuited cell by the marked difference in color of the plates or of the specific gravity of the electrolyte, as compared with the other cells. No particular damage will be caused, if the trouble be discovered and removed before these symptoms become too marked.

If a foreign substance has become lodged between the plates, it may be removed by a wood or glass instrument.

If some of the active material has scaled off, it may be forced down to the bottom of the jar. If excessive sediment be found, the jar and plates should be washed carefully, and reassembled.

A cell that has been short circuited may be disconnected from the battery and charged and discharged several times separately, which may remedy the trouble.

Batteries Used but Occasionally.—If a battery is not to be used for several days, it should first be fully charged before standing; if it continue idle, a freshening charge should be given every two weeks, continuing the charging when the cells begin to gas freely.

In standing idle for some time, a battery loses part of its charge, due to local losses in the cells, which the freshening charges may not entirely overcome; so that several discharges may be required to regain full capacity.

Lack of Capacity.—Should there be a decrease in the speed or mileage of a vehicle, the falling off may be due to trouble in the running gear, in the motors, in the connections or in the battery.

If the current consumption, as shown by the meter, be greater than normal, the vehicle is running "hard," and it should be overhauled. If, however, the current consumption be normal, there may be poor connections or trouble in the battery.

Falling off in the capacity of the battery can always be traced to some cause, and when it gives indications that something is wrong, take it out of the vehicle and look for the trouble.

There may be a dry cell, due to a leaking jar; some or all of the cells may be in a state of incomplete charge, due to the battery having been run too low and not sufficiently charged; or the plates may be short circuited, either by the sediment (deposit in the bottom of the jar) getting up to the bottom of the plates or by something that has fallen into the cell.

Short circuits in a cell are indicated by short capacity, low voltage and low specific gravity, excessive heating and evaporation of the electrolyte.

If the trouble cannot be located by the eye, connect the battery in series, and discharge it at the normal rate, through suitable resistance. If a suitable rheostat be not available a water resistance may be used.

This consists of a receptacle (which must not be of metal) filled with very weak acid solution or salt water in which are suspended two metal plates, which are connected by wires through an ammeter. The current may be regulated by altering the distance between the plates or by varying the strength of the solution. As the discharge progresses, the voltage will gradually decrease and it should be frequently read at the battery terminals; as soon as it shows a sudden drop the voltage of each cell should be read with a low reading voltmeter.

While the readings are being taken, the discharge rate should be kept constant and the discharge continued until the majority of the cells read 1.70 volts; those reading less should be noted. The discharge should be followed by a charge until the cells which read 1.70 volts are up; then the low cells should be cut out, examined and the trouble remedied.

If the electrolyte be low in specific gravity, assuming that there are no short circuits, due to sediment or other cause, it is evidence:

1. Of sloppage or a leaky jar, the loss having been replaced with water alone;

2. Of insufficient charge, overdischarge, standing in a discharged condition or a combination of these abuses; any of them mean that there is acid in combination with the plates, which should be brought out into the electrolyte by a long charge at quarter the normal discharge rate.

The low cells should be grouped by themselves and charged as a separate battery, care being taken that the positive strap of one cell is connected to the negative strap of the adjoining cell and that the charging connections are properly made. If there be not sufficient resistance in the charging rheostat to cut the current down to the proper point, use water resistance.

While a cell is being treated, when possible, the cover should be removed (if sealed, the compound can be loosened by using a hot putty knife).

Disconnecting Cells.—The best method of disconnecting cells assembled with pillar straps, for the purpose of replacing broken jars, cleaning or taking out of commission, is to use a five-eighth inch twist drill, in a carpenter's brace, boring down into the top of the pillar about one-quarter inch; then pull off the connector sleeve from the pillar. By following this method, all parts may be used again.

When cells are equipped with top straps, the straps should be cut with a sharp knife or chisel midway between the cells.

Taking Batteries out of Commission.—Where a battery is to be out of service for several months, and it is not convenient to give it the freshening charge every two weeks, it should be taken out of commission.

To do this, proceed as follows: Charge the battery in the usual manner, until the specific gravity of the electrolyte of every cell in the battery has stopped rising over a period of one hour (if there be any low cells, due to short circuits or other cause, they should be put in condition before the charge is started, so that they will receive the full benefit of it). Disconnect the cells, remove the covers (if sealed, loosen compound with a hot putty knife), remove the elements from the jars, place on their sides with the plates vertical, slightly spread the plates apart at the bottom, withdraw the separators and pull the positive and negative groups apart. Play a gentle stream of water on them, to wash off the electrolyte, and then allow them to drain and dry.* The positives, when dry, are ready to be put away. If the negatives, in drying, become hot enough to steam, they should be again rinsed or sprinkled with clean water and then allowed to dry thoroughly.

When dry, completely immerse the negatives in electrolyte (of about 1.275 specific gravity), and allow them to soak for three or four hours. The jars may be used for this purpose. After rinsing and drying, they are ready to be put away. The rubber separators should be rinsed in water. Wood separators, after having been in service, will not stand much handling and had better be thrown away. If it be thought worth while to keep them, they must be kept immersed in water or weak electrolyte, and in reassembling the electrolyte must be put into the cells immediately, as wet wood separators must not stand exposed to the air for an unnecessary moment, especially when in contact with plates.

When putting the battery into commission, it should be treated in the same manner as if it were new, and the regular instructions for assembling and putting into commission a new battery followed.

---

* If the active material in the negative plates extend beyond the ribs of the grid (the supporting frame), it should be at once pressed back into place, care being taken to prevent the plates from drying before this is done. The most suitable and convenient method for pressing is to place between the plates smooth boards of a thickness equal to the distance between the plates and then put the groups under pressure.

Cleaning Jars.—The jars should be thoroughly cleaned with fresh water, no sediment being allowed to remain.

Condensed Rules for the Proper Care of Batteries.—The following general instructions should be followed in the care and maintenance of batteries:

1. A battery must always be charged with "direct" current and in the right direction.

2. Be careful to charge at the proper rates and to give the right amount of charge; do not undercharge or overcharge to an excessive degree.

3. *Do not bring a naked flame near the battery while charging or immediately afterwards.*

4. Do not overdischarge.

5. Do not allow the battery to stand completely discharged.

6. Voltage readings should be taken only when the battery is charging or discharging; if taken when the battery is standing idle they are of little or no value.

7. Do not allow the battery temperature to exceed 110° Fahr.

8. Keep the electrolyte at the proper height above the top of the plates and at the proper specific gravity. Use only pure water to replace evaporation. In preparing the electrolyte *never pour water into the acid.*

9. Keep the cells free from dirt and all foreign substances, both solid and liquid.

10. Keep the battery and all connections clean; keep all bolted connections tight.

11. If there be lack of capacity in a battery, due to low cells, do not delay in locating and bringing them back to condition.

12. Do not allow sediment to get up to the plates.

Mercury Arc Rectifier.—This is a device for obtaining direct current from alternating for use in charging storage batteries. This transformation of current is obtained at a low cost, because the regulation is obtained from the alternating side of the rectifier, while the current comes from the direct current side.

The theory is as follows: In an exhausted tube having one or more mercury electrodes, ionized vapor is supplied by the negative electrode or cathode, when the latter is in a state of "excitation." This condition of excitation can be kept up only as long as there is current flowing towards the negative electrode.

If the direction of the voltage be reversed, so that the formerly negative electrode is now positive, the current ceases to flow, since in order to flow in the opposite direction it would require the formation of a new negative electrode, which can be accomplished only by special means. Therefore, the current is always flowing towards one electrode, the cathode, which is kept excited by the current itself. Such a tube would cease to operate on alternating current voltage after half a cycle if some means were not provided to maintain a flow of current continuously towards the negative electrode.

The construction and operation of the General Electric Company's rectifier is as follows:

There are two graphite electrodes (anodes), and one mercury cathode.

Each anode is connected to a separate side of the alternating current supply and also through reactances to one side of the load.

The cathode is connected to the other side of the load. As the current alternates first one anode and then the other becomes positive and there is a continuous flow of current towards the cathode, thence through the load and back to the opposite side of the supply through a reactance.

At each reversal the reactances discharge, thus maintaining the arc until the voltage reaches the value required to maintain the current against the counter electromotive force of the load, and also reducing the fluctuations in the direct current. In this way a true continuous current is produced with very small loss in transformation.

A small electrode, connected to one side of the alternating current circuit is used for starting the arc.

A slight tilting of the tube makes a mercury bridge between the mercury cathode and the small electrode and draws an arc as soon as the tube returns to a vertical position.

CHAPTER FORTY-FOUR.

METHODS OF CIRCUIT-CHANGING IN ELECTRICAL MOTOR VEHICLES, AND THEIR OPERATION.

Varying the Speed and Power Output of a Motor.—The methods employed to vary the speed and power output of an electric vehicle motor consist briefly in such variation of the electric circuits as will modify the pressure of the batteries on the one hand and the operative efficiency of the motors on the other. This is a very simple matter and may be expressed in a few words. As is well known, there are two general methods of connecting up both electric batteries of any description and electric motors. They are the series-wiring and the multiple-wiring, or parallel-wiring. In series-w:ring, various cells of a galvanic battery, or the several units of a battery of dynamos, are connected in line. At one terminal of each is the negative pole, at the other the positive—each unit in combination having its negative pole connected to the positive pole of the one next following. In the parallel method of wiring the various units are each separately connected at their positive and negative poles to two lead wires, one of which is the positive pole of the battery, the other the negative.

Effects Obtained by Varying the Circuits.—Electric motors, lights and other electrically effected devices are similarly connected in circuits, either in series or parallel. Now, in the matter of circuit arrangements on this plan, one general principle may be laid down, which is that a connection of a number of electrical generators in series involves an increase in the power pressure of the battery, which is equal to the sum of the individual voltages. Connecting a number of generating units in parallel or multiple has the effect of producing a pressure only equal to the voltage of one of the units. Thus, if four generators of 10 volts each be connected in series, the pressure is equal to 40 volts. If, however, they be connected in parallel or multiple, the pressure is equivalent to but 10 volts, the effect in the latter case being the same as if but one unit were in circuit, so far as the voltage is concerned. On the other hand, where four motors are connected in series the efficient pressure of the circuit is reduced to very nearly $\frac{1}{4}$ for each motor, the C. E. M. F., generated by their operation, serving to cut down the average of efficiency; but when four motors are connected in parallel, which is to say, bridged between the limbs of the circuit, the greatest available pressure of the battery is able to act upon each one of them.

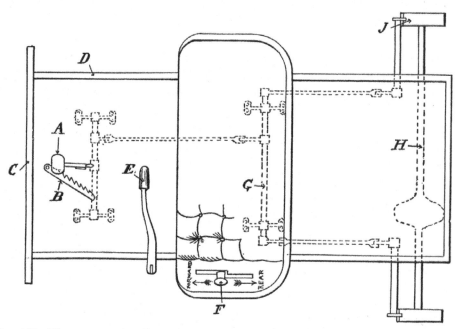

FIG. 439.—Diagram of the Controlling Apparatus of a Columbia Light Electric Vehicle. A, brake pedal; B, ratchet retaining pedal in place, operated by left foot; C, dash board; D, body sill; E, steering handle; F, controller handle; G, rocker shaft for setting hub brakes; J, brake band on wheel hub; H, rear axle.

Arrangement of the Batteries and Motor Parts.—In an electric vehicle the storage batteries are arranged so as to form a number of units, the circuit wiring being so arranged that by the use of a form of switch known as a controller the connections may be varied from series to multiple, or the reverse, as desired. The same arrangement for varying the circuit connections is used for the field windings, and, with some manufacturers, for the brush connections also. In the accompanying first diagram of the connections of an electric vehicle this fact is indicated. The dotted lines on each figure indicate the circuits that are cut out, or open, and the full lines those that are active, or closed. In fig. 440 showing the first speed, we have the two units of the battery, *B*, connected in multiple, which means that the voltage is reduced to the lowest point. The wire, *C*, connected to the bridge between the positive poles of the battery, leads the current to the field windings, *H* and *J*, which, in this figure, are connected in series-multiple, which

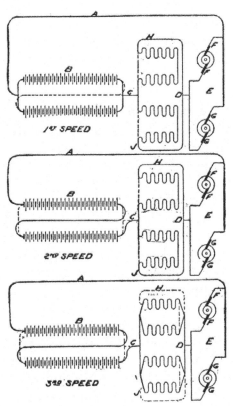

FIG. 440.—Diagram of the Circuit-Changing Arrangements of a Typical Electrical Venicle. The full lines in these plans indicate the closed, or active, circuits; the dotted lines the open, or inactive, circuits. As may be readily understood, the whole scheme of circuit-changing depends on employing several different circuit connections between battery and motor, which may be opened and closed, as desired. Here A and C are the lead wires between battery, B, and motor brushes, F F and G G, and the field-windings, H and J, and wire, D.

gives the lowest speed and power efficiency of the motors. By the wire, *D*, the current is carried to the brushes, *FF* and *GG*, which, according to this scheme, are permanently connected in multiple, the return path to the negative pole of the battery being through the wire, *A*.

In the second figure of the diagram the circuit is varied so as to connect the two units of the batteries, so as to give its highest pressure efficiency. But, since the field windings of the motors are also connected in series, or in series-parallel, as in this case, the efficiency in speed and power is reduced nearly one-half.

In the third figure the two units of the battery are connected in series, which, as in the former case, indicates the greatest efficiency in power output; but the field windings are connected in parallel, which means that the C. E. M. F., generated by their operation, is equivalent to the C. E. M. F. of only one motor, with the result that the speed and power efficiency is raised to its highest point.

Diagram of Battery, Motor and Controller.—In the second diagram, illustrating a typical method of shifting the circuits, we have the same general scheme applied, so far as the first, second and fourth speeds are concerned, the connections of the controller being laid out in rectangular form between the broken lines. When the controller is rotated, so that the row of terminal points, A, B, C, D, E, F, G, are brought into electrical contact with the row of terminal points, on the controller, A', B', C', D', E', F', G', we have the first speed forward, which, as may be readily discovered by tracing the connections throughout, involves that the two-unit battery is connected into multiple and the field windings of the two motors in series. Tracing the connections indicated for the second speed, we see that the terminal points, A, B, C, etc., are brought into electrical contact with A^2, B^2, C^2, etc., and we have the batteries in multiple and the fields in series-multiple. Tracing the connections indicated for the third speed, we have the terminal points, B and C, connected to the terminal points, B^3 and C^3, and the terminal points, E and F, connected to the terminal points, E^3 and F^3, which means that the batteries are connected in series and the fields in series. Similarly, by tracing the connections for the fourth speed, we find the terminal points, B and C, connected to terminal points, B^4 and C^4, and the terminal points, D, E, F, G, in electrical connection with the terminal points, D^4, E^4, F^4, G^4, which means that the batteries are in series and the fields in multiple. The connections between the battery, the armature brushes and the motor fields, are made as indicated through the

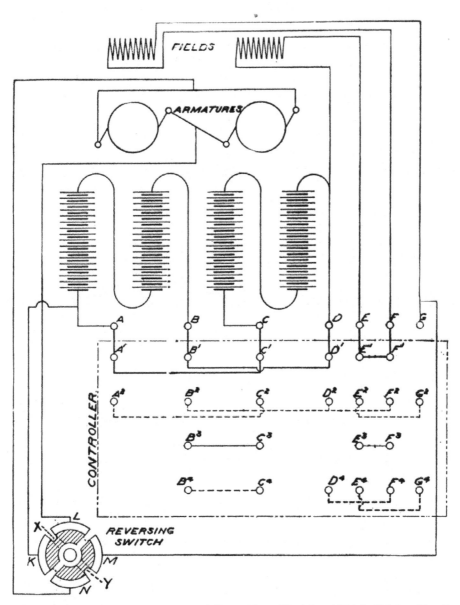

FIG. 441.—Diagram Plan of the Several Parts of an Electric Vehicle Driving Circuit. The field-windings and armatures are shown projected, the proper wiring connections being indicated. The periphery of the controller is laid out within the broken line rectangle, the contacts and connections through it for varying the circuits through four speeds being shown. A, B, C, D, E, F, G are the terminal contact points of the various speed circuits, to be made as the positions of the controller contacts are varied. A′, B′, C′, D′, E′, F′ are the controller contacts, which, with those already mentioned, make the proper circuits for the first speed. Similarly, A², B², C², etc., when brought into contact with A, B, C. etc., give the second speed circuits; B³. C³, E³, F³, in contact with A, B, C, D, etc., give the third speed; and B⁴, C⁴, D⁴, in the same manner, the fourth speed. The reverse switch gives the backward movement, as described.

rotary reversing switch, by the terminals, *K, L, M, N*. This switch may effect the reversal of the motors by giving a quarter turn to its spindle, which means that the contacts of segment, *X*, will be shifted from *L* and *K* to *K* and *N*, and the contacts of segment, *Y*, shifted from *M* and *N* to *L* and *M*, thus reversing the direction of the current.

Electric Vehicle Company's Circuits.—Some leading manufacturers of electric vehicles, notably the Electric Vehicle Co.,

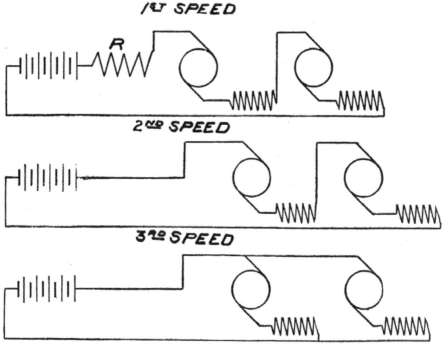

FIG. 442.—Diagram of a Typical One-Battery-Unit, Two-Motor Circuit. The first speed shows the two motors *in series*, with a resistance coil interposed; the second, the motors *in series*, without the resistance; the third, the motors *in multiple*.

vary the scheme shown in the last two figures by connecting the armature brushes and fields of each motor into series, and shifting the circuit connections, where two motors are used, from series to series-parallel. In the figure showing the combination of one battery unit with two motors, the connections for the three speeds obtained are obvious. Since only one unit is used, the lowest pressure of the battery can be obtained only by inserting a resistance coil, *R*, in the circuit, with the armature brushes, field windings and both motors connected in series. For the second speed the resistance is simply cut out, allowing the full current of the battery to pass through the armatures and windings of both motors, still connected in series. For the third speed the connections of armatures and motors are shifted to multiple, or series-multiple. With the use of a two-unit bat-

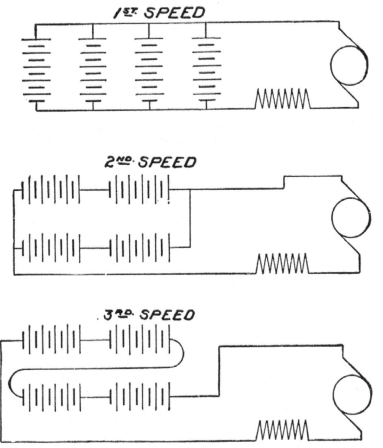

FIG. 443.—Diagram of a Typical Four-Battery-Unit, Single-Motor Circuit, showing combinations for three speeds. The only changes made in these circuits are in the battery connections. For the first speed the battery units are *in multiple;* for the second, *in series-multiple;* for the third, *in series.* The motor connections are not varied.

tery and two motors, it is possible to eliminate the resistance coil altogether and depend entirely upon circuit shifting regulating the voltage and power. Accordingly, for the first speed we have the batteries connected in multiple, and the armatures and windings of the two motors in series. For the second speed, the series connections are adopted for both batteries and motors, while for the third speed the batteries are in series, with the motors in parallel.

A Four-Battery-Unit, One-Motor Circuit.—In the diagram indicating the use of four-battery-units with one motor, which, as shown in an accompanying cut, is used to drive both rear wheels of the wagon through a single reduction, it is possible to obtain

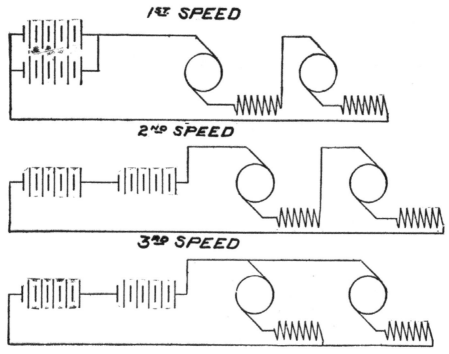

FIG. 444.—Diagram of a Two-Battery-Unit, Two-Motor Circuit, showing combinations for three speeds. The first speed is obtained with the battery units *in multiple*, and the motors *in series;* the second, with the battery units *in series*, and the motors *in series;* the third, with the battery units *in series*, and the motors *in multiple.*

a still greater range of variation by the simple shifting of the battery circuits, without alteration of the armature or field connections. Accordingly, for the first speed we have the four units connected into parallel, which gives a total voltage equivalent to the voltage of any one of them. For the second speed, the battery units are connected into series, the two pairs thus formed being joined in multiple, with the result that the total voltage of the battery is equivalent to the sum of the voltage of two of the units, or twice the voltage used in the first speed. For the third speed, all four units of the battery are connected into series, thus doubling the voltage again, and realizing the highest speed and power efficiency possible in the combination.

Vehicle Circuit Arrangements.—The next two figures illustrate different methods of arranging the circuits of an electric

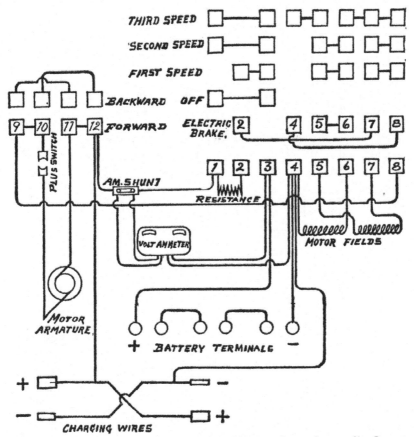

Fig. 445.—Diagram of Controller Connections of a One-unit, One-motor Circuit, with Variable Fields.

vehicle in actual practice. In the first, which shows the arrangements used on light Waverley carriages, the one-unit battery in three trays is shown connected in an invariable series circuit, giving the first, or lowest, speed through the resistance coil between controller contacts, 1 and 2, the motor-fields being in series; the second speed with the same circuit without the re-

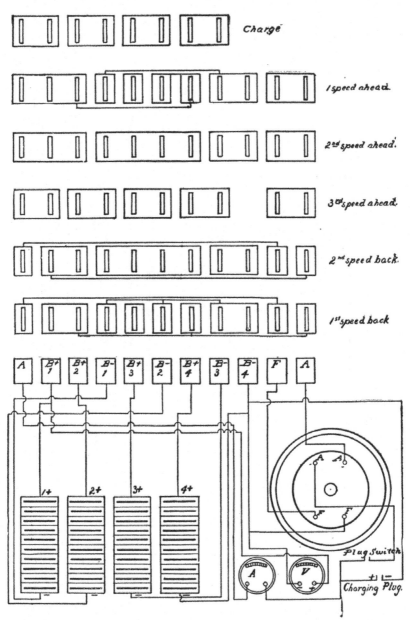

Charge

1 speed ahead.

2nd speed ahead.

3rd speed ahead.

2nd speed back.

1st speed back

FIG. 446.—Diagram of Controller Connections of a Four-unit, One-motor, Circuit, with Constant Series Connections for Fields and Armature in Forward and Backward Speeds.

sistance, and the third speed with the motor-fields in parallel. The motor used on these carriages is of the six-pole type, the field coils being divided into two halves of three coils each, each half being independently connected to the controller contacts, as shown in the cut. Reversal is by a form of rotatable switch, and an electric brake is also used, which operates on the principle of reversing the polarity between the armature and field windings. In the second diagram is shown the connections of a series motor, in which the field and armature windings are in invariable series connections for all forward speeds. The first, or lowest, speed forward is obtained with three units of the bat-

Fig. 447.—A Typical Electrical Vehicle Controller, or Circuit-changing Switch. The circuit terminals of battery and motors are shown at the jack-springs, which are arranged to be engaged by the fins on the periphery of the controller-cylinder. The connections within the controller, between the fins, are the same as those shown in Fig. 446. except for the fact that the four rings at the right hand end provide constant voltage connections for use with a shunt motor. The gaps at the rear of the rings show means for cutting out the shunt field at top speed.

tery in series-multiple; the second, with the four units in series-multiple; the third, with the four units in series. In reversing, the first and second speeds backward correspond to the forward speed arrangements similarly numbered, with the exception that the connections of field and armature are reversed, as may be readily understood from following out the indicated connections. In the charging position, the three contacts at the right side of the controller are cut out, leaving the battery to be charged in series from the charging plug connections to contact, *A,* at the left of the controller, to the similar connections with the negative pole of battery, 4.

The Controller of an Electric Vehicle.—The controller of
an electric vehicle consists of a rotatable insulated cylinder, carrying on its circumference a number of contacts, arranged to
make the desired connections with the terminals of the various
apparatus in the circuit through a wide range of variation. As
shown in fig. 441, illustrating the arrangement of battery and controllers in an electric vehicle, it should be noted that for the

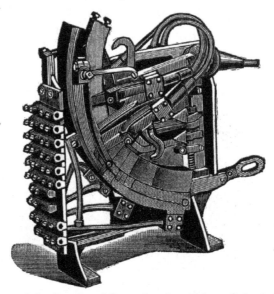

FIG. 448.—Controller of the Rauch and Lang electric vehicles. It is of the flat radial type.
Two movable copper leaf contacts of ample size make all commutations necessary to
obtain the various speeds. Five speeds forward and reverse are provided. All speeds
being obtained on the same voltage permits a constant torque working where at no
speed, from the lowest to the highest, is the circuit open for an instant, and the motor
is doing work at every position of the controller handle.

first speed, in which the batteries are connected in multiple, the points, A', C', are in electrical connection, as indicated
by the lines between them, so that the points, A, C, connected to
the like poles of the two battery units, are directly connected,
thus bringing the two units into multiple. The battery circuit
is completed by the electrical connection on the controller between the points, B' and D', when they are brought into contact
with the points, B and D, which connect to the two other poles
of the battery. Furthermore, the points, E' and F', being in
electrical connection through the body of the controller, connect
points, E and F, direct, thus throwing the field windings of the

motors into series. As may be understood from the last two diagrams of vehicle circuits, the contacts may be arranged to make any of several schemes of circuit variation, although, as must be obvious on examination, a specially arranged controller is necessary for each separate scheme.

Construction of a Controller.—The accompanying cuts show the general appearance and construction of several types of controller for electrical vehicles. As may be seen in the first cut,

FIG. 449.—Chassis of a Heavy Wagon of the Electric Vehicle Co., showing arrangement of controlling apparatus.

the connections of the terminals of the batteries, of the field windings, and other elements of the circuit, are made at the binding posts at the front base of the instrument. From each of these binding posts, which are electrically insulated from one another, jack-springs rise to a position convenient to make connections with the switch blades arranged along the periphery of the controller cylinder. These switch blades, as may be seen, are secured to the controller cylinder by screw connections, being arranged singly, or several of them together on one plate. In the case of a pair of blades, shown in contact with the spring at either extremity of the controller cylinder, it is evident that there is an electrical contact, through the base plates, between the two terminals, represented by the contact springs in engagement. Between these two end plates, as may be seen, there are several switch blades arranged singly upon the circumference. At one point there is no contact whatever, showing that the terminals represented by the contact springs at that point are out of circuit. These several blades that are arranged singly on the controller surface have such electrical connections as the scheme of circuit variation adopted demands, made through insulated wire connections arranged between any pair it is desired to connect. This is the arrangement indicated in the diagram of connections already described. It is perfectly easy to understand, therefore, how the circuit arrangements of battery units and motor windings may be varied through any desired range of connections, by simply connecting their terminals through properly arranged and connected controller contacts.

Varieties of Controller.—The controller shown in the cut, already described, represents only one type of this machine. Some controllers are constructed simple, with a perfectly cylindrical surface, upon which bear single leaf springs, the desired electrical connections being made by suitably connected conducting surfaces on the cylinder circumference, and cut-outs being similarly accomplished by insulating surfaces, bearing against the spring contacts at the desired points. This type of controller is shown in the second cut, and is one of the most usual forms for motor vehicle purposes. As is perfectly obvious, it is possible to so arrange the electrical connections on the controller surfaces, that by proper contacts with the terminal springs, reversal of the motor may be accomplished, as shown on the last circuit diagram. This is done in a number of controllers, the reverse being accomplished at a definite notch on the quadrant of the shifting lever.

CHAPTER FORTY-FIVE.

AUTOMOBILE RUNNING, CARE AND REPAIR.

Introductory.—In the handling of a car on the road, it would be hard to find two drivers who would adopt the same methods. This is due to the varied experience the drivers have had, and to their knowledge of the theory and principles of the automobile. Under suitable conditions, the gas engine will run for a long time without attention. However, a slight fault will often cause considerable trouble, the symptoms of which may not be plain enough to enable the trouble to be located directly, and the whole system must be gone over sometimes before it is located. It is, therefore, necessary to know just what is happening under the bonnet, and just when some things should happen, that reasonable satisfaction may be derived from the car.

There is no car that can be expected to be free from trouble, for even the best workmanship and material may give way sometimes.

An inexperienced driver will find that he cannot get as much out of a car as the demonstrator for some little time, or till he is thoroughly accustomed to the car and knows how to handle it, whether traveling uphill or on the level.

To handle a car intelligently, the driver should, 1, be well acquainted with the carburetter and ignition system, 2, understand the management of the spark, throttle and control levers under varying road conditions, 3, give proper attention to the lubrication of the various parts, and 4, be able to make repairs resulting from the ordinary mishaps likely to be encountered on the road.

The control of a steamer or electric vehicle is not so complicated, but the driver should have a good knowledge of the principles of operation of the motive power in either case and understand any peculiarities that may be inherent in the system.

Before Starting the Car.—In the chapter on engine operation, detailed instructions are given for its management and care, hence, it will suffice to say little here on this phase of the subject.

Before taking a car out on the road, the driver should first make himself familiar with the instructions given in the above

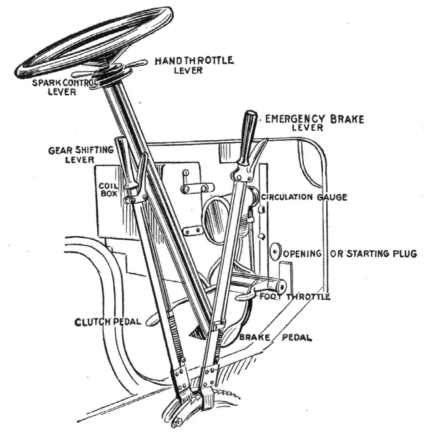

Fig. 450.—Control levers and dashboard appliances on a gasoline automobile. Located at the side of the car are the two levers which operate the brake and shift the change speed gears. As shown, the throttle and spark levers are just below the steering wheel; a number of cars have the levers placed on top of the wheel. The arrangement of foot pedals illustrated in the figure is to be found on nearly all makes of cars.

mentioned chapter and also with the "control" system which will now be explained.

Control.—The term *"control,"* relates to the various levers and devices used in running the car and which are conveniently located on the dash, steering column and foot board. A typical arrangement is shown in fig. 450. They are marked in the figure and their location should be carefully noted.

The Throttle Levers.—It will be seen that there are two throttle levers, most cars being provided with this number. In running a car through crowded streets where frequent speed changes are to be made, this is done most conveniently with the

FIG. 451.—The Holsman high-wheeled gasoline surrey. This vehicle is fitted with either a two or four-cylinder engine, developing respectively 12¾ and 26 horsepower. The transmission for both low and high speed is direct from the motor shaft to the wheels through a steel friction chain. One control lever of rack and pinion type operates the high and low gear and reverse. The vehicle starts and runs on all ordinary roads from zero to twenty-five or thirty miles per hour by friction of the steel chains operating on grooved sheaves on the ends of the motor shaft to the sheaves on both rear wheels. The reverse is accomplished by pushing the grooved pulleys on the ends of the motor shaft back into engagement with the steel channels or rims of the wheels, by the same control lever. The driving chains are wholly and automatically raised from engagement whenever the tension on them is relieved or the brake is set, or whenever the reverse is in action.

foot. A downward pressure of the foot opens the throttle; it closes automatically when released by the action of a spring. The foot throttle is also used when shifting the transmission gears, as one hand is required to operate the gear shifting lever, while the other is engaged in steering the car.

The running conditions on an open or country road are such that the hand throttle lever may be used to advantage since it need not be moved so often. The hand throttle may be set at any desired opening and it will remain in any position, whereas if the foot throttle be used, it is necessary to retain it in position by the foot against the tension of the spring. The latter operation naturally becomes tiresome if continued for any length of time, hence, the hand throttle furnishes a ready relief.

Each throttle is arranged so that when the lever is in the closed position, the supply of fuel mixture to the engine is not entirely shut off but just sufficient to keep the engine in motion.

As shown in the illustration, the throttle lever is placed below the steering wheel, however, in many cars it is placed above the wheel. A notched segment is provided to retain the throttle in any setting.

The Spark Control Lever.—This is usually placed near the throttle lever where it can be conveniently operated while steering. Both the spark and throttle are placed either below or above the steering wheel. The latter arrangement seems most in favor as the two levers can be operated without removing the hands from the rim of the steering wheel.

The Brake Levers.—When two sets of brakes are provided it is usual to have one set controlled by the foot brake pedal and another by the emergency lever.

The running or service brake, is operated by the foot pedal and is released by a spring when not held down. The construction is such that when this pedal is depressed to apply the brake, the clutch is simultaneously released. This arrangement prevents an inexperienced or confused driver, applying the brake without releasing the clutch—a proceeding which would strain or bring heavy stresses on the engine and driving gear.

Sometimes the emergency brake is arranged to simultaneously release the clutch when applied, but this construction has been criticised by some authorities as undesirable in handling the car on a hill.

It is pointed out, that if it be necessary to stop the car in ascending a hill, the brakes must be released before the clutch can be thrown in, with the possibility of the car starting down hill backward before the power can be applied. The chance of stalling the engine through this and the

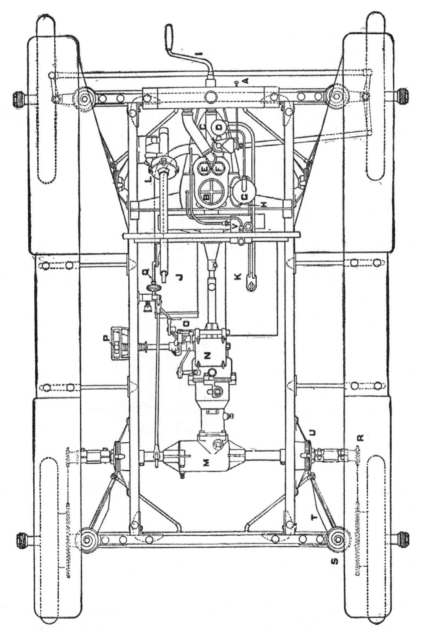

FIG. 452.—Plan of the Brush Runabout. Parts are as follows: A, priming push rod; B, cylinder head; C, carburetter gasoline adjustment; D, carburetter fuel cup; E, removable cap over exhaust valve; F, spark plug cap over inlet valve; G, gasoline pulsation pump; H, removable plate on crank case; I, starting crank; J, muffler; K, gasoline tank; L, steering gear; M, differential gear; N, transmission case; O, interlocking device; P, gear and clutch lever; Q, brake foot pedal; R, driving sprocket; S, spring; T, radius rod; U, adjustable friction joint of radius rod.

danger of the combination to any but an experienced driver, it is contended, make it advisable to have the emergency brake separate from any connection with the clutch.

The emergency brake lever is provided with a pawl and notched segment for retaining it in position when set. This segment is concentric with the segment of the transmission gear shifting lever, the brake lever being always placed outside. On some cars the segment has a hole drilled to receive a padlock. When the

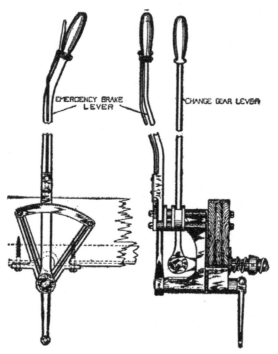

EMERGENCY BRAKE LEVER   CHANGE GEAR LEVER

FIG. 453.—Franklin emergency brake and transmission levers, as applied to models having progressive transmissions.

lever is drawn past this hole and padlock inserted, the clutch is out and the brake applied, so that the car is protected against unauthorized use or theft.

The Clutch Pedal.—The usual location of this device is to the left on the floor board to be operated by the left foot. By pressing down this pedal the clutch is released which allows the engine to run free by disconnecting it from the transmission.

As previously mentioned, there is a connection between the clutch and brake pedals, such that if the latter be pressed down the clutch is released at the same time the brake is applied for reasons already explained.

There is a simplified arrangement· on some cars in which a single pedal operates both clutch and brake. Pressure on this pedal first throws out the clutch while continued movement of the pedal applies the brake. This arrangement leaves the right foot free to operate the foot throttle.

The Transmission Gear Shifting Lever.—This lever is located beside the emergency brake lever but is always the inner

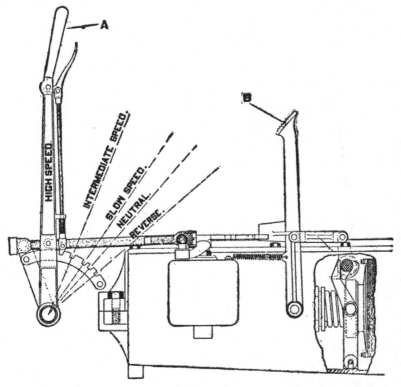

FIG.. 454.—The Maxwell transmission lever, showing the several positions of the lever in making the speed changes. The transmission is of the progressive type.

one or that one nearest the driver. On most cars it is further distinguished by the construction as is shown in fig. 453, the brake lever being provided with an external latch while the transmission lever has a press button on top, the latch link passing down through the handle.

The shape of this segment must be such that the proper movements may be given to the lever in shifting the gears, according to the type of transmission used.

When the car is fitted with a progressive transmission a simple linear movement of the lever is sufficient to affect the different gear changes, the lever being rotated through the proper arc. This type of transmission control as applied to the Maxwell car, is shown in fig. 454. The positions for the different speed changes are shown by the dotted lines, the latch segment having notches in the proper places to retain the lever in position.

The selective type of transmission requires, instead of the simple latch segment, a compound form of segment, known as a *selector*, since with selective transmissions it is necessary in shifting the gears, to give in certain cases both a linear and a lateral movement to the lever. A selector is simply a compound segmental guide for the transmission lever, having two slots for a three speed transmission, three slots for four speed transmissions, and a central gate to provide for the necessary lateral movement of the lever in passing from one slot to another. Fig. 455 shows the position of the selector with respect to the lever. The brake lever is also shown on the outside, the whole forming a structural unit which is attached to the side of the car. In shifting the gears for the several speed changes, the lever is moved to the various slot terminals, the central position at the gate corresponding to the neutral position.

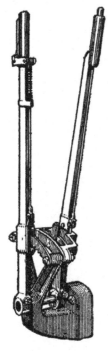

Fig. 455.—Characteristic side lever control. The two levers have distinctive constructions, the brake lever having an external latch mechanism and the transmission lever being provided with a press button at the top of the handle and connection running through same to the latch.

There seems to be no standard arrangement of the slot terminals for the different speeds. A great diversity exists, as is shown in the accompanying cuts.

Figs. 456 to 461 are examples of three speed selectors, and figs. 462 to 468 are four speed selectors, showing the varied slot arrangements to be found on different makes of cars. The numerals 1, 2, 3 and 4 indicate the position of the lever for the different speeds forward, R being the position for reverse.

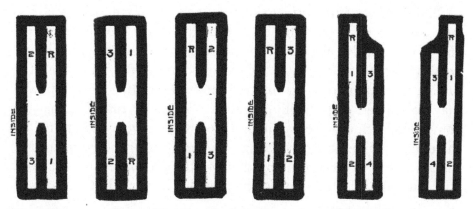

FIGS. 456 to 461.—Types of three speed selectors as used on well-known American automobiles in the greatest proportion. Fig. 456, Franklin; fig. 457, Columbia and Corbin; fig. 458, Apperson, Cadillac, Elmore, Knox, Oldsmobile, Walter, Winton and Thomas; fig. 459, Buick model five; fig. 460, Locomobile; fig. 461, Thomas.

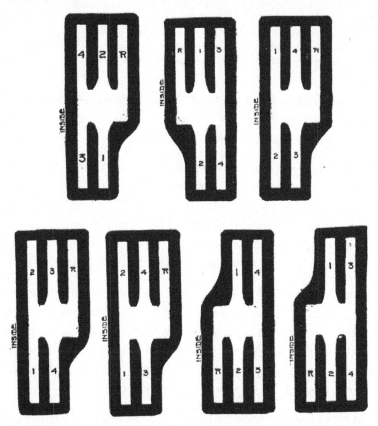

FIGS. 462 to 468.—Types of four speed selectors as used on American automobiles, showing wide variation; fig. 462, Lozier model G; fig. 463, Peerless and Stearns; fig. 464, Studebaker; fig. 465, Lozier model H; fig. 466, Matheson; fig. 467, Toledo; fig. 468, Simplex.

631

The Muffler Cut Out.—Since the action of a muffler tends to increase the back pressure of the exhaust and thereby diminish the power of the engine, it is desirable, in running over heavy road or ascending a hill, to switch out the muffler and allow the engine to exhaust directly into the atmosphere, that its full power may be applied in propelling the car. In order that this may be conveniently done, a cut out or three-way valve is connected to the exhaust pipe between the engine and muffler. The operation of this valve is controlled by a press button placed on the foot board usually located conveniently to the driver's left foot.

Foot Whistle Control.—In addition to the usual horn signal, a chime whistle is sometimes fitted to four and six cylinder cars.

The whistle is operated by the exhaust from the engine and produces a pleasing sound, especially on a six cylinder car, the rapid variations of the exhaust pressure producing a trembling tone.

The whistle is connected to the exhaust pipe with a Tee, and its valve operated by a push button located on the foot board near the muffler cut out button.

Other Dash and Foot Board Attachments.—In addition to the various levers and control devices already described, there are other attachments that are placed within reach of the driver.

The Coil Box.—In the absence of a high tension magneto, an induction coil is a necessary part of the ignition system, and this is usually located on the dash at the left side. With synchronous ignition the coil is a small affair, when a multi-unit coil is used, its casing assumes larger proportions. The vibrators being placed at the top are conveniently located for adjustment.

Ignition Cut Out Plug.—In order to prevent any one operating the car without the owner's consent, especially when left standing in a public place, a plug switch is inserted in the primary circuit of the ignition system and located on the dash or some other convenient yet non-conspicuous place, so that the plug is easily removed by the driver on leaving the car.

Self Starter.—A number of cars are now fitted with self starting devices, thus eliminating cranking. The method employed by the Winton Company on their six cylinder car is as follows:

Attached to cylinders 1 and 6 are outlets through which a small portion of the pressure of each power stroke passes to a pressure tank placed between the left frame rail and the driving shaft. Here the pressure is stored until required to start the motor, when a cock is opened, allowing the pressure to flow through the distributor to one of the cylinders. The pressure forces this piston down, and at the same time another piston passes the firing point and the motor starts. However, if for any reason the first cylinder should fail to fire, the distributor sends the pressure to the cylinder next in order, and forces the next piston past the firing point, and so on, if necessary, through the series of cylinders.

The control of the self-starter is shown in fig. 469, consisting of a push button, which allows pressure to flow from the tank to the cylinders. Immediately above the press button is the pressure gauge which indicates the amount of pressure in the tank. In addition, there is a shut off valve

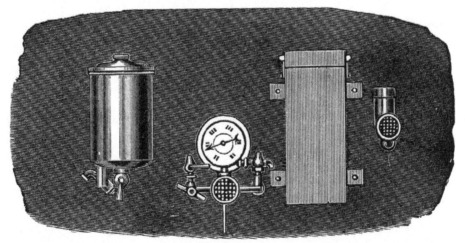

FIG. 469.—Winton six dash assemblage, showing from left to right, the auxiliary gasoline tank, the shut off, push button and gauge of self starter, the spark coil and oil sight feed.

for use when the car is to remain long idle, preventing loss of pressure from the storage tank. The other devices shown in the dash assemblage are; 1, the auxiliary gasoline tank at the left, 2, the spark coil, and 3, the oil sight feed.

Starting the Car.—After performing the preliminary operations, as set forth in Chapter Thirty-three the driver takes his position at the steering wheel and is ready to start the car. These preliminary operations may be briefly summarized as follows:

1. Supplies: { the gasoline tank must be filled;
the radiator supplied with *clean water;*
the lubricators filled and bearings oiled.

2. Before Cranking :

- the brake should be set, which releases clutch;
- the gasoline valve should be opened and carburetter primed;
- *the spark fully retarded;*
- the throttle placed at starting position or about one-quarter opening.

3. Cranking:

In the absence of a self starter, the operation of cranking the engine should be performed with care, as directed in Chapter Thirty-three *to avoid personal injury.*

4. After Cranking :

- the throttle should be closed;
- the spark advanced.

Having performed the above operations, the driver now takes his seat and starts the car as follows:

1. The engine speed must be increased by slightly retarding the spark.

The throttle and spark adjustments made immediately after cranking were for the slowest engine speed, just sufficient to keep it turning until the driver has mounted his seat and is ready to start the car.

2. Before any load is put on the engine, its speed must be increased in order to store up in the fly wheel sufficient momentum to keep it going between power strokes, against the added resistance of the load. This increased speed, as stated, is secured by spark adjustment rather than by changing the throttle position— the latter method being reserved for any additional increase of speed that may be necessary.

3. The clutch pedal is fully depressed and held down;

4. The emergency brake released.

It should be remembered that the emergency brake and clutch are so connected that when the brake is set, the clutch is automatically released, it being thrown into engagement with the transmission upon the release of the brake. Hence to prevent the clutch being thrown in, when the brake is released, the clutch pedal is held down before releasing brake.

5. With clutch still disengaged, the transmission lever is moved to *first speed position.*

The transmission lever is assumed to be in its neutral position, *to which position it should always be brought when the car is stopped.*

6. The right foot is placed on the throttle pedal, or *accelerator* as it is sometimes called, ready to press down and increase the throttle opening should the engine show any tendency to diminish its speed or stop.

7. The clutch pedal should then be *slowly released,* which will allow the clutch to engage gradually and start the car easily and without jerk.

FIG. 470.—The American Traveller with 40 inch wheels. An example of the underslung frame type of car. Four cylinder engine, bore 5⅜ in.; stroke, 5½ in., 50 H. P. Double ignition system—Bosch high tension magneto and single unit coil.

To Change to Second Speed.—In making a speed change there are three things to be done and it is important to remember the order in which these operations should be performed, viz.:

1. The clutch must be detached by pressing down on the clutch pedal with the left foot.

2. AFTER WAITING ONE OR TWO SECONDS, *in order that the two gears to be meshed shall be revolving at nearly the same speed,* quickly move the transmission lever to *second speed position.*

During the wait, the speed of the engine may be accelerated by the foot throttle if necessary, as is very often the case when running over a heavy road.

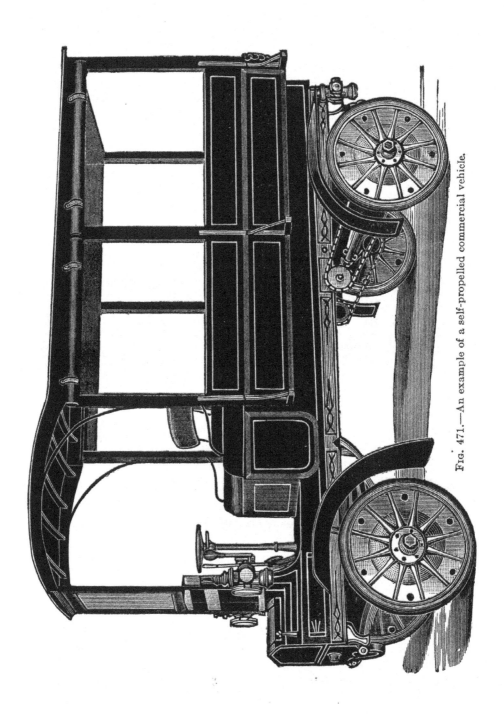

FIG. 471.—An example of a self-propelled commercial vehicle.

To Change to High Speed.—This is the speed of direct drive and in shifting the gears for this speed, the driver proceeds in the same manner just described for changing to second speed, that is, *after* releasing the clutch, the transmission lever is moved to the high speed position, and then the clutch is gradually re-engaged or thrown in again.

In the four speed transmission there is an additional speed to pass through, but the same operations as just described are performed.

In some four speed transmissions the direct drive is the fourth speed, while in others the construction is such that the direct drive is on the three speed, the fourth speed gearing the engine to run slower than the propeller shaft.

Throttle and Spark Control.—In running the car, the speed is almost entirely regulated by the throttle, the accelerator, or foot pedal being used mostly.

The hand throttle lever is used occasionally as a relief, to prevent fatigue of the ankle muscles, or where the car is run considerable distances without speed changes, as on open country roads.

To properly manage the spark under varied running conditions, the driver should have an understanding of ignition and carburetter principles together with extensive experience in operating the car. The spark control will depend somewhat on the kind of ignition used.

When a vibrating spark coil is used, no such advance of the spark is possible as would be indicated by the position of a timer apparently capable of a movement of 90 degrees or more. This is due to the lag in vibrating spark coils. Hence, it should be remembered that with a vibrating coil, the spark position as indicated by the spark lever is always in advance of its true position—the difference increasing with the engine speed.

With a high tension magneto, no such difference exists since the mechanically operated interrupter is positive in its action.

The car should always be run with the spark at least partially advanced and the speed controlled with the throttle. The spark should never be advanced to its highest point suddenly, nor should it be put at full advance before picking up speed, the advance being made gradually as the speed of the car increases.

The spark position is dependent to some extent on the quality of the fuel mixture. The mixture at low speeds should be richer than at high speeds on account of heat and compression losses.

In this connection it should be remembered that a lean and highly compressed charge burns faster than a richer one and the spark position should be modified to suit the immediate conditions of combustion.

A late spark, especially with a rich mixture causes the engine to heat up and results in an increased consumption of gasoline.

When on the road the best results are usually obtained by advancing the spark lever as far as possible without the engine pounding.

Rules for handling the spark lever cannot be laid down, as conditions vary with the kinds of roads being traveled, difference in motors, etc., but a good driver will not allow the engine to pound. The general practice among drivers, when desiring to keep the engine running slowly, is to retard both spark and throttle levers as much as possible, the adjustments being usually set to allow the engine to just keep running under these conditions. This practice is responsible for the need of grinding in valves at short intervals. With the spark lever retarded, the gas is ignited so late in the stroke that the exhaust valve opens before the charge is burnt, consequently the gas at a very high temperature is passing between the valve and its seat.

The cool gas, coming in on the suction stroke, will help the water-cooling system to keep the valve cool, but even with this help it will not withstand the heat very long and is soon warped, allowing leakage during the compression stroke. The remedy is to adjust the throttle so that the engine may be run as slowly as desired with the spark advanced so that ignition does not take place so near dead center.

To Stop the Car.—When making a gradual stop, 1, the throttle may be closed allowing the compressional resistance of the engine to act as a brake, until the car has reduced its headway, 2, the left pedal is now depressed throwing out the clutch, and 3, the foot brake applied with the right pedal.

To made a quick stop, both the clutch and brake pedals may be pressed simultaneously and the emergency brake set. In making a stop, the transmission lever should always be placed in the neutral position; the throttle should be closed and spark advanced so that the engine will not race.

To Reverse the Car.—After the car has come to a standstill, 1, the clutch is held out with the left pedal, 2, brakes released, 3, the transmission lever moved to the *reverse position,* and 4, the clutch *gradually* thrown in.

Shifting the Speed Change Gears.—The proper handling of the transmission lever, on a sliding gear system, can only be obtained by practice. One of the best tests of a driver's skill is to notice the way he handles the change speed gears.

A skillful man, accustomed to a car, will pass through all speeds, either up or down, noiselessly, unless for the click caused by the lever bringing up against the quadrant.

In shifting the transmission lever for the speed changes, if the transmission be of the selective type, the two movements necessary to give the lever may offer some difficulty to the beginner.

In moving the lever, the driver gives it a slight lateral pressure as it approaches the neutral point. With a little practice, the change may be made with practically one motion, the lateral movement requiring no separate action.

In the mind of the average demonstrator and that of his pupil, for the latter has it ground into him, there are but two things to do in gear changing, release the clutch and push or pull the lever.

The beginner pushes or pulls the lever mechanically, and it is usually not until long after he has graduated from his novitiate that he comes to learn what actually happens in the gear box when he moves the lever.

If a knowledge of the principles of operation of a transmission were first acquired, there would be less difficulty in learning to handle the lever correctly.

In the operation of the change speed gears, it will be evident that unless the teeth of the two pinions, that it is desired to mesh, happen to be in a position where they correspond, they cannot be slid together. Then if both shafts be idle and the gears do not happen to be in a position where their teeth will go together, they must be moved. But, taking the speeds in their usual order, which makes the operation of starting the first thing to be considered, it is evident that only the clutch shaft can be moved as the car is standing still. This gives a condition where one shaft is idle and the other is revolving at a high speed.

The fundamental requirement in every case is that the two gears to be meshed shall be revolving at as nearly the same speed as possible, therefore when going into first speed the necessity for waiting a moment or two after declutching in order to allow the clutch shaft to slow down must be plain. If the lever be moved, immediately the clutch is disengaged, it is practically the same as if an attempt were made to mesh the gears without going through the very necessary preliminary of taking the clutch out of engagement.

Just how long it is necessary to wait must be a matter of experience on different types of cars.

The old conical clutch with its comparatively great diameter is apt to hold its momentum much longer than other types such as the multiple disc, in which the discs are very small and very light, although improvement along these lines has also made a vast difference in the earlier type which is still adhered to by a surprising number of prominent builders.

In any case, the wait will not exceed a few seconds, but the difference in the result at the end of that time will be very perceptible as the gears are easily slid into mesh without any noise when the pinion on the clutch shaft is just about to come to rest.

Waiting too long is not as bad as delaying the operation for too short a time, as the noise and damage will be proportioned to the relative speeds of the shafts, whereas in the former case, it is merely a matter of try again, and a word of advice here should not come amiss.

Gears should not be forced into mesh. If they do not engage without being forced together, there is something radically wrong, and jamming down hard on the lever is only liable to aggravate the trouble or spring the shifting arm or lever.

The noise or growl so frequently heard is caused by the attempt to force the gears together while they are traveling at different rates of speed. This serves to grind and chip the edges, occasionally breaking the teeth. No matter how easy an entrance has been provided by the designer of the car, the pinions cannot be slid together unless they happen to be revolving at something approximating the same rate of speed, and the closer they are to this, the better.

Observation shows that the average driver seldom takes the precaution of waiting before engaging the first speed to start, and noise and damage inevitably ensue.

On increasing to second speed, very similar conditions obtain. The clutch shaft is revolving at a comparatively high rate of speed and the countershaft is going at a considerably slower rate. Hence, it is impossible to make the latter go any faster and therefore an immediate and noiseless change is not possible.

The usual method is to move the side lever simultaneously with the release of the clutch, and the result is to bring the speed of the clutch shaft down to that of the countershaft by the friction thus created between the sides of the pinions, to their resultant damage. The same result can be much better accomplished by a momentary halt between the operation of pulling the lever out of one speed and placing it home at the other, keeping the clutch fully disengaged in the interval. Here skill and experience in the handling of the make of car that one happens to be driving count, for if the wait be prolonged, the result will be the same as if none had been indulged in and the stop is apt to compel the momentary re-engagement of the clutch to again set the clutch shaft in motion.

With the progressive gear the system is usually arranged so that reverse is in mesh with the lever at the extreme rear and high speed at the forward end of the quadrant, the intermediate speeds proportioned in between. The lever usually has a button on top, controlling a latch that locks it in place at any desired speed by fitting into a slot cut in the quadrant.

The easiest method of securing the proper amount of travel, from one speed to another, is the following: Press the button or finger clasp that releases the latch from its slot, and while holding it released move the lever far enough to prevent its slipping back into the slot when the button is released. The latch will now be pressing against the quadrant bar, and the lever can be moved until the desired gear is properly meshed, where the influence of the spring will pull the latch into the slot and lock the lever. If the latch be held released the result may be that the lever will be carried too far into the following neutral. If this occur the best thing to do is to stop and come back to first speed again.

The progressive gear, as worked out by the Packard Company, does not have a locking device on the lever, the same result being obtained by a device in the gear box. When shifting from first to second, or from third back to second, the lever should be carried rapidly forward or backward until the gears are felt to engage. The locking device, though not automatic, will check the travel of the lever, and if the gears are properly in mesh will provide sufficient resistance to the movement of the lever to assure the operator that the gears are correctly in mesh.

Drivers handling the selective system have two things to remember. The first is to keep it well oiled that the lever may slide freely sideways. The second is to keep their hands off the button unless it is desired to enter reverse.

Some cars have appeared on the market with speeds arranged as follows:

R 2 4

1 3

If on a hill and conditions demand a change to a lower gear, say, third back to second, the driver will have no trouble if he handle the lever without touching the button. If he does, he is almost sure to enter reverse, with possibly serious consequences.

The clutch should be thrown as far forward as possible before any attempt is made to engage the gears. (Some cars have appeared with only one pedal so arranged that the clutch is first released and further travel of the pedal applies the running brakes.) The different types of clutches in use and the care bestowed on them has much to do with the ease with which the gears may be engaged.

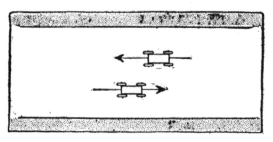

Fig. 472.—When two cars are going in opposite directions, the safe procedure is for each driver to keep well to the right of the crown of the road, thus avoiding the possibility of a collision.

The cone clutch, with its comparatively large diameter, is likely to spin longer than the multiple disc. Any attempt to mesh the gears while the clutch is spinning will result in the gears growling, possibly chipping the teeth.

Occasionally the shaft will stop so that the teeth of one gear will strike the teeth of the other and prevent them meshing. If this occur, the clutch should be engaged again for an instant, thus letting the clutch shaft spin, and after giving them time to slow down, another attempt may be made to mesh the gear.

City Driving.—In driving an automobile in the city, there are certain fixed rules of the road that must be observed, and rightly, too, if one is to avoid trouble, but the motto of every driver should be: *"Always be prepared for everyone else doing the wrong thing."* By observing this rule, the driver will find himself armed for whatever may occur on the city streets.

The first thing a new driver should do is to become familiar with the rules of the road. In some places they are unwritten rules, but in most of the big cities the police have framed up regulations for the control of traffic, which, unfortunately in most cases, apply only to motor cars, the bluecoats being singularly near sighted when it comes to noting infractions of the rules by drivers of horse drawn vehicles.

In driving a car the first rule is to *keep to the right in passing a vehicle going in the opposite direction.*

In England the traffic stays on the left side of the road, but this is the exception. It is only by everyone observing this rule that traffic can be handled in any kind of a manner, and accidents avoided.

In passing a vehicle going in the same direction the rule is to *pass to the left.*

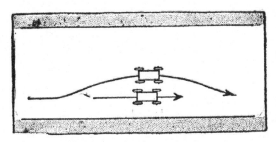

Fig. 473.—The driver should not pass to the right of a vehicle going in the same direction He has no recourse in case of an accident caused by the other driver turning into the curb.

Numerous accidents have been caused by failure to observe this rule. The driver who disregards this rule is liable for damages in case of accident, as a vehicle has the right to swing to the right at any time.

The non-observance of the above rule is sometimes due to the presence of electrics whose drivers generally stay in the middle of the street and run at about eight or ten miles an hour, which often compels others to invade forbidden territory to get by or else swing to the left directly into the path of the vehicles coming from the other direction. Cases are seen daily where drivers have had to go almost to the left curb in order to pass.

In turning corners, the driver should not cut diagonally across the street by beginning to turn before reaching the corner.

It is evident that such a procedure will cut off traffic coming from the other direction.

Road Signals.—As laid down by the makers of road rules, *the driver raises a hand or whip, when he is about to turn a* *corner or stop;* the right arm extended means that it is unsafe for the man behind to come up on that particular side, because the signaler is preparing to turn a corner and needs room.

The arm extended to the left means caution on that side.

The right arm raised so the arm is above the level of the head, with the forearm vertical and the shoulder portion horizontal, means that speed is about to be slackened, possibly because of the traffic or because of some maneuver the driver wishes to make.

It may be a case of reverse; then the horn should be sounded to call attention to the signal.

Another signal that is sometimes used when a driver desires the car behind to pass him or he has consented to give the right

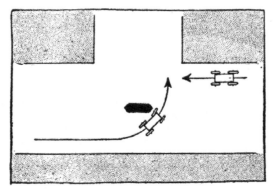

Fig. 474.—In turning corners where there are pedestrian refuges drivers should use signals, a wave of the hand to the right asking the other driver to pause, while one to the left gives the right of way.

of way is to hold the right arm downward outside the body of the car, and wave it forward.

Operating the Brakes.—The life of tires may be prolonged by the judicious and moderate handling of the brake lever. The brake should never be applied with such force as to cause the tires to slip.

If the wheels be locked, much of the retarding effort is lost and much rubber is ground off the tires, or if traveling on muddy roads or pavements all control over the car will be lost.

On long grades the brakes should not be depended on to hold the car. The ignition should be cut out, and, depending on the length and steepness of the grade, a suitable gear should be meshed and the car allowed to coast under compression, the brakes supplying any further retarding effort necessary.

In driving in a hilly country, it is desirable, not to have the emergency brake lever interconnected with the clutch, as this prevents the use of a very efficient brake.

Some brakes are intended to be lubricated, others are useless if oil gets on the friction surfaces. When this happens the best thing to do is to squirt a little gasoline on the drum. This will cut the oil and restore the efficiency. If one brake be adjusted tighter than the other it will throw the end of the car on that side around.

Friction surfaces of metal to metal, or steel to camel's hair or asbestos, will give little trouble with ordinary care.

If leather be used, its life will be prolonged by releasing the brakes for an instant while in use. This will allow a current of air to pass between the surfaces and carry away a great deal of the heat generated. The friction of the brake leather on the drum always generates heat, and the leather may be heated enough to be burnt or charred until useless unless the brake be used with moderation.

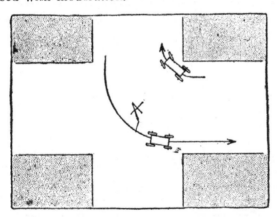

Fig. 475.—In turning corners the driver of a vehicle turning to the left from the right hand side should pass the center of the street intersection before making a turn. In case he is seeking to make a right hand turn he should hug the curb as closely as possible in turning the corner.

Trolley Lines.—As a rule, the track is laid on one side of the road, but there appears to be no recognized plan as regards location, and the autoist must keep a sharp lookout, not only for surprising changes in the location of the line but also for the cars themselves.

In regard to the track itself, strict watch should be kept for rails which are elevated above the level of the road, for switch tongues and differences in level between the bed of the track and the surface of the road.

Any of the above may interfere with the steering of the automobile if the wheels come in contact with them, and if the road be at all greasy, side slips are likely to occur.

The rails are a source of trouble when slippery and care should be taken that the tires do not get into the rail channels, as they will be badly wrenched or even torn off when a change of direction is desired.

One of the commonest mistakes made is in running the car with all four tires in the channels, which undoubtedly makes smooth riding but which also renders it difficult for the autoist to steer out of them again when he wishes to do so by any movement of the steering gear.

When the rails are dry, only a short time will elapse before the tire will ride over the rail head and get clear, but with wet rails sometimes hundreds of feet are traversed before the tires are clear.

Crossing Railroad Tracks.—All railroad tracks should be treated as if trains were likely to be due at the crossing at any moment and the car should be driven across at the greatest angle and at the best speed possible. A sharp lookout should be kept in both directions and the car slowed down on approaching the crossing, taking absolutely no chances.

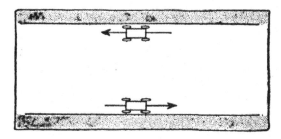

Fɪɢ. 476.—In making a stop, avoid facing the car in the wrong direction. The rules of the road call for a machine or vehicle stopping with the right wheels to the curb.

In case a collision is imminent, the steering wheel should be turned sharply in the direction in which the train is moving so that the car will be struck a glancing blow and the occupants will have some chance of escape.

Negotiating Turns.—The procedure on approaching a turn is exactly similar to that on approaching a road crossing. The car should keep to the center of the road and its speed should be reduced somewhat until the road is seen to be clear when the turn can be made. In taking a right hand turn, the autoist should keep well away from the corner, describing as large an arc as possible and gradually gaining the center of the other road. There are numbers of drivers who habitually shave corners; who start to make the turn before reaching the proper point and cut diagonally across the road, obstructing traffic coming in the opposite direction, and hugging the left hand corner of the intersecting road. Their desire is evidently to travel from one point to another in the shortest possible space of time, and to save distance cut the corners without regard to the rights or safety of others.

Because of the presence of reckless classes of drivers, special caution has to be exercised at all times by those in charge of vehicles of every kind.

The difficulty of taking a car around a corner which has to be turned to the right is sometimes acute, since the driver must keep to his own side, and on that the camber of the road adds seriously to any danger that

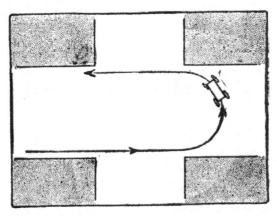

FIG. 477.—A good rule to observe and one that will prevent accidents is to go to the next corner before turning in a street. The turn should not be attempted until the farther corner has been reached, then a wide swing should be made, caution being observed, of course, to avoid rigs going in both directions.

may exist owing to mud or slime. Even when the surface is quite dry, the camber is sometimes sufficient, with the acuteness of the turn, to cause the rear of the car to swing, and it is because of this that many heavy cars are fitted with metal non-skid covers all the year round.

Where the presence of an acute turn of this description is known, or is indicated by a warning sign, the driver can be relied upon to reduce his speed, so as to be able to take it without unduly stressing his running gear. But it is when the situation suddenly presents itself that matters assume a critical phase.

If the car be still running in a straight line when the nature of the corner becomes apparent, the engine should be switched off and the brakes judiciously applied without taking out the clutch, but if the corner has been entered upon the greatest care should be exercised in using the brakes, as to lock the driving wheels would probably make a violent side-slip inevitable.

If the corner has been entered upon, it will be wise to withdraw the clutch and trust to gentle braking with the side lever and good steering to get round. Every broken bit of road surface should be taken advantage of to assist the driving wheels to hold to the road.

To take a greasy corner, turning on the off or right hand side is easy enough since, the driver being on his own side, can put the innerside wheels in the gutter—where they act as non-skids against the slope of the latter—and run round cautiously.

It is best to run free for the sake of the differential gear if the corner be sharp, and if the rear of the car shows an inclination to swing, gently letting in the clutch will cause the inside wheel to "bite," and the car will answer the helm.

Country Driving.—On a country road the farmer will either give the motorist the whole road or won't move until he has to. He isn't a bit particular whether he turns to the right or left.

Fig. 478.—The American Motor League "caution signs." Background and posts white, symbols black; 1 indicates approach to a steep descent; 2, approach to a railroad crossing; 3, approach to a branch road (to right); 4, approach to a branch road (to left); 5, approach to cross roads; 6, approach to a ditch or abrupt depression in the road; 7, approach to a hummock; 8, approach to a city, village or other collection of inhabited dwellings; 9, is a general caution signal indicating the proximity of any danger or obstruction not scheduled above, or any other condition requiring caution; 10 (not shown in cut) is a plain white sign and can be improvised in emergent cases by using a sheet of white cloth fastened upon a board of proper shape. Each sign is placed at a distance of not less than 200, nor more than 300 yards from the point to which it refers.

Similarly when following and trying to overtake another automobile on the road, the driver of the leading machine may try to prevent the other car passing him, or may take that side of the road that looks best to him regardless of rules or laws. When passing little breaks in the road caused by water running off and carrying the road material with it, holes in pavement, etc., the shock of striking the edges is rather severe on tires and may be lessened by releasing the clutch for the moment and allowing the car to coast, always taking "waterbreaks" and similar rough spots straight on, so as not to strain the car unnecessarily.

On approaching a point where the road forks or branches off, the autoist should hold well over to the proper side of the road in order to avoid cars coming along the branches.

Should he be traveling along one of the branches toward the fork, however, he should keep in the center, as when approaching an ordinary turn.

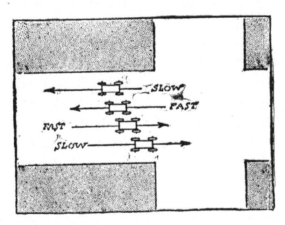

Fig. 479.—Slow moving vehicles should keep as near the curb as possible, leaving the left side of that side of the road for faster moving rigs.

Skidding and Side Slipping.—Although both the terms skidding and side slipping are used freely, their meanings are often confused.

Skidding implies a continued forward movement of the car after the wheels have been locked by the brakes.

Side slipping relates only to a lateral motion of the car due to the wheels sliding bodily sideways.

Nothing but experience can teach the autoist how to evade side slip when the roads are in a slippery state. He may be forewarned of the various kinds of side slips and skids and the proper procedure under the circumstances, but he must actually experience each kind in order to distinguish one from the other and to acquire the instinct necessary to counterbalance every tendency in that direction immediately the first symptoms are perceptible.

There are certain kinds of surface on which the tires cannot obtain a firm grip, places in which lateral strains are brought to bear on the car, and acts on the part of the driver which either reduce or increase the adherence between the tires and the road.

Deft manipulation of the steering wheel by an expert operator often will neutralize a well developed skid, by maintaining the car in approximately its original line of onward movement.

Thus, if the front wheels be steered in the direction in which the rear wheels are skidding, the tendency of the vehicle is to stay parallel to its original line of movement, ready to resume it as the skidding terminates.

Operating a Car at Night.—Objects at night are deceiving to the eye. What appears as a dark patch in the road may be either a pool of water or a depression, and light colored objects by the side of the road may even be taken for the road itself. The road, too, apparently disappears a short distance ahead and the autoist sets the brakes, only to find himself deceived. Due to the combination of deep shadows and strong lights with the general gloom of the night, all sorts of objects created in the imagination seem to spring up, causing doubt and anxiety.

Powerful lamps should be used for comfortable night driving as well as for the safety of the occupants of the car.

Running in city streets or on lighted roads is of course much easier than running on dark roads, but in such cases the eyes are constantly accommodating themselves to the changes in light as the car approaches and passes a street lamp.

With the powerful arc lights in use in many cities, the view will be obscured for a short time as the car passes out of the circle thrown by the light and a feeling of blindness will result, soon passing off, however, as the eyes adjust themselves to the change in quality of the light. It is due to this effect on the eyes that a number of the minor accidents occur at corners, not only to autos but to horse vehicles and foot passengers.

When emerging from light into what seems total darkness, as when leaving the last light of a city and going along the unlighted road, an involuntary sensation of being lost is experienced and even with powerful headlights the feeling of blindness occurs for a short time.

Goggles to be Avoided at Night.—Except when absolutely necessary, goggles should not be worn nor should the wind shield be raised when driving at night, as the reflections from street-lamps or other sources of light on the glass surfaces of the goggles and shield appear as direct lights and obscure objects on the road, with unhappy results.

Lamp Equipment.—For properly illuminating the road and objects surrounding it the lamp equipment should consist of:

1. One or two headlights;
2. Pair of side lamps;
3. Tail lamp;
4. Swivelling searchlight.

The headlights should be carried low down and well forward, not only to better illuminate the road but to cease to dazzle other road users.

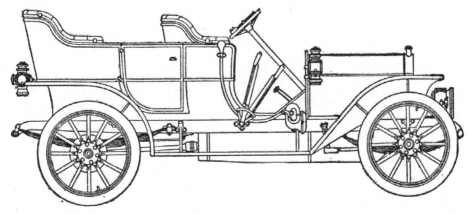

FIG. 480.—The Pullman four cylinder car (model K); engine 4½x4½ water cooled, rated at 30 horse power; selective transmission; shaft drive; two double high tension ignition system—Bosch magneto and dry cells.

Overhauling the Car.—A thorough overhauling of the entire car is occasionally required, that the needed repairs may be made. It is only by this thorough overhauling that the owner can get a good idea of the car's condition, ascertain what parts show wear, and correct wrong adjustments which may have been previously made.

The principal reason for taking an engine apart is to find the exact condition of the pistons and bearings, as well as to clean out thoroughly any carbonized oil that may be found adhering to the cylinder walls.

Each part as it is removed should be cleaned. As soon as one part is unjointed or uncoupled, insert its pins or screws in their proper place before laying aside. This will prevent any small parts being misplaced.

Confusion is to be avoided by providing a sufficient number of boxes to accommodate the several units of the car, and keep everything pertaining to a certain part in its respective box.

In overhauling the car, the carburetter, pump, wiring, spark plugs and any other movable parts fastened to the engine should be removed.

When removing the magneto, the gear wheels of the engine and the driving pinion of the armature shaft should be marked with a punch at the point where they mesh, if not marked already. By taking this precaution the magneto may be assembled on the car in its proper place without disturbing .he original ignition timing of the car. Each valve should be marked as it is taken out, that each may be replaced in its proper seat. It will be convenient to number them 1, 2, 3, etc., by punch mark.

The cylinder castings may now be lifted off the pistons and removed to the work bench. Some workmen prefer to lift cylinders and pistons off together; this is a good plan if a helper be at hand, but more difficult for one man than lifting the cylinder alone. In assembling, however, without assistance, and especially when the cylinders are cast in pairs or *en bloc,* the weight of the cylinder casting is considerable, and it is much less laborious first to assemble the cylinders with the pistons in their respective places, and so avoid holding up the heavy casting while fitting the pistons.

The connecting rods should be uncoupled from the crank shaft, the rods and pistons being removed together.

Before taking down any other part of the car, it is a good plan to first clean out the cylinders with kerosene to remove any oil and so soften deposits of carbon adhering to the walls. If the deposit be light, this soaking may be all that is necessary, but where a considerable amount of carbon has gathered in the combustion chamber, the walls must be scraped either with a suitable carbon scraper sold for this purpose, or with a file bent and sharpened to a cutting edge.

All the piston rings should be clean and bright; if any black streaks be found, it is a certain indication of leakage. All worn piston rings should be replaced. Examine the piston pin with a view to possible looseness and wear. It is important that this pin should be a tight fit, otherwise it may work out and injure the cylinder walls. A loose piston pin may be due to the set screw becoming loose, or it may be caused by wear. In the latter event, the pin should be replaced with a new one of the proper diameter and length.

The valves should be ground. A good grinding mixture is one composed of emery of the grade known as 120 mixed with kerosene and a few drops of heavy lubricating oil to give the mixture body.

The camshafts in most cars are removed by taking off the cover of the case which encloses the timing gears and pulling the camshafts through this opening.

All modern cars have the crankshaft gear marked, and another mark between the two teeth of the timing gear on the camshaft. When assembling, the single marked tooth should be inserted between the two teeth as designated. Breakage or undue wear of the cams is a matter which only the factory experts can handle.

Cleaning the radiator of grease or any scale that may have accumulated is best done after the car is reassembled and in running order. In cleaning the radiator a cleaning mixture is made by dissolving one-half pound of lye in a bucket of water, stirring until dissolved. This should be strained and the radiator filled with the mixture. The engine should now be run for five minutes and then allowed to stand for one-quarter of an hour. The mixture may now be drained off and the radiator filled with *clean water*. The engine is again run for a few minutes after which the radiator is drained and refilled with a fresh supply of water. The foregoing treatment will remove any grease deposits in the radiator.

The transmission cover should now be removed and the gears examined. As most transmission systems are fitted with annular ball bearings, only a good cleaning to remove old grease will be required. In case any gears are badly worn and their edges chipped, they should be replaced with new ones.

The clutch may next be taken down. The exact mode of procedure differs in different car clutches. In most cars using clutches of the multiple disc type it may be removed as a unit; in other forms, the shaft connecting the shifting sleeve may be uncoupled, which gives sufficient room between clutch and gear box to take the clutch apart. If the latter be of the cone type, it may be found that the leather face is badly worn and that a new leather is necessary. This is not a very difficult job, but requires painstaking work.

The leather of a cone clutch is removed by cutting off the rivets on the underside and driving the rivets through to the outside. The old leather should be kept for use as a pattern by which to cut the new piece. It will be much better, however, to purchase from the factory a new leather of the proper width and thickness. As a new leather will have considerable "give," it must be stretched tightly over the cone. One end of the leather should be cut square and fastened to the cone with two rivets; the other end brought around to meet the fastened end, and, after tightly stretching it over the small end of the cone with a single rivet, the leather is then forced up onto the cone, holes drilled out and countersunk and the leather riveted.

The only knack in the operation is to keep the leather tight that it may be a snug fit on the cone. A loose leather will, naturally, be a dead failure. After the leather has been forced into its place the uncut end should be trimmed to make a good joint. Any unevenness may be trued up with a file. The new leather will readily absorb several applications of castor oil before it becomes smooth and pliable.

Care should be taken that the rivet heads are countersunk below the surface of the leather. In case they work flush, owing to the wearing down of the leather face, they should be again riveted. The "biting" or jerky action of a cone clutch may often be traced to the rivets working out, and this will frequently prevent the clutch being readily disengaged. Reriveting will prove an effective remedy in this case, and considerable additional service may be had from the leather before it wears down to the rivet heads.

The differential gear should be tested with a view to locating any wear or side play. This may be done by jacking up the rear axle and shaking one wheel forward and backward while the other is held stationary, and noting how far the wheel must be turned before the movement is taken up by the flywheel of the engine. Any noticeable play will generally be found either in the center pinions or studs of the differential gear, in the large and small bevel gears, in the clutch sleeve, or in the universal joints. The differential gear and live axle of modern cars seldom give trouble if kept properly lubricated, and the car's mileage should run up into many thousands before any considerable amount of play is evident.

The joint pins of the propeller shaft may become loose through wear, in which case a knocking noise in the transmission gear will indicate the cause and location of the trouble. These pins may be readily replaced with new ones at small cost. If the play be found in the bevel gears, the small gear should be adjusted to mesh deeper with its larger mate. This may be done by means of the adjustable locking ring or by inserting a washer of the proper thickness. It may be found, however, that no adjustment is necessary, and a thorough cleaning with gasoline to remove all oil and grease will be all that is required. The case should then be refilled with the quantity of oil and grease recommended by the manufacturers.

Oil pipes or "leads" which conduct the oil to the bearings should be removed and all oil washed out by forcing gasoline through them. Care should be taken that the passages of all oil leads are clear and unobstructed.

The oil pump should be taken apart and given a thorough cleaning with gasoline.

The sight feed lubricator on the dash should also be cleaned out and the glasses wiped and washed out with gasoline.

The steering gear should be taken down, given a thorough cleaning and examined for possible wear. In case the steering action be stiff and the wheel turn hard, the ball joint may be out of adjustment due to wear; the steering link may be bent, or the cause may be insufficient lubrication.

If there be any considerable amount of backlash, the cause may be looked for in the joints of the levers, in the swivel pin, in loose bearings, or in wear of the worm and sector. Another common cause of backlash is often found in the wheels, which work out of alignment. It is essential that all moving parts of the steering gear be well lubricated.

The distance rod is easily bent, which throws the front wheels out of line. This is a common cause of "side slip" and rapidly wears out the tread of the tire. The bent rod should be uncoupled and carefully straightened. On many cars, however, the rod is designed to be bent, in order to clear other parts.

Each wheel should be removed and examined at the hub to see if the spokes have become loosened through shrinkage. Although this is not a common fault, it is, nevertheless, worth looking for. If slightly loose, tighten up the bolts which secure the two side flanges together, clean out bearings with gasoline and renew any ball or roller which is found damaged. If rust has accumulated, scrape or sandpaper it off (a painter's wire brush is a handy tool), and when perfectly clean, coat the rim with beeswax. This may be applied with a clean paint brush if the wax be heated to a liquid state. This will effectually prevent further rusting of the metal, and will do much to preserve the life of the tires.

The brakes should be examined to ascertain if the lining be in good condition. If worn, the old lining should be replaced with new. If the brakes be of the internal expanding type, the shoes may have become worn, in which case they should be renewed. Toggle joints and adjusting nuts should be inspected and any looseness taken up. Brakes should be adjusted on the road, as any improper adjustment of the equalizer bar will have a strong tendency to make the car skid. Both brakes should be adjusted alike, that the braking force applied by the equalizer may be transmitted to the wheels equally.

The tires should be cleaned of the old chalk on the inside of the shoe. If they be badly worn on the treads, but otherwise in good shape, send them to the factory to be retreaded. A tire should never be kept on the car after the rubber tread wears down so as to expose the fabric. Any small cuts and holes should be washed out and filled with rubber solution.

Inner tubes should be tested for leaky valves and patches attended to at once. The old casings and tubes may be made to give considerable additional mileage by using them on the front wheels, where the strain is not so severe.

In overhauling the ignition apparatus, worn wires should be replaced with new ones to guard against *breaks* or *partial breaks*. A timer should be cleaned with gasoline and lubricated with light oil.

The magneto need not be taken apart, as it will probably only need a little surface cleaning, a few drops of oil, and the amateur had better not meddle with its internal mechanism.

The storage battery should be examined, and if the brown deposit collect in any quantity at the bottom, the electrolyte should be poured out into a glass bottle and the battery washed out with clear water (rain water preferred). Clean the top of the battery and make it a point to keep it clean and free from acid. Clean the terminals of any corrosion and see that the air vents are not clogged up. If the accumulator has been neglected, either in the electrolyte having been allowed to get below the proper level or in not giving it the regular monthly "charge," it may get a bad case of sulphating.

To get the battery into its normal condition the electrolyte should be emptied and the case thoroughly washed with soft water. The case is then refilled with about seven-eighths of the electrolyte and the remainder with soft water. In case the plates are broken down or "buckled," or if the paste has dropped out of the pockets in the grids, the accumulator should be sent to the manufacturers for repair.

The contact points of the coil will probably require adjusting. This is easily accomplished by trimming up the points with emery paper. Do not rub away the metal unnecessarily, only removing enough to true the points so that they make a good contact. In adjusting the vibrator, remember that a light tension is much better than a stiff tension. A light flexible vibration with a moderately high pitched buzzing note will not only give a better spark, but will keep the points in better shape. A heavy tension will make the coil less responsive and will pit the contact points and exhaust the battery more quickly. As a coil will render the most efficient service only when the vibrators are adjusted as nearly alike as possible, a special ammeter is often used to determine the current consumption of each unit. The ammeter should show a reading of 6-10 amperes.

Assembling after Overhauling.—This should be done as soon as possible after taking down and cleaning, to guard against the loss of any of the parts.

In assembling the car, the engine had best be put together first. When putting the pistons in their respective cylinders see that the splits or joints in the piston rings are not in line, but are spaced evenly around the piston. See that all parts are thoroughly clean and that no grit or stray strands of waste remain on any projection.

All nuts and bolts should be screwed tight and the jaws of the wrench should be properly adjusted to them, that the corners of the nuts and cap screws may not be rounded off. Insert the cotter pin after each nut has been screwed home. In joints where packing is required the old packing may be used if it be in good shape. Joint faces should, of course, be perfectly clean. A stout grade of manila wrapping paper soaked in linseed oil will make an excellent packing for crankcase and other joints having a good contact surface.

While the engine is being reassembled it will be found advantageous to check up the valve timing. To do this, turn the fly-wheel until the inlet valve plunger of No. 1 cylinder just touches the lower end of its valve stem. At this point the line on the fly-wheel indicating "Inlet No. 1 Open" should coincide with the pointer on the engine base. If the contact between the valve stem and the plunger be made before the mark on the fly-wheel lines up with the pointer, the valve opens too early.

In most cars the adjustments may be made by the screw cap and lock nut on the plunger.

As the valve stems are lowered by repeated grindings of the valves, the plungers require adjustment occasionally to compensate for this movement. Insert a piece of paper between plunger and valve stem, and by lightly pulling on the paper the time of contact and the moment of release may be determined to a nicety. When the paper is held tightly, a good contact is assured, and the moment the paper becomes loose and can be moved about, the contact is broken. In many cars the reference or index mark on the engine bed is omitted; in this case the markings on the fly-wheel must be brought directly to the top. The other inlets and the exhaust valves should then be similarly checked up and adjusted.

Most cars base the valve setting on a 1-32-inch clearance space between valve stem and plunger rod when the valve is closed. This may be taken as the minimum amount, and should not be increased. A larger amount of clearance will cause the exhaust valve to open too late, and, the exploded gases not being entirely expelled, the power of the motor will be impaired. This clearance is necessary to allow for the expansion of the valve stem when it becomes heated.

Too much stress cannot be laid on the necessity of going about the work in an orderly and methodical manner. A mechanic who leaves parts lying about carelessly will rarely be found a good one, and certainly he is not a proper model for the amateur to copy. With the proper circumspection, then, and with a little "horse sense" in applying the directions to his particular make of car, the amateur owner should have no difficulty in making a good job of overhauling, thus bettering the condition of his machine and at the same time acquiring a valuable stock of knowledge for the future.

Accident Preventer.—Attached to the wall at the corner of a narrow street leading into the market place of Woodbridge, Suffolk County, England, is a mirror which makes it possible for automobilists coming from either direction to look around the corner and thus avoid collisions. The idea is being copied quite extensively.

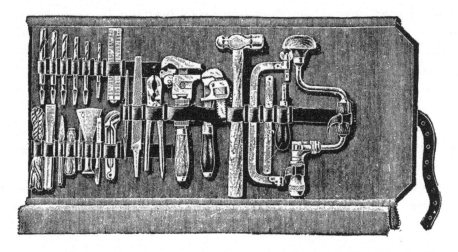

Fig 481.—Kit of tools as usually carried on an automobile. With this outfit, the driver can make adjustments and repairs such as arise from the ordinary mishaps likely to be encountered on the road.

WORDS OF CAUTION.

A plea for sanity and moderation.—Moderation,

says Charles Clifton, President of the Ass'n of Licensed Automobile Manufacturers, is the great decreaser of expense and
augmentor of enjoyment.   He writes as follows:

Quotation.—"Automobile owners, as a rule, in discussing their
costs generally name the great item of expense as being tires,
and in that connection they are quite inclined to arraign the
makers of pneumatic tires as being responsible for this condition. These statements are an individual expression of opinion
based on more or less experience, and doubtless justified in
part by the records of bills paid by those who buy tires."

"These remarks, in the same sense, are an individual expression of opinion based upon the same facts, and are contributed in the hope that they may suggest a way of reducing
the sum total of tire bills, as well as leading in the direction
of safer and saner methods in driving, and in the last analysis,
greater pleasure from motor cars."

"There are three prime factors responsible for short tire
life. First, excessive speed, especially during the warm
months. Second, changes of direction at a high rate of
speed; and third, excessive and unnecessary use of mechanical
brakes. My experience has gone to prove that—punctures ex-
cepted—the life of tires is enormously prolonged by avoiding
the above three cardinal enemies of the pneumatic tire's lon-
gevity. So much for the direct money cost, but if these three
cardinal principles are insisted upon by owners, the liability
of accident will be reduced to a minimum, and all the high
costs incident to property and personal damage."

"Accidents will also be reduced, as well as wear and tear mentally on an owner in connection therewith. In other words, sanity in the use of the motor car is an incalculable money value which no owner should ignore; and the reverse of the proposition is an unnecessary extravagance, which, if indulged in, should not carry with it an invective against the tire manufacturer or the manufacturer of the motor car."

"In other words, the responsibility for high costs in running expenses is absolutely in the hands of the owner, or, perhaps, more directly in the hands of the driver. Excessive speed, under all conditions, is done at high cost, which abnormal cost can only be reduced by the adoption of sane methods."

"To go a step further in this line of reasoning, I wish to plead for saneness in the use of highways. Not only in the matter of excessive speed, but also in the relation which should subsist between those who ride in cars and those who use it in other and older ways. The antagonism of the farmer against the automobile is mainly the result of a series of circumstances which to "the other fellow" seems like a succession of outrages. It is well for the driver of a motor car to realize that the other fellow used the highway, more or less unmolested, ever since there were highways. That, while he may feel he has pre-emption, that pre-emption goes no further than the joint use. For the driver of a motor car to assume to use more than his share of the road to make of his vehicle a menace, or at the very least a nuisance to other users, is a very natural cause for antagonism."

"The users and drivers of motor cars can, by sane driving, do the larger part in accomplishing a reversal of this sentiment, and in any event only fair play will eliminate the present friction which none may truthfully deny exists."

Other books from CGR Publishing at CGRpublishing.com

1939 New York World's Fair: The World of Tomorrow in Photographs

San Francisco 1915 World's Fair: The Panama-Pacific International Expo.

1904 St. Louis World's Fair: The Louisiana Purchase Exposition in Photographs

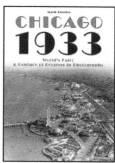

Chicago 1933 World's Fair: A Century of Progress in Photographs

19th Century New York: A Dramatic Collection of Images

The American Railway: The Trains, Railroads, and People Who Ran the Rails

The Aeroplane Speaks: Illustrated Historical Guide to Airplanes

The World's Fair of 1893 Ultra Massive Photographic Adventure Vol. 1

The World's Fair of 1893 Ultra Massive Photographic Adventure Vol. 2

The World's Fair of 1893 Ultra Massive Photographic Adventure Vol. 3

World War 1: A Dramatic Collection of Images

Magnum Skywolf #1

Ethel the Cyborg Ninja Book 1

Ethel they Cyborg Ninja 2

How To Draw Digital by Mark Bussler

How To Draw Pandas by Mark Bussler

Other books from CGR Publishing at CGRpublishing.com

Ultra Massive Video Game Console Guide Volume 1

Ultra Massive Video Game Console Guide Volume 2

Ultra Massive Video Game Console Guide Volume 3

Ultra Massive Sega Genesis Guide

Discovery of the North Pole: The Greatest American Expedition

Chicago's White City Cookbook

Official Guide to the World's Columbian Exposition

How To Grow Mushrooms: A 19th Century Approach

The Great War Remastered WW1 Standard History Collection Vol. 1

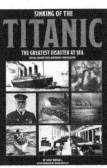
Sinking of the Titanic: The Greatest Disaster at Sea

All Hail the Vectrex Ultimate Collector's Guide

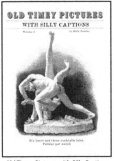
Old Timey Pictures with Silly Captions Volume 1

The Art of World War 1

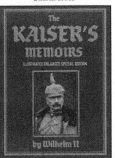
The Kaiser's Memoirs: Illustrated Enlarged Special Edition

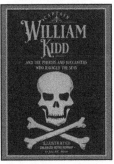
Captain William Kidd and the Pirates and Buccaneers Who Ravaged the Seas

Robot Kitten Factory Issue #1

Antique Cars and Motor Vehicles:
Illustrated Guide to Operation, Maintenance, and Repair
by James E. Homans

Cover Design by
Mark Bussler

More History Books at
CGRpublishing.com

Made in the USA
Monee, IL
24 January 2022

89761602R00365